Canto is a paperback imprint
which offers a broad range of titles,
both classic and more recent,
representing some of the best
and most enjoyable of Cambridge
publishing.

The Order of the Temple was founded in 1119 with the limited aim of protecting pilgrims around Jerusalem. It developed into one of the most powerful corporations in the medieval world which lasted for nearly two centuries until its suppression in 1312. Despite the loss of its central archive in the sixteenth century, the Order left many records of its existence as the spearhead of crusading activity in Palestine and Syria, as the administrator of a great network of preceptories and lands in the Latin west, and as a banker and ship-owner.

Because of the dramatic nature of its abolition, it has retained its grip on the imagination and consequently there has developed an entirely fictional 'after-history' in which its secret presence has been evoked to explain mysteries which range from masonic conspiracy to the survival of the Turin Shroud. This book offers a concise and up-to-date introduction to the reality and the myth of this extraordinary institution.

THE NEW KNIGHTHOOD

THE
NEW KNIGHTHOOD

A HISTORY OF
THE ORDER OF THE TEMPLE

MALCOLM BARBER

Reader in Medieval History,
University of Reading

CAMBRIDGE
UNIVERSITY PRESS

PUBLISHED BY THE PRESS SYNDICATE OF THE UNIVERSITY OF CAMBRIDGE
The Pitt Building, Trumpington Street, Cambridge, United Kingdom

CAMBRIDGE UNIVERSITY PRESS
The Edinburgh Building, Cambridge CB2 2RU, UK
40 West 20th Street, New York, NY 10011–4211, USA
477 Williamstown Road, Port Melbourne, VIC 3207, Australia
Ruiz de Alarcón 13, 28014 Madrid, Spain
Dock House, The Waterfront, Cape Town 8001, South Africa

http://www.cambridge.org

First published 1994
Canto edition 1995
Reprinted 1996, 1998, 2000, 2003

Printed in the United Kingdom at the University Press, Cambridge

A catalogue record for this book is available from the British Library

Library of Congress Cataloguing in Publication data
Barber, Malcolm
The new knighthood: a history of the Order of the Temple/Malcolm Barber.
p.   cm.
Includes bibliographical references and index.
ISBN 0 521 42041 5
1. Templars – History. 2. Civilization, Medieval. I. Title.
XR473.B27   1993
271'.7913–dc20
92–33821   CIP

ISBN 0 521 42041 5 hardback
ISBN 0 521 55872 7 paperback

Cover illustration: map of Jerusalem c. 1170 (detail),
Ms 76 F5 fol. 1r, Koninklijke Bibliotheek, The Hague

To Bernard Hamilton

CONTENTS

LIST OF PLATES

LIST OF FIGURES

PREFACE

This study was undertaken to meet the need for a concise and modern introduction in English to the history of the Order of the Temple, and to be a companion, albeit rather belated, to my *Trial of the Templars* (Cambridge University Press, 1978). It is not comprehensive; in particular, there remains considerable scope for examination of the Order in specific regions, for which there is insufficient space here. Unlike the trial, the earlier history of the Order is beset by problems stemming from lack of evidence, the most obvious gap being the loss of the central archive, probably in the sixteenth century. I have nevertheless tried to present a coherent picture from the material available without dwelling excessively upon what we would like to know, but cannot find out.

No book can be completed without help from one's friends and I would particularly like to thank Michael Biddiss, Gary Dickson, Bernard Hamilton, George Hintlian, Denys Pringle, Louise Robbert, Elizabeth Siberry, Frank Tallett, Jan Troska, and Judi Upton-Ward, for their advice and encouragement. I am, too, very pleased to thank the staff of the British Library, the Bibliothèque Nationale, the Archivo de la Corona de Aragón, and the University of Reading Library. A grant from the Research Board at the University of Reading made a significant contribution towards the cost of microfilm. Above all, the award of a British Academy Research Readership between 1989 and 1991 provided me with a unique opportunity to concentrate upon shaping a large mass of material collected over many years into a manageable structure, and for this I am very grateful.

ACKNOWLEDGEMENTS

The author is grateful to the Hakluyt Society for permission to quote from *Jerusalem Pilgrimage 1099–1185*, ed. J. Wilkinson, 1988; to the Boydell Press for the extracts from *The Rule of the Templars*, tr. J. Upton-Ward, 1992; and to Secker & Warburg for the extracts from U. Eco, *Foucault's Pendulum*, trans. W. Weaver, 1989. Figures 4, 5, 6 and 8 are based on versions which appear in P. Deschamps, *Les Châteaux des Croisés en Terre Sainte*, vol. III, 1973, published by Librairie Orientaliste Paul Guethner, Paris. Figure 9 (i) is based on a version in C. N. Johns, *Guide to 'Atlīt*, 1947, published by the Department of Antiquities, Government of Palestine. Figure 9 (ii) is based on Deschamps, *Les Châteaux des Croisés en Terre Sainte*, vol. II, 1939, publisher as above. Figure 10 is based on F. Laborde, 'L'église des Templiers de Montsaunès (Haute-Garonne)', *Revue de Comminges*, 92 (1979); figure 11 on D. Jacoby, 'Crusader Acre in the Thirteenth Century: Urban Layout and Topography', *Studi Medievali*, 20 (1979); and figure 12 on E. Baratier, G. Duby and E. Hildersheimer, eds., *Atlas Historique. Provence. Comtat Venaissin. Principauté d'Orange. Comté de Nice. Principauté de Monaco*, 1969 (map 68), published by Librairie Armand Colin, Paris.

LIST OF ABBREVIATIONS

AOL	*Archives de l'Orient latin*
BEC	*Bibliothèque de l'Ecole des Chartes*
BEFAR	*Bibliothèque des Ecoles françaises d'Athènes et de Rome*
BN	*Bibliothèque Nationale, Paris*
Cart.	*Cartulaire général de l'Ordre des Hospitaliers de Saint-Jean de Jérusalem, 1100–1310*, 4 vols., ed. J. Delaville Le Roulx, Paris, 1894–1905
CG	*Cartulaire général de l'ordre du Temple 1119?–1150. Recueil des chartes et des bulles relatives à l'ordre du Temple*, ed. Marquis d'Albon, Paris, 1913
Cont. WT	*La Continuation de Guillaume de Tyr (1184–1197)*, ed. M. R. Morgan, Documents relatifs à l'histoire des Croisades publiés par l'Académie des Inscriptions et Belles-Lettres 14, Paris, 1982
DOP	*Dumbarton Oaks Papers*
EHR	*English Historical Review*
Eracles	*L'Estoire d'Eracles Empereur et la Conqueste de la Terre d'Outremer*, in *RHCr. Occid.*, vols. I, II, Paris 1859
Ernoul-Bernard	*Chronique d'Ernoul et de Bernard le Trésorier*, ed. L. de Mas Latrie, Paris, 1871
JMH	*Journal of Medieval History*
MGH SS	*Monumenta Germaniae Historica, Scriptores*
MS	*I Templari: Mito e Storia. Atti del Convegno Internazionale di Studi alla Magione Templare di Poggibonsi-Siena, 29–31 Maggio 1987*, ed. G. Minnucci and F. Sardi, Siena, 1989
MSB	*Mélanges S. Bernard, 24e Congrès de l'Association Bourguignonne des Sociétés Savantes*, Dijon, 1953

NAL	*Nouvelles Acquisitions Latines*
OR	*Obituaire de la Commanderie du Temple de Reims*, ed. E. Barthélemy, in *Mélanges historiques. Collection des Documents inédits*, vol. IV, Paris, 1882, pp. 301–41
PL	*Patrologiae cursus completus. Series Latina*, ed. J. P. Migne, vols. 214–16, Paris, 1890–1
Potthast	*Regesta Pontificum Romanorum*, ed. A. Potthast, Berlin, 1873–5
Procès	*Le Procès des Templiers*, ed. J. Michelet, 2 vols., Paris, 1841
Provins	*Histoire et cartulaire des Templiers de Provins*, ed. V. Carrière, Paris, 1919.
RCI	Regestum Chartarum Italiae
RHCr.	*Recueil des Historiens des Croisades*
RHCr. Lois	*RHCr. Les Assises de Jérusalem*
RHCr. Occid.	*RHCr. Historiens Occidentaux*
RHCr. Or.	*RHCr. Historiens Orientaux*
RHG	*Recueil des Historiens de Gaul et de France*
Règle	*La Règle du Temple*, ed. H. de Curzon, Société de l'histoire de France, Paris, 1886
RIS	Rerum Italicarum Scriptores
ROL	*Revue de l'Orient latin*
RRH	*Regesta Regni Hierosolymitani*, ed. R. Röhricht, 2 vols., Innsbruck, 1893–1904
RS	Rolls Series
TOI	*Templari e Ospitalieri in Italia. La chiesa di San Bevignate a Perugia*, ed. M. Roncetti, P. Scarpellini, and F. Tommasi, Milan, 1987
TRHS	*Transactions of the Royal Historical Society*
WT	Guillaume de Tyr, *Chronique*, ed. R. B. C. Huygens, Corpus Christianorum. Continuatio Mediaevalis 63 and 63A, Turnhout, 1986

CHRONOLOGY

CHRONOLOGY

LIST OF GRAND MASTERS OF
THE TEMPLE

Hugh of Payns, 1119–*c.*1136
Robert of Craon, *c.*1136–1149
Everard des Barres, 1149–1152
Bernard of Tremelay, 1153
Andrew of Montbard, 1154–1156
Bertrand of Blancfort, 1156–1169
Philip of Nablus, 1169–1171
Odo of Saint-Amand, *c.*1171–1179
Arnold of Torroja, 1181–1184
Gerard of Ridefort, 1185–1189
Robert of Sablé, 1191–1192/3
Gilbert Erail, 1194–1200
Philip of Plessis, 1201–1209
William of Chartres, 1210–1218/19
Peter of Montaigu, 1219–1230/2
Armand of Périgord, *c.*1232–1244/6
William of Sonnac, *c.*1247–1250
Reginald of Vichiers, 1250–1256
Thomas Bérard, 1256–1273
William of Beaujeu, 1273–1291
Theobald Gaudin, 1291–1292/3
James of Molay, *c.*1293–1314

CHAPTER ONE

ORIGINS

In about 1340 Ludolph of Sudheim, a German priest on a pilgrimage to the Holy Land, came upon two elderly men on the shores of the Dead Sea. He entered into conversation with them and discovered that they were former Templars, captured when the city of Acre had fallen to the Mamluks in May 1291, who had since then been living in the mountains, cut off from all communication with Latin Christendom. They had wives and children and had survived by working in the sultan's service; they had no idea that the Order of the Temple had been suppressed in 1312 and that the Grand Master had been burnt to death as a relapsed heretic two years later. The men were from Burgundy and Toulouse and, within a year, were repatriated, together with their families. Despite the scandal of the suppression, they were honourably received at the papal court, and were allowed to live out the remainder of their existence in peace.[1] These two Templars were the almost forgotten remnants of what, barely a generation before, had appeared to be one of the most powerful monastic orders in Christendom. During the thirteenth century the Order may have had as many as 7,000 knights, sergeants and serving brothers, and priests, while its associate members, pensioners, officials, and subjects numbered many times that figure. By about 1300 it had built a network of at least 870 castles, preceptories, and subsidiary houses, examples of which could be found in almost every country in western Christendom. The extent of the Templar empire can be gauged from the fact that in 1318 pensions were being paid to former Templars in twenty-four French dioceses, as well as in York, London, Canterbury, Dublin, Tournai, Liège, Camin, Cologne, Magdeburg, Mainz, Castello, Asti, Milan, Bologna, Perugia, Naples, and Trani, in Nicosia in Cyprus, and in the kingdoms of Aragon and Mallorca.[2] In turn this network sustained fighting forces for the holy war in Palestine, Syria, Cyprus, and Iberia, together with some of the most formidable and impressive castles ever built. By the late twelfth century and during most of the thirteenth century the Order probably had about 600 knights and 2,000 sergeants on active service in the east[3] and by the 1230s it had built up a Mediterranean fleet capable of transporting men and supplies to Spain, Italy, and the Morea, and ultimately to 'Outremer', the lands beyond the sea. Moreover, its international structure and large resources had made the Templars ideal financial agents, whose expertise and capital were utilised by popes, kings, and nobles.

For medieval chroniclers, who were fond of discoursing upon the transitory nature of life on earth and the fleeting and illusory mirage of success, the rise and fall of the Templars was indeed an ideal paradigm, for this great corporation had found its origins in circumstances almost as humble as those of the two men discovered by Ludolph of Sudheim. In 1095, at Clermont in the Auvergne, Pope Urban II had urged Christians to take up arms to aid their brethren in the east, who were allegedly being harassed, tortured, and killed by a race of new barbarians called the Seljuk Turks. The call had been answered by several thousand warriors and peasants who had combined into the armies of the First Crusade. After many hardships and horrific experiences the better-equipped of the crusaders had managed to fight their way across Asia Minor and into Syria and thence southwards to Jerusalem, which they captured with terrible bloodshed in July 1099. But from the outset the Latins were bound to be at a severe numerical and logistical disadvantage in the east, a disadvantage exacerbated by the unwillingness of many of them to stay once Jerusalem had been taken. Moreover, the fragmented nature of the crusading forces obliged them to adopt *ad hoc* solutions to immediate governmental and ecclesiastical problems. Nevertheless, by the end of the second decade of the twelfth century much had been achieved: the states of Antioch, Tripoli, and Jerusalem, along the coast, and Edessa, inland to the north-east of Antioch, had been established; most of the vital coastal cities had been captured, leaving only Tyre and Ascalon in Muslim hands; and under the forceful King Baldwin I, who had seized power in 1100 after the early death of his brother, Godfrey of Bouillon, a solid monarchical power had been created.

Yet, although a framework had been erected, many problems remained and nowhere were they more evident than in the conquerors' inability to secure the safety of travellers and pilgrims in the regions supposedly under Frankish control. Fulcher of Chartres, chaplain to Baldwin I and a participant in the First Crusade, chose to make his home in Outremer, and his honest and observant chronicle offers invaluable evidence of conditions in the east under the first generation of settlers. At no time between 1100 and Fulcher's death in about 1127 were the roads around Jerusalem and the adjacent holy places secure. In 1100 the route between Ramla and Jerusalem was infested by robbers who hid in the caves along the way and preyed upon the pilgrims coming up from the port of Jaffa. A quarter of a century later anybody who ventured out of a fortified place around Jerusalem was still in severe danger of ambush either from the Egyptians and Ethiopians in the south or from the Turks in the north. According to Fulcher, the populace lived in a state of perpetual insecurity, always attentive to the trumpet blast which warned them of danger.[4]

Visitors to the kingdom were naturally deeply apprehensive (see figure 1). A Russian abbot called Daniel was one of those who described the dangers and hardships during his pilgrimage in 1106 and 1107. He was a man determined to see all that he could, an ambition which exposed him to even greater perils. The church of St George at Lydda was only about six miles from Jaffa, but was very vulnerable to sorties of the Egyptians from Ascalon. 'And there are many springs here; travellers rest by the water but with great fear, for it is a deserted place and nearby is the town of Ascalon from which Saracens sally forth and kill travellers on these roads. There is a great fear too going up from that place into the hills.' If the traveller reached Jerusalem, he might later wish to visit the River Jordan, but 'it is a very difficult road and dangerous and waterless, for the hills are high and rocky and there are many brigands in those fearful hills and valleys' (see plate 1). On another occasion, returning to Jerusalem after a visit to Hebron, about twenty-three miles to the south, he says: 'there is a very high rocky mountain and on it a great dense forest and there is a way over that terrible mountain but it is difficult to pass along it because the Saracens have a great fortress there from which they attack. And if anyone in a small party tries to travel that road he cannot, but God granted me a good and numerous escort

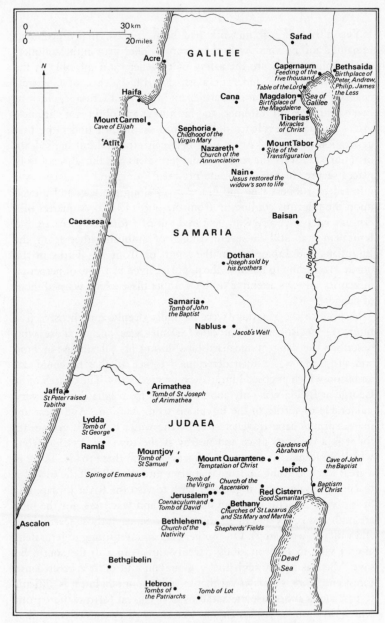

Figure 1 Popular pilgrim sites in the crusader period.

4

Plate 1 Maldoim (The Red Cistern) and the road between
Jerusalem and Jericho. The Templars instituted regular patrols
along this route to protect pilgrims visiting the Jordan.

and thus I was able to pass that terrible place without hindrance.' Most striking of all is the abbot's description of his visit to Galilee, in the course of which he had to pass near the town of Baisan. Here he conveys a sense of brooding menace which is eloquent testimony to the feelings of vulnerability experienced by pilgrims like himself:

And this place is very dreadful and dangerous. Seven rivers flow from this town of Bashan and great reeds grow along these rivers and many tall palm trees stand about the town like a dense forest. This place is terrible and difficult of access for here live fierce pagan Saracens who attack travellers at the fords on these rivers. And lions are found here in great numbers. This place is near the River Jordan and a great watermeadow [?] lies between the Jordan and the town of Bashan and the rivers flow from Bashan into the Jordan and there are many lions at that place.[5]

The formation of the Templars arose from a desire to provide protection for such pilgrims. No contemporary thought them sufficiently significant to record their first establishment, but three chroniclers of the second half of the twelfth century, William, Archbishop of Tyre (died c. 1186), Michael the Syrian, Jacobite Patriarch of Antioch (died 1199), and Walter Map, Archdeacon of Oxford (died between 1208 and 1210), writing in the light of the Order's later importance, gave their versions of how this came about.[6] William is by far the most important of these. He was born in the east in about 1130, but was absent in the west between about 1146 and 1165. Nevertheless, he diligently investigated events which occurred before his lifetime by reading the sources and questioning those who might know. However his view of the Templars is coloured by the development of an acute dislike of what he saw as their unfair manipulation and exploitation of their privileges in his own time. Michael the Syrian included details not found in William of Tyre, but is generally regarded as less reliable than William when describing matters outside his own experience and times, while Walter Map – the farthest removed from the events – is known as a man for whom a good story usually took precedence over historical inquiry.

Under the year 1118 William says that 'certain noble men of knightly order, devoted to God, pious and God-fearing', the two most important of whom were Hugh of Payns (in Champagne) and Godfrey of Saint-Omer (in Picardy), took vows of poverty, chastity, and obedience at the hands of Warmund of Picquigny, Patriarch of Jerusalem. They promised to devote themselves to God's service in the manner of regular canons, and King Baldwin II, who had succeeded his cousin at Easter 1118, gave them a base in his palace, to the south side of the Temple of the Lord, which was the name given by the Franks to the Dome of the Rock. At this time the king was resident in the al-Aqsa mosque at the southern end of the Haram al-Sharif or Temple platform in Jerusalem, for the crusaders believed this to be the site of Solomon's Temple and therefore an appropriate dwelling for the king. In addition the canons of the Temple of the Lord gave them a square near the al-Aqsa where they could follow the monastic offices, while a number of benefices were granted to them by the king and his nobles and the patriarch and other prelates, the income from which was intended to feed and clothe them. The distinctive feature of this fraternity, however, was the duty 'enjoined on them by the lord patriarch and the other bishops for the remission of their sins', which was that 'they should maintain, as far as they could, the roads and highways against the ambushes of thieves and attackers, especially in regard to the safety of pilgrims'.

It is not clear from William's account who originally had the idea of using these men for this purpose, although the implication is that at first they intended simply to adopt a penitential way of life as a kind of lay confraternity, and that later a more active role was suggested to them. Michael the Syrian says that it was the king, a man acutely aware of the deficiencies of the military establishment, who persuaded Hugh of Payns and thirty companions 'to serve in the knighthood, with those attached to him, rather than becoming a monk, in order to work to save his only soul, and to guard these places against robbers'. Walter Map creates a vignette about a knight called Paganus from a village in Burgundy, who took it upon himself to protect pilgrims whom he frequently saw attacked at a horse-pool not far from Jerusalem. When the numbers of the enemy became too great for him on his own, he obtained a hall from the canons of the Temple of the Lord and devoted himself to recruiting more men from among the knights who came on pilgrimage to Jerusalem. They lived frugal, chaste, and sober lives. Finally, nearer to the events than any of these chroniclers is a charter of William, Castellan of Saint-Omer, and perhaps a relative of Godfrey, in 1137, 'to the knights of the Temple, whom divine providence deputed to the defence of the land of Jerusalem and the protection of pilgrims with the counsel of the Patriarch Warmund and the barons'.[7]

Certainly the creation of a permanent guard for pilgrim travellers must have seemed to both king and patriarch an ideal complement to the activities of the Hospitallers, who provided shelter and medical care for pilgrims. They had been formed as an annex to the monastery of Santa Maria Latina in about 1080, and after the Frankish conquest in 1099 quickly gained royal favour, grants of property and, in 1113, papal recognition. While it seems certain that the Templars influenced the Hospitallers to take on a military role during the 1130s, it is equally likely that initially the Hospital provided Hugh of Payns and Godfrey of Saint-Omer with an effective example of what could be done to help pilgrims. Templars, indeed, appear on only four charters in the Kingdom of Jerusalem before 1128 and two of these are concerned with the affairs of the Hospital. In December 1120, Hugh of Payns was a witness to Baldwin II's confirmation of the privileges of the Hospital, while Robert, 'knight of the Temple', is among the witnesses to a charter of Bernard, Bishop of Nazareth, dated October 1125, exempting the Hospital from payment of tithe in his diocese.[8] Further indirect evidence of the links, at least in the minds of contemporaries, can be found in a charter of Fulk, Count of Anjou (who was very familiar with the Kingdom of Jerusalem), which can be dated soon after 22 September 1127, at Saumur, where among the witnesses is 'Rotbertus Burgundio, miles Sancti Stephani Jerusalem'. This is almost certainly Robert of Craon, who succeeded Hugh of Payns as Master of the Order in about 1136. Here, however, he is associated with St Stephen's Church, outside Jerusalem near the Damascus Gate, which was in fact a dependency of Santa Maria Latina.[9]

It is possible to be more precise about the date of the establishment of the Templars. Among the early grants to the Order was one by Thierry, Count of Flanders, dated 13 September 1128, which states that it was made in the ninth year from the Order's foundation.[10] As this grant was actually made in the presence of Hugh of Payns, it must be more reliable evidence than the year 1118 given by William of Tyre, whose reputation for faulty chronology is well known and who was writing over half a century later.[11] Nor is William consistent, for he says later in the same passage that the Council of Troyes,

8

at which the Templars received official papal recognition, occurred in their ninth year. Jean Michel, the scribe who wrote down the council's proceedings, dates his record as the Feast of St Hilary (13 January) 1128, 'the ninth year from the beginning of the aforesaid militia', information which, like Count Thierry's scribe, he must have obtained from Hugh of Payns himself, since he was present at the council.[12] As it has been shown by Rudolf Hiestand that this date should be corrected to January 1129, in accordance with the contemporary French practice of beginning the year on 25 March,[13] the official date of the foundation, according to information gained from the Templars themselves, must fall between 14 January and 13 September 1120.

The most likely occasion for their acceptance in the east was, as Hiestand suggests, at the assembly of prelates and secular leaders held at Nablus in January 1120, which issued a series of decrees on the 23rd of the month. The supposition is reinforced by the fact that the Christian settlers in Outremer were experiencing a period of severe crisis at this time, and the assembly at Nablus had been called in an atmosphere heavy with contrition and penitence.[14] A dramatic letter from the Patriarch Warmund and Gerard, Prior of the Holy Sepulchre, written at about this time, appealed to Diego Gelmirez, Archbishop of Compostella, and his people, to send help in the form of men, money, and food as soon as possible. They were, said Warmund, being attacked on all sides by Saracens from Baghdad, Ascalon, Tyre, and Damascus. The kingdom had become so unsafe that no one dared to venture outside the walls of Jerusalem without an armed escort, while the Saracens had become so bold that they came up to the gates of the city itself.[15] The group may well have first been formed in the course of the previous year, perhaps in reaction to a particularly shocking incident at Easter when a large party of about 700 pilgrims had been attacked in the barren and mountainous region between Jerusalem and the Jordan. Having witnessed the famous miracle of the holy fire at the Church of the Holy Sepulchre, they set out, according to the German monastic chronicler, Albert of Aachen, 'in joy and with a cheerful heart', but when they reached an isolated place they were ambushed and, since they were unarmed and weakened by fasting and the journey, they were an easy target. Three hundred were killed and sixty captured. Although King Baldwin quickly sent out a posse of armed knights,

9

they failed to make contact because the attackers had already retreated to Tyre and Ascalon.[16]

However, despite the evident support of king and patriarch, according to William of Tyre the early Templars did not have much initial success, having recruited only nine members by the time of the Council of Troyes, and remaining so poor that they were able to dress only in the clothes donated to them by the pious, which meant that they had no distinctive 'occupational' garments of their own. Moreover, according to Fulcher of Chartres, the Franks did not have sufficient resources to maintain 'the Temple of Solomon' properly and the building became dilapidated,[17] so the adjacent area given over to Templar accommodation probably had the same cast-off air as their clothing. It was indeed a formidable and stressful undertaking and there are signs of failing morale and loss of belief in the legitimacy of their mission among the Templars at this time which hint at very real difficulties. The tradition of humble and poor beginnings was certainly accepted by the later Order as established fact, as can be seen by the symbolic representation of poverty on their seal which shows two knights riding on one horse (see plate 7), although the asceticism of the Cistercians, channelled through St Bernard, the famous Abbot of Clairvaux, may also have contributed to this self-image. So too was the idea of nine original founders, which seems still to have been embedded in the Order's collective memory in the middle of the thirteenth century. In the lunette of the apse inside the important Templar church of San Bevignate at Perugia, built and decorated between 1256 and 1262, nine stars are shown around the three crosses painted in the upper register.[18]

Nevertheless, there is an element of topos in these representations. William of Tyre had reasons of his own for stressing the initial humility, for he draws a moral from this when he compares it to the allegedly proud Order of his own day. Although for a long time, he says, they carried out their proper functions, eventually they neglected humility, 'which is known to be the guardian of all the virtues'. Moreover, there is a suspicious symmetry about the nine members in nine years, which is contradicted by Michael the Syrian's figure of thirty and by the intrinsic improbability that the papacy would have allowed a new order which had failed to attract larger numbers than this to be confirmed. They had, as well, regular if modest incomes: a charter of the Holy Sepulchre of 1160 records that the Templars exchanged an annual allowance of 150 *besants* that they had been accustomed to receive from the canons for three *casalia*.[19] It is evident too that they quickly attracted the attention of powerful visitors to the kingdom in the persons of Fulk V, Count of Anjou, who seems to have become a kind of associate of the Templars during his pilgrimage in 1120, and Hugh, Count of Champagne, who actually joined as a full member, probably late in the year 1125. According to the chronicler of St Evroult, Orderic Vitalis, on his return home, Fulk granted them an annual revenue of thirty *livres angevines*, and his example was followed by several other French lords.[20] The connections with the Count of Champagne were even stronger, for Payns is only about eight miles north of Troyes, and Hugh can be identified as its lord in 1113. He was a member of 'the old aristocracy' of the county, who witnessed the count's charters, filled his offices, and took part in his assemblies and military expeditions.[21] Hugh of Champagne, in turn, had close ties with Bernard of Clairvaux. Although Bernard regretted the loss of the count's presence and support, he nevertheless congratulated him on exchanging his position as count for that of an ordinary knight and for shedding his riches to become a pauper.[22] Less prominent but nevertheless of high social standing was William of Poitiers, from the family of the Counts of Valentinois in Lower Provence. In what may be the earliest surviving charter in the west involving the Templars, perhaps dating from 1124, this young man, supported by older relatives, acted on behalf of the Templars by granting the church of St Bartholomew of La Motte-Palayson to the church of St Mary of Palayson and the monks of St Victor, but retaining an annual revenue for the Order of eight *setiers* of grain from the church's incomes. This transaction was presumably made because the Templars in the east did not feel capable of holding such a church at this time.[23] Such influential connections suggest greater early support than William of Tyre allows.

In Jerusalem itself King Baldwin II remained a strong supporter, for their objectives fitted well into his plans. Since at least 1126 he had been pursuing with some vigour a 'western policy', designed to overcome two immediate and fundamental problems: the lack of a male heir to succeed him and the military weaknesses of the kingdom. Baldwin had four daughters but no sons, and in an assembly, probably held early in 1127, he and the barons had decided to offer in marriage the hand of his eldest daughter, Melisende, to Fulk of Anjou. William of Bures, Prince of Galilee, and Guy of Brisbarre, Lord of Beirut, were deputed to lead an embassy to negotiate with the count.[24] According to William of Tyre, the king also sent Hugh of Payns to the west specifically to recruit *potentes* for a campaign against Damascus.[25] Hugh is last recorded in Outremer at Acre in May 1125, where he was witness to the extremely important royal confirmation of the grant of privileges to the Venetians at Tyre which had previously been made by the Patriarch Warmund when Baldwin II had been in Muslim captivity. Here, for the first time, he is designated 'Master of the Temple'.[26] Since both William of Bures and Hugh of Payns were in Le Mans by mid April 1128, it is probable that the embassy to Fulk and the Templar group sailed together during the autumn passage of 1127.

This was a policy the king had tried before. Just as the patriarch had written to Archbishop Diego Gelmirez, so too, in 1120, following the defeat and death of Roger of Antioch at the 'Field of Blood' (near al-Athārib, between Antioch and Aleppo) in June, 1119, Baldwin had sent to Pope Calixtus II and the Venetians for help, and had been rewarded with the capture of Tyre in 1124, as well as by a small influx of crusaders from France, Germany, and Bohemia.[27] But the crusader states remained short of manpower. Baldwin himself had suffered captivity between April 1123 and June 1124, while his three-month siege of the strategically important city of Aleppo, at the end of the year, failed in the face of a numerically superior Muslim coalition.[28] In the same way he may have prepared the ground for the recruiting tour of Hugh of Payns by writing to Bernard of Clairvaux before October 1126. He explained to him that the brothers of the Temple 'desired to obtain apostolic confirmation and to have a certain rule of life', and that he was sending two knights, Andrew and Gondemar, 'in order that they might obtain approval of their order from the pontiff, and incline his spirit to initiating subsidy and help for us against the enemies of the faith'. These enemies were rising up 'in order to supplant and subvert our kingdom'. He added that he would be grateful if Bernard could use his influence similarly with the secular rulers of Europe.[29] The king may well have had reason to believe that Bernard would be sympathetic. In late 1124 or early 1125, in a letter to Pope Calixtus II, Bernard had voiced his opposition to a plan by Arnold, Abbot of the

Cistercian house of Morimond, to travel to the Holy Land. Among other objections he had told the pope: 'If, as has been related to us, he says that he wishes to propagate the observances of our Order in that land, and for that reason to lead a multitude of brothers with him, who cannot see that the necessities there are fighting knights not singing and wailing monks?'[30]

The meeting at Troyes was therefore preceded by a vigorous campaign to solicit donations and to attract recruits and other crusaders. Hugh of Payns and his colleagues naturally handed over their own possessions; in the words of Joscelin, Bishop of Soissons, who assisted at the Council of Troyes, they devoted 'not only their patrimonies, but their souls to the defence of Christianity'.[31] At the same time the network of contacts was activated to enable the Templars to lay the foundations of a secure landed base in the west. As early as October 1127, at Provins, Theobald, Count of Blois, the nephew and successor of Count Hugh in Champagne, granted the Templars a house, grange, and meadow, together with a tenement of one carucate, at Barbonne, near Sézanne to the north-east of Provins, as well as conceding to his own vassals the right to make gifts from their own lands, provided this involved no loss of service.[32] At about the same time, William Clito, Count of Flanders, conceded to the Templars the right to feudal reliefs in his lands.[33] Both counts were men of significance in the politics of northern Europe, for Theobald, holder of two great fiefs, was the most powerful of the Capetian tenants-in-chief,[34] while William Clito, the son of Robert Curthose, former Duke of Normandy and leading participant in the First Crusade, had been supported in his claims to Flanders by King Louis VI himself. Although William Clito lasted a little more than a year, for he was killed in battle on 27 May 1128, his successor, Thierry of Alsace, was equally favourable to the Order and quick to make a similar grant of reliefs in September 1128.[35] Hugh of Payns himself went to Anjou, where he and William of Bures witnessed the taking of the cross by Fulk on 31 May. At the same time Hugh mediated in a quarrel between Hugh of Amboise, a leading vassal of the count, and the monks of Marmoutier, thus facilitating the departure of Hugh of Amboise on crusade.[36] The Master also received grants from various individuals in Poitou – two marks of silver on the port of Beauvoir, horses and armour, and a salt-marsh – but it is not clear where these grants were made.[37]

13

It seems probable that Hugh was still in Le Mans on 17 June, on the occasion of the marriage of Geoffrey, Fulk's eldest son, to Matilda, heiress to Henry I, which was part of the comprehensive settlement of the affairs of Normandy, Anjou, and Jerusalem. This, among other consequences, made Fulk's future accession to the throne of Jerusalem possible. At this time Hugh may have made contact with Henry I, or his representatives, for the Anglo-Saxon Chronicle says that the king 'received him with great honour and gave him great treasures, consisting of gold and silver'. He was sent to England where further donations were received and he even visited Scotland. 'He summoned people out to Jerusalem, and then there went with him and after him so large a number of people as never had done since the first expedition in the days of Pope Urban.'[38] The chronology of Hugh's movements is not entirely clear, but it seems probable that his visit to England and Scotland took place in the summer of 1128 and that he had returned to Cassel in Flanders by mid September, where, together with Godfrey of Saint-Omer, he received the grants of Thierry of Flanders and his vassals.

The convocation of the Council of Troyes in January 1129 was the climax of this tour. Although the date of the council has generally been given as January 1128, it was presided over by the papal legate, Matthew du Remois, Cardinal-Bishop of Albano, whose itinerary Rudolf Hiestand has convincingly related to the year 1129. Hiestand also shows that it was almost impossible for the agenda to be prepared and the protocols sent out in time for a meeting at the beginning of 1128. The reference to the Patriarch of Jerusalem as Stephen of Chartres in the Rule drawn up at Troyes points to the same conclusion, for his predecessor, Warmund of Picquigny, did not die until July 1128.[39] Moreover, a meeting in 1129 gives more time for news of the Order to spread and for contacting those important secular and ecclesiastical lords so essential to the launching of the Order in the west. This is reflected in the distinguished attendance. St Bernard himself speaks of the heavy pressures upon him to come, despite the fact that he was suffering from an acute fever.[40] In all there were seven abbots (including Stephen Harding of Cîteaux), two archbishops (those of Sens and Reims), and ten bishops, as well as Count Theobald and William II, Count of Nevers.

Hugh of Payns described 'the manner and observance' of his *militia* in a speech before the council on the Feast of St Hilary, 13 January. Basically they adhered to a small number of simple precepts: attendance at the offices of the choir together with the regular canons, communal meals, plain clothing, unostentatious appearance, no contact with women. They differed from the canons, however, in that they were frequently on outside service and therefore knights were allowed one horse, later increased to three, and a small number of servants, while at such times attendance at the offices was replaced by the recitation of set numbers of paternosters. All owed obedience to the Master, although the Order as a whole was under the jurisdiction of the Patriarch of Jerusalem.[41]

These informal regulations formed the raw material of the Latin Rule, which consisted of seventy-two clauses. According to Jean Michel, who describes himself as 'the humble scribe of the present pages', the fathers at the council critically assessed the Master's account, praising or rejecting as seemed appropriate. This was a process to which even the seculars present, whom Jean Michel describes as 'non-literate', contributed by 'scrutinising with the most intense care that which was best, [and] condemning that which seemed to them absurd'.[42] Therefore, although St Bernard was the guiding hand in the drafting, content, and, very evidently in places, the actual wording of the new Rule,[43] it was clearly subject initially to a fairly exhaustive process of committee discussion. In this a vast weight of experience of the religious life was brought to bear, but there was comparatively little understanding of the exigencies of campaigning in the east. The result is a monastic Rule which very much reflects the contemporary ascetic drive and anti-materialistic longings which had created the reformed orders of the late eleventh century, in particular the Cistercians, but which is less successful in adapting these precepts to the Templars' struggle with the infidel. The beginning of the Rule, which lays down how the Templars should hear the divine office, encapsulates the outlook of these men and of St Bernard in particular:

You, indeed, renouncing your own wills and others with you fighting for the high King for the safety of souls to that end with horses and arms, in pious and pure affection should strive universally to hear matins and the whole of the divine service, in accordance with canonical institution and the custom of the regular masters of the holy city. For that reason it is especially owed by you, venerable brothers, since despising the light of the present life, being contemptuous of the torment which is of your bodies, you have promised in perpetuity to hold cheap worldly matters for the love of God: restored by the divine flesh, and consecrated, enlightened and confirmed in the Lord's precepts, after the consumption of the divine mystery no one should be afraid to fight, but be prepared for the crown.[44]

A secular knight could petition to join, having given proof of his seriousness, the period of probation depending 'upon the consideration and foresight of the Master in accordance with the honesty of his life'. Boys, though, were not to be promised in the way that was customary in the older Benedictine Orders; instead their parents should wait until they were of an age at which they could carry arms against 'the enemies of Christ in the Holy Land'. White vestments were conceded to all professed knights, symbolising that they have placed 'the dark life' behind them and have entered a state of perpetual celibacy, 'for unless each knight perseveres in chastity, he cannot come to perpetual rest nor see God, as is testified by St Paul'. Otherwise their general lifestyle reflected the modesty of the early customs: plain and undifferentiated clothing, tonsured heads, a pallet, blanket, and coverlet each for bedding, communal and silent meals during which there should be a holy reading. Particular abhorrence was expressed for what Bernard evidently despised in contemporary knightly fashion: excessive hair, immoderately long clothes, and pointed, lace-up shoes, a theme to which he was later to return. Knights were to sleep in shirt and breeches and there was always to be a light during the hours of darkness. Diet was closely regulated. There were two main meals a day, in the late morning and the evening, although a light collation could be authorised by the Master before compline, the last of the monastic hours, at sunset. Since it 'is known to be a corruption of the body', meat was allowed three times a week only, except for the great festivals and the recognised periods of fasting. Otherwise vegetable dishes or what is called 'cooked pottage' were thought sufficient. After the meals thanks were to be rendered to the Lord, while anything left over was to be distributed to the servants and paupers, although untouched loaves were to be kept back. In addition to such informal hand-outs, the Rule laid down that a tenth of all daily bread should be given in alms, for 'to the poor is the first place in the Kingdom of God'. Conversation was strictly limited to functional needs and 'scurrilous and shameful words' and laughter were altogether prohibited, regulations especially relevant to a recurring theme in the Rule: the need to avoid displays of anger, malice, or grumbling, or reminiscences about past sexual conquests. 'Every idle word is known to generate sin.'

Joining the Order represented an abrogation of will, and individual freedom of action was therefore closely circumscribed: casual discussions with outsiders, personal possessions, letters or gifts sent or received, were among the activities allowed only with the Master's permission. Discipline was enforced by a system of penances in the monastic fashion ranging from minor transgressions dealt with by the Master to actions which could lead to expulsion. 'It is necessary', says the Rule, 'that the unwholesome sheep be removed from the society of the brothers of fidelity.' Rigid as this structure might seem to be, however, there was room for discretion for, as an experienced abbot, Bernard recognised the need for some flexibility. Allowances were made for brothers who were tired, ill, or aged; major issues were discussed and decided upon in chapter, presided over by the Master; and brothers obliged to travel outside the house were to 'try to preserve the Rule as far as their strength permits'. Although the Master would soon become one of the leading members of the military establishment in the Kingdom of Jerusalem, in 1129 he was presented very much in terms of the traditional Benedictine abbot, enjoined by his Rule to exercise moderation in all things: 'The Master ought to hold the staff and the rod in his hand, namely the staff by which he sustains the weaknesses of other men, also the rod by which with zeal for rectitude he strikes the vices of those who err.'

In matters such as these Bernard and his colleagues could draw on their own experiences, but in tackling the regulation of the military functions of the Order they were breaking new ground, and while they were aware that such responsibilities would be costly they had little to offer in the way of practical military injunctions. Each knight was allowed three horses and a squire, but his equipment should not be decorated with gold, silver, or elaborate coverings, 'for the splendour of the colour and decoration should not be seen by others as arrogance'. The traditional aristocratic sports of hawking and hunting were forbidden, excepting only hunting the lion, seen as a symbol of evil. St Bernard had devoted his whole adult life to the diminution of such materialistic attitudes, but he nevertheless did recognise that the Temple was 'a new type of Order in the holy places', one which mixed knighthood with religion, and that, unlike the Cistercians, it needed to possess houses, lands, serfs, and tithes, and was entitled to proper legal protection against what the Rule calls 'the innumerable persecutors of the holy Church'.

Bernard evidently saw professed knights as the core of the Order, for the Rule has relatively little to say about other elements. It is clear, though, that provision was made for knights to serve *ad terminum*, that is, for a set period before returning to secular life, as Fulk of Anjou appears to have done informally just after the Order was founded. *Fratres conjugati*, or married brothers, were also permitted, although if such a man died before his wife she was entitled to a proportion of their property for her sustenance. Neither group was supposed to wear the white mantle, brown or black being considered more appropriate; nor were those called by the Rule *famuli*, who were persons apparently linked to the Order so that they could obtain certain spiritual benefits. One clause refers to the provision of victuals and clothes of chaplains serving the Order, but they do not seem to have been regarded as full members at this time. Two passing references are made to the existence of *clientes*, translated in the French version as *sergens*, the sergeants or serving brothers who were in the future to form such a substantial element in the Order. These too wore brown or black mantles and, like the knights, could join *ad terminum*. No sisters were to be admitted, 'since the ancient enemy expelled many from the right road to Paradise by the society of women'.[45]

With papal approval secured and the drafting of the Rule under way, Hugh of Payns was in a position to return to Jerusalem. He probably accompanied Count Fulk in the spring of 1129 and would therefore have been able to witness the count's marriage to Melisende before Whitsun (2 June).[46] He was certainly back in the kingdom by November 1129, when he and the men he had brought with him took part in the siege of Damascus.[47] The establishment of the Templars in the west reflects an evident perception of the need to create a regular network of support which would provide the crusader states with fresh forces, a steady income, and supplies of food, clothing, and arms. In the 1120s and 1130s it may well have seemed to the Latins of the east that an expedition on the scale of the First Crusade would never occur again and that the continued existence of their settlements needed the creation of permanent logistical support systems rather than bursts of crusading enthusiasm.

During the half century which separates the great expeditions of the First and Second Crusades the typical crusader arrived in the east as part of a relatively small unit, perhaps linked to a particular lord or kin group, or drawn from a specific geographical area.[48] Moreover, the distinction between crusader and armed pilgrim was seldom very evident or perhaps even very conscious. The incorporation into the Templar structure of provision for such crusader/pilgrims to serve for set periods was a recognition of contemporary realities and an attempt to harness such forces and individuals within a more systematic framework. The acceptance of the Order at Troyes in 1129 was the central event of the Templars' early history, but at the same time it was as much part of Baldwin II's policy for the east as his invitation to Fulk of Anjou.

Donations in the west took the form of estates and buildings, together with dependent populations, as well as financial and jurisdictional concessions. These laid the foundations of a provincial structure which, during the next twenty years, took shape under a growing hierarchy of officials. The basis of this landed power remained in areas where the Order was first established in Francia, Provence, Iberia, and England (as the titles of the earliest officials show), although the Templars were established in Rome by 1138,[49] and during the thirteenth century the Order's preceptories in Italy became increasingly important, while it also held possessions in Germany, Dalmatia, and the Morea. Just as there was no established Rule for a military order, so too there was no organisational model which the Templars could follow, for the monasteries of the early middle ages were individual houses which, although they might have dependent priories on outlying estates, did not conceive of themselves as a unified order like the Templars. It is true that by the late eleventh century Cluny had developed a vast monastic empire, but it had been created so haphazardly that, although it was theoretically centred upon Cluny itself, the complex interrelationships of its houses almost defy description and it had nothing to offer the Templars by way of example. The Cistercians were more consistent, for their system of affiliation between abbeys and their daughter houses established distinct 'families' within the larger structure. In this way they may have had some influence on the Templars, for as their estates expanded there is evidence that they too formed their houses into groups. Nevertheless, the Cistercian system was quite unsuitable for adoption in its entirety, since mother houses were often far removed from their daughters. This would have been impractical for an order which needed to organise its establishments to act as conduits for the supply of those regions directly facing Islam in Outremer and Iberia.[50]

Although under the first generation of leaders the titles and duties of the Templar officials were sometimes inconsistent and vague, it is clear that from the outset a decision was taken to organise the Order on a provincial basis largely determined by geopolitical realities. Here again the influence of the Hospital is evident, for this was the only other order which had a comparable structure at this time, having established its first province by about 1120.[51] In 1130 Payen of Montdidier, one of Hugh of Payns' early companions and a participant at Troyes, is described as 'a devoted knight of the Temple of the Lord, to whom Hugh, Master of the knighthood of the Temple, had at that time committed the care of their things in these parts'.[52] The grant was at Noyon (Oise) on the northern edge of the Ile-de-France and 'these parts' seems to have meant 'France' as it was then understood, that is north of the Loire. Farther south, in Provence, Toulouse, and Aragon many grants were made to Hugh of Rigaud who by 1133 is being described as 'procurator' of the Order.[53] He had received property on behalf of the Order as early as November 1128 at Douzens in the Aude Valley, east of Carcassonne; by 1132 he was associated with another Templar called Robert, who is described as 'seneschal' or 'butler' of the Order.[54] In 1136 Hugh of Rigaud seems to have been succeeded by Arnold of Bedocio, who is called master, minister, or *bailli*, and received numerous donations in the counties of Barcelona, Toulouse, and Provence down to 1139.[55] The relationship of these men to William of Baudement, called 'Master of the Temple' in a grant which is not later than 1132, and William Falco who in the next year is described as having had custody of 'the alms of the knighthood of the Temple beyond the sea' in the grant of a village near Provins in the County of Champagne,[56] is by no means clear. Nevertheless a broad division of authority between northern France and Provence and north-east Spain seems to be emerging. By 1141, in a grant made in Brittany, William Falco had become 'Master of the Temple', and may possibly have taken over the role of Payen of Montdidier. From 1138 Payen himself was operating in England, where the rate of acquisitions had increased markedly since Stephen of Blois had gained the throne in 1135.[57]

By this time the overall north–south divison was quite clear, with the Master in France apparently regarded as the senior official in the west. The major grant made by Raymond Berenguer, Count of Barcelona and ruler of Aragon, at Gerona in November 1143, was received 'into the hands of the lord Everard, Master of France, and the venerable Peter of Rovira, Master in Provence and in certain parts of Spain'.[58] Everard des Barres held this position until he became Grand Master in 1149 during the Second Crusade, while Peter of Rovira was very active as Master in Provence, Aragon, and Barcelona, until 1158, his area of authority now apparently partly determined by the political union of Aragon and Catalonia which had occurred in 1137.[59] Even so, titles remain ambiguous: in 1146 Peter of Rovira and his brother Berengar are described as 'masters of the knighthood on this side of the sea', while a brother Oliver makes a single appearance as Master in Spain.[60] Moreover, terms like master, minister, and bailli were widely used, but without specific designation of an area of responsibility. In practice, Templars described in this way do seem to have had wider responsibilities than the preceptors of particular houses, but to rank below provincial masters like Everard des Barres and Peter of Rovira. In Portugal, where the Order had received donations as early as 1128, there is a reference to a brother Suerio as 'minister' in 1145, and to Galdinus as 'master' in 1148.[61] Berengar of Rovira, although at various times described as minister, bailli, and servant, as well as 'master on this side of the sea' and 'master of the knights', acted almost exclusively at Douzens and in the County of Barcelona, the place of his origin.[62]

Preceptors of local houses and convents also begin to appear in the late 1130s. By this time, for example, a house had been established at Coulours in Burgundy to the east of Sens, where the preceptor is rather ponderously described as 'Raymond, who had been sent by the Knights of the Temple and placed in authority at the aforesaid place'.[63] This suggests that a resident administrator was established once enough property had been accumulated in a particular area. Between 1139 and 1150 preceptors were placed at Marmoutier, near Tours; farther up the Loire at Orléans; at La Neuville in the diocese of Châlons-sur-Marne; at Richerenches and Roaix in Provence, north-east of Orange; at Rodez in the County of Toulouse; at

Willoughton c.1150
Temple
Cowley
c.1139
Temple
Guiting
1147
Temple
Dinsley c.1147
Cressing
1137
London c.1128
Shipley
1134-9
Sommereux 1150
Laon 1140-1
Beauvais
1140-1
Paris 1146
Coulours 1135-42
La Neuville
1132-42
Nantes
1141
Orléans
1148
Marmoutier 1144
La Rochelle
1139-40
Richerenches 1136
La Sèlve
c.1150
Rodez
1150
Roaix 1138-41
Avignon
c.1150
Albenga
1143-5
Saint-Gilles c.1150
Pézenas 1140
Arles 1143-6
Siena
1148
Montsaunès
c.1140
Douzens 1133
Braga
1148
Monzón 1143
Chalamera 1143
Mas-Deu 1137
Rome
1138
Grañena 1130
Novillas 1739
Palau 1140
Ambel
1141
Remolins
1143
Barbará
1132
Soure
1128
Corbins
1143
Santarém
1147

0   1000 k.
0   500 miles

Figure 2 Templar preceptories and castles in the West to 1150.

22

Novillas on the River Ebro in Aragon; at Palau, near Barcelona; and at Braga in Portugal.[64] There are similar signs of the Templar presence in Italy, where, although the terminology seems rather archaic, the Templars concerned are unmistakably holders of delegated authority. Near Albenga, on the Ligurian coast west of Genoa, for example, Oberto, described as a *missus* of the Temple of Jerusalem, bought half a manse from Lombarda, daughter of Oddo of Legeno, in April 1143. This seems to have been used to form the nucleus of a preceptory, for the Order made further purchases in the area and, in 1145, its two representatives, Hugh and William Normanno, are designated *missi de casa Templi* (see figure 2).[65]

The presence of an embryonic hierarchy of officials was necessary because the new Order had attracted a wide base of support, both socially and geographically. Clerics ranging from archbishops and abbots to simple priests set a prominent example. Probably late in 1131, Raymond, Archbishop of Reims, wrote to Milon, Bishop of Thérouanne, to tell him of a charitable concession made to the Order in the latter's diocese:

In a council recently held at Reims [19 October, 1131] by the common counsel and assent of our venerable brothers the bishops, the abbot of Clairvaux and many other religious persons, we established and confirmed that, in the chapel of Ypres, in the place which is called Obstal, every year on the three rogation days [Monday, Tuesday and Wednesday before Ascension Day] and the five other days continuously following, solemn masses should be celebrated, and whatever is made in oblations during these eight days, will be for the knighthood of the Temple of Jerusalem; however, at other times no other divine offices will be celebrated there, except by the canons of the church of St Martin of Ypres.[66]

The Bishops of Soissons and Angers granted them burial privileges. In 1133 Joscelin of Soissons conceded that in front of the church at Cerches the Templars 'should have free burial without parish jurisdiction, in the consecrated atrium there', as well as two separate sets of *cens* (annual payments) which the bishops drew from the incomes of this church. Ulger, Bishop of Angers, in an undated grant which can, however, probably be placed between 1144 and 1149, allowed the Templars to ignore any interdict in his diocese once a year both by celebrating the divine office and by burying their dead. He encouraged others to give by relaxing a fifth part of any penance for confessed sins to all who granted benefices to them.[67] These privileges were granted from existing churches, but Walter,

Abbot of Saint-Vaast in the Pas-de-Calais, in a charter given during his abbacy between 1141 and 1147, also allowed the Templars to promote a colonisation project on the abbey's land at Hesdin which entailed the building of a completely new church. The plan included the establishment of a hamlet and a chapel, 'in which they and their subjects, namely those who have turned their backs on the secular life, might observe the divine offices, both in death and burial as well as in life, saving all our other rights in the parish of Hesdin'.[68] This grant formed the basis of a later Templar house. At the other end of the clerical hierarchy a priest called Wither of Barbonne (near Provins) gave 'all his vines and land and meadow of Cleeles and his books, namely the breviary and the missal, and after his death, his house and all his manse'. He seems to have been planning eventually to join the Order himself, at which time he intended to concede his entire property; meanwhile, he granted them a gold coin as recognition of his future commitment.[69]

Lay grants encompassed a similarly wide social spectrum from kings downwards. In England, for example, although Henry I seems to have facilitated early recruiting, it was King Stephen (1135–54) who really established the foundations of Templar landed possessions.[70] A typical concession was that of the royal manor at Cowley in Oxfordshire, together with the easement of adjacent forest lands, in 1139.[71] A concession of similar size was made in 1141, by Conan, Duke of Brittany, when he granted the Order the island of Lannia, as well as an income of 100 *solidi* from his rents in the city of Nantes and a square in which to build their house.[72] The Templar preceptories at Cowley and Nantes found their beginnings as a consequence of this princely generosity. Ordinary laymen could not make donations on this scale, but in the course of the twelfth and thirteenth centuries the Templars nevertheless benefited from the cumulative effects of many hundreds of individual donations. They were not dissimilar to those made in the following charter from the Toulousain, dated sometime between 1128 and 1132.[73] Most important of these grants was the one made by the family of Raymond Rater of Toulouse of 'all that honour which we have from the church of Saint Mary of Delbate up to the road and to another road which crosses in front of the church of Saint Rémi', which heads the document, but this is followed by the donations of forty-three individuals, which include small pieces of land, sums of money as low as one *denier*, horses, arms, shirts, breeches, and mantles. A man called Rorritus, for instance, gave twelve *deniers*, to which would be added at his death his best horse and arms, or if he did not possess a horse at that time, thirty *solidi* instead. The knightly culture which stimulated this kind of donation was equally powerful in Italy, despite the higher degree of urbanisation.[74] At Treviso, in 1140, Bertaldo Bozzolino, the bishop's advocate, left his destrier, bridle, leg armour, spurs, helmet, and lance, to the Temple there.[75]

While it may be assumed that all the benefactors of the Temple had a general interest in supporting the cause of the crusade, some grants are quite explicitly connected with crusading. In 1134, William Peter, another inhabitant of the Toulousain, granted part of his allod to the Templars of Douzens, with the proviso that the whole of it would fall to the Order 'if I remain in Jerusalem by death or another way'.[76] 'Another way' may imply that he was contemplating joining the Order in the east, for the same charter made provision for his heirs, as well as a range of grants to the Temple dependent upon whether he returned or not. A similar idea prompted the brothers Gerard and Garin of Bouzonville, probably in the spring of 1147, when they commended their allods at Rispe and Bouzonville (northeast of Metz) on the understanding that they would be restored if both or either of them returned from the crusade upon which they were about to embark. The influence of the preaching of Bernard of Clairvaux to 'the army of Christ' is clearly implied in the document, suggesting that the Templars first began to make some impression in imperial lands at the time of the Second Crusade and that again St Bernard's support was of key importance.[77] It was his experiences in the course of that expedition that influenced Louis VII's grant of the town of Savigny after his return from the crusade in the summer of 1149. He acknowledged a special devotion towards the Templars (whose financial and military aid had helped sustain the king through the agonies of this expedition) and recognised that they incurred great costs in their work for the Church in the east. He therefore granted them Savigny (just to the south of Melun in the royal demesne), together with an annual income to be drawn on his *cens* at Etampes. Any surplus from this was to be returned and any deficit to be made up by the royal *prévôt* of Etampes.[78]

Interest in the Order was not exclusively male.[79] Eleanor of Aquitaine, wife of Louis VII, and a great fief-holder in her own right, created the base for the very important Templar house in the rapidly growing port of La Rochelle. In her charter of 1139 she conceded mills granted to the Templars by one of her vassals; she declared the buildings and enclosures already occupied by them in La Rochelle to be 'entirely free and quit of all custom, infraction, and *tolte* and *taille*, [arbitrary seigneurial levies] and the violence of our officials, except for our toll'; and, provided that she did not herself lose any service by it, she granted freedom to her vassals to make any donation they wished to the Order. Finally, and particularly important in a port like La Rochelle, she allowed the Templars to transport anything of their own throughout all her lands 'freely and securely, without all customs and all exactions, either by land or by water'.[80] More modestly, in the 1140s, under the auspices of Bartholomew, Bishop of Laon, the lady Ermentrude granted a clutch of properties to make up a benefice to support a chantry priest in the Temple church at Laon, situated near the church of St Geneviève.[81]

As an active crusading frontier the situation in Iberia differed markedly from France and England; here the evident potential of the Templars as a fighting force was recognised almost immediately, particularly in Aragon and Catalonia, and in Portugal, although it was some time before the Order was able to transform this potential into a practical military role. The situation in Aragon had recently been transformed by Alfonso I, 'the Battler' (1104–34), through whose military skills and crusading fervour the centre of Aragonese power had moved south from the Pyrenees and the Upper Ebro valley. Between 1118 and 1120 alone he had taken Zaragoza, Tudela, Tarazona, Daroca, and Calatayud.[82] The extremely rapid expansion of Aragon in the last two decades of Alfonso's reign posed great problems of absorption for the king. To some extent he was forced to alleviate these by granting lands to powerful barons (with all the potential that this contained for the weakening of royal power), but his own original contribution seems to have been the creation of fraternities of knights devoted to the war against the Moors: in 1122 he founded the confraternity of Belchite, followed soon after (probably 1128–30) by the establishment of a similar militia at Monreal del Campo. Members of Belchite served for variable periods, but they did not take vows as such, having a status more akin to that of lay associates of the Temple rather than fully professed knights. They were, however, explicitly committed 'never to make peace with the pagans', unless they were under Christian lordship.[83] The role envisaged for Monreal particularly reveals Alfonso's caste of mind. Sometime in the late 1120s William, Archbishop of Auch (1126–c. 1170), became an associate of this militia, at the same time granting a remission of forty days' penance to whoever contributed one *denier* for one month to the knights. Although ultimately the confraternity failed to take root, it is evident from the archbishop's description in this document that Alfonso's intentions were very serious and that he had gone to considerable trouble to endow it. In the lands between Daroca and Valencia, which were 'unconquered and uncultivated and uninhabitable places', the king built a city called Monreal, 'that is the habitation of the celestial king, in which the militia of God might have its own seat'. This concession was supported by a wide range of revenues in cash and kind, and by the king's wish that it 'be expressly freed and exempt, in the same way as the confraternity of Jerusalem', a phrase which appears to signify that the Templars were already established in Aragon and that the institution of Monreal had been influenced by this.[84]

In this context Alfonso's generosity to the Canons of the Holy Sepulchre, the Hospitallers, and the Templars in his famous will of October 1131, becomes more explicable. In comparison with the provisions of this will, other contemporary grants to the military orders pale into insignificance and, consequently, the circumstances have been examined closely by historians seeking to explain a unique event. The core of the bequest is as follows:

Therefore, after my death I leave as heir and successor to me the Sepulchre of the Lord which is of Jerusalem and those who observe and guard and serve God there, and to the Hospital of the poor which is of Jerusalem, and to the Temple of Solomon with the knights who keep vigil there to defend the name of Christendom. To these three I concede my whole kingdom. [I concede] also the lordship which I have in the whole of the lands in my kingdom, both over clerics as well as over laity, bishops, abbots, canons, monks, magnates, knights, burgesses, peasants and merchants, men and women, the small and the great, rich and poor, also Jews and Saracens, with such laws as my father and I have had hitherto and ought to have.

The three beneficiaries were to hold the kingdom in equal parts.[85]

The king had no direct heirs; his marriage to Urraca of Castile had been dissolved in 1114, ending a possible union with Castile. He did not marry thereafter and indeed may have been sterile, as he had no known offspring.[86] He needed therefore to take account of possible outside intervention after his death, in particular by Alfonso VII of Castile (who had gained full power in 1126), as well as to make provision for the protection and extension of the frontier with the Moors. However, when Alfonso I died in September 1134, interested parties moved swiftly to secure their own positions, irrespective of the fact that the king had confirmed the will shortly before his death.[87] Castile occupied Zaragoza; the Navarrese nobles elected their own ruler, García Ramírez (an illegitimate descendant of the Navarrese royal family) thus ending the union between Navarre and Aragon which had existed since 1076; and Alfonso's younger brother, Ramiro, a monk at San Pedro de Huesca, left the monastery, married, and fathered a daughter, Petronilla. In 1137 she was promised to Raymond Berenguer IV, Count of Barcelona and ruler of Catalonia (they were eventually married in 1150). Ramiro then retired to his monastery, leaving Aragon to Raymond Berenguer, even if Petronilla were not to survive into adulthood, thus founding what became an enduring union of Aragon and Catalonia. Alfonso VII of Castile remained in a position to exert pressure: in 1135 he had been crowned emperor at León, and both García Ramírez and Raymond Berenguer had become his vassals. The actions of Ramiro II and Raymond Berenguer, however, prevented any direct Castilian takeover of Aragon.

There remained, nevertheless, the problem of the original will, whose beneficiaries had been effectively excluded by these manoeuvres. The process of unravelling took Raymond Berenguer until 1143 and left the Templars with vast interests in the new political entity of Aragon-Catalonia. Neither Ramiro II nor Raymond Berenguer made any attempt to carry out the provisions of the will, but equally neither wished to alienate an order which could possibly have much to contribute to the reconquest. Therefore, within a month of his brother's death, Ramiro had granted the town of Grisenich to the 'cavaleatores of Zaragoza'.[88] In Catalonia, Raymond Berenguer's father, Raymond Berenguer III, had actually joined the Order, probably shortly before his death in July 1131, when, at the same time he granted them 'a certain very fortified castle, called Grañena, in my march against the Saracens'.[89] Raymond Berenguer IV himself became an associate for one year in 1134 (probably in April, before the death of Alfonso I), when he promised

28

to maintain ten knights in the Order on a permanent basis, and his
example was followed by twenty-six other Catalan nobles, each of
whom made a commitment to the indefinite support of one Templar
knight.[90] He seems to have followed this up soon after his agreement
with Ramiro II in 1137, when he wrote to the Grand Master
requesting that he send ten knights to Aragon to be supported from
the kingdom's resources. He proposed too that the Order should
receive the city of Daroca and the castles of Osso and Belchite,
together with other revenues and jurisdictional rights. As a further
inducement he conceded the Order a tenth part of all future
conquests.[91]

There is no evidence that these plans came to fruition, but the offer
does presage the much more comprehensive settlement that Raymond Berenguer made with the Templars at Gerona in 1143.[92] By
this time the former beneficiaries seem already to have accepted that
the will would not be implemented. The Hospital and the Canons of
the Holy Sepulchre had formally acknowledged this in 1140; Raymond Berenguer's charter of 1143 represents the definitive agreement
with the Templars as well.[93] In this document, Robert of Craon,
Grand Master since the death of Hugh of Payns sometime between
1133 and 1136, specifically renounced the Order's claims and, in
return, received 'in perpetual right' the possession of six major
castles, together with their dependent territories: Monzón, Mongay,
Chalamera, Barbará, Belchite, and Remolins, as well as Corbins,
'when God will have deigned to render it to me'. One of these,
however – Belchite – was subject to the Order reaching an agreement
with its lord, Lope Sanchéz, which it failed to do,[94] while another –
Barbará – had already been granted to the Templars in 1132 by the
Count of Urgel, who had held it from the Counts of Barcelona.[95] As
well as the castles, the Templars were granted a tenth of royal
revenues, an annual sum of 1,000 *solidi* from Zaragoza, a fifth of
proceeds from *chevauchées* or expeditions conducted in Spain, and
freedom from tolls and customary exactions throughout Raymond
Berenguer's lands. Anticipatory concessions were also included: a
fifth of any lands conquered and permission to build castles against
the Moors. The acceptance of these responsibilities suggests that the
Templars were strong enough, financially and numerically, to take a
leading role in the *reconquista*, which they had probably not been able
to do in the 1130s.[96] Raymond Berenguer III's grant of Grañena, for

instance, had been made together 'with the knights who have this castle on my behalf and with the people living there', which implies that although the Templars obtained formal overlordship of the castle, they were not expected to garrison it themselves at that time. Indeed, if the situation in Iberia was at all similar to that in the east, even after 1143 fully professed Templars would have made up only a small proportion of the manpower of a castle.[97]

The problems created by Alfonso's will therefore took nearly ten years to resolve, but the king's own motives remain a matter of controversy. Alfonso I had been a tough and resourceful ruler who had reigned successfully for thirty years. During that time he had transformed his kingdom from little more than a collection of Pyrenean lordships, largely restricted to the region north of the River Aragon, into a major Iberian power, strong enough to rival Castile-León in the struggle for the spoils of the *reconquista*. For this reason historians have found his will hard to accept at face value, since its provisions appear to them to stem from quite uncharacteristic political naïvety. In an attempt to explain these apparent contradictions, Elena Lourie argued that the king intended the will to be a device to block the claims of Alfonso VII of Castile while allowing time for Alfonso's brother, Ramiro, to divest himself of his religious habit and establish himself in power. The pious nature of the grant reduced the efficacy of papal intervention, almost certain since Aragon was a papal fief.[98] The argument is ingenious and subtle, but largely speculative. It takes insufficient account of the seriousness of a clear and unambiguous concession supported by the oaths of more than sixty witnesses and confirmed shortly before the king's death. It was made, he said, for the safety of the souls of his father and mother and for the remission of his own sins, 'that I might merit a place in the life eternal'. It seems highly unlikely that a king who had shown himself deeply committed to the cause of the crusade and who had already established two military fraternities of his own would have risked his immortal soul in an attempt to orchestrate such a complex political manoeuvre from beyond the grave. Certainly, Pope Innocent II saw the will as a genuine expression of the king's wishes, for in 1135/6 he pressed for its enforcement,[99] while the division of a patrimony among co-heirs was typical Spanish practice at this period. Although no one can be sure, the balance of evidence therefore suggests that Alfonso I was neither simple-minded nor insincere, but was expressing his piety in a way quite typical of contemporary mental attitudes, reflected in grants made by many others. The only difference was one of scale.[100]

One further consequence of the failure of Alfonso I to leave heirs of his own body was the disintegration of the union of Aragon with Navarre. Therefore, the kings of Navarre made their own grants to the Temple, independently of their neighbours, although the potential military value of the Order in the kingdom diminished during the twelfth and thirteenth centuries as Navarre became increasingly isolated from a frontier dominated by Castile, Aragon, and Portugal. The most significant (and probably the earliest) grant made by García Ramírez was the cession, in 1135, of the castle and town of Novillas, jointly to the Hospital and the Temple.[101] The previous year, García, Bishop of Zaragoza (1130–6), had conceded to the Templars all his episcopal rights over the church at Novillas, 'except only that they come to our council and receive the oil of chrism and recognise the see of Zaragoza, in such a way that each year, on the Feast of St Michael, the aforesaid knighthood give to us and our successors twelve *deniers* to be delivered at regular intervals to the aforesaid see'.[102] By 1139 the Templars had established a preceptory there,[103] and during the 1140s they consolidated their hold through donations, purchases and, above all, by exchanges of buildings within the walls, presumably aimed at establishing a distinct quarter of their own. Since, in 1132, the two Orders had also received joint possession of the nearby village of Mallén from Alfonso I, in 1149 they agreed upon a mutual renunciation of rights, which left Novillas to the Templars and Mallén to the Hospitallers.[104] Like the Abbot of Saint-Vaast in the Pas-de-Calais region, King García also used the Order for colonisation purposes. In a charter which can only be placed within the limits of his reign, between 1134 and 1150, he extended juridical and commercial concessions to those 'who populate and will populate' a place called 'Villa Vetula', situated on land granted to the Templars, to whom they owed an annual *cens*.[105] Leading churchmen adopted the same approach: Lope, Bishop of Pamplona (1142–59), in 1149 gave the Order the right to build a church at Ancessa for the population that they were establishing there. The church was to be freely held, except that the bishop would retain a quarter of the *cens* and his jurisdiction over the clergy. However, he waived his claim to the quarter of the revenue for the first two years in order to allow the church to be constructed.[106]

At the same time as the Count of Barcelona was beginning the process of developing the new entity of Aragon-Catalonia, on the other side of the peninsula a completely new political structure was taking shape. In 1128 Afonso Henriques forced his mother, Queen Teresa, to relinquish power in the lands lying to the south of the River Miño and, from this time, began a long and successful reign which, by his death in 1185, had founded an independent kingdom of Portugal. Teresa was the daughter of Alfonso VI of Castile (died 1109), the conqueror of Toledo in 1085 and, despite the setbacks of the later years of his reign, regarded as the most powerful ruler in the peninsula. When Teresa married Henry of Burgundy in 1094, Alfonso granted him the lordship of the lands centred on the region between the Miño and the Duero, evidently intended as a base for further southward expansion, although equally evidently as a dependency of Castile. Their son, Afonso Henriques, devoted himself to the first of these objectives, but had no intention of allowing the continuation of the second, and during the 1130s began to overcome the Muslim powers along the Tagus valley. In 1139 he even defeated the Almoravides at Ourique, far to the south, and after this he began to call himself king. Although, like Raymond Berenguer, he accepted Alfonso VII's imperial pretensions in 1135, he skilfully protected himself against the Castilian king's direct intervention by becoming a papal vassal in 1143. The establishment of the military orders, in particular the Templars, was therefore as valuable to him as it was to Raymond Berenguer, for their commitment to the cause of the crusade made them ideal recipients of the castles and newly colonised lands along the frontier with the Moors.

Even before Afonso Henriques' assumption of power, Queen Teresa had granted the Templars the castle of Soure, to the south of the River Mondego, just below Coïmbra, in March 1128, and this was confirmed a year later by Afonso himself, when he gave his reasons as being for the remedy of his soul and those of his kindred and 'for the love which I have in my heart for you [the Templars] and since I am a brother in your fraternity'.[107] The parallels with the situation in eastern Spain are striking. Like Raymond Berenguer, Afonso seems to have become an associate of the Order and, as with the castles of Grañena and Barbará, it seems inconceivable that the Templars could have garrisoned Soure, given to them even before the Council of Troyes. However, circumstances may have changed by 1145 as Afonso geared himself up for a further drive southwards. In that year, Fernand Menendiz, Afonso's brother-in-law, in association with the king, made over the castle of Longroiva in the underpopulated region of Estremadura.[108] The main objective, however, remained the Tagus valley and in 1147 Afonso succeeded in taking Santarém, and then, in October, with the help of crusaders en route for Outremer, Lisbon itself. Among the careful preparations which the king had made were anticipatory grants to the Templars, ensuring the Order's support without touching existing resources and making a genuine appeal for God's help through pious donations. This is how Afonso's charter of April 1147 expresses it:

beginning my journey to that castle which is called Santarém, I made a proposition in my heart, and I took a vow, that if God in his mercy brought that to me, I would give all the churches to God and to the military brothers of the Temple of Solomon, established in Jerusalem for the defence of the Holy Sepulchre, part of which [Order] was established with me in the same county. And since God made such honour to me and well fulfilled my wish, I Afonso, above-named king, together with wife, Matilda, make the charter to the above-mentioned knights of Christ for every church of Santarém, that they and all their successors might have and possess [them] in perpetual right, so that no cleric or layman can question anything in them. But if by chance it happens that at any time God, in his mercy, gives to me that city which is called Lisbon, they are to agree with the bishop on my advice.[109]

By this time the Order had already established an important house farther north at Braga, where it had received particular favour from the archbishops. The significant grants took place in 1145 under Archbishop John of Braga (1138–75), but his charters make clear that he was largely carrying out the wishes of his predecessor, Pelagius (died 1137). In August 1145, Archbishop John granted the Order a house originally set up by Pelagius as a hospital for the poor, as well as providing a means of support by conceding half of the tithe from all revenues and fairs which the archbishop had inside and outside the city.[110] Although it is not absolutely certain that he is referring to the same hospice it seems likely that the account given in a charter of the following year in which the king presents himself as the prime mover in the revival of the property is in fact referring to this house. According to this, Pelagius built a certain house, namely a dwelling-place for pilgrims, as a remedy for his soul and those of his parents, in the archiepiscopal city which is called Braga, to the sustenance of which house he brought with generous hand, vines, landed property, many benefices, [and] many incomes. After his death, however, those wanting many of the perishable riches of this world, and forgetting the true crimes which arose, seizing for themselves the rights of the aforesaid, as for example its landed property, destroyed it, reducing it altogether to nothing. Afterwards, however, I, Afonso, King of Portugal, saw the above-mentioned house to be so destroyed and diminished, wishing to reform it for the better, established a charter of testament and stability for it, together with John, Archbishop of Braga, with God and the knights of the Temple of Solomon, namely residing in Jerusalem for the defence of the Holy Sepulchre. I give and concede it to them, with all its appurtenances which now it has and used to have on the day of the death of the aforesaid Archbishop Pelagius, that they might have and possess it, and do whatever they wish with it in the service of the Temple.[111]

The long-term prominence of the Templars in Aragon and Portugal reflected their early establishment in these regions; even at the time of the trial in 1308 the rulers of these kingdoms were reluctant to obey papal orders to act against them and after the Temple was suppressed in 1312 the new order of Christ created by King Diniz of Portugal in 1319 was largely based upon Templar property and personnel. The Templars never gained such an important position in Castile-León, although they had considerable indirect influence upon the foundation of the specifically regional military orders of Calatrava, Alcántara, and Santiago, confirmed respectively in 1164, 1175, and 1176. Even so, like his colleagues, Alfonso VII saw their value as lords of the underpopulated areas so frequently encompassed by the *reconquista*. In 1146, at a great gathering of Spanish rulers at his court, Alfonso granted them the deserted village of Villa Sicca, situated on the wind-swept plateau between Soria and Almenar de Soria.[112]

With developments on this scale taking place in France, Iberia, and England, it might be expected that the Order would quickly rise to a new prominence in Outremer, especially given the success of Hugh of Payns' recruitment and the evident favour of both Baldwin II and, after his death in 1131, his successor, King Fulk. However, there is little evidence to support such an idea. In the Kingdom of Jerusalem the Hospitallers seem to have been the first to be trusted with important military responsibilities, when they received the guard of the castle of Bethgibelin (Bait Jibrīn), newly built in 1136 to threaten the port of Ascalon, still held by the Egyptians.[113] This is nearly fourteen years before the first similar grant was made to the Templars, that of Gaza, also just constructed to increase the pressure on Ascalon, in 1149–50.[114] Similarly, in Tripoli in 1144 Raymond II made sweeping concessions to the Hospital which encompassed five fortresses (including Krak des Chevaliers) and two towns, making them a key element in the county's eastern defences.[115] Yet the Hospitallers were militarised only rather slowly at a time which appears to postdate the appearance of the Templars as a military force.[116] The Templars apparently took over fortresses much earlier in the north, when in about 1136–7 they were made responsible for the guard of the passes into Antioch from Cilicia through the Amanus Mountains.[117] Otherwise there is little sign of Templar activity. In the period before the arrival of the Second Crusade in 1148, William of Tyre mentions the Templars in connection with only two military actions: the siege of Damascus in 1129 and a minor skirmish near Hebron ten years later. Both ended in failure: in 1129 many men from the considerable force Hugh of Payns appears to have recruited were killed while foraging in territory unfamiliar to them, while the 1139 engagement cost the life of a well-known Templar, Odo of Montfaucon.[118] A western source, Orderic Vitalis, says that they were involved in the campaign to defend Montferrand (in the County of Tripoli) against Zengi, Atabeg of Mosul, in 1137. Here too they were defeated and the Franks sustained heavy losses. Among those who escaped were eighteen Templars.[119] Between 1129 and the attendance of the second Grand Master, Robert of Craon, at the war council of crusaders in June 1148, held near Acre, there are references to only nine Templars in the surviving charters of the crusader states: the Grand Master, Robert of Craon (1137/8), William, Seneschal of the Order (1130), and the brothers Goscelin (1137/8, 1140), Drogo (1140), Ralph Caslan (1143), William Falco (1144), Geoffrey Fulcher (1144), Osto of St Omer (1145), and Ralph of Patingy (1145).[120] All these are in the Kingdom of Jerusalem, except for Goscelin and Drogo in 1140 (Antioch) and Ralph Caslan (probably Tripoli). To these can be added Odo of Montfaucon referred to by William of Tyre, and probably Andrew of Montbard, uncle of St Bernard, mentioned in the abbot's letters.[121] This compares with references to 210 named Templars in the west during the same period and with the figure of 130 knights who attended a chapter-meeting in Paris in April 1147, prior to the departure of the Second Crusade.[122]

There are, however, a number of reasons for believing that this cannot be a true reflection of the order's position in the east during the 1130s and 1140s. Fulk of Anjou was as favourable to the Order as his predecessor, and it is not surprising to find that when Hugh of Payns died on 24 May, probably in 1136,[123] an Angevin, Robert of Craon, was elected as his successor. Robert, who seems to have joined the Order by 1127, can be seen acting on Fulk's behalf from 1113 onwards, and his appointment was in keeping with Fulk's policy of filling important positions in the kingdom with his own men.[124] William of Tyre provides a brief pen picture of this man, whom he says came from Antioch to Jerusalem in 1139 and whom he describes as 'a man of pious memory in the Lord; an excellent knight and vigorous in arms, noble in the flesh and in his conduct'.[125] If Fulk was prepared to entrust Bethgibelin to the Hospitallers in 1136, there is equally good reason to expect that he would have used the Templars in the same way. Moreover, given the increase in the landed holdings of the Hospitallers during this period, it is reasonable to assume that the Templars would have made similar advances,[126] especially in the context of the many grants received in France and England, the cession of the lordship of important castles in Aragon and Portugal, and the anticipatory concessions made by Raymond Berenguer which are not dissimilar to those offered to the Italian maritime cities in the east to enable the capture of key ports like Tyre. It is not therefore surprising to find that, in certain circles in the west, there was an evident realisation of the importance of the Templars; as early as the middle of the twelfth century, the Cluniac, Richard of Poitou, wrote that some said that if it had not been for the Templars the Franks would have lost Jerusalem and Palestine a long time ago.[127]

The problem therefore lies in the sources, both in the lack of contemporary crusader chronicles and in the loss of many charters, including those of the Temple and of the nobility of Jerusalem.[128] William of Tyre later researched this period, but he himself was only a child at the time; in contrast the Templars seem to have been well known to contemporary Muslims such as the Damascene chronicler, Usāmah Ibn-Munqidh, who describes their position in the al-Aqsa Mosque in about 1140.[129] There are only seven charters in which Templars are named between 1129 and 1148, of which six are concerned with the affairs of the canons of the Holy Sepulchre. Only one bears directly on the affairs of the Temple and since this is the grant of William of St Omer of the churches of Sclippes and Leffinges and has therefore been preserved in the west, the extent of the lacunae of Templar documents can be readily understood. There is a hint of the position achieved by the Templars in the east in a grant of Alfonso-Jordan, Count of Toulouse, to the Order, in 1134. Alfonso-Jordan was probably better informed about the east than most rulers, since he was the son of Raymond of Toulouse, one of the leaders of the First Crusade, and was related to the Counts of Tripoli, who were descended from his half-brother, Bertrand. He had been born in the east shortly before his father's death in 1105 and, although he had been taken to Toulouse by his mother in 1108 and there accepted as count, in adult life he retained an interest in Outremer and perhaps even cherished a desire to reclaim Tripoli for himself.[130] His description of the position of the Temple in the crusader states therefore carries some weight. Here he offers to the Templars

such power and permission in all my lands, as they have in eastern parts from the king of Jerusalem, the prince of Antioch, and the count of Tripoli, namely that whoever wishes to give to them in all my provinces either his own person or money or land or town or castle or also city or any of those things which they hold from me in fief (*feualiter*) can give, without dispute, and they can freely receive, so that the house of the knighthood at Jerusalem might possess it and hold it in perpetuity as by hereditary succession, serving no-one for this except God alone.[131]

CHAPTER TWO

THE CONCEPT

By the time of the Second Crusade the idea of a militarised monastic order had been absorbed into the structure of Latin Christian life. The Hospitallers, with whom the Templars had been so closely associated in their early days, had themselves in turn taken on a military function, although it never predominated in the way that it did in the Temple. Localised military orders followed in Castile in the 1160s and 1170s, and in 1198 the Teutonic Knights established themselves at Acre, modelling their Rule upon that of the Templars. The much smaller Order of St Lazarus, probably founded in the 1130s at Jerusalem as an order for both leprous and healthy brothers, seems to have had close links with the Templars. It was possible for leprous brothers from the Temple to transfer to St Lazarus and by the 1230s the brothers of St Lazarus were themselves taking part in military actions in the east, usually together with the Templars.[1]

The acceptance of such an idea had been possible because it was fundamentally compatible with contemporary mores. In the late eleventh and the early twelfth centuries many men had felt a call to redirect their lives along ways which would free them from what they discerned to be the increasingly corrupting influences of the world around them. They were influenced by a papacy which, since the middle of the eleventh century, had itself attempted to cleanse the Church of the abuses of simony and clerical unchastity which were widespread in the tenth and early eleventh centuries, and to disentangle its personnel and property from the tentacles of lay control. This movement had been particularly associated with Pope Gregory VII (1073–85), whose strident leadership had given the clerical order a new identity within western society. Moreover, signs

38

of economic change, in turn propelled by population growth, although not quantifiable, were equally evident, promoting much more active monetary circulation and a much stronger and more widespread market economy. The problems created by economic upheaval, in themselves unsettling, were therefore brought into sharp focus by a reforming Church, driven by the moral imperatives of its papal leaders. The tensions thus arising encouraged the search for a new direction and were a major reason for the great monastic reformation of the time which, among others, produced new orders like the Carthusians and the Cistercians, saw the reform and establishment of the regular canons like the Augustinians and Premonstratensians, and led the papacy to recognise the Hospitallers as an independent order in 1113.

However, while the Hospitaller vocation was a well-established form of charitable activity whose origins went back to the time of the early Church and the first pilgrimages, the concept of an order of monks dedicated to the use of force in the Christian cause certainly was not, and the establishment of the Templars would not have been possible without the climate of opinion which had promoted the First Crusade. Although the eleventh-century Church contained strong personalities who spoke out against the use of violence in any circumstances, St Augustine himself had accepted that under certain specific conditions it might be necessary for a Christian to use force.[2] Moreover, during the early middle ages the admission of the warlike and aggressive Germanic tribes into the Christian family of peoples had inevitably forced the Church to compromise on this issue, seeking to control and channel violence rather than pursuing the impossible dream of its complete abolition. From the late tenth century, in areas particularly affected by noble lawlessness, this sometimes took the form of peace movements in which leading clerics sought to mobilise popular support for the imposition of restrictions upon those who wielded the sword, trying to limit the times at which they should fight and to protect selected categories of the populace. These peace movements, while not very effective in a practical sense, nevertheless raised the level of popular consciousness, so that in some cases the initiatives resulted in the formation of secular confraternities, which aimed at collective action in support of the objectives of the peace campaigners. After 1050 the reform popes had taken more positive steps than any of their predecessors to redirect men's warlike impulses towards what they regarded as their own higher goals. Gregory VII had spoken of 'the soldiers of Christ' who would fight for the Church's cause, no longer using the phrase to describe a monastic battle against the forces of evil, as in the past, but applying it to lay warriors whose notion of fighting was literal and physical.[3] Urban II's call to combat against the Turks was a more developed version of this idea, having the double advantage of combating a perceived Muslim threat and of reducing the high level of internecine warfare at home. By the time that the first Templars took their vows, 'holy violence' had achieved a high level of general acceptance, and the idea that laymen might achieve salvation in such a cause was well established. Indeed, the crusaders believed that the indulgence granted to them by the papacy meant a direct passport to Heaven for those who were killed in battle or who succumbed to the hardships of the journey. These circumstances help to make comprehensible what at first sight seems anomalous: the development of a fighting order of monks representing what was supposedly a pacifist religion.

Like the crusading movement itself, therefore, it is possible to identify the generating elements of the military order in the attitudes prevalent in western Christian society in the late eleventh and early twelfth centuries. Nevertheless, while the crusade was initiated by the pope, preaching at a council in France, the Templars found their origins in the frontier society of Outremer, where they came into daily contact with Muslims, and it has been suggested that they may have been influenced by an exterior institution as well, that of the Islamic *ribāt*. *Ribāts* had been established from the seventh century on Islamic frontiers, where they formed centres for devout Muslims who wished to combine a life of prayer with military activity on behalf of their faith. Service in them was for set periods rather than for life.[4] This idea opens intriguing possibilities, especially as there are evident parallels between *ribāts* in Iberia and the confraternity of Belchite, founded by Alfonso of Aragon in 1122,[5] which in turn bears some similarities to the Templars. Acculturation was characteristic of medieval Spanish society, but there is no direct evidence to connect the *ribāt* with the early Templars in Jerusalem, nor do crusader sources suggest that the Franks knew of these Muslim communities. Indeed, it has been pointed out that it is not even clear that *ribāts* existed in those parts of the Muslim world adjacent to the crusader states in the early twelfth century,[6] a point reinforced by the apparent inability of contemporary Palestinian and Syrian Muslim powers to combine against the Franks under the auspices of the *jihad*. Even so, by the same token, the application of such stringent standards of proof to the Christian influences already discussed could result in an equally negative answer; in the end the arguments for the contextual background to the formation of the Temple (as opposed to the specific circumstances) rest more on the balance of probability than upon concrete links.

The absorption of the concept of a military order into Christian society should not, however, be too readily assumed, whatever the apparent sources for the idea. Although approval of the Temple was widespread by the middle of the twelfth century, before this time there were, in some quarters, deep misgivings and, even after 1150, a small number of individuals persisted in voicing their doubts. Even those like the famous Cluniac abbot Peter the Venerable, who accepted their value, sometimes seemed distinctly uneasy. Although he expressed his 'special and unique affection' for them, praising them as 'the army of the Lord of Sabaoth', he never seems to have regarded them as equal in status to more conventional orders of monks and canons.[7] It is clear too that there was a deep-seated hostility to the idea of monkish participation in crusades or pilgrimages – a hostility incidentally shared by St Bernard himself – and that even the relaxation of restrictions on monks established by Innocent III during the first decade of the thirteenth century did little to change ecclesiastical or legal opinion on the matter.[8] It is not therefore difficult to imagine that some contemporaries, brought up to believe in a functional division of social orders, might find Templar duality a quite bizarre idea. In about 1145, Henry, Archdeacon of Huntingdon, described Henry of Blois, Bishop of Winchester, as 'a certain new monster composed from purity and corruption, namely a monk and a knight'.[9] Although he was not referring to the Templars, the inference is clear: such a combination was against nature.

The clearest evidence of the existence of contemporary criticism powerful enough to induce doubt even among the Templars themselves, comes from a sermon or letter addressed directly to the brothers. The writer says that:

we have heard that certain of you have been troubled by persons of little wisdom, as if your profession, to which you have dedicated your life, to carry arms for the defence of Christians against the enemies of the faith and of peace, as if, I say, that profession is either illicit or pernicious, that it is either a sin or an impediment to a greater achievement.

Neither the identity of the author nor the date is certain. It has been thought that the writer was Hugh of Payns himself, but both the content and the style make this improbable. Another candidate is the theologian Hugh of St Victor, of the Augustinian house in Paris, since the manuscript is headed by the rubric, *Prologus magistri hugonis de sancto victore*, although the text itself refers only to *Hugo peccator* and there is no particular reason to connect Hugh of St Victor with the Templars.[10] It seems to have been kept with copies of the Latin Rule and St Bernard's famous treatise about the Order, *De laude novae militiae* (*In praise of the new knighthood*), possibly in the Hospitaller house at St Gilles, which had presumably inherited the material when the Templar properties were transferred to the Hospital after the suppression of the Templars in 1312. This provenance, together with the letter's content, suggests a date around 1130. As the letter was found between the Rule and *De laude*, it is tempting also to conclude that this indicates a chronological order as well, but there is no solid evidence for this.

The writer begins by warning the brothers to be on their guard against the machinations of the Devil, 'for the first labour of the Devil is to lead us into sin'. He attempts this both by corrupting men's motives in undertaking good works and then by weakening the resolve to carry them out at all, but they should heed the Apostle, who said, 'Each should remain in the vocation to which he was called' (I Cor. 7:20). Drawing upon the familiar clerical functional view of society (which suggests that the Order had indeed been challenged on the grounds that it fitted into no known category), he asks how the body as a whole could subsist if all its members attempted to perform the same function. 'Do not deceive yourselves: each receives recompense in accordance with his labour. The roofs of the houses receive the rain and the hail and the wind; but if there were no roofs, how would the walls be protected?' Moreover, the Devil is a subtle tempter, for he knows that a direct assault upon their virtue will not succeed, so he attempts instead to corrupt their innermost thoughts by suggesting hatred and fury when they are killing, cupidity when they are taking the spoils. Yet their hatred is not of the man but of the iniquity and what they take in the course of these actions is just recompense for their sacrifices. Having failed to persuade the Templars that their activities were reprehensible, the Devil tacitly admits their merit, but tries to induce them to desert their position in order to chase the phantom of a higher good. This too is a delusion, for God desires a patient acceptance of the gifts which one has received. 'If the place could save, the Devil would not have fallen from Heaven. On the other hand, if the place could damn, Job on his dungheap could not have conquered the Devil. Therefore reflect upon this, since neither the place nor the appearance is anything to God.'

The writer therefore stressed to the Templars the importance of examining their interior state rather than being dazzled by the exterior world. But while this may have been sound advice for members of a more usual contemplative order, it could be objected that the nature of the Templars' occupation necessarily involved them in the cares of the world, diverting them from such internal self-examination. The author meets this by admonishing them to remember that a place with Christ needs to be earned. The Church of God could not survive otherwise: even the hermits in the desert needed to obtain the basic necessities of earthly life. 'If the Apostles had said to Christ: "We wish to rest and to contemplate, not to run to and fro, not to work, [but] to be far from the quarrels and contentions of men", if the Apostles had spoken to Christ in this way, where would Christianity be now?' A true servant of God therefore understands the need to be content with his lot and goes about his ordained function in a tranquil frame of mind. This was not of course easy for ordinary mortals, for the Devil's assault was unremitting. Those who have the responsibilities of leadership are persuaded that they cannot be saved unless they abandon their position; those who play an inferior role are agitated by the sugges-tion that they do all the work and yet are ignored. All this is trickery: there is no doubt that all those who participate in Christ's work will receive their recompense. 'If you feel thus, most dear brothers, and you serve your society in peace, the God of peace will be with you.'

The circumstances which led to the writing of this exhortation remain hidden, as do any effects which it may have had. It might be thought that the success of Templar recruitment and the growth of donations after 1129 would largely have eradicated these fears, which could place it in the mid 1120s, or at any rate before the Council of Troyes. However, it seems very unlikely that a relatively small band of knights, protecting pilgrims in a limited part of the Kingdom of Jerusalem, should be the subject of the kind of debate implied in this letter. The proceedings at Troyes, on the other hand, would have brought them to wider notice and this in turn could have provoked criticism. Moreover, unless the much-better-known tract of St Bernard, *De laude novae militiae*, is also to be placed as early as this, it seems that the voices of inner doubt (and perhaps those of external critics) were not stilled even after 1129.[11] In the prologue to *De laude* Bernard says that he has written this sermon because he has three times been asked by Hugh of Payns. He cannot delay further without exposing himself to the accusation that he was unwilling to produce a work which he regarded as being 'very necessary', whereas, he says, the real reason was a lack of confidence in his own ability to do it effectively. These comments have led historians to believe that the tract must have been written by 1136, the supposed year of Hugh of Payns' death. However, if they are not to be dismissed as mere rhetorical form, they also imply that not only were there contemporary critics willing to say that there was no real justification for such a hybrid, but that Bernard himself had also feared that there might be some truth in such an allegation. Moreover, the evidence that the Rule, the letter of 'Hugo peccator', and *De laude* were apparently kept together in a Templar house suggests that the brothers saw all three manuscripts as a guide to their vocation, to be preserved for necessary consultation. *De laude* may, therefore, have been written in circumstances similar to those which produced the letter of 'Hugo peccator' and should be seen as a genuine exhortation and spiritual guide rather than simply a means of creating publicity, for the Templars seem already to be quite well known at the time that it was written.

De laude is crafted with St Bernard's customary skill and literary flair, cleverly exploiting the currents of opinion which had been a precondition of the calling of the crusade and which in turn had made the establishment of the Templars possible. As a consequence, even though the fundamental purpose was to advance the Templars' own spiritual development, the first part of the tract appeared as a panegyric in favour of the Templars which, directly or indirectly, exercised a profound influence upon the minds both of his contemporaries and those of later generations. The success of this part of the treatise was in the creation of an image. They were, he said, a new species of knighthood, previously unknown in the secular world, pursuing a double conflict against both flesh and blood and the invisible forces of evil. Strong warriors, on the one hand, and monks waging war with vice and demons on the other, were not unusual, but the combination of both was quite unique, creating a body of men who need have no fear. Since they fought with a clear and pure conscience these men had no dread of death, confident in the knowledge that in the sight of the Lord they would be his martyrs.[12] The gulf between them and contemporary secular knights, driven by anger or greed and seduced by superficial appearances, was plain, as was the difference in their respective fates when this brief sojourn on earth came to an end. Through the Templars the pollution of the holy places could be cleansed and the Christians returned to their true home. 'Rejoice Jerusalem', cried Bernard, 'and know already the time of your visitation.' In Bernard's presentation the conduct of the Templars was completely in keeping with this holy mission: disciplined, ascetic, sober, hard-working. Rank was of no consequence, for it was a man's intrinsic quality which really mattered. Moreover, so great was God's gift in furnishing Christians with such an Order, that he had even endowed it with the capability of converting sinners, for men previously regarded as criminals and a menace to society were transformed into faithful defenders within the Templar community.[13] The underlying theme is that the Templars have put aside the superficialities and temptations of secular life for the service of the Lord; 'they arm themselves not with gold, but inside with faith'. This, as he had already demonstrated in his *Apologia* to William of St Thierry in 1125, was what Bernard regarded as the true monastic vocation.[14]

It has been said that the spirituality of the Incarnation was at the heart of Bernardine theology and that for Bernard the Holy Land was not the Promised Land of Moses, but the land of Jesus Christ. He saw the crusade as a form of pilgrimage in which Christians became participants in the Passion of Christ and therefore his heirs. Conversely, Muslims were unjustified invaders of Christ's patrimony.[15] Bernard could therefore present the Templars as the perfect realisation of this Christian role: living in the Holy Land in the places of Christ's life and sacrifice and defending those places from infidel pollution. These attitudes are strongly developed in the later chapters of *De laude* where he sets out a few of 'the abundant delights' of the Holy Land to 'the praise and glory' of its name, reviewing in turn the meaning and importance of Bethlehem, Nazareth, the Mount of Olives and the Valley of Josaphat, the Jordan, Mount Calvary, the Holy Sepulchre, Bethpage, and Bethany. Here, on the face of it, he is less directly concerned with the Templars, seemingly abandoning the exhortation of the first part of the treatise for a detailed discourse upon the meaning of these holy places. Consequently this section of the work has seldom received the attention which has been devoted to the first. Yet it was important to the Order because of the unique nature of its membership and the functions they performed. As 'Hugo peccator' had realised, its essentially active function in the world might be thought to militate against the pursuit of that repose and reflection which was supposedly the key to medieval monasticism. In this part of the treatise St Bernard gives overt recognition to these problems and attempts to adapt his message to the needs of the new Order and to the type of members which it attracted.

The Templars lived and worked in the physical environment of the holy places and they could become familiar with them in a very literal way. But St Bernard wished to provide a further dimension by explaining their inner meaning. The concept of a 'spiritual sense which lay beneath the written letters', as he put it, was fundamental to Bernard and his fellow intellectuals, but it needed explanation and amplification for the laity, the 'non-literates' whom he envisaged as being the majority of Templar recruits. If they could be shown how to contemplate the holy places in the manner of sacred exegesis the Templars might be able to transcend mere outward appearance and thus be encouraged to search for a deeper spiritual meaning. Those knights actually based in the Temple itself, for example, had a daily view of the Valley of Josaphat and the Mount of Olives beyond and on many occasions must have made this relatively short journey from the Temple Mount. The physical act of descending into the valley and then climbing the mountain could itself be the occasion to remind the Christian that in contemplating the riches of divine mercy he should equally retain an appropriate dread of divine judgement. The journey was in itself an allegory, for 'the proud man rushes headlong into this valley, and is shattered; the humble descends, and is not endangered in the least'. A similar moral can be drawn from his description of Bethany where Martha and Mary came from, and where Lazarus was brought back to life. Following Jerome, he interprets Bethany as 'the house of obedience', and in this the Templars can see the virtue of obedience and the fruits of penance. As monks the Templars are vowed to obedience, which reminds them that they can achieve nothing without the strength of the Lord, in whom they must put their trust.

Even more fundamental is the discourse upon the Holy Sepulchre, which occupies about half of Bernard's entire review of the meaning of the holy places. Here he moves from the sight of the physical place in which Christ's body rested to a contemplation of Christ's life and death and its relationship to sinful man. 'The life of Christ was for me a model for living, his death a redemption from death.' Towards the end of this section his purpose and his method are made quite explicit. Seeing the Holy Sepulchre with one's own eyes strikes the deepest sensibilities of the Christian and from this in turn he can contemplate that this is his resting place too. According to St Paul: 'For by baptism we are buried in death that just as Christ rose from the dead by the glory of the Father, so we may walk in the newness of life. For if we have been planted with him together in the likeness of his death, so we shall be resurrected' (Romans 6:4–5).

While the Templars lacked the opportunity and the means for much of the solitary reflection and reading available to the more traditional cloistered monks, they had the advantage of physical proximity to the holy places which might inspire them to search for a deeper truth. Bernard had perhaps too a secondary purpose, for as protectors of the pilgrim routes the Templars would come into contact with an almost constant stream of visitors to the holy places and it must be assumed that many would need instruction and explanation. Although there were other ecclesiastics who could fulfil this role, the Templars themselves must often have been called upon to provide answers and De laude could furnish them with the means to do this, so that they could offer the pilgrim a deeper understanding of what he was seeing and experiencing. A favourite pilgrim destination was the River Jordan, a fact acknowledged by the special section in the French version of the Templar Rule devoted to the arrangements which the Templars needed to make to protect and provision pilgrims along this dangerous route.[16] Bernard's short section on the Jordan can be read in this light. Pilgrims wanted to bathe in the waters, 'which gloried in consecration by the baptism of Christ himself', but Bernard explained further how the waters had parted to leave a dry path for Elijah and Elisha and how they had enabled Joshua and his people to cross. No river could claim superiority over this one, 'which the Trinity dedicated to itself by a manifest presence'. Quoting Luke 3:22, Bernard explained that, 'The Father was heard, the Holy Spirit was seen, and the Son baptised.' Again, he takes his reader from the literal to the inner meaning: as by bathing in the Jordan Naaman was restored in his body at the behest of the Prophet, so the whole population of the faithful undergoes spiritual cleansing on the order of Christ. The lengthy section on the Holy Sepulchre is more complicated, but can equally be read as instruction, for here St Bernard sets out the issues in a series of pertinent questions. The answers he provides can in turn be used by the Templars not only for their own edification, but for that of the pilgrims for whose care they were responsible. The Holy Sepulchre was, as Bernard saw it, the central goal of their entire pilgrimage and needed appropriately detailed treatment.

How sweet it is to the pilgrims, after the great fatigue of a long journey, after the many dangers both on land and sea [2 Cor. 11:26], finally to rest there, where they know that their Lord had rested! I know that already on account of their joy they do not feel the labour of the journey nor reckon the burden of their expenses, but claiming both the recompense of their labour and the reward of their journey [1 Cor. 9:24], according to the meaning of Scripture, 'they rejoice exceedingly when they find the Sepulchre' [Job 3:22].

These strands are brought together at the conclusion of *De laude*, for the defence of the holy places which Bernard has so carefully elucidated was the responsibility of the Templars who, he must have hoped, would be imbued with a stronger sense of their own mission having understood the full meaning of their role. These last sentences provided a theme and a motto for the Templars thereafter:

However, then, you suffice to guard the trust of Heaven securely and faithfully, if you never rely upon your own judgement and strength, but everywhere only upon the help of God, knowing 'since no man is strengthened by his own fortitude' [1 Sam. 2:9], and in the same way saying with the Prophet: 'The Lord is my support, my refuge, and my deliverer' [Ps. 18:2], and that 'I guard my strength in you, since God is my protector; my God, whose mercy goes before me' [Ps. 59:17], and again: 'Not unto us, Lord not unto us, but give to your name the glory' [Ps. 115:1], so that he might be blessed in all things, who instructs your hands in battle and your fingers in war' [Ps. 144:1].

Even if this new Order had not attracted much attention, St Bernard's close involvement ensured that the Templars would be the subject of wide interest in monastic circles. Not only was Bernard the most famous monk of his time, but he was also a tireless correspondent, so that the recipients of his letters were bound to hear of it, even if the news had not reached them by other means. One such contact was Guigo, fifth prior of La Grande Chartreuse, a position he held from 1109 until his death in 1136. Guigo commanded deep respect for his profound knowledge of the history and development of monastic life, especially of the varied rules which had been followed, and it is not surprising to find that, like 'Hugo peccator', he too felt constrained to write direct to the Templars about the nature of their vocation.[17] Guigo was no supporter of warfare conducted on behalf of the Church and, on occasion, did not hesitate to say so,[18] and his letter to Hugh of Payns suggests that, perhaps like Bernard of Clairvaux and Peter the Venerable, he had also faced up to and eventually overcome considerable spiritual and intellectual doubts about the concept of a military order.

Guigo seems to have written soon after Hugh of Payns had returned to the east in 1129, for he says that he regrets having missed the opportunity to enjoy a conversation with him during his recent visit. He writes out of an evident need to warn Hugh of potential danger. 'It is useless indeed for us to attack exterior enemies', he says, 'if we do not first conquer those of the interior.' Dominion over vast territories was a vain pretension while still in 'shameful servitude' to that minuscule lump of clay which was one's own body. 'Let us first purge our souls of vices, then the lands from the barbarians.' In a letter replete with the imagery of warfare, but applied to spiritual struggle rather than actual combat in a manner reminiscent of pre-Gregorian monasticism, he urged the Templars to protect themselves with spiritual armour so that 'the stewards of the darkness of this world' (Ephesians 6:12) cannot penetrate it. Although he wished the Templars success in their temporal wars, there is a deep vein of anxiety here, for he believed that their occupation might all too easily undermine the achievement of that inner purification without which he evidently considered their worldly conquests to be worthless. Guigo was so concerned that his message should reach its destination that he sent the letter by two different messengers, 'in case because of some impediment – God forbid – they should not manage to reach you', and he asked Hugh of Payns to ensure that it was read out to all the brothers.

It was, however, St Bernard who was best known and his treatise had a double value to the Templars in that it clearly influenced others to accept the idea when, without his authority, they might have been less susceptible. One such writer was Bishop Anselm of Havelberg, who found space to consider them in his *Dialogues*, written about 1145. While his grasp of the chronology of their foundation is unsteady (Urban II is substituted for Honorius II), his image of the Order and the language in which he expresses it is permeated by *De laude*:

Similarly, a little after this time a new religious institution began in Jerusalem, the city of God. There were assembled some laymen, pious men who called themselves knights of the Temple: having abandoned their fortune, they live and fight under the obedience of a master alone; they have renounced superfluity and luxury in clothing; they have sworn to defend the glorious tomb of the Saviour against the Saracens; peaceful at home, outside they are valiant fighters; at home obedient to regular discipline, outside obedient to military discipline; at home enveloping themselves in sacred silence, outside imperturbable in the fracas and violence of war; and to say everything, perfect for the execution of all the orders they receive, inside or outside, in the simplicity of obedience.[19]

Anselm believed in the value of new orders (he himself was a Premonstratensian),[20] but even he hints that he had felt disquiet in that perhaps their path to salvation was not as clear as the more traditional routes. 'It was declared there [at Troyes] that all those who joined their society in the hope of eternal life and who persevered there faithfully would obtain the remission of all their sins. It affirmed that their merit was not inferior to that of the monks and the canons who lead a communal life.'

However, simultaneously, images were also forming in the public mind, reflected particularly in the charters of the early donors. As might be expected, ecclesiastics are most reminiscent of St Bernard. Ulger, Bishop of Angers, in a charter which probably dates from the mid 1140s, ordered his clergy to receive 'our brothers' kindly and affectionately and allow them into the churches to preach and to collect dues.

For these are the messengers and officials and soldiers of the knighthood of Christ, in the sacrosanct Temple of the Lord in Jerusalem, whose militia is without doubt true and most pleasing to God, who turning aside from all worldly desires, namely the joys of marriage and all kinds of pleasures, devoid of property of their own, professing an arduous religion, in order that there might follow an eternal blessedness, have chosen to fight against the enemies of God, who persecute the holy city of Jerusalem and other oriental places, nor do they hesitate to give their souls and to shed their blood, until they have destroyed and exterminated the impious pagans from the most holy places, which the Lord chose for his activity and passion and abode.[21]

The descriptions in the charters of secular donors are simpler, but encompass a variety of names and functions for the Templars nevertheless, suggesting that a settled picture of the meaning and role of a military orders was still emerging during the 1130s and early 1140s. Many are expressed in very general terms: 'to Christ and his knights of the holy city' (Troyes, 1129); 'to the knighthood of St Mary which is in Jerusalem' (Mas-Deu, 1137); 'to the glorious knighthood of the Temple of Solomon, established in Jerusalem' (Richerenches, 1138); 'to the knights of the Temple of God' (Foix, 1145).[22] Those with strong connections with the east, especially those who actually went there as pilgrims and crusaders, were more fully informed. Alfonso-Jordan, Count of Toulouse, made his grant 'to God and the Christian knights who serve God in the Temple of Solomon and guard the Holy City and its inhabitants, [and] also defend those travelling to and from there' (1134). In a grant actually made in the Kingdom of Jerusalem, William of St Omer and his son Osto conceded their incomes from churches in Flanders 'to the knights of the Temple, whom divine providence deputed through the lord patriarch Warmund and the advice of the barons to the defence of the land of Jerusalem and the guard of pilgrims' (1137). Thierry, Count of Flanders, who in 1139 completed the first of his four expeditions to the east, spoke of 'the knights of the Temple perpetually fighting for God by strongly defending the Oriental Church from the filth of the pagans' (1144). King Louis VII of France, freshly returned from the Second Crusade, explained that he was granting them the town of Savigny because he wished to augment their wealth 'from which they do not cease to sustain both paupers and pilgrims daily with copious charity' (1149).[23]

Crusaders to the east seem therefore to have observed that the military activity of the Templars was not confined solely to the guard of pilgrims. This wider military role was appreciated in Catalonia and Aragon at an equally early date. In 1131 Raymond Berenguer III's grant of Grañena was 'to the defence of Christendom, in accordance with the institution of the Order'. His son, Raymond Berenguer IV, in making his great cession of six frontier castles in 1143, was more grandiloquent. He was

moved by the strength of the Holy Spirit on high by the power of the knighthood to defend the western church which is in Spain, to lay low and to conquer and to expel the people of the Moors, to exalt the faith and religion of holy Christianity, to [follow] the example of the knighthood of the Temple of Solomon in Jerusalem which in its subject and obedience defends the oriental church, in accordance with the rule and *milicia* of this knighthood instituted in blessed obedience you have decreed to be established.[24]

The grant of these castles was in part a consequence of the problems arising from the will of Alfonso of Aragon in 1131. In this document Alfonso appears to have believed that he was leaving his kingdom to three communities which would perform complementary roles: the canons who undertook religious and liturgical duties, the Hospitallers who looked after the poor, and the Templars who mounted the defence of Christendom. Three years later, his brother, Ramiro, said unequivocally that the Templars 'go against the Moors for the defence of Christians and to the confusion of the Pagans'.[25]

Whatever their individual views of the nature of the Order of the Temple, such donors were untroubled by the heart-searching of the monastic world and clearly had confidence that their material sacrifices would ultimately be efficacious. Many of the charters explain (or purport to explain) the motives of the donors; indeed, in some cases there is a manifest anxiety to record in written form the reasons for such grants. In a minority of cases there is a direct connection with pilgrimage to Jerusalem. In August 1143, Poncius Chalveria gave mill-stones for working his mill at Roaix on the River Ouvèze (which runs into the Rhône at Avignon), which the Templars were already using, 'wishing to set out for Jerusalem in order to visit the Sepulchre of the Lord, that almighty God might put aside my sins and concede to me the good fortune to return to my own land'.[26] Three years later, not far away, at Richerenches, two brothers, Raymond and William of Balmis, made a grant of a manse to the Templar house there, 'on account of the indulgence of our sins, wishing to go to Jerusalem and put aside all malice', while a third brother, Gerald, although apparently not intending to make the journey, gave his part too, 'that our Lord might indulge my sins and ordain that my soul and those of my relations be warmed in the perfection of Paradise'.[27]

In most cases, however, these desires and hopes are not directly connected with pilgrimage as such, although the choice of this new Order as recipient must reflect an admiration for its work as protector of pilgrims and a conviction that support for such work was a particularly meritorious act. Fairly typical is the grant of 1133 in the County of Barcelona by Bernard Amati, describing himself as viscount, together with his wife and sons, 'on account of the remission of our sins, in all the year through any week, one *somada* of salt, that the omnipotent Lord might deign to be more well-disposed to the sins and crimes of our sons and ourselves and deign to grant to us the reward of eternal life, and direct our acts in all our work, while we are in this life'.[28] In a more elaborate form in the same year in Roussillon, Açalaidis gave her body and soul to God and the Templars as well as her allod in the county:

And this gift I make because my Lord deigned to be a pauper for me: just as he was a pauper for me, so I wish to be a pauper for him; that he might cause me to come to true repentance and true confession and make me arrive at his holy paradise; and he might have mercy on the souls of my mother and father and all my relations, and he should induce all my children into his holy service, that they might come to a good end.

The gift was made with the advice and consent of her children and concludes with a formula (not uncommon in various forms) aimed at preventing them reneging on this in the future. 'If any of my children or my relations should despoil or infringe the above-written allod, may he be separated from the Book of Life until he has made amends.'[29] In contrast, in 1146, when Bardonas and his wife gave lands at Gerona, they said simply and succinctly that this was done 'in order that we might have eternal rest in the future'.[30]

This preoccupation with future salvation is underpinned by a strong sense of human mortality and of the decay of material things.

In his will of 1131 Alfonso of Aragon said that he had been 'reflecting and drawing together in my mind that nature generates all mortal men' and that therefore he wished to make these provisions 'while I still have life'.[31] Eight years later, on the other side of the peninsula at Avida in Portugal, Bona Soariz and her daughter, Mandreona, made their testaments under the inspiration of the Gospel of St Matthew (25:13): 'For since the Lord said: "Be vigilant and pray since you do not know the day or the hour", he certainly gave a sign to summon us, by the renunciation of corruptible things.' Otherwise there was a danger that a love of perishable things might have dire consequences for 'suddenly wretched man is taken from this life while he is not yet sustained with the fruit of good works'.[32] In 1145, Fernand Menendiz, in granting his castle of Longroiva in Estremadura, came to the same conclusion, 'seeing the riches of this world quickly go to ruin, it is pleasing to me, that from these transitory things I should expend some in the service of God'.[33] Sometimes personal circumstances brought this sense of impending death into even sharper focus. In 1144, one knight gave not only his allodial estates and his best horse and equipment to the Templars of Mas-Deu, but his body to be buried there as well. 'I, Raymond of Montesquieu, lie in illness and I fear lest unexpected death might suddenly come upon me; therefore I caused this my testament to be written, that if death happens to come to me, I have distributed all movables and immovables, as is here written.'[34]

It may be, of course, that both the sentiments uttered and the manner of expressing them owe more to the clerics who drew up the charters than to the donors themselves, especially when there is direct appeal to New Testament precept. The preamble of the charter of John, Archbishop of Braga, shows very clearly this clerical mode of expression, again drawing on Matthew, chapter 25, as a source:

Although in the Christian religion there are many works by which it is believed one can attain the promise of eternal life, nevertheless it is incumbent upon the office of piety that it should lead the quest for this life by offering solace to the knights of Christ, who not only take care of the poor, but also lead the protection of Christians. Moreover, since the gospel says 'what you have done for one of the least of mine you have done for me' [v.40], he who piously bestows the solace of necessity upon the least doubtless establishes for himself the debt of eternal remuneration in Christ.[35]

54

Along with the Gospel of St Matthew, the injunctions of St Paul provided a ready source of inspiration. One of the earliest grants to the Order by William, Castellan of St Omer, in September 1128, wove in a quotation from the Epistle to the Galatians (6:10): 'Considering indeed what the apostle said that "while we have time, we must devote ourselves to the good of all, especially however to the servants of the faith", for the remission of my sins by which I confess myself to be dreadfully burdened, I make this gift to the knighthood of Christ of the Temple of the land of Jerusalem, legitimately fighting against the Pagans.'[36] In the late 1130s, Gerard of Montségur, who by 1142 had himself become a Templar in the house at Richerenches, granted the house the properties held by him and his wife at Bourbouton, taking his lead from the Epistle to the Ephesians (4:7): 'Every man has this example as the Apostle says: "Each of us is given grace, in accordance with the measure of the gift of Christ."'[37] Such documents reflect evident clerical influence, but too much stress can be given to this. Simply because laymen and women lacked the skills to express their feelings in written Latin it does not follow that the preambles to their grants are pious formulae unrelated to the realities of their lives. Indeed, if this were so the whole reason for the existence of such donations would be called into question.

Hugh of Payns and his companions had, however, aimed not only at soliciting donations, but also at gaining recruits, for, even if William of Tyre's figure of nine recruits only need not be taken literally, their numbers were evidently too small both for the kind of role which Baldwin II appears to have envisaged in the east and for the administration of properties now rapidly accumulating in the west. Charters recording the property brought to the Order by the new recruit often describe his motivation and feelings as well. As with the more conventional monastic orders, the sense of the abrogation of the will is powerfully manifest, as the two following examples show. In 1140 Raymond of Luzençon (near Rodez) prefaced his donation: 'I, renouncing secular life and its pomp, relinquishing everything, give myself to the Lord God and to the knighthood of the Temple of Solomon of Jerusalem, that, as long as I shall live, in accordance with my strength, I shall serve there a complete pauper for God.'[38] Further south, at Mas-Deu in Roussillon, Arnold of Sournia, who joined in 1142/3, began with an equally unequivocal declaration: 'I, wishing to come to the joys of Paradise, surrender my body and my soul to the Lord God and the Blessed Mary and the brothers of the knighthood of the Temple of Solomon in Jerusalem.'[39]

The cement for all these separate stones in the edifice was provided by the papacy in three definitive bulls of privileges issued between 1139 and 1145.[40] These bulls, known as *Omne datum optimum*, *Milites Templi* and *Militia Dei*, underwrote the new order so unequivocally that henceforth doubts about the validity of the concept no longer found a place in the mainstream of thought in the western Church. This support was maintained throughout the rest of the Order's history, for the bulls were many times reissued. After Troyes the ability of the papacy to provide the Order with positive help had been severely hampered by the schism between Anacletus II and Innocent II, making the 1130s an acutely difficult period for the papacy. The support given by St Bernard and the French clergy to Innocent II inevitably connected the Temple to his cause, an allegiance repaid at the Council of Pisa when Innocent granted the Order a mark of gold each year, his chancellor, Aimeric, contributed two ounces of gold, and each of the archbishops, bishops, and abbots, and 'other good men' a mark of silver. Others made similar donations.[41] Since 113 bishops attended, this made a substantial contribution to the Order's resources, as well as setting an example for other clerics not present.

After Anacletus' death in 1138 it was possible for Innocent to return to Rome and at the Lateran on 29 March 1139, he promulgated the fundamental bull of Templar privileges known as *Omne datum optimum*. Taking his theme from the Epistle of James, the pope quoted, 'Every best gift and every perfect gift descends from above from the father of lights in whom there is no change nor shadow of alteration' (1:17). Innocent described this gift in terms of the contrast between secular knights and the *militia* of the Temple made by St Bernard. They had been transformed from men who were 'by nature the children of wrath' (Ephesians 2:3), given over to secular pleasures, into 'true Israelites', who fought 'divine battles'. By this means they truly 'kindled the flame of charity'. In the words of the Gospel of John: 'No man has greater love, who lays down his life for his friends' (15:13). Innocent therefore gave official sanction to their role as defenders of the Catholic Church and attackers of the enemies of Christ, for which he enjoined the remission of their sins, 'on the authority of God and the blessed Peter, prince of the apostles'. All legitimate acquisitions could be harnessed to such a worthy end. Spoils taken from the infidel could be converted to their use; any attempt to force them to give them up was prohibited by the pope. All donations made to them were placed under the protection of the Holy See.

In taking the Templars directly under the papal umbrella, Innocent recognised them as a legitimate order of the Church whose members were directly answerable to their Master. The Master himself could be drawn only from among those 'professed in the vows of your habit', elected either unanimously or 'by the sounder and purer part'. No ecclesiastical or secular person could licitly infringe 'the customs established in the observation of your religion and offices' from this time onwards; only the Master and Chapter could effect changes to these customs. A concomitant was that no 'fealties, homages or oaths or safeguards on sacred relics' should be made to any secular person. Nor should any Templar transfer elsewhere, 'for God, who is immutable and eternal, . . . wishes that a sacred proposal once begun be carried through to the end of the obligation taken on'. Using the same reference as 'Hugo peccator' the pope ordered: 'each of you remain in that vocation to which you are called' (1 Cor. 7:20). No longer was there room for doubt about the legitimacy of the Templar calling, for it had been set down with the authority of the see of St Peter.

Independent and permanent, the Templars needed the means to sustain themselves. As defenders of the goods of the Church it was appropriate to exempt them from the payment of tithes, while at the same time giving them the right to acquire them, provided that they had the assent of the bishops and their clergy. Moreover, such a structure needed not only material resources, but spiritual guidance as well, and the bull granted the Order its own priests for the first time. Once in the Order, these priests were as much under the control of the Master as the knights and sergeants, despite the fact that the Master was not ordained. The Order was similarly allowed its own oratories, where divine office could be heard undisturbed by seculars, and around which they and their associates could be buried.

In this bull Innocent II provides a detailed definition of the Order of the Temple as it was conceived in the late 1130s. His successors, Celestine II and Eugenius III, built upon this foundation by providing it with the means to take full advantage of the imperium the Order was in the process of creating. The bull *Milites Templi* (1144) was addressed to the prelates of Christendom. Celestine explains how, through the Templars, 'God liberates the eastern church from the filth of the pagans'. These men 'do not fear to place their lives at the disposal of their brothers', but they do not have sufficient resources and therefore 'you should admonish the people committed to you by God to make collections'. Contributions were a partial substitute for crusading: helping to establish a Templar house brought an indulgence of a seventh part of the penance enjoined on the donor. Templar brothers could themselves make their own collections, for which purpose they were allowed the special privilege of opening churches once a year in a place under interdict. For their part, it was the duty of the clergy to protect their persons and goods from 'any damage or injury'. *Militia Dei* (1145) established this Templar presence very visibly in the dioceses. Eugenius told prelates that while 'by no means wishing to diminish the rights of your parishes', he nevertheless gave the Templars permission to take tithes, obligations, and burial fees in places where they had oratories and to bury members of their own *familia* there, 'for it is shameful and a danger to the soul to mix the religious brothers on the occasion of their going to church next to the disturbances of men and the places frequented by women'. It was the obligation of the prelates to consecrate these oratories and to bless the cemeteries, when asked to do so by the brothers.

As might be expected, the jurisdictional and economic independence granted in *Omne datum optimum* does not seem to have been implemented immediately, since in practice the reality of daily relations inevitably led to compromise. In a document which originally dates from 1152 the Templars seem to be continuing to accept the authority of the patriarch of Jerusalem as well as the pope, while the limitations placed upon the sweeping tithe exemption by Adrian IV in 1155, when he defined it as applying specifically to the produce of demesne lands, only seem to have been a confirmation of what was happening in practice anyway. On the other hand, the provision of their own priests and oratories had a more rapid effect: in the Templar agreement with the Bishop of Tortosa in 1152 all churches in the Order's hands, both in the parishes and castles, were free of episcopal jurisdiction.[42] It may indeed have been during the period when these privileges were beginning to have some visible effect that St Bernard, anticipating potential problems, wrote to the Patriarchs of Jerusalem and Antioch urging them to give their support to the Templars.[43] The ultimate importance of the papal privileges, therefore, was to inaugurate a significant shift in society's perception of the Order of the Temple. The Order's importance to the papacy under Alexander III, for instance, has been compared to that of the Cluniacs in the era of Urban II.[44] From now on the Temple was established as a powerful element in the religious establishment, a position which had profound effects upon both the outlook of its leaders and the attitudes of outside observers towards it.

Two of the most important of these observers were dismayed by the changes. In his *Policraticus*, completed in 1159, John of Salisbury offers what amounts to a critical commentary upon the papal privileges.[45] In the section of the work devoted to hypocrites, he warns that such people are most likely to be found in the company of communities of sincere and worthy men, since under this cover they can most easily conceal their ambitions. The evident virtues of new orders, like the Templars, who follow the example of the Maccabees in laying down their lives for their brethren, exercise a strong attraction for these men and, in consequence, communities which had originally rejoiced in poverty are now 'favoured with privileges which, ceasing to be necessary and snubbing charity are deemed to be instruments of avarice rather than of religion'. Pope Adrian had restricted their scope, particularly in regard to the payment of tithes, but he had made serious omissions.

Although he does not refer to the bulls by name, his references to the Templar privileges are quite clear. For John, the provisions of *Omne datum optimum* were quite wrong and contrary to 'the right order' of society as conceived by the leaders of clerical opinion since the beginning of the reform movement in the middle of the eleventh century:

For the Knights of the Temple with the pope's approval claim for themselves the administration of churches, they occupy them through surrogates, and they whose normal occupation it is to shed human blood in a certain way presume to administer the blood of Christ. Not of course that I would call those – almost alone among men – who wage legitimate war 'men of blood', since even David was called a man of blood not because he engaged in wars which were legitimate but on account of Uriah, whose blood he criminally shed. For as is provided by the canons, none of the power of the ecclesiastical sphere may be seen to be ascribed to laymen, even if they are religious men. Above all it would be a sign of true religion if they refrained from the administration of those things which by God's prohibition it is not permitted for them to touch.

John's acceptance of the legitimacy of the shedding of blood by Christians in certain circumstances was only possible if the knights did not take on clerical functions: for him the two were completely incompatible. Nor did he think that the Order should be allowed to perform the duty of hospitality 'from the spoils of plunder', even though it was taken from the infidel, 'because God hates the bread of sacrilege, and spurns sacrifices which are offered out of blood; and as often as He is called upon by such means, He closes His ears so that He is not open to their supplications'.

The contents of *Milites Templi* and *Militia Dei* deepened his disgust:

Still it is entirely wicked that, enticed by the love of money, they open churches which were closed by bishops. Those suspended from office celebrate the sacraments, they bury the dead whom the Church refuses, and they act once a year so that during the rest of the year the erring people are deaf to the voice of the Church; and he who cannot be coerced seems to be corrected. Therefore, they travel around to the churches, they praise the merits of their own Orders, they bring absolution for crimes and sometimes they preach a new gospel, falsifying the word of God because they preach living not by grace but by a price, by pleasure and not by truth. And in the end, when they convene in their lairs late at night, 'after speaking of virtue by day they shake their hips in nocturnal folly and exertion'. If one moves in this fashion towards Christ, then the doctrine of the Fathers which teaches that the narrow and steep path heads towards the true life of man is false and vain.

For John of Salisbury these privileges were an encouragement to avarice, one of the two worst cardinal vices of the age.[46] The other was pride, characterised by the knightly warrior, mounted on his horse, high above the rest of the populace, which he could so easily scatter before him. In *De laude*, St Bernard had pointed up the difference between the pride of these secular knights and the humility of the Templars but, as has been rightly said, in reality the Church had great difficulty in convincing this class that pride was a sin worth considering.[47] William of Tyre, although sympathetic to the ideals of the early founders, believed that the Order had failed to curb this characteristic among its members, like John of Salisbury, claiming that their privileges had led them to forget the humility of their founders.[48]

The attitudes of John of Salisbury and William of Tyre towards the Templars were shaped by what they believed the Order had become, but for two other writers, Isaac of L'Etoile and Walter Map, they were determined by the belief that they should not have been established in the first place.[49] These two observers were very different from each other, for Isaac was the abbot of the isolated and obscure Cistercian house of L'Etoile in Poitou, while Walter, Archdeacon of Oxford and courtier of Henry II, was an active participant in the varied affairs of the secular and ecclesiastical worlds. As abbot, Isaac regularly preached to his monks, drawing on a profound knowledge and wide culture acquired over twenty years of study under men like Peter Abelard and Gilbert de la Porrée. He probably entered L'Etoile when it was still a daughter house of Pontigny before this monastic network was absorbed by the Cistercians in 1145 and, although an admirer of the sanctity of St Bernard, cannot be seen as an uncritical follower of his views. For Isaac, 'the new knighthood' which had arisen was in fact 'a new monstrosity'. It was, he says, quoting an unnamed source with approval, 'The Order of the Fifth Gospel', apparently meaning that he saw no place for it within the Church. These knights forced the infidel to the faith with lances and clubs, 'so that those who do not have the name of Christ, they freely despoil and religiously massacre'. However, if they themselves are killed in the process, they are pronounced martyrs of Christ. He wondered what the unbelievers thought of a Church which behaved in this way and asked why they were not shown the gentleness and patience of Christ instead. Will it not be asked, he said, what kind of Church it is that does such things? While the abbot stopped short of actually condemning 'the new knighthood', conceding that it might not be altogether bad, he does nevertheless warn his monks that evil can arise from good intentions, for 'virtues can nourish vices', clearly implying that whatever may have been the original idea, the very nature of the occupation carried within it an immense danger of corruption.[50]

In contrast, Walter Map wrote from the point of view of the secular clergy and, not unexpectedly, criticised the Templars for their abandonment of their early humility for pride and avarice. 'Since, owing to their services, they are held dear by prelates and kings, and are high in honour, they take good care that the means of their exaltation shall not be wanting', he says cynically. His hostility to all exempt orders, especially the Cistercians, is, however, well known, so his complaint is predictable, almost routine. But this initial dissatisfaction seems to have led him to reflect more deeply than this. Christ had denied Peter the use of the sword: 'There Peter was taught to ensue peace by patience: who taught these [the Templars] to overcome force by violence I know not.' They could not even justify their existence on the grounds of effectiveness, for 'we see that under their protection our boundaries in those parts are always being narrowed, and those of our enemies enlarged'. Moreover, if eventually, 'all the ends of the world remember themselves and are turned unto the Lord, as the prophet says, what will these do? If peace comes, what is to become of the sword?'[51]

Isaac of L'Etoile's view is the more considered, both because of its greater consistency and because, unlike Map, it was not written with the benefit of hindsight derived from the fall of Jerusalem in 1187, but neither writer represented the mainstream, nor indeed did they have much in common with each other. Nevertheless, they do show that the doubts which had gnawed at the consciences of the first Templars had not been entirely dispersed by St Bernard's rhetoric. Moreover, although Bernard's monastic contemporaries had recognised that the first Templars were good men with righteous intentions, properly authorised in a just cause, and that they therefore fulfilled the Augustinian criteria, the unease of the leaders of more contemplative orders was undisguised. The immense changes in the Christian world during the twelfth and thirteenth centuries, both intellectual and socio-economic, gradually accustomed men to novelty, so that the essentially defensive attitudes displayed by the clerical reformers of the early crusading era had, by the time of the Franciscans, been replaced by a much more positive appreciation of the value of at least some innovations.[52] But this readjustment of mental horizons was not sufficiently advanced during the early years of the Temple for the Order to be universally accepted as a valuable new vocation, beneficial to the Church. Indeed, during the first half of the twelfth century, there was a most intense debate about the nature of monastic orders in general, a debate which inevitably carried implications for the military orders. It is no coincidence that the Hospitallers, for their part, felt it necessary to justify themselves by claiming a completely spurious existence in apostolic times.[53] There is perhaps some irony in the fact that, in 1306, 187 years after the foundation of the Temple, James of Molay, the last Grand Master, faced with the idea of a union of the military orders, can be found grumbling that *novitas* was rarely, if ever, anything but dangerous.[54]

Nor did the resonances ever fully die away, despite the unequivocal statements of papal bulls, for the feeling that the Templars were an unnatural hybrid persisted. Despite the change in the position of the Master of the Temple in witness lists and other records after 1129, when he moves from the laity to a place among the ecclesiastics,[55] in 1308 Philip the Fair's ministers still considered that there was an issue here worth exploiting. The king's lawyers, ever alert to spot an opening, must have been encouraged by the knowledge that the scholastics had hitherto failed to give any definitive consideration to the proper social and legal position of the military orders.[56] One of the questions which they therefore asked the masters of theology at the University of Paris was whether they considered that the Templars had forefeited any privilege of immunity they might claim, not only because of their heresies, but also since they were 'a college of knights and not principally of clerks'.[57]

CHAPTER THREE

THE RISE OF THE TEMPLARS IN THE EAST IN THE TWELFTH CENTURY

> On the morning of May 17 rabi 'II, two days after the victory, the Sultan sought out the Templars and Hospitallers who had been captured and said: 'I shall purify the land of these two impure races.' He assigned fifty *dinar* to every man who had taken one of them prisoner, and immediately the army brought forward at least a hundred of them. He ordered that they should be beheaded, choosing to have them dead rather than in prison. With him was a whole band of scholars and sufis and a certain number of devout men and ascetics; each begged to be allowed to kill one of them, and drew his sword and rolled back his sleeve.[1]

'Imād-ad-Dīn, secretary and chancellor to Saladin, was an eye-witness of the treatment of the brothers of the military orders after the comprehensive Christian defeat at the battle of Hattin on 4 July 1187, and in this passage he dramatically encapsulates the Islamic view of their role in the crusading wars. While St Bernard had seen the Templars as the instrument of God driving out the Saracens who had defiled the holy places, Saladin and the holy men in his entourage were equally convinced that the real causes of pollution were the military religious brotherhoods of Christian warriors. For the normally merciful Saladin, his face full of joy as he watched the executions according to 'Imād-ad-Dīn, there was only one solution.[2]

Saladin's reaction was based upon a correct assessment of the ideological commitment and the military importance of the orders. For without them, despite their faults (and there were many prepared to point these out during their history), the precarious Latin settlements in Outremer could not have survived until 1291, and the many thousands of pilgrims infused with the desire to visit the holy places would have been frustrated. Although Edessa was lost to Zengi,

Atabeg of Mosul, in 1144, and the Second Crusade – led by King Louis VII of France and King Conrad III of Germany – neither recovered the county nor offset its loss, nevertheless until Hattin the Latins succeeded in retaining most of the 600 kilometres of territory along the coast which made up the remaining three states of Antioch, Tripoli, and Jerusalem. Until 1174 the key figures were the vigorous and effective kings of Jerusalem: Fulk of Anjou (died 1143), and Fulk's sons, Baldwin III (died 1163) and Amalric (died 1174). They never captured the important inland cities of Aleppo and Damascus, but they did gain all those along the coast with the help of blockades from the Italian maritime cities. Tyre was taken in 1124 and even Ascalon, the most stubborn, fell in 1153. In the 1160s Amalric made a series of determined, but ultimately unsuccessful, attempts to conquer Egypt, a strategy which, if it had worked, would have greatly increased crusader resources and effectively blocked off the Muslim encirclement which Saladin had achieved by 1187.

Nevertheless, the position of the crusader states remained difficult. The stability of the Kingdom of Jerusalem was from time to time shaken by internal dissension, especially in the revolt against King Fulk of 1134 and during the struggle for power between Queen Melisende and her son, Baldwin, between 1149 and 1152,[3] while at the same time in Syria the rise of powerful Turkish leaders, first Zengi (died 1146) and then his son, Nūr-ad-Dīn (died 1174), placed immense external pressure on the Christians. By 1157 Nūr-ad-Dīn was established in both Aleppo and Damascus and ten years later his lieutenant, Shīrkūh, Saladin's uncle, was contesting Egypt with Amalric. The deaths of Nūr-ad-Dīn and Amalric in 1174 increased the strains upon the crusader states, since Amalric's successor, Baldwin IV, was sick with leprosy, a disease which was to kill him in 1185, aged only twenty-four. First his youth and then his illness made Baldwin a ruler only fitfully effective and the underlying factional tension which had occasionally disrupted the rule of his house now surfaced quite overtly. On the other hand Saladin, freed from the restraints imposed by an uneasy relationship with Nūr-ad-dīn, was now able to expand his conquests relatively unhindered. The defeat of the Christians at Hattin had been preceded by an extensive and carefully planned military and diplomatic offensive in the Muslim and Byzantine worlds which had left the Christians isolated. William of Tyre, while complaining about what he believed to be a contemporary decline in morality and fighting skill among the Christians, put his finger on the fundamental problem when, writing early in the 1180s, he contrasted past divisions in Islam with the contemporary situation in which 'now all the kingdoms neighbouring us have been brought under one power, God willing it thus'.[4]

During these years the Templars moved from a role so marginal that they are not even mentioned by Fulcher of Chartres, the chronicler who was the contemporary of Hugh of Payns in Jerusalem, to the very centre of the action. A measure of the extent of this change can be obtained by observing the role of the French Templars in the crusade of King Louis VII in 1147–8. The Templars were able to assemble 130 knights at the chapter in Paris on 27 April 1147,[5] before the departure of the crusade, presumably intending that this contingent should travel to the east with the French army. It seems unlikely that there would have been fewer sergeants or serving brothers accompanying them. Present at the chapter were Pope Eugenius III, King Louis VII, and four archbishops, persons so eminent that, in rank if not in numbers, the gathering was comparable to that brought to St Denis by Abbot Suger for the consecration of the new choir of the abbey church, three years earlier.[6] According to William of Tyre it was under Eugenius III that the Templars received the right to wear the characteristic red cross upon their tunics, symbolising their willingness to suffer martyrdom in the defence of the Holy Land,[7] and this chapter meeting would have been the most appropriate setting for this event.

During the journey itself Everard des Barres, Master in France, emerged as one of the king's trusted counsellors. He was one of the three ambassadors (together with Bartholomew the Chancellor and Archibald of Bourbon) sent ahead to Constantinople by the king to conduct the difficult negotiations with the Byzantine emperor, Manuel I, who was nervous about the presence of such a large army in the vicinity of the city. Although at first there were clashes between the French and the emperor's Patzinak and Cuman troops, negotiations by the envoys eventually brought a truce and the market facilities that the crusaders required.[8] The French army crossed the Bosporus in late October and began the dangerous journey through Asia Minor, pushing on through the late autumn and winter, despite news of the defeats suffered by the German army which had preceded them and the deteriorating weather. When on the move crusaders were almost as vulnerable as pilgrims and the most obvious extension of the Templars' role was as guardians of the mobile columns. From the outset the army found the attacks of the Turkish light horsemen difficult to counter, for their skill at firing from the saddle and then rapidly retreating from range was quite new to the western knights. A particularly severe reverse took place at Cadmus Mountain between Laodicea and Attalia in January 1148, by which time supplies were running low and there was a severe shortage of horses. 'Like a beast which becomes more savage after tasting blood', says the Saint-Denis chronicler, Odo of Deuil, the Turks attacked all the more fiercely when they realised the crusaders' weakness.[9] In these circumstances the king handed over responsibility for the defence of the army to the Templars who had, in contrast to most of the crusaders, carefully conserved their supplies. Everard des Barres, 'who should be revered for his piety and who furnished the army an honourable example', according to Odo of Deuil, organised the army into units of fifty, each under an individual Templar, in turn responsible to an overall commander, a Templar knight called Gilbert. These units were intended to provide a focal point for the various sections of the army within the column, as well as acting as a body when any manoeuvre was undertaken. This seems to have achieved a modicum of order, although the army was considerably undermined by the damage it had already sustained, and at Attalia the king took advantage of shipping supplied by the Byzantines to sail to Saint Symeon in the Principality of Antioch.[10]

By the time the king arrived in Antioch in March 1148, he had spent so much money on supplies and shipping that he needed to borrow to keep his expedition in being. Again the Templars proved their value. On 10 May, Everard des Barres travelled from Antioch to Acre, where he raised the necessary money either directly from the Order's resources or by borrowing on the security of the Order's possessions. When, later in the year, the king wrote to his regents in France ordering them to repay the Temple, Abbot Suger was told to find 2,000 marks of silver and Raoul of Vermandois, Count of Péronne, 30,000 *livres parisis*. Louis told Suger that only the help which he had received from the Temple had enabled him to sustain his crusade and that the sums paid out by the Order had brought it close to bankruptcy.[11] The repayments were presumably taken from the extraordinary taxation levied for the crusade, but an idea of the size of the Templar loan can be gauged from the fact that, even in the 1170s, Capetian demesne revenues were unlikely to have been more than 60,000 *livres* per annum, a sum which represents a good return for the monarchy at this date.[12] Comparison with the manpower and resources available to the Order on the eve of the Council of Troyes shows how the foundation of the military and financial power of the Temple was laid in the years between 1129 and 1148.

However, the new high profile of the Order of the Temple brought it under scrutiny from potential critics as well as admirers, and the Second Crusade is also significant for the Temple in that its failure offered a vehicle for such critics to articulate their views. At Palmae, near Acre, on 24 June 1148, a great assembly of the leaders of the crusade, including Kings Conrad, Louis, and Baldwin III of Jerusalem, decided to direct their forces against Damascus. Robert of Craon and Raymond du Puy, the Masters of the Temple and the Hospital, were present, and must have taken part in the discussions, although the advice they gave is not known.[13] However, Otto, Bishop of Freising, who, as Conrad III's half-brother and a participant in the crusade, was well informed about these events, says that Conrad stayed at the palace of the Templars in Jerusalem for a few days in Easter week (Easter Sunday was 11 April) and that by the time he returned to Acre he had agreed with the patriarch and the Templars that they should attack Damascus in the following July.[14]

In the event, the choice of Damascus proved to be a disastrous mistake. After some initial success besieging the city from a well-supplied position on the western side, the crusader attack stalled and a decision was made to switch the main effort to the east. Here it was known that conditions for a sustained siege were much less favourable, but it seems to have been argued that the defences were weaker and therefore that a quicker victory could be expected, making the question of supply much less crucial. When the city did not fall as rapidly as had been hoped, the Franks had no alternative but to retreat. The failure of the crusade astonished contemporaries, for it had been inspired by the preaching of St Bernard and executed by the powerful king of Germany and the pious king of France. It was a massive blow to the prestige of all three men and, inevitably, it was followed by recriminations.[15] Treachery was the favourite explanation, hinted at but not specified by Conrad himself in a letter to his regent, Wibald, Abbot of Corvey,[16] and accepted too by William of Tyre who, however, says that he had often spoken to men with clear recollections of the campaign, but was still unable to pin down its source.[17] Others were less reticent. In particular they blamed the resident Franks who were known to have been in alliance with Unur, ruler of Damascus, before the crusade, and to have received payments from him in the past. Some German writers, prompted by the desire to explain Conrad's failure, claimed that the Templars had deliberately engineered the retreat. According to the anonymous Würzburg annalist, the attack would have succeeded had it not been for the 'greed, deceit, and envy' of the Templars, who had accepted a massive bribe to give secret aid to the besieged.[18] This was later picked up by John of Würzburg, a priest who visited the Holy Land, probably in the late 1160s, and wrote a description of its sites and their inhabitants. According to him, the reputation of the Templars had been undermined by an accusation of treachery, although he did not know if the charge were true or false. Nevertheless, he was quite certain that it had been 'manifestly proved' at Damascus, when they were there with King Conrad.[19]

John of Salisbury, from his observation post at the papal court, also heard these rumours, perhaps from the returning French crusaders who, in October 1149, together with Louis VII, visited Rome on the way back to France. John accepted the view that must have been strongly pressed upon him, that Louis had been 'betrayed and deceived', but stressed that the king himself, as might be expected after all the military and financial support he had received, 'always endeavoured to exonerate the brothers of the Temple'.[20] It does, indeed, seem unlikely that the Templars had undermined the crusade, since all the concrete evidence about their participation contradicts such a view, but the existence and evident circulation of the belief is significant. It is the first suggestion that the ambiguous feelings about the formation and existence of the military order might be translated into specific discontents. The Franks of Outremer increasingly found that their inability to maintain the defence of the holy places without constant subsidy and military aid from the west fostered a resentment which was not always overcome by the emotional appeal of the holy places.[21] In a remarkably short time the Order of the Temple had come to epitomise the struggle with the infidel and while this brought widespread interest and support, equally, when money and lives seemed to have been wasted, as in the Second Crusade, this could sometimes rebound against it.

Whatever the truth of the Damascus episode – and it seems most likely that there was no definable treachery[22] – the Franks of the east were left to face the consequences of the failure of the crusade. Robert of Craon did not long survive it, dying on 13 January 1149; he was succeeded by Everard des Barres, one of the few participants whose reputation had been enhanced.[23] Evidently, too, the choice was influenced by Everard's close connections with Louis VII, for the Order would need to exploit its contacts and resources in France to maintain its new importance in the east. For this reason the new Master did not stay in Outremer, returning to France with the king in the autumn of 1149. Louis, for his part, imbued with the idea of raising a new crusade, possibly aimed at the Byzantines as well as Islam, must have seen the Templars as part of these plans.[24]

This is certainly the implication of a letter written to Everard in late 1149 or early 1150, by Andrew of Montbard, Seneschal of the Order, who was acting as his deputy:

Although we submitted to your departure at the petition of the lord king of the Franks, as you have heard, we are constrained on all sides by lack of knights and sergeants and money, and we implore your paternity to return to us quickly, so that, with God's help, supplied by this means with arms and money, knights and sergeants, we can relieve our mother, the Oriental Church, miserably weighed down.

The urgency was caused by a crisis in Antioch where Nūr-ad-Dīn, Zengi's successor in Aleppo, had already made inroads into the principality before the arrival of the Second Crusade. On 29 June, he had taken advantage of the crusaders' departure to advance towards Inab, where he had defeated a substantial Christian force, killing Prince Raymond in the battle. On hearing of the disaster, the Templars had gathered 120 knights and 1,000 squires and sergeants in support of Baldwin III's relief expedition to the north. Heavy borrowing had been necessary to equip them: 7,000 besants raised in Acre and another 1,000 in Jerusalem. The journey north had only been accomplished with difficulty; once there they had discovered that Nūr-ad-Dīn's forces were ravaging the countryside with impunity and that Antioch was heavily besieged. Most of the men he had taken to Antioch were now dead. Consequently, 'you will never have a better reason for returning nor at any time will your arrival be more pleasing to God, and more useful to our house and the land of Jerusalem'. The seneschal said that he could spare only a small number of brothers to bring this message; once in France their orders were to assemble all the men, knights, and sergeants, that the Templars could muster. He asked too that the pope, the king of France, and all the princes and prelates be made fully aware of the situation in the hope that they would either appear in person or send subsidies.[25]

In fact, the presence of Baldwin III's forces seems to have deterred Nūr-ad-Dīn temporarily, but the situation remained critical. Everard returned to the Kingdom of Jerusalem himself soon afterwards: in April 1152, together with Andrew of Montbard, he was witness to the royal confirmation of the possessions of the Abbey of St Mary of the Valley of Josaphat at Tyre.[26] He probably brought men and supplies with him, for the Templars took a leading role in the siege of Ascalon the following year. However, soon after this, later in the year 1152, for reasons unknown, he resigned his position. Since he ultimately became a monk at Clairvaux, where he was still living in 1176, he may have become convinced by St Bernard's view that the only true Jerusalem was Clairvaux.[27]

As well as writing to the Grand Master, Andrew of Montbard was in a particularly strong position to make known the plight of the crusader states among influential leaders in the west, for he was St Bernard's uncle and a man in whom the saint said he placed especial trust.[28] Aleth, St Bernard's mother, was an elder sister of Andrew, although as Andrew was the sixth child of Bernard, Lord of Montbard, and Humberge of Ricey, he was in fact younger than his nephew. The eldest surviving brother, Rainard, succeeded to the lordship, while two other older brothers, Miles and Gaudry, had entered Cîteaux.[29] Andrew may have joined the Temple soon after the Council of Troyes, although there is no definite evidence of his presence in the east until 1148.[30] No letter of his to St Bernard has survived, but it is evident from letters received by Peter the Venerable, including one from St Bernard, that news of the problems faced by the Templars at Antioch was effectively circulated in the west during the year 1150.[31] Moreover, three of St Bernard's own letters (one to Andrew himself and two to Queen Melisende) show that the two men were in regular correspondence. Bernard's letter to Andrew, possibly written in 1153 shortly before the saint's death, refers quite directly to 'your letters which you have most recently sent'. The real point of these letters was to elicit aid for the Holy Land, for Bernard's reply reflects his concern at 'the danger to the land, which the Lord honoured by his presence, and the danger to the city which he consecrated by his blood'.[32]

The two letters to Queen Melisende almost certainly predate this, since they apparently belong to the period of her direct rule between the death of King Fulk in 1143 and her effective removal from power by her son, Baldwin III, in 1152. Both stress the good reports of her rule and character sent to him by Andrew of Montbard, although, in what appears to be the second letter, Bernard seems less confident of their accuracy, having heard, as he says, some adverse comment about her.[33] This appears to be an oblique reference to the growing rift between Melisende and her son, caused by the determination of the queen to retain the grip on the conduct of policy and the distribution of crown offices which she had gained when Fulk had died in 1143. At that time Baldwin had not yet reached his majority, but when he came of age in 1145 the queen took little cognisance of the fact. Consequently, the period after the Second Crusade saw the crystallisation of two distinct parties in the Kingdom of Jerusalem. As institutions of some standing within the crusader states, both military orders were now, for the first time, obliged to face directly the political and military problems caused by internal conflict among the Franks. Although in this instance they seemed to have avoided taking a partisan line, it is evident that they would be drawn directly into such quarrels and that in turn this would have its effects upon their reputations. Hans Mayer had argued from charter evidence that Andrew of Montbard might be seen as a supporter of the queen,[34] a view which is given credence by the contents of St Bernard's letters. Nevertheless, too much can be read into a limited number of charters and Mayer points out that once Baldwin had excluded the queen from power (which he achieved during April 1152), Andrew of Montbard immediately appears on his charters, while, soon after, the Bishop of Tortosa conceded the Templars land in the city on which to build a castle to oppose Nūr-ad-Dīn, a grant which could not have been made without the king's approval.[35]

Once fully established in power, Baldwin moved against the one coastal city which had held out against the Christians longer than any others, that of Ascalon. So stubborn was its resistance, backed by

Egyptian resources, that the Franks had built forts around it to hem it in. Fulk's grant of Bethgibelin on the eastern side to the Hospitallers was part of this policy, and during the winter of 1149–50 the Templars received Gaza, sixteen kilometres to the south, completing a formidable blockade in conjunction with Ibelin to the north and Blanchegarde to the north-east.[36] Gaza had been a great city in the time of the Philistines and there remained many reminders of its splendid past. However, because of the conflict between the Franks and the Egyptians, it was uninhabited at this time and its buildings were in ruins. William of Tyre says that the Franks realised that they did not have the resources to rebuild the entire city, but they did erect strong walls and towers on part of the small hill upon which it stood. This was the fortification handed over to the Templars, although in the years that followed Frankish settlers built a much weaker enclosure on the rest of the hill, adjacent to the Templar fortress. This was the first major castle in the kingdom which the Templars are recorded as receiving, and its value is attested by William of Tyre who, although no friend of the Templars, found nothing to criticise in this case:

These men, brave and vigorous in arms, have kept the commission prudently and faithfully up to the present day. They have struck hard against the aforesaid town [Ascalon] with frequent attacks both secretly and openly, so that those who previously terrorised us by overrunning and plundering the whole region, now regard themselves as most happy if, through prayers or payment, they are permitted to live in peace within the walls and quietly go about their business, temporarily untroubled.

In the spring of 1150 a determined attempt by the Egyptians to seize Gaza failed and 'from that day their strength was so weakened and their ability to inflict harm so reduced, they completely gave up attacking the surrounding region'. From this time, too, the Egyptians abandoned the attempt to supply Ascalon by land and brought aid only by sea, 'fearing ambushes from the garrison along the way and having great suspicion of the knights'.[37]

The reward for this forward planning was the fall of Ascalon on 22 August 1153, opening the way for Amalric I's invasions of Egypt during the 1160s. The Templars were prominent in this long-awaited triumph, but in the one account of the siege from the Frankish side – that of William of Tyre – the price they paid in damage to their reputation was heavy. On 25 January 1153, Baldwin III assembled the secular and ecclesiastical leaders of the kingdom before Ascalon, including the Master of the Hospital, Raymond du Puy, and the new Master of the Temple, Bernard of Tremelay. Bernard of Tremelay was probably from a Burgundian family which had its origins near Dijon, so he was again drawn from this region of rich monastic recruitment.[38] He may have come to the east with the Second Crusade, but his name is not recorded in any of the surviving charters of the crusader states. The attack on Ascalon was pursued with great vigour into the summer months and particular damage was inflicted by a moveable wooden assault tower which the Franks had constructed. On the night of 15 August,[39] the defenders attempted to set fire to the tower, but a strong easterly wind blew the flames back against the city, causing part of the wall to collapse. According to William, the whole army was awoken by the noise and rushed to the breach, only to find that the Templars, presumably manning that section of the wall, had already reached it, led by Bernard of Tremelay. William claims, however, that the Master allowed no one to enter except the Templars: 'It was said that they prevented the others from approaching for this reason, that the first to enter obtain the greater part of the spoils and the more valuable booty.' This gave the Egyptians time to shore up the wall and to attack the forty or so Templars who had entered the city. The next day their bodies were hung over the walls in a gesture of contempt for the Franks. 'Sordid pillage', said William, paraphrasing Ovid, 'has no good consequences.' In William's account this set-back came close to causing the abandonment of the siege; only the determination of the Patriarch Fulcher, supported by the Hospitallers, persuaded the Christians to continue.[40]

It is impossible to determine the truth of this matter. No Muslim source mentions the role of the Templars, although the Damascene chronicler, Ibn al-Qalānisī, describes both the wooden tower and the breach in the wall as if they were preliminaries to the fall of the city.[41] William of Tyre, although giving an extraordinarily vivid and detailed account of the siege, had nevertheless obtained his information second-hand, for he was studying in France at the time. Historians have therefore been left to pursue their own speculations: the two extremes are perhaps represented by Grousset, who saw this as the beginning of a long career of greed and violence by the Templars, and Lundgreen, who portrays William's interpretation as an example of his prejudice against the Order.[42] It may be significant that the bull *Omne datum optimum* had granted the Order the right to convert spoils seized from the infidel for its own use, but it is equally possible to interpret the Templar action as an unsuccessful attempt to hold open a breach which had unexpectedly appeared until the rest of the army came up. Rather, as Ibn al-Qalānisī implies, it does seem as if the city was on the brink of capitulation, for it fell less than a week later, on 22 August, which suggests that the Franks had suffered a much less serious reverse than William implies.

Whatever Bernard of Tremelay's motives had been, the attack cost him his life; he was succeeded as Master by Andrew of Montbard. The incident had no obvious repercussions for the Templars remained entrenched at Gaza, from which they were able to mount attacks and organise patrols in the direction of the routes passing to the south and south-west, some of which were taken by those travelling between Egypt and Damascus. The Templars and Hospitallers at Gaza and Bethgibelin respectively were now in a position to create spheres of influence centred on these castles, often at the expense of secular lordships, and sometimes in competition with each other. The Templar presence and policy in the south is shown most clearly in the capture and ransoming of Nāsir-al-Dīn, son of ʿAbbās, the vizier of Egypt in 1154, which is described in two Latin sources, William of Tyre and Walter Map.[43] During 1153 and the early months of 1154 there was a power struggle in Cairo, during which the vizier, ʿAbbās, murdered the caliph, apparently with the intention of replacing him with his son, Nāsir-al-Dīn. But he failed to consolidate his position, revolt broke out, and they were forced to flee, taking with them what treasure they could pillage. They took, says William, a route 'towards the desert, intending to go to Damascus, it was said'. But although they outdistanced their Egyptian pursuers, according to the Syrian chronicler Usāmah ibn Munqidh, who was actually in the party attacked but managed to escape, on 7 June 1154 they were ambushed by a Christian force at al-Muwaylih (in the mountains between Sinai and Arabia Petraea).[44] ʿAbbās was killed and Nāsir captured. Great booty was obtained, but the Templars, because they had more knights than anybody else, carried off the greater part of the spoils, including Nāsir himself. After keeping him prisoner for many days, they sold him to the Egyptians for 60,000 pieces of gold. Once back in Egypt, he was torn to pieces by the mob. However, according to William, before the Templars sold him, Nāsir had allegedly been 'asking most eagerly to be reborn in Christ, had already learned Roman letters, [and] was being instructed in the first rudiments of the Christian faith'.

It is not clear what interpretation William intends his readers to put on this story. Defenders of the Temple, like Lundgreen, assumed that it was intended to show the Order in a bad light and accordingly dismissed it as untrue,[45] but in fact William, so prone to moral tags and quotations elsewhere, makes no actual judgement on the matter. The Templars were not an Order dedicated to conversion nor, as will be seen in the case of the murder of the Assassin envoy in 1173, did they readily believe in changes of heart among Muslims. Certainly, Nāsir had strong reason to affect an interest in Christianity, whereas the Templars for their part saw the opportunity to acquire a large sum towards their never-ending expenses. There does seem to have been some exaggeration on William's part: Usāmah, who knew the Templars well, says that his party had lost most of what they had intended to bring in the fighting in Cairo,[46] while it seems unlikely that Nāsir had advanced very far with his Christian studies during the time that he was imprisoned by the Templars.[47]

Although Walter Map seems to have obtained the story independently, his version contributes no information on the events themselves, but instead concentrates upon making overt the implied criticism of the Templars seen in William of Tyre. He seems to have included it to show that the Templars were devoted to war to the exclusion of all else. Nāsir is presented as a man of culture and nobility who had already come to the conclusion that 'his own religion had no stability or faith', even before his capture. But when the Templars were told of this they refused to listen, even when he offered to obtain the city of Cairo for them. Hearing of the proposed surrender, the Egyptians paid heavily for him to be handed over to them, but even then they still hoped to make him their leader. The stumbling block was his belief in Christianity, a constancy, as Map describes it, which led to his condemnation as an apostate. 'He was led therefore to the stake, and bound to it, and, like those noble martyrs, King Edmund and blessed Sebastian, was shot with arrows and sent to Christ.' The chief interest of the story here therefore lies in its existence and not in its credibility.

Gaza therefore functioned as a base for a substantial Templar presence, from which the knights could exercise some control over movements to the south of the kingdom. After the middle of the twelfth century there is evidence of an increasing reliance upon the military orders to maintain and guard important castles and their dependent lands in this way (see figure 3). In 1306, in a report on the idea of a union of the Orders of the Temple and the Hospital, James of Molay argued that such a union was unnecessary in that the two orders complemented one another in their military roles. The orders, he said, formed the advance and rear guards of the moving columns, so that they enfolded visitors to the east within their protective arms 'like a mother does her child'.[48] This phrase could equally well have applied to their guard of the fortified places which provided the structure around which the crusader states were built. While it is clear that the Franks did not – indeed, could not – operate to any grand strategic plan, for both the piecemeal and sometimes individualistic nature of their conquest and the need to utilise the fortifications built by previous occupants, both Byzantine and Muslim, with very different political and strategic objectives, mitigated against this, nevertheless survival was ultimately dependent upon the possession and retention of these fortified places.[49] The military orders had both the resources and the disciplined and celibate warriors to fulfil these functions.

The Templars' enclave in the extreme south of the crusader lands was matched by their position in the far north. Precise dating is not easy, since the evidence mostly indicates when the Order was already established in a particular place, rather than describing a specific grant as William of Tyre does with Gaza. A wholesale concession of rights in the Amanus Mountains by Raymond of Poitiers, the ruler of Antioch, seems to have occurred soon after he had established himself in the principality in April 1136.[50] According to the Byzantine imperial secretary, John Kinnamos, the Templars and the Hospitallers formed a quite distinct element in Raymond's army when the Emperor John Comnenus besieged Antioch in 1137.[51] But if the Templars had been granted any specific fortresses by this time, then it seems likely that their occupation was short-lived, for the emperor successfully forced Raymond to submit, and re-established Byzantine control in the places north of Antioch. He consolidated his position in a further expedition in 1142. There were, however, Templar contingents operating in the area in the mid 1150s, while the extreme

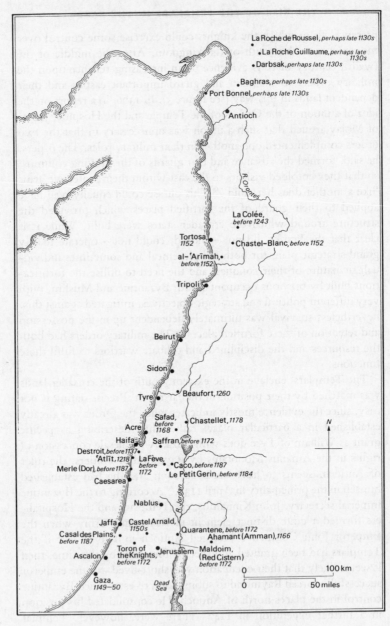

La Roche de Roussel, *perhaps late 1130s*
La Roche Guillaume, *perhaps late 1130s*
Darbsak, *perhaps late 1130s*
Baghras, *perhaps late 1130s*
Port Bonnel, *perhaps late 1130s*
Antioch

R. Orontes

La Colée, *before 1243*
Tortosa, 1152
Chastel-Blanc, *before 1152*
al-ʿArīmah, *before 1152*
Tripoli
Beirut
Sidon
Tyre
Beaufort, 1260
Safad, *before 1168*
Chastellet, 1178
Acre
Haifa
Saffran, *before 1172*
Destroit, *before 1137*
ʿAtlīt, 1218
La Fève, *before 1172*
Merle (Dor), *before 1187*
Caco, *before 1187*
Le Petit Gerin, *before 1184*
Caesarea
R. Jordan
Nablus
Jaffa
Castel Arnald, 1150s
Quarantene, *before 1172*
Casal des Plains, *before 1187*
Ahamant (Amman), 1166
Toron of the Knights, *before 1172*
Ascalon
Jerusalem
Maldoim, (Red Cistern) *before 1172*
Gaza, 1149–50
Dead Sea

N

0   100 km
0   50 miles

Figure 3 Principal Templar castles in Syria and Palestine.

78

anxiety of the Order's leaders about the situation in the north, exhibited not only by Andrew of Montbard in 1149/50, but also by his successor as Grand Master, Bertrand of Blancfort, in his letters to the west during the 1160s, is strong evidence of the Order's interest in the region at this period.[52] The leaders' worries were fully justified, for William of Tyre says that Malih, a brother of King Thoros of Armenia and apparently an ex-Templar himself, seized all the Order's possessions in Cilicia about 1169/71, and the Templars do not seem to have regained them until after Malih's death in 1175.[53]

The Order's castles in the region can be identified by the masonry patterns and the techniques of construction, which are quite distinct from the fortifications of Armenian Cilicia.[54] As this suggests that they were entirely or substantially built by the Templars themselves, it argues against placing too early a date upon them; in the 1130s, for instance, it is unlikely that they possessed sufficient resources or manpower, although in the case of Baghras it is possible that they occupied existing fortifications which they altered at a later date. Baghras (or Gaston, as the Templars called it), which stood on the Belen Pass (the Syrian Gates), about twenty-six kilometres north of Antioch, was the key fortress. The German pilgrim (later bishop), Wilbrand of Oldenburg, travelling through the region in 1212, was impressed by its towers and the three lines of very strong walls (see plate 2).[55] As well as Baghras, they held Darbsak (Trapesak), which guarded the northern approach to the pass, about fifteen kilometres further north, and two other castles, more northerly still, known to contemporaries as La Roche de Roussel and La Roche Guillaume. One of these was situated at modern Çalan in a commanding position 1,200 metres above sea level, where it was able to overlook the east–west route to the Gulf of Alexandretta. Further south, on the coast, they had access to the sea through Port Bonnel (Arsouz).[56] Robert Edwards has shown that the Armenians created a defensible political entity in Cilicia by building a whole series of interlinked forts around the gorges and passes which cut through the ring of mountains surrounding the Cilician Plain.[57] Before Saladin took Baghras and Darbsak in 1188, these Templar castles performed the same function for the Latin Principality of Antioch, forming a screen across the northern frontier and establishing the Templars as virtually autonomous marcher lords.[58]

The Templar presence in the County of Tripoli, centred upon

Plate 2 Aerial view of Baghras. This was the most important Templar castle in the Amanus March, north of Antioch.

their castles at Tortosa (Tartūs) and Chastel-Blanc (Sāfīthā), was created almost contemporaneously with their establishment at Gaza. Not long before April 1152, William, Bishop of Tortosa, granted the Order land in Tortosa on which they could build a new castle, following the temporary capture and burning of the city by Nūr-ad-Dīn, which had left Tortosa 'deserted and destroyed'.[59] The original castle had been held from the bishop by a secular lord, Raynouard of Maraclea,[60] but after the destruction wrought by Nūr-ad-Dīn he appears to have given it up, presumably because he lacked the resources to make it viable again. The bishop ceded land 'from the entrance to the port to the house of William of Tiberias and reaching on all sides to the Gate of St Helen', which appears to have been at the north-west corner of the city, showing that the Order planned to build a much larger complex than that held by Raynouard. Its heart was a large keep, about 35 metres square, which, with its associated buildings, including two flanking towers, occupied a sea-front site 54 metres long. A postern gate enabled revictualling from ships. The keep was set into a large talus and separated by a fosse from two complementary rings of walls which, when Wilbrand of Oldenburg saw them in 1212, incorporated eleven towers set along them, as he imagined it, like precious stones in a crown (see figure 4). The strategic importance of such coastal cities is obvious but, in this case, the installation of the Templars was particularly appropriate in view of the considerable pilgrim traffic, attracted by the cathedral of Notre-Dame, revered as the place of St Peter's first mass and as the keeper of a painting of the Virgin which was believed to have been executed by St Luke.[61]

It is clear also from the bishop's grant that they already held Chastel-Blanc, south-east of Tortosa, about 380 metres up in the Nusairi Mountains, where they constructed a keep set upon a high mound and protected by an oval perimeter wall, 165 × 100 metres at its extremities (see figure 5). The keep was rebuilt at least twice by the Templars after earthquakes in 1170 and 1202; in its surviving form it is a formidable structure on two floors with base dimensions of 31 × 18 metres (see plate 3). Defenders positioned on the top could see the Hospitaller Krak des Chevaliers to the south-east and a third important castle held by the Templars, that of al-ʿArīmah, situated between Chastel-Blanc and the coast. The site at al-ʿArīmah was occupied three times by Nūr-ad-Dīn, in 1148, 1159 and 1171, as

Figure 4 Plan of the castle and town of Tortosa.

well as being damaged by the earthquake that shook Chastel-Blanc
in 1170, and it is not clear when the Templars were first established
there. It was a ridge castle, set along a relatively narrow spine of
rock 300 × 80 metres, about 171 metres above sea level. Apart from
the visual contact with Chastel-Blanc, there were extensive views
towards the sea and across the plain of Akkar to the south. The castle
rose up the ridge in a series of three steps from the western end,
where the slope was the least formidable. At the third stage there
was a rectangular enclosure with strengthening towers on each corner
(see figure 6).[62]

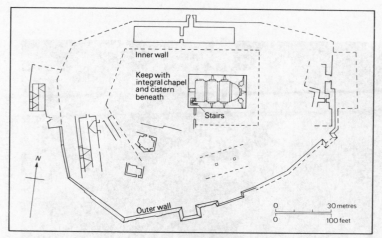

Figure 5 Plan of Chastel-Blanc.

Extensive ecclesiastical privileges gave the Templars control of the churches in the lands they held in the diocese of Tortosa, as well as the tithe exemption on produce from their own demesne land. Although no document survives recording their secular rights, it seems certain that the counts of Tripoli, Raymond II (d. 1152) and Raymond III, would have ceded privileges very similar to those enjoyed by the Hospitallers around Krak des Chevaliers in the east of the county. Here, during the period between 1144 and 1186, they were allowed to establish what Jonathan Riley-Smith has rightly described as a 'palatinate', which included full lordship over the population of their estates, the right to share spoils, and the freedom to have independent dealings with neighbouring Muslim powers.[63] This package of rights and castles meant that between the 1140s and the 1180s the two military orders came to dominate a large slab of territory extending right across the County of Tripoli from the prosperous and ancient cities of the coast into the long chains of mountains which dominate the inland region. Control of the transverse east–west valleys ensured that communication between the interior and the coast was maintained. This part of the county was particularly important, for here it was at its widest, extending some sixty kilometres to the River Orontes.[64]

During the 1160s the Order took over further castles in two other

Plate 3 Chastel-Blanc, the keep; Templar castle in the southern part of the County of Tripoli.

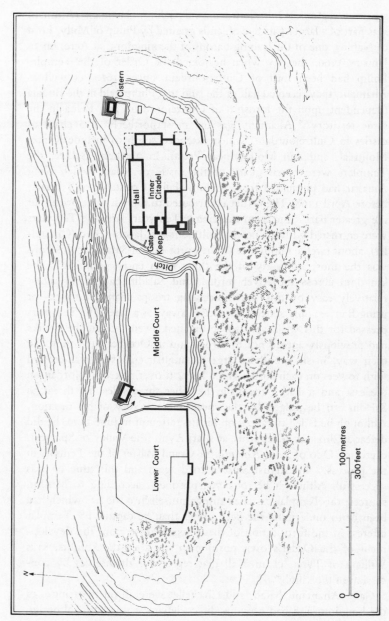

Figure 6 Plan of al-ʿArīmah.

sensitive regions, Oultrejourdain and Galilee. Ahamant (Amman) was part of a larger package of lands granted by Philip of Milly, Lord of Nablus, one of the leading barons of the kingdom, at Acre, on 17 January 1166, the day when he joined the Order of the Temple. Philip had been lord of Oultrejourdain since 1161. As well as Ahamant, they received half of the land that Philip held in the Buqaia (dependent upon the lordship of Oultrejourdain) and Belqa in the same territory.[65] Ahamant was the most northerly of a chain of castles in Oultrejourdain, which extended south to include Kerak, Montréal, and Aïn Mousa (near Petra). In northern Galilee, the Templars were given guard of the castle of Safad, which King Amalric had purchased from its lord, Fulk, Constable of Tiberias, before April 1168. The Order contributed to the purchase price, but the greater part came from the king.[66] Ten years later the Templars were entrusted with the newly built *castrum* at Jacob's Ford (Chastellet), about twelve kilometres to the north-east of Safad. Jacob's Ford was the most northerly of the three main entry points into the kingdom across the River Jordan, and Saladin had found access relatively easy by this route, bringing troops from Damascus or using Banyas, only sixteen kilometres away, as a base. The Templars pressed for this weak spot to be fortified, even though the Franks had previously agreed not to do so, and in October 1178 they had their way. In six months a large rectangular enclosure was erected with towers on each corner and a keep. It overlooked the Jordan on the east and it had a fosse on the other three sides. Its threat to Saladin can be judged by the speed and intensity of his reaction. Although he failed to take it on his first attempt in June 1179, he did defeat a Christian relief army at Marj Ayun (the Valley of Springs), capturing Odo of Saint-Amand, the Grand Master of the Temple, in the process.[67] In August Saladin tried again and this time he was successful. Although he took 700 prisoners, according to Muslim sources, the Templar castellan threw himself into the fire which had been lit to undermine the keep rather than be captured.[68] Templar interest in the fortification of the crossing arose from the development of the Order's own position in the area; the knights, says William of Tyre, 'claimed all that region for themselves by concession of the king'.[69]

Gaza, Ahamant, Safad, and Chastellet were all on the fringes of the kingdom and had obvious direct defensive functions, although equally they could be used as bases for *chevauchées* into Muslim territory, as the attack on the perpetrators of the failed coup in Egypt demonstrates. Much more centrally placed was the castle of La Fève (al-Fūla), probably built by the Templars themselves as, among other functions, a supply depot. Its situation at the crossroads of the routes running north and south between Tiberias and Jerusalem and north-west to south-east from Acre to Baisan in itself invited fortification, but it had other evident natural advantages. An artificial mound dating from the Bronze Age already stood there and, in the generally arid region of the Jezreel valley, water was obtainable from a marsh which at certain times of the year filled to become a small lake, some 150 metres to the north-west of the mound. The Templars certainly occupied a rectangular enclosure here by the early 1170s, when it was described by the German monk, Theoderich, on pilgrimage at that time, but they may have received the site as many as thirty years earlier. The enclosure was about 120 metres by ninety metres and was protected by a ditch about thirty-four metres wide. Running along the inside of the walls were long vaulted chambers, rather like those of the larger Hospitaller fortress at Belvoir, overlooking the Jordan to the east, and below were further vaulted cellars. There may have been a cistern within the castle in addition to the large wheel, probably driven by a donkey, which drew subterranean water from the marshy area to the north-west. The Templar garrison was, by contemporary standards, of considerable size, amounting to between fifty and sixty knights, reflecting the importance of La Fève as a storage centre for arms, tools, and food. Twice in 1183 it was used as an assembly point for the army of the kingdom and it was from here that the Grand Master, Gerard of Ridefort, led a mixed force of Templar, Hospitaller, and secular knights to a terrible defeat at the nearby Springs of Cresson, north-east of Nazareth, on 1 May 1187, an ominous prelude to the disaster at Hattin two months later. Among the knights who died there were reinforcements summoned by the Grand Master from another Templar castle in the vicinity, that of Caco (Kh. Qara), which was 6.5 kilometres to the east of La Fève, from which he seems to have drawn about another thirty knights.[70] The size of the garrisons of the two castles combined suggests a Templar presence as important as those in Gaza and Safad.

These castles were major centres for the Order, making up a formidable part of the defensive strength of the crusader states, but the Templars did not forget their original mandate to protect pilgrims, especially along the crucial routes from the ports of Jaffa, Haifa, and Acre to the holy places, and from Jerusalem to the Jordan. Casal des Plains was built just outside Jaffa on the road leading to Lydda, while in the vicinity of Jerusalem in the Ayalon valley, which was the most important route from the coast to Jerusalem, the Order held Castel Arnald and Toron of the Knights. Castel Arnald had originally been built by King Fulk (probably at Yalu, south-west of Bait Nūbā) in 1132/3, specifically for, as William of Tyre says, 'the safety of pilgrims passing along', and was an obvious place to entrust to the Templars, who seem to have held it from the 1150s.[71] Toron of the Knights complemented Castel Arnald. Built some time between 1150 and 1170, it was situated on the southern side of the same ridge.[72] Travellers landing at Acre and Haifa often took the road south, which at Haifa passed along a narrow section next to Mount Carmel. As early as 1103 the Franks had built a castle just to the south at Destroit, as even armed men had sometimes experienced difficulty in forcing a passage along this road. Under the Templars, the castle took the form of a keep about sixteen metres square with two storeys, around which was an enclosure large enough for stabling and two cisterns. It was probably capable of holding a garrison of between fifteen and twenty men and their horses.[73] Further south, at Merle (Dor), the Templars had another refuge on the coast, situated at the southern end of a long mound on which stood a modest settlement. The Templar fort was probably square, with four corner towers, and it overlooked a small harbour to the north which had a jetty and a protected entrance cut out of a nearby reef.[74]

Once they had visited Jerusalem and the adjacent holy sites, most pilgrims wished to bathe in the Jordan and perhaps also to see Mount Quarantene, 'the Mount of Temptation', where the Devil offered Christ the material riches of the world. William of Tyre describes the road between Jerusalem and Jericho and the Jordan as being 'very defective and dangerous, with rocky and precipitous places so that even when there is nothing to fear, and passage can be freely achieved, it has always proved to be a troublesome journey in both its ascents and descents' (see plate 1).[75] About halfway along this route the Templars held the castle of Maldoim, sometimes called the Red Cistern, situated above the Jericho Road. It was a rectangular enclosure, protected by a rock-cut ditch. Inside the walls were a keep and some vaulted buildings, which presumably included stables.[76] Overlooking Jericho itself was a fort on the west of Mount Quarantene, where the Order kept supplies of victuals and arms. According to the German monk, Theoderich, who visited the Holy Land between 1169 and 1174, at the foot of the mountain was a great spring around which was a place known as the Garden of Abraham, often used as an overnight stopping place for pilgrims, who were guarded here by Templars and Hospitallers. As well as this, the Templars had a castle near the Jordan at the place of Christ's baptism, not only to protect pilgrims, but also to prevent a repetition of the massacre by Zengi of the six monks who had lived at a church which had been erected there.[77] One of the duties of the Templar commander of Jerusalem was to keep ten knights on standby to protect pilgrims going to and from the Jordan, as well as a string of pack-animals to carry food and exhausted travellers.[78]

The rising proportion of castles in the possession of the military orders was matched by the acquisition of lands which helped to support them, particularly evident in the Templars' case around Baghras, Tortosa, and Safad. The loss of the Templar archive means that only glimpses of the Order's role as landlord are possible, but settlements of disputes with the Hospitallers and other powers in the crusader states show that the Temple must have held many *casals* or villages, mills, and adjoining agricultural lands. The comprehensive agreement between the two Masters in 1179, for instance, settled their respective rights to the three *casals* of Terre Galifa, Banna, and Bertrandimir, situated in the very sensitive area between the Orders' enclaves around Tortosa and Krak des Chevaliers, as well as disputes about lands near Castel Arnald and Gaza.[79] Research by Steven Tibble shows just how rapidly the Hospital was making inroads into the possessions of what were formerly powerful secular lordships and he convincingly argues that the Templars must have been adding properties at a similar rate. The example of the lordship of Caesarea is instructive, particularly as this has been seen as one of the stronger lordships which survived in secular hands right down to 1291. Using Hospitaller acquisitions as a basis, it seems that the military orders together held nearly 18 per cent of the lordship even before the middle of the twelfth century, while by the time of Hattin this had almost doubled to about 35 per cent.[80]

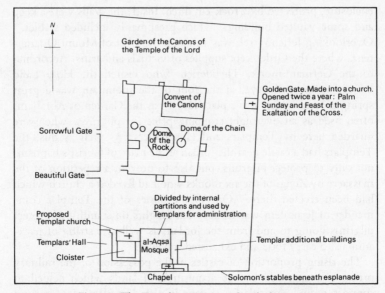

Figure 7 The Temple area in Jerusalem before 1187.

Until 1187 the headquarters of the Order remained the Temple area in Jerusalem, where they had received their first small grants in 1119–20. At some point in the 1120s King Baldwin II had moved out of the al-Aqsa mosque and had erected a royal palace next to the 'Tower of David', the citadel of Jerusalem, overlooking the Jaffa Gate on the west side of the city. This left the Order free to develop the Temple area in a manner which deeply impressed western visitors. Theoderich's description is the most detailed and is particularly valuable because it reflects the state of Templar building some fifty years after they had first established themselves adjacent to the decrepit al-Aqsa (see figure 7).[81] Pilgrims normally entered the Temple area on the western side by what they understood to be the 'Beautiful Gate' at the end of the Street of the Chain. Theoderich's account begins after he had described the Dome of the Rock, occupied by the Canons of the Temple of the Lord, to the north of that entrance (see plates 4 and 5).

One follows to the south, and there is the Palace of Solomon. Like a church it is oblong and supported by pillars, and also at the end of the sanctuary it rises up

Plate 4 The Temple area, Jerusalem, from the north. The Templars occupied the area around the al-Aqsa mosque at the southern end of the platform.

Plate 5 Solomon's stables beneath the south-east corner of the
Temple platform.

to a circular roof, large and round, and also like a church. This and all its
neighbouring buildings have come into the possession of the Templar soldiers.
They are garrisoned in these and other buildings belonging to them. And with

stores of arms, clothing and food they are always ready to guard the province and defend it. Below them they have stables once erected by King Solomon. They are next to the Palace, and their structure is remarkably complex. They are erected with vaults, arches, and roofs of many varieties, and according to our estimation we should bear witness that they will hold ten thousand horses with their grooms. A single shot from a cross-bow would hardly reach from one end of this building to the other, either in length or breadth.

Above them the area is full of houses, dwellings and outbuildings for every kind of purpose, and it is full of walking-places, lawns, council-chambers, porches, consistories and supplies of water in splendid cisterns. Below it is equally full of wash-rooms, stores, grain rooms, stores for wood and other kinds of domestic stores.

On the other side of the palace, that is on the west, the Templars have built a new house, whose height, length and breadth, and all its cellars and refectories, staircase and roof, are far beyond the custom of this land. Indeed its roof is so high that, if I were to mention how high it is, those who listen would hardly believe me. There indeed they have constructed a new Palace, just as on the other side they have the old one. There too they have founded on the edge of the outer court a new church of magnificent size and workmanship.[82]

Somewhere close by the Templars also maintained a cemetery, not only for the brothers themselves, but also for laymen closely associated with the Order. Otto of Freising says that when Frederick, Advocate of Regensburg, died during the Second Crusade at Easter 1148, he was buried in this cemetery, described by Otto as 'not far from the ancient Temple of the Lord'.[83] Below the city wall to the south, the Order had protected all this by strengthening the outer defence works. This probably represents the fullest development of the area while it was under Templar control, for the new church was never completed and the living-quarters set against the west side of the al-Aqsa were demolished by Saladin's men after they captured Jerusalem in October 1187.[84]

The Templars had therefore made the southern part of the Haram al-Sharif into a combined religious, administrative, and military centre, conveniently provided with a vast stable beneath the main buildings. No definitive evidence of the numbers of men needed for such an operation is available, but both William of Tyre, who was resident from the mid 1160s, and Benjamin of Tudela, a Jewish traveller from Spain who visited Jerusalem in about 1168, said that the Order had 300 knights.[85] This figure is in rough accord with the losses claimed by Terricus, the Templar commander after Hattin, who wrote to the brethren in the west to tell them that 230 Templars had been executed by Saladin while another sixty had been killed at the Springs of Cresson in May.[86] William of Tyre gives no figure for the sergeants or serving brothers, saying only that 'the number of the other brothers is almost infinite', but a ratio of about three to one may be taken as reasonable, given the much greater expense of maintaining fully armed knights, and therefore it seems likely that the Order had about 1,000 sergeants in the Kingdom of Jerusalem. Knights serving with the Order for a set term were a common sight too, further augmenting Templar strength, while the availability of resources to hire mercenaries was particularly valuable in an age when specialist skills were becoming increasingly important in warfare as in other fields. The complexity of the military hierarchy described in the Rule, the number of castles garrisoned, the proportion of the secular lordships which they held, and the escort duties carried out, therefore make an establishment much below William of Tyre's figure of 300 unlikely to have been viable. They needed not only men but horses. The Second Crusade showed the priority that they gave to these: despite appalling losses in the army as a whole, according to Odo of Deuil, the Templars 'kept their chargers, even though they were starving'. Consequently, King Louis VII was able to persuade the Turks that they still had plenty of excellent horses by placing the Templars in a prominent position during attacks.[87] In the Rule, leading officials were allowed up to four, depending upon their work, function, and status, knights had three, and sergeants one. Even if a full quota of horses was maintained, however, this does call into question Theoderich's claim that 10,000 were kept under the Temple platform. Indeed, less than ten years before, another German pilgrim, John of Würzburg, had estimated the capacity of the stables at about 2,000 horses or 1,500 camels. These figures may be nearer the mark, but it is improbable that they were all kept under the Temple platform, since the present area would seem unlikely to be able to accommodate more than about five hundred horses, especially if allowance is made for space for squires, grooms, and perhaps even pilgrims sleeping there.[88] Similar figures are likely for the Order's strength in Tripoli and Antioch, since the military resources of the lay powers in these two states were roughly equivalent to those of the Kingdom of Jerusalem,[89] while the maintenance of the Templar 'palatinates' around Tortosa and Baghras were heavier responsibilities than those borne by any single individual lordship. During the 1170s and 1180s, therefore, an establishment in the east of about 600 knights and 2,000 sergeants seems a not unreasonable estimate.

Not surprisingly, a force of this size and nature was prominent in almost all the important military encounters with the Muslims from the late 1140s, but contrary to popular belief the Templars were not accustomed to deploying their armed strength in a rash or fanatical fashion. From the beginning they were generally conservative in their approach to warfare, an attitude in keeping with contemporary military practice in both east and west. Indeed, the author of the Anglo-Saxon Chronicle complained that when the men who had been recruited by Hugh of Payns in 1128 actually arrived in the east they found that he had been lying in telling them that a great war was raging between the Christians and the pagans.[90] Battles were always a risk, even if conditions were favourable, while in Outremer in particular patience was usually rewarded by the break-up of the uneasy coalitions which formed the basis of most Muslim armies in the twelfth century. The fate of two Grand Masters showed the risk of direct clashes. Bertrand of Blancfort had been Master for barely a year when, on 18 June 1157, he was captured along with eighty-seven other Templar knights. The Franks were returning from the relief of Banyas which had been attacked by Nūr-ad-Dīn, but as they moved south along the Jordan they were surprised by a Muslim attack. The Master's release was not obtained until the end of May 1159, when the Byzantine Emperor Manuel secured a truce with Nūr-ad-Dīn.[91] Odo of Saint-Amand was not so fortunate. He too had been captured in 1157, when he was royal marshal and not yet a brother of the Temple, but he had been released by March 1159.[92] However, in June 1179 he led an attack on Saladin's forces and was taken again, at Marj Ayun, near Jacob's Ford. He was never released, dying in a Muslim prison within a year.[93] According to the later Damascene chronicler, Abū Shāmā, his body was handed over in exchange for the release of a Muslim leader held by the Christians.[94]

The most evident example of Templar caution in this period can be seen in Bertrand of Blancfort's refusal to take part in King Amalric's campaign to Egypt in the autumn of 1168. The control of Egypt had been an issue which had preoccupied the Franks since they had taken Ascalon in 1153, for the unstable caliphate seemed almost to invite outside intervention and the establishment of a preponderant Frankish influence in Cairo, perhaps under the cover of an Egyptian puppet regime, had the double advantage of increasing resources and securing the southern approaches to the Kingdom of Jerusalem. But Nūr-ad-Dīn was equally aware of the opportunities, especially after his capture of Damascus in 1154. Neither power could afford to let the opportunity pass through inaction and, in 1164, the situation came to a head when both Shīrkūh, Nūr-ad-Dīn's Kurdish general, and Amalric, mounted campaigns to Cairo. Amalric succeeded in forcing Shīrkūh's withdrawal and, in 1167, when Shīrkūh attempted another invasion, made a very favourable treaty with the Egyptian vizier, Shawar, who agreed to provide the Franks with lavish resources to oppose Shīrkūh. It seems certain that the Templars took part in the expeditions of 1164 and 1167, for the chief negotiator of this treaty, Hugh, lord of Caesarea, was accompanied on the mission by Geoffrey Fulcher, a leading Templar since at least 1156.[95] The Templars were still supporting the king's Egyptian policy in May 1168, when Bertrand of Blancfort and Geoffrey Fulcher were signatories to a royal grant to the Pisans in Acre in return for their help against Alexandria.[96]

However, in October 1168, the king mustered his forces for a new expedition into Egypt, this time apparently with the intention of achieving outright annexation.[97] William of Tyre was not present when the army left, having been sent to Constantinople to negotiate a Byzantine alliance, but his narrative leaves no doubt that he strongly disapproved of the campaign, believing that it violated the treaty with Shawar. He saw the forced withdrawal of the Christians in January 1169, which was followed by Shīrkūh's successful seizure of control, as an appropriate consequence of actions motivated largely by avarice.[98] As a writer, William was very much a child of his time for, in keeping with the preoccupations of the French schools in which he had received much of his education, he was always deeply interested in motive and never more so than in this case. He thought that one of the chief supporters of the invasion, perhaps even the instigator, was Gilbert d'Assailly, Master of the Hospital, whom he describes as 'magnanimous . . . but with an unstable and rambling mind'. He had led the Order into a financial crisis of such depth that he seems to have regarded the Egyptian campaign as the only way he could bail himself out. When it failed, he resigned, leaving a debt of 100,000 pieces of gold, and creating a controversy within the Order so serious that it led to a schism in 1170.[99] The Templars, on the other hand, refused to participate either because 'it seemed against their conscience' in that it broke the treaty with Shawar, or because 'the master of a rival (emule) House seemed to be the originator and leader'.[100] In view of the later image of the two Orders as being in constant competition, this suggestion that the Templar withdrawal was a consequence of jealousy has sometimes been accepted as a possible explanation for an action which brings out very starkly the power and independence achieved by the Order since 1129.[101] But William himself had moral objections to the expedition and he accepted that this was an equally valid motive for the Templars, whose Master, Bertrand of Blancfort, he describes elsewhere as 'religious and God-fearing'.[102] Moreover, there are solid strategic objections. The Order had been preoccupied by the threats to the north since the time of Andrew of Montbard's support for the campaign to help Antioch in 1149; the letters of Bertrand of Blancfort and Geoffrey Fulcher show that this concern had by no means diminished.[103] In August 1164, Geoffrey Fulcher's appeal for help to King Louis VII of France was buttressed by the information that on the tenth of that month sixty brothers had died fighting in the army of Bohemond of Antioch at Hārim (not counting associate brothers and turcopoles) and that only seven Templars had escaped from this battle.[104] Two months later Bertrand of Blancfort wrote to tell Louis that Nūr-ad-Dīn had taken Banyas.[105] On both occasions the bulk of the Templar forces had been with Amalric on campaign in Egypt. A final consideration can be surmised if not proven. Financial misman-agement had brought the Hospital to the verge of bankruptcy; there must have been a possibility that further expensive campaigns in Egypt undertaken while sustaining heavy losses in Antioch and Tripoli might have brought the Templars to a similar crisis. By the 1160s the Templars were an integral part of any large-scale expedition, but at the same time they recognised only too well that they were responsible for the defence and upkeep of castles ranging from the Amanus Mountains in the north to Gaza in the south.

In this context the tactics adopted by the Franks in the summer of 1180, when Saladin invaded the County of Tripoli, are quite consist-ent with usual Templar practice and indeed represent a typical response of the Latins to outside attack. Here is William of Tyre's description of how the Muslim army positioned itself in the northern part of the county between the coast at 'Arqah, the Templars at al-

'Arīmah and Chastel-Blanc, and the Hospitallers at Krak des Chevaliers, precisely in those lands that had been sufficiently valuable to both Orders to be the subject of a dispute between them, only settled the year before.[106] Yet the Orders' response was essentially passive:

The count had gathered his men in the town of Arqah [to the north-east of Tripoli], looking for an opportunity to combat the enemy without serious danger. Moreover, the brothers of the Temple, since they were in the same region, were kept closed up in their castles, expecting almost every hour that they would be besieged, nor did they dare rashly to commit themselves to attacks; the brothers of the Hospital, influenced by similar fears, assembled in their castle, which is called Krak, judging it to be sufficient if, in such a crisis, they could protect the aforesaid castle from damage by the enemy. Therefore the enemy's troops were mid-way between the aforesaid brothers and the forces of the count, so that they could not bring help to each other nor even send messengers, who could inform them about each other's situation. But Saladin, moving through the fields and especially through the cultivated places and, with nobody to oppose him, wandering freely everywhere, set fire to the harvest, some of which was already gathered in for threshing, some of which was already collected in the fields in sheaves, and some of which was still standing, stole cattle as booty, and depopulated the entire region.[107]

The policy of the Templars towards Amalric's Egyptian campaign of 1168 underlines a fundamental point: decisions on military activity cannot be isolated from their political implications. The acquisition of fortresses, *casalia*, and landed estates and the ability to raise money and men on both sides of the sea was now apparently coupled to an ability and a will to act independently of the monarchy if it was thought necessary. Moreover, the privileges embodied in the papal bulls issued between 1139 and 1145, while they did not completely remove the Templars from under the wing of the patriarch,[108] nevertheless formed the basis of an independence from the ecclesiastical power in the east as well, which, in William of Tyre's opinion, fundamentally changed the nature of the Order. Here is the key passage, subtly incorporated into his favourable description of the initial foundation:

When they had, for a long time, maintained themselves in this honourable manner, fulfilling their profession prudently enough, neglecting humility, which is known to be the guardian of all the virtues and, voluntarily sitting on the ground consequently does not have to suffer a fall, they withdrew from the Patriarch of Jerusalem, from whom they had received both the foundation of their order and their first benefices, denying to him the obedience which had been shown to him by their predecessors, and they became very irksome to the churches of God, taking tithes and first-fruits for themselves and disturbing their possessions without just cause.[109]

The archbishop's conclusion has become highly influential, since it emanates from a man who was both a very effective historian and unchallenged in his interpretation of events in the Kingdom of Jerusalem down to the mid 1180s by any other contemporary Christian chronicler. Yet William's view of the Templars was naturally moulded by his own experiences in the kingdom. He was originally commissioned to write by King Amalric himself, and therefore might be expected to have some sympathy with the king's point of view; he was himself an active participant in local politics in the two decades before Hattin; and, as an archbishop, he would certainly feel strongly about any diminution of the rights and powers of the secular clergy. Any examination of the position of the Templars in the Latin states of the east in the twelfth century must therefore take account of the fact that the agenda has largely been drawn up by William of Tyre.

By 'a long time' William seems to have meant until the early 1150s, when, in his description of the siege of Ascalon in 1153, he first places an unfavourable construction on the motives of the Templars.[110] The next incident seems to have occurred in 1166, when, at the end of a chapter describing the disasters that had befallen the Kingdom of Jerusalem, William adds a section describing a direct conflict between King Amalric and the Templars. He says that a Templar garrison had surrendered an allegedly 'impregnable' fortified cave, situated in an unspecified place beyond the Jordan, to Shīrkūh. Amalric had heard that it was under siege and had hastened to relieve it with a large force, but when he had reached the Jordan he was told that it had already fallen. 'When he heard this, the lord king, confounded and inflamed with anger, caused about twelve of the Templars who had surrendered the castle to the enemy, to be hung from gallows.'[111]

This incident highlights the problems of analysing William's treatment of the Templars in his chronicle. The imprecision of both location and dating, together with the lack of any apparent direct connection with other material in the chapter, convey the strong impression that this section has been tacked on at a later date. Moreover, in a period when the Church was becoming acutely sensitive about encroachments upon its legal immunities (the incident is contemporary with the quarrel between Henry II and Thomas Becket), William says nothing about any further repercussions arising from the king's arbitrary action. Yet it is unlikely that the story is complete invention, for there is a possible context. When Philip of Nablus had joined the Temple in January 1166, the king had approved the grant of a major part of his fief of Oultrejourdain to the Templars. If, as seems likely, the lost cave fortress was part of this grant, Amalric's anger at its loss so soon afterwards, apparently without any really determined resistance, is understandable.[112]

This was not the only *cause célèbre* of Amalric's reign, according to William. In 1173 the archbishop includes an extended description of an even more dramatic conflict, which culminated in the arrest and imprisonment of a Templar by the king, an action clearly seen by the Master, Odo of Saint-Amand, as a violation of the Order's privileges.[113] The central event in this story was the murder of an envoy from the sect of the Assassins by the Templars while the envoy was travelling under royal safe-conduct.

The Assassins were one of the products of the schisms which had appeared in the Islamic world after the death of Muhammed in 632. The most fundamental of these divisions was that between the Sunnites, who recognised Abū Bakr, one of Muhammed's earliest converts, as the Prophet's true successor, and the Shī'ites, who adhered to a line descended from Ali, Muhammad's cousin and son-in-law. According to the Shī'ites, this was the one legitimate line of imams, from which at some unknown time would appear the Mahdi, 'the guided one', who would overthrow the existing tyrannical order. Within the Shī'ites therefore there existed a messianic element, which expressed itself with particular force and urgency among those groups impatient with the pace of change and commitment of the ruling political elites. The Assassins were one such group, setting themselves up in the fortress of Alamut in Persia in the late eleventh century and, in 1094, splitting from the prevailing Shī'ite regime of the Fātimids of Cairo. Soon afterwards they established themselves in the Lebanese Mountains as well, where their leader was known to the Franks as the 'Old Man of the Mountain'. Although relatively weak in territory and numbers, their devotion to the cause and their belief in 'tyrannicide' as an instrument of policy made them an effective and feared force in the Muslim world.[114]

It was with this group that, in 1173, Amalric seems to have been attempting the unlikely feat of negotiating an alliance, a condition of which, so William alleged, was that the Assassins 'would join with the faith of Christ and be baptised'. Such a union seems, on the face of it, incongruous, but the Assassins had seldom directed their deadly skills against the Christians, while about ten years before, Hasan II, their leader at Alamut, had formally abrogated the law of the Prophet, believing that the appropriate time had come, an action in keeping with the messianic nature of the sect. Moreover, the territories of the Syrian Assassins, situated between al-Marqab and Shaizar, formed an enclave within Christian lands, so that at the least Frankish neutrality would have been advantageous (see figure 8).[115] In these circumstances it is possible that both sides believed that they could arrive at a mutually advantageous accommodation, and it was for this reason that Abdullah, the Assassin negotiator, visited King Amalric. He was travelling back to his leader with the Christian proposals, protected by a royal safe-conduct, when, according to William of Tyre, he was suddenly ambushed and killed by some Templar knights in the region just beyond Tripoli. As William saw it, this was an act of treason and he described the king as beside himself with anger. Amalric sent his representatives to demand that the Templars hand over the culprits, in particular the actual murderer, a one-eyed knight called Walter of Mesnil, whom William designates 'a worthless individual'. But Odo of Saint-Amand would do no such thing. 'Indeed, on behalf of the lord pope, he ordered that no one should dare to lay violent hands upon the aforesaid brother.' The king himself therefore went to Sidon, where the Grand Master was at the time, and actually had the knight concerned seized by force and thrown into prison at Tyre. William claimed that the matter brought the kingdom to the edge of 'irrevocable ruin' and that the king had not been prepared to let the matter rest there. 'It is said, indeed, that if he had recovered from that final illness he had proposed to explore that question, by means of envoys of the highest rank, with the kings and princes of the lands of the world.'

The way that William tells the story, the king's jurisdiction had been violated and his integrity thrown into question. Only strenuous diplomacy convinced the Assassins that Amalric had not been involved in the murder, while the chance of an advantageous alliance had been irretrievably lost. Moreover, probably since 1152, the

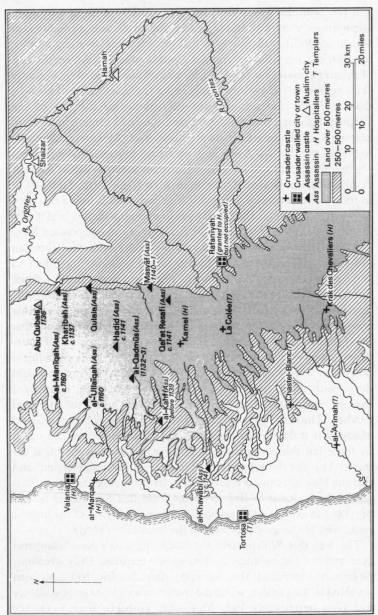

Figure 8 The military orders and the Assassins.

Templars, with their powerful enclave around Tortosa, not far from the bases of the Syrian Assassins, had been receiving an annual tribute of 2,000 *besants* from them, as a kind of 'protection money'. The Temple, as an undying corporation, was not vulnerable to an organisation which relied upon the murder of individuals to achieve its ends. When William refers to a possible offer of compensation by the king for the loss of the tribute which would follow an alliance, he implies that the murder was prompted by a financial motive. The two deadly sisters of greed and pride, therefore, had taken hold of an Order which, only a generation before, had been marked by the purity of its aims and the humility of its demeanour. A further dimension is provided by Walter Map, writing in 1182, and therefore the one source of the incident independent of William. Walter was no more a friend of privileged orders than was William, having a particular hatred for the Cistercians, and it is not surprising to find that he too suggests a base motive for the murder. Moreover, as the story of the fate of Nāsir-al-Dīn in 1154 immediately precedes this incident in his work, it appears that he was looking for a theme through which he could demonstrate the failings of privileged monastic orders. In this case it was Templar indifference to the greater good of Christianity. In Walter Map's version the issue is purely religious. The Old Man of the Assassins, 'who is the fountainhead of the cult and faith of the paynims', had sent to the Patriarch of Jerusalem for a copy of the Gospels. The patriarch responded by providing both the Gospels and an interpreter, and the Old Man was so impressed that he planned to be baptised. The envoy who was murdered was his representative, who had been sent to the patriarch in order to bring back priests and deacons for this purpose. The Templars, he says, killed the envoy 'lest (it is said) the belief of the infidels should be done away and peace and union reign'.[116] In other words, the Order, like other military machines, was determined to prevent peace breaking out.

It is difficult to believe that a man as worldly as Walter Map really expected that the whole Muslim world was about to succumb to Christianity, but William of Tyre needs to be taken more seriously, since he must have had access to the king's version of the matter and his account is presumably an accurate reflection of the royal point of view. Pro-Templar writers of the modern era, however, have been anxious to refute what they see as the archbishop's evident bias.

Lundgreen, for example, believes that the Templars were consulted beforehand, but would not give up their tribute because they doubted the good faith of the Assassins. This infuriated William, who could see only that an opportunity for conversion had been lost because of the Grand Master's mercenary greed. As Lundgreen sees it, the Master was not prompted by greed because the Order was in no need of money, having just received a substantial donation from Henry the Lion, Duke of Saxony.[117] This interpretation goes so far beyond any known facts that it cannot be accepted; it seems perfectly plausible, for instance, that Abdullah did indeed carry confidential information as William says, which would mean that the Templars were not fully aware of the exact nature of the alliance proposed.

There are alternatives to an explanation based on avarice; the grounds of objection could have been religious rather than economic, for the Templars may have regarded an alliance with the Assassins as incompatible with the Christian cause, or they may not have believed that the conversion of the Assassins was genuine or at least that they interpreted the Christian faith in the same way as the Franks. The Templars were presumably aware of Hasan's proclamation of the millennium. This could have prompted the negotiations by the Syrian Assassins, but their reading of Christianity was likely to have been in allegorical terms related to their own history and traditions. The only other form of pressure which might have led the Assassins to make such a move might have come from orthodox Islamic leaders such as Nūr-ad-Dīn. But they apparently survived his reign without difficulty (he died in 1174). In these circumstances the Templars may have been concerned about their image in the west. They had been granted important castles adjacent to the Assassin enclave and fighters for the faith who accepted the word of such a sect would have lacked credibility, especially in a world characterised by a lack of understanding of the military and diplomatic problems faced by the Franks of Outremer.[118] The Templar attitude was not as isolated as William of Tyre makes it appear. One reason for the failure to reopen negotiations after Amalric's death in July 1174, was the distrust of the Assassins harboured by the regent, Raymond III, Count of Tripoli, whose father had been one of the few Christians murdered by the sect.[119]

However, the arrest of Walter of Mesnil by two royal knights and his imprisonment by the king raised another fundamental issue.

According to William, Odo of Saint-Amand refused to hand over the knight when the king demanded it on the grounds that he had given him a penance and now intended to send him to Rome for judgement. The bull *Omne datum optimum* could certainly be interpreted in this way, but the hanging of the twelve Templars in around 1166 shows that the king was not prepared to concede this. Nor indeed do the thirteenth-century legal texts of the Kingdom of Jerusalem and Latin Greece. The *Assises de la Cour Bourgeois* did not see the military orders as having full ecclesiastical immunity, while the *Assises de Romanie* left the position vague, recording only that 'some say' that they had 'a voice like the bishops'.[120] The matter, then, was still far from clear-cut even in the thirteenth century, and this perhaps explains the attitude of the French translator of William of Tyre, whose work, known as the *Eracles*, probably dates from the mid thirteenth century. He glossed the archbishop's words in such a way as to make Amalric's position seem even more forceful than in the original version. Here, Amalric's plan to explore the issue with other monarchs comes out as an intention to warn them of the damage that the Order had done to the Christian faith, especially in Syria, so that the princes might then take action against the Templars in their own lands.[121]

The reign of Amalric was a crucial one in the development of the Order in the east, for he was a king determined to impose his own authority, as a recent reinterpretation of the *Assise* of liege homage has emphasised.[122] He was, too, the progenitor of an aggressive expansionist policy, as well as a politician prepared to exploit any alliance – Byzantine, Egyptian, or Assassin – to counter the continuing rise of Nūr-ad-Dīn. Yet he needed the resources of the military orders and, like his predecessors, granted castles and lands in the hope that they would be more effectively guarded and maintained than would be possible under the relatively poorer secular lords. But this only served to increase the importance of the Temple, which had already far outstripped the concept of a community of pious laymen essentially subordinate to the patriarch and the king and now saw itself as independent of local authority and responsible only to a distant papacy. The consequence had been direct conflicts, in two instances leading to the use of force by the king to impose his will. However, the surrender of the cave fortress in about 1166 and the withdrawal of military support in 1168 must have suggested to the king that reactive policies were insufficient and that a more effective method would be to secure the appointment of royal nominees as Masters of the Order. Bertrand of Blancfort died in 1169; both his immediate successors were drawn from the king's own circle.

Bertrand of Blancfort was succeeded by Philip of Nablus, the only one of the Order's Masters to have been born in the east and to have come from the local baronage of the Kingdom of Jerusalem. He was the eldest son of Guy of Milly (in Picardy), whose name appears frequently on the charters of the kingdom in the years between 1108 and 1126, and who attended important baronial assemblies during this period. Although Guy held lands at Nablus and near Jerusalem, it appears that Philip gained the lordship of the important fief of Nablus by inheritance from his uncle Pagan the Butler, who died in the late 1140s.[123] During the 1140s, Philip took a prominent role in military activities on behalf of Queen Melisende and, as the schism between the queen and her son became more overt after 1150, it was evident that, together with Amalric, the queen's younger son, and Rohard the Elder, he was one of Melisende's strongest supporters, a stance which put him on the losing side when Baldwin III removed the queen from power in April 1152. He was, however, too powerful to be pushed aside and it was not until 1161 that Baldwin was able to take advantage of the queen's last illness to exchange his fief of Nablus for the less well-favoured lordship of Oultrejourdain.[124] Baldwin III died in 1162, bringing to power Amalric, who, as another former member of Melisende's party might be expected to see Philip of Nablus as an ally. Philip himself joined the Templars on 17 January 1166, probably after the death of his wife, and when Bertrand of Blancfort died three years later he became Grand Master. It seems an obvious inference that his appointment was the consequence of royal pressure, although an apparent delay between Bertrand's death on 2 January and Philip's accession some time in August, might suggest resistance within the Order.[125] Philip of Nablus had already been prominent in Amalric's earlier Egyptian campaigns, especially in 1167,[126] and it may be that his election was perceived within the Order as a means to force it back into the fray against Egypt. As the new Master appears immediately on charters directly connected with the Egyptian campaign of the winter of 1169, it must be assumed that this perception was correct.[127] Early in 1171, Philip led an embassy to Constantinople on the king's behalf, resigning his post as Master in order to do so. He died on 3 April 1171, during the course of this mission.[128]

The king's successful insertion of his own candidate led him to repeat the process after Philip's death, although in the second instance, like Henry II and Becket in England, the policy rebounded on him. Unlike his predecessor, Odo of Saint-Amand did not hold extensive fiefs, but he had made a long career in the royal service. In 1155 he appears at the head of those listed *de hominibus regis* and then, between 1156 and 1164, he held the posts of marshal, castellan of Jerusalem, and butler, under Baldwin III and Amalric.[129] Between 1165 and 1167, he accompanied Hersenius, Archbishop of Caesarea, on the extremely important mission to Constantinople which resulted in Amalric's marriage to Maria Comnena, grand-niece of the Emperor Manuel I, in August 1167.[130] The signs of royal pressure in his appointment as Grand Master are evident: he was in post by 1173 at the latest, but he was not even a member of the Order in 1169.[131]

Under Amalric, therefore, relations between the Temple and the monarchy had become an issue of crucial importance, but William of Tyre was equally concerned to draw attention to what he saw as the iniquities of Templar conduct towards the secular church, whose incomes and jurisdiction he believed they had violated.[132] Indeed, it has been surmised that the issue of a decree at the Third Lateran Council of 1179, intended to put a check on the extent to which the military orders could exploit their privileges, owed much to William's presentation of the case against them. William did attend the council, but there is no actual record of his active participation.[133]

That the distribution of incomes and the control of churches were important issues can clearly be demonstrated by the situation in the dioceses of Tortosa and Valania in the County of Tripoli. Here the establishment of the large Templar enclave around the city of Tortosa inevitably meant a diminution in the power and resources of the bishops, for they could not avoid some kind of *pariage* with their new neighbours, especially after the privileges granted in *Omne datum optimum*. The agreement with the bishop of Tortosa in 1152 is the most extensive of its kind which survives for the Templars in the east. In the diocese the Templars had full authority over churches and chapels in their castles and over all churches outside Tortosa itself, except in seven specific places. They were, too, exempt from paying tithes on produce raised from their own demesnes in the diocese, on their animals and gardens, and on any booty taken. With the exception of Chastel-Blanc, where all the tithes went to the Templars, and Maraclea, where they all went to the bishop, other tithes were shared equally by the two parties.[134] The agreements with the bishop of Valania, in his much smaller diocese just to the north, might well have been a by-product of the extensive Templar rights around Tortosa, for they probably date from the same period. In 1163, Bishop Anterius and Bertrand of Blancfort confirmed an agreement previously made between the Temple and Gerald, the predecessor of Anterius in the see, to divide in half the tithes deriving from the hospital at Valania and the orchards and goods possessed by the Templars in the diocese, tithes previously belonging to the bishopric. Six years later, they confirmed another agreement over *casalia* and villeins appertaining to the Canon Walter, although here the document makes specific mention that this had been done in order to resolve various quarrels.[135] As Jonathan Riley-Smith has pointed out, the Tortosa agreement does not represent such a sweeping tithe exemption as is implied in *Omne datum optimum*, coming closer to the more restricted privilege enacted by Adrian IV in 1155; nevertheless, it must have bitten deep into diocesan revenue, especially as the Hospitallers enjoyed a similar position in their lands around Krak des Chevaliers. If similar pressures were at work in William's province at Tyre, it explains the archbishop's resentment. The price of handing over responsibility for large parts of the defence of the crusader states to the military orders was paid not only by the secular rulers and their vassals, but by the ecclesiastical authorities as well.

The personalities of the Masters, therefore, vitally affected relations with other institutions. The mastership of Odo of Saint-Amand demonstrates that, even within a generally conservative tradition, it is not easy to stifle the activities of a headstrong and highly strung individual. Indeed, strong discipline and the habit of obedience to higher authority make such a person all the more dangerous if he can reach a position of power within the hierarchy, and it seems likely therefore that in large part the public reputation of the Templars for reckless bravery regardless of the consequences derives from the actions of two men: Odo of Saint-Amand and Gerard of Ridefort, Grand Master between 1185 and 1189. William of Tyre had a particular detestation of Odo of Saint-Amand, and his portrait of him is one of the most striking of the many vignettes which he produced of the leading figures in the Kingdom of Jerusalem in the 1170s and early 1180s. In the affair of the Assassin envoy in 1173, William described his response to the king's demand for the culprit to be handed over as 'dictated by the spirit of pride, of which he had an excess'. In his description of the Christian defeat at Marj Ayun in 1179, during which the Grand Master was captured, William is even more outspoken. He was, he says, 'a worthless man, proud and arrogant, having the spirit of wrath in his nostrils, neither fearing God, nor having reverence for man'.[136] William held him responsible for the defeat, his bitterness intensified by the fact that his brother Ralph was killed in the engagement.[137]

Odo of Saint-Amand's successor was Arnold of Torroja, an experienced Templar who had been Master in Spain and Provence since 1167, where he had been particularly active in Aragon.[138] After the turbulence of Odo's mastership it might have seemed prudent to appoint an outsider, not previously involved in the politics of the east, and indeed the chief record of his activity in the crusader states is as a mediator in the increasingly factionalised politics of the east.[139] Meanwhile, the threat posed by Saladin's build-up of diplomatic and military alliances continued to increase and, in 1184, together with the Patriarch Heraclius and Roger des Moulins, Master of the Hospital, he set out on an embassy to Italy, France, and England intended to impress upon men of influence in these lands the imminent danger to the Christian states of the east. But he did not survive the journey, dying at Verona on 30 September 1184.[140]

Arnold of Torroja's death brought the election of Gerard of Ridefort, probably early in 1185. He was a knight of Flemish or Anglo-Norman origin, who had probably arrived in the east in the early 1170s.[141] In 1179 he was marshal of the Kingdom of Jerusalem,[142] but the crucial influence upon his later career arose from his relationship with Raymond III, Count of Tripoli. Raymond apparently promised him a fief in the county when one became available, and when William Dorel, lord of Botron, died in about 1180, he expected to be given his daughter, the sole heiress. Botron was a small coastal town between Jebail and Nephin, from which a steady income in revenues from trade could be expected, but to Gerard's anger, Raymond, who was probably in debt to the Hospitallers at the time, sold the heiress to a Pisan merchant called Plivain. According to an account which appears to have been derived from the lost chronicle of Ernoul, Gerard was particularly insulted because the recipient was an Italian, drawn from a class of men whom he despised as usurers and merchants. This, says the chronicle, was the reason for the hatred between the Master and the Count of Tripoli.[143] Soon after, Gerard joined the Templars, perhaps influenced by his recovery from a serious illness, but perhaps, too, seeing this as a more likely means of advancement than he would now expect to find in secular life; indeed, by 1183, he had become seneschal, a post he was still holding in August, 1184.[144]

His rise to prominence coincided with the culmination of the factional disputes which had dogged the kingdom under the sick king, Baldwin IV. Baldwin died in March 1185, and his successor, his nephew, the child-king, Baldwin V, outlived him by little more than a year. In 1183, Baldwin IV had laid down that, should his nephew die before the age of ten, Raymond of Tripoli should remain in the position which he had held in the past, that of *bailli* or regent, and that a new ruler should be chosen through the arbitration of the pope, the emperor, and the kings of France and England.[145] But instead these deaths left the way open for the seizure of the throne by Sibyl, Baldwin's sister, and her husband, Guy of Lusignan, a coup achieved in September 1186, with the aid of Gerard of Ridefort, who helped force the reluctant Roger des Moulins, Master of the Hospital, to give up his key to the treasury where the crowns were kept. Gerard is alleged to have said that the coronation was well worth the marriage of Botron.[146] The crystallisation of two parties was now complete: a 'court' party centred upon Sibyl, her mother, Agnes of Courtenay, and their relations by blood and marriage, on the one hand, and the more important local barons, led by Raymond of Tripoli and supported by the leading noble family, the Ibelins, on the other.[147]

William of Tyre, whose chronicle stops in 1184, makes no mention of Gerard of Ridefort, which suggests that he was of little importance in the factional conflicts of the early 1180s which had so engaged William's attention. He is, however, given a central role in the years 1185 to 1187 by the anonymous Old French compilations which are the chief narrative sources for the events which led to the Frankish disaster at Hattin in July 1187. One of these, the manuscript known as Lyon 828, has been shown to be the one which most closely relates to the lost chronicle of Ernoul, thus making it an invaluable source, for Ernoul was a member of the entourage of Balian of Ibelin and an eye-witness to the most crucial incidents of these years.[148] The factionalisation of politics during the 1180s had tested even William's objectivity; Ernoul was inevitably strongly pro-Ibelin in his sympathies and, consequently, his view of Gerard of Ridefort, as one of the most prominent members of the opposing camp, was bound to be unfavourable. It is, nevertheless, an interpretation which most modern commentators have been inclined to accept.

In this presentation, Gerard's nature showed itself most dramatically in the war with Islam, where political rivalries became fatally entangled with military events. In the winter of 1186–7, the Grand Master encouraged King Guy to take up arms to force Raymond of Tripoli to come to terms, and Raymond, in response, negotiated a truce with Saladin to cover Tripoli and Galilee. Gerard wanted Guy to march north and capture Raymond's town of Tiberias on the Sea of Galilee, and only the intervention of Balian of Ibelin prevented this from being carried out.[149] Balian now tried to reconcile the two factions and, together with Josias, Archbishop of Tyre, and the two Grand Masters, set out on an embassy to Tiberias. They stopped on the night of 29 April at Balian's castle of Nablus, where Balian himself was delayed for a short time, leaving the rest of the embassy to continue north. They were to meet Balian at the Templar castle of La Fève. Meanwhile, Saladin's son, al-Afdal, asked Raymond for permission to send a scouting party into the county, and under the terms of his private truce Raymond could only agree, allowing them in for a day only and on condition no harm was done to either property or inhabitants. Raymond then sent a message to the members of the embassy telling them of the situation. Gerard of Ridefort reacted at once, sending to the nearest Templar garrison at Caco, just to the east, for reinforcements, and the next morning, 1 May, they set off for Nazareth, where they were joined by some of the royal garrison there. They found the Egyptians to the north at the Springs of Cresson, where it became clear that the Muslim forces were far larger, perhaps as great as 7,000, in comparison with a Christian force of 140, of which 90 were Templars. James of Mailly, the Marshal of the Temple, and Roger des Moulins, urged retreat, but Gerard would not hear of it, and taunted the marshal with cowardice. The charge upon the Mamluks which followed resulted in a nearly complete massacre of the Christians; only Gerard and two other Templars escaped. The proposed reconciliation between the Grand Master and Raymond of Tripoli never took place, for Gerard said that his wounds were too serious for him to travel farther. 'This was the beginning of the loss of the kingdom', says the compiler of the Lyon manuscript, presumably directly reflecting his source.[150]

Saladin, meanwhile, was assembling his forces for a great onslaught upon the kingdom. Accordingly, the king proclaimed the *arrière-ban*, mustering all able-bloodied men, and the Christians assembled at Acre, where they were joined by Gerard of Ridefort, apparently recovered from his wounds, who released money deposited with the Temple by Henry II as penance for the murder of Becket. The reason given by the Old French compilations is that the Master did this 'to avenge the shame and damage which they [the Saracens] had done to him, and to Christianity'.[151] On 2 July, the army settled in a defensive position based on the well-watered site at Sephoria, with the object of sitting out the invasion, as had been done in the past. Although Saladin had taken his city of Tiberias and his wife was trapped in the citadel, at a meeting of the barons called by the king at Vespers on the evening of 1 July, Raymond of Tripoli advised the Christians to stay where they were, for Saladin's forces were too strong. It was Gerard of Ridefort who, later that night, changed the king's mind and precipitated the great defeat at the Horns of Hattin on 4 July, when the Christian army was trapped in waterless country, still short of Tiberias. The following passage, derived from Ernoul's account, shows the manner in which the Grand Master is alleged to have convinced him:

Lord, do not believe the advice of the count. For he is a traitor, and you well know that he has no love for you, and wishes you to be shamed, and that you should lose the kingdom. But I counsel you to start out immediately, and we with you, and thereby overcome Saladin. For this is the first crisis that you have faced in your reign. If you do not leave this pasturage, Saladin will come and attack you here. And if you retreat from his attack the shame and reproach will be very great.

A longer version can be found in the compilation attributed to Bernard the Treasurer, put together at the monastery of Corbie in 1232. Here, there is stress on the dishonour to the king if he allowed a city only six leagues away to be lost, and the point is emphasised by the claim that the Master threatened that 'the Templars would put aside their white mantles, and sell and pawn [what they have]', if the shame of what the Saracens had done to him and his Order were not avenged. The king dared not contradict him, 'for he loved and feared him because he had made him king, and had handed over to him the treasure of the king of England'.[152]

Ernoul's chronicle has been called an apologia for the Ibelins and may even have been written as a defence of the family's actions during this period; certainly an outside observer might have wondered how the Ibelins emerged from the debacle relatively unscathed, even escaping from the battle itself.[153] Somebody had to take the blame for the fall of the kingdom; the Ibelins and Ernoul wanted to make sure that it was Guy of Lusignan and Gerard of Ridefort, leaving the historian with a problem in interpretation no easier to solve than that presented by William of Tyre's stories about the Temple. Ernoul's version is very persuasive, for it is difficult to build a case for the Grand Master in view of the aftermath of the defeat, but the outcome was perhaps not so obvious before the battle as hindsight now makes it appear. Ibelin 'prudence' might well have looked like 'treachery' to some contemporaries. There is, moreover, a consistency about Ridefort's actions which, even in the Lyon manuscript, are clearly shown to be based upon a French chivalric code which held in contempt any compromise with the Muslims. His personal grudge against Raymond of Tripoli therefore reinforced his conviction that the count shared the values of *vilains*, which he despised, but it is likely that Ridefort would have given the king the same advice whatever position the count had taken. Moreover, the Templars themselves seem to have tried to develop their own counter-propaganda. If the author of the first book of the chronicle of Richard I's crusade, known as the *Itinerarium*, was indeed an English Templar,[154] then his obituary of Gerard of Ridefort, who died at the siege of Acre in October, 1189, should be seen as part of such a campaign. According to this account, which was probably written in about 1192, the Grand Master was crowned with the laurel of martyrdom, 'which he had merited in so many wars'.[155]

Saladin's victory at Hattin created a chain reaction. Acre fell less than a week later, and Jerusalem in October, including the Templar headquarters in the al-Aqsa. Tripoli and Antioch survived, as did the Templar and Hospitaller enclaves around Tortosa and Krak des

Chevaliers, but the only important city left in the Kingdom of Jerusalem was Tyre, saved by the chance arrival of a fleet under the German crusader, Conrad of Monferrat. In Jerusalem, the same powerful sense of the need for purification as he had been seen in the execution of the knights of the military orders is described in a letter from Terricus, the acting commander of the Templars, to Henry II, early in 1188:

After Jerusalem had been captured, Saladin had the Cross taken down from the Temple of the Lord and, beating it with clubs, had it carried on display for two days throughout the city. Then he caused the Temple of the Lord to be washed with rose water, inside and out, above and below, and, with an astonishing commotion, had his law acclaimed from on high in four places.[156]

CHAPTER FOUR

HATTIN TO LA FORBIE

Few Templars escaped the battle of Hattin, but among those who did was Brother Terricus, the Grand Commander. With Gerard of Ridefort in captivity and most of his companions executed by the Muslims, he assumed command of the remnants of the Order. In two dramatic letters, one written between 10 July and 6 August 1187, and the other in January 1188, he provides a vivid commentary upon the events seen from the Order's point of view.[1]

The first letter was intended for as wide a circulation as possible, being sent specifically to Pope Urban III and to Philip of Alsace, Count of Flanders, the one important western leader to have visited the east during the previous decade, and generally to all Christians and all the brothers of the Order itself.

How many and how great the calamities with which the anger of God has permitted us to be scourged at this present time, as a consequence of our sins, we can explain neither by letters nor by tearful voice. O sadness! For the Turks, assembling an immense multitude of their people, began fiercely to invade our Christian territories, against which we brought together phalanxes of our men, fighting them during the octave of the Blessed Apostles Peter and Paul [the week following 29 June]. To begin with we set out for Tiberias, which they had captured, having abandoned their camp. When they had pressed upon us in some very bad rocks, they attacked us so fiercely, that they captured the Holy Cross and the king and killed a great number of our men, so that in truth we believe on that day 230 of our brothers were beheaded, not counting the sixty who were killed on the first of May [the battle at the Springs of Cresson]. The lord count of Tripoli, the lord Reginald of Sidon, and the lord Balian of Ibelin, and ourselves, were scarcely able to escape from that pitiable field. Then the pagans, raging without control in the blood of our Christians, did not delay in coming to the city of Acre, with all their multitude, and when they had violently captured it, they invaded almost the entire land. Only Jerusalem, Ascalon, Tyre, and Beirut remain to us at the present time. Moreover, we can in no way retain these cities, in which almost all the inhabitants have been killed, unless we immediately receive divine aid and your help. They do not cease to attack us violently by day and by night, for the city of Tyre is being unrelentingly besieged at the moment, and so great is their army that they cover the entire face of the land from Tyre to Jerusalem and beyond to Gaza, like ants. Therefore deem it worthy to send help as soon as possible to us and to the Christians of the East, at present all but lost, so that through God and the distinction of your brotherhood, the remaining cities may be saved by means of the support which you provide.

Worse was to come. In his letter of January 1188, to King Henry II, he had to tell of the fall of Jerusalem itself, which had taken place on 2 October, and he described how Saladin had ordered the Cross to be taken down and carried through the streets for two days, where it was publicly beaten with sticks as a preliminary to the purification of the city. Saladin, however, had allowed the Syrian Christians custody of the Holy Sepulchre until the fourth day after the Feast of St Michael (presumably until 3 October 1188) and had also allowed the Hospitallers to keep ten brothers in their house to look after the sick for up to a year. Despite the loss of Jerusalem, nevertheless, resistance continued: the Hospitallers at Belvoir had counter-attacked and seized two Muslim caravans, in one of which they found the arms and equipment taken from the Templar castle of La Fève, which, being so close to Hattin, had fallen shortly after the battle. Moreover, Montréal, Kerak, Safad, Krak des Chevaliers, al-Marqab (Margat), and Chastel-Blanc still held out. Nor had the determined siege of Tyre by Saladin in November and December succeeded; indeed, Conrad of Montferrat, helped by the Hospitallers and Templars, had won a significant sea battle just off-shore, capturing eleven Muslim galleys. According to Terricus, Saladin had been so dismayed that he burnt the surviving ships and 'moved by grief beyond measure, cutting off the ears and tail of his horse, he rode through the whole army, in the sight of all'. The survival of Tyre was indeed crucial, but of the castles listed by Terricus four had been lost within the year, those of Belvoir, Montréal, Kerak, and Safad.

In his second letter, Terricus refers to himself as 'former' Grand Commander of the Templars, for Gerard of Ridefort had reappeared in the Christian ranks. It is not known why he was the only Templar spared after Hattin, but presumably Saladin had seen his value as a bargaining counter, for in September 1187 he obtained his freedom in exchange for the Templar castle at Gaza, which obeyed his command to surrender.[2] His movements after this are not clear, but certainly he was with the army assembled by King Guy in late August 1189, in order to besiege Acre. Guy had been released in the summer of 1188, and it has been argued that he needed a success to re-establish his now shaky position as king.[3] Nevertheless, it was a rash undertaking, characteristic of Gerard of Ridefort, and it is possible that the Grand Master's hand lay behind the move. At any rate, it cost him his life, for he died fighting near the city on 4 October 1189.[4]

The fact was that, despite increasingly frantic appeals for help in the early 1180s, no substantial military aid from the west had then been forthcoming, but Hattin so shocked Christian opinion that pious promises and conscience-salving monetary donations were at last replaced by the armies of the Third Crusade. Although the German emperor, Frederick Barbarossa, died in June 1190, while crossing Asia Minor, the French king, Philip II, and the Angevin, Richard I, arrived in the east in April and June 1191 respectively, and their combined forces retook Acre on 12 July. Although Philip departed for France within three weeks of this success, Richard stayed on in the hope of regaining Jerusalem, defeating Saladin in a great battle at Arsuf in September. During the march south from Acre along the coast, the Christian army had been especially hard-pressed, and here the experience of the military orders in defending the columns – an experience which went back to the days of Louis VII's march across Asia Minor – proved vital. Despite heavy losses, especially of horses, the Templars maintained their position at the rear, while the Hospitallers usually formed the van. The orders proved indispensable, collecting oxen and fodder, recovering bodies, and beating off the constant Turkish attacks. On the day of the battle of Arsuf, 7 September, the military orders were assigned a key role in Richard's military formation. According to the author of the *Itinerarium*, who seems to have had access to a good eye-witness account, he established twelve squadrons, which were then divided in appropriate proportions into five battle-lines. The Templars were to hold the front rank and the Hospitallers the rear.[5] The essential feature here was the imposition of discipline and group coherence; the king could not have used the military orders in this way if he had believed that they would be reckless in their battle conduct. In the end, it was the Hospitallers, pressed to breaking-point at the rear of the column, who finally charged, but the king was able to maintain sufficient control to ensure that the Frankish assault made maximum impact.

These successes partially resurrected the kingdom, restoring the coastal cities as far as Jaffa, including Acre, which now became the most important city with all the leading powers, including the Templars, establishing their main bases there.[6] They failed, however, to regain Jerusalem. Although in January 1192, Richard was within sight of the city at Bait Nūbā, he finally accepted local advice that an attack would be impractical, showing that with the death of Gerard of Ridefort in 1189 the Templars had reverted to their traditional caution. The author of the *Itinerarium* describes the situation in this way:

But the wiser heads did not express agreement with the incautious wish of the common people. For the Templars and Hospitallers, as well as the Pullani of that land, looking more acutely at what might happen in the future, dissuaded King Richard from going on to Jerusalem at that time. For, if the city were besieged and they pressed their attack with full strength against Saladin and those who were enclosed with him, the army of the Turks which was outside, stationed not far away in the mountains, would make sudden attacks upon the besiegers, putting the campaign in the greatest danger, on the one hand from those outside and on the other from forays from those besieged within. Even if they succeeded in their desire and gained the city of Jerusalem, this did not seem to be expedient either, unless the strongest men were assigned to guard the city. This, however, they did not think could easily be done, especially since they considered that the people, who were most keen to complete their pilgrimage, would each without delay return home, for they were already wearied beyond measure by the pressures of everything.[7]

It was decided instead to retreat to the coast and rebuild Ascalon, 'so that there they could keep a watch on the Turks bringing food from Egypt to Jerusalem'.[8] By June, the crusaders felt strong enough for another attempt, but the basic strategic situation had not changed, and once again local advice, in which the Templars and Hospitallers were prominent, persuaded them that it would not be practical. Equally, the king failed to gain sufficient support to implement an alternative plan to attack Egypt. These moves are significant. Saladin was dependent upon Egypt for supplies; the time spent on the rebuilding of Ascalon showed the Christians' recognition of this. It also demonstrates the importance of the concession of Gaza by

Gerard of Ridefort in 1188; it had been a heavy price to pay for his release.

Throughout his crusade Richard relied heavily on the Templars, a trust reinforced when, almost certainly through the king's influence, Robert of Sablé, a leading Angevin vassal of the king, became Grand Master in 1191.[9] Robert of Sablé's patrimony had been based upon a cluster of important lands in the valley of the River Sarthe to which he had succeeded in the 1160s. His earlier career had been fairly typical of the turbulent baronage of Anjou: in 1173 he had supported the unsuccessful revolt of Henry, the Young King, against his father, Henry II, while the amends which he made to monastic houses in the region in the course of 1190 before his departure on crusade show that he had not been over-sensitive to their rights in the past.[10] His close association with Richard can be seen in his involvement in the king's preparations for the crusade in Anjou and Normandy during the spring and summer of 1190, and his appointment in June as one of the five justiciars in command of the crusading fleet. When Richard stayed in Sicily en route to the east during the winter of 1190–1, Robert of Sablé acted as his emissary in negotiations with King Tancred and he was also one of his representatives on a committee established by Kings Richard and Philip to decide on the disposal of property of men who died during the crusade.[11]

It may have been this connection that led the Templars to purchase the island of Cyprus from the king, who had captured it from its Byzantine governor in June 1191, on his way east. Richard's governors found the island difficult to control and it was arranged that the Templars should buy it for 100,000 Saracen *besants*, of which the Order initially paid 40,000, a sum which shows the depth of the Templars' financial resources considering their losses and expenses since 1187. If this had been successful, the Templars would have been the first of the military orders to establish their own independent state, a feat later achieved by the Teutonic Knights in Prussia by 1283, and by the Hospitallers in 1309 when they moved their headquarters to Rhodes. In the event, the project proved too ambitious, for the Templars committed only twenty brothers to its garrison, while at the same time alienating the population with their heavy taxation and arbitrary rule. On 5 April 1192, a rebellion broke out in Nicosia, where the garrison was said to have treated the population like 'villeins' and only a desperate charge from the castle saved the Templars. In May 1192, therefore, Richard sold the island to Guy of Lusignan, who, the previous month, had been displaced as King of Jerusalem by Conrad of Montferrat.[12] Even so, during the thirteenth century the Templars remained a force on the island with their own quarters in Famagusta and Limassol and castles at Gastria, Khirokitia, Yermasoyia, and Limassol. As a final service to the king, when Richard began his journey back to the west in October 1192, a group of Templars was chosen to accompany him. According to Bernard the Treasurer's compilation of the Old French sources (Ernoul-Bernard), Richard actually set out disguised as a Templar in an effort to avoid the many enemies who he knew barred his way.[13] Whether or not the story is true, it does emphasise how closely the Templars were associated with the king in contemporary minds. In fact, as is well known, just before Christmas 1192 Richard was captured near Vienna by Leopold of Austria and then sold to the Emperor Henry VI. He was not released until February 1194.

As an exercise in damage limitation, the Third Crusade had achieved more than any expedition since the late eleventh century and when Saladin himself died in 1193, leaving the Aiyūbids quarrelling among themselves, the survival of the mainland settlements, at least for the immediate future, was assured. Nevertheless, for the Franks of Outremer, the task of rebuilding their position after the Third Crusade had left was hard and expensive. The prolonged struggle by the Templars to re-establish themselves in their key northern fortress of Baghras provides a telling demonstration of the point, at the same time showing how difficult it had become in the complicated politics of the east for the Templars to act simply as straighforward champions of the faith against Islam. Darbsak and Baghras had fallen to Saladin in September 1188, destroying the heart of the great Templar marcher lordship. Baghras had been well stocked, but apparently lacked sufficient defenders, probably as a consequence of the manpower losses during the previous fourteen months. It was indeed a massive fortress, which was difficult to maintain, and Imād ad-Dīn, who was an eye-witness to Saladin's siege, was not at all surprised when 'Alam-ad-Dīn, Lord of 'Azāz, to whom Saladin granted Darbsak and Baghras, abandoned Baghras after having made what profit he could from its contents.[14] In 1191, when he was preoccupied with the siege of Acre, Saladin sent men to dismantle the fortress, but they had not apparently completed the job when they fled on the approach of Leo, Roupenid Prince of Lesser Armenia (Cilicia), a state independent of Byzantium since 1172/3. When the Templars returned to reclaim Baghras they found that Leo had refortified the castle and had no intention of handing it over. Indeed, it seems clear that he intended this as a stage in a campaign to take over Antioch itself, to whose princes he was, in theory, a vassal.

The Armenians were settled in a band of territory which stretched from Cilicia in south-east Asia Minor to the River Euphrates, largely because of the forcible resettlement policies of the Byzantines in the eleventh century and the incursions of the Turks into Asia Minor after the battle of Manzikert in 1071. The Byzantines regarded them as monophysite heretics, but in 1184, after a long period of amicable relations in ecclesiastical affairs, the Armenian Church entered what the papacy understood to be communion with Rome.[15] The situation was, however, greatly complicated by Leo's war with Antioch, since Leo's move into the Templar lands constituted a direct threat to Bohemond III, Prince of Antioch. Although Bohemond and Leo were reconciled in 1194, when Bohemond died in 1201 the conflict flared up again in the form of rival claims to his inheritance from Raymond-Roupen, Leo's great-nephew and grandson of Bohemond III, and Bohemond of Tripoli, who was a son of Bohemond III. The papacy became entangled in this web because in 1197 Leo had brought Lesser Armenia into full union with the Catholic Church, following his acquisition of a crown for Cilicia from a representative of the Emperor Henry VI. Innocent III supported the Armenian claim because he was attracted to the idea of a strong Cilician–Antiochene state.

This was how the Templars came to be allied to Bohemond of Tripoli in the bitter war which followed, for they could not accept any settlement which did not restore Baghras to them. Matters came to a head in 1211, for the Templars had been bringing pressure to bear on the pope, perhaps through their representatives at the curia, who may have been estabished there by this time as they were later in the century. This may well have inclined Innocent to take their side in 1211 after Leo had made a series of destructive attacks upon Templar possessions in the region, which included the ambush of a party of Templars in a narrow pass, in which one brother was killed and the new Grand Master, William of Chartres, seriously wounded.[16] In the autumn of 1211, the Templars mounted an attack in reprisal, reinforced by fifty knights sent by John of Brienne, King of Jerusalem. Leo himself had been excommunicated by Innocent III as a result of his attacks on the Templars, and this may have been a reason for his conciliatory policy in 1213, when he restored Templar lands. Even so, the Order did not regain Baghras until 1216, after a new series of political upheavals not directly connected with them allowed Leo finally to instal Raymond-Roupen in Antioch.[17]

In these circumstances it was as well for the survival of the crusader states that the departure of the Third Crusade and the death of Saladin left a stalemate. After Saladin the Muslim world reverted to that endemic disunity which had allowed the establishment of the Latins in the first place. Despite the efforts of al-ʿĀdil, Saladin's brother, Cairo and Damascus were frequently in conflict, and it was often convenient for both Muslims and Christians to arrange truces and enter into tacit understandings over spheres of influence. On the Latin side no figure of the stature of King Amalric emerged to provide a guiding policy for the crusader states; after Sibyl's death in 1190, the government of the Kingdom of Jerusalem devolved upon the husbands of Isabel, Sibyl's half-sister, Conrad of Montferrat (died 1192), Henry of Champagne (died 1197), and Aimery of Lusignan, younger brother of Guy. Aimery, who had inherited Cyprus after the death of Guy in 1194, was the most effective of these, but when he died in 1205 he left no direct successor, so that the inheritance of the kingdom fell to Maria, Isabel's daughter by Conrad of Montferrat. Not until a husband was found for her in 1210, in the person of John of Brienne, did the kingdom once more have a central figure on which to focus. Not surprisingly, therefore, there was little to divert the energies of the major interests within the crusader states from complicated and enduring conflicts such as that over Baghras.

Richard's Grand Master, Robert of Sablé, died on 28 September, in either 1192 or 1193.[18] His successor was Gilbert Erail, who had formerly served in the east, for he was Grand Commander at Jerusalem in 1183, but between 1185 and 1190 he had been Master in Provence and Spain, and thereafter in overall charge of the western provinces as Master in the regions beyond the sea.[19] Although Grand Master from 1194, he was still in Spain in August 1197, and is not recorded in Outremer again until the following year. On 5 March 1198, he was a prominent member of the council, held at the

Templars' house at Acre, at which the Teutonic Knights were accepted as an order of the Church. The Teutonic Knights had developed from a German hospital established by visitors from Lübeck and Bremen in 1190; when they became a military order in 1198 they modelled their statutes on those of the Temple.[20]

Gilbert Erail appears to have been a long-serving 'career' Templar, but his successor, Philip of Plessis in Anjou, came to the east as a layman with the Third Crusade, as Robert of Sablé had done. The castle of Plessis was about eight miles north-east of Angers and there were already powerful lords established there in the eleventh century. Philip was a younger son, but had married and had sons of his own. Initially, he had tried to raise money for his crusade by offering the monks of St Nicholas of Angers an estate and wood at Linières, in exchange for thirty *solidi* to help him make the journey to the east. The monks did not agree, and Philip was therefore forced to pawn his property to his brother Fulk in order to raise the money. But the monks gained the property in any case, since Fulk granted it to them to ensure the safety of the pilgrim's soul.[21] He presumably departed on the Third Crusade in the company of other Angevin lords like Robert of Sablé, but there is no further record of him until his appearance as Grand Master of the Temple in 1201.[22] He seems to have been eager to promote the crusade. Although King Aimery had negotiated a truce with al-ʿĀdil in July 1198, to last for five years and eight months, nevertheless Philip of Plessis reports that sporadic fighting still occurred. In a letter to the abbots of the Cistercian houses in Europe, he described two attacks made by al-ʿĀdil on 11 November 1201 and 2 June 1202. Al-ʿĀdil raided into Tripolitan territory with, according to the Grand Master, troops from most of the Muslim world. They came from Egypt, Jerusalem, Damascus, and even from beyond the Euphrates, putting the population to flight and destroying property.[23] This experience might explain the Grand Master's attitude when, in July 1209, in the absence of an adult ruler, a council met to discuss the renewal of the five-year truce established by Aimery in September 1204. All except Philip of Plessis and the prelates wished the truce to continue, but the Grand Master argued that any new king could not be bound by it. By this time, John of Brienne had been chosen to marry Queen Maria, but had not yet arrived. Philip's view prevailed, but little serious fighting followed.[24] The Grand Master, perhaps concerned to maintain the Order's reputation and role, may have been mindful of Innocent III's letter of 1199 to the important leaders in the east, in which he complained that westerners lacked enthusiasm for the crusade because the barons of Outremer constantly made truces with the Saracens.[25]

There was some truth in the pope's accusation, for the Christians of Outremer were as much preoccupied with internal conflicts as they were with the war against the infidel. The Templars' often uneasy relations with the secular Church resurfaced in 1196, when Pope Celestine III reminded the Order that it had broken its agreement over the division of tithes with the prior and canons of the Holy Sepulchre.[26] More serious were the consequences of the dispute with the Bishop of Tiberias over the revenues from his diocese. Innocent III named the Bishops of Sidon and Gibelet as mediators and Gilbert Erail sent two brothers as his representatives. Eventually the matter was settled by the patriarch, but the Bishop of Sidon was not satisfied, and when the Grand Master refused to concede his point he excommunicated him. Innocent III, however, supported the Templars, suspending the bishop and ordering the Patriarch, the Archbishop of Tyre, and the Bishop of Acre, to rescind the excommunication on the grounds that this represented a usurpation of papal power.[27]

The wide-ranging agreement with the Hospital in 1179 had also demonstrated how, as the two Orders took over an increasing proportion of the crusader states, they needed to define their own interests in relation to each other. Inevitably disputes arose in areas where those interests intersected. The northern parts of the County of Tripoli were a particularly sensitive region, for, despite the disasters of 1187–8, both orders retained extensive lands and castles stemming from the grants made to them in the early 1150s. At Krak des Chevaliers, the Hospitallers had weathered the storm of Saladin's siege of July 1188, and the Templar fortresses of Chastel-Blanc and al-ʿArīmah had also survived the crisis. Tortosa, although damaged by Saladin, had not been properly taken over because the Templars had stubbornly held on to one of the main towers of their complex. Further north, the Hospitallers had made a new acquisition in 1186, the great castle of al-Marqab, near the coast just south of Valania, a fortress so formidable that Saladin had made no serious attempt to take it. As the 1163 tithe agreement with the bishop shows,[28] the Templars were established in and around Valania, and in 1198 it is not surprising to find them in dispute with the Hospital over a fief lying between Valania and al-Marqab. The dispute necessitated a conference between the leaders of the orders in December 1198, which was followed by a sharp reminder by the pope the next February that they should remember the agreements made in the time of Alexander III. The pope said that he would arbitrate between Templar representatives sent by Gilbert Erail, named as brothers Peter of Villaplana and Terricus, and the Hospitaller brothers, Disigius, Prior of Barletta, and Ogier, Preceptor of Italy.[29] In 1201 the agreement between the Masters of the Orders over the use of ovens in Valania – the Templars were to use only the public oven and the Hospitallers and the bishop their own private ovens – suggests that the need to define their respective rights had affected the town itself.[30]

These interventions were typical of Innocent III, who believed very firmly in the exercise of the authority claimed by the papacy, which included direct jurisdiction over exempt orders. The rescinding of the excommunication of Gilbert Erail by the Bishop of Sidon was a demonstration of this belief; equally, it seems unlikely that Innocent could have accepted Amalric I's arbitrary action against Walter of Mesnil in 1173.[31] But for the Templars such interventionism was double-edged. On the one hand the pope issued a stream of bulls demanding that the Templars and their privileges be protected by the clergy. He reminded the clergy of the Templars' rights to their own burial grounds and their freedom to erect churches on land donated to them (1199, 1200); he issued a general warning against doing any violence to Templars, their men, or their property, and he reaffirmed that they were to retain bequests exempt from tithes, repeating this four times between 1198 and 1210. He condemned bishops who, by their provocation, had forced Templars to fight other Christians, and even imprisoned members of the Order, also issuing this four times between 1198 and 1205; and he told the clergy not to interfere with the Templars' annual collection of tithes, not to put Templar churches under excommunication or interdict, and to make sure that justice was done to those of their flock who broke into Templar houses and committed robbery (1198).[32] Between 1204 and 1209 he forbade clergy to take tithes from estates cultivated directly by the Templars for their own use, he renewed *Omne datum optimum*, he ordered clergy to prevent those engaged to serve in the

Order for a set period from freeing themselves before time, and to protect the property and privileges of the Temple against usurpers and to excommunicate those who would not submit to their injunction.[33]

However, while Innocent III made clear to the clergy and to society as a whole that the Order was directly under papal protection, at the same time he left the Templars themselves in no doubt about his views in regard to the abuse of these privileges. In 1207 he wrote to Philip of Plessis telling him that he had frequently been disturbed by complaints against the Templars and he accused them, as William of Tyre had done, of the sin of pride. He complained that they gave their cross to any vagabond who had a few pence and then asserted that he was entitled to Christian burial and ecclesiastical services, despite the fact that he might be under excommunication. In this way the Templars were ensnared by the Devil and, although he did not wish to dwell on these errors, he hoped that the Order would reform itself. He concluded the letter by accusing the Templars of lack of respect for papal legates, which was probably a reference to the continuing dispute over Baghras.[34]

Innocent's concerns about the Templars reflect his wider determination to promote a new crusade for, although the Third Crusade had ensured the survival of the crusader states, the papacy could hardly be expected to view the crusades as some kind of pragmatic exercise in power sharing. In particular, the exclusion from many of the most revered holy places continued to rankle. Therefore when Innocent III ascended the papal throne in 1198 he determined to make the revival of the crusade his first priority. The main objective was to be Egypt, the most important seat of Aiyūbid power, since without a secure southern frontier the defence of Jerusalem, even if the Christians did manage to recapture it, was extremely difficult. Even the relatively ineffectual Fātimids had been able to damage the kingdom from their base in Ascalon in the first half of the twelfth century. But Innocent's ability to stimulate crusading activity was not matched by any means of controlling it once it was set in motion. The members of the Fourth Crusade, contracted to Venice for sea transport but unable to pay for it, allowed themselves to be diverted to Constantinople in 1204. Admittedly, new crusader states were set up, even though at the expense of the Byzantines rather than the Muslims, but the creation of a Latin empire at Constantinople, Latin states at Thessalonica and in the Morea, and a string of Venetian ports and island bases, did not compensate for the failure to attack the Muslims. Moreover, neither the official crusade against the Albigensian heretics in southern France, which began in 1209, nor the so-called 'Children's Crusade' in 1212, an unofficial outburst of popular enthusiasm in Germany and France, brought any help to Outremer.

It was not until 1217 and 1218, after Innocent's death, that the pope's tireless planning and promotion of the crusade produced a series of expeditions to the east which resulted in the campaign in Egypt known as the Fifth Crusade. Sums towards the crusade were channelled through Haimard, the Templar treasurer at their house in Paris.[35] When Innocent died in July 1216, his successor, Honorius III, carried on with the plans, writing in July 1217 to the Patriarch of Jerusalem and the two Grand Masters of the Temple and the Hospital, telling them to meet the first of the crusading leaders, King Andrew of Hungary and Leopold, Duke of Austria, in Cyprus.[36] Although this idea was abandoned, the two princes nevertheless arrived separately in the east in the autumn of 1217, enabling the Christians to plan their campaign. Philip of Plessis had died on 12 November 1209, and had been succeeded as Master of the Temple by William of Chartres, who came from a family with close associations with the Temple.[37] About October, William wrote to Honorius III explaining that the Christians intended to use the new forces to attack Damietta, a plan probably developed at discussions held at Acre that month.[38] According to William, before the arrival of the crusaders, the king, the patriarch, and the Hospitallers and Templars, had planned to attack al-Muʿazzam of Damascus, a son of al-ʿĀdil, but it was now agreed to use the main army against Egypt, while leaving a few men in Palestine as a diversion. Nevertheless, although he assured the pope that the sultan was afraid of their forces, he still appealed for more troops, as many problems remained, especially of supply.[39]

Although the Grand Master's point was underlined by the ineffective nature of the campaigns in Palestine in November 1217, and by the departure of King Andrew early the next year, nevertheless the arrival of a fleet from Frisia in April 1218, and the news of further reinforcements on their way, stiffened Christian resolve. On 24 May 1218, John of Brienne, together with the military orders under their

Grand Masters, sailed from Acre to ʿAtlīt and then to Egypt, landing at Damietta six days later.[40] William of Chartres died here on 26 August, either in 1218 or 1219. He had been ill in the autumn of 1217 and may not have recovered properly before setting out for Egypt.[41] The Templars, though, had committed considerable resources to the campaign and the Grand Master's death did not affect this. The new Master, Peter of Montaigu, was a highly experienced Templar who probably originated in the region of Clermont in the Auvergne. His family was heavily committed to the crusades: one brother, Garin, had been Grand Master of the Hospital since 1207, and another, Eustorge, was Archbishop of Nicosia.[42] Peter's background was not dissimilar to that of Gilbert Erail, having been Master in Provence and Spain between 1206 and 1212, and thereafter Master *citra mare*. In July 1212, he had taken part in the famous Christian victory at Las Navas de Tolosa.[43] He had probably arrived in Acre in May 1218, with the German fleet which had helped in the successful siege of Alcacer do Sal, just to the south of Lisbon, in the previous autumn, although he cannot be identified with certainty in the east until September 1220.[44]

In November 1219 the combined forces of the Fifth Crusade, made up of western crusaders under the papal representative, Cardinal Pelagius, and the Latin settlers themselves, including royal forces under the regent, John of Brienne, and the military orders, succeeded in capturing Damietta on the Nile Delta. So alarmed was al-Kāmil, the Aiyūbid sultan, that both before and after the city's fall he had offered to cede Jerusalem in exchange for Frankish withdrawal. But the offer was rejected by Pelagius, a man imbued with a strong belief in his own manifest destiny, and by many of the Franks, including the Templars, who believed that the defence of Jerusalem was not viable without possession of the lands beyond the Jordan, not included in the deal.[45] Oliver of Paderborn, master of the cathedral school at Cologne, and a participant and eye-witness, was particularly enthusiastic about the military contribution of the Templars. In the network of waterways which made up the delta, much of the fighting was amphibious, demanding the use of techniques which must seldom have been needed in Palestine and Syria. The Templars' deployment of their ships, their construction of pontoons, their handling of horses in mud and swamp, deeply impressed Oliver, and were of major importance in the encirclement of Damietta which led to its fall. Once the city was taken, the Templars raided the coastal town of Burlus and brought back a large quantity of spoils, including 'about 100 camels, [and] as many captives, horses, mules, oxen and asses and goats, clothing and household utensils'.[46]

The capture of Damietta might have been regarded as a vindication of the rejection of al-Kāmil's peace offer, but by the autumn of 1220 it is nevertheless clear that the Templar leaders were having doubts about the wisdom of continuing the campaign in Egypt. In many ways the dilemmas of the 1160s had once more arisen, for al-Muʿazzam presented a sufficiently serious threat to the Frankish possessions in northern Palestine, including the Templar castle of ʿAtlīt, newly built in 1218 with crusader help, for Peter of Montaigu to gain permission from Pelagius to leave Egypt to attend to the matter.[47] In a letter to Nicholas, Bishop of Elne, written at Acre on 20 September 1220, the Master explained the situation as he saw it. Since the capture of Damietta and Tanis, a new arrival of pilgrims had given the Christians sufficient men both to garrison Damietta and to defend the castles. As a result Pelagius, supported by the clergy, wanted to advance, but most of the baronage, whether from the west or from Outremer, did not believe that their forces were yet large enough. Peter of Montaigu evidently agreed with the barons: 'For the Sultan of Babylon with an infinite number of infidels encamped not far from Damietta built bridges on both branches of the river to impede the Christians, [and] was waiting there with such a large number of armed men that the greatest danger would have threatened any of the faithful who had pushed forward.' The Christians therefore decided to dig in and wait for help, although Saracen harassment continued, especially from the sea. At the same time, the problems of defending Palestine were mounting every day. Al-Muʿazzam had taken Caesarea and had done much damage to Acre and Tyre, as well as threatening ʿAtlīt several times. Another brother, al-Ashraf, had gathered his forces together and had overcome several Saracen emirs to the east, and if he defeated them all, then the Christians in Antioch, Tripoli, Acre and even Egypt, would find themselves in the greatest danger. Meanwhile, the crusaders were still anxiously awaiting the arrival of the Emperor Frederick and the Germans; if they did not come by the following summer, then the whole Christian position in Palestine, as well as in Egypt, would be in doubt. Money was running low and they would not be able to sustain the crusade for much longer.[48]

In June 1221, al-Kāmil put forward new peace proposals. They did not differ materially from those of October 1219, but this time the Templars were in favour. Pelagius, though, still believed that Frederick II was about to sail and turned them down. This was to be the crusaders' last chance, for the disaster which overcame them in August justified Peter of Montaigu's fears. In a letter written at Acre to Alan Martel, Preceptor in England, in September 1221, Peter described what had happened the previous summer. He himself was an important participant, having returned from Palestine some time before al-Kāmil's peace proposals. The crusaders had been much criticised, both in the west and in Outremer, for making no further advance after the capture of Damietta until the arrival of Louis, Duke of Bavaria, who, as representative of the emperor, announced that 'he had come to this place to attack the enemies of the Christian faith'. A council was therefore held, attended by all the leaders, and it was unanimously agreed to advance. John of Brienne, who had been in Palestine since February 1220, returned to Egypt and joined an orderly advance, which began after the Feast of the Apostles Peter and Paul [29 June]. The sultan retreated to his camp beyond the River Tanis, while the Christians attempted to cross the river by building bridges. However, according to the Master, as many as 10,000 Christians deserted at this time. It was then that the Egyptians cut off communication with Damietta by opening the sluice-gates which they controlled and water flooded along previously prepared courses, in places which the Christians had not known about. Muslim shipping down river blocked the arrival of any new provisions. An attempted retreat during the night was a complete disaster, supplies were lost, pack-horses and waggons abandoned, and many men were drowned. 'Destitute of provisions, the army of Christ could neither proceed further nor retreat nor flee anywhere, nor could it fight with the sultan on account of the lake between the waters. It was trapped like a fish in a net.' Under this pressure the Christians were forced to agree to the return of Damietta and the exchange of prisoners. Peter of Montaigu was among those sent to Damietta to explain the terms, but they found that the Bishop of Acre, the Chancellor, and Henry, Count of Malta (who had just arrived), wished to defend the city. 'We very much approved if it could be done effectively, indeed we would rather have been thrust into perpetual prison, than the city be returned by us to the unbelievers to the shame of Christendom.' But, although a careful search was made, nothing could be found to make such a defence viable. The proposed eight-year truce was therefore accepted. As had been agreed, the sultan then supplied the army with loaves and flour for fifteen days. The letter ends with an appeal to the Master in England to send what assistance he could.[49] Such appeals did have some effect: in 1222, Philip II of France left the Hospital and the Temple 2,000 marks each, plus a sum of 50,000 marks on condition that they kept 300 knights in service for three years in the Holy Land, beyond their own establishment.[50]

Frederick II's failure to arrive in Egypt was a major reason for the demise of the Fifth Crusade, but even so efforts continued to prepare the way for the emperor's arrival. In March 1223, a meeting was held at Ferentino attended by leaders from the east, including Garin of Montaigu, Grand Master of the Hospital, Hermann of Salza, Grand Master of the Teutonic Knights, and William Cadel, Commander of the Temple, as well as John of Brienne.[51] Here it was decided that the crusade be postponed for two years, but agreed that Frederick was to marry Isabel, daughter and heiress of John of Brienne, an arrangement which the eastern leaders obviously hoped would increase Frederick's commitment to the proposed expedition. The marriage took place in 1225, but Frederick had still not appeared two years later when the patriarch and masters of the military orders wrote to Pope Gregory IX complaining about the continued delay.[52] In September 1228 they had their wish, for Frederick II finally arrived in Cyprus. But now a substantial body of the Franks of Outremer found his presence less than welcome. In his Sicilian kingdom, Frederick's style of government was distinctly autocratic; in the east the Christian leaders, including the patriarch, the masters of the military orders, the barons, and the maritime communes, had become accustomed to a more corporate approach to government, within which, in practice, many of them pursued their own specific interests. In particular, the baronage often justified their attitude by reference to the alleged legal rights of their class, rights which they had developed with assiduity both in oral pleading in the courts and, in the course of the thirteenth century, in the form of written treatises. Such a legalistic class was not unaware that with the death of his wife, Isabel, in May 1228, Frederick was technically no longer king, for this now devolved upon his infant son, Conrad. Not surprisingly, therefore, Frederick almost immediately came into conflict with one of the leading figures among the barons, the Ibelin John of Beirut, whose stewardship he challenged and whose fief in Beirut he threatened to confiscate.

Although the quarrel with John of Ibelin was patched up, and the leaders of the military orders were among those who swore to maintain the peace,[53] new tensions arose after Frederick landed at Acre in September 1228, for news had reached the east that Gregory IX had excommunicated the emperor for his most recent postponement of the crusade the previous year, when sickness in the fleet had forced him to turn back. Despite this, the initial welcome for Frederick was fulsome – the Templars and Hospitallers are described as falling at his feet and kissing his knees[54] – but the arrival of letters from the pope forbidding all contact with the emperor seems to have led to the withdrawal of clerical support, especially that of the patriarch and the military orders.[55] This was the beginning of a feud in which the Templars came to play a leading part and which had repercussions for the Order long after Frederick's departure from the east the following year.

The stages in the degeneration of relations are by no means clear. According to Bernard the Treasurer's compilation, the Temple contained a number of Apulian lords who, after rebelling against Frederick, had fled from Italy and joined the Order in the east,[56] and this element must have reinforced Templar willingness to comply with the papal ban. There may, too, have been resentment at the close links between Frederick and the Teutonic Knights under Hermann of Salza, since the Templars saw the German order as at best a junior partner, formed originally in imitation of their own order. Certainly, the Templars had always been more closely associated with the Capetians rather than the Hohenstaufen, and had far fewer houses in Germany than in their vast empire in French lands.[57] Indeed, the idea of Templar 'treachery' found its earliest manifestations in German commentators upon the Second Crusade.[58] For his part, Frederick seems to have tried to assert his authority by marching to 'Atlīt and demanding that the Templars hand over the fortress to a German garrison.[59] This action was in keeping with his policy of monopolising castles in the Kingdom of Sicily, but, as the description of it in Bernard the Treasurer's compilation as 'great treason' shows, underlines the emperor's lack of understanding of the realities of the situation in the east. Not surprisingly, the Templars barred the gates and the emperor returned to Acre empty handed.

Therefore, when, in November 1228, the emperor set out on campaign by marching south from Acre towards Jaffa, the military orders followed at a distance equivalent to a day's journey,[60] a luxury none of the parties could have afforded in the days of Richard I and Saladin. By the time Frederick had reached Arsuf, both sides had decided to compromise, and the military orders rejoined him, apparently after agreeing a formula which avoided the appearance that they were under the emperor's command.[61] It is not clear whether scrupulousness about the papal ban or their sensitivity about their independence was uppermost in their minds. This fragile unity was broken most decisively when Frederick, under pressure to return to Italy as news of further progress by the papal armies was received, and al-Kāmil, still struggling with his enemies in Damascus, negotiated a ten-year truce, of which the centrepiece from Frederick's point of view was the recovery of Jerusalem. However, the patriarch and the leaders of the military orders took an extremely jaundiced view of this apparently sensational achievement, since it ignored their interests entirely. Not only was Jerusalem to be left unfortified, connected to the sea by no more than a narrow strip of land extending to Lydda and Jaffa, but the Temple area was to remain under Muslim control, and the military orders were forbidden to provide any further support or make any improvements to their great castles in the County of Tripoli, Krak des Chevaliers and al-Marqab of the Hospital, and Chastel-Blanc and Tortosa of the Templars.[62] While Frederick celebrated with a great crown-wearing ceremony in the Church of the Holy Sepulchre, the patriarch put Jerusalem under interdict.

Frederick, though, had little time left, for the situation in his Sicilian kingdom urgently required his presence, but when he returned to Acre he found the patriarch and the Templars gathering troops on the grounds that the truce covered only the Sultan of Egypt and not the Sultan of Damascus. The emperor responded by calling a great open-air assembly outside the city at which, according to the Patriarch Gerold, he 'began to make serious complaints about us, piling up false accusations. Then, turning his speech to the venerable man, the Master of the Temple, he attempted to blacken his reputation to no small degree with various vain declarations; and by this means he intended to place his own culpability, which was already manifest, upon others, adding finally that now we were retaining mercenary soldiers to his prejudice and damage.'[63] The pro-Ibelin chronicler, Philip of Novara, claimed that 'many men said that he [Frederick] wished to capture the lord of Beirut, his children, Sir Anceau de Brie, and others of his friends, the master of the Temple and other people, and that he wished to kill them at a council to which he had called and summoned them, but they became aware of it and came in such strength that he did not dare to do it'.[64] It was a short step to open violence, and shortly before his departure from the east on 1 May 1229, the emperor laid siege to the house of the Temple at Acre. According to the patriarch, he posted crossbowmen at strategic points in the city in order to cut off all communications with the Templars.

News of the vendetta between Frederick and the Templars soon became common knowledge, picked up by, among others, the St Albans chronicler, Matthew Paris. Matthew presumably obtained his information from Richard of Cornwall who, as Frederick's brother-in-law, fed him a Hohenstaufen view of the conflict. In a reverse image of Philip of Novara's story, the military orders are presented as plotting to kill the emperor. They wrote to al-Kāmil telling him that Frederick intended to visit the River Jordan. As this would be in the nature of a pilgrimage he would have only a small escort and this would give the sultan his opportunity. Al-Kāmil, supposedly shocked by such treachery, informed the emperor, who thereafter was bitterly hostile to the two Orders.[65] The famous Muslim preacher, the Sibt Ibn al-Jawzī (died 1257), who, as a friend of the Aiyūbids was well informed about Frederick's crusade, also believed this, explaining that Frederick stayed only two nights in Jerusalem before returning to Jaffa, 'for fear of the Templars who wanted to kill him'.[66] Further apparent confirmation can be found in the pro-Hohenstaufen chronicler Bartholomew of Neocastro, who included a letter from Gregory IX, supposedly written at the beginning of 1229, in his *Historia Sicula*. In it, the pope tells the Masters of the Temple and the Hospital and the sultan of Egypt that the emperor should be captured and killed.[67] That the pope should commit such thoughts to writing, even had he considered such an idea, seems intrinsically unlikely and indeed there are serious doubts about the letter's authenticity.[68] It does not appear that Frederick ever made the accusation himself,[69] but, whether true or not, the circulation of the story in places as far apart as Damascus, Sicily, and St Albans can only reflect a virulent propaganda war arising from an intense conflict.

Relations had certainly reached a low ebb by the time of Frederick's departure from the east. When he returned to Italy he confiscated the property of the Hospital and Temple and, despite the reconciliation with the papacy under the Treaty of San Germano of July 1230, still had not returned it all in 1239.[70] According to Bernard the Treasurer's compilation, he not only seized the houses of the Templars, but also imprisoned the brothers themselves.[71] By 1239 papal–imperial relations had again deteriorated so far that Gregory excommunicated the emperor for a second time, giving as one of his reasons the failure to restore the orders' property. Matthew Paris says that the emperor defended this policy on the grounds that the orders had helped his enemies in the days when he was struggling to gain control of his Sicilian kingdom, and that the lands withheld were those they had received at that time, not the ones they held before the death of King William II in 1189.[72] This would have been quite consistent with Frederick's policy in Sicily, for, in 1220, he had refused to recognise any title to property acquired since 1189.[73] For their part, the Templars seem not to have changed their attitude because of the treaty. In February, 1231, in response to complaints from the emperor, Pope Gregory wrote to the Grand Master condemning him for disobeying the commands of the imperial *bailli* and for provoking war contrary to the emperor's peace.[74]

Frederick's departure from the east was forced on him; it did not mark an end to his interest in the affairs of the crusader states. Although he was never again free to visit the east in person, from the autumn of 1231 he was represented there by his *bailli*, Richard Filangieri, the imperial marshal, who brought with him a large force of knights and foot soldiers, ostensibly for the defence of the Holy Land.[75] Filangieri failed to seize Acre, but he did establish himself at Tyre, with the consequence that intermittent factional conflict persisted among the Christians until 1243, when the baronage succeeded in driving the imperial forces out of Tyre.

As the Templars had proved to be among the most obdurate of his opponents in the east, it might be expected that Frederick, like other strong rulers before him, including Fulk of Anjou, Amalric, and Richard I, would try to influence the election of the next Grand Master. Peter of Montaigu probably died in 1231,[76] and was succeeded by Armand of Périgord, Preceptor in Sicily and Calabria. Although, as the name suggests, he was evidently from Guienne, he was the first Master to have held a provincial post outside France or Spain, and it is tempting to ascribe his election to imperial pressure. This is difficult to prove, however, since, unlike previous Masters appointed in this way, there is no evidence to connect him to the emperor before this time. The only reference to his position as Preceptor in Sicily and Calabria comes from a document apparently from September 1230, given at Frederick's castle near Avellino, in which the emperor, at Armand of Périgord's request, confirmed the Templars in their possessions at Lentini, Paterno, Butera, Syracuse, and Aydone, as well as the privileges received from various nobles. The charter is, however, ambiguously dated, and just possibly can be placed in 1229, rather than 1230 or 1231. While the first date might suggest imperial influence, since the emperor was otherwise in confrontation with the Order at that time, the placing of the document in 1230, which is by far the most likely, means that it probably reflects the papal–imperial agreement of the previous July rather than any special relationship between Armand of Périgord and Frederick II.[77]

In fact, during the 1230s the Templars do seem to have taken a less militant line in the struggle between the imperialists and the baronage than under Peter of Montaigu, although it may nevertheless be significant that John of Ibelin, the chief opponent of the Hohenstaufen, chose to end his days as a Templar in 1236.[78] In late February or early March 1232, Armand of Périgord was one of a group of leading members of the establishment of the kingdom to attempt to mediate in the quarrel. Together with the patriarch, the constable, the Grand Master of the Hospital, and Balian of Sidon, he rode up from Acre, but Filangieri proved intransigent and they were forced to return with nothing accomplished.[79] By 1233, the Ibelins, supported by most of the barons of Outremer, had gained the upper hand. After the fall of Kyrenia in April 1233, imperial troops were driven out of Cyprus and, on the mainland, Filangieri was restricted to Tyre.[80]

Not until the crusade of Richard of Cornwall in 1241 do the Templars again appear overtly in opposition to the imperial party, and by this time the situation in the Muslim world may have been a more decisive factor in Templar policy than the desire to take an anti-imperial stance.

Fortunately for the Latins, the crusader states were not directly threatened during the 1230s, although at times tension was high because of news of two nomadic powers that had arisen in the east, creating a potential threat which appeared to transcend that of the quarrelling Aiyūbids. The more immediate problem seemed to be posed by the Khorezmian Turks, who had established themselves in a wide area between the Indus and the Tigris. Letters written by Pope Gregory IX in 1231 to the prelates of the west and to the kings of France and England show that the Christian leaders in the east, including the masters of the military orders, were alarmed at the rise of what Gregory described as 'the King of the Persians'.[81] However, even as Gregory wrote, the Khorezmian empire was beginning to fall apart, its leader, Jalāl-ad-Dīn, assassinated in August 1231, and its power undermined by attacks by the Aiyūbids from the west and the Mongols from the east. The Mongols were the second of the new powers to appear and were to prove much more formidable. In 1206, scattered tribes of Asiatic nomads originally from the region of the upper River Amur, north of China, were united under a single leader, Chingis Khan. Chingis had inaugurated a massive expansion of the Mongols, southwards into China and westwards towards Iran, to which they had been drawn partly by what they saw as provocation on the part of Khorezmians.

However, although in the second half of the thirteenth century the presence of the Mongols added a completely new dimension to the policies of the Middle East, Templar military activity during the 1230s was much more concerned with immediate local problems. In 1233 the Templars and Hospitallers led contingents of knights from Jerusalem, Cyprus, and Antioch, against the Sultan of Hamah, apparently because he had defaulted in payment of 'protection money' owed to the Hospital in the form of an annual tribute. In an eight-day campaign, this raid accomplished its aim, laying waste the sultan's territory, and forcing him to pay up.[82] Much more serious for the Templars was a campaign led by Armand of Périgord in 1237, when a large company of 120 Templar knights attacked

Muslim bands foraging in the region between 'Atlīt and Acre, a region seen as very much within the Templar sphere of influence. They ran up against a larger force than expected and, despite warnings from Walter of Brienne, Count of Jaffa, risked battle and were badly defeated. According to Alberic of Trois-Fontaines, only the Grand Master and nine Templars managed to escape.[83]

These two conflicts can probably be best described as *chevauchées*. Neither side intended to achieve permanent conquest of territory by this means, for the primary aims were profit and plunder. But the situation could not solidify into an indefinite stalemate. Gregory IX was aware that the peace between Frederick II and al-Kāmil would expire in 1239 and was busy sending out agents to preach a new crusade. Theobald, King of Navarre and Count of Champagne, was the most eminent of the French nobles to respond, and he seems to have begun to plan his expedition by sending a series of questions to the Christian leaders in the east. Their reply urged him to leave as soon as possible, for the Saracens never respected a truce and many pilgrims might be killed if there was a delay. Crusaders could leave from Marseille and Genoa and sail to Limassol in Cyprus, where they could consult with the prelates, the masters of the orders, and the barons concerning the objective of the crusade. They would need to decide whether to attack Egypt, either Damietta or Alexandria, or Syria, but in both cases care would have to be taken to organise provisions, as the export of foodstuffs from the Holy Land was forbidden.[84] In the event, they seem to have decided to concentrate on the Holy Land, taking advantage of the civil wars in the Muslim world following the death of al-Kāmil in March 1238. In the summer of 1239, Armand of Périgord, writing to Walter of Avesnes, who had helped to build 'Atlīt during the Fifth Crusade, described what he evidently saw as the opportunities presented by the divisions of the Aiyūbids. The new Sultan of Egypt (al-'Ādil II) was a coward and worthy only of contempt; he was at war with the Sultan of Hamah (al-Muzaffer Mahmūd). The Lord of Kerak (al-Nāsir Dā'ūd) was at war with the Sultan of Damascus (al-Sālih Aiyūb). Several Aiyūbid lords had promised to submit to the Christians and receive baptism. He concluded that Christian control of the land would then become possible again.[85]

Although the Grand Master's view of the situation was over-optimistic, it does nevertheless show that the relations between the powers of the Near East were far more complex than western commentators like Matthew Paris were willing or able to grasp. The hesitation of Theobald of Champagne after his arrival on 1 September 1239, is therefore not surprising, while the decision in November to move first against the Egyptian fortresses of Gaza and Ascalon, and then against Damascus, is comprehensible in terms of sudden changes in the Muslim world which occurred at that time. In September, al-Salīh Ismā'īl, Aiyūb's uncle, had seized Damascus, and soon after, Aiyūb himself had been captured by al-Nāsir of Kerak. To Theobald, the Aiyūbid world was a confusing kaleidoscope, the changes of which were inevitably open to differing interpretations: the conflicts which a few months before had looked so promising to Armand of Périgord had now rearranged themselves in such a fashion as to threaten the encirclement of the crusader lands.[86]

The expedition to the south did nothing to help the situation, for there occurred an incident typical of the problems seen in the past when visiting crusaders and resident Franks attempted to co-operate with each other. Henry, Count of Bar, together with a few friends, apparently believing that the Egyptian force consisted of only about 1,000 men, decided to make a foray of their own. When the other leaders discovered this, they tried to dissuade them, but the count refused to listen and his force was nearly annihilated at Gaza.[87] As had happened before, western opinion was quick to accept adverse reports of the behaviour of the eastern Franks, especially concerning the military orders, whose conduct they inevitably judged in the light of an over-simplified view of their function as fighters for the faith. This time the Templars and Hospitallers were blamed for refusing to support the Count of Bar. Simon of Montfort, who came to the east soon after with Richard of Cornwall's expedition, even claimed that the King of France had withdrawn his cash deposits with the Temple because of the Order's behaviour.[88]

This incident was symptomatic, for it presaged a new series of problems which the military orders – and in particular the Templars – were about to experience in the projection of their image in the west. The idea that the military orders fatally undermined the Christian position in the Holy Land by their endemic and sometimes violent conflict owes much to the opposing policies adopted by them during the years 1240 to 1244.[89] The dominant role played by the Templars in this ensured that ultimately the Order received the strongest criticism. In fact, as the history of the crusader states in the twelfth century had shown, it was inevitable that there would be some rivalry between the orders over their respective rights, and it was all the more likely that such quarrels would recur as the surface area of the crusader lands shrank while at the same time an increasingly large proportion of what was left came into the orders' possession. Steven Tibble has shown, for example, that by the period 1229–41 nearly 70 per cent of the lordship of Caesarea was in religious hands, among which the Templars were the most important, holding possibly as much as a quarter. Based at 'Atlīt and, by 1264, holding at least four other fortified sites, their power completely overshadowed that of the lord of the fief, who by that time held only one of the twelve fortresses still thought to be in Christian hands.[90]

In these circumstances, the recorded examples of direct conflict in the crusader states as a whole are not notably high before 1240. One controversy occurred over the possession of the port of Jabala (Gibel), situated in the sensitive area north of Tortosa, where the orders had already been in dispute over their respective rights in Valania. The region was dominated by Hospitaller possessions, and it is probable that quarrels arose from Templar attempts to intrude into a Hospitaller enclave. In October 1221, the papal legate, Pelagius, succeeded in arbitrating over the city of Jabala, which, largely as a consequence of the long conflicts over the Antiochene succession, the Templars claimed they had received as a gift from Bohemond of Tripoli, while the Hospitallers based their claim upon a grant from Raymond-Roupen. Pelagius awarded them half each, although a more detailed and definitive agreement was not made until 1233.[91] Two years later, in July, the orders also settled a long-standing dispute over the exploitation of the water and mills on the River Na'aman, which flows into the sea just to the south of Acre. The dispute arose from the use made of the waters on which the Hospital held Recordane, where the river found its source, while the Templars worked various mills further downstream at Doc, dependent upon the flow from this source.[92]

However, it was the differences over policy towards their Muslim neighbours that were significant in the wider world. Ironically, they occurred because the Frankish position was actually improving, for in the spring of 1240 al-Nāsir suddenly decided to ally with Aiyūb against Egypt, apparently in return for help in recovering Damascus, which he had himself ruled between 1227 and 1229. Ismā'īl, as current ruler of Damascus, was quickly persuaded that he needed Frankish help in these new circumstances, an attitude reinforced when Aiyūb and al-Nāsir gained control of Cairo in June. Agreement between Ismā'īl and the Franks was accordingly reached in July or August. The Templars favoured this alliance and indeed took a leading part in the negotiations. They were rewarded with the fortress of Safad which, although in a poor condition, was situated in a key position in Upper Galilee, thus re-establishing the Order in an area which it had seen as its own special sphere of interest in the years before Hattin.[93] Soon afterwards, Armand of Périgord wrote to Robert of Sandford, the Order's Preceptor in England, to tell him of this success: 'when the Christian army had lain for a long time on the sand, affected by weariness and inactivity, . . . the Lord, rising on high, visited it, not because of its few merits, but from the clemency of his customary mercy'. The result was that the Sultan of Damascus had now allied with the Franks and had restored all the lands up to the River Jordan. The messenger carrying the letter met the fleet of Richard of Cornwall, then on his way to crusade in the east, and told him the news, adding that the sultan 'most certainly intended to receive the sacrament of baptism'.[94] Theobald appears to have consolidated the position by negotiating a truce with al-Nāsir as well, for the ruler of Kerak had found Aiyūb disinclined to honour his promises to help him regain Damascus. Theobald was not, however, prepared to contemplate an invasion of Egypt, a policy apparently advocated by some of the local Franks, especially as Aiyūb still held important Christian prisoners taken at Gaza, and disagreement over this may well have precipitated his rather abrupt departure from the east at the end of September 1240.[95]

Armand of Périgord claimed in his letter to Robert of Sandford that the agreement with Damascus had been accepted 'unanimously', but if he really believed this he was soon to find that he was mistaken. It seems evident that the Hospitallers under their Grand Master, Peter of Vieille Bride, were among those who favoured instead an accommodation with Egypt and that from this time at least the two military orders represent opposing poles of policy.[96] Temporarily, the Templar view had been predominant, but soon after Theobald's departure Richard of Cornwall sailed into Acre (11 October 1240), and stayed in the east until May 1241. As Frederick II's brother-in-law, his sympathies lay with the policy of negotiation with Egypt and by early 1241 he had reached an agreement with Aiyūb which included the release of the Frankish prisoners. He was supported by the Hospitallers, now apparently reconciled to Frederick II and inclined to take a pro-imperial line.[97] Richard of Cornwall was well aware of the discord in the Holy Land, but his claim that he had tried to heal it was somewhat disingenuous.[98]

According to Matthew Paris, after Richard's departure the Templars had their revenge. In a particularly rancorous passage, clearly dependent upon sources close to Richard of Cornwall, Matthew denounced the Templars for being 'roused by the pangs of envy', which led them to break Richard's truce, and to besiege the Hospitallers in their house at Acre, 'so that they were not able to supply themselves with food, nor even bring their dead from their houses for burial'. They also drove out some of the Teutonic Knights, 'in contempt of the emperor', causing them to leave the east and lay complaints before the emperor. As a consequence, 'a serious scandal arose, that those who had stuffed themselves with so many revenues in order to be able powerfully to attack the Saracens, were impiously turning violence and venom against the Christians, indeed against their own brothers, thus most gravely bringing God's anger down upon them'. Richard of Cornwall was aware of 'the pride of the Templars', and therefore had not entrusted Ascalon to them before he left, but had handed it over to imperial representatives.[99]

Like all of Matthew Paris's material on the Templars, the account needs to be treated with caution. There was indeed a bitter conflict after Richard's departure, during which Filangieri tried and failed to seize Acre, using the house of the Hospitallers as a base. The subsequent siege of the Hospitaller building between October 1241 and March 1242, referred to by Matthew Paris, seems to have been supported by the Templars, but it is clear that it reflected the wider conflict between the baronage and the imperialists rather than simply a quarrel between the two military orders.[100] Nevertheless, Matthew Paris' account is important as an indication of some western opinion, while the underlying point that the Templars and Hospitallers had pressed opposing policies upon Richard of Cornwall is confirmed by Philip of Novara.[101] Moreover, Armand of Périgord lent strong support to the election of Alice, Queen-Dowager of Cyprus as

Regent of Jerusalem, in June 1242, on the grounds that she was the nearest heir, despite the fact that, in April 1243, Conrad, Frederick's son, would come of age and would therefore be the legal ruler.[102] Conrad himself did not appear, but sent Thomas of Aquino, Count of Acerra, in his place, a choice which may have strengthened Templar opposition, as the Order had an old grudge against him dating back to 1228. At that time, according to Gregory IX, who must have received his information from the Templars, he had allegedly deprived them of booty worth 6,000 marks seized from the Saracens, returning part of it to the Saracens and retaining the rest for himself.[103] The Hohenstaufen position was finally undermined in the summer of 1243 when, with the help of the Venetians and the Genoese, the baronage ejected the imperial forces from Tyre, on what has now been shown to be the spurious legal grounds that Conrad had not personally arrived in the east to claim the rulership.[104]

These circumstances permitted Armand of Périgord to revive Templar policy towards the disunited Aiyūbids. The Templars, for instance, took a leading role in a major attack upon Nablus in October 1242, apparently in revenge for a previous massacre of Christian pilgrims by al-Nāsir, an expedition of which the Order was sufficiently proud to commemorate in a striking fresco in its church at Perugia.[105] Matthew Paris incorporates into the *Chronica Majora* a new letter by the Grand Master to Robert of Sandford, probably written late in 1243, in which he explained his policy. According to Armand, the Sultan of Egypt could not be trusted to keep the terms of any truce, for he had not returned Gaza, Hebron, Nablus, and Daron, as promised, and he had kept Templar emissaries sent by the Master in a state of virtual captivity for more than six months. 'But we, through divine inspiration, observing his cunning and perfidy', saw the real motive for this delay, which was to gain time which he would use to establish control over the other Muslim rulers, thus enabling him to overcome the Christian states which were 'so weak and small'. For this reason the Templars, supported by the prelates and 'some of the baronage', entered into negotiations with al-Nāsir and Ismā'īl and gained from them all the land west of the River Jordan except for Hebron, Nablus, and Baisan. 'Therefore, there should be rejoicing among angels and men, that the holy city of Jerusalem is now inhabited exclusively by Christians, all the Saracens having been expelled, and that in all the holy places, restored and cleansed by the prelates of the church, where for fifty-six years the name of God had not been invoked, now, God be praised, the divine mysteries are celebrated daily.' Safe access to these places was now possible for everybody. Nor did the Master have any doubt that this situation would last if only the Christians would be 'of one heart and mind'. By this he appears to be referring to those who opposed Templar policy, whom he describes as motivated by hatred and envy. In consequence, the whole burden of defence fell on the Templars, supported by the prelates and 'a few of the barons of the land'. He had also been trying to regain Gaza, 'the entrance to the land', under conditions of great difficulty and expense, but in another reference to opposition to his policies, he warned that God would take heavy vengeance on those who were 'idle and rebellious in this matter'. As well as this, the Templars proposed, if they could find sufficient backing, to build 'a very strong castle', north of Toron of the Knights (al-Atrūn), situated near the route between Jerusalem and Jaffa. Through this he hoped that 'the whole land can more easily be retained and defended against our enemies for ever'. Even so, none of this would be permanent unless the Christians offered strong support, for the Sultan of Egypt 'is a most powerful and cunning man'.[106]

Matthew Paris' main reason for copying the letter seems to have been to discredit it, for it is followed by a diatribe in which he says that the letter was scarcely to be believed, for the Temple and the Hospital had such bad reputations, 'because, it is said, they always provoke discord between Christians and Saracens, so that during the war they might collect money from pilgrims arriving from all parts; both because of their mutual discord and because of this they were plotting the capture of the emperor'.[107] But Frederick II was well aware that his policy had indeed been overthrown, since both the return of the Temple area to the Christians and the proposed fortress near Toron were quite contrary to the treaty which he had negotiated in 1229. He wrote angrily to tell the Master and brothers that this was contrary to his honour and that if they did not desist he would confiscate all Templar property in Germany and Sicily.[108]

Early in 1244 a new war broke out between al-Sālih Aiyūb and Ismāʿīl of Damascus. Christian support for Ismāʿīl suggests that the Templar view continued to predominate.[109] Aiyūb retaliated by renewing an alliance with Khorezmian Turks, who, although no longer the power they had been in the 1220s, were still dangerous. Newly established near Edessa, they were encouraged by Aiyūb to attack Damascus and invade Palestine. A collective letter of the Christian leaders to Innocent IV, dated at Acre, 21 September, described the calamity which this alliance brought upon Jerusalem, for the Khorezmians had swept south and, on 11 July, had sacked the city, treating the population in a far more brutal fashion than any previous infidel ruler. The Christians could muster little strength to oppose them, for there were only about a hundred overseas knights and foot-soldiers in the east, and local knights were scattered all over the region preparing to defend their castles. So far, no help had been forthcoming from the King of Cyprus or the Prince of Antioch, the latter being especially frightened in case the Mongols, whose threat had temporarily abated, should return. They did not think it advisable to engage the Khorezmians in battle, since their numbers were estimated at about 12,000 fighting men.[110]

Despite their apparent reluctance to seek a confrontation with the Khorezmians, within two weeks these same leaders had gathered togather a large army at Acre, reinforced by troops from Homs, Damascus, and the Transjordan provided by their Muslim allies, including al-Nāsir, who would otherwise have found himself isolated. These forces confronted the Egyptians and the Khorezmians on 17 October at La Forbie (Harbīyah), near Gaza, faced with the same dilemma as their predecessors at Hattin (see plate 6). Once again they chose battle, urged on by Walter of Brienne, Count of Jaffa, a past enemy of the Templars, which suggests that Armand of Périgord was probably among those who counselled restraint.[111] The opposing forces were too strong for the Franks, al-Nāsir deserted, and the Egyptians won an overwhelming victory. Armand of Périgord was among those missing, either killed in battle or dying in captivity, while, according to the acting Master of the Order, William of Rochefort, only thirty-three Templars, twenty-six Hospitallers, and three Teutonic Knights survived the battle.[112] In a letter to Richard of Cornwall, Frederick II had no doubt where to point the finger of blame. The Templars, by their unjust and foolish war with the Sultan of Egypt, had forced him to seek an alliance with the Khorezmians, stirring up a conflict in utter contempt of the emperor's treaty. The alliance with the rulers of Damascus and Kerak was a naïve and childish folly, like using oil to extinguish a great fire. But

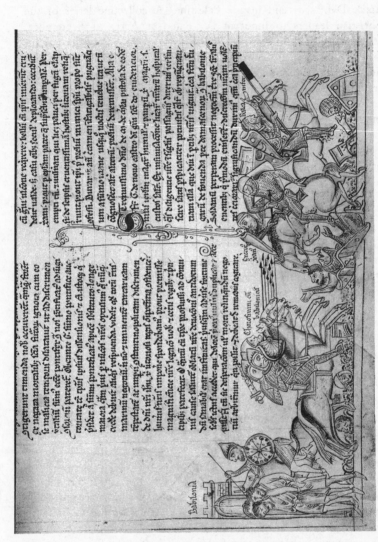

Plate 6 Battle between the Latins and the Khorezmians at La Forbie, 1244, Matthew Paris. On the left, Christian prisoners are being taken to Egypt, while on the right, the Templar standard-bearer is fleeing from the field

the Templars had received these Muslims in their house and provided them with lavish entertainment, and they had allowed them to perform their superstitious rites and to invoke the name of Muhammad. The result of this foolish policy had been the desertion of these false allies in the time of crisis.[113]

If the disaster at La Forbie was the outcome of Templar policies, then the Order certainly paid for its mistakes. The loss of between 260 and 300 knights was compounded by the disappearance of the Grand Master, probably captured. According to a report recorded in Matthew Paris' chronicle, an attempt to ransom him in 1246 was rejected by the sultan.[114] The new Master of the Templars, William of Sonnac, Preceptor of Aquitaine, was not therefore elected until 1247 at the earliest, probably arriving in the east in the autumn of that year.[115] He found the remnants of the Kingdom of Jerusalem in a precarious state, for Aiyūb had followed up his victory by wresting Damascus from Ismāʿīl in 1245, and capturing Christian territory and castles at Tiberias, Mount Tabor, Belvoir, and Ascalon in 1247.

CHAPTER FIVE

THE LAST YEARS OF THE TEMPLARS
IN PALESTINE AND SYRIA

La Forbie did not provoke a response on the scale of Hattin, but it did strengthen the resolve of Louis IX of France to fulfil a deep desire to crusade which had been maturing ever since his recovery from serious illness in 1244. After extensive preparations lasting over three years, Louis IX was able to sail from his new port of Aigues-Mortes for Cyprus on 25 August 1248, the first European king to crusade in the east for twenty years. When the king arrived at Limassol on 17 September 1248, the Master of the Temple was among those who had sailed from Acre to greet him.[1] However, old habits died hard, for the Templars had become accustomed to conducting their own policies towards the Muslims. Shortly afterwards the Master received overtures from an emir representing the sultan, who proposed a negotiated peace, but when he informed the king of this he was sharply told not to meet any such messengers again without royal permission.[2]

King Louis' crusade attacked Egypt in the summer of 1249, making the first landing on 5 June. On that day they met fierce resistance, but the next morning they found that Damietta had been evacuated. Soon afterwards, William of Sonnac wrote to Robert of Sandford in England, describing how the city had been taken on the Sunday morning of 6 June, with the loss of only one man on their side. The king, he said, now proposed to march against either Alexandria or Cairo.[3] The death of Aiyūb on 23 November 1249 seemed to increase the chances of the Christians even more and, towards the end of November, they began to advance inland towards Cairo, the Templars forming the van. They were held up for a month by a branch of the Nile known as the Ashmūn-Tannāh, but a local Bedouin showed them the ford and on 8 February 1250 they began to cross.[4]

This inevitably took time and the Templars, together with Robert of Artois, the king's brother, and William Longespée, Earl of Salisbury, reached the other side some time before the rest of the army. This was the prelude to the disastrous attack on Mansurah, which became so notorious that it was still remembered at the time of the Templars' trial sixty years later.[5]

There are two major versions of what happened, by John of Joinville and Matthew Paris.[6] Joinville says that the Count of Artois at once attacked the Turks and put them to flight, but that the Templars, who had been placed in their traditional position in the van by the king, were seriously affronted by what they saw as the count's usurpation of their role. However, Foucaud du Merle, a knight holding the bridle of the count's horse, was completely deaf and did not hear what the Templars were saying to the count, and he continued to urge the company after the Turks. Consequently, the Templars 'thought that they would be dishonoured if they allowed the count to go before them', and charged after him. The whole company thereupon hurled itself into the narrow streets of the town of Mansurah. Many of the Muslims escaped out of the other side, but the Christian knights were trapped in the town, their way blocked by great beams flung into the streets by the inhabitants. Their losses were huge, including the Count of Artois, about 300 knights, and 280 Templars.[7]

Matthew Paris gives a different version, complete with verbatim conversations from the participants. Having crossed the river the count, who 'was excessively proud and arrogant, and strove after vainglory', immediately attacked the Muslims, even pursuing them into Mansurah itself until he was forced to retreat by a volley of rocks and stones. The count then held counsel with William of Sonnac and William Longespée to try to persuade them to attack again while they had the enemy on the run. But the Grand Master, described here as 'a discreet and circumspect man, who was also skilled and experienced in the affairs of war', commended the count's courage, but advised caution, for they were tired and many horses were wounded. Moreover, if they attacked, the enemy would soon find out that the numbers of Christians were relatively small and would launch the main strength of their army against them. On hearing this, the count became very angry, claiming that this proved the truth of a past prophecy, which said that the whole region would long ago have fallen to the Christians had not their efforts been impeded by the military orders, who hindered the crusade for their own profit. If the crusaders overcame Egypt, he said, the military orders would no longer be able to dominate the land from which they drew such large revenues. 'Is not Frederick, who has experienced their deceit, a most proven witness upon these things?' This provoked the Grand Master, against his better judgement, to make ready for an attack, only for the Earl of Salisbury to intervene in an attempt to calm the situation, advising that they listen to William of Sonnac, whose experience of eastern affairs was so much greater than their own. He too was then treated to a volley of the count's insults, who, according to Matthew Paris, was 'bellowing and swearing disgracefully as is the French custom', and he too was so incensed that he made ready for attack. Matthew Paris maintains that Robert of Artois was motivated by pride and by the desire to win glory for himself, and because of this did not inform the king of his intentions. But Muslim spies knew all this and the sultan had brought together a large force ready to take advantage of the Christian weakness. Very soon, the Christians were surrounded by the Muslims 'like an island in the sea': William Longespée was killed in the battle, Robert of Artois drowned by the weight of his armour while trying to swim the river to safety. Only two Templars and one Hospitaller escaped the massacre.[8]

Joinville's account is probably the more reliable. He was a friend and later biographer of the king and a participant in the crusade, and the circumstantial detail which he provides appears authentic. He was, however, writing many years afterwards, between 1305 and 1309, and he was not actually present, being with the main body of the army on the other side of the river. Matthew Paris was clearly trying to show the heroic role of the Earl of Salisbury, which he emphasised by a chauvinistic description of English superiority over the French. However, his story cannot be entirely discounted, despite the long fictitious speeches, as he certainly had information from members of the crusading army, perhaps transmitted through Richard of Cornwall. Neither source blames the Templars, whose usual caution in warfare is shown once more, and both agree that the chief instigator was Robert of Artois. For the Templars, the losses must have been a massive blow to sustain less than six years after La Forbie.

Despite this defeat, the Christian army succeeded in fording the river, establishing itself in front of Mansurah. Even then, there was no respite for William of Sonnac who, although already wounded, helped Joinville fight off a group of Saracens trying to steal a tent on that same evening.[9] The pressure was relentless. On 11 February the Egyptians made another major onslaught, and it was only with great difficulty that the Christians resisted them. William of Sonnac did not survive this battle. According to Joinville:

Next to the troops of Walter [of Châtillon] was brother William of Sonnac, Master of the Templars, with those few brothers who had survived Tuesday's battle. He had built a defence in front of him with the Saracen engines which we had captured. When the Saracens came to attack him, they threw Greek fire onto the barrier he had made; and the fire caught easily, for the Templars had put a large quantity of deal planks there. And you should know that the Turks did not wait for the fire to burn itself out, but rushed upon the Templars among the scorching flames. And in this battle, brother William, Master of the Templars, lost an eye; and he had lost the other on the previous Shrove Tuesday; and that lord died as a consequence, may God absolve him! And you should know that there was at least an acre of land behind the Templars, which was so covered with arrows fired by the Saracens, that none of the ground could be seen.[10]

This battle, although not in itself decisive, proved to be the turning-point of the campaign, for thereafter the army made no further advance. By the beginning of April, Louis decided that he would have to negotiate, for the army was slowly being worn down by Muslim attack, famine, and disease. Joinville says that the king realised that he and his people could only remain there to die. But the Christian offer was rejected, clearly having been made from a position of weakness, and on 5 April the crusaders were forced to begin a retreat, described by Joinville in terms not dissimilar from the battles in the mud of the First World War. In the course of this retreat, the Muslims caught up with the army and, although there was fierce resistance, slaughtered several thousand of the Christians. The military orders, who seemed to have formed the rearguard, again sustained heavy losses: it seems unlikely that more than fourteen survived, of whom three were Templars.[11] Most of the remainder of the army, including the king, were captured, a coup which enabled the Muslims to dictate terms. Damietta was to be handed over in exchange for the person of the king himself and the rest of the army was to be ransomed for 500,000 *livres*, later reduced to 400,000 *livres*.[12] On 2 May, Tūrān-Shāh, Aiyūb's successor, was murdered by members of his Mamluk bodyguard, elite troops of slave origin who had featured in Egyptian armies since the twelfth century, but who, at this time, began a prolonged and bloody struggle for direct power. Nevertheless, their leader, Aybeg, agreed to abide by the treaty, but demanded that 200,000 *livres* of the ransom be paid before the king left Egypt. As the terms of the peace demanded, Damietta was given up and on 6 May the king was released. His brother, Alphonse of Poitiers, was to be kept in captivity until the payment was made.[13]

The royal officers began to accumulate this sum on Saturday 7 May and counting went on until Sunday evening, when it was discovered that they were still 30,000 *livres* short. The king agreed to Joinville's suggestion that the balance should be borrowed from the Templars, only for Joinville to find that Stephen of Otricourt, the Templar commander, refused to help, maintaining that the Order could not lend other people's money which had been entrusted to it. 'There were many hard and abusive words between myself and him', says Joinville, until Reginald of Vichiers, Marshal of the Temple, suggested that Joinville should take the money by force and that in this way the knights would not be breaking their oath. Having received permission from the king to take this course of action, Joinville went on board the chief Templar galley, where the treasure was kept in the hold. Stephen of Otricourt refused to have any part of this, but Reginald of Vichiers agreed to act as witness. The Treasurer of the Temple, however, would not hand over the keys, partly, Joinville thought, because of his haggard and unprepossessing appearance after the sufferings of the retreat. Joinville reacted by threatening to break open one of the chests with a hatchet, at which point Reginald caught hold of his wrist, saying that since it was evident that force was about to be used, the keys would have to be given up.[14]

The dispute over the ransom money reflected the lack of a single leader in the Order since the death of William of Sonnac the previous February, and it is clear that Louis IX determined to see that a new Master was elected as soon as possible after his arrival in Acre on 13 May 1250. Like other powerful rulers before him, the king decided who that man should be. Reginald of Vichiers 'became master of the Temple', says Joinville, 'with the aid of the king, because of the *courtoisie* which he had shown to the king when he was in prison'.[15] In fact, Reginald had been closely associated with the French monarchy since well before this time, for he had been Preceptor of the Temple in France between 1241 and 1248, and he had helped to negotiate shipping for Louis' crusade from the syndics of Marseille in August 1246.[16] As well as this, he had had previous eastern experience, for he was Preceptor of Acre in 1240, and he was made Marshal of the Order in 1249, soon after his arrival in Cyprus.[17]

The mutual support of the king and the military orders paid off handsomely in 1251 when Assassin envoys arrived at Acre intent on blackmailing the king, claiming that Louis should pay tribute to the Assassins, as others did. The envoys alleged that the Emperor of Germany, the King of Hungary, and the Sultan of Cairo, were allowed to live only because they paid tribute to the Old Man of the Mountain. On the other hand, if Louis did not wish to pay, they would instead accept the cancellation of the tribute they themselves paid to the Temple and the Hospital. Louis did not give a definite reply, but adjourned the interview until the afternoon, and when he reappeared he was supported by the two Grand Masters. Joinville says that 'they did not at all fear the Assassins, because the Old Man of the Mountain could gain nothing if he had the Master of the Temple or the Hospital killed; for he knew that if he killed one, he would be replaced by another just as good'. At first the envoys refused to speak in the presence of the Masters, but both commanded them to do so. On hearing the demands, the Masters organised a private meeting for the following day, at which they took a very hard line. The envoys were insolent to come with such demands and they were fortunate not to be drowned 'in the filthy sea of Acre'. They should return to the Old Man and bring back valuable gifts for the king. The ultimate result was that the Old Man entered into a non-aggression pact with the king, for Joinville was quite right in his perception that the undying corporation was not susceptible to Assassin threats.[18] The Templars continued in the king's favour throughout the year 1251. The fortification of Caesarea, the king's main project at that time, was undertaken with the advice of the Templars and Hospitallers, while a new son, Peter, Count of Alençon, was born to the king in the Templar castle of 'Atlīt and Reginald acted as godfather.[19]

However, in 1252, there arose a serious conflict between Louis and the Templars, in the course of which the king left no doubt that he believed his authority to be superior to that of the Order. Reginald of Vichiers had shown signs of an independence of spirit even before he became Master. In December 1249, under provocation, he had led a successful charge against the Muslims while helping to form the van of the army moving south from Damietta, despite royal orders expressly forbidding it.[20] There were no overt consequences that time, but in 1252, unknown to the king, he attempted to revive the old Templar policy of alliance with Damascus.[21] Conditions were favourable, for the Aiyūbids were anxious to gain revenge for the assassination of Tūrān-Shāh, and al-Nāsir Yūsuf of Aleppo, who had taken over Damascus in 1250, was willing to listen to Frankish proposals. The master therefore sent Hugh of Jouy, Marshal of the Order, who negotiated an equal division of a large area of land once held by the Templars. The agreement was completed subject to royal approval and the marshal returned from Damascus, bringing with him a representative of the sultan, and a document embodying the terms.

When told of these negotiations by the Master, the king became very angry because he had not been consulted, just as he had done when William of Sonnac had received envoys from Egypt in 1248. Louis had good political reasons for his attitude, since the Egyptians still held many Frankish prisoners and the threat of the Damascene alliance could have been used as a lever. Conversely, an alliance with the Mamluks (which had already been offered by Aybeg) would have enabled the Franks to attack Damascus, gaining land from both sides in the process.[22] The king therefore insisted that the Templars make reparation and the lower ranks of the army were assembled to watch the master and knights of the Temple walk barefoot through the camp. The king then sat Reginald of Vichiers and the sultan's envoy in front of him and ordered the master to tell the envoy that he regretted making the treaty without first consulting the king. For this reason, the sultan was to be released from the agreement and to have all the documents relevant to the matter restored to him. Then all the members of the Order were obliged to kneel before the king, while the Master held the hem of his mantle towards Louis and formally surrendered all the Order's possessions to him. From them, the king could take whatever compensation he had decided upon.

Hugh of Jouy was banished from the kingdom, a sentence which, Joinville says, neither the queen nor Reginald of Vichiers could prevent from being carried out. Three years later, in 1255, Hugh of Jouy was to be found serving in Spain.[23]

Louis IX provided strong government and financial help, but he could not remain in the east indefinitely. His departure in April 1254 not only removed both these supports, leaving the Franks prey to faction and bankruptcy, it also coincided with the rise of the Mamluks in Egypt. Although their path to power was by no means smooth, by the end of 1259 Saif-ad-Dīn Kutuz, the leader of the Mamluk company known as the Bahrī, had established himself as sultan. However, although it was the Mamluks who were finally to drive the Christians off the mainland of Syria and Palestine, the full potential of their threat was by no means evident at this time, and the Franks could be excused for feeling more concerned about the Mongols. Indeed, in 1255 the Mongols had demanded that the Temple and the Hospital recognise their suzerainty. Templar letters and military activities strongly reflect their apprehension. On 4 October, probably in 1256, the Templar commander, Guy of Basainville, wrote to the Bishop of Orléans, telling him that the Mongols had devastated many of the lands of the Saracens and were now close to threatening Jerusalem.[24] It must, therefore, have been about the same time that Thomas Bérard, who had succeeded Reginald of Vichiers as Grand Master after the latter's death on 20 January 1256,[25] ordered the twelve brothers who were stationed at Jerusalem to leave and go to Jaffa where they would be safe from the Mongols. Some argument followed, as four of the brothers tried to obey the master's command, only to find that the local commander refused to abandon the brothers of the Hospital who were with them.[26] Fear of the Mongols probably also lay behind the agreement between Thomas Bérard, Hugh Revel of the Hospital, and Anno of Sangerhausen of the Teutonic Knights, who, on 9 October 1258, promised to keep the peace among themselves in the territories of Jerusalem, Cyprus, Armenia, Antioch, and Tripoli.[27] The agreement was made in the wake of the damaging civil war of the previous two years, which had been sparked off in 1256 by a dispute between the Venetians and the Genoese over the possession of the monastery of Saint Sabas, near Acre. Although the prime movers in the affair were the maritime cities, the warfare had escalated, drawing in the military orders with the Templars and Teutonic Knights supporting the Venetians and the Hospitallers behind the Genoese.[28]

Although the Mongols had shown a certain tolerance towards Christians, it was not easy to divine their intentions. Moreover, it was obvious that they would let nothing stand in their way. In February 1258, Hulagu, Ilkhan of Persia, had sacked Baghdad and by September 1259, he was ready to invade north-west Syria. Aleppo fell in January the next year, and in March Damascus capitulated to the army of Kitbogha, Hulagu's most important general. By the spring of 1260 the Mongols were close enough for military contact to be made, perhaps initially provoked by Julian, Lord of Sidon and Beaufort, who was deeply in debt to the Templars and may have been hoping to recoup some of his losses by a raid into the Mongol-held territory of the Beka Valley (al-Biqāʿ). A small force sent by Kitbogha, including his nephew, according to the Armenian chronicler, Hayton, was wiped out by Julian's raiders, provoking Mongol retaliation in the form of a damaging attack upon Sidon.[29]

The Christian leaders now tried to raise help by bombarding the west with letters describing the imminent danger. On 4 March 1260 Thomas Bérard wrote to his leading officials. The sheer scale of the Mongol devastation had made a deep impression on him; even Baghdad, which was the city of the caliph, 'the pope of the Saracens', had been subjugated. The rulers of Aleppo and Damascus had been conquered and refugees were streaming away from these regions, while the Antiochenes had sent embassies bearing gifts so that they might be spared. The Order needed money to meet the danger, as most of the reserves had been spent on fortification, while credit was no longer readily available, since the Genoese and other merchants could no longer be found in Acre. The Master said that there were only three castles fit to resist the Mongols in the Kingdom of Jerusalem, two of which were Templar (presumably ʿAtlīt and Safad) and one of which belonged to the Teutonic Knights (Montfort). In the north the Templars had three fortresses ready in Antioch and two in Tripoli, while the Hospitallers also had two in Tripoli. In order to achieve the maximum coverage in the west, the orders had pooled their resources: brother Stephen of the Temple had gone to Spain, a Hospitaller brother to France, and a brother of the Teutonic Knights to Germany.[30]

Bérard's letter reached Guy of Basainville, now Visitor of the Temple in the West, on 10 June, and Guy then sent messengers on to Francon of Borne, Preceptor of Aquitaine, and to the pope. In turn, Alexander IV set 28 June as the date upon which he would examine five matters: the Holy Land, the Mongols, the Kingdom of Sicily, aid to Constantinople, and the position of princes such as Bohemond of Antioch, the King of Armenia, and the King of Russia, who had entered into treaties with the Mongols.[31] On 16 June, the master's letters reached London where, according to the St Albans chronicle, the *Flores Historiarum*, they had a dramatic impact:

A certain Templar, coming at that time in haste from the Holy Land, arrived in London on the vigil of the Feast of St Botulf, bringing several letters to the king and to the Master of the Temple in London [Brother Amadeus] and others, and he brought many more to magnates on both sides of the mountains [the Alps]. This man covered so great a distance with such a speed that, compelled by intolerable necessity, he took thirteen weeks from the day he left the Holy Land to the day he entered London, travelling from Dover to London in one day, which he said that he had done in a similar fashion at other times. However, when they had read these letters, both the king and the Templars, as well as the others who heard them, gave way to lamentation and sadness, on a scale no one had ever seen before. For the news was that the Tartars, advancing with an innumerable force, had already occupied and devastated the Holy Land almost up to Acre. And what was astonishing to hear, they intended to occupy all of that land with their army for forty days, so that having laid it waste in this way, they could more easily and more widely extend their destruction of the great majority [of the population]. And the same messenger added that they exposed all foreigners fleeing to them or captured by them in the first line of battle, and when fighting, men and women shot arrows as well behind them as they did in front. Nor will Christendom be able to resist them, unless supported by the aid of the powerful hand of God. Also, they have already killed almost all of the Templars and Hospitallers there, [and] unless help is quickly brought, God forbid, a horrible annihilation will swiftly be visited upon the world. This same message, as was said, had been brought to all the other powerful rulers around the sea of the Greeks.[32]

Letters from the papal legate, Thomas Agni, Bishop of Bethlehem, of 1 March, and from the leaders in the east collectively, including the masters of the military orders, of 22 April, testify to the dangers described by Bérard.[33]

The Mamluks were equally aware of the threat posed by the Mongols; indeed, as the letters of the Christians show, Islamic powers had been their greatest victims. In July 1260, therefore, Kutuz led his army into southern Palestine. He requested that the Franks gave him free passage through their territory and also apparently asked for aid against the Mongols. In a council held at Acre the first request was agreed, but through the influence of Anno of Sangerhausen, the second was declined.[34] This decision was of the greatest importance, for Kitbogha's position had been weakened by dissension within the Mongol empire, and on 3 September 1260, the Mamluks defeated the Mongols at ʿAin Jālūt, south of Nazareth, and Kitbogha was killed in the battle. The Christians had in effect helped the power which, within a generation, was to drive them out of Palestine altogether, but they could not have discerned these consequences in 1260. Their letters show that they were almost entirely preoccupied with the Mongols, who appeared a superhuman and terrifying force which had destroyed everything in its path, whereas the Christians were quite used to living with the changing powers of Egypt, including the Mamluks, who had been a familiar element in Muslim armies since Saladin's time.[35]

This attitude was well illustrated by the Christian attempt to take advantage of ʿAin Jālūt when, in February 1261, they assembled a formidable force for an expedition east of the Sea of Galilee. The most prominent lay lords were John of Ibelin and John of Gibelet, Marshal of the Kingdom, but the backbone of the force seems to have been Templars gathered from their main bases in the region at Acre, Safad, ʿAtlīt, and Beaufort. According to Abū Shāmā, the Frankish army amounted to 900 knights, 1,500 turcopoles, and about 3,000 foot-soldiers. They directed their attack against Turcoman tribesmen who had apparently taken refuge from the Mongols in the Jaulan region, but were so severely mauled that they lost most of their men, killed or captured. Among the leaders, only Stephen of Sissey, the Templar marshal, escaped.[36] The military orders were still underestimating the Mamluk threat in 1263, when, in February, John of Ibelin conducted negotiations with Baybars, who had seized power after the assassination of Kutuz in October 1260, soon after ʿAin Jālūt. A truce and exchange of prisoners were agreed, but the Temple and the Hospital refused to release the Muslims they held because these men were skilled craftsmen from whom they were making great profit.[37]

The very real danger of the Mamluks, however, was forcibly brought home early in April, when Baybars retaliated with a major

attack which brought him within sight of Acre. A collective letter of
4 April 1263, from the leaders to Henry III, while stressing that the
Mongols were still very much feared, shows a marked change of
emphasis, describing how the Sultan of Egypt had broken his word
and had occupied the country up to the gates of Acre. Thomas
Bérard added his own brief note, in which he said that the only hope
now lay in the Kings of France and England.[38] In July 1264, Urban
IV wrote back, telling them that a crusade was being prepared, as
did his successor, Clement IV, in 1265. However, perhaps more
significant was a further letter from Clement in February 1266, in
which he explained that crusades would be able to pass more easily
to the east when the Kingdom of Sicily had been recovered from the
papal enemies.[39] The fact was that the papacy was deeply preoccupied
with Sicily, having managed to recruit Charles of Anjou, brother of
Louis IX, as its champion to fight against Frederick II's descendants.
In the short term papal policy was successful: between 1266 and 1268
Charles overcame both Manfred, Frederick's son, who was killed in
battle, and Conradin, his grandson, who was executed at Naples.[40]

More practical help came from Louis IX, whose interest in the
crusade had been sustained despite all the setbacks and who still
hoped that he could lead another expedition to the east. He made use
of the financial networks of the military orders to provide a loan of
4,000 *livres tournois* for his representatives in the east, Geoffrey of
Sargines and Oliver of Termes. In order to put the money to use as
soon as possible, these men told the Grand Masters of the Temple
and the Hospital to negotiate the loan with local merchants at Acre
and the merchants would then be reimbursed by the royal treasury
at Paris through their factors in France. The two masters received the
money in this way on 24 June 1265.[41] But so great was the pressure
that more money was constantly needed. In the summer of 1267, the
Patriarch, William of Agen, wrote to Amaury de la Roche, Preceptor
of the Temple at Paris, setting out in detail the money urgently
needed for the payment of soldiers; Amaury was to explain the
situation to the pope.[42] Appeals to the west continued in an almost
unbroken stream. In May 1267, for example, a letter from all the
leaders to Theobald of Champagne, while ostensibly written to
explain the long absence of Hugh of Brienne, Theobald's vassal, in
the Holy Land, laid out in detail the devastation caused by the
Mamluks in the plain of Acre.[43]

However, it was precisely during this period, when the papacy was most heavily involved with its Sicilian project, that Baybars made his greatest inroads upon crusader territory. Although his successes were not quite as rapid as those of Saladin, they were equally damaging. In 1265 he took Caesarea, Haifa, and the Hospitaller fortress of Arsuf; in 1266 the Templar castle at Safad; in 1268 Jaffa, and another Templar castle, that of Beaufort. Even more significantly, Antioch fell on 18 May, and thereafter Thomas Bérard seems to have decided that it would be useless to try to defend the Templar castles in the region. Baghras, La Roche de Roussel, and Port Bonnel were abandoned.[44] In 1271 the great enclaves of the military orders in northern Tripoli began to crumble, including the Templar castle of Chastel-Blanc and the Hospitaller fortresses of Krak des Chevaliers and Akkar. Further south, in the Galilean hills, the headquarters of the Teutonic Knights at Montfort, established in the late 1220s, fell in June, the last of the great inland castles of the military orders.[45] Pinned into their coastal defences, the Franks of Outremer were at last given a respite in April 1272, when the crusade of Prince Edward of England persuaded Baybars to agree to a ten-year truce.

Between 1265 and 1271 Baybars had dismantled the whole basis of the Templar establishment in the east, which the Order had so painstakingly and expensively reconstructed since the debacle of 1187–8. Even before Hattin the military orders were gaining control of an increasing number of castles and a growing proportion of the secular lordships of the Frankish states.[46] During the thirteenth century it became evident that only the military orders had the resources even to maintain existing defences, while local secular lords could not hope to undertake new building on any scale. Recognition of this fact can be seen in the construction of the two best publicised castles of the crusader era: 'Atlīt, built on a promontory along the coast midway between Haifa and Caesarea in 1218, and Safad in northern Galilee, previously held by the Order between 1168 and 1188, and rebuilt between 1240 and 1244. These became the most important Templar castles in the thirteenth century, but both owed their existence to the drive of outsiders rather than to Frankish initiative.

During the twelfth century the Templars had improved the fortress at Destroit, built to protect the coast road along the foot of Mount

Carmel, near Haifa.[47] Late in 1217 Walter, lord of Avesnes, in the east as part of the Fifth Crusade, combined with the Templars and the Teutonic Knights to begin the building of ʿAtlīt, Destroit's much grander and more modern replacement (see figure 9 (i)). Participation by visiting crusaders and pilgrims was on a scale sufficient for Walter to name it Pilgrims' Castle. Progress must have been rapid, since by October 1220, although it had not been completed to the full height intended,[48] it was strong enough to withstand a very serious attack by al-Muʿazzam, ruler of Damascus, who was trying to take advantage of the fact that a large proportion of the Latin forces was still campaigning in the Nile Delta. According to Oliver of Paderborn, the Templars had begun to dismantle the now deserted castle of Destroit, but al-Muʿazzam was upon them so quickly that they were forced to retreat into ʿAtlīt before they had finished. They had done enough to render it useless to the Muslims, however, and al-Muʿazzam completed its destruction, as well as cutting down the neighbouring orchards. He then began a prepared assault with a formidable collection of eight siege engines. Peter of Montaigu, Master of the Templars, and a select group of knights, rushed back from Damietta, and reinforcements arrived from Acre, Beirut, Tripoli, and Cyprus. Oliver claims that the Templars fed 4,000 warriors within the castle at this time, not counting those who took part in the defence at their own expense. It took less than a month to convince al-Muʿazzam that his attack was fruitless and, at the beginning of November, after firing his own camp, he lifted the siege.[49]

Oliver of Paderborn, who also calls it 'the Castle of the Son of God', apparently deriving the name from the idea that the Virgin and Child had once hidden in a cave in the nearby hills, was so impressed by the castle that he described its position and importance in some detail. He explained that it was built on a piece of land projecting into the sea, so that it was protected on three sides by water, just as inland castles, strung out along narrow ridges, used the surrounding ravines. Not only the road, but the region around, was well worth protecting. According to Oliver, there were fisheries and salt-pans, as well as woods, pastures, vines, and orchards, but these could not be properly exploited while the populace feared attack. Indeed, he even thought that its effects were felt as far away as Mount Tabor, on the other side of the Jezreel Valley, since in 1218 al-ʿĀdil decided

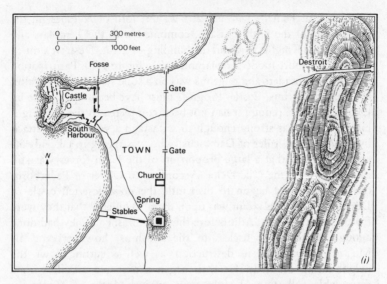

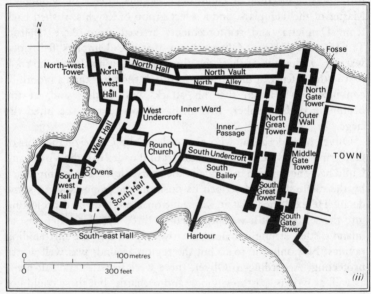

Figure 9 ʿAtlīt: (i) environs; (ii) plan.

to dismantle his fortifications there, thus making the plain from there to the Carmel range much safer for cultivation.[50] After six weeks' work digging the foundations, the Templars found the remains of previous occupation in the form of a wall and coinage unknown to them, for the area had been settled since at least the time of the Phoenicians, and soon after a source of fresh water.[51] Oliver's account suggests that some of the stone which was dug up was put to secondary use, just as had been done in the past at castles like Belvoir. Oliver was particularly impressed by the two large rectangular towers which dominated the inner wall, and the curtain wall which joined them which 'by marvellous ingenuity armed horsemen can ride up and down inside'. In front of this was another wall with three towers, giving the Templars two lines of co-ordinated defences on the landward side. Between the outer wall and the mainland was a moat which could be flooded if necessary. This structure, says Oliver, has a naturally good harbour, which 'will be improved by skilful additions', an especially valuable asset along a coast where few such harbours existed. Archaeological evidence has added to the information supplied by Oliver. C. N. Johns' survey of the outer wall showed it to have been four metres thick. Two lines of archers would have been deployed to cover the area in front of the moat, firing through the casemates on the gallery and from the top of the wall, amounting to between 120 and 140 men in all. Each of the three towers along this wall controlled a separate entrance to the interior and was therefore self-contained with its own portcullis and machicolations (see figure 9 (ii)).[52] The Templars took good care to ensure that visitors knew about the castle, for the sight of such work attracted donations from pilgrims and crusaders and helped to enhance the Order's reputation in the west. Burchard of Mount Sion, a German Dominican who visited the east in the early 1280s, was one such witness. Pilgrims' Castle, he says 'is sited in the heart of the sea, fortified with walls and ramparts and barbicans so strong and castellated, that the whole world should not be able to conquer it'.[53] Indeed, although in 1265 Baybars managed to destroy the small town which had grown up in front of it, the castle itself never did fall to siege, for the Templars abandoned it in August 1291, after the fall of Acre.

Great castles like 'Atlīt did not stand in isolation. Just as they had done in the northern parts of Tripoli and Antioch, the Templars created a dependent zone around it. Much of this was acquired at the expense of the lords of Caesarea; they had, for example, originally held the fortified village of Cafarlet, south of ʿAtlīt, but by 1255 it was in the hands of the Templars.[54] In 1232 the Templars had made a similar purchase to the south-east, buying the strategically placed village of Arames for 15,000 *besants* from John of Ibelin, thus giving themselves a position at the entrance to the pass through Mount Carmel to the Jezreel Valley.[55] These transactions give only a glimpse of the real position, for under the terms of a treaty with the Mamluks in 1283, ʿAtlīt is described as having sixteen dependent 'cantons'.[56]

While the construction of ʿAtlīt shows the determination of the Franks to hold on to the coast and the vital communications with the west, the rebuilding of Safad in Galilee from 1240 was begun in circumstances which suggest that they were hoping to re-establish control of considerable parts of inland Palestine. Safad is the subject of the most detailed description of crusader castle-building in the east, although its author is unknown and it is therefore particularly frustrating that it is not accessible to detailed archaeological investigation which would complement the documentary source.[57] The central figure in the story and the inspiration behind the project was Benedict of Alignan, Bishop of Marseille (1229–67), and the author was probably in his entourage. Whatever his provenance, he had close contacts with the Templars, for whom the treatise was splendid propaganda. According to the author, some crusaders from the army of Count Theobald of Champagne, anxious to relieve their guilt at the defeat, death, and capture of many of their companions at the hands of the Egyptians near Gaza in 1239, proposed to contribute 7,000 marks towards the rebuilding of Safad, but their promised donation never materialised. At the same time Bishop Benedict had taken advantage of the truce with Damascus to visit Our Lady of Surdenay, near the city, and while waiting there for an escort, learned how much local Damascenes feared the rebuilding of Safad. If this happened, they told him, 'the gates of Damascus would be closed'. On his return the bishop found that Safad was now only 'a large heap of stones without any building, where once had been a noble and famous castle'. The small Templar garrison lived frugally in these diminished surroundings. Yet he noted that the only substantial Muslim castle in the region was Subeibe, near Banyas. It seemed that if Safad was rebuilt the sultan would lose his income from the surrounding villages, 'since he would not dare to cultivate the land for fear of the said castle', and his expenses would rise since he would need to pay for mercenaries to defend Damascus.

The bishop therefore went to the Master, Armand of Périgord, at that time confined to bed by illness, and despite the Master's doubts about its viability, persuaded him to consider the idea. In a rousing speech before the assembled chapter of the Order the bishop is then presented as convincing the Templars of the overwhelming urgency of the project, especially while the truce lasted. Great numbers of workers and slaves were gathered and strings of pack animals organised. The bishop himself came and 'placed his tents where there had been a synagogue of the Jews and a mosque of the Saracens, in order that by this he might give a sign and openly show that the castle of Safad was built to expel the infidelities of the unbelievers and to strengthen and defend the faith of our Lord Jesus Christ'. The bishop celebrated mass, followed by a short sermon and, on 11 December 1240, 'invoking the grace of the holy spirit . . . he placed the first of the stones to the honour of our Lord Jesus Christ and to exaltation of the Christian faith, and offered upon the stone a gilded cup full of money to help in the subsequent work'. Once building was started, God's approval was shown when, in exchange for a tunic, an elderly Muslim led the bishop to a source of fresh water within the precincts, previously covered by a pile of rubble. By the time Benedict set out for home, he had the satisfaction of seeing Safad fortified, and as a parting gift he gave to the castle, 'as to a most dear favourite little son', all his mounts, tents, and bedding.

Twenty years later the bishop returned to the Holy Land and naturally his first concern was the condition of Safad. He found that the castle's 'exquisite and excellent construction seemed to be done not by man alone, but rather through the omnipotence of God'. What he saw was a double line of walls shaped in an ellipse in accordance with a site 'enclosed on every side by mountains and hills and steep precipices and crags and rocks'. According to the best modern estimates it had an overall size of 330 metres by 170 metres with a circumference, including the outer ditch, of 850 metres, making it the largest castle in the kingdom.[58] Cylindrical or round towers stood along the outer wall, while rectangular towers seem to have been built along the inner ward. There was probably a large round keep in the south-eastern part of the inner court. The castle was stocked with a full range of war machines and crossbows, and needed a peacetime complement of 1,700 men, increasing to 2,200 in time of war. Fifty of these were Templar knights and thirty were serving brothers or sergeants. They were reinforced by fifty turco-poles (light mounted troops, often recruited from the local popula-tion) and 300 crossbowmen. Other staff totalled 820, while there were 400 slaves who would have been captured Muslims. In the first two-and-a-half years the building had cost 1,100,000 Saracen *besants* over and above the normal revenues drawn from its surrounding dependent lands. 'And they spend there annually more or less 12,000 mule loads of barley and grain, apart from the other victuals and stipends which are given to mercenaries and hired persons, and the horses and mounts and arms and other necessities which are not easy to compute.' Supplies were drawn from the surrounding agricultural lands and from the food gathered by the castle's own hunters and fishermen. Fish were brought in fresh and salted on a daily basis from the Sea of Galilee and the River Jordan. Among the equipment for processing food were wind, water, and animal-powered mills. The dependent lands included a burg or large village on the western side of the castle, which had its own market, and more than 260 other *casalia* or villages which the writer claimed contained some 10,000 able-bodied men.

Although it was difficult, if not impossible, for any single castle to block a route completely in the manner of some modern defences, Safad's rebuilding had dramatic effects upon the safety and well-being of the region. Whereas previously frequent incursions were made by 'the Saracens, the Bedouins, the Khorezmians, and the Turcomans' the castle of Safad 'placed there a defence and an obstacle so that they did not dare to do harm by openly crossing the River Jordan as far as Acre, unless they had a very large army, and from Acre to Safad the loaded pack-horses and waggons go safely, and agriculture and the cultivation of the land are freely undertaken by all'. In contrast, the territory beyond the Jordan towards Damascus lay waste, subject to the frequent *chevauchées* of the Templar garrison. Perhaps most important of all to the bishop was the fact that the Christian faith could be freely preached in a region previously subject to 'the blasphemy of Mahomet' and the famous places of Galilee with which the faithful had become familiar through the Bible could now be again accessible. These included the cistern where Joseph was sold by his brothers; Capernaum, where Jesus preached and Peter found the tribute money in the mouth of the fish and where Matthew left the custom-house to join the apostolate; the hillside where Jesus fed the 5,000 'from which there still remain twelve buckets full of fragments'; and the 'Table of the Lord' where Jesus manifested himself to the disciples after Easter. Next to the Sea of Galilee itself was Bethsaida, birthplace of Peter, Andrew, Philip, and James the Less, and Magdalon, 'which is said to be the birthplace of the Magdalene'. Moreover, Nazareth, Mount Tabor, and Cana of Galilee could now be freely visited again. The value of the castle to the Franks is confirmed by Muslim sources: the fourteenth-century Egyptian chronicler, Ibn al-Furāt, who compiled his history from contemporary sources, described it as 'an obstruction in the throat of Syria and a blockage in the chest of Islam' until Baybars brought about its downfall.[59]

Benedict's second visit to the Holy Land lasted until 1262 and he himself died in 1267. He must have lived long enough, however, to hear the news of the fall of 'this most inaccessible and impregnable castle'. Three times during July 1266 Baybars attempted to take it without success, until he decided upon the tactic of sowing dissent between the Templars and the Syrian Christians inside. This was a shrewd move given the relatively small size of the Templar garrison in comparison with the large number of native troops and servants, and soon so many Syrians had been persuaded to desert by a promise of free passage that the viability of continuing to defend it was called into question. This persuaded the Templars to send a Syrian sergeant brother called Leon Cazelier to negotiate, since he knew Arabic, and he was apparently successful in arranging the castle's evacuation and safe-conduct to Acre for the Christians. However, when the gates were opened, Baybars sent the women and children into slavery and, like their predecessors eighty years before, had the Templars decapitated. Leon, says the chronicler known as 'The Templar of Tyre', who had a good knowledge of events since he seems to have worked for the Order's secretariat in the east, 'for fear of death made this treason'.[60] Burchard of Mount Sion had been as stirred by Safad as he had by 'Atlīt. This was a shameful betrayal of 'in my judgement, the fairest and strongest of all the castles which I have seen'. Its loss opened up not only Galilee, but all the land as far as Acre, Tyre, and Sidon.[61] Hugh Revel, Master of the Hospital, was less adulatory, remarking tartly that Safad, 'about which the Templars had talked so much', was unable to last more than sixteen days.[62] The news was quickly disseminated in the west. The anonymous chronicler of St Martial of Limoges says that it was the loss of Safad that convinced King Louis IX that he should renew his crusading vow, while the chronicler of the monastery of St Peter at Erfurt, in Saxony, believed that Baybars was able to subjugate the whole land because he had captured this castle.[63]

No secular lords could match this in the thirteenth century – indeed, secular control of formerly important lordships like Caesarea and Galilee had been thoroughly eroded as early as the 1170s[64] – but even those lords more successful in maintaining the integrity of their lands succumbed soon after the middle of the century. Julian, Lord of Sidon and Beaufort, had been able to keep the core of his patrimony in his own hands, despite selling off some of the more outlying parts to the Hospitallers and the Teutonic Knights, but his position was completely undermined, first by Aiyūbid attacks on Sidon in 1249 and 1253 and then by his losses in a foray against the Mongols in 1260. The damage caused by the Mongols was the final blow and in that year he was forced to sell his main lordship of Sidon, together with its spectacular castle of Beaufort, to the Templars.[65] According to Eracles, the sale enraged Hetoum, King of Armenia, whose daughter was married to Julian, causing 'great hatred . . . between the King of Armenia and the Temple.'[66] Beaufort had upper and lower castles protected by a rock fosse, and its elevated position gave it commanding views across the Beka Valley in southern Lebanon. The Templars attempted to secure its economic support by agreement with the Hospital in 1262, renouncing long-held claims in the region around Valania and al-Marqab, which was dominated by the Hospital, and ceding their *casal* at Cafarsset, near Tiberias, in exchange for all the property possessed by the Hospitallers in Julian's old lordship.[67] But in the end they too were unable to hold it. Although they built about 250 metres of additional fortifications on the southern side, Beaufort fell to an overwhelming attack by Baybars in April 1268, during which he deployed as many as twenty-six siege engines.[68]

The breathing-space offered by Prince Edward's truce allowed time for the intrusion of a new power into the politics of the Levant, a power significant enough to deter the Mamluks from applying what in 1271 might have been the final and fatal blow to the remnants of the crusader states. By 1268 Charles of Anjou had gained control of the Kingdom of Sicily and within three years he had begun to take a serious interest in the crusader states. His ambitions were far-reaching for, like other Sicilian rulers before him, he imagined that he could create for himself a Mediterranean empire encompassing both Byzantium and Jerusalem, and he worked throughout his reign to achieve these goals. His execution of Conradin in October 1268, ended the Hohenstaufen connection with Jerusalem, and the eastern Franks chose in his stead Hugh III, King of Cyprus, already in a strong position following his acceptance as *bailli* in 1264, after protracted legal arguments. However, he was opposed by Maria of Antioch who, as granddaughter of Isabel I, through whom the kingship had been transmitted after the death of her half-sister, Sibyl, in 1190, was one generation closer to Isabel than Hugh. She was not accepted by the High Court, but did receive the support of the Templars and, having made a formal challenge to Hugh's right, she left Outremer to place her claim before the papal curia.[69] When she arrived in Italy, Charles of Anjou stated that his previous, tacit recognition of Hugh did not prejudice her claim, and after several years of bargaining she eventually sold her rights to Charles, confirmed in a contract of March 1277.

By this time the Order of the Temple had become an integral part of the structure of power which Charles had been erecting for himself in the Mediterranean. When Thomas Bérard died on 25 March 1273,[70] he was succeeded by William of Beaujeu, Preceptor of southern Italy and Sicily.[71] William was the fourth son of Guichard of Beaujeu, Lord of Montpensier, and Catherine of Clermont, Dame of Montferrand. Guichard himself was the second son of Guichard IV of Beaujeu and Sibyl of Hainault, younger sister of Isabel, first wife of Philip Augustus, which explains why Charles of Anjou habitually refers to the Grand Master as *consanguineus* in his documents, and why the Templar of Tyre, who acted as William's secretary when he became Grand Master, speaks of him as *parent dou roy de France*.[72] There seems little doubt, therefore, that Charles had secured the appointment, but it is possible that the Templars had been looking in this direction as early as 1268 when they had supported Maria of Antioch.[73] William was in any case well known in the east, for he probably took part in Louis IX's campaign in

Egypt, during which his uncle Humbert V of Beaujeu, was killed;[74] he had joined the Temple by 1253 and was certainly in the Kingdom of Jerusalem in 1261, when he was captured during the raid conducted by John of Ibelin. He was ransomed soon afterwards and by 1271 he had become Templar Preceptor in the County of Tripoli.[75] There were strong reasons for the Templars' pro-Angevin policy, for Capetian commitment had always formed the bedrock of support in the west for the crusader states, and the evident interest of such a powerful cadet of the French royal house, whose base was the rich and powerful Kingdom of Sicily and who was assured of papal backing, must have seemed the only realistic hope after the battering which the crusader states had received from Baybars. As for Charles, the military and financial services which the Templars had provided for the Capetians ever since the time of Louis VII, were an obvious channel through which he could make his presence felt in Outremer.

William was elected master on 13 May 1273, and brothers William of Ponçon and Bertrand of Fox at once set out from Acre to fetch the new leader. He did not, however, immediately return to the east, for he spent the greater part of two years visiting the preceptories of the Order in France, England, and Spain. His secretary says that, in the course of these visits, 'he amassed a great treasure' for use in Outremer.[76] William had another reason for delaying his departure, for in May 1274, he led a group of Templar representatives at the Council of Lyon, called by Pope Gregory X primarily to examine the prospects for a new crusade. The Templars were closely associated with this pope, for Tedaldo Visconti, Archbishop of Liège, had been elected in 1271 while on crusade, and Stephen of Sissey, William of Beaujeu's predecessor as Preceptor in Apulia, and Fulk of Letrie, a follower of Charles of Anjou, had been sent to collect him from the east.[77] At the council William of Beaujeu was one of those who, on 1 May, met James of Aragon, the only king to attend, outside the city of Vienne, and escorted him to the papal palace at Lyon. When Gregory opened the first session of the council in the cathedral of St John on 7 May, the Grand Master sat in a prominent position to the right of the pope.[78]

In the days that followed, from 8 to 17 May, the assembly engaged in detailed discussions about the proposed crusade. By his own account, James of Aragon proposed sending 500 knights and 2,000 foot in advance, to be followed by the main expedition in two years' time, led by the pope himself and accompanied by the king together with 1,000 knights. The lack of response to this offer led King James to ask sarcastically if any of the representatives of the Christian kings and princes present were prepared to shame him by offering more men. The pope then turned to William of Beaujeu for an opinion, but the master said that Brother John of Carcella would speak, as he had had sixty years' service in the Temple. Brother John, however, replied only that it was not a question of years of service. According to the king this led to the following exchange with the Grand Master:

Then the pope told the master to speak, which he did; but though he ought to have said that the pope thanked me for what I had said concerning the expedition beyond sea, the master said nothing of the kind; nor that himself and the others thanked me for my offers: he only observed that an expedition to the land beyond sea required great consideration in matters of arms, and food, and especially of men disposed to the work. People, he said, had not there what they needed of all that. Still, he gave as his opinion that from 250 to 300 knights, with 500 footmen, would be wanted at first. When I heard him say so, I could not refrain from answering, 'Master, if the pope is willing to send 500, how many will be there under you?'

The pope then asked the master the size of the sultan's navy and was told that the Muslims could not fit out more than seventeen ships of various sizes. The pope thought that the Christians would therefore need about twenty, but King James said that ten ships from Aragon would be enough to deal with the enemy. General opinion seemed to favour the view of the Grand Master, so the king asked permission to leave the session, which was granted. In the end, nothing came of James' plans, for he was further offended by the pope's refusal to crown him unless he was prepared to pay tribute to the papacy as his predecessors had done, and on 31 May he left for Aragon.[79] It is clear that James of Aragon thought that the Templars were unenthusiastic about the crusade, a view which had already gained some popular credence from writers like Matthew Paris. However, it seems more likely that William of Beaujeu saw Charles of Anjou as a more reliable long-term support than James of Aragon, and did not wish to provoke a Mamluk attack while Charles was still negotiating with Maria of Antioch. The Council showed that there were no other obvious heavyweight crusaders in prospect.

William of Beaujeu eventually arrived at Acre in September 1275.[80] Under his leadership the Templars proved to be consistent supporters of the policies of Charles of Anjou and therefore leading opponents of King Hugh, whose authority the Order was not prepared to recognise. In October 1276, for example, the Templars purchased the village of La Fauconnerie, near Acre, without any reference to the king. Hugh was apparently so angry that he left for Cyprus almost at once, and only after pressure from the patriarch, the Hospitallers, and the Teutonic Knights was he persuaded to appoint a *bailli* in the person of Balian of Ibelin.[81] Although it is evident that the Templars were not his only antagonists, it does seem that the king felt particularly bitter towards them. According to the Templar of Tyre, Hugh had abandoned the kingdom, and on his arrival in Cyprus, wrote letters to the pope telling him that the land was ungovernable because of the Temple and the Hospital. He added that he had heard that Maria of Antioch had ceded the kingdom to Charles of Anjou, who was sending his representative, Roger of San Severino, to seize it.[82]

Roger of San Severino did indeed arrive in September 1277, bringing letters from Charles of Anjou, Maria of Antioch, and the pope saying that Charles was now the rightful King of Jerusalem.[83] He took up residence in the house of the Temple at Acre. Balian of Ibelin and the other barons were now caught between rival rulers, but William of Beaujeu suggested that messengers be sent to King Hugh in Cyprus before any action was taken, rightly believing that they would receive no satisfaction from the king. The barons appear to have thought that they had no alternative but to submit to Roger of San Severino, who at once set up a pro-Angevin administration. Thereafter, Charles of Anjou evidently regarded Roger of San Severino and William of Beaujeu as his representatives in the east, sending supplies of food, clothing, horses, and equipment through them, and making use of the Templar financial system. On 24 March 1279, for example, Charles instructed his treasurers to repay 4,000 *onces* to the Templar Peter of Fontaines, procurator of the Preceptor in Sicily and Apulia, 2,800 of which had been loaned by William of Beaujeu to Roger of San Severino 'in order to sustain him and our people'.[84] The same policy was maintained even after Charles' power had been shaken by the revolt of the Sicilian Vespers at Easter 1282: in February 1283, William of Beaujeu and Odo Poilechien, who succeeded Roger of San Severino as *bailli* in 1282, were informed that they were about to receive a quantity of grain for sale in the kingdom.[85]

Hugh of Cyprus twice tried to regain his position on the mainland, in 1279 and 1283, but on neither occasion was he able to overcome the Angevin–Templar alliance. Although in 1277 William of Beaujeu succeeded in negotiating a peace between John of Montfort, Lord of Tyre, one of Hugh's strongest supporters, and the Venetians, whose access to Tyre John had previously blocked,[86] Hugh was still able to land at Tyre with John of Montfort's aid two years later. But the Templars prevented him from gaining control of Acre and he was forced to retreat to Cyprus again. He took his revenge by dismantling the Order's castle at Gastria and wrecking the Templar houses at Limassol and Paphos. The property which he seized was not regained until after his death in 1284.[87] His second attempt occurred after the Vespers had shaken Angevin power, when, in August 1283, he landed at Beirut. Once again he made no progress, although it is not clear from the sources what part the Templars played in the opposition to him on this occasion.[88]

While the role of the Templars in supporting the Angevin position can be seen to have some credibility as a means of protecting the crusader states as a whole, the intervention of William of Beaujeu in the civil war in the County of Tripoli between 1277 and 1282 seems to have had little wider justification, and the Templars' actions during this period must have contributed to the lack of trust in the Grand Master shown by other Christians in the east in the crucial years between 1289 and 1291. The problems seem to have arisen from rather specific personal enmities. Between 1275 and 1277 Tripoli was administered in the name of its under-age heir, Bohemond VII of Antioch, by Bartholomew, Bishop of Tortosa. He, however, was opposed by Paul of Segni, Bishop of Tripoli, who seems to have become friendly with William of Beaujeu at the Council of Lyon, and when Bohemond came of age in 1277, he found that he had inherited the opposition of the Templars. The *Estoire d'Eracles* says that 'this was the beginning of the great war between the prince and the Temple, from which much evil arose'.[89] The Templars exacerbated the quarrel by receiving Guy II Embriaco of Gibelet, a former friend and vassal of Bohemond, who had quarrelled with him over what he regarded as a broken promise to his brother, John. The Templar of Tyre says that Guy went to Acre and became a *confrere* of the Order and that William of Beaujeu 'promised to help him as much as he could',[90] a commitment which led to five years of intermittent fighting.

In a world overshadowed by the Mamluks and the Mongols, this purely local dispute within the scattered remains of the crusader states takes on a distinct air of unreality. Bohemond attacked the Templars' house at Tripoli and began destroying property such as the Order's woodland at Montroque, while the Templars retaliated by setting fire to Botron and besieging Nephin. In a battle between Guy Embriaco and Bohemond near Botron, Guy was supported by a contingent of thirty Templars sent by the Master. The next year there was further fighting at sea, with Templar galleys being sent to Tripoli and Bohemond's ships attacking the Templar castle at Sidon, which the Order had acquired at such expense in 1260. The culmination of the conflict came in 1282 when, in an attempt to take Tripoli by surprise, Guy and his forces set themselves up in the Templar house in the city. However, the absence of the local preceptor, the Spanish Templar, Reddecoeur, made them suspicious, and in a panic they took refuge with the Hospitallers. When they surrendered to Bohemond, believing themselves to have a safe-conduct, they were savagely put to death.[91]

The weakening of Angevin power as a consequence of the revolt of the Vespers at Easter 1282, and Charles of Anjou's death in January 1285, seems to have persuaded the Templars to take a less partisan line. After the brief reign of John, King Hugh's eldest surviving son, in June 1285, the next son succeeded as Henry II. He was acknowledged in Cyprus, but he needed Templar support if he were to establish himself on the mainland, and he therefore sent an envoy, Julian le Jaune, to negotiate with William of Beaujeu. Henry himself landed in June 1286. At this point, the three masters of the Templars, Hospitallers, and Teutonic Knights tacitly committed themselves to Henry's support by persuading Odo Poilechien to give up the citadel at Acre to the military orders, who handed it over to the king four days later. William of Beaujeu's name appears on a safe-conduct offered to the French by Henry II on 27 June.[92] The Master was equally conciliatory when a dispute broke out between the Pisans and the Genoese early in 1287. Although he was unable to stop this conflict from escalating into a sea battle, he and Theobald

Gaudin, the Commander of the Temple, did prevent some fisher-men, apparently of Pisan origin, from being sold into captivity.[93]

The respite from Mamluk attacks which had followed Prince Edward's truce of 1271 continued throughout the 1270s and into the early 1280s. Charles of Anjou, being preoccupied elsewhere, pursued a policy of non-provocation, while the Mamluks themselves concentrated their efforts on the other regions. Moreover, despite 'Ain Jālūt, they remained wary of the Mongols, while the death of Baybars in July 1277 embroiled them in a succession dispute from which his ultimate successor, Kalavun, took time to emerge. William of Beaujeu's policies in these circumstances reflect Angevin caution. Two letters written in 1275 display the same worries as his predecessor, but in general he seems to have been less concerned to stimulate a large-scale expedition than Thomas Bérard, placed under extreme pressure by Baybars, had been. In September he wrote to congratulate Rudolf of Habsburg, King of the Romans, on his elevation to the throne, and hoped that he would soon be bringing help to the Holy Land.[94] A second letter, in October, probably in the same year, went to Edward of England. The sultan was in the region of Damascus with a large army and it was also rumoured that the Tartars were approaching. The Temple was burdened with expenses for the repair of fortifications, nor did it have sufficient men for safety. The master therefore asked for royal support in this time of great danger.[95] Nevertheless, new truces were made in 1281 and 1282: in the second of these William of Beaujeu agreed with Kalavun to a peace intended to last for ten years and ten months, one condition of which was that 'in the territory of Tortosa mentioned in the treaty no fort or fortification is to be repaired, nor any reinforcement, entrenchment or the like built'.[96]

Truces left the Mamluks free to tackle the renewed Mongol threats, but ultimately they did not prevent Kalavun from turning against the Christians. His attacks began in 1285, before the expiry of the truces, and now the coastal defences began to go the way of the inland cities. Latakia was captured in April 1285, and the very strong Hospitaller fortress of al-Marqab fell in May. In February, 1289, Kalavun moved against Tripoli. William of Beaujeu had a contact in the Mamluk army, an emir called al-Fakhri, who, in return for annual presents, supplied him with information about the movements of the Mamluks. Al-Fakhri duly told him about Kalavun's next objective and

William at once sent a messenger to warn the inhabitants of Tripoli. He was not believed and it was only when the master sent Redde-coeur to Acre with a second message that reinforcements were rushed up. But they were too late, for Tripoli fell in April and Botron and Nephin soon after.[97] The initial refusal to accept the truth of the Grand Master's message is significant. His political activity during the previous fourteen years had created an image of him as untrust-worthy and partisan, an image which in turn came to be reflected in some of the later judgements of him and of the last years of the Templars in Palestine.

Letters from the west show that the leaders in Outremer were now desperately seeking help. Two replies from Pope Nicholas IV in September 1288 and October 1290, did little more than exhort them to be vigilant.[98] Some rulers offered more practical help: in April 1290, Alfonso III of Aragon wrote to William of Beaujeu to tell him that, despite wars in his own lands, he was allowing the export of materials to aid the Holy Land in its present misfortune.[99] Some crusaders did arrive, for in August 1290 twenty galleys from northern Italy reached Acre. Their numbers, however, proved great enough to provoke, but insufficient to deter. Soon after their arrival, they caused a riot in the city in which a number of Muslims were killed, largely *les povres vilains* who brought their goods into Acre to sell, according to the Templar of Tyre.[100] This provided Kalavun with a pretext and he demanded reparation. At a council called at Acre to discuss the matter, William of Beaujeu suggested that all the prisoners in the city held by the orders and the maritime powers should be handed over as the culprits. As he saw it, it would make little difference as these men were under sentence of death in any case. But he was overruled and the Christian leaders contented themselves with explaining to the sultan that these crusaders were strangers to Outremer and did not understand the law. Kalavun at once began to prepare for an attack on Acre and, as before, William of Beaujeu received advance warning from al-Fakhri, but again he was not believed.[101]

According to Ludolph of Sudheim, writing some sixty years later on the basis, he claimed, of truthful men who remembered the events well, at the request of William of Beaujeu, the sultan made one last offer: he would restore the truce if every man in Acre paid one Venetian penny. But when the Grand Master urged this on the populace, assembled in the Church of the Holy Cross, the proposal was rejected out of hand, and he barely escaped with his life, for the people regarded him as a betrayer of the city.[102] The story seems unlikely to be literally true – the Templar of Tyre, who is the best informed writer on the Order in the east at this period, makes no mention of such an offer – but it does perhaps reflect the way that the leadership of the Order was perceived on the eve of the fall of Acre. No advice coming from the Grand Master was likely to be seen as disinterested, while the Templars' contacts with the Muslims seem to be too close for honest Christians.

Although Kalavun died in November, 1290, his son, al-Ashraf Khalīl, continued the preparations. Frankish envoys, including some Templars, were thrown into prison and, in March 1291, the new sultan wrote to William of Beaujeu telling him of his intention to attack Acre 'to avenge the wrongs done'. On 5 April, his army appeared before the walls of Acre.[103] All available men were organised for the defence of the city, with the Templars and Hospitallers stationed along the walls of Montmusard. On 15 April, William of Beaujeu led a night attack on that section of the Muslim camp occupied by troops from Hamah. Surprise gave an initial advantage, but the Christians became entangled in the tent ropes in the darkness and were beaten back, losing eighteen dead in the process. On 15 May, the Hospitallers and Templars fought off an attack on St Anthony's Gate, but three days later the Muslims broke in at the 'Accursed Tower', farther to the south, and street-fighting began. William of Beaujeu was resting at the time, but rushed out, only lightly armed. Badly wounded, he was carried back to the Templar complex where he lingered thoughout the day and died that evening, aged about sixty.[104] There was panic in the harbour area and some of those with access to ships made fortunes, including, it is thought, a Templar captain called Roger of Flor, who seems to have used the profits to finance a later military career quite independent of the Temple.[105] Meanwhile, the Mamluks had captured most of the city until only the Templar fortress remained in Christian hands, filled with refugees. On 25 May, Peter of Sevrey, Marshal of the Templars, agreed to surrender in exchange for a safe-conduct for those inside, but as they entered, some Muslim troops began to pillage and to molest women and children, provoking an attack from the Templars and ending all thoughts of surrender. That night, the commander,

Theobald Gaudin, was sent out of the fortress with the Order's treasure and sailed to Sidon. The Templar building fell three days later and all those left were slaughtered.[106]

The Templars now held only Sidon, Tortosa, and 'Atlīt. At Sidon the remaining knights elected Theobald Gaudin as master. He was probably the most senior Templar left, for he had served in the east for over thirty years, as both commander and turcopolier.[107] The Templars stayed at Sidon for a month, until a large Mamluk army appeared, when they prudently retired to the Castle on the Sea, situated on the north side of the harbour about 100 metres from the coast and connected to the town only by a long, narrow bridge.[108] After consulting the brethren, Theobald Gaudin set sail for Cyprus with the intention of bringing back reinforcements, but he did not return, and some of the brethren there sent a message to the defenders of Sidon, advising them to give up. Deeply discouraged, they abandoned the castle during the night of 14 July. Left with only Tortosa and 'Atlīt, the garrisons had no alternative but to evacuate them, departing on 3 and 14 August respectively.[109] 'Atlīt, more than any other castle, had symbolised the Templar commitment to the Holy Land; it had never been taken by storm and thereafter the Mamluks dismantled it to ensure that it would never need to be.[110] 'This time,' says the Templar of Tyre, 'everything was lost, so that the Christians no longer held a palm of land in Syria.'[111]

CHAPTER SIX

TEMPLAR LIFE

The Templars are most excellent soldiers. They wear white
mantles with a red cross, and when they go to the wars a
standard of two colours called balzaus is borne before them.
They go in silence. Their first attack is the most terrible. In
going they are the first, in returning the last. They await the
orders of their Master. When they think fit to make war and
the trumpet has sounded, they sing in chorus the Psalm of
David, 'Not unto us, O Lord', kneeling on the blood and
necks of the enemy, unless they have forced the troops of the
enemy to retire altogether, or utterly broken them to pieces.
Should any of them for any reason turn his back to the enemy,
or come forth alive [from a defeat], or bear arms against the
Christians, he is severely punished; the white mantle with the
red cross, which is the sign of his knighthood, is taken away
with ignominy, he is cast from the society of brethren, and
eats his food on the floor without a napkin for the space of
one year. If the dogs molest him, he does not dare to drive
them away. But at the end of the year, if the Master and
brethren think his penance to have been sufficient, they restore
him the belt of his former knighthood. These Templars live
under a strict religious rule, obeying humbly, having no
private property, eating sparingly, dressing meanly, and
dwelling in tents.[1]

In many ways this description of the Templars, by an unknown
pilgrim who visited Jerusalem some time before 1187, encapsulates
the popular view of the Templars both then and since. The extent to
which this picture was embedded in the contemporary consciousness
can be seen in the writing of the poet Guiot of Provins who, in
contrast to the earnest seriousness of the anonymous pilgrim, surveyed the monastic scene with an amused cynicism. Towards the
end of his life he in fact entered a Cluniac house, but in his *Bible*,

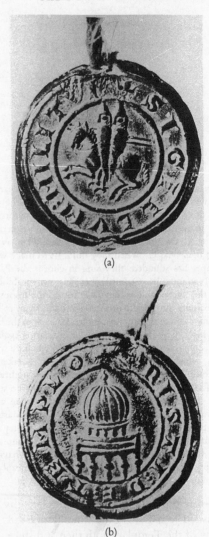

(a)

(b)

Plate 7 Seal of Bertrand of Blancfort, 1168: (a) obverse; (b) reverse.

written between 1203 and 1208, he considered the possibilities of other orders. In many ways the Templars seemed the most attractive, but there was an insuperable obstacle:

The Templars are greatly honoured in Syria; the Turks fear them terribly; they defend the castles, the ramparts: in battle they never flee. But this is exactly what upsets me. If I belonged to this order I know very well that I should flee. I would not wait to be struck, for I am not fond of such things. They fight too bravely. I have no desire to be killed: I would rather pass for a coward and remain alive than experience the most glorious death in the world. I would readily go to sing the hours with them; that would not bother me at all. I would be very exact in the service, but not at the hour of battle; there I should be completely wanting.[2]

Twelfth- and thirteenth-century illustrations present the same image: the Templar seal with the two knights mounted on one horse suggesting frugality and humility (see plate 7); the Templars doing battle with the infidel in the frescoes of the churches at Cressac and Perugia; the black-and-white banner carried by the Templars in the drawings of Matthew Paris. Nineteenth-century engravings are equally evocative: the bearded warrior with white surcoat and flowing cloak carrying a long shield emblazoned with a red cross.[3]

St Bernard had been the first to establish this image in *De laude novae militiae*, giving the Templars a standard against which, despite the fact that it was more rhetorical than realistic, they would later be judged. When they join battle 'at last putting aside former restraint, as if they say: "Have I not hated those Lord, who hated you and languish upon your enemies?" charging their adversaries, they repute their enemies like sheep, by no means, although they be few, fearing barbarian savagery, or the numerous multitude'.[4] While the treatise itself did not have as wide a circulation as many of St Bernard's other works, its ethos does seem to have permeated Templar society, leading some knights to present themselves in this way to outsiders. Indeed, Gerard of Ridefort apparently acted directly upon it, for his charge against impossible odds at the Springs of Cresson bore more relation to St Bernard's claim that 'one chases a thousand, two put to flight ten thousand' than to the pragmatic and often devious ploys used by most other contemporary warriors.[5] Consequently some, like James of Molay, joined in the expectation of such action and took time to adjust to the realities of life in Outremer. In 1309, when he was in his late sixties, Molay recalled how, when he and other young knights had first been sent to the east in the 1270s during the Mastership of William of Beaujeu, they had grumbled about him among themselves because of his apparently pacific attitude towards the Mamluks. However, they had finally come to accept that the maintenance of the truce made by Edward was the only practical policy.[6]

Although Molay, like many others before him, found that Templar life in Outremer was not all blood and glory, it was nevertheless true that in addition to the usual monastic vows of poverty, chastity, and obedience, all entrants swore, in the words commonly used by Templars during the trial, always to 'help as far as you can to conserve what is acquired in the Kingdom of Jerusalem, and to conquer what is not yet acquired'. It was necessary, therefore, to provide a disciplined framework within which to accomplish this, and during the twelfth and thirteenth centuries the Order evolved a detailed set of regulations which by the early 1260s ran to 686 clauses.[7] These were written in French and included a translation of the original Latin Rule, which would not have been readily comprehensible to many recruits, whose Latin seldom extended beyond the set formulae of documents recording property transactions.[8] More importantly, the Latin Rule had been composed when the Templars were still little more than guardians of the pilgrim routes and had relatively little to say upon the increasingly important subject of the duties, responsibilities, and authority of the military hierarchy, nor about the ways that discipline should be imposed. Two hundred and two additional clauses covering these aspects of Templar life were therefore set down, probably by the mid 1160s, expanding a largely monastic Rule into a military manual as well.[9] However, the rapid growth of military functions did not mean that the fundamental monastic vocation was ignored thereafter: a further 107 clauses regulated conventual life, followed by 158 clauses describing the holding of a chapter and the nature of the penances which could be handed out there. Although these sections cannot be dated, the appearance of one significant difference in the list of offences for which a Templar could be expelled suggests that they are not exactly contemporaneous with the hierarchical statutes or *retrais*.[10] It seems unlikely, though, that they were written down much later, since they would be equally necessary for the functioning of the Order by this time. Another 113 clauses on penances were added in the middle of the thirteenth century: internal evidence shows that they can be dated to the decade between 1257 and 1267. They did not create any new regulations, but were written in a form which suggests that an

experienced and senior Templar had been asked to show the operation of the penance system in practice, drawing upon specific
examples known to him. As a kind of coda or appendix there is a
description of the ceremony of reception. Again this cannot be dated,
but it must have been used from an early date, even if it was not
written down immediately. The Rule continued to grow even after
the middle of the thirteenth century. A manuscript found in the
archives of the Aragonese crown in Barcelona contains a version of
the Rule in Catalan which, since it incorporates an account of the fall
of Baghras in 1268, postdates the last clauses of the French Rule.[11] It
seems probable that, had the Order not been suppressed in 1307, the
Master and Chapter would have continued to add such further
clauses as seemed necessary, a power which they were allowed to
exercise under the terms of the bull *Omne datum optimum* of 1139 and
which all new entrants swore to accept at their reception.[12] The
French and Catalan Rules have, for instance, little to say about
activities at sea, but these were becoming increasingly important
during the 1290s after the Templars had been forced to retreat to
Cyprus, and, had the Order survived into the fourteenth century,
more clauses would have been needed to take account of them. The
Templars lacked any real impulse to reform, a trait which made them
vulnerable to criticism, especially after 1291,[13] but these additions
perhaps partially offset this, since they did take account of changing
circumstances. Further development seems all the more likely given
the preoccupation with eastern affairs shown in the Rule; even in the
Catalan version the events of northern Syria receive more prominence than those of Iberia.

The application of this Rule lends no support to those who like to
believe that the Temple was a secret Order, guarding esoteric rites
which their accusers at the trial were attempting to expose. Not only
does the translation of the original Rule from Latin into French and
the exclusive use of the vernacular for all subsequent clauses contradict such a notion, but it is also clear that both the leadership and the
rank and file needed it for day-to-day use. Receptions are a case in
point. As the trial records show, there were few Templars who had
not been present at a reception ceremony at some time or another,
and many who had actually conducted proceedings or who played a
significant role in them, including ordinary chaplains and serving
brothers. The condition of the Catalan version of the Rule underlines

this; Delaville Le Roulx pointed out that the sections dealing with receptions show the most signs of wear, suggesting that these were the parts consulted most frequently.[14] Not surprisingly, therefore, all Templars were required to know its contents: one of the preconditions of entry was that the Rule must be read to the new recruit,[15] while the existence of a variety of extant copies of the Rule, as well as reference to copies no longer in existence, suggests that copies were made when and where they were needed.[16] The Catalan version is a case in point, for it was apparently kept for the Master in Catalonia and Aragon,[17] and it must be assumed that other regional officials were similarly equipped. The Rule was, after all, a practical tool, not the repository of heretical doctrine. Although there are evident lacunae in the Catalan manuscript, it is significant that the parts which were important for the administration of a province in the west are to be found here, including the procedures for chapter-meetings, the penance system, and the instructions for receptions, rather than the hierarchical statutes with their almost exclusive concern with the situation in the east.

The Templars were not, of course, unaware of the need for confidentiality and security in certain circumstances. The disclosure of the proceedings of chapter-meetings, for example, was punishable by expulsion, apparently in order to prevent idle or malicious gossip within the Order about confessions of sins made by individuals or about discussions of other sensitive topics.[18] Clause 326, on the other hand, expressly forbids ordinary brothers from keeping a copy of the *retrais* (that is, the hierarchical statutes) and the Rule, on the grounds that 'the squires found them once and read them, and disclosed them to secular men, which could have been harmful to the Order'.[19] This prohibition cannot have been to protect individuals, nor to cover up secret blasphemies, since there are none in the Rule. Moreover, this clause comes from a section which is unlikely to date from later than the 1160s, a period in which even the lawyers of Philip IV of France did not claim corruption. The most obvious potential damage would have been the disclosure of military information; the axiom that loose talk costs lives was as relevant to the Templars as it has been in many other wars since that time.[20]

At the head of the whole structure was the Grand Master who, by the 1160s, held an office of power and prestige. No longer an ordinary knight humbly guarding pilgrims, too poverty-stricken to keep sufficient horses and equipment, he had become a great man, entitled to four horses and an entourage which included a chaplain, two knights, a clerk, a sergeant, and a servant to carry his shield and lance. He had, too, his own farrier, a Saracen scribe to act as an interpreter, a turcopolier, and a cook.[21] At the end of the thirteenth century James of Molay had a serving brother to look after his harnessing and animals, another to supervise the provisioning of his household, and two more to guard his chamber.[22] When the Order received a fresh consignment of horses from the west, the Master was entitled to select any of them for himself, as well as one or two others which he could give 'to worthy secular men, who are friends of the house'. On any overnight journey he was assigned two pack horses, increased to four on campaign or in dangerous regions. In time of war he could select a group of between six and ten knights to accompany him personally. Equally, he was expected to act out the symbolism of humility in the manner of Christ: every Maundy Thursday he washed the feet of thirteen paupers and distributed to each of them a shirt, breeches, and shoes, as well as two loaves of bread and two *deniers* in cash.[23] His prestige in life was reflected in his treatment after death. At a period when in the west the burial rites of many monarchs were only just beginning to take a settled and dignified form,[24] the funeral and interment of the Grand Master were attended by all the prelates and distinguished men of the land. A great lighting of candles marked the service, an honour unique in the Order, and all the brothers present and throughout the *baillie* were required to say 200 paternosters over the following seven days. One hundred paupers were fed 'for the sake of his soul'.[25]

Elaborate procedures governed the election of his successor. It was the responsibility of the Marshal to arrange the funeral service and to summon all the provincial officers in the east to assemble, if possible, at Jerusalem. There they would choose a Grand Commander to govern the Order in the interim, and then a group of 'the worthy men of the house' selected one of their number to act as presiding officer. After a night of prayer, he, together with a designated companion, chose two further brothers, and the group in turn added another two, until they reached twelve, in honour of the twelve apostles, before finally co-opting a chaplain, 'to take the place of Jesus Christ'. This made an electoral college of thirteen, consisting of eight knights, four sergeants, and one chaplain, as far as possible reflecting the diverse countries from which the membership was drawn. A majority decision was acceptable, having the usual aim of selecting someone already living in Outremer, although the history of the Order shows that this did not invariably happen. When the name was announced, the new Master was acclaimed by the brothers and then, while the chaplains sang the *Te Deum*, they carried him to the chapel before the altar, as a means of offering him to God.[26]

All but two of the Masters died in office, six of them in battle or in captivity following a battle, one of them at the stake as a relapsed heretic. Presumably the same procedures were necessary after the resignations of Everard des Barres and Philip of Nablus in 1152 and 1171 respectively, although there is no specific provision for this eventuality in the Rule, despite the appearance of this problem at such an early date in the Order's history. In theory these elections were structured in accordance with papal will: the bull *Omne datum optimum* of 1139 stated that only professed brothers of the Order could be elected, chosen 'by all the brothers together or by the sounder and purer part of them'.[27] Nevertheless, as with most institutions of the Church which mattered to the lay powers, it was not always as straightforward as this; at least seven of the twenty-two Masters were appointed through the direct influence of a secular ruler.

Even so, everything that occurred during the election was supposed to be kept secret and, until the time of the trial, there are no extant accounts. It seems likely that the correct procedure was followed even when there was outside pressure; like many cathedral chapters in a similar position, the Templar electors were well aware of the result required. However, in 1311, a knight called Hugh of Faure claimed that James of Molay had forced the Order to accept him as successor to Theobald Gaudin against the wishes of the majority. In this man's version, Molay had been given the key position of Grand Commander on the understanding that he had no ambition to be Master himself, and had taken an oath to this effect before John of Villiers, Grand Master of the Hospital, and the famous crusader knight, Odo of Grandison, to this effect. The majority had then expected to see the election of Hugh of Pairaud, the Visitor and senior Templar in the west, but Molay had forestalled them by declaring himself to be the new Master on the grounds that the Grand Commander was in effect the head of the Order. 'And thus by oppression it was done', alleged Hugh of Faure.[28] This witness needs to be treated with some scepticism, for his deposition shows a strong tendency to repeat gossip and embroider stories, but he had had experience in the east and it is possible that he had picked up rumours of a disputed election, even if events did not follow the course which he describes. As the Rule says, such discussions should be kept secret, otherwise 'great scandal and great hatred may spring from it'.[29]

Once elected, considerable power lay within the Master's discretion, although within strictly defined limits. He could, for instance, redistribute resources between the various castles and houses if, in his judgement, it was necessary, and indeed the Rule lays down that he was to pay close attention to the condition of these places as he rode from one to another. Donations made to the house as alms and presents sent from the west to Templar brothers who had since died were distributed at his discretion. Nevertheless, he was not an autocrat. Major decisions over whether to make war or agree to a truce, whether to alienate land or acquire a castle, who should be appointed to positions of command, who should be sent to the west either because of illness or for administrative reasons, or who could be received into the Order, could only be taken in consultation with the Chapter. Similarly, although he was entitled to withdraw up to 3,000 *besants* from the treasury if he was intending to go to Tripoli or Antioch, he could do so only with the permission of the Commander of the Kingdom of Jerusalem, 'who is Treasurer of the convent and who should keep and guard the keys of the treasury'. The Chapter was made up of a range of senior officials: the Seneschal, the Marshal, the Commander of the Kingdom of Jerusalem, the Commander of the City of Jerusalem, the Commander of Acre, the Draper, and the Commanders of Tripoli and Antioch. In addition, by this time, provincial masters had been designated for the regions which, by the 1160s, were considered to be the main centres of Templar strength: France, England, Poitou, Aragon, Portugal, Apulia, and Hungary. It seems unlikely, though, that these men made much contribution to the deliberations of the General Chapter; indeed, the Rule lays down that they must not come to the east except when instructed to by the Master and Chapter.[30] Occasionally, a matter went beyond the Master and Chapter to the pope, as in the case of Stephen of Sissey, who, as Marshal, had led the Templar contingent which had been so disastrously defeated by the Turcomans in 1261.[31] It may be significant that the Marshal was the only senior Templar to escape, but whatever the reason the Grand Master seems to have held him responsible for the defeat. Thomas Bérard took away his habit and sent him to Rome for judgement. Although the Marshal resisted papal jurisdiction, both Urban IV and his successor Clement IV insisted on their ultimate right and, in 1265, he was eventually obliged to submit to papal authority.[32]

The Seneschal acted as the Grand Master's deputy. He carried the black-and-white banner, represented in the thirteenth-century drawing of Matthew Paris as a simple oblong, attached vertically to a pole or spear.[33] Sometimes, the white ground had superimposed upon it the characteristic eight-pointed red cross of the Order, as shown in a frieze of a great battle depicted in the church of San Bevignate at Perugia.[34] Like the Master, he had his own staff and horses. The Marshal was almost as important, for he was head of the military establishment, responsible for the individual commanders, the horses, arms, and equipment, and possessor of wide powers of purchase, requisition, and distribution. The Commander of the Kingdom of Jerusalem was treasurer of the Order, in charge of the strong room, his powers shared with the Grand Master in such a way as to prevent either of them having too much control over funds. The Grand Master, for instance, could keep a lockable strongbox in the treasury, but was not allowed to hold the key to the room as a whole. Anything received by the Commander was first seen by the Master and then recorded in writing, so that the list was available for inspection. All the non-military booty, such as pack-animals and slaves, was controlled by the Commander, as well as the houses, villages, and *casals* which the Templars held, and their ships and storage vaults at Acre. The Draper issued clothes and bed linen and he could also distribute gifts made to the Order. Equally, he would withdraw and remove items when he considered that an individual Templar had more than was proper, for he was not simply a keeper of the robes, but also had the duty of ensuring that the brothers were dressed 'decently', as the Rule puts it. These five officials seem to have been 'the high men' of the Order, although their exact relationship in the chain of command is not completely clear. The Draper, for example, was obliged to obey the Commander of the Land of Jerusalem when that official required something from him, but he is also described as being 'superior to all other brothers' after the Master and the Marshal.[35]

Beneath these officials stood commanders with specific regional responsibilities: the Commander of the City of Jerusalem, whose knights protected pilgrims going to and from the Jordan and guarded the True Cross when it was transported, and who was in charge of those secular knights serving the Order for a set term, and the Commanders of Tripoli and Antioch with overall responsibility for their regions, especially for ensuring that their castles were in a proper state of readiness. In addition, there was a Commander of the Knights, who acted as deputy to the Commander of the Land of Jerusalem, and a number of knight commanders who administered specific houses in the east.[36] Other specialist officials were the Turcopolier, in charge of the light turcopole cavalry who acted both as auxiliaries and scouts, the Under-Marshal, who managed those whom the Rule calls 'the craftsmen brothers of the stable', the Standard Bearer, responsible for the engagement and discipline of the squires, and the Infirmarer, who looked after the welfare of the sick and aged brothers. All these men seem to have been drawn from the knightly class, except for the Under-Marshal and the Standard Bearer, whose tasks were essentially concerned with the Order's artisans, the craftsmen and the squires.[37] A sergeant could also command a specific house or fortress, provided this did not place any knights under his control and, under the name *casalier* brother, could act as administrator of the villages and farms of the Order.[38]

Generally, this theoretical structure seems to have been implemented in practice. Andrew of Montbard, for example, Seneschal from about 1149, commanded the Order in the east while the Grand Master, Everard des Barres, was in France between 1149 and 1152, and he duly became Grand Master after Bernard of Tremelay's death in 1153.[39] However, some individuals are less easy to place in the hierarchy. One of the most interesting is Geoffrey Fulcher, who had probably joined the Temple by 1144, and had risen to senior rank by the mid 1150s when, in a document which can probably be placed in 1156, he appears without title, but immediately after the Grand Master in the list of signatories. In two further documents, probably from 1164, he is described as 'procurator' and 'preceptor' respectively. He acted as an emissary to Louis VII of France in 1163 and to the Egyptian caliphate in 1167. He was still alive in the 1170s, when he served as Commander of the Order's houses in the west, but neither his functions nor his rather general titles accord very closely with the offices set out in the Rule, even though it seems to have been written up at about this time.[40]

The rank and file of the Templar army were either knights or sergeants, their status largely depending upon their social standing in secular life before entry. New entrants handed over their outside clothes to the Draper and were then provided with a standard set of armour, clothing, and equipment. For knights, armour ranged from a helmet and a mailed hauberk covering the head and body down to the iron hose and *solerets* which protected the legs and feet. The mail was reinforced by *espaliers* which appear to be metal shoulder protectors, and the whole outfit was worn over a padded jacket, probably made of leather. Weapons consisted of a sword, shield, lance, a 'Turkish' mace (apparently with a fixed metal head with spikes at the end of a long haft), as well as a dagger, a bread-knife, and a pocket-knife for more everyday use. In addition, the basic clothing issue included two shirts, two pairs of breeches, and two pairs of hose, a small belt to tie over the shirt, a jerkin, two white robes (one with fur for winter use), a heavy cloak like a cape, a short-sleeved tunic worn on top of the shirt, and a leather belt. Each knight was allowed three horses and a squire and, at the Master's discretion, an additional horse and squire. Horse blankets and a ration of barley for the mounts were provided.[41] The allocation of a squire was essential, for his function was to support the fighting knight by looking after his armour and equipment and horses. This was not a chivalric role, but a relationship of master and servant, for although bound by a specific set of regulations and subject to a disciplinary regime which could include being placed in irons and flogging, they were not members of the Order as such, but outsiders hired for a set period.[42] As well as providing him with this essential back-up, great care was also taken to ensure that the knight possessed the right equipment, especially for campaigning, when he might spend many days and nights in the field. All knights were required to carry portable bedding, including a straw-filled bag to use as a mattress, blankets, sheets, a rug, and storage bags. They needed, too, cooking and eating utensils, as well as the vital drinking flasks and cups, without which any prolonged *chevauchées* would have been impossible in a climate in which temperatures even in Jerusalem, which is relatively cool compared to many other places in this region, often reach 35°C (95°F) in high summer. Moreover, rainfall is so low in many areas to the east and south of Jerusalem that desert conditions prevail.

Unlike the knights, granted the privilege of white mantles, the sergeants wore a black tunic with a red cross on the front and back and a black or brown mantle. Their armour was less elaborate, consisting of an iron cap, a sleeveless coat of mail and hose without feet, reflecting their actual military function which rarely involved the cavalry actions of the knights. Only the five sergeants who held positions of authority in the east – the Under-Marshal, the Standard Bearer, the brother Cook of the convent, the Farrier, and the Commander of the Vault of the Sea at Acre – were entitled to two horses and a squire. Ordinary sergeants had one horse each. They appear to have been more racially mixed than the knights, who were drawn exclusively from the Latin Christians, whereas there were sergeants of Armenian and Syrian birth, as well as those of mixed parentage.[43] The most important distinction between knights and sergeants was, however, one of social background, and indeed as the role and legal status of knighthood became more clearly defined within society as a whole in the course of the twelfth and thirteenth centuries, the Templar knights hardened almost into a caste. It was necessary to be of knightly descent to wear the white mantle even in the middle of the twelfth century;[44] by the 1260s the community in which St Bernard had claimed that there was no distinction of persons had made lying about one's social position in secular life at the time of entry an offence punishable by expulsion. The Templar who drew up the examples of the application of the penance system at the end of the Rule cited the following case:

It happened that we had a knight brother, and there were brothers from his country who said that he was neither the son of a knight nor of knightly lineage, and these words were so serious for the house that it was fitting they should come before chapter. And these same brothers said that if he were present he would be found guilty; so the brothers agreed to send for him, for he was in Antioch. And the Master sent for him, and when he had come to the first chapter he attended, he rose and said before the Master that he had heard the words which were said about him. And the Master ordered those who had said the words to rise, and they rose, and he was found guilty of the fact that his father was neither a knight nor of knightly lineage; so his white mantle was taken from him and he was given a brown mantle.

The offence was seen as sufficiently serious for the receptor to be summoned from the west to explain himself, and he avoided expulsion only by showing that he had acted on the orders of the Commander of Poitou.[45]

Among the sergeants themselves there may possibly have been a further gradation. The Rule shows that they were intended to form an integral part of the Templar fighting force, but this did not necessarily apply to all of them. The trial depositions demonstrate that, in the west, there was an extensive class of artisan Templars, identified by the trial notaries as *serviens* or serving brothers, often of an age and physical condition which would have precluded serious military activity.[46] The term *serviens* is not used in the Rule, but references to 'the craftsmen brothers of the stables' and 'mason brothers', as well as to blacksmiths and cooks, underline the obvious fact that such functions were equally necessary in the east as well,[47] a difference apparently recognised in the use of the terms *frere sergent* and *frere de mestier*.[48] Even so, the designations *sergens* and *serviens* do not seem to have been used to indicate two separate groups within the sergeant class, as they were in the Hospital.[49] In the proceedings against the Templars in Cyprus in 1310, only three Templars are described as *serviens* and two of these are called *sergens* as well, with no attempt at consistency; one of them, Abraham of Chastel-Blanc, is actually called a *faber sergens*, a sergeant blacksmith, a function he apparently performed at the Order's castle in the County of Tripoli.[50] Generally, the term *sergens* is used in the east, and *serviens* in France, a difference which may be one of notarial and scribal usage rather than a reflection of hierarchy.

Most knights were trained in individual fighting skills and many were very experienced warriors when they joined the Order, often honed in the many tournaments which particularly characterised French and English society, and in long-running conflicts such as those between the Angevins and Capetians and the Hohenstaufen and the Italian cities. They were perhaps less familiar with the needs of disciplined and sustained communal action, except when led by commanders of exceptional ability and strength of character such as Richard the Lionheart or William Marshal. Not surprisingly, therefore, the practical nature of a Rule (which even specified the need to carry a spoon among the knight's equipment) was particularly evident in the methods set down for pitching camp, organising knights into squadrons, and controlling the cavalry charge. For the purposes of setting up camp, each knight with his squires, horses, and equipment formed a unit, placing his tent in relation to the chapel, which acted as the assembly point if the alarm were raised. No movement away from the camp was allowed, unless the Templar concerned was within earshot or had express permission. All military manoeuvres from loading up to the actual cavalry charge were strictly subject to orders from the Marshal. Once assembled they were divided into squadrons from which no brother was allowed to leave without permission, even if he was wounded, except 'if it happens by chance that any Christian acts foolishly, and any Turk attacks him in order to kill him', in which case he could go to the rescue, returning to his squadron as unobtrusively as possible afterwards. Once the time for a cavalry charge drew near, the Marshal took up the banner, which was vital to the Templars' battle order especially during the mêlée which usually followed a charge. So important was the banner that a special guard of ten knights was placed around it and the precaution was taken of carrying a second folded banner, which could be raised if anything happened to the first one. In no circumstances should it be lowered to be used as a weapon; any Templar who did this ran the risk of losing the habit and being put in irons. No Templar should ever leave the field while the piebald banner was still to be seen, whatever the overall military situation; disobeying this fundamental tenet meant 'he will be expelled from the house for ever'. If the banner was eventually brought down, the Templars should seek to rally first to that of the Hospitallers and, failing that, to any Christian banner. Only after all these had disappeared could they leave the field without fear of consequent punishment.[51]

The anonymous pilgrim who so admired the skill and bravery of the Templars in battle was, however, equally impressed by their submission to a rigorous monastic rule. Indeed, faced with the problem of defining the Templars, St Bernard had decided that they were both monks and knights, since they combined the balancing qualities of monastic mildness and knightly strength.[52] According to the reports of the pilgrims John of Würzburg and Theoderich during the 1160s and 1170s, the Templars were laying the foundations of a large new church at right angles to the north end of the al-Aqsa mosque.[53] Although the loss of the Temple area in 1187 meant that this project was never completed, it seems that they intended to build here on a lavish scale. The church would have run across the Temple platform to the west of the al-Aqsa and, together with the vaulted halls along the western and southern sides, would have enclosed a large square or cloister, an arrangement which could not have failed to impress western visitors. The discovery in this area of the remains of limestone blocks with Templar inscriptions which were probably part of a vertical wall face, together with the existence of a flourishing workshop on the Templar platform capable of producing very high quality sculpture, suggests decoration in the manner planned for the contemporary Church of the Annunciation at Nazareth.[54]

The failure to complete their great church was partially offset by the building of important churches in the great castles, where they formed the focal points of the communities established there, just as the temporary churches and portable altars did when the Templars were on campaign. At Chastel-Blanc, where the chapel was appropriately dedicated to St Michael the Archangel in keeping with his image among Latin Christians as the smiter of the Devil and his minions, the church was in the centre of the enclosure, built into the walls of the formidable keep on the ground floor. It was 23.6 metres in length, divided into three bays each with a cylindrical vault, with a nave 10.2 metres wide, vaulted to a height of 13.5 metres. The end of the apse and the two square sacristies which flanked it were embedded in a wall four metres thick, pierced by loopholes at the end of the apse and along the sides of the nave, an arrangement which eloquently affirmed the dual nature of the Templar profession. It appears to have been built in the last quarter of the twelfth century, with some restoration after the earthquake of 1202.[55] Early in 1217, during a preaching tour aimed at re-creating the spirit of the First Crusade, James of Vitry, Bishop of Acre, gave a sermon there, before going on to the Templars' castle by the sea at Tortosa, where he celebrated mass and baptised two Muslims.[56] Unlike Chastel-Blanc, the chapels at both 'Atlīt and Safad were built in the knowledge of the loss of the Templar area at Jerusalem, knowledge which may have influenced their scale and design. At 'Atlīt the builders incorporated a large round church more than thirty metres across in the south-west corner of the inner enceinte. The shape was formed from twelve sides built around a central pillar from which the vaulting fanned outwards, creating a structure not unlike the Constantinian rotunda in the Holy Sepulchre, which it appears to have been broadly imitating.[57] At Safad the chapel stood on one of the most elevated positions within the castle, built inside the circular tower on the south-eastern part of the inner ward. It seems to have been octagonal in shape and covered by a dome by means of which it was lit. Around the walls were niches containing statues, the most prominent of which represented St George, seen by the victorious Mamluks in 1266 as idols to be smashed.[58]

The tower at Safad needs detailed archaeological investigation before the exact nature of the chapel can be known, but it probably did not differ greatly from the polygonal and round churches built by the Templars in many of their western preceptories. At Tomar in Portugal and at Segovia in Castile they had striking round chapels, each of which had a central lantern within which was the sanctuary. At Segovia, this lantern enclosed an upper floor which formed the chapel in which a fragment of the True Cross was kept. On a smaller scale, at the preceptory at Laon, north-east of Paris, a narthex with open arches leads into an hexagonal chapel dating from the twelfth century (see plate 8). Both the great centres at London and Paris had large round churches, later extended with rectangular choirs. Although the Parisian example no longer exists, the Temple Church just off the Strand in London, consecrated in 1185 by Heraclius, Patriarch of Jerusalem, remains an elegant example of the English Transitional style. The Templars did not build as lavishly as this in every preceptory, but they did attempt to provide a chapel to enable the members of the local house to observe the canonical hours as laid down by the Rule, rectangular in shape and plain in decoration in the Cistercian manner. Many of these were in small rural preceptories where they formed one side of a square, with the refectory, domestic buildings, and stabling on the other sides, not dissimilar to a small version of a Cistercian monastery.[59] In the walled enclosure which formed the Templar house at Montsaunès, at the confluence of the Sarlat and the Garonne in the Pyrenees, the church divided the military and domestic offices to the north from the cemetery and presbytery garden to the south. Public access to the church, which served the parish as well as the Order, was by the west door, while the Templars had a separate entrance to the north side. A smaller south door led into the cemetery (see figure 10).[60]

After 1139, when the bull *Omne datum optimum* permitted the

Plate 8 Chapel of the Templar preceptory at Laon (Aisne).

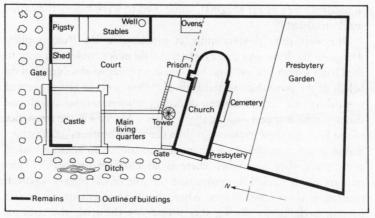

Figure 10 Plan of the Templar house at Montsaunès
(Haute-Garonne).

Templars to have priests both 'in your principal house as well as in the dependencies and places subject to you',[61] these churches were served by the Order's own clergy. The chaplains wore a closed robe and were clean-shaven, and they were given an honoured place in the house: the best robes, a place next to the Grand Master at table, the privilege of being served first. For lesser offences their penances were moderated: while other brothers did menial labour, they said the psalter, 'instead of working'.[62] In these circumstances any misrepresentation of status was commensurately serious. Among the examples of transgressions given in the later part of the Rule was one of a brother who had himself made a sub-deacon, an offence for which he was expelled from the Order.[63] These chaplains conducted services, heard confessions, gave absolution for certain offences, and buried the dead. Some became preceptors of local houses, especially in France. However, given the nature of the Order, they never gained the kind of influence which made the clerical element so important in other monastic orders, nor did many of them progress far in the Church as a whole. Examples of Templar priests who reached archiepiscopal or episcopal rank are very rare,[64] a sharp contrast to the numbers of Cistercians, Franciscans, and Dominicans who became prelates of the Church. There are signs of discontent, for even among the priests serving a fixed term (which was possible in the same way as for knights), some tried to leave before their time was completed.[65]

Nor were their powers quite as extensive as the Rule implies. Although the Rule says that brothers should make confession only to the Order's own priests, who had 'greater power to absolve them on behalf of the pope than an archbishop',[66] they were in fact prevented from absolving major offences, including murder, serious assault and simony, which appertained to the diocesans. Moreover, the insistence of the Rule on their exclusive right to hear the brothers' confessions was in practice modified by permission to confess to another 'out of a great necessity and when there is no chaplain brother'.[67] Thus military needs tended to marginalise the role of the priests, again in contrast to most other orders, where the clerical element was in fact gaining in influence during this period. At the trial, the issue of confession became a matter of extreme interest to the Order's accusers, for if it could be shown that the Templars never made confession to outsiders, then the allegation that the Order maintained tight secrecy to cover up its heresy would be strengthened. In fact, the Templars claimed that they confessed to a variety of other clerics, including the Patriarch of Jerusalem, local bishops, Franciscans, and Austin canons. Naturally, the Templars would be anxious to show this in the face of the accusation of secret heresy, but if the convincing description of the close links which the Templars maintained with the Carmelite friars during the thirteenth century is any guide, then the claims appear to be true. The Carmelites, whose convent was in the valley of Nahal Siah, south of Haifa, on the western slopes of the Mount Carmel ridge, were situated only about twenty-five kilometres from the castle of 'Atlīt, and these links emerge very clearly in the depositions made by the Templars before the Bishop of Clermont in 1309. A priest, Bernard of Villars, correctly told his questioners that, when they were available, the Templars confessed to the Order's own priests only. Otherwise, they turned to the Carmelites because 'as he heard, they had great friendship in parts beyond the sea with brothers of the Order'. Another witness, the sergeant, John Cenaud, who had seen service in Outremer, said that 'beyond the sea the Carmelite brothers received a tenth part of the victuals that the brothers of the Temple expended at Pilgrims' Castle ['Atlīt], on account of which they held these brothers friends and confidants'.[68]

Unlike the Cistercians, however, from the beginning, the Templars needed to publicise their activities both to gain recruits and to attract donations, for the defence of the holy places was prodigal with manpower and hugely expensive. James of Molay was proud of this public face, claiming that he did not know of 'any other Order in which the chapels and churches . . . had better or more beautiful ornaments and reliquaries relating to the divine cult and in which the divine service was better performed by its priests and clerics, except for cathedral churches'.[69] Molay had some justification for this boast, for the Order had considerable appeal to connoisseurs like Henry III of England, who initially had planned to be buried in the Temple Church at London before his attention was captured by the rebuilding of Westminster Abbey.[70] His interest can be seen when, on Ascension Day, 1240, he attended the dedication of the choir extension of the Round Church and the festivities which followed, including a lavish banquet laid on by the Hospitallers.[71]

These churches were often the focus of highly visible religious cults, for the Order, with its extensive eastern connections, built up a large collection of relics. In Outremer it held some particularly powerful specimens. On Holy Thursday, Templar priests held aloft the Crown of Thorns to show it flowering in their hands. At 'Atlīt, among other relics, they kept the heart and body of the virgin and martyr St Euphemia of Chalcedon (d. 303), whose miraculous properties drew in many pilgrims travelling south along the coast road from Acre on their way to Jerusalem.[72] According to tradition, these remains had been miraculously translated to 'Atlīt, a belief which must have added to their potency in the eyes of the faithful, although in fact the dedication of a church to the saint near Caesarea as long ago as the seventh century suggests that the region had been associated with her for many centuries before the time of the crusaders.[73] The Templars also brought out their relics during periods of crisis. In adverse weather conditions, like prolonged drought, they carried their most precious relic, a cross made from a tub or trough in which Christ supposedly bathed, through the streets of Acre in penitential procession. The cross was believed to have curative properties and many sick people came to the Temple church at Acre for this reason.[74] Both these relics were rescued in 1291 and taken to Cyprus. One witness said at the trial that he had seen two reliquary heads decorated with silver at the Temple church at Nicosia, one of which he believed was that of St Euphemia.[75] When the goods of the Temple were transferred to the Hospitallers in 1312, the relics were taken over as well. In the late 1330s, Ludolf of Sudheim saw the large collection held by the Hospitallers at Rhodes which had once belonged to the Templars, including a bronze cross which was believed to have been derived from the bowl used by Jesus Christ to wash the feet of the apostles.[76]

Relics were also used to strengthen links with potential patrons in the west and to maintain interest in the affairs of the Holy Land. In 1247 it was a Templar who brought to London a crystalline phial containing Christ's blood, shed on the Cross, which had been sent by the Masters of the Temple and the Hospital and authenticated by the seals of the Patriarch of Jerusalem and the other prelates of the Holy Land, while in 1272 Thomas Bérard sent to London pieces of the True Cross, together with relics of saints Philip, Helena, Stephen, Laurence, Euphemia, and Barbara.[77] In Castile, the Templars had the church of Segovia built in a striking position in open country outside the north wall of the city specifically to house a fragment of the True Cross (see plate 9), and in Paris on feast days the Order exhibited the relic collection kept at the house, including remains of the famous 11,000 virgins of Cologne.[78] Moreover, because of their role as money-lenders, the Templars often held relics as pledges for loans, and these are not infrequently found in the treasuries of local Templar houses. The reliquary bust of St Policarp appears to have been acquired in this way, pledged by the Abbot of the Temple of the Lord and never reclaimed, while the commune of Zara on the Dalmatian coast handed over a large collection of reliquary arms of saints and crosses to the Master of Hungary and Slavonia in return for a loan, finally redeemed as late as April 1308.[79]

The Templars were particularly well established in those parts of central Italy where there was a strong popular religious sensitivity: the meticulous work of the notaries who recorded the proceedings against the Templars in the Papal State and the Abruzzi in 1309 and 1310 reveals that the Order held twenty-one churches in the region, from Chieti in the east to Rome in the west and north to Gubbio, with a particular concentration of eight around Viterbo and Orvieto.[80] At Perugia in Umbria the church of San Bevignate, built between 1256 and 1262 just outside the Porta Sole under the auspices of the papal chamberlain and Templar brother, Bonvicino, was the

Plate 9 Templar chapel at Segovia, Castile.

assembly point for the great processions of flagellants with which the city became associated from 1260 onwards. San Bevignate was believed to be the patron of penitential flagellation, and inside the church, at the foot of a fresco of the Last Judgement on the south wall, a group of *disciplinati* or flagellants is depicted, among whom is thought to be Raniero Fasani, their leader. The concept of pilgrimage and crusade as penitential activities was given particular focus in Perugia both by the strong desire for peace in the midst of the internecine strife caused by the Guelphs and Ghibellines and by the fears which were generated by news of the Mongol invasions, perhaps channelled into central Italy through the Templar network.[81]

The decoration of the churches often attracted similar attention. In some, like Cressac in the Charente, colourful frescoes dating from the 1170s show Templars and other crusaders riding out to do battle with the Saracens. The scenes may record the victory over Nūr-ad-Dīn near Krak des Chevaliers in 1163, in which two local barons, Hugh of Lusignan, Count of La Marche, and Geoffrey Martel, brother of William Taillefer, Count of Angoulême, took part. The message is reinforced by the depiction on the west wall of the militant St George overcoming the dragon and the symbolic representation of the Church Triumphant welcoming the Emperor Constantine in the form of a woman greeting a knight whose horse is crushing a grimacing figure.[82] The dedication of other churches to St George, as at Ydes in the Auvergne, and the depiction of the martyrdom of St Catherine, as at Metz and Montbellet, suggests that these themes of Christian militancy and sacrifice for the faith were frequently used in Templar churches. The story of St Catherine, indeed, was often reproduced in France and England, having been popularised by the crusaders, who had come into contact with the cult at Mount Sinai, where it had begun in the ninth century.[83] The painting and sculpture on Templar churches was not confined to crusading subjects, but there are recognisable connections with the Order's self-image reflected in an interest in the cult of the Virgin (which went back to the Temple's early links with St Bernard), Christ triumphant, and the apostles and saints of the New Testament, especially those who had suffered martyrdom.[84] The church at Montsaunès is a case in point. Although part of a relatively modest preceptory, it was situated close to the important route between Toulouse and Bayonne, and the Order seems to have gone to considerable trouble to provide sculpture for the portals and frescoes for the interior. On the west portal, that is, the public face of the church, the archivolt has a striking collection of fifty-two human heads: at the top of the arch, beneath a labarum, the faces are severe, but on either side they become progressively more grotesque and tormented, apparently because they are farther from God, perhaps even damned. The capitals above the door jambs show the martyrdom of the apostles: on the left the decapitation of Paul, the crucifixion of Peter, and the stoning of Stephen, and on the right, scenes of miracles from the life of Christ, themes which in combination illustrate the Christian triumph over death. The north portal, used by the brothers themselves, is devoted to the Virgin, presenting a chronological sequence from the Annunciation to the Adoration of the Magi, culminating in the Virgin and Child in majesty. The frescoes of the interior are badly damaged, and it is less easy to discern overall themes. Many of the motifs are geometrical rather than figurative, but there is nevertheless a depiction of the Last Judgement, as well as images of a wide range of prophets, apostles, and saints, each framed individually by round arches painted on the walls.[85]

The great fortress-like church of San Bevignate at Perugia, with overall dimensions of 39.5 metres by 17.5 metres and a maximum height of 27 metres, offered particular scope for an extensive programme of fresco decoration (see plate 10). Although much of this has been lost, sufficient survives to form a good idea of the impact that these images would have had upon a local populace accustomed to use San Bevignate not only for the Flagellant gatherings but also as their parish church. San Bevignate is a characteristic Templar church, built as a large rectangle, very open internally, and finishing in the east with a square apsidal chapel, adjacent to which was a large campanile. It seems to have replaced a smaller church, dedicated to St Jerome, which was at or near this site. Initially it was one of two Templar centres in Perugia, but some time between 1283 and 1285 the Order lost its other base at San Guistino d'Arno in a dispute with the local Benedictines, and was obliged to develop the San Bevignate site with a large complex of monastic buildings on the south side, all of which was probably enclosed by a perimeter wall.[86]

Possibly four different hands can be discerned in the fresco decoration, three of whom worked on the church during the initial

Plate 10 The Templar church of San Bevignate, Perugia.

phase of construction at the site.[87] The frescoes reflect the dual aspects
of Templar life. The religious themes are particularly striking and
suggest that in this region at least the idea that the Temple was an
order which lacked much spiritual content needs reassessing. At the
top of the main wall of the apse are shown the Virgin and Child
enthroned, flanked by angels, and below them, on either side of the
window, the signs of the Four Evangelists. At the base in the centre,
directly behind the altar, is the Crucifixion, with the body of Christ
twisted and suffering in the contemporary Umbrian and Tuscan
manner. On the left wall of the apse is the Last Supper, while the
large expanse of the right wall, which is not interrupted by window
openings, is dominated by the Last Judgement. Around 1280,

perhaps under the influence of William Charnier who, as *hostarius* to Pope Nicholas III and administrator of Templar property in the region, was Bonvicino's natural successor, the Order had a new series of figures of the twelve apostles painted at intervals around the walls of the apse and the nave. Liturgical activities more specifically related to the Order can be seen in illustrations of revered Christian figures such as Mary Magdalene and the saints Laurence and Stephen on the left wall beneath the Last Supper, whose feast days were among those which the Rule lays down should be observed within the Order.[88] The particular local connections are shown in the bottom right hand corner of the apse wall which depicts a scene from the life of the hermit San Bevignate himself, where he is shown being blessed by a bishop who is apparently granting him the site where his church will be built. As well as this, above the pointed arch at the east end of the nave which leads into the apse, amid an elaborate set of decorative patterns, appear fragments of a story of a miracle attributed to the hermit, who revived a child savaged to death by a wolf.

The west wall, often reserved for the Last Judgement elsewhere in Italian churches, is more overtly Templar propaganda. Three scenes stand out from the surviving images. To the left of the window is a dramatic painting of a Templar galley at sea, its provenance marked by the two black and white banners on the prow (see plate 11). Pilgrims travelling to the Holy Land are in the care of a watchful crew, including three men crowded into the crow's nest at the top of the mast. Above the ship to the right is a closed book held in the talons of an eagle, evidently symbolising the protection of St John for those who embarked on Templar ships. At another level the ship can also be seen to represent the Church which, even though tossed in the storms of the material world, is able to offer the opportunity of salvation to those who will put their trust in her.[89] Below this scene, amid waving palms, a lion raises itself towards a group of white-robed monks standing on a loggia in their convent (see plate 12). The point may be to show that the Order could withstand the assaults of the enemies of the faith, symbolised here by the lion. In the Latin Rule hunting is forbidden to the Templars as being a frivolous occupation; the one exception is the lion since 'he goes around seeking whom he can devour' and 'his hand is against all, and the hand of all is against him' (1 Peter 5:8).[90] Moreover, since the

Plate 11 Templar ship, third master of San Bevignate, west wall.
Fresco showing Templars transporting and protecting pilgrims.

leading monk is reaching out towards the lion in a manner reminiscent of St Jerome who, when he lived at Bethlehem had extracted a thorn from a lion's paw, the Order may have intended to reinforce the point through an evocation of the saint to whom the original chapel had been dedicated. Then, finally, in the long frieze stretching right across the west wall beneath the window, is a dynamic battle scene, as at Cressac, with crusaders and Muslims in fierce combat, and Templar shields and banners much in evidence. The battle in this case may have been the attack by the Templars upon Nablus in 1242, in which they sacked the town and burnt the mosque there, an exploit to which the Templars gave considerable publicity in the west.[91]

Plate 12 Templar convent, third master of San Bevignate,
west wall. Fresco symbolising the role of the Templars in the
defence of Chritendom.

However, the Templars' need for a high profile had to be balanced
with their objectives as monks. To a greater or lesser extent, all
religious orders reflected a desire by their entrants to enhance their
chances of salvation by escaping from the temptations and corrup-
tions of secular life. Cistercians and Carthusians tried to achieve this
by seeking out isolated places, free from the clamour of men's daily
concerns. The Templars, too, were mindful of the problem. Oliver
of Paderborn believed that the Order had established itself at 'Atlīt
not simply for military purposes, but also to retreat from what the
community saw as the sin and filth of Acre.[92] Inside 'Atlīt, their

oratory and associated buildings made up a monastic complex encased by the defensive shell of the castle. Here they followed the pattern of the monastic round as laid down by the Rule, just as they had done in the Temple at Jerusalem and, according to Oliver, intended to do again when the holy city was recaptured.

When the Templars were not on campaign or were established in preceptories in non-combatant areas in the west, therefore, the Rule laid down a manner of conventual life centred upon the canonical hours not dissimilar from the daily round of other monks. Clause 279 sets out this obligation without ambiguity:

Each brother of the Temple should know that he is not committed to anything so much as to serve God, and each one should apply all his study and understanding to this, and especially to hearing His holy office; for none should fail or be lacking in this, as long as he is content in it. For as our Rule says, if we love God, we should willingly hear and listen to His holy words.[93]

The day began with attendance at matins which in the summer would have been at about 4.00 a.m., where the brothers heard or recited thirteen paternosters, followed by prime at 6.00 a.m. and the hearing of mass, terce at 8.00 a.m., and sext at 11.30 a.m. A brief sleep was permitted between matins and prime, provided everything had been attended to, at the end of which they would be summoned by the bell which determined the divisions of the day. By late morning each brother should have said sixty paternosters for the benefactors of the house 'that is to say thirty for the dead, that God may deliver them from the pains of Purgatory and place them in Paradise, and the other thirty for the living, that God may deliver them from sin and pardon them the sins they have committed, and lead them to a fine end'. Sext was followed by the first meal of the day, usually taken in two sittings, the first for knights, the second for sergeants. Whenever possible, a priest gave the blessing and during the meal a clerk read a holy lesson, while the brothers ate in silence. Afterwards they went to the chapel to give thanks. Nones at 2.30 p.m. and vespers at 6.00 p.m. divided the afternoon, followed by supper, the second meal of the day. The final office was compline, where the assembled brothers drank communally, either water or diluted wine. Sleep followed and silence was observed from compline to matins the following morning. During winter the offices were compressed, for matins could not begin before daybreak and compline then usually took place about 6.15 p.m.[94] The only brothers exempted from immediate attendance in the chapel at the ringing of the bell were the sick, the brother in charge of the oven, 'if he has his hands in pastry', the brother in charge of the large forge, 'if he has iron burning in the fire', and the blacksmith, if he was preparing to shoe a horse. Even so, as soon as they had finished they were required to go to the chapel and listen to the hours being sung or say them to themselves if they were unable to do this.[95]

In many of the Order's houses, therefore, the Templar's day differed little from that of his Benedictine counterpart; indeed, as in the Rule of St Benedict, there was even provision for him to be released from a command if he felt unable to do it, or that it was unreasonable.[96] Nevertheless, in the east and in Spain he remained simultaneously a monk and a soldier on active service. Attendance at the hours was not only necessary for the purposes of devotion, but was essential for practical reasons, 'because it is customary in the Order that appeals or commands are issued at the end of the hours, except compline'.[97] Fitness was also important. While extensive fasting might have been appropriate for the Cistercians, it would have left members of the military orders too weak to fight. Archaeological evidence does not suggest that the Templars had a lavish diet,[98] but it needed to be good enough to ensure that the Templar did not appear on the battlefield in the enfeebled condition of the knight satirised by James of Vitry in his *exempla*, who had fasted so much on bread and water that he was useless for combat.[99] The Rule mentions beef, mutton, veal, goatsmeat, trout, eels, cheese, and vegetables – including beans, lentils, and cabbage – as being part of the diet at one time or another, and as the Order kept pigs and hens, and cultivated kitchen gardens, they must have consumed the products from these too.[100] Combat readiness equally meant care and attention to horses and equipment; after matins and compline the knight was obliged to check these, consult his squire if necessary, and to attend to any repairs that were needed. Strict rules concerning the use and treatment of the animals were imposed, for horses were not for racing or galloping, nor should a knight favour one horse over another. Consequently, the Templars' reputation for expertise in the care of horses was high, for outsiders sent their own sick animals to be treated by them.[101] The nature of Templar life in the combat areas is brought home very clearly by the regulations on conduct during meals; among the limited number of reasons for leaving meals without permission were disturbance among the horses and a call to arms.[102] During the trial, one serving brother, Bertrand Guasc from Rodez, described how he was actually being received into the Order at Sidon when the ceremony was interrupted by a Saracen attack to which the brothers immediately reacted, while even those brothers undergoing penance were obliged to join the troop when an emergency threatened, although the penance still had to be completed afterwards.[103] But the conflicting demands of monastic and military life were most acute on the occasions when the Templars were not in the house at all, but out on campaign, away from the bells and the regular incantations of the hours. At such times they recited a set number of paternosters as a substitute, but as far as possible 'they should behave in eating, rising, reading the lesson and in everything else' as they would in the convent.[104] But nowhere is the difference between the military orders and their Benedictine contemporaries brought out more clearly than in the injunctions on how to spend spare time. Both see idleness as a tool for the Devil: 'the Enemy assails more boldly and more willingly with evil desires and vain thoughts and mean words, a lazy man than he does one whom he finds busy in good work', says the Templar Rule. But, while the Rule of St Benedict encourages the monks to use their time in quiet contemplation and reading, the Templars, having fulfilled all their duties, including any repairs needed to armour and equipment, 'should make tent-posts or pegs or anything else that befits their office'.[105]

All this occurred within the overall structure of the Christian year, in which the key periods of Advent, Christmas, Lent, and Easter, and the important saints' days, necessarily modified the usual daily pattern, both by the addition of extra services and the imposition of fasts.[106] Set rituals were followed on special occasions. On Ash Wednesday, 'all the brothers should receive ashes on their heads; which ashes the chaplain brother should place there, or another priest if they cannot have a chaplain brother, in remembrance that we are ashes and to ashes we shall return'.[107] Maundy Thursday was similarly marked out. When mass and vespers had been sung the Almoner supplied thirteen paupers with hot water and towels:

And the brothers should wash the paupers' feet and dry them with the towels, and afterwards kiss their feet humbly. And let it be known that the Almoner should ensure that those paupers who are washed do not have any vile diseases on their feet or legs; for perhaps it could bring illness to a brother's body. And while this service is performed, the priest and the clerk should wear the surplice and carry the cross, and say such prayers as are customary in the house on that day. And afterwards, the commander of the house, if there is no one more senior, should give each pauper who has been washed two loaves of bread, a pair of new shoes and two deniers.

This was done before the brothers ate and then, when it was nearly time for compline, a rattle was shaken:

at the sound of this rattle the brothers should assemble in the palace just as they would if the bell were rung; and the priest and the clerk should also go to the palace, and should carry the cross. And then a priest or clerk should read the gospel to the palace, that which it is customary to read on that day, and he should read it without a title; and he may be seated while he reads if he wishes, but he should be fully dressed; and when he has read for a while he may rest. And the sergeants should bring wine to the brothers, and the brothers may drink if they wish; and when they have drunk, the one who is reading should read what remains of the gospel. And when the gospel is finished, the brothers and the priest and clerk should go to the chapel; and the priests should wash the altars, and afterwards they should sprinkle wine over the altars. And then it is customary in the house for all the brothers to go and pray at the altars and kiss them, and each brother should wipe a little of that diluted wine which is sprinkled on the altars, over his lips, and he should drink it.[108]

Then they reached the climax of Good Friday, when 'all the brothers should pray at the cross with great devotion; and when they go to the cross they should be barefoot. And on that day they should fast on bread and water and eat without a napkin.'[109]

Nobody was supposed to enter this society without proof of serious intent and, indeed, if a brother was found to have lied about his status during his reception, this was considered to be as serious as the nine specific offences listed in the Rule which could lead to his expulsion.[110] At the end of the Rule there is a self-contained section setting out 'how a brother should be made and received into the Temple'. This was probably written down about 1260, but it is unlikely that reception ceremonies had been substantially different during the Order's earlier history. As in the marriage ceremony, the rituals of the reception were designed to emphasise the gravity of the undertaking. The receptor, who was sometimes the local commander, sometimes a higher official on circuit like the Visitor, assembled the brothers of the house in chapter and asked if they knew of any reasons why the postulant should not be admitted. If there were no objections, then the entrant was taken to a separate room, where two or three of the experienced men of the house explained to him the hardships that he would have to undergo if he entered the Order:

And if he says that he will willingly suffer all for God, and that he wishes to be a serf and slave of the house for ever, all the days of his life, they should ask him if he has a woman as wife or fiancée; or if he has ever made a vow or promise to another order; or if he owes a debt to any secular man which he cannot pay; and if he is healthy in his body, and has no secret illness; or if he is the serf of any man.

When both the chapter and the postulant had once again been asked to confirm their wishes, the man entered the chapter room, knelt before the receptor with hands clasped in the common gesture of homage, and requested admission. The receptor then said:

Good brother, you ask a very great thing, for of our Order you see only the outer appearance. For the appearance is that you see us having fine horses, and good equipment, and good food and drink, and fine robes, and thus it seems to you that you would be well at ease. But you do not know the harsh commandments which lie beneath; for it is a painful thing for you, who are your own master, to make yourself a serf to others. For with great difficulty will you ever do anything that you wish; for if you wish to be in the land this side of the sea, you will be sent the other side; or if you wish to be in Acre, you will be sent to the land of Tripoli or Antioch, or Armenia; or you will be sent to Apulia, or Sicily, or Lombardy, or France, or Burgundy, or England, or to several other lands where we have houses and possessions. And if you wish to sleep, you will be woken; and if you sometimes wish to stay awake, you will be ordered to rest in your bed.

In the case of a sergeant, 'he may be told to carry out one of the basest tasks that we have, perhaps at the oven, or the mill, or in the kitchen, or with the camels, or in the pigsty or several other duties that we have'. Throughout the reception the emphasis was upon the negation of will for the greater good of the Order and for the salvation of the individual's soul. After this the entrant left the room and the receptor asked a third time if there were any reasons why he should not be admitted. The entrant returned and was put through the same series of questions again, great emphasis being placed on the serious consequences should he be lying, for this time he swore on the Gospels. There followed the vows of obedience, chastity, and poverty, and the promise to conquer and defend Jerusalem. He promised never to leave the Order, nor to be the instrument by which any Christian was wrongfully or unreasonably deprived of his property:

And then the one who holds the chapter should take the mantle and should place it round his neck and fasten the laces. And the chaplain brother should say the psalm which is said, *Ecce quam bonum,* and the prayer to the Holy Spirit, and each of the brothers should say the paternoster. And the one who makes him a brother should raise him up and kiss him on the mouth; and it is customary for the chaplain brother to kiss him also.

The postulant then sat before the receptor who explained in more detail the offences for which he could be expelled or given penances and the manner of life he would be expected to follow. 'Now we have told you the things which you should do and what you should guard against, and those which lead to expulsion from the house, and those which lead to loss of the habit, and the other punishments; and we have not told you everything we should tell you, but you will ask it. – And may God let you say and do well.'[111]

The community to which he was being admitted was composed almost entirely of adult males. The admission of women was deemed inappropriate, as was quite unambiguously stated in both the Latin and French Rules.[112] The reception ceremony reinforced this. 'Nor should you ever use the services of a woman, except for an illness of your body, or with the permission of the one who may give it to you; nor should you ever kiss a woman, neither mother nor sister nor any relative you may have, nor any other woman.'[113] There were, therefore, no female houses as in the Hospitaller order in the thirteenth century, despite the evident interest shown in the Temple by female donors.[114] Wives of men who joined the Temple were expected to become nuns, but 'in another order'.[115] The wording of some charters of donation occasionally implies that the women concerned intended to live under the Rule of the local Templar house,[116] but it seems unlikely that these mean more than a wish to live a celibate life as a dependant in the neighbourhood. Nevertheless, complete isolation from the world was not always possible, especially when dealing with the very powerful. Despite Oliver of Paderborn's belief that the Templars had built 'Atlīt as a place of monastic seclusion, it was in this castle that Margaret of Provence, wife of King Louis IX, gave birth in 1251.[117]

The traditional Benedictine orders had admitted children, many of whom were handed over to the monastery while still very young and grew up knowing little of any other life. These oblates were educated in the monastery and benefited from the sustenance and support of the community, even though they were deprived of family life. The monastic reformation of the early twelfth century, of which the military orders were an important part, was not, however, favourable to such a system. The Cistercians prohibited oblates as a distraction, while the Templars needed recruits who had attained the requisite physical strength. Clause fourteen of the Latin Rule allows a theoretical commitment to the Order while under age, but insists that the boy be brought up by his parents until he is of an age when he is able to bear arms with sufficient strength to destroy the enemies of Christ in the Holy Land.[118] Such arrangements can be seen in practice in local Templar preceptories. In 1241, for instance, at the house of Provins, in the County of Champagne, Renaud, son of Odelina, 'healthy and sound and sane in the head, arriving at the years of puberty and free from the tutelage of his parents', confirmed that he wished to enter the Order as his mother had promised when he was still a child.[119] Rates of physical development of course varied. The Provins charter does not state Renaud's age, simply that he had reached adulthood, but the definition of such a state was clearly open to varied interpretation. At the trial one Templar claimed that he was eleven when he joined, and two others that they were only thirteen.[120] Moreover, in April 1148, Alfonso-Jordan, Count of Toulouse, on crusade in the Holy Land, left his fourteen-year-old son, Raymond, in the care of the Templars at Jerusalem, not apparently with the aim of joining him to the Order, but more likely as a way of training him in the martial arts, while he himself took part in the main crusade. The Templars' attitude towards such boys is unknown, but it is clear that they could not afford to offend a man like Alfonso-Jordan, who had granted the Order extensive privileges in his western lands in 1134. Whatever the implications of this situation, it was quickly upset by Alfonso-Jordan's unexpected death on about 15 April, which left Raymond as the new count and necessitated his rapid return to Toulouse.[121] While these boys may have been taller and stronger than average, there is evidence that in relatively isolated preceptories like that of Vaour in Rouergue the rules were broken and children were taken into the house, either for sustenance or in the expectation that they would join the Order when they grew up.[122]

A concomitant of this seems to have been dispensation with a novitiate. During the trial most witnesses said that they had professed at once, presumably because entrants were expected to have reached an age of sufficient maturity to know their own minds. The system of allowing secular knights to serve for a specific term must have been an acceptable alternative in many cases. Clause twelve of the original Latin Rule, however, makes provision for a probationary period and, when, in 1139, the Order had been allowed to take its own priests, the bull *Omne datum optimum* set down that they should be 'proven in your society for the space of one year' before making profession.[123] However, the practice seems to have been dropped quite early in the Order's history. The equivalent clause in the French translation of the Rule omits the sentence on probation, moving it instead to the end of clause fourteen, which forbids the reception of children, and altering the wording from 'term of probation' to 'be put to the test'.[124] This is much less specific and may in fact refer to the rigorous questioning of the reception ceremony rather than a novitiate. This suggests that if any formal system had ever existed, it disappeared during the 1140s and 1150s.

Age was less of a barrier among entrants who might be thought to have passed beyond the stage where they could be active soldiers. Many men joined while middle-aged or even elderly, and were never sent to the east but worked in the Order's western houses.[125] Some, especially those of high social standing, postponed entry until near death with the intention of making 'a good end', as was the custom in more traditional monastic orders. This was sufficiently common for the Rule to allow the Master to admit, 'for the love of God', a worthy man who was 'so ill that it is believed he cannot escape death', the prohibition on admission without consent of the chapter notwithstanding.[126] One of the most famous cases, planned well in advance, was that of William Marshal, Earl of Pembroke and Regent of England during the infancy of Henry III. William was a close friend of Aimery of Saint Maur, Master of the Temple in England and, some years before his death in 1219, he had had a mantle made for the occasion.[127] His recumbent effigy and those of his sons,

Plate 13 Effigies of associates of the Templars in the Temple
Church, London.

William and Gilbert, occupy prominent places in the Round Church
in London (see plate 13). The Templars served the same purposes in
Outremer as well, despite the fact that it was an active crusading
frontier. In 1236 John of Ibelin, 'the Old Lord of Beirut', having
made appropriate arrangements for his dependants and goods, chose
the same path as William Marshal. The pro-Ibelin chronicler, Philip

of Novara, who was present at John's deathbed, described the event in this way:

After this he made himself a brother of the Temple as he had vowed. His children offered great opposition and all the people of the country felt great sorrow therefor, but nought did it avail, for he entered the Temple in spite of them, and that most tranquilly, and had himself taken to Acre. Not long did he remain a brother and at his death so fine an end did he make that only with marvel could one believe the truth which all attested. When he had to surrender his soul he asked that the crucifix be brought to him. Philip de Novare carried it before him and he held out his hands, and he kissed the feet of Our Lord Jesus Christ and said as well as he was able: 'In manus tuas, Domine, commendo spiritum meum.' And thus he rendered his spirit to God. The body did not change in death, and if one believes that good souls go before God, one can be certain that his soul went there to paradise.[128]

Others grew old or ill in the Templars' service. When they felt themselves no longer capable of bearing arms, it was their duty to hand over their equipment and horses, in exchange for which the Marshal should give them 'a gentle, ambling horse'. They should set a good example in all things 'so that especially the young brothers should be mirrored in them, and from the behaviour of the old men the young should learn what behaviour they should adopt'.[129] Sometimes, after due consideration, they were sent back to end their service in one of the Order's western houses.[130] While it was an offence punishable by expulsion to conceal serious illness on entry, especially leprosy and 'that evil disease called epilepsy',[131] the Rule makes extensive provision for those who became ill or were wounded once they were in the Order. Sick brothers were given over to the care of the Infirmarer, who was granted considerable discretion in exempting them from the Order's dietary regulations and from attendance at services. Quartan fever (malaria), dysentery, vomiting, and delirium, as well as serious wounds, were recognised as requiring special treatment, including a separate room if necessary, and outside doctors could be brought in to visit and advise.[132] Leprosy was sufficiently common for afflicted brothers to be offered the opportunity of transfer to the Order of Saint Lazarus, specifically formed as a community of lepers in the 1130s in close association with the Templars, although in the French version of the Rule they were not to be forced to do so. However, by the 1230s the Order of Saint Lazarus had itself assumed military functions, serving as a respectable refuge for both laymen and members of the Order in various stages of the disease.[133] Perhaps both because of this and because of hardening attitudes towards the presence of lepers in society as a whole in the thirteenth century, by the time of the Catalan Rule in the late 1260s it had become obligatory for any Templar judged to have contracted the disease to transfer to Saint Lazarus.[134] The Catalan Rule also takes account of brothers who became 'sick with the disease of demons', who were to be placed apart from the others until cured. There was less tolerance, however, for those who had gone 'out of their senses'. Apparently, the Order could think of no solution other than restraint. They were to be put into irons and placed where they could do no harm to anyone, again until such time as they were judged to be cured.[135]

Although not primarily a charitable order like the Hospital, Templar care was not confined exclusively to its own membership. According to the Rule, 'wherever the Master is, three paupers should eat of the brothers' food, four in each major house or castle, for the love of God and the brothers'.[136] It was customary, too, to feed paupers from the remains of the brothers' own food, the portions being fixed on a generous scale not 'in order that the brothers or sergeants could fill their stomachs, for they could easily abstain, but primarily they were established so large and fine, for love of God and the poor, to give to alms'.[137] The Order also maintained permanent establishments for the poor: at Valania in the County of Tripoli, for example, they provided them with 'bed, fire and water' in their hospital there.[138] John of Würzburg, despite his suspicion of the Order, admitted that they were generous providers of charity to the Christian poor, although in his estimation this did not amount to a tenth of that done by the Hospitallers.[139] While the proportions may be wrong, John was undoubtedly correct in perceiving that the Hospitaller role was much greater, for, as James of Molay pointed out, the Hospital 'had been founded upon hospitality', while the Temple was specifically a military knighthood. Nevertheless, he said that the Temple gave alms three times per week in its *bailliages* and donated a tenth of its bread to paupers. One of his objections to a union was that the quantity of alms would be diminished.[140] The Templars at the trial, questioned closely on this point, generally confirmed this practice,[141] although in one case, at a time of acute famine, this apparently caused a dispute among the brothers.[142] The serving brother, Bertrand Guasc, even claimed the Order had admitted himself and his friends to its ranks when, as pilgrims in the east, they had run out of money, although since the year was 1291, this may reflect the desperate circumstances of the time.[143]

The whole pattern of Templar life was enforced by a detailed schedule of penances, imposed after confession or successful accusation in weekly chapter-meetings.[144] In the most serious cases the Rule lays down the penalty of expulsion. Nine offences justified this: simony, disclosure of the affairs of the chapter, killing a Christian man or woman, certain types of theft, leaving a closed castle or house by an exit other than the one prescribed, conspiracy against other brothers, desertion to the Saracens, heresy, and abandonment of the banner in the course of a battle.[145] In the list of penances which could be imposed at chapter-meetings, which is probably slightly later in date, these are reordered so that the provision concerning secret exit from a closed castle is incorporated under the general heading of theft, a sin which has 'so many branches'.[146] In its place, a new offence was defined, that of sodomy.[147] When the offence was considered to have justified it, the Order's justice could be savage. In the section of the Rule added some time between 1257 and 1267 several examples of actual incidents are given to demonstrate the application of the Order's disciplinary system. Three brothers who had murdered some Christian merchants at Antioch were apprehended and asked why they had done it. They replied that 'sin had made them do it'. After judgement by the convent they were therefore sentenced 'to be expelled from the house and flogged throughout Antioch, Tripoli, Tyre, and Acre. Thus they were flogged and cried, "See the justice which the house exacts from its wicked men", and they were put in perpetual imprisonment at Château Pèlerin and died there.'[148]

Ritual was as important for expulsion as it was for entry:

If a brother does anything for which he should be expelled from the house for ever, before he is given leave from the house he should go naked in his breeches, a rope around his neck, to the chapter in front of all the brothers; and he should kneel before the Master and should do just as is commanded of one who is put on penance for a year and a day; and afterwards the Master should give him a letter of dismissal so that he may go and save himself in a stricter order.[149]

As many Templars found after the suppression of the Order in 1312, vows once taken could not be undone, even when the original order no longer existed,[150] but in the case of expulsion there was apparently some doubt as to what was meant by a stricter order. Mutual agreement with the associated Orders of Saint John and Saint Lazarus forbade acceptance into either of these, but there was some support in the Temple for transfer to the Benedictines or Augustinians. 'We do not agree with this', says the writer of this section of the Rule, who evidently did not see these as fitting his concept of a stricter regime.[151] His worry stemmed from the possibility that a man expelled from the Order might thereby be seen to have gained a passage to an easier life, or worse, was left free to act in a way which would harm the reputation of the Templars. Therefore those reluctant to enter a stricter order were to be detained in irons until they had thought again.[152] Such traffic was not all one way, for the Templars themselves took on members of other military orders and even of the Franciscans. A notable case was that of Gerard of Malberg, Grand Master of the Teutonic Knights between 1241 and 1244, who was accepted into the Templars in 1245 with papal approval. He had apparently caused a financial scandal during which he had incurred considerable personal debts, but Innocent IV evidently considered that the Templars' disciplinary system was sufficiently rigorous to cope with men like him.[153]

Less final but still 'the hardest and harshest after being expelled from the house' was to be sentenced to lose the habit. This could be imposed for a wide and varied range of offences: displays of anger and violence; sexual intercourse with women; lying, especially malicious accusation against other brothers; misuse or loss of the Order's property in anything from slaves to cats; disobedience to a command; breaking the Master's seal; reception of unworthy entrants; building without permission; and staying away from the house for one night without permission.[154] Loss of habit meant both deprivation of those things which defined a brother's position within the Order and the obligation to undergo a series of regular and humiliating penances. He was therefore required to hand back his armour and horses, and take up the role of the penitent, fasting three days per week on bread and water, working with the slaves and eating on the ground. Each week he received corporal punishment before all the other brothers during attendance at Sunday chapel. This regime normally lasted for a year and a day, but even then he was not entirely quit of the offence, for he could never again bring an accusation against another brother, carry the seal or purse, command knights, carry the piebald banner, or give advice.[155] In practice, he had lost all chance of making any kind of career in the Order, for his reputation clung to him for the rest of his days. Leaving the Templars for another Order without permission amounted to the same thing, for he had voluntarily given up the Templar habit and readmission was possible only after an elaborate display of contrition.[156] The loss of the habit cancelled out all other penances: 'it was established in this way because the penance is very heavy, and harsh the great misfortune and the great misery and shame that he suffers when he loses his habit, and all the honour that he will never have in the house'.[157]

Below these major penalties was a series of graded penances, imposed upon a brother for three, two, or one day per week, 'until God and the brothers show him mercy'. Three days per week signified an offence for which he would have lost the habit had it not been for that mercy, and two days 'for the slightest failing by which he transgresses the commandment of the house'.[158] A Templar undergoing penances of three or two days 'should lead an ass or do any other of the basest duties of the house, that is to say wash the bowls in the kitchen, or peel garlic and chives, or make the fire'. On Sundays he received corporal punishment:

When the Master or the one who has authority wishes to put a brother on penance, he should say to him, 'Good brother, go and undress if you are well.' And if he is well, he should undress and afterwards come before the one who holds chapter, and should kneel. And then the one who holds chapter, or who should give the punishment, should say, 'Good lord brothers, see here your brother who comes to his punishment, pray to Our Lord that He pardon his sins.' And each brother should do this and say one paternoster, and the chaplain brother, if he is present, should also pray to Our Lord for him in such a way as seems good to him. And when the prayer has been said, the one who holds chapter should give the brother his punishment with a whip if he wishes, as he sees fit, and if he does not have a whip he may use his belt if he wishes.[159]

Towards the end of chapters it was the duty of the Master or whoever was holding the chapter to exhort the brothers to follow the path of righteousness:

Before he leaves there, [he] should instruct the brothers and teach them how they should live; and he should teach them and recount to them a part of the rules and customs of the house, and should ask and command them to be wary of evil thoughts and even more of evil deeds, and to strive and take care to conduct themselves in such a way in their riding and in their speech and in their judgement and in their eating and in all their actions, so that no excess or folly may be noted, and to take special care in their haircut and their clothing, so that there is no untidiness.[160]

The elaborate list of offences and their accompanying penances show very clearly the contemporary awareness that since mankind carried the burden of original sin there was no way of avoiding transgressions. Indeed, in the Rule some concessions were made to the kind of men who were attracted to the Temple. Despite St Bernard's picture of paragons who had no interest in any worldly activity, jousting was allowed, provided life and limb were not endangered by the throwing of lances; in very specific circumstances wagers could be made, as long as they used objects like pieces of candle rather than actual money; and they were permitted certain types of board game (although not chess and backgammon, two of the most popular games in Outremer).[161] There was, too, provision for discretion in the application of the penance system, in the tradition of the Benedictine Rule: the section of the Rule added in the middle of the thirteenth century is especially concerned with the interpretation and treatment of specific cases in order to show in what kind of circumstances this discretion could be exercised. Summing up this long section of case-law on penances, the writer says that the examples are given for two reasons: firstly, that the brothers may see the importance of obedience, without which all kinds of other problems arise, and secondly, that those who have to administer the rules have a better idea of how best to apply them in a just fashion.[162]

However, the penance system and the limited concessions to human frailty were not excuses for fatalism; positive effort was needed to overcome man's weakness, especially among God's dedicated elite. The question therefore arises as to the extent to which the Templars actually managed in practice to be wary of evil thoughts and deeds. The aristocratic and knightly ethos reflected in indulgence towards limited forms of secular activity is equally apparent in the type of minor offence committed by Templars. The Rule, for example, recounts the case of a brother who, while out walking with others near Casal Brahim in the County of Tripoli, saw a bird on a river bank, casually threw a mace at it, missed, and lost the weapon in the water. Theoretically, wilful loss of the mace was a serious transgression, but in this case the brothers exercised discretion and he was allowed to keep the habit.[163] The temptation to take on the colour of local secular society must have been even stronger in the western preceptories. It was not resisted by brother John of Mohun who, in 1293, was acquitted of a fine of 100 shillings by King Edward I, following an appeal by the Master in England, because he had kept running dogs without warrant in the royal forest in Huntingdon-shire.[164] The Rule, too, gives concrete examples of more serious offences, including wagering of Templar habits, brawling among themselves, and sleeping with a woman.[165] The most serious category of offences, however, were those which could lead to expulsion. It is not possible to assess how frequently these occurred, but by selecting three of those regarded as the most grave – simony, desertion, and homosexuality – it is possible to show that the penance system described in the Rule was not simply based upon a theoretical view of possible problems.

Of these three, simony seems to have been the most common, partly because it could be committed unwittingly. It is clear that, although the health of entrants mattered more to the Templars than it did in conventional monastic orders, nevertheless any idea that the membership could consist exclusively of a cadre of fit men of fighting age quickly disintegrated in the face of the social and economic pressures of practical crusading.[166] Charters of donation and associa-tion therefore show that arrangements for entry often differed little from the usual Benedictine practice. There is an implicit expectation that an entrant would bring a gift with him or that the prayers for an associate and his burial in Templar ground merited a donation in return. This attitude helped create the Templar empire, but it took no account of the important changes which the reform papacy and its canon lawyers had been trying to implement on the issue of simony. By the late twelfth century, Walter Map was claiming that both the Templars and the Hospitallers accepted advowsons of churches from knights who entered their orders, often under the pressure of debt. This was a device, he alleged, by means of which 'they evade simony'.[167] Matters came to a head in the early thirteenth century, when the papal legate, Robert of Courçon, advised Innocent III that Templar practices amounted to simony as it was then being defined, although, unlike Walter Map, he understood this to have been done through ignorance rather than wilful disobedience. The pope therefore initially confined himself to a warning. In 1213 he told the Master and brethren that 'nothing be demanded for the reception of anyone . . . Not even under the pretext of an "aid".' The treatment of past offenders could be left to the Master's discretion, but anyone who did this in the future should be expelled and forced to enter a stricter order.[168]

The problem had arisen partly because of the development of canonistic opinion in the second half of the twelfth century, but executive order and wide publicity could not easily provide the answer in the case of the Temple, since the arrangements of mutual convenience into which many local houses had entered since the 1130s were built into a system which depended upon constant injections of new men and resources if it were to function at all. The case of Bernard Sesmon of Albedun, for example, is one of many which demonstrates how this worked at local level and underlines how difficult it had become for the Order to extricate itself. Bernard Sesmon remitted his body and soul to the Templar house of Douzens (in the Aude region, east of Carcassonne), asking that he be associated in the alms and prayers owed to dead brothers and that if he died while still in secular life 'they should receive him like a brother' and bury him in their cemetery. He then made a very large donation of 1,000 *sous*, for the remedy of his own soul and those of his father and mother. The Templars, for their part, gave him charge of their honour at Espéraza, together with its revenues, with the proviso that it would revert to the Order on Bernard's death.[169] The phrasing of the document makes no real attempt to cover the fact that Bernard Sesmon, although genuinely making a pious donation, nevertheless received in exchange, firstly, an important role in the management of Templar estates and, secondly, the guarantee of either late entry to the Order or at least treatment at his death which amounted to the same thing. While the economic development of Cistercian houses, for example, was a by-product of the Order's success in attracting recruits, it was the *raison d'être* of the Templars' western structure. Many Templars may have been guilty of simony through *simplicitas*, as Innocent III put it, but the fact remained that in those clauses of the Rule which probably date from about 1165, simony is the first crime listed as justifying expulsion from the Order. Here the definition is quite straightforward: 'simony is committed by gift or promise to a brother of the Temple or to another who may help him to enter into the Order of the Temple'.[170] The problem was less one of *simplicitas* than of the pressures exerted by the needs of the crusades. Indeed, Innocent III himself had succumbed to this pressure. Desperate to produce new crusaders, he made significant changes to canon law governing the circumstances under which the cross could be taken – for example abrogating the wife's right of veto[171] – and thereby gave explicit recognition to the priority of crusading needs.

The result was a heightened awareness of the danger of simony within the Templar hierarchy, but an apparent inability to make any fundamental change. The later clauses of the Rule, put together some time between 1257 and 1267, show the realities of the problem in practice, for under the mastership of Armand of Périgord (*c.*1232–1244/6), it manifested itself in a severe crisis of conscience among some of the leading members of the Order in the east.[172] After some agonising, they decided that they had entered the Order through simony and, although the Rule does not say so, they had almost certainly done so through one of the western houses:

So they were very sick at heart, and came before Master Brother Hermant de Pierregort and told him with many tears and in great sadness of heart, and disclosed all their deeds. And the said Master was in great distress, for they were worthy men who led lives of goodness, religion and purity. And the said Master took counsel privately with the old and wisest men of the house and those who knew most of this matter; and he commanded them in virtue of obedience not to speak to any man of this matter, and to advise him in good faith and to the benefit of the house.

The Master's advisers considered that, as these men had led such virtuous lives, 'great harm and serious scandal could come to the house if they were expelled', and it was therefore decided to send a representative to the pope to ask if he would put the matter under the jurisdiction of the Archbishop of Caesarea, 'who was a friend and confidant of the house'. As this was probably Peter of Limoges (1199–1237), this places the affair in the mid 1230s, during the pontificate of Gregory IX. The pope granted this and therefore Armand of Périgord sent the brothers, together with a selected group of his private advisers, to appear before the archbishop. The Master's delegates advised the archbishop that the brothers concerned should make a formal renunciation of their habits and then be readmitted to the house, 'as if they had never been brothers', and this the archbishop duly enacted. The brother who wrote up this section of the Rule explains that this happened only because they 'were wise and worthy men, who had led good and religious lives', and that such leniency would not have occurred if they had been men of bad behaviour. It seems not to have blighted their careers within the Temple, for one of them later became Grand Master.[173]

Armand of Périgord's fears in this case are clear, although unspoken. Scandal and harm would have arisen in that if expulsion applied to these men, how many others would then have found their position untenable? Just as the Church had had to reject the donatist idea that the validity of the sacrament depended upon the moral state of the priest who administered it, so too the Templars needed to evade the problem of simony if the Order was to continue as a viable organisation. The concluding line of clause 549 is significant, for the writer says that the same treatment was later given to 'a worthy man of the house because of his goodness', suggesting that this crisis by no means eliminated the problem. The fact remained that a strict interpretation of the rules on simony would have prevented the Order raising the resources for the relentless demands of warfare in the east.[174]

While some men were apparently sufficiently anxious to enter the Order as to run the risk of simony, others were equally determined to escape. Although the problem did not match that of simony in scale, nor can any chronological pattern be discerned, vigilance was needed to minimise the perennial military problem of desertion. Some Templars in western houses simply took off, for reasons unexplained. In 1305, for example, the sheriffs of Kent, Sussex, and Southampton were ordered to keep watch for brother Richard of Feckenham, who was known to be 'wandering about the country in secular dress'. If they found him, he was to be delivered to the Master in England 'to be chastised in accordance with the Rule of the Order'.[175] Sometimes, motives were more evident. The elaborate regulations laid down in the Catalan Rule concerning Spanish Templars who left for the east without permission suggest a frustrated desire to participate in the fight for the Holy Sepulchre, rather than desertion from the Order as such.[176] However, some of those already there were not so enthusiastic. According to William of Tyre, the Armenian Malih, brother of King Thoros, had once been a member of the Order, but had deserted, and when Thoros died in 1168, had seized his lands, using them as a base for attacking Templar properties in Cilicia.[177] A century later, another important recruit, the bankrupt Julian of Sidon, who sold his main castles to the Temple in 1260, left the Temple to join the Order of the Trinity where he died in 1275.[178]

In the east the possibility that desertion would become apostasy was a further danger. The Rule cites the case of a Templar mason called Jorge, who left Acre and went over to the Saracens, 'and the Master knew it, so he sent brothers after him, and he was found guilty, and they found the clothing of a secular man under his own clothing; so he was sent to Château Pèlerin, where he was put in prison and died'.[179] No reason is given for Jorge's drastic step, but he may have been alienated by some action against him within the Order. Matthew Paris claimed to know of a Templar called Ferrand who had changed sides at Damietta, 'in consequence of a valuable horse having been forcibly taken from him'.[180] Apostasy, though, was not always voluntary. Roger the German, captured at La Forbie in 1244, was forced to renounce Christianity and apparently to proclaim Muhammad a prophet, although he said that he did not know what he had been made to say. This did not, however, prevent him from being expelled from the house.[181]

The offence about which the framers of the Rule express most horror, however, is when a brother was 'tainted with the filthy, stinking sin of sodomy, which is so filthy and so stinking and so repugnant that it should not be named',[182] and was seen as more serious than sexual intercourse with a woman or entering a brothel.[183] The mid thirteenth-century section of the Rule does indeed cite the case of three Templars at 'Atlīt who were discovered to have engaged in what are described as acts 'against nature'. They were summoned to Acre by the Grand Master who had them put in irons, although one of them, a brother Lucas, escaped at night and went over to the Saracens. Of the other two, one tried to escape, but appears to have been killed in the attempt, while the other was imprisoned at 'Atlīt.[184] Moreover, during the trial at an episcopal hearing at Clermont in 1309, the knight William of Born provided the most explicit description of homosexual activity in the whole of the trial records, suggesting that this was indeed a justifiable accusation to level against an Order whose members professed strict celibacy. Here is the relevant passage:

he said that he had lived with four brothers of the Order, namely, with brother Stephen of Bosco, of the diocese of Cahors, and whom he believed to be in Cahors, and with three other brothers now dead whose names he could not remember, saying that when he lay with them and knew them, those with whom he was having intercourse placed their mouth towards the ground and supported themselves with the feet and hands, and the witness climbed upon the one whom he wished to know carnally and introduced his penis through the anus of the one who was prostrate in this way, saying also that he had carnal intercourse with the above persons more than fifty times.[185]

It has often been argued that homosexual acts must have taken place within all monastic orders and that there is no reason to believe that the Templars were any different.[186] The accusers at the trial seem to have believed the same, claiming that active participation was a ritual obligation upon all entrants. In fact, despite a large number of confessions to the denial of Christ and spitting on the cross, admission of homosexual acts is relatively unusual.[187] Given the pressure to confess placed upon the Templars during the trial, this imbalance may suggest that the Templars had taken seriously the dramatic prohibition of the Rule. The questions during the trial were presented in such a way as to place the blasphemies as an integral part of the reception ceremony, while the homosexual acts were seen as an obligation to be fulfilled at some unspecified time in the future, after entry into the Order. Within this context, the Templars may have seen the blasphemies as carrying less blame for them as individuals, since they were coerced into them at their reception, than consent to homosexuality. To say that homosexuality existed within the Order was not the same as admitting that it was widespread or was part of a cult which was 'the rule of the Order'.

CHAPTER SEVEN

THE TEMPLAR NETWORK

Among the Templars brought before the papal inquisitors at Paris in October and November 1307 was a serving brother called Odo of Wirmis. His demeanour and appearance bore little relation to the modern stereotype of the bloodstained Templar Knight, dressed in white surcoat with its red cross, heavily armoured, and mounted on a powerful warhorse. The setting of such a knight is the dust of the Palestinian highlands and deserts; his function the relentless war against the Saracens. But Odo was aged sixty and described himself as a master carpenter; he had been past his prime when he had joined the Order, for he was already forty-four years of age.[1] Clearly he had not been recruited to fight and, indeed, it seems unlikely that he had ever ventured outside the rolling green countryside of his native landscape, for he had originated in the diocese of Beauvais and had joined the Order at its house in Paris. Yet such a man was not untypical of those seized by the royal officials from the houses of the Order in France in the early morning of 13 October 1307, for, apart from their leaders, on a temporary visit to France as part of the perennial process of activating support for the Holy Land, most of those arrested were the administrators, craftsmen, and agricultural workers who manned the Order's preceptories in the west.[2] They were part of a huge monastic enterprise which, as early as the 1160s, had needed seven large provinces ranging from England to the Dalmatian coast; by the era of Odo of Wirmis, the area which encompasses present-day France had on its own been subdivided into eleven separate *baillies*.[3]

Not surprisingly, this elaborate organisation had been forced to sustain much criticism, for the contrast with the 'poor knights' of the early 1120s was indeed stark. Matthew Paris' treatment of the letter of the Grand Master Armand of Périgord, written to the Order's preceptor in England late in 1243 or early in 1244, is a case in point.[4] Here the Master explains how his policy of negotiating with Damascus and opposing Egypt had paid splendid dividends by enabling the Christians once more to gain safe and secure access to Jerusalem. But Matthew Paris, echoing Walter Map's cynical observation of half a century before,[5] chose to present Templar opposition to Egypt (which disrupted the peace made by Frederick II in 1229) as simply one more method of perpetuating the wars between Christians and Saracens, wars in which the military orders appeared to him to have a vested interest. The orders, he claimed, actually had adequate resources to achieve victory over the Saracens, for the Templars had 9,000 manors and the Hospitallers 19,000, besides their other revenues and privileges, and every manor could furnish a fully equipped knight for the Holy Land. Yet, since victory had not been achieved, despite the participation of 'many vigorous western knights' in the crusades, Christians had come to believe that the military orders must be perpetrating some kind of fraud.[6]

Such views are understandable, for the Templars seen by most western Christians were precisely those who seemed most remote from fighting for the cross, yet at the same time they apparently consumed a considerable proportion of the almost infinite amounts of money which the crusades seemed to need. But the admission of men devoid of fighting skills and already of mature age reflects the kind of organisation which had become necessary to sustain the Order's responsibilities after 1129. Without an extensive network of support in the west, the Templars would have vanished with the first major defeat they suffered. As a non-renewable force, they would have been taken over like the Order of Mountjoy in southern Aragon, which was absorbed by the Temple itself in 1196, or even wiped out completely as a fighting body as happened to the much smaller Order of St Lazarus at La Forbie in 1244.[7] The deployment of perhaps 300 knights in the Kingdom of Jerusalem alone in the twelfth century, or the building, maintaining, and garrisoning of castles like 'Atlīt and Safad in the thirteenth century, would have been unthinkable. Moreover, costs escalated throughout the period. In about 1180 a Burgundian knight needed about thirty manses (equivalent to about 300 hectares or about 750 acres) to equip and maintain himself as a mounted warrior; by about 1260 he could not manage on less than 150 manses. This was matched by the rise in the cost of horses: the average price tripled between 1140 and 1180, and had doubled again by 1220.[8] Most landlords were affected, for these problems were becoming acute by the later years of the thirteenth century,[9] but the position of the military orders was exacerbated by the growth of their responsibilities in the east, as more and more of the secular nobles found that they could no longer shoulder the burdens of maintaining and defending their castles and fiefs.[10]

Examples from more recent experience of warfare are instructive. The effectiveness of eighteenth-century armies was tightly constrained by the difficulties of moving and supplying large numbers of men and horses. According to Marshal Saxe, writing in 1732, even a single battalion on the move 'is like some ramshackle machine which is on the verge of disintegrating at any moment, and which moves only with infinite difficulty'. Apart from the organisational problems there was a crucial need to conserve expensively trained soldiers. Direct confrontations between eighteenth-century armies could lead to the loss of up to a third of such men within a few hours, which meant that two or three battles could bring warfare almost to a standstill.[11] Modern warfare illustrates a closely related consideration. At the end of the Second World War, only three out of every ten soldiers in the US army had a combat role, while what was described as 'service support' accounted for about 45 per cent of the army's manpower. In the Vietnam war every infantryman was backed by between four and five personnel.[12] In addition, in both wars, many thousands of civilians in the USA itself were employed in supplying equipment, clothing, food, and transport, who never came closer to actual combat than the radio or the television screen. Although the more sophisticated the army, the more elaborate is the logistical and technological back-up needed, nevertheless the labour-intensive nature of most production in the twelfth and thirteenth centuries meant that the relative effort required to keep soldiers in the field was just as great.

Amleto Spicciani's study of the relations between Pope Innocent IV (1243–54) and the Templars underlines this point.[13] The pope was acutely aware of the financial burdens of the defence of the crusader states and was concerned lest the Order in the east should fall into the hands of usurers.[14] Therefore, despite his own desperate financial problems, Innocent made great efforts to ensure that the houses of the military orders in the west would be able to supply the eastern command with as little hindrance as possible. He justified his exemption of these houses from crusading taxes imposed by the Church on the grounds that they already contributed to the aid of the Holy Land and that any imposition would simply reduce this capacity.[15] Two specific practical measures, early in 1253, demonstrate the papal concern.[16] On 27 January he acceded to the Templar request to sell and lease some of its property in Provence up to the value of 2,000 silver marks, as well as making similar provision for England (up to a limit of 4,000 marks sterling), Poitou (up to 3,000 silver marks), and the Kingdom of France (up to 6,000 marks). On 30 January, in every country except Germany, he assigned to the Templars the proceeds from the commutation of crusading vows, from restitutions made for the crime of usury, and from wills in which the testator had made provisions for the Holy Land. He set the very high limit of 10,000 marks on these concessions.

In this context, the reasons for the reluctance of most Templar commanders to risk troops in frontal clashes are obvious; on the occasions when they did, losses could be proportionately much higher than those of up to a third which occurred in eighteenth-century European battles. It was a lesson forced upon them from the beginning. During the first decade after the Council of Troyes, all three engagements in which the Templars are known to have been involved ended in defeat with heavy losses.[17] This experience was repeated many times. At Hārim in 1164 they had sixty dead from a contingent of sixty-seven; in the space of a little over two months in 1187 they lost 290 knights at the Springs of Cresson and at Hattin; in 1237, while besieging Darbsak, the Templars of Baghras were heavily defeated by Aleppan troops, leaving them with only twenty survivors from a force of 120 knights; at La Forbie, in October 1244, they emerged with only thirty-three knights from the 300 they had contributed to the army; less than six years later, at Mansurah, the Grand Master told Joinville that 280 of his knights had been killed.[18] It is natural to see such losses in human terms, but at the same time it should not be forgotten that each of these knights represented a large financial investment. In 1267 the cost of maintaining a knight for the defence of Acre for a year was ninety *livres tournois*.[19] As a good estimate of the average annual income of the French monarchy at the time of Louis IX's first crusade is approximately 250,000 *livres tournois*, this means that even if each knight killed at La Forbie represents only a year's investment of Templar resources, the total loss was still little short of a ninth of the annual Capetian income.[20]

Crises like these provoked a flurry of activity as all resources were strained to make up the deficits. As early as 1150 the seneschal, Andrew of Montbard, wrote to the Grand Master, then in France, asking urgently for more money and men and describing the debts incurred in assembling the force of 120 knights and 1,000 squires and sergeants for Baldwin III's expedition to Antioch. Even these were now mostly dead and he asked the master to bring back all the able-bodied men he could gather and to sell what he could 'in order that we can live'.[21] An idea of the chain reaction such a letter could cause in the Order's organisation in the west can be seen in the chapter-meeting held by Everard des Barres in Paris on 14 May 1150, apparently in response to this appeal. Part of the business transacted there was the grant of a house and a meadow at Aunis, near Liège, to Suger and the Abbey of St Denis. The Templars had acquired the property from three brothers who had now joined the Order, but the brothers had previously held it from St Denis on payment of an annual *cens*. The wording of the charter clearly reflects the exigencies described in the seneschal's letter, even though the transaction concerned turned out to be of little practical help. 'Although, impelled by the oppression of the eastern church, we have sold certain of our possessions, we have conceded [these] as a gift . . ., judging [it] unworthy to sell this to anyone else, who might in some ways trouble the town and men of St Denis there, especially since the same venerable abbot loves us and augments our possessions very much, and zealously assists us in our affairs as if they were his own.'[22]

The disasters of 1187 and 1244 left even bigger gaps to be filled. After the massacre at the Springs of Cresson in May 1187, Gerard of Ridefort appears to have written direct to the papacy asking for help, explaining that, although the Muslims were always striving to destroy the Christians in the east, they were especially dangerous at that time because they had discerned dissensions among the Christian leaders. The Cresson defeat had caused the deaths of fifty knights and ten sergeants, as well as heavy losses of horses and arms. Early in September, apparently unaware of the much greater defeat at Hattin, Pope Urban III wrote to the Archbishop of Canterbury and the prelates of England to order them to use every available means to activate military help among the princes and barons, as well as assisting the Templars with horses and arms 'by which they may better defend the land'.[23] Just over half a century later, after La Forbie, Matthew Paris described the very public reaction of the military orders in the west to the disaster:

In order to wipe away the tears from the cheeks of our mother Church, weeping for recently dead sons, the King of France, and also the Hospitallers and the Templars quickly sent novice knights (milites neophitos) and a force of armed men, together with no small quantity of treasure, for the consolation and help of those living there [the Holy Land] and to sustain them against the daily attacks of the Khorezmians and other infidels.[24]

Numbers were also continually eroded by old age, infirmity, and disease, as well as by the need to send some of the more experienced leaders to administer important western provinces. Even when there was no obvious immediate crisis, therefore, there was a routine and regular transfer of men to maintain the establishment in Outremer. Testimonies in the trial throw some light on this process. James of Molay described how he was received into the Order in 1265 at Beaune in Burgundy and was sent to the east, along with other recruits, in the mid 1270s.[25] Among the lower echelons, a serving brother, Stephen of Troyes, recalled how he had been one of a large group of 300 brothers sent overseas at a general chapter-meeting held at Paris in 1297, less than a year after his reception.[26] Analysis of the age structure of 115 Templars examined at Paris in 1307 shows that a high proportion of men in their twenties was still being sent overseas in the late thirteenth and early fourteenth centuries, while the depositions of seventy-six Templars examined in 1310 in Cyprus, by then the front-line crusader state, show that only five had entered the Order in the east, the remainder having arrived from preceptories in the west.[27] The Rule hints at the problems involved. A man who was married or in debt could be reconsidered if he could arrange for his wife to enter a religious order or his debts to be settled in such a way that the creditor had no claim on the Order. Moreover, although lying about one's status on entry was an offence punishable by expulsion, nevertheless the possibility that a man who had pretended that he was a knight and been found out could be readmitted as a sergeant brother was left open for consideration by 'the worthy men of the house', provisions which show an evident reluctance to lose potential recruits despite such misrepresentation.[28]

The Templars were faced with problems of similar magnitude in the provision of horses and supplies. Horses were as crucial as manpower and highly expensive, which was why there were such detailed regulations on their care in the Rule. If the precepts of the Rule were followed concerning the numbers allowed to officials, knights, and sergeants, the Templars would have needed to maintain about 4,000 horses in the east, apart from camels and pack animals.[29] This was a huge undertaking. It is estimated that, in the nineteenth century, a standard hay and grain ration for each horse was about 25 pounds (11.4 kilograms) per day, a figure which, in contrast to the armies of the mechanised era, hardly diminished if the force was immobile. A rough calculation was that a horse consumed about five or six times as much as an average man, and, even in the climate of western Europe, drank six gallons of water a day.[30]

Major crusades made even greater demands. During the march across Asia Minor in the winter of 1147–8 Odo of Deuil was particularly impressed by the fact that, although the secular knights had lost so many horses during the journey, the Templars 'had kept their chargers even though they were starving'.[31] This was indeed a considerable achievement, since horses were particularly vulnerable on the march and in battle, especially in the twelfth century when they were relatively unprotected. Turkish archers were well aware that they represented the soft under-belly of the knight. According to 'Imād-ad-Dīn, the Frankish knight was so well protected by his armour that he was impossible to overcome, but once his horse had been killed it was relatively easy to capture him. He commented how, despite the large number of knights taken prisoner at Hattin, hardly any horses had survived.[32]

The description of Richard I's march south from Acre in the autumn and winter of 1191–2 by the author of the *Itinerarium* highlights the problems. Fodder was essential and risks had to be taken to obtain sufficient food for the horses and pack-animals. On 6 November 1191, Templars guarding foragers were attacked by a large company of Turks and a routine operation quickly escalated into a fierce fight, from which the Christians were only extricated when the king brought up extra help. Such an army was often caught in a vicious circle, since horses were vital to achieve the mobility and range needed to find supplies for both men and animals; in the Holy Land there was seldom sufficient food or pasture within easy reach, especially during the months when this march was conducted. When the army was encamped between Ramla and Lydda in late December, for example, the Hospitallers and Templars had set out at midnight on Holy Innocents' Day (28 December) on a raid into the mountains around Jerusalem, returning to Ramla at dawn with a booty of 200 oxen. Bad conditions and disease also took their toll of both men and animals. A few days after this raid, at the end of December, Richard's army had advanced within sight of Jerusalem at Bait Nūbā, but on the advice of the military orders decided to go no further at this time. One of the reasons given was that the heavy rain, the storms, and the cold had caused the deaths of a large number of the horses and beasts of burden, as well as the effects such weather had had upon men and equipment.[33]

New animals and supplies were therefore continually needed, not only because of the pressures of war, but also because the average equine life-span was only about twenty years. Moreover, horses were vulnerable to diseases ranging from influenza to swamp fever; their skin could be infected with parasites; and sores, abscesses, and eczemas could occur unless they were very carefully looked after. They suffered, too, from intestinal and digestive disorders, particularly during the hot weather encountered in crusader lands, and from lameness caused by too much exertion on hard surfaces such as the rocky desert that characterises the territory between Jerusalem and the Jordan.[34] So important were these animals that a Templar who killed or wounded any 'equine animal or mule through his own fault', ran the risk of being deprived of the habit of the Order, a punishment second only to complete expulsion from the house.[35] To some extent replacements could be acquired in the east, since it was possible to buy horses and pack-animals there, and the Templars themselves kept foals, some perhaps bred on their own lands.[36] However, purchase from local markets and villages was not adequate in itself, especially in a bad year; 1217 was such a year. On the eve of the Fifth Crusade, in the autumn, the Grand Master, William of Chartres, wrote to the pope with the news that the harvest had been poor, food sent from the west inadequate, and there were so few horses available that it was impossible to buy any.[37] The Templar network in the west was essential to make up these deficits, either by supply direct from the Order's estates or as a channel for secular contributions. The Rule shows that both horses and food were regularly imported. Horses were first placed in the care of the Marshal before being distributed, while an official called the Commander of the Vault was responsible for receiving and storing wheat.[38]

Most of the imports came by sea. In the twelfth century it seems that the Templars contracted with regular commercial operators; in 1162, for example, Romano and Samuele Mairano of Venice carried a large consignment of iron for the Order.[39] Horses presented greater problems, since they did not always travel well. Joinville says that they were loaded into the hold and the door then carefully caulked since it was submerged during the voyage,[40] a method which must have risked respiratory diseases or even pneumonia. Even so, losses seem to have been kept low enough to make the operation practical, perhaps as early as 1113 and certainly by 1123.[41] Possibly Hugh of Payns brought back a limited number of horses for the Damascene campaign in 1129; by the 1170s the transport of horses across the Mediterranean was relatively common.[42] From 1207 there are references to the Templars' own ships, which indicate that the Order was beginning to build up a fleet of its own.[43] The most important port for them in the western Mediterranean at this time was Marseille where, in 1216, both the Hospital and the Temple had been granted the right to carry pilgrims and merchants virtually without restriction, but by 1233 the consuls of Marseille had become dissatisfied with the situation, for they believed that their own shippers were being undercut. A new agreement in that year limited the orders to two sailing each per annum at Easter and in August, rather than the apparently unlimited activity permitted in 1216.[44] Comparison of the two agreements suggests that the military orders had developed their shipping resources very rapidly in the period between 1216 and 1233, leading the consuls to believe that their original privilege was being abused. Part of the problem seems to have been that Marseille merchants never achieved a commanding position in the Levantine trade, even when at their most active in the middle of the thirteenth century, but the port was an important embarkation point for pilgrims, and the competition from the orders for passengers might explain why the consuls had become particularly sensitive on this point.[45] Nevertheless, the port's notarial registers show that the

Templars continued to operate out of Marseille throughout the thirteenth century, while in the trial depositions there is a reference to a Templar official called the 'Master of Passages', who was based in Marseille.[46]

The growth in traffic through Marseille may also have been related to the problems faced by the Templars in Apulia and Sicily during this period, for the bitter quarrel between the Order and Frederick II must have limited the value of the Adriatic ports to the Templars from the late 1220s onwards. This area was crucially important to the Holy Land, as it was situated in a key position in the Mediterranean, and was a major producer of both wheat and horses.[47] The Catalan knight, Ramon Muntaner, writing later in the century, who had a good knowledge of the region, thought that Brindisi was particularly useful as a conduit for the Holy Land. Many ships taking pilgrims and provisions to the east spent the winter there and all the commercial houses had large establishments in the port. Templar ships were among those who called there:

And so the ships which winter there begin to load up in the spring to go to Acre, and take pilgrims and oil and wine and all kinds of grain of wheat. And, assuredly, it is the best fitted out place for the passage beyond sea of any belonging to Christians, and in the most abundant and fertile land, and it is very near Rome; and it has the best harbour of the world, so that there are houses right down to the sea.[48]

The Templars had a preceptory at Brindisi as well as in the other ports of Barletta, Trani, and Bari, while they could draw on the produce of their inland possessions, especially from their lands around Foggia and Torremaggiore. In Sicily their house at Messina acted both as a channel for produce from the island and as an entrepôt for shipping arriving from Provence and Catalonia.[49] The Order also had its own ships constructed in the region; in 1242 the Venetian sea-captain (later doge) Ranieri Zeno saw carpenters working on a vessel for the Temple in a dry dock at Zara on the Dalmatian coast.[50]

However, Frederick II was determined to re-establish monarchical power in the *Regno* following its dissipation in the years after his father's early death in 1197. In 1220 he had stated that the military orders could not be allowed to acquire lands freely and without restriction since 'in a short time they would have bought and acquired all the kingdom of Sicily, which among the regions of the world is reputed to be the most suitable for them'.[51] Although the emperor could obviously see the potential value of the region for the orders, he was not discriminating against them: all his subjects in the *Regno* were being called to account at this time.[52] In 1221 and 1223, indeed, he duly confirmed the privileges granted by his predecessors and the papacy, while in the past he himself had conceded property and confirmed the grants of others to the house at Messina on the grounds that these donations contributed to the support of the Order in Outremer.[53] But the climate changed after the development of overt hostility between Gregory IX and Frederick, which led to the emperor's excommunication in September 1227, and then to the clashes in the east during the imperial crusade of 1228–9.[54] Despite the papal–imperial agreement of 1230, Frederick did not return all Templar property which he had confiscated after his crusade, while the Order continued to finance pro-papal opposition and to attempt to extend its lands in contravention of imperial mortmain legislation.[55] In these circumstances it is unlikely that the Templars were able to use the Adriatic ports at all effectively for the aid of the Holy Land; indeed, in 1244, Innocent IV complained to the Apulian bishops that the barons, counts, and *cittadini* had no regard for the labour and expenses needed for the Templars to maintain their eastern province.[56]

This situation changed little under Frederick's successor, Conrad IV (1250–4), but relations began to improve once Manfred, Frederick's illegitimate son, had seized power in 1258, largely through the personal intervention of Albert of Canelli, Templar preceptor in Apulia between 1262 and 1266. In March 1262, Manfred forbade interference with the Templars in his lands, placing the Order under his protection.[57] However, the real importance of the region to the Order became evident after the defeat and death of Manfred by Charles of Anjou at the battle of Benevento in 1266. The Templar alliance with the Angevins was apparent almost at once. In June 1267, Charles granted Baldwin, Master in Apulia, the right to export food for the Holy Land from Bari free of taxes.[58] Thereafter, during the late 1260s and 1270s horses, wheat, vegetables, barley, armaments, and cloth were sent from the Apulian ports, sometimes in the Order's own ships, for use in the east, and horses and ships from Catalonia passed through Messina en route to the Templars in the

Holy Land. The crusading aim of Charles's export licences is quite clear. The goods and animals were not usually for resale, but were specifically for the Order's own use.[59]

Among the cargoes carried in the opposite direction were slaves, whose labour contributed to the running of the Order's western houses, at least in southern Italy and Aragon.[60] They seem to have been used on a considerable scale. Among Gregory IX's many complaints about the conduct of Frederick II in 1227 was that 'he collected a hundred slaves which the Hospitallers and Templars had in Sicily and Apulia, and returned them to the Saracens without any compensation to the orders'.[61] They were probably channelled through the port of Ayas in Cilicia, which was a centre of the slave trade in the late thirteenth century and a convenient place for loading Turkish, Russian, Circassian, and Greek captives.[62] Ayas gave access to the vast hinterland opened up after the Mongol conquests of 1243, especially to the route leading to Tabriz, the hub of oriental commerce in the second half of the thirteenth century.[63] During the 1270s and 1280s the Templars shrewdly established a wharf here, perhaps taking advantage of their knowledge of Cilicia acquired during their long occupation of the northern marches of Antioch.[64]

Details of Templar shipping in the Apulian ports are quite limited, mostly because of the destruction of the Angevin archive in 1944, but some insight into the world can be gained from Ramon Muntaner's sketch of the life of the Templar sea-captain, Roger of Flor. One of the ships which overwintered at Brindisi was commanded by a Templar sergeant from Marseille, whom Muntaner calls 'Frey Vassayll'. While he was taking on ballast and having repairs done, a young boy called Roger 'ran about the ship and the rigging as lightly as if he were a monkey, and all day he was with the sailors, because the house of his mother was near to where the ship was taking in ballast'. Roger was the son of a German falconer, Richard of Flor, who had been killed at the battle of Tagliacozzo in 1268, and Vassayll offered to take him on. In time he grew up into an expert mariner and the Templars made him a sergeant brother, giving him command of a ship called The Falcon which the Order had bought from the Genoese and which was, according to Muntaner, 'the greatest that had been built at that time'. The Falcon seems to have been actively involved in trade and perhaps even in piracy, for 'the Templars did so well with this ship that they liked none so well as this one'. All this came to an end in May, 1291, when Acre fell. *The Falcon* was in the harbour at the time and rescued many 'ladies and damsels and great treasure and many important people' by taking them to 'Atlīt. Muntaner says that Roger of Flor gave a large part of the profits of this enterprise to the Order, but envious people told the master that he had cheated the Templars, since he had still more. The Master therefore wanted to apprehend him, but Roger was too quick. He took the ship to Marseille, where he abandoned it, left the Temple, and sought employment elsewhere. This was the beginning of a second career, which eventually led to the command of the mercenary troop known as the Catalan Company, where he served the Byzantines until he was murdered in 1305.[65]

The presence of *The Falcon* in the harbour at Acre reflects the importance of the port to the Templars, especially after 1191, when the city replaced Jerusalem as the headquarters of the military orders. All the major powers of the kingdom were represented here, since the tongue of land on which the city was built provided good protection for the double harbour established in its lee.[66] The maritime powers had their own quarters within the city, originally based upon special royal grants, and often delineated by their own walls. The Templars dominated the area in the south-west corner, although they had no direct access to the harbour, which was controlled by the 'Court of the Chain', or the royal custom-house. In Theoderich's time, in the early 1170s, they had what he describes as a large and wonderfully built house on the seashore,[67] and by the middle of the thirteenth century this had expanded into a complex of buildings, although it does not seem to have been a self-contained, walled enceinte like the Italians quarters (see figure 11).[68] The Templar of Tyre, who must have worked there, knew it well:

The Temple was the strongest place of the city, largely situated along the seashore, like a castle. At its entrance it had a high and strong tower, the wall of which was twenty-eight feet thick. On each side of the tower was a smaller tower, and on each of these was a gilded lion *passant*, as large as an ox. These four lions, [together with] the gold and the labour, cost 1,500 Saracen *besants*, and were a noble sight to look upon. On the other side, near the Street of the Pisans, there was another tower, and near this tower on the Street of St Anne, was a large and noble palace, which was the Master's. In front of the house of the nuns of St Anne was another high tower, which had bells, and a very noble and high church. There was another ancient tower on the sea-shore, which Saladin had built one hundred years before, in which the Temple kept its

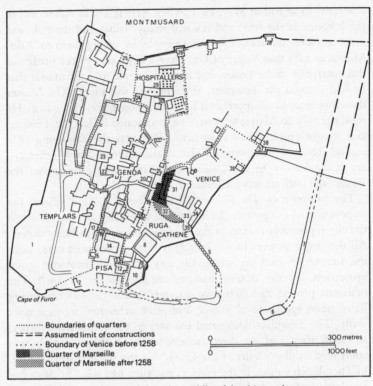

Figure 11 Plan of Acre in the middle of the thirteenth century.

Crusader sites: 1 Castle of the Templars. 2 Church of St Andrew. 3 Southern breakwater.
4 Northern extension of no. 3. 5 Chain closing a section of the harbour. 6 Tower of the Flies.
7 Eastern breakwater. 8 Court of the Chain (khan al-'Umdān). 9 Round tower.
10 Abu Christo coffee-house. 11 *Porta ferrea* ('Iron gate'). 12 Pisan (?) warehouses.
13 Pisan eastern gate and 'old' tower. 14 Pisan *fondaco (khan ash-Shūna)*. 15 Pisan western gate.
16 Pisan 'new' tower. 17 Templar fortified gate. 18 Fortified gate of the southern Genoese
district. 19 Main thoroughfare (present Market Street). 20 Lamonçoia, main Genoese tower.
21 Corner house of the Genoese quarter. 22 Church of San Lorenzo, northern district of the
Genoese quarter. 23 Genoese 'Old tower of the Commune'. 24 Hospitaller corner house.
25 *Porta balnei* ('gate of the Bathhouse'), renamed *Porta nova* ('New gate'). 26 *Porta Hospitalis*
('gate of the Hospital'). 27 *Porta Domine nostre* ('gate of Our Lady'). 28 Tower to the
east of the royal *Castellum* and the connection with the inner wall of Montmusard.
29 Hospitallers' fortress. 30 Hospitaller bathhouse (later Turkish bathhouse, at present
Municipal museum). 31 Venetian *fondaco (khan al-Ifranj)*. 32 Church of St Mary of the
Provençaux, in the quarter of Marseille 33 Venetian church of San Marco. 34 Venetian
tower on the shore. 35 Church of St Demetrius. 36 Venetian fortified tower (*Burj as-Sultān*).
37 House of the Constable (?). 38 Royal Arsenal.

treasure, and it was so close to the sea that the waves washed against it. Within the Temple area there were other beautiful and noble houses, which I will not describe here.[69]

Although Acre remained the most important port for western supplies to the Templars, the Order had a substantial presence in most of the coastal cities, including Caesarea, Tyre, Sidon, Gibelet (Jubail), Tripoli, Tortosa, and Jabala, as well as controlling Port Bonnel, north of Antioch. After 1218 Acre was also supplemented by the harbour at 'Atlīt, similarly situated on the south side of the promontory. C. N. Johns' survey suggests that the south bailey acted as a receiving area for supplies like timber, iron, and victuals, which could then be stored in the south undercroft just behind it.[70]

The supply of men, horses, food, and equipment from the west was underpinned by the obligation upon western houses to make regular payments in cash of a third of their income, known as responsions, which went specifically to help operations in the east. Although it is only a fragment covering less than sixteen months, the record of the sums paid into the Temple treasury at Paris in 1295–6 offers a brief glimpse of this operation. It shows deposits made by thirty-eight preceptors, ranging from those with responsibility for entire provinces like Aquitaine and Normandy, to the commanders of minor houses like La Villedieu-en-Dreugesin (Eure-et-Loire) and Montbouy (Loiret). Eighty per cent of the payments were made in July or between December and February, implying a relationship between the gathering of resources and the spring and late summer passages to the east.[71] These payments were equivalent to the taking of ordinary taxation by secular rulers, but in times of crisis or extreme financial pressure houses were also expected to contribute additional 'extraordinary' taxes, just as secular rulers and popes taxed for warfare and crusades. During the 1290s, for example, when the Templars in Cyprus were striving hard to put some pressure on the Mamluks both by naval raids upon the Egyptian coast and by maintaining a garrison on Ruad, off Tortosa, James of Molay ordered additional sums to be provided over and above the usual responsions.[72] Money was also raised for specific projects. A special levy was imposed to find the purchase price of Sidon, acquired from its lord, Julian, in 1260, as is shown by the efforts made by Roger, Preceptor of San Gimignano in Tuscany. In June 1261, he confirmed that he had received a loan of ten *livres* for the specific purpose of paying his house's share of the levy imposed by the Master at Acre upon all preceptories to pay for the purchase of the city of Sidon.[73] Only the Iberian lands were treated more leniently, since here too the Order was obliged to maintain castles and troops ready for combat, but even these contributed about a tenth of income upon a regular basis.[74]

The dissemination of news and information was an essential part of this process. The continuous movement of regional officials from house to house formed the arteries which made this possible, for they often carried the letters or accompanied the emissaries sent from the east. Thomas Bérard, Master during the crucial years between 1256 and 1273, made particular use of this system, for he faced both the Mongol and Mamluk threats during the period after Louis IX had returned to France but before Charles of Anjou had begun to take a serious interest in the Holy Land. Bérard's urgent need to mobilise resources and opinion in the west may explain the appointment of Guy of Basainville, Preceptor in the east in the mid 1250s, as Visitor in the west at this time, for the Master thereafter used him as an important channel of communication. His letter to Guy of Basainville of March 1260, received at Châteaudun on 10 June, was sent on very rapidly, probably within a week, both to the pope and to Francon of Borne, Preceptor of Aquitaine.[75]

From the time of the appointment of Payen of Montdidier as the official in overall charge of the Order's French lands, the whole system had been founded upon the organised structure of the Templars' western properties. The section of the French Rule which seems to date from the mid 1160s lays down that the Grand Master needed to obtain the consent of the General Chapter before appointing 'commanders in the houses of the kingdoms', a phrase which presumably refers to regional preceptors. This General Chapter might include not only the leading specialised officers such as the Seneschal, the Marshal, the Commanders of the Kingdom of Jerusalem and of the City of Jerusalem, but also the most important regional commanders, seen at that time as the Preceptors of Tripoli, Antioch, France, England, Poitiers, Aragon, Portugal, Apulia, and Hungary.[76] The reasons for this provincial structure are obvious from the pattern of the early donations,[77] assuming that Poitiers encompassed most of the lands in south-west France and Apulia applied to the Kingdom of Sicily as a whole. The reference to a Hungarian province is the most problematical, for the Order never seems to have established itself very extensively in the Kingdom of Hungary as such, if that is taken to consist primarily of the Carpathian Basin centred upon the Danube, but in 1097 the Hungarians expanded into Dalmatia, where they continued to dispute control with the Venetians during the twelfth and thirteenth centuries, and it is probably these lands which are meant. Information on the Order's shipping in the thirteenth century shows a strong Templar presence in the Adriatic, which appears unlikely without an established base of houses and lands from an earlier period. New provinces were then created as they became justified, making the list in the Rule at least partially out-of-date by the later thirteenth century. By this time the Preceptors of Aquitaine, Normandy, and the Auvergne were among the leading dignitaries of the Order,[78] none of which had originally been designated as separate provinces. Moreover, the increasing importance of the Italian lands saw the creation of important regional subdivisions, similar to the French *baillies*, in Lombardy, Tuscany, the Patrimony of St Peter *in Tuscia*, Rome, Spoleto, Campania and Marittima, the Marches of Ancona, and Sardinia during the thirteenth century under the overall command of a grand preceptor.[79] His responsibilities in Italy were shared with the Order's commander in Apulia and Sicily, who probably remained the most important official in the peninsula. During the thirteenth century, a Master with overall charge of the western provinces was appointed. In about 1250 this post was split into two with a Visitor for the Iberian provinces on the one hand, and a Visitor for France, England, and Germany on the other, reflecting the different nature of these groups of provinces in the west.[80] In the crusader lands, Cyprus became a major base from the 1190s and the Order's headquarters after 1291, and here too there was a regional commander. After the Latin conquests which followed the capture of Constantinople in 1204, a limited number of houses were also established in Latin Greece. The initial attempts were not very successful, for the Emperor Baldwin's grant of Sattalia in 1205 proved abortive, while his successor, Henry, confiscated their establishment at Ravennika in 1207 following the Templars' involvement in a rebellion. Nevertheless, the Order had not been driven out of the region, for it was still in conflict with Henry in 1211, and it retained its castle at Lamia on the island of Euboea, acquired some time before 1210.[81] The Templar holdings must never have been extensive, however. According to the Greek

THE NEW KNIGHTHOOD

version of the Chronicle of the Morea, the Templars and Hospitallers were each responsible for four knights' fees in the region, which was equivalent to an individual bishop, and modest in comparison with the largest fief of Akova, which owed twenty-four.[82]

However, unlike England, France, or Italy, Iberia and eastern Europe remained crusading frontiers, comparable in the papacy's eyes to that of the Holy Land. With the break-up of the Caliphate of Córdoba in the early eleventh century, Muslim Spain distintegrated into a series of petty emirates, a situation exploited by the Christian kings of the north to expand their power at Muslim expense. Particularly significant was the capture of Toledo by Alfonso VI of Castile in 1085. But the Christian reconquest was to prove far from easy, for invasions by powerful religious brotherhoods from north Africa, the Almoravides in 1086 and the Almohades in 1147, not only checked but at times reversed the Christian advance. It was not until the Christian victory at Las Navas de Tolosa in 1212 that the papacy felt confident of ultimate victory, and even then vast areas of southern Spain remained in Muslim hands. Valencia was not taken until 1238 and Seville not until 1248. During this period the Christian effort had focused upon the development of three front-line powers, Castile-León in the centre, Aragon-Catalonia to the east, and Portugal to the west. The Templars were more prominent in the lands of the smaller monarchies on the flanks, where they had received recognition soon after the Council of Troyes, rather than in Castile-León, where, from the 1160s the powerful local military orders of Calatrava, Santiago, and Alcántara were established. The Order's Iberian houses were therefore likely to be fortified as they were in the east: Miravet on the River Ebro in Aragon, established in 1153, and Almourol on the River Tagus in Portugal, held from 1171, reflect the prolonged conflict with the Moors (see plates 14 and 15).[83] As in the crusader states, this ensured that the Templars played a much more overt political and military role than in the non-combatant areas of the west. During the minority of James I of Aragon, for example, following the unexpected death of his father, Peter II, at the battle of Muret in 1213, the Aragonese notables chose William of Montrodon, a Catalan who was Master of the Temple in Aragon and Catalonia, to take care of the boy. He was protected in the great fortress of Monzón until, according to James' own account, in 1217, at the age of nine, he decided that he wanted to take a more

Plate 14 Templar castle at Miravet, Aragon.

Plate 15 Templar castle at Almourol, Portugal.

positive role in the swirling aristocratic conflicts of his kingdom. James' version of these events seems to imply that initially the Templars were reluctant to release him at this point, but whatever the truth of this they remained prominent members of his entourage, providing military advice and resources throughout a long reign of crusading during which the king made vast gains against the Moors both in the Balearic Islands and in the rich Kingdom of Valencia.[84]

Under James, the Templars were able to build upon the gains of the past. After the capture of Mallorca in 1230, the Templars were among the beneficiaries of the *repartimiento* which followed, often settling Muslim families on lands acquired in this way. This practice annoyed Popes Gregory IX and Innocent IV, whose demand that all such Saracens be treated as slaves implies that the degree of dependence of some of the Templars' Muslim subjects was by no means absolute. Evidently, for the Spanish Templars, the colonisation and exploitation of these lands took precedence over religious prejudices.[85] Although careful study of James I's methods of rewarding those who aided him shows that the Order's gains in Mallorca and Valencia were relatively smaller than they had been in the twelfth century,[86] nevertheless, at the time of the trial in the early fourteenth century, James' grandson, James II, was faced with a series of fortresses which his predecessors had granted to the Order, which could be reduced only by siege. In the past Peñíscola, Miravet, Monzón, Ascó, Cantavieja, Villel, Castellote, and Chalamera, had all been regarded as integral to the defence and expansion of Aragon, as well as forming part of the wider Templar network.

In contrast to Aragon and Portugal, the Templars were established in central and eastern Europe relatively late in their history and they played no significant part in the eastern crusades.[87] Their very limited penetration of the Polish principalities illustrates the point.[88] They did not receive their first grant there until 1227, when Henry the Bearded, Duke of Silesia, conceded Mala Olesnica, near Olava in Lower Silesia, to them,[89] but, although this developed into a precepttory, it did not serve as a basis for large-scale expansion. By the end of the thirteenth century they had at the most eight (possibly only five) houses in the vast area of Poland and three of these, at Lesnica, Suleçin, and Chwarszczany, passed into the sphere of the rulers of Brandenburg in the second half of the century. In 1239 they did receive some villages near the Prussian frontier, but this was short-lived, for the Teutonic Knights, favoured by Frederick II and the local ruler, Conrad of Mazovia, were already established as the dominant military order in the region. Maria Starnawska calculates that the maximum number of personnel at the end of the thirteenth century was between sixty-six and eighty-eight, of whom between twenty-one and thirty-two were knights. The Templar command does not seem to have appointed a separate regional master and these remained under the control of the provincial master responsible for Germany, Bohemia, and Poland. Most of them were drawn from north-east Germany, Silesia, and Pomerania, and they made a modest contribution to the Christian forces at the battle of Legnica against the Mongols in 1241, where they lost six dead while three escaped.[90] Those who fought there seem to have been known to the Preceptor of France, since they apparently attended chapter-meetings in Paris, but otherwise their orientation was largely local.

Donations to the houses within this structure were necessarily random, but in areas where the Templars received substantial numbers of gifts from an early date, such as northern France and Provence, the very public presence of the Order must have kept it in donors' minds, encouraging further grants. Once a landed base in a given region had been created, it was possible to consolidate and to rationalise through land transactions and careful management. Therefore, when they are plotted on a map, patterns of Templar property emerge which suggest that, within certain limits, attempts were made to create a structure related to the overall aims of the Order (see figure 12). Particular attention was paid to the major land routes and to the ports. The routes from England and northern France along the valleys of the Saône and Rhône and thence to the Provençal coast, and across the Alps to Venice, central Italy and Rome, and the Angevin kingdom, were well covered. The Order had houses in most of the important ports, maintaining a presence along the Atlantic coast and the Channel in Bordeaux, La Rochelle, Nantes, and Dover, which was an increasingly important region for maritime trade from the middle of the twelfth century onwards, as well as in the key ports for embarkation to the east in the Mediterranean, centred upon Marseille. Although the Order's French possessions remained the bedrock of its western empire, the relative importance of its Italian bases seems to have increased from about the middle of the thirteenth century, especially once the Apulian and Sicilian ports were more fully utilised during the period of Angevin rule. The Order also had a house at Venice, although a serious dispute with the Venetians, some time before 1248, led to the burning of the Dalmatian town of Segna by the Templars. In 1259, however, all concord apparently restored, the Great Council of Venice granted the Templars 5,000 Venetian pounds for 'the extension and improvement' of their house in the city.[91] In central Italy Brother Bonvicino, promoter of the Flagellants in Perugia, was a key papal agent in Umbria, faithfully representing the political interests of the Holy See against the Hohenstaufen under five popes between the 1230s and the 1260s.[92] Further south they had a house at Vetralla, near the important Via Cassia, from which they could reach Rome or their preceptory on the coast at Civitavecchia. Indeed, in the region south of Lake Bolsena their close links with the papacy strengthened their position even further, especially in and around Viterbo, which was frequently used as a papal residence.[93] Indicative of the change is that in 1198, when Innocent III arbitrated between the Temple and the Hospital over a disputed fief situated between al-Marqab and Valania, the Templars needed to send representatives from the east to Rome, while the Hospitallers already had appropriate officials on the spot. However, in the late thirteenth and early fourteenth centuries, Peter of Bologna, who emerged as an eloquent defender of the Order during the trial, was a trained lawyer appointed to the position of full-time procurator of the Order at the papal curia.[94]

The extent to which the Order in the west engaged in a conscious policy of land management can be seen in the remarkable survey made by the Templars in England some time between 1185 and about 1190.[95] Using the method of collecting evidence through local juries in a manner similar to the English crown, they made a detailed record of the extent and value of their many varied rural estates and urban holdings throughout the country. According to Geoffrey Fitz Stephen, the Master in England who presided over the survey, the purpose was to ensure that future disputants could be refuted, and indeed specific questions aimed to establish donors and possessors of land, churches, and mills. However, there is throughout an emphasis on revenue, especially on the returns from the demesne and the rented lands, which suggests a more direct crusading connection. It is possible that the survey was begun after the mission from the Holy Land of 1184–5. Although Arnold of Torroja, the Master, had died

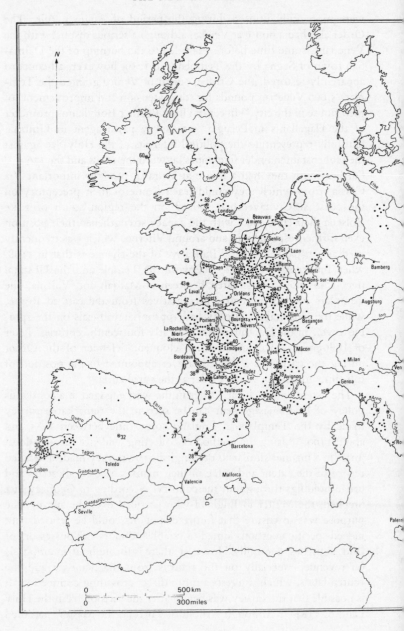

Figure 12 Distribution of the Templar houses in the late thirteenth century.

KEY

1	Fuste	33 Montsaunès
2	Paleopolis	34 Vaour
3	Lamia	35 Le Puy
4	Syracuse	36 Valence
5	Messina	37 Agen
6	Taranto	38 Romestaing
7	Brindisi	39 Angoulême
8	Bari	40 Gentioux
9	Troia	41 Civray
10	Penne	42 Nantes
11	Vanna	43 La Guerche
12	Perugia	44 Baugy
13	Siena	45 Prunay
14	Lucca	46 Provins
15	Albenga	47 Troyes
16	Hyères	48 Coulours
17	Marseille	49 Epailly
18	Roaix	50 Bure-les-
19	Richerenches	Templiers
20	Saint-Gilles	51 Bertaignemont
21	Montpellier	52 Arras
22	Douzens	53 Ivry
23	Carcassonne	54 Sommereux
24	Mas-Deu	55 Oisement
25	Monzon	56 Abbeville
26	Huesca	57 Gombermond
27	Zaragoza	58 Sandford
28	Tortosa	59 Willoughton
29	Tomar	60 Clontarf
30	Pombal	61 Tempelhof
31	Soure	62 Mala Olesnica
32	Segovia	63 Wielka Weis

before this embassy reached England, the rest of the company, under the leadership of the Patriarch Heraclius, would have explained the growing problems faced by the defenders in the east, and may, consequently, have alerted the English Templars to the need for a more accurate and detailed knowledge of the varied properties which had been acquired since the 1130s.

Control of such estates was centred upon the local house or preceptory, where the Templars and their associates lived as a community. Study of the houses in Provence suggests that, where practical, these houses were grouped around the largest preceptory in the vicinity (see figure 13). One such 'mother house' was Richerenches in the Vaucluse region which, in the second half of the twelfth century, had between ten and twenty Templars resident, and eight dependent houses, manned by perhaps two or three Templars each.[96] The same system can be found in the late thirteenth century. At the time of the trial, the important house of Mas-Deu in Roussillon (a region which at that time remained within the lands of the Aragonese kings) had seven dependent houses, with a Templar staff of twenty-five under Ramon Sa Guardia, the preceptor. Most of these houses were established on rural estates and managed by one or two Templars only, but in the city of Perpignan the Order had its own fortified quarter with six or seven Templars resident.[97] As Perpignan was an expanding financial centre at this period,[98] this preceptory was well placed to maintain links with this sector of the local economy. The purpose of such grouping may have been to provide access to communal life for the guardians of the smaller, outlying houses, as well as enabling the Order to make more efficient use of its resources (see figure 14). Apart from the men themselves, the most vital resource was horses and pack-animals, for which large areas of pasture and vast quantities of fodder were needed, so it is reasonable to suppose that the clustering of houses was organised to facilitate this. Horses were frequently donated to the Order, while the existence of commercial stud farms in the secular world suggests that the Templars would have bred their own stock as well. It is clear that the grant of a war-horse or its equivalent in money represented an important gift in medieval aristocratic society, both as a sign of devotion to the Order and in terms of its high intrinsic value.

The great majority of Templar houses in the west were rooted in the local community. Like other monastic foundations, the original

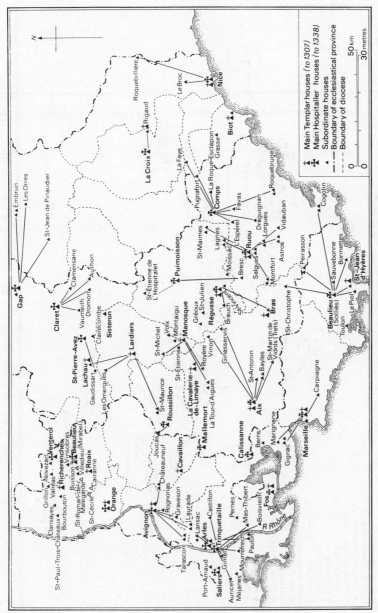

Figure 13 The Templars and Hospitallers in Provence.

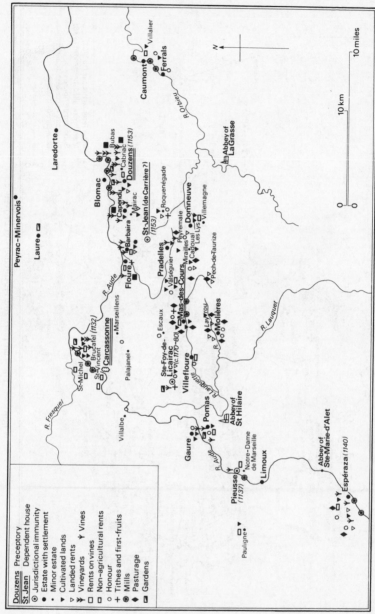

Figure 14 Possessions of the Temple in the region of the Preceptory of Douzens (Aude), 1132–1180.

nucleus of the site or buildings was often donated by a prominent local lord or prelate, usually with a particular interest in crusading. If the donor was a secular lord, sometimes he or his relatives became Templars, sometimes they served in the east with the Order for a set period, and almost always they gave their bodies for burial in the Order's cemetery, receiving in exchange the daily prayers for their salvation laid down in the Rule.[99] Obituary rolls such as that for the preceptory at Reims are a good reflection of the relationship with the locality, for they list the anniversary dates of those for whom prayers should be said. That of Reims is particularly valuable, since the house was situated in a busy urban environment and the roll appears to have been kept continuously from its foundation during the 1160s right down to October 1307, when its members were seized by Philip the Fair's officers.[100] By that time the list ran to forty-two pages of parchment and included Philip II of France, an archbishop, a bishop, a count, and a countess, as well as thirty-four other clerics of various kinds, a minter, and a baker. Fifteen of the Order's Grand Masters were recorded and eleven other Templars. Nor was this an exclusively male world. Women were closely involved not only as wives of men associated with the house, but as donors in their own right, individually remembered. Sixty-seven of the 197 non-Templars listed are female. Prayers for these had become a major task of the house, involving 223 persons remembered on 154 days of the year. Except for the Grand Masters and some of the Templars, the beneficiaries of the house's prayers had all either made a donation or their relatives had done so on their behalf.

Some of the entries are laconic, but others offer additional detail which throws light both on the house itself and those who were associated with it. Among these were two key figures in the establishment of the preceptory, Archbishop Henry of Reims and Brother Stephen, the first commander. The archbishop had provided the Templars with their original church, the eleventh-century church of the Trinity, 'on account of the remedy of his soul and those of his parents', and was accordingly remembered on the anniversary of his death, 13 November. Brother Stephen had developed the house from this base, adding a dormitory and stables, and restoring and refurbishing the church. The house had then built up its holdings through the donations of families like those of Gunter and his wife Heliadis, both buried in the cemetery of this church. Their son, Henry, a canon in Reims, gave the Templars half a house which he had near the Porta Martis. Here there was a direct link with the structure which supported the Templars' crusading activity, for the share in the house was sold and the proceeds divided four ways: one part went to the aid of the Holy Land, a second was distributed in bread for the poor, and the other two quarters in pittances (small allowances) for the brothers of the Temple who prayed for Gunter and Heliadis and Henry on their respective anniversaries of 11 September and 10 October.

Neither Gunter nor Henry actually joined the Temple, but in many cases such family associations were a direct source of personnel for the Order. The Templar charters show how such decisions affected not only the individual concerned, but had repercussions throughout his whole family. On Christmas Day 1144, Ermessende, 'who was the wife of Berengar of Rovira and mother of Raymond of Rovira', gave the Temple her wedding-gifts (*sponsalicia*), which 'were formerly made to me by my reverend husband, Berengar, who is now brother and knight, by grace of God, of this good *milicia*'.[101] Berengar had joined the Order three or four years before, but he had been planning to enter the Temple from at least 1136. In that year, in association with Ermessende and Raymond, he had made a grant of a manse at Moral (Vallense). 'For I, the aforesaid Berengar, humbly pray present and future knights and *baillis* of the aforesaid knighthood, that when, on the inspiration of God, I will wish to renounce this secular life and to be of their society and order and religion, they will accept and receive me to fight for the will of God.'[102] Berengar was therefore drawn from that class of married knights for which provision had been made in the Rule of 1129 and from which, following the example of Hugh of Payns himself, the Temple drew many of its recruits. Indeed, adult renunciation of this kind was sufficiently common for Gratian to elucidate the position in canon law in the *Decretum* of about 1140: the wife's consent for her husband to join a monastic order was just as necessary as if he were taking a crusading vow.[103] However, in Ermessende's case it is unlikely that she was in any position to oppose her husband (even had she wished to), for the family as a whole was linked to the Templars from the earliest years after Troyes. The 1144 grant was made into the hands of Peter of Rovira, Berengar's brother, who had been a Templar since at least 1136 and was already an important provincial administrator with wide responsibilities,[104] while Raymond of Rovira, who in 1143 had dictated his testament as he lay dying of wounds, had left his dwelling and half his movable goods to the Temple.[105]

The model for such family association had been set up by the relatives of Godfrey of Saint-Omer, Hugh of Payns' co-founder. It seems almost certain that Godfrey came from the family which held the castellany of Saint-Omer in Picardy, and was possibly a brother of William II, castellan between 1128 and about 1145. Probably as a consequence of a personal visit by Godfrey, in September 1128, William conceded to the Temple the right of relief on his fief and castellany of Warrêton-Bas.[106] This first grant was followed by others, clearly intended to make comprehensive provision for the salvation of the family by means of the intercession of the Templars. In 1137, William and his son Osto conceded

what is to be had from the altars, chapels, oblations and tithes of Sclippes and Leffinges, both in corn and in cattle and in other things, and their appurtenances that they might freely and quietly dispose from these things, excepting those things which the knights are known to possess there in fief. If anyone wishes to grant from these things in charity to the Templars, we concede it to remain no less fixed and stable. To this moreover we add two measures of adjacent land, which I, William, have not forgotten that I joined from my own property a long time ago to the places where annually the aforesaid tithes are attached. However, making this gift with both prayer and devotion we decree that [it] remain in perpetuity, for the safety of our souls and those of my father and mother, together with my wife and children and all my predecessors and our relations, all of whom also held the aforesaid tithes, [and] we concede [it] in such a way that when the brothers wish, the chaplain is employed to celebrate the divine office for our souls and all those whose memory is contained in this page, offering daily the wafers of the host, who nevertheless is regulated by the wish of the knights and what they judge to be appropriate.[107]

This patronage seems to have influenced the castellan's vassals, three of whom made grants to the Order at Ypres in 1142.[108] By 1140 Osto had himself joined the Order and can be seen acting on its behalf, not only in north-west Europe but also in Catalonia and in Jerusalem.[109] William of Saint-Omer died in about 1145, and was succeeded by his son, Walter, who in turn witnessed a grant to the Temple together with Osto soon after his succession.[110] Walter maintained the family's crusading tradition, for he was in the Kingdom of Jerusalem by 1151, took part in the siege of Ascalon two years later, and then, through his marriage to the heiress, Eschiva of Bures, became prince of the important fief of Galilee in 1159. This lordship had in fact once been held by Hugh of Saint-Omer, who may have been a great-uncle, in the early years of the kingdom between 1101 and 1106.[111]

Even more closely connected to the Temple was the family of Bourbouton, whose estates lay to the east and south of Richerenches in the Vaucluse region. This family was instrumental in establishing the preceptory at Richerenches; the head of the elder branch, Hugh of Bourbouton, entered the Temple in 1139 and had become master of the house by 1145, while his son, Nicholas, followed his father's example in joining the Order that year. Most of the family patrimony was donated to the house, whose association with the Temple is recorded in 119 charters preserved in the cartulary of Richerenches extending from about 1136 to 1183.[112] According to the preamble of his charter, Hugh had joined the Templars in direct response to Christ's injunction in Matthew 16:24: 'If anyone wishes to come after me, he should deny himself and bear his cross and quickly follow me.'[113] The circumstances were fully explained by Nicholas of Bourbouton on the occasion of his own entry in December 1145:

I, Nicholas of Bourbouton, . . . wish to relate that my father Hugh, by the name of Bourbouton, with the advice of our bishop, Pons [of Grillon, Bishop of Saint-Paul-Trois-Châteaux] and many other noble men whose names it would take too long to enumerate, surrendered to the knighthood of the Temple of Jerusalem himself and his wife and myself, Nicholas, his son, and all the honour which he possessed by the arrangement of our relatives and everything else which at that time he seemed to possess, thus he conceded to the above-mentioned brothers of the Temple to possess and to do with whatever they wished. Then my mother who, on the advice of Robert, Master of the said knights, and other brothers of the Temple, had remained in this honour, after a short time, with the advice of Peter of Rovira and others who were brothers with him, assuming the monastic habit, in the same way as my father, conceded the honour to the above-mentioned knights. Now, however, through the truth which says: 'unless you renounce everything that you possess, you cannot be my disciple' [Luke 14:33], wishing to obey, I, Nicholas, give and surrender in order to render to the possession of Peter of Rovira, Master of the aforesaid knighthood, and other brothers, both present and future of this same knight-hood, the honour of my mother and father, all and whole, cultivated and uncultivated, lands, vines, meadows, woods, pasturage with all its exits and entrances, waters and irrigation channels and mills and whatever plots there might be, houses and sheds and all their furnishings, horses and mares, oxen and asses, wine and grain, all male and female *rustici*, with all their children, and all their tenements, and to the last of my possessions without fraud, to possess in perpetuity, I surrender to the said brothers of the Temple, excepting the sheep therein, all of which I mercifully lease to my mother; I render myself to the same knighthood of God and the Temple to serve as servant and brother, although unworthy, all the days of my life, that I might merit the indulgence of my sins and by inheritance [be] with the elect in eternity.[114]

When Hugh died, some time in the first half of 1151, the entire seigneurie of Bourbouton had been conceded to the Templars.[115] The families of Rovira, Saint-Omer, and Bourbouton were drawn from a social stratum within the aristocracy which seems to have found the Order of the Temple particularly attractive and which provided the backbone of the Order's structure in the west. These were substantial lords below the level of counts, but nevertheless often castellans with vassals of their own, like those of Saint-Omer, or *nobiles*, as the men of the Bourbouton family are described.[116] Both Hugh of Payns and Godfrey of Saint-Omer belonged to the same milieu, as indeed did Bernard of Clairvaux.

Flexible forms of association with the Order seem to have been devised particularly with this class in mind. In 1172, for example, the Order was prepared to accept a type of provisional membership, apparently to please William VII, Lord of Montpellier. In his will William stipulated that the Templars should 'support and keep' his son, Guy, for six years, after which Guy would join the Order, provided that his elder brothers were still alive. If either of them died within this period, however, Guy would return to secular life and be provided with the necessary fiefs, and the Order would receive 1,000 *sols* instead.[117] Moreover, the Latin Rule recognised from the beginning the status of 'married brothers', provided the man and his wife both agreed. Their property would be conceded to the Order, although if the husband died first, his wife retained a part for her support during her lifetime. Such brothers were not entitled to wear the white mantle nor live in the same house as the fully professed brothers, but it is likely that in many of the smaller western houses there was little distinction in practice.[118] Many of these men seem to have occupied a position which has been compared to that of the lay brothers or *conversi* in the Cistercians or Carthusians.[119] Sometimes individuals gave themselves to the Order for sustenance as well as from piety. Typical of such associates were Bartholomew of Milagro and his wife, Inés, who, in May 1199, gave themselves to the house of the Temple at Huesca in northern Aragon. They brought with them houses and fields in Huesca and 100 *solidi* to pay for their burial in the cemetery of the house. Their commitment was total and irrevocable, for they offered themselves body and soul, 'so that it would not be licit in life to transfer to another order nor in death to choose to be buried elsewhere without permission of the house and brothers'. The Templars, in return, received them as *socios et participes* in all the benefits of the house and granted them a means of support in the form of set measures of wheat, wine, and cheese, as well as an annual sum of eleven *solidi* in cash.[120] All these donors had some form of property to present, but there were others with nothing to offer except their own bodies; these entered a position of dependence in which the documents make few allusions to spiritual motivation or benefits, for they were driven largely by economic necessity.[121] The overall effect of these links was to create powerful socio-economic units focused upon the local Templar house. Most of these associates hoped eventually to share in the spiritual benefits, while the Templar house itself established a web of local relationships and patrons which increased both its material wealth and its political security, and thus strengthened its ability to function within the wider network upon which the warriors in the east depended.

Nevertheless, despite the attempts to mould the Templar possessions into a coherent structure, there was no typical preceptory, modelled on a preconceived plan like that of the Cistercians. Examples from different regions can serve to illustrate this. One of the Order's most important preceptories in northern France was at Provins in the County of Champagne where, by the end of the twelfth century the Templars had two houses.[122] The Order had had links with the region since the 1120s and had received one of its earliest grants not far to the north-east at Barbonne, near Sézanne, in October 1127.[123] The date of the foundation of a preceptory in Provins itself is not known, but the presence of local officials as witnesses to a charter of 1171 suggests that at least one of the houses was fully established by that date.[124] Here, the brothers were well placed to take advantage of the proximity of the great cycle of trade fairs in Champagne. Provins itself held such fairs three times a year, as well as a weekly market in the upper town. The Templars steadily increased their share of the taxation levied on sales at these fairs, gaining rights on wool and yarn in 1164, on animals destined for slaughter in 1214, and, probably most valuable of all, given the large-scale tanning industry of thirteenth-century Provins, on hides in

1243.[125] Their presence was evident almost everywhere in the town, where they eventually held about seventy properties, including a square and many shops. Two acquisitions, forty years apart, reflect this ubiquitous activity. In the first, an agreement made with one Henry la Borde in 1171, they received his stone house near the church of St Mary, together with other buildings appertaining to it, in exchange for another house of their own and a payment of sixty *livres*. This appears to have been a business transaction with no religious overtones; the high price paid probably reflected the importance of the site for trade. In his confirmation, Count Henry of Champagne conceded that 'all merchants, whoever they are, should conduct business freely there'.[126] In contrast, the second charter shows a modest grant by Ansell of Quincy and his wife, Aaliz, of 'two retail stalls where fruit is sold', made in 1211, for the remedy of their souls and those of their ancestors.[127] This was of purely local significance compared to the mercantile centre created at the house of Henry la Borde, but it underlines the range of business in which the Templars of Provins had an interest. But the preceptory was not simply a commerical house; in addition, the Templars exploited mills and fishing rights on the River Varenne, leased a tile factory to a tenant, and were heavily involved in money-lending against the security of real estate. Outside the city they were prominent landlords, especially in the countryside to the north and south, farming their own estates, including vineyards and managed woodland, and they drew tithes, rents, and incomes from the exercise of monopoly rights on mills, ovens, and wine-presses.

Their position seems to have been largely established in the twelfth and early thirteenth centuries. They were especially favoured by Henry II of Champagne, Count of Troyes, who, in 1191, during the siege of Acre, gave them wide-ranging privileges which enabled them to acquire all types of property within his lands, stopping short only of the lordship of the city or castle.[128] Count Theobald IV was less generous, for he had considerable debts, and his attempt in 1228 to repossess all the property acquired since the death of his father, Theobald III, resulted in a major quarrel. After appeals both to Rome and to Queen Blanche, arbitration confirmed that the seizure was contrary to the terms of Count Henry's charter,[129] but the incident was symptomatic. From about this time the evidence suggests a decline in local generosity towards the houses at Provins, while for their part the Templars themselves seem to have been quite prepared to use the full range of ecclesiastical and temporal sanctions to enforce their rights, often making them disagreeable neighbours.[130] Cause and effect are difficult to disentangle here, for the Templars' attitude may in turn reflect greater pressure on the Order as a whole exerted by the needs of Outremer. Frederick II's confiscations in the 1230s must have meant that compensatory incomes were needed to offset losses from Apulia, while the military disasters of 1244 and 1250 and the inroads of the Mamluks in the late 1260s left little respite.

The preceptory was headed by a commander and a chaplain, who in the case of Brother Gerard during the 1280s were one and the same person. Other recorded personnel were an almoner, whose duties were the administration and distribution of alms; a marshal, in charge of requisitions, buildings, and stables; and a steward, who held the keys. Certain specific positions reflected the economic interests of the house, including a money-changer, a receiver of tolls from the town of Provins, and a vendor of wines.[131] Ordinary brothers are listed much less frequently than in the preceptory at Richerenches, but it seems unlikely that these two houses would have managed their wide range of functions within such a busy urban environment with fewer than the average of eighteen brothers seen at Richerenches. In addition, a large number of ancillary workers and serfs were necessary, many of whom – like Constant the cordwainer and his family in 1225 – were valuable acquisitions, received in the same manner as grants of property.[132] As at Richerenches, Provins seems to have been a major house around which a number of smaller preceptories were grouped, in this case in the *bailliage* of Brie. At various times these subsidiary houses included Champfleury, Chauffour, Chevru, La Ferté-Gaucher, Tréfols, Coulommiers, Lagny-sur-Marne, Chrisy, Lagny-le-Sec, and Sennevières. Two other large houses, Moisy and Mont-de-Soissons, seem also to have been dependent upon this *bailliage*, and one of these, Moisy, seems in turn to have governed four small houses at La Sablonnière, Nanteuil-les-Meaux, Viffort, and Montaigu.[133] Working on the basis of a personnel of three in the larger houses and two in the smaller ones, this would suggest that the Order's houses in the *bailliage* needed at least fifty Templars to fulfil their functions.

An apparent contrast is one of the Order's minor preceptories, that situated near the village of Frosini in the hills of southern Tuscany not far from the point where the route from Siena to Massa Marittima crosses the River Féccia.[134] Since 1138, when the Order had received its first donation in Tuscany, near Lucca,[135] the Templars had built an impressive network of preceptories in the region. Houses were established at Siena (by 1148), Lucca (by 1157), and Pisa (by 1163). During the thirteenth century the Order held further preceptories at Colle di Baggiano (between Pisa and Pistoia), Florence, San Gimignano, Arezzo, Vignale, Grosseto, Montelopio, and Frosini. Most of these were on or near the main routes leading to the pilgrimage centres at Rome and Monte Gargano and to the Adriatic ports of embarkation for the east. Many pilgrims received hospitality at these houses and, for this reason, they have been seen as offering a service in the west comparable to the Order's function of protecting pilgrims in the Holy Land.[136] On the face of it, the house at Frosini was one of the more obscure parts of this network, for it was not situated in a major city, but Tuscany was one of the most economically advanced regions of western Christendom and in fact Frosini too was profoundly affected by the tempo of this activity. Routes from San Gimignano and Poggibonsi (where the Templars may have had another house) and Siena converged here, giving access to the coast in the west and Grosseto and Rome to the south. Moreover, the hills between Frosini and Massa had a strong intrinsic attraction of their own, for they were rich in copper, iron, and alum, all of which were excavated and worked during this period, while saffron and grain added further to local prosperity. The metal industry in particular attracted investment from Sienese and Pisan merchants. It is not therefore surprising to find that, before 1239, the Templars had installed a preceptor at Frosini, presumably supported by an appropriate staff. Frosini was, of course, much smaller than Provins and its history is less well documented, but it is clear that within its locality it too served the Templar network, both as a hospice for pilgrims and merchants and as a subsidiary financial centre.

The adaptation to the immediate environment seen at Provins and Frosini is equally evident at Huesca in the foothills of northern Aragon. Here the Templars were particularly preoccupied with the rationalisation and consolidation of donations by active participation in the local property market. The Order was established at Huesca before 1148 and its cartulary, which includes documents down to 1273, shows the Templars constantly involved in buying and selling vineyards, orchards, olive groves, pasture lands, mills, and even a pigeon loft. In an area like this, the control and exploitation of water was more than usually important; the Templars of Huesca were anxious to obtain river frontages, especially on the Alcanadre and the Aragon, as well as entering into agreements and settling disputes over the water courses themselves. In 1180, for example, the Lady Orbellito, widow of García of Yesa, allowed the Templars to run water for irrigation through her orchard, on condition that she could use a fourth part of it for her own crops. It may be significant that the Templars' own orchards were established on two sides of her property.[137] Within the city itself, the cartulary shows that the Order possessed a large number of houses and shops, and was consequently keen to round off its control of areas of the city in which it was already predominant. As early as 1157 the Templars bought houses which are described as already having Templar properties to the east, south and north, the remaining side giving access to the public road. In 1213, the grant of a large house or palace (*palacium*) by the Lady Altabella seems to have been precipitated by a similar situation, for it is apparent that it was adjacent to the preceptory complex itself. Her charter says that it bordered on the cemetery of the knights in the east and their church to the north, so that, as these buildings enclosed the palace on all sides, she conceded it to the brothers.[138]

The development of banking and financial services arose quite naturally from this structure. Monastic houses had traditionally acted as depositories for precious objects and documents and, with the growth of pilgrimage and crusade, were often called upon to provide loans and to hold mortgage pledges. But the Templars were better equipped than individual monastic houses to provide these services, since their web of preceptories made them convenient for crusaders from many regions and their possession of the equivalent of 'branch offices' at both ends of the Mediterranean, as well as large complexes in northern Europe in Paris and London, meant that they could make specie available where and when it was needed and in the form which was locally acceptable. During the great crisis in the east caused by the conquests of Baybars during the 1260s, it was to Amaury de la Roche, the Templar commander in Paris, that William of Agen, Patriarch of Jerusalem, turned with a wide variety of requests for finance, which he intended would be arranged through the Paris Temple. William's shopping list included the deposit of money at

Acre for crossbowmen, financial help to enable the retention of fifty knights who had been provided by various French lords, and the reimbursement of loans contracted both by Louis IX's representative, Geoffrey of Sargines, and by himself, in order to pay the wages of soldiers being used to defend Acre.[139] It was the obvious place for the patriarch to use, for the Paris Temple had become one of the key financial centres of north-west Europe. It was situated to the north of the city, outside the walls built during the reign of Philip Augustus, and was fortified with a perimeter wall and towers. Inside was an impressive array of buildings. When Henry III visited Paris in 1254 he chose to lodge there because it was the only place in or near the city sufficiently spacious to accommodate his huge entourage. Some time between 1265 and 1270, the Order added a powerful keep which, judging by later illustration, had a pointed roof and a tower on each corner. This keep, which was about fifty metres high and had four floors, was at the heart of the Templar bank in the late thirteenth century.[140]

The Templars' experience in financial administration also meant that they acquired a body of expertise of particular value to both secular rulers and the papacy, all of whom were, to a greater or lesser degree, seeking to improve their governmental systems in order to maximise their revenue from taxation. As a consequence, financial services which had begun as an ancillary to crusading soon developed as activities in their own right. The most basic facility (and probably the most widely used) was the use of Templar houses for protection of important documents (including treaties, charters, and wills), and the guard of funds and precious objects, all of particular concern to the pilgrim or crusader who might be away for several years. Throughout their history the Templars held documents associated with forthcoming crusades, perhaps left as security for a loan which made the expedition possible in the first place or as a pious donation, always in the forefront of the mind of the departing crusader who wished to set in order his relationship with the ecclesiastical world.[141] But pilgrimage and crusade were never safe, and the prudent man made his will before he set out; it was natural for the Templars not only to look after the document, but also to act as executors of its provisions. The testament of Pierre Sarrasin of Paris, dated June 1220, made when he was about to set out upon a pilgrimage to Santiago de Compostella, provides just such an example.[142] Under the terms of the will the Templars held his capital, from which they were to distribute various sums as directed: 600 *livres parisis* to the Abbey of St Victor with which they were to buy rents from corn and from whose revenues, amounting to 200 *livres* annually, they were to make a daily charitable distribution of bread, an act intended to be of benefit to the souls of the donor, his relatives, and friends; in addition, a further series of charitable gifts; various legacies to particular individuals, the most important of whom was his mother, who was to receive 100 *livres*; and finally, the residue of the estate to be kept by the Templars for his heirs until they were of age. Some legators made direct provision for the Holy Land. In 1281, William of Lege, Preceptor of the Temple at La Rochelle, was one of the executors of the will of Guy of Lusignan, Lord of Cognac, charged with the specific duty of making an annual payment of 250 *livres* to the Templars in Outremer from a captial sum of 1,500 *livres* left for the defence of the Holy Land.[143] The administration of this will fits easily into the normal functional role of the Order, but the Templars also made deposit facilities available when the client's activities had no crusading connotations at all. In such cases there were often distinct political implications. The thirteenth-century English kings found the Order valuable in this way. King John used the London Temple as a repository for the crown jewels, but in 1261, his son, Henry III, in trouble with baronial opposition in England, felt that they would be safer if transferred to the Templar fortress in Paris, well away from his opponents and considerably more secure than its London equivalent. The jewels were sent to Queen Margaret of France (his wife's sister), who had them inventoried and placed in two chests in the care of the Parisian Templars. Three years later, Henry used these as security for a loan needed to finance his conflict with the opposition under Simon of Montfort.[144]

The most obvious extension of the facility for guarding crusaders' documents and money was to make funds available during the expeditions themselves. Joinville, although evidently unused to the idea, gives a valuable description of how the Templars kept such an account during Louis IX's crusade. After the disaster in Egypt in 1250, the king decided to sail to Palestine, where he spent the next four years. Necessarily this placed a great strain on the finances of his entourage, for a campaign which under most leaders would have amounted to a season or two actually resulted in six years away from home. The system cannot be said to have been at its most efficient in Joinville's case, but nevertheless he does provide an insight into how contemporary crusaders were able to use the Templar 'bank'. During the summer of 1250, while the army was at Acre, Joinville had received a sum of 400 *livres* owed to him in pay. He kept forty *livres* for current expenses and deposited the rest with the Templars. However, when he sent one of his men to withdraw another forty *livres* the Templar commander claimed that he had none of his money, nor did he even know who he was. Joinville made no further progress when he complained to the Grand Master, Reginald of Vichiers. 'When he heard that, he became very agitated, and said to me: "Lord of Joinville, I like you very much, but know for certain that if you do not wish to withdraw this demand, I will love you no more, for you wish people to believe that our brothers are thieves."' Nevertheless, Joinville insisted that his claim was valid, and four days later the Master came to him and told him that he had recovered the money. During that time Joinville says that he suffered acute anxiety, and he was apparently so relieved to get his money back that he asked no further questions. All he knew was that the original commander had been transferred.[145]

It is difficult to discern whether incompetence or dishonesty lay behind this incident, since in contemporary Paris the Templars had a highly organised system for handling such accounts, based upon meticulous record-keeping. One of the Order's most eminent clients was the Queen Mother, Blanche of Castile. Three times a year, at the beginning of the accounting terms of Candlemas, Ascension, and All Saints, the Templars sent her a summary of the movements within her account. In an extract printed by Léopold Delisle for Candlemas 1243, the statement is not simply a chronological list of undifferentiated items, but begins with the sum carried forward from the previous accounting term and then sets out the credits and debits, with the origin and destination of each item carefully recorded. Incomes are shown to be derived from the revenues collected by the *baillis* and *prévôts* who administered the queen's demesnes, while the outgoings are largely destined for a variety of religious institutions in the form of gifts or loans, or are expenses incurred by the queen's household.[146] Joinville's 360 *livres* would not simply have 'disappeared' had the Templar official with whom he had dealt at Acre been equally conscientious.

Delisle has shown the mechanics of this system in his analysis of a surviving fragment of the daily records of the cash desk at the Temple in Paris during the period between 19 March 1295 and 4 July 1296.[147] Only eight parchment sheets survive, but these contain 222 entries set out in a consistent pattern, each showing the date and the name of the Templar cashier on duty. This is followed by concise descriptions of the various transactions of that day: the amount of the payment, the name of the depositor, the origin of the money deposited, the name of the person to whose account the sum should be credited, and a record of the register in which the receipt would ultimately be recorded. Deposits were made not only by Templar officials, but also by a wide range of individuals and institutions from outside the Order. Most of the items recorded are receipts, for payments of any size were made through a special desk reserved for this. The total receipts for each day were then taken to the equivalent of a central office within the house, which seems to have been the great tower built during the administration of Brother Hubert, probably during the late 1260s and early 1270s, and from which the last two treasurers, both called John of Tour, seem to have taken their names. More than sixty accounts can be seen in operation during this period and Delisle discerned five categories of client: officers of the Temple itself, ecclesiastical dignitaries, the king, other members of the royal family, and important nobles and bourgeois. In the Templar record most of these were represented by their agents or officials. The entries show too that the Order kept parallel records of the sums received, for the desk clerk methodically noted the appropriate register at the time of receipt. In the surviving folios from 1295–6 it can be seen that the Order kept at least ten separate ledgers for this purpose. All sums were therefore categorised so that, for instance, some registers recorded revenues from their own preceptories, others deposits made in the name of important clients like the *prévôt* of Paris or the *bailli* of Vermandois.

It is tempting to imagine that the *Journal du Trésor* is a record of the transactions of an accessible cash desk, not dissimilar to a modern bank, open at specified times, at which account holders or their representatives could present themselves without notice. It is, though, impossible to be certain of this from the limited evidence provided by the *Journal*, which does not cover two complete years and shows activities in consecutive years for the months of April,

May, and June only. Business was not conducted on the key feasts of Easter, Ascension, and Christmas, the three feasts of the Virgin, the Feast of St John the Baptist, and on the saints' days of particular interest to the order, such as those of Matthias, George, Stephen, James, Michael, Laurence, and Simon and Jude, all of whom had associations with militancy or martyrdom.[148] Beyond this framework, the pattern of the bank's activity seems to reflect quite closely the needs of its clients. November, December, and July were the busiest months, when the Templars were receiving deposits collected on or near All Saints' Day (1 November) and the Feast of St John the Baptist (24 June), the days most frequently designated in charters and agrarian surveys for payments. In November 1295, for example, the desk was open for twenty-three days, completing fifty-seven transactions, in contrast to August, the quietest month, when it was open for only six days, during which eight transactions took place. Normal opening seems to have been between three and five days a week, but when the need arose the Temple responded to pressure of demand: in December 1295, in one period of the month, the desk conducted business on eleven consecutive days.

A concomitant of such close involvement with the finances of Latin Christendom, especially those of crusaders, was the provision of loans. The Order's potential as a major creditor had first been utilised by Louis VII of France during the Second Crusade, an operation which the king admitted brought the Order close to financial ruin.[149] A hundred years later Louis's great-grandson, Louis IX, was faced with an even more serious crisis, following the disastrous retreat of his forces in the Nile Delta which culminated in the capture of the king in April 1250.[150] By this time, however, unlike the period of the Second Crusade, the practice of holding money specifically for individual clients had become common, and the Templar treasurer had difficulty in reconciling the principle that appears to have been followed – that these deposits were sacrosanct and not to be touched by anyone except the client concerned – and the evident emergency created by the need to raise further money for the king's ransom. This attitude is understandable, for, although Templar financing of the crusades could often be remarkably flexible, there were distinct physical limitations when actually on campaign. The money needed for the ransom would have had to be drawn from the deposits kept on board the Templar galleys off the Egyptian coast; given the dire condition of the French army, these depositors might themselves have needed their money at short notice. If this had happened, the Templars would surely have had considerable difficulty in gaining rapid access to further funds held either in Palestine or the west. Moreover, the Order no longer tolerated the *ad hoc* arrangements of the Second Crusade which had brought it close to bankruptcy: by the middle of the thirteenth century it was accustomed to lend on proper security, which was conspicuously lacking in Egypt. When, ten years before, they advanced what was described as 'an immense sum of money' to Baldwin II, Latin Emperor of Constantinople, a man who was known to have almost insoluble financial problems, they took as security the priceless relic of the True Cross.[151]

While in the twelfth century loans with a direct crusading interest were most common, in the thirteenth century the growth in the scale of the economy and the military and political commitments of rulers meant that the Templars became an integral part of the European financial system. It is not surprising to find, for example, that the Templars were one of the many sources of finance to which King John of England had recourse. Sometimes these loans were quite small: in 1213 the king had apparently been unable to find nine marks of gold for an offering on the day of his absolution following the lifting of his excommunication, so he had borrowed it from the Master of the Temple in England. But in 1215 he was borrowing on a much larger scale, both before and after Magna Carta in June. In May, he wanted two loans of 1,100 and 2,000 marks, and in August another 1,000 marks, this time specifically to pay for soldiers from Poitou and Gascony.[152] Loans were not made exclusively to seculars. During the thirteenth century many abbeys, caught up in an economy in which the leading participants played for much higher stakes than in the past, fell into debt. These included establishments as famous as Cluny, whose abbot, Girold, on 1 April 1216, borrowed 1,000 marks of silver from the Temple to be repaid to Brother Haimard, Treasurer of the Order in Paris, within two months. The Countess of Champagne stood as guarantor.[153]

Activities like this made the Temple an important player in the financial markets of the thirteenth and early fourteenth centuries, and almost inevitably it became involved in the web which the Italian merchants and bankers had spun across Europe and the Levant. Two transactions in London in 1304 and 1305 illustrate the point. In the first, William de la More, Master in England, lent 1,300 marks to two merchants from the society of the Mozi of Florence, which he claimed that they promised to repay in Paris at midsummer 1304. According to William, the Parisian representatives of the society had defaulted on the debt, and he had therefore taken the matter to the royal courts to seek an order distraining their goods in England. The Master also feared that the London merchants of the society were about to renege on another debt, due the following year, of 700 marks owed for wool supplied to them by the Temple. In a separate loan in 1305, the Templars had provided the societies of the Galerani of Siena and the Frescobaldi of Florence with the sum of 879 marks 6s. 8d., although in this case the debt was repaid on time.[154]

Neither document makes overt mention of crusading activity and it is likely that in the second case there was no direct link. This may also be true of the money owed in 1304. It would have been easy to conceal the loan interest in the currency change, since it was common practice in such transactions to set a low valuation on the foreign currency and thereby profit from the repayment. However, since on this occasion William de la More had already departed for the front line in Cyprus, where the Templars were increasingly desperate for supplies, it seems likely that he had intended to travel via the Paris Temple, collecting repayment en route for use in the east. Moreover, the provision of wool on credit seems to show that the ability of the English Templars to make such loans stemmed directly from the commercial exploitation of sheep-farming on their estates, which, in this rather indirect way, was ultimately channelled into the crusading cause.

Rulers needed the financial expertise which these operations engendered as much as the money itself. Two powers particularly made use of Templar administrators: the kings of France and the cadet branches of their house, and the papacy. When Louis VII incurred his debts to the Order during the Second Crusade, the repayments were made by the regents in Paris, presumably directly into the Paris Temple, thus beginning an association with the French monarchy which was to endure until the early fourteenth century. Under Philip II, the Order became a key part of a financial structure which by the end of the reign in 1223 had increased annual ordinary revenues by close to 120 per cent since the king's accession in 1180.[155] The

Templars had been heavily involved in these changes even before the reorganisation of Capetian demesne finances during the 1190s, for before Philip left on crusade in July 1190, he ordered that receipts from his lands be paid into the Paris Temple.[156] By 1202–3, the year for which the first Capetian 'budget' is available, the demesne accounts were being rendered at the Paris Temple three times per annum at each accounting term. Brother Haimard, the Treasurer, was one of a select inner circle of advisers to the king, presiding over the Exchequer in Normandy after the conquest of 1204, and acting as executor of the wills of both Philip and Queen Ingebourg in 1222.[157] Haimard was the first of a continuous line of Templar treasurers to serve the Capetian kings during the thirteenth century: there were at least eight such men between Haimard (1202–27) and Brother John of Tour, seized with the other Templars in France in 1307.[158] Royal influence ensured that the Paris Temple was controlled by the man chosen by the king. In 1263, for example, Louis IX wrote to Pope Urban IV asking for Brother Amaury de la Roche as Preceptor in France. The pope passed on the king's request to the Grand Master, Thomas Bérard, who in turn gave his assent. Amaury, formerly Grand Commander in the East, held the post from 1265 until 1271.[159] Special meetings of the curia at the Temple were maintained throughout the thirteenth century, although, as Joseph Strayer pointed out, these sessions did not look in any detail at the accounts, which were prepared for them beforehand.[160] It may be that the political heavyweights of the curia attended such sessions only once a year in any case. It seems that at least one Templar sat on this committee, presumably to give technical assistance. One such brother was the Fleming Arnoul of Wisemale, Preceptor of Reims, who is recorded at a meeting at Breuil in 1289. His death is remembered in the Reims obituary roll with the comment that 'he was a great man in the curia of the lord king of France'.[161]

The association between the French monarchy and the Templars established a model closely followed by other members of the Capetian house. The Templars were bankers not only to Louis IX, but to his mother, brothers, and sons. The most formidable and ambitious of these brothers, Charles of Anjou, who became King of Sicily in 1266, used a Templar treasurer, Brother Arnoul, while his purchase of a claim to the kingship of Jerusalem in 1277 led him into frequent co-operation with the Order in exporting needed supplies to the east. Indeed, when Charles acquired his claim from Maria of Antioch, as part of her compensation he granted her an income of 4,000 *livres tournois* from his rents in the County of Anjou which she could draw annually from the Templars in Paris.[162] The rather different interests of Queen Blanche were also accommodated. Apart from leaving the administration of her demesne finances to the Templars, the queen made them responsible for the funding of one of her favourite projects, the building of the monastery of Maubuisson. Between 1236 and 1242, almost 24,500 *livres* passed through the hands of the Templars for this purpose.[163]

Just as Philip II utilised the Temple in his remodelled financial structure, so too did the papacy increasingly employ Templar officials to help implement its policies both in Outremer and in Italy itself. The failure of the Fourth Crusade to provide the Holy Land with much practical help had profound effects upon Innocent III, and he determined to reorganise the crusading machinery as thoroughly as Philip II had overhauled his administration in the 1190s.[164] In 1198, the pope had taken the significant step of imposing proportional taxes upon the clergy to help pay for the crusade; thereafter the papacy used both the Temple and the Hospital as depots for the accumulation of these funds and as agents to transmit them to the east.[165] The Templars seem to have been undertaking these responsibilities from at least 1208, but it was under Honorius III, who inherited Innocent's crusading plans in the form of the Fifth Crusade (1218–21), that the operations really intensified. In 1220, for example, the pope sent orders to Pandolf, his legate in England, to gather the tax of a twentieth and the payment of Peter's Pence, and send it to the Temple in Paris. In turn, the Templars were to make the money available to Pelagius of Albano, the papal legate in Egypt. A letter of 24 July shows the pope deploying Templars in France, England, Hungary, and Spain to transfer the proceeds of the twentieth and the redemptions from crusading vows.[166]

But the popes always had the difficult task of balancing this wider vision of the needs of the Church as a whole against their own particular problems. Alexander III seems to have been the first pope to make extensive use of Templar financial expertise; for most of the pontificate until the reconciliation after the battle of Legnano in 1176, Frederick Barbarossa's rival line of popes created a schism which meant that access to many of the usual sources of papal revenue was at best fitful. Templar *cubicularii* can be seen administering Pope Alexander's revenues and arranging loans from 1163 onwards, enabling him to continue to operate in often adverse political circumstances.[167] Equally, such men were prominent at the thirteenth-century papal court and throughout the papal states, especially helping to finance the pro-papal Guelphs in the long struggle with imperial forces in central Italy. The ubiquitous Brother Bonvicino combined his political activities on behalf of the papacy with the role of papal *cubicularius* from at least the 1230s until his death in the mid 1260s. He appears particularly prominent in acting on behalf of Alexander IV in the conflict with the Hohenstaufen King Manfred, especially in his efforts to ensure that his native city, Perugia, gave no support to Manfred after the victory of the Ghibellines at the battle of Montaperti in 1260.[168] Not surprisingly, political problems faced by the papacy in Italy took precedence over crusading needs. When this occurred, as it did during the pontificate of Martin IV (1281–5) in particular, the practice of gathering funds for the crusade at a central depot like the Temple treasury in Paris proved extremely convenient. During 1281, for instance, the Temple received crusading money which included the tithe levied on Cistercian houses in France and the sums paid for redemption by crusaders who had failed to fulfil vows made for St Louis's expeditions. Most significant of all were the funds accumulated for a proposed crusade by the French king, Philp III, amounting to 100,000 *livres tournois*. But Martin IV was faced with a rebellion in the Romagna, and in December 1282 he drew on these deposits in the form of a loan in order to pay for troops raised in France intended to re-establish papal authority. The sum eventually borrowed seems to have fallen not far short of 155,000 *livres tournois*.[169] The link was maintained even during the trial. In 1307 and 1308, when the Templars throughout France were being held in custody by the royal officials, the *cubicularii* working for Clement V at Poitiers were exempt, being left directly under papal jurisdiction.[170]

The benefits accruing to the Temple from such services can be measured in a number of ways. Co-operation with rulers was necessary to obtain the freedom to function effectively in their lands. In England, for example, extensive privileges were conceded by Henry III in 1227 and confirmed by Edward I in 1285, by means of which the Order had full jurisidiction over its estates and their inhabitants.[171] The goodwill of such rulers was especially important in the second half of the thirteenth century when the growing crisis in Outremer made the unimpeded export of needed goods from the west absolutely imperative. Nevertheless, it is evident that the Order made specific administrative charges. Delisle has drawn attention to such items in the accounts of Philip IV with the Order between 1290 and 1293,[172] and it is equally clear that interest payments were made upon loans even though this is not always overtly stated in the documents recording the transactions. Medieval strictures on interest were not, in fact, always as rigid as they appear in Gratian's formulation of about 1140,[173] since canonists came to accept so many subtle variations on the theme of legitimate 'expenses' that the provision of credit was not hindered to anything like the extent to which it has sometimes been presented. There is no doubt, too, that the Templars genuinely incurred expenses, especially in the complicated matter of financing crusaders. Moreover, the Order was better placed than most creditors to make profit from the variations in the relative value of currencies, given that loans made at one end of the Mediterranean were often repaid some time later at the other. Even so, on occasions the payment of interest is clearly stated. In August 1274, for example, Edward I of England reimbursed the Templars the large sum of 27,974 *livres tournois* borrowed during his crusade of 1272, together with 5,333 *livres*, 6 *sous*, 8 *deniers* for 'administration, expenses, and interest'.[174]

A major reason for the Templars' success in this field was the degree of objectivity which they brought to the administration of the items entrusted to them, for in serving, in particular, the kings of France and England simultaneously, their role might otherwise have been seen as politically contradictory.[175] This reputation proved particularly valuable to King John who, by 1214, could find few who would place much credence in his promises. Therefore, when he wished to subsidise his allies in Poitou through the payment of pensions, he gained their confidence by depositing the money in the Templar treasury at the Order's house at La Rochelle, with instructions that the pensions be paid out from there for a set number of years.[176] Moreover, although there were isolated financial scandals, as well as a case in Catalonia during the 1260s in which a brother made a false seal which he then used on letters, their reputation for probity and for punishing wrongdoers generally stood up to examination.[177] The Rule was uncompromising on this issue. Each brother 'should assiduously take care that he does not keep money for himself, neither gold nor silver; for a person of religion should not have anything of his own, as the saint said, "a man of religion who has coppers is not worth a halfpenny"'. Any brother found with unauthorised money on his person when he died would be denied Christian burial, for the money was considered to have been stolen. It was obviously necessary for Templars to carry money on occasion, and this was permissible, but 'as soon as the brother is where he is to stay, he should give back what remains of the money to the treasury or to the one who gave it to him', whether the amount was great or small.[178]

But the Order remained a religious community formed to fight the infidel and ultimately it could never adopt the disinterested posture of a Swiss bank whose clients' morality was not its concern. Therefore, money deposited by King Henry II with the Order as part of his atonement for the murder of Becket was utilised by Gerard of Ridefort in the crisis which preceded Hattin in 1187 in order to raise troops.[179] The king was not apparently offended, for the next year the Templars were among those authorised to collect the so-called 'Saladin tithe' in England. Nor, on the other hand, were many rulers consistently able to resist the temptation to seize Templar assets, especially under the pressure of political or military needs. Templar houses in France and England were by no means secure – only the treasury in Paris seems to have presented a really formidable obstacle to a determined assailant – and even the London Temple succumbed on occasion. In June 1263, when royal fortunes were at a low ebb in the conflict with Simon of Montfort, Prince Edward, despite Templar opposition, entered the treasury and broke into a number of strong-boxes kept there. He seized nearly £10,000 belonging to various barons and merchants and took the money away with him to Windsor Castle.[180] His son was no more restrained. Soon after his father's death in July, 1307, Edward II and Piers Gaveston seized money, jewels, and precious stones from the London Temple, worth about £50,000.[181] Such violations were not unique to England. In 1285, Peter III of Aragon invaded Roussillon, held by his younger brother, James, King of Mallorca, whom he suspected of collaboration with the French crusaders who were about to invade his lands. During the course of his campaign, he gained entry to the city of

Perpignan, where his brother was staying, and there he broke into the Templar preceptory. According to the Aragonese chronicler, Bernat Desclot, he found not only treasure left by his brother for safekeeping, but also a series of incriminating documents which, Desclot claimed, showed that James was indeed plotting against him, having been promised the Kingdom of Valencia by Philip III of France when the crusaders had overcome Peter.[182]

In the end, the chief deterrent for anyone, king or common thief, was moral rather than physical. In the same way that rulers hesitated before breaking their feudal obligations to vassals, knowing that their own credibility rested on the maintenance of the system, so too did they exercise restraint when attracted by the ideas of despoiling Templar property. Nevertheless, that temptation remained, even though some form of justification was usually deemed necessary. In October 1307, the officials of Philip IV of France found just such a cover-story.

CHAPTER EIGHT

THE END OF THE ORDER

During the twelfth and thirteenth centuries the Order of the Temple appeared to be an integral part of the body politic of Latin Christendom, indispensable in the fight against the infidel, in the servicing of the crusades, and in financing popes and monarchs. Yet, in the bull *Vox in excelso* of 22 March 1312, Pope Clement V announced to the Church fathers assembled at his great council in Vienne in the Dauphiné that the Order was abolished 'by an inviolable and perpetual decree'. Serious scandal had arisen against it according to the bull, which could not be restrained while the Order remained in existence.[1] The two Templars found by Ludolph of Sudheim, whose last memories of the Order had been the slaughter of their companions by the Mamluks in the devastated city of Acre, came back to France to find that the papacy had achieved by decree what the Muslims had never been able to do by force, which was the complete destruction of their Order. Both at the time and in the centuries since, a huge and controversial literature has developed in the attempt to explain how a society of men which St Bernard had seen as invulnerable – their bodies protected by iron, their souls clothed in the breastplate of faith, as he said – could meet such a fate.[2]

De laude novae militiae is a potent and dramatic work, made all the more effective by the linguistic skill of the man who was the foremost communicator of his age. Its inspiration extended far beyond Bernard's lifetime. Almost a century later, James of Vitry, Bishop of Acre between 1216 and 1228, a man who was often scathing about what he regarded as the lethargy of the local Palestinian Franks, heaped praise upon the fervency of the Templars. In his *History of Jerusalem* he describes them as 'Lions in war, mild as lambs at home; in the field fierce knights, in church like hermits or monks; unyielding and savage to the enemies of Christ, benevolent and mild to Christians.' He claims that they were beloved by all because of their piety and humility, and that their fame had penetrated every corner of the Church.[3] He is equally enthusiastic in his *exempla*, a series of stories written down to provide clerics with material for sermons and therefore adapted to appeal to the general populace. In the following *exemplum* he uses the faith of the Templars to draw his moral:

That those of us who die for the defence of the Church are reckoned martyrs, we read in ancient histories, since when the King of Jerusalem had been besieging Ascalon for a long time and could in no way take it in the face of Saracen resistance, certain very brave knights of the Temple were captured by the Saracens and, in contempt of the name of Christ, all of them were seen to be hung above the city-gate. When the king and the brothers of the Temple saw this and, troubled in sadness of mind to an almost desperate extent, they wished to retreat from the siege, the Master of the Temple, a distinguished man of great faith, prohibited them, saying: 'You see these martyrs suspended on a gibbet, know that they have gone before and have proceeded to God in order that they might render the city to us.' Which proved to be the case; for in the space of two days against the hope of the whole city they took that which in no way they believed that they could capture.[4]

It is not surprising, therefore, to find that in his *Parzival* the great German poet, Wolfram von Eschenbach (died 1225) should translate these paragons into defenders of the Grail: pure warriors, disciplined and steadfast in the defence of the sacred territories which contained the Grail, just as in Bernard's vision the real Templars defended Jerusalem and the holy places. In Wolfram's version of the story the Grail is a stone rather than a vessel, but its central place as the object of true Christian struggle remains. The role of the Templars is explained to Parzival in the following way:

'It is well know to me', said his host, 'that many formidable fighting-men dwell at Munsalvaesche with the Gral. They are continually riding out on sorties in quest of adventure. Whether these same Templars reap trouble or renown they bear it for their sins. A warlike company lives there. I will tell you how they are nourished. They live from a Stone whose essence is most pure. If you have never heard of it I shall name it for you here. It is called "Lapsit exillis". By virtue of the Stone the Phoenix is burned to ashes, in which he is reborn.'[5]

These are all striking images, but they do not belong to real life; no body of men, however devoted, could be expected to match such idealisation in practice. Wolfram's Templars, although men of flesh and blood, have overcome the temptations of the carnal world, but the Templars who lived in everyday society could not always act out their assigned literary role. The important canon lawyer, Vincentius Hispanus (died 1248), for example, attacked a papacy which, in his view, while it promoted the importance of clerical celibacy, protected privileged groups from the consequences of their transgressions. He specifically named the Templars as being among those groups who said that they could not be punished by anyone, since the papacy reserved them for its own judgement.[6] Herein lay the nub of a serious problem, for the papacy's enthusiastic patronage created an organisation whose position and activities increasingly came to chafe upon the society within which it needed to function. The friction generated by the growth of this large corporation was exacerbated when critics judged that the crusading performance of the Order did not justify the vast sums of money which it appeared to consume. During the thirteenth century, as the military orders steadily took over the defence of the crusader states, so too their expenses continued to rise. To build an ʿAtlīt or a Safad needed the mobilisation of all possible resources, and there is some evidence to suggest that Templar anxiety to exploit their lands and rights in the west to the fullest extent possible created enemies in regions where a century before there had been only donors. Yet the results were meagre. The crusader states continued to shrink, and new disasters, like those of La Forbie and Mansourah, replaced Hattin in the public consciousness. The military orders offered a convenient focus for complaints which would otherwise have lacked a real target.

In the last quarter of the thirteenth century potential critics gained a much more solid platform than ever before. Consideration of the best methods of crusading had been brought to the top of the papal agenda by Pope Gregory X at the Council of Lyon in 1274, but the loss of Acre in 1291 stimulated an even more powerful and widespread debate, made manifest in the production of a number of detailed treatises.[7] Inevitably the role of the military orders came under intense scrutiny. The Templars had faced sporadic accusations against the integrity of their military operations from as early as the 1160s, but this was a situation which had not occurred before and, although the recent trend of crusading historiography had been to play down the significance of the events of 1291 as a turning-point,[8] it is arguable that for the Templars at least it was the most important in their history. More than any of the other military orders the Temple was associated with the defence of the crusader states and the holy places. The decision to abandon first ʿAtlīt and then, in August 1291, Tortosa as well, although forced upon the leaders by strategic realities, was a portentous step, the repercussions of which were certain to be profound both inside and outside the Order.

The Templars were not, of course, alone in their predicament after 1291. Neither the Hospitallers nor the Teutonic Knights had been able to prevent the Christian defeat and, indeed, the most frequently discussed proposals concerned not the Temple alone, but the reform of all the military orders. This was in fact an important question, which the military orders had never really seriously addressed. The closest the Templars had come to this was in about 1260, when they had added 113 clauses to the Rule, in which examples of specific Templar transgressions were described and their significance and punishment discussed. But this was not a systematic reform; nor was it intended for public consumption. It does not compare with that of the Cistercians, for example, who were capable of a high degree of self-examination and internal renewal, nor with the Franciscans, who, during the thirteenth century, had evolved within the context of a highly volatile debate about their life-style and objectives. The most persistent idea was that the military orders should be merged into a single organisation, possibly under a strong outside leader, which, it was argued, would eliminate their alleged rivalry and pool their resources, thus making them a more efficient tool in the crusade to regain the Holy Land.[9]

Not surprisingly, no evidence of enthusiasm for this proposal can be gleaned from Templar sources. Nevertheless, in 1306 the matter was forced upon the masters of both the Hospital and the Temple by Pope Clement V, who ordered them to produce *mémoires* summarising their views on the idea of a union. The arguments put forward by the Templar Grand Master, James of Molay, purport to present the case for and against, but in fact are heavily weighted in favour of the latter.[10] Molay recalled that the idea had been seriously discussed as long ago as 1274 at the Council of Lyon, but had foundered on the objections of the Spanish kings, who wished to preserve their own Iberian orders.[11] It had then been revived by Nicholas IV in 1291, in Molay's view largely as a sop to those elements critical of the papacy for failing to do enough to prevent the catastrophe. The pope considered the matter, says the Grand Master, 'In order that it might appear that he wished to apply a remedy concerning the matter of the Holy Land', but 'at length nothing was done'.[12] Boniface VIII had also talked a great deal about it, but 'for all that, having considered everything, entirely for the better, he ceased, as you can be told by some cardinals of that time'. Far from being advantageous, Molay believed that union would eventually lead to a diminution of the good that the two orders were able to achieve separately, which included the giving of alms, the passage of men and supplies across the sea, the protection of pilgrims and crusaders, and the battles against the Saracens. As Molay saw it, the two orders were similar but not duplicates; indeed, a man chose to join one or other because of perceived differences, and it would not be right to compel him 'to choose another order unless he wishes'. What recruits realised was that the ethos of the orders was not quite the same, for with the Hospital charitable work took precedence, while the Templars 'were founded especially as a knighthood'. Rivalry between the orders could therefore only be beneficial, providing a stimulus for each to strive to outdo the other.

Molay was of course well aware that the orders were operating in a different climate, claiming that in the past people had been devoted to the orders, but that now 'many more are found who wish to take from the orders rather than to give', and he does suggest that a united order might be better able to defend its rights against those who would do them harm. Clearly, though, he did not feel that this argument was decisive. The military orders remained the best means for promoting the crusade. 'Beyond this, holy Father, I have heard it recounted to you that the orders, who submit in obedience, are more apt and useful in the recovery and guarding of the Holy Land than other persons.'

In fact, Molay's account is somewhat disingenuous, for the discussions about a union of the orders were much more lively and persistent than his outline history suggests. One of the strongest supporters was the Mallorcan writer, Ramon Lull, who, since about 1263, had devoted his life to the study and promotion of the best ways of converting the Muslims, in particular by means of Christian missions. Lull had initially thought in terms of peaceful relations with Islam, but the losses of 1291 seem to have persuaded him that this was no longer practical and from this time he accepted the need for a crusade, even though it was only as a means of clearing the way for missions. This necessarily meant that he needed to consider the position of the military orders and, in 1292, he put forward the idea of a united order under the leadership of a so-called *Bellator Rex*, or Warrior King. Thereafter, he remained a consistent advocate of this plan until, in the course of 1308, he came to accept that the Templars were guilty of the accusations made against them and that therefore his scheme could not be fulfilled as he had orginally conceived it.[13]

Lull was not a negligible force, for he was a tireless advocate of his plans at the papal curia and at the courts of Aragon, France, and Sicily, as well as a prolific writer, and his advocacy of the idea of a unified order led by the son of a king in his *Liber de fine*, which he finished in 1305, may well have influenced Philip the Fair of France.[14] According to a report dating from the spring of 1308, shortly after the death of his wife in 1305 Philip had asked the pope to unite all the military orders into one, at which point he would renounce his kingdom and assume the leadership of this new force in a new guise as king of Jerusalem. Under the name of the 'Order of the Knighthood of Jerusalem', it would thereafter be ruled by a son of the king or, if he had no son, by a royal appointee.[15] Molay may, of course, have seen the idea of union simply as a threat to his own position as Master, since a merger would inevitably have meant a reorganisation of the hierarchies, a problem to which he alludes in his *mémoire*. However, if there is any truth in the report of Philip IV's ideas, then his opposition perhaps derived not simply from an innate conservatism or even from fears about his own career, but from an awareness of the form such a union might take if it were dominated by the French court.

Molay's evident belief that the idea of a union was a hardy perennial from which nothing had come in the past was shaped by the context within which he wrote. It has been justly argued that the period between 1291 and the Council of Vienne in 1311–12 was more productive of theories than of practical action;[16] indeed, despite the attention given to it by historians, the idea of the *Bellator Rex* remained far-fetched, whether led by the French or the Aragonese. In contrast, Molay was essentially an active crusader whose experience in the east went back to the early 1270s, a man more at home with the details of military planning and execution than grandiose theory. This mental set is reflected in another *mémoire*, requested by the pope at the same time, in which he made a much more effective presentation of what he regarded as the most important preconditions for an assault on the Holy Land.

Just as, during the last quarter of the thirteenth century, the function of the military orders had come under close examination, so too had the nature of crusading expeditions. Large-scale ventures, even when led by a king like Louis IX, amply endowed with both genuine commitment and large resources, had failed to justify the human and material costs involved. Since the Council of Lyon it had therefore become fashionable to talk of the *passagium particulare*, the advance force intended to establish a bridgehead before the arrival of a more general crusade.[17] Clement V seems, therefore, to have asked Molay for his opinion of such schemes.[18] The Grand Master, however, was quite adamant that the *parvum passagium* 'would cause the loss of all those who crossed'. It would have no base upon which it could rely, since the mainland possessions of the Christians had been totally lost, and it would simply not have the strength to confront the Mamluks directly in battle. Molay wrote from bitter experience: in 1302 a Templar force established on the island of Ruad, just off Tortosa, for what appears to have been a similar purpose, had been totally wiped out.[19]

The alternative sometimes put forward was a landing in Christian Armenia, that is, Cilicia in south-east Asia Minor. This, too, Molay viewed with deep scepticism; to do battle even with the Muslim forces occupying Jerusalem would require between 12,000 and 15,000 horsemen and 40,000 or 50,000 archers, and this would still leave the main Mamluk force in Egypt, which could easily be deployed against them. Moreover, there were additional problems in the Cilician landing, for the climate was so unsuited to westerners that Molay thought that it would be a miracle if more than fifty horsemen from 4,000 could survive there for more than a year, even though they were strong and healthy when they set out. The Armenians them-selves could not be trusted, both because they were unreliable in battle and because they suspected the Franks of trying 'to take their kingdom from them', and would not therefore allow them to enter any of their castles and strong-points. Again, Molay spoke from Templar experience; the long and debilitating conflict between the Order and the Armenians in the Amanus March had sapped the strength of both sides.[20] Finally, the mountain passes which would need to be traversed in northern Syria would be very difficult to break through, not only because of the nature of the country, but because they were inhabited by peoples ranging from Turcomans to Bedouin, none of whom would be prepared to give the Franks a friendly reception.

Molay therefore asked the pope to try to promote a large general expedition as soon as possible, involving 'the lord kings of France, England, Germany, Sicily, Spain, and the other lords of the land great and small, whose hearts God might illuminate in that affair so pious and laudable'. Transport should be provided by the Genoese, Venetians, and other maritime powers in the form of large carriers, which had a capacity four times that of a galley, but could be provided at only a third of the cost. Galleys for fighting at sea would not be needed, since the Mamluk naval forces were negligible. Again Molay had cause to know, for Templar ships had been prominent in raids on the Egyptian and Levantine coasts since the early 1290s.[21] Basing his estimate on the numbers which Baybars was supposed to have said would have forced him to retreat, as well as on conversations with veterans of St Louis' campaign, Molay thought that a general passage would need between 12,000 and 15,000 knights and 5,000 footsoldiers. The assembly-point would depend upon the kings involved, but it was crucial that thereafter the crusade should first adopt Cyprus as a base and then attack the mainland from there. Secrecy should be maintained about the ultimate destination; the Master was prepared to furnish the pope with a confidential list of the best places. Meanwhile, he wanted the pope to send ten galleys immediately, to be placed under the command of Rogeron, son of the late admiral, the famous Roger of Lauria (died 1305), apparently less for the purpose of attacking the Muslims than in order to prevent illegal trading by the maritime cities. For this reason Molay did not want this fleet led by a member of the military orders, since he foresaw likely clashes with Venice and Genoa, which could have far-reaching repercussions. A concomitant of this was that the ban on trading with Egypt be strictly enforced in such a way 'that they [the maritime powers] could not be easily absolved from the said sentence on their return as they had become accustomed to do at other times'. He was, he explained, much better able to present these matters in conversation than in writing, and it appears that one of the purposes of his visit to the west in 1307 was to elaborate upon these arguments.

The *mémoire* ends with what amounts to a kind of prayer for the future of the crusade. 'Therefore I ask the Omnipotent God that he gives to you the grace of ordaining upon these things what will be best and the power of recovering in your time the holy places, in which Our Lord Jesus Christ deemed worthy to be born and die for the salvation of the human race.'

There is no reason to doubt the conviction behind these sentiments, since Molay had been a rigorous promoter of crusading action ever since he had first arrived in Palestine, over forty years before. Moreover, Theobald Gaudin had died on 16 April, in either 1292 or 1293,[22] so Molay was therefore the real heir to the problems of 1291. He was a Burgundian of wide experience, who had joined the Order at Beaune (in the diocese of Autun) in 1265. His receptors were Humbert of Pairaud and Amaury de la Roche, Masters in England and France respectively, and therefore two of the most important Templars in the west, which suggests that his family already had good connections with the Temple. He had seen at least ten years' service in the east and indeed had probably been in Palestine for over twenty years. According to a witness at the trial, he was present at a chapter-meeting at Nicosia 'in that year in which Acre was lost',[23] although the reference does not make it clear if this was before or after the event, and therefore it is not known if he was at the siege in May 1291.

In view of the suppression of the Order, it is natural that historians should pay particular attention to the character and attitudes of the last Grand Master in order to see if herein lies any part of the explanation for the Order's sudden demise. To some extent this leads to a seductive, but nevertheless dangerous, circular argument. His reputation has undoubtedly suffered from the very existence of the trial, the pressures of which forced him into a series of vacillations which undermined the Order's defence and credibility, but which may well represent a serious distortion of his character in more normal circumstances. In addition, witnesses whose voices would otherwise have never been heard and who themselves might in any case have spoken differently without the stress of imprisonment and torture, were placed in a position where they believed that to denounce the Master might gain them relief from their own tribulations. Thus, according to one knight, Molay fraudulently manipulated the election procedure in order to become Master, while a serving brother in his immediate entourage claimed that he had had homosexual relations with him, and another (who seems never to have been to the east) maintained that it was common talk that he loved one of his personal servants, a young man called George.[24] On the other hand, not all those critical of him were involved in the trial. The Templar of Tyre, who did not believe the Order guilty of the charges brought against it and who admired William of Beaujeu, for whom he had worked as a secretary, clearly did not like Molay. He describes him 'as mean beyond reason', and claims that he offended Philip IV by dismissing a treasurer of the Order who had loaned the king 400,000 gold florins without the Master's knowledge. Despite pressure from both king and pope, Molay refused to reinstate him, even throwing the letter from the pope into the fire.[25] This story is also found in the *Chronique d'Amadi*,[26] and is a popular one with historians in that it seems to suggest a motive for the French king's attack. In fact, the treasurer of the Temple at Paris, John of Tour, was in post right up to the time of the actual arrests, but it is possible that the author intended to demonstrate his contention that Molay's attitude was damaging to the Order, and that to do this, even so well informed an observer as he was not above repeating stories of this kind.

In one respect, however, Molay was very similar to William of Beaujeu, the Templar of Tyre's patron, for he could not free himself from the partisan postures which had bedevilled the politics of the crusader states during the thirteenth century. Molay inherited the feud between the Temple and the Cypriot kings, arising from Beaujeu's commitment to the Angevin cause,[27] a feud made all the more intense because the Templars were forced to base themselves in Cyprus itself after 1291. Molay was as determined as his predecessor to maintain the Angevin link, for the supply of Cyprus through the Apulian ports was indispensable to the Order, and it is not therefore surprising to find Henry II, Hugh's son, who succeeded his brother in 1285 as King of Cyprus, complaining to the pope about the Temple's continued opposition.[28] Boniface VIII tried to mediate, reminding the king of the value of the military orders to the kingdom, and Molay of the fact that Henry had taken in the Templars after the loss of the Holy Land,[29] but he failed to effect a permanent reconciliation. Tensions within the island came to a head in April 1306 when, led by Amaury of Lusignan, Lord of Tyre, the king's brother, an assembly of Cypriot lords succeeded in deposing Henry, and establishing a regency in his place. In February 1310, Amaury engineered his brother's exile to Cilicia. By this time James of Molay was held in prison in Paris, struggling to maintain his self-respect in the face of the accusations brought by the French government, but in the spring of 1306, while not the instigator of the move against Henry II, he was certainly heavily involved. A sixteenth-century chronicler, Florio Bustron, says that Amaury's declaration that he had taken over as governor was drawn up by Molay and by Peter of Erlant, Bishop of Limassol, while the *Chronique d'Amadi* claims that the Templars had recently loaned Amaury 50,000 *besants*, a statement which carries the implication that the Order had financed the coup.[30] According to *Amadi*, Amaury argued that Henry II was incapable of governing because he suffered from epilepsy, backing up his point by alleging that the country had been inadequately defended and supplied, and that justice had not been properly administered.[31] The military orders and the clergy were said to be among the chief losers by this and, indeed, Fulk of Villaret, Grand Master of the Hospital, is listed among the adherents of this protest, together with Molay himself.

This, indeed, may be the key to the Grand Master's attitude for, whether or not the criticisms emanating from the trial witnesses and the Templar of Tyre are taken seriously, Molay's record from the early 1290s shows a consistent determination to implement the crusade in the manner of past Templar masters. No explanation for the Order's demise arising from an alleged neglect of the traditional functions of the Temple can be given much credibility, even though it may have served the purposes of a theorist and place-seeker like the Norman lawyer, Pierre Dubois.[32] The Order was faced with two problems: how to maintain and increase its supplies of men, food, and clothing from the west, and how to conduct campaigns against the Saracens in a way which would show the world that the Templars were continuing to prosecute the holy war with as much vigour as in the past, even though the mainland bases had been lost. The most immediate gap was in manpower, for the losses of 1291 must have been very heavy. But the Templars had rebuilt before, notably after Hattin and again after the defeats of the 1240s, so that the testimony of John Cenaud, Preceptor of La Fouilhouze (in the diocese of Clermont) at the time of the trial but serving in the east between

1285 and 1291, that he had seen 400 brothers at a chapter-meeting at Nicosia in the year that Acre was lost, may well be true.[33] Although he is vague about the time of year, this figure does suggest that it was an assembly gathered by Theobald Gaudin towards the end of the year and that many of these men were reinforcements from the west sent to replace those killed in the defence of Acre. The Order continued to draw on its western preceptories in this way down to the trial in 1307: seventy-one of the seventy-six Templars interrogated in Cyprus in 1310 had joined in the western preceptories (including the Morea) and at least fifty-nine of these had been recruited since 1291.[34]

Molay sought to build on the Order's contribution by travelling to the west and making a personal appeal to key rulers. In a letter to James II of Aragon, he told that king that he was at the papal curia at Rome at the time of the abdication of Celestine V and the accession of Boniface VIII in December 1294, and he appears to have stayed in central Italy for a further six months before travelling to Paris and London.[35] Another letter, to Peter of St Just, Preceptor of the Aragonese house of Graynane, explained that 'he had come from beyond the sea to these parts on behalf of the Christian community and for the advantage of our house'.[36] During the journey, which may have lasted until 1297, but was more likely to have taken about a year, he seems to have made contact with Boniface VIII, Charles II of Naples, Philip IV of France, and Edward I of England, either directly or through their representatives, as well as with James II.[37]

The concrete results of this activity can be seen both immediately and over the following decade. In July 1295, Boniface VIII issued a bull confirming that the privileges of the Temple in Cyprus would be the same as those enjoyed in the Holy Land.[38] Even more quickly, in January, Charles II of Naples had responded by ordering his port officials in Apulia to exempt shipments of food produced by the Templars on their own lands in the province and destined for Cyprus or the Holy Land from export taxes, provided they did not exceed a certain level and that they were directed through the ports of Barletta, Manfredonia, or Brindisi. The levels were 2,000 *salmae* of wheat, 3,000 of barley, and 500 of vegetables, and, as had been the case under his father, were specifically 'for the sustenance of the persons and men of the said house', that is, they were not intended for resale.[39] In 1299, Henry of Herville, Portulan of Apulia, ordered the royal officials at Manfredonia to allow wheat purchased by various persons, including the Italian banking society of the Bardi, for the Hospital, to be exported, which implies a relaxation of the restriction limiting exports to produce from the Orders' own estates. This cargo was to be carried on a Templar ship, itself already loaded with grain for the Order in Cyprus.[40]

On the same day as his general confirmation of the Templar privileges in Cyprus, Boniface VIII also wrote to Edward I of England, asking him to permit the free export of goods by the Templars in order to sustain them in Cyprus.[41] Edward was the only reigning monarch who had personally been on crusade to the east but, preoccupied with his own immediate problems in Gascony and Scotland, he had been unable to fulfil his intention of following up his expedition of 1272. He was, however, ready to make the same concessions as Charles II. In 1296, at Berwick, he issued two orders to Stephen of Pencestre, Constable of Dover Castle, to permit both Guy of Foresta, former Master of the Temple in England, and Brian of Jay, the current Master, to cross to Cyprus. Guy of Foresta was taking three horses worth six marks each, and worsted cloth for the brethren's robes, while Brian of Jay was bringing the responsions due from the Order's English province. Brian of Jay was travelling specifically to confer with the Grand Master.[42] These privileges were extended to the next Master in England, William de la More, as well. The king himself was still fully stretched campaigning in Scotland (this time the order came from Stirling), but on 10 May 1304, he ordered Richard of Burghersh, Constable at Dover, to allow the Master to travel to Cyprus with his household, horses, arms, and other things, and to take money with him for his expenses, despite the king's general prohibition on the export of money from the kingdom. In a separate communication with Molay three days later, the king praised William de la More for his services to the crown and asked that the Grand Master send him back as soon as possible. He also explained that he had been prevented from going on crusade by various wars, but that once these were settled he had every intention of fulfilling his vow. For this reason William de la More was to bring back information on the state of the Holy Land and advice from the Templars on the proposed expedition.[43]

In lieu of a major crusade the men, money, and supplies helped fuel the Templars' own efforts to take the war to the Saracens. Henry of Herville's order of 1299 shows that they continued to maintain their own freight carriers in Apulian ports; in 1293 they had also acquired warships in the form of six galleys from Venice 'for the guard of the island of Cyprus', to add to the two which they already had.[44] The period of the most intensive effort, though, seems to have been between 1300 and 1302, partly because it was believed in some quarters that there was a genuine possibility of an alliance with the Mongols. Both Pope Innocent IV and King Louis IX had sent representatives to the Mongols, but neither had found much to encourage them. However, the rise of Mamluk power and the defeat at 'Ain Jālūt in 1260 seems to have persuaded the Mongols to take a more positive attitude towards the Christians and, from 1267, embassies came to the west reasonably regularly in the hope of organising a joint campaign. The idea was not therefore new in 1300, but the attempts at practical implementation were to show that the logistical and political difficulties which had wrecked previous initiatives still existed.

The course of these campaigns shows how the Christians of Outremer were beginning the transition from land-based armies to sea powers, successfully completed by the Hospitallers in the later middle ages. In July 1300, the military orders, the king, and Amaury of Lusignan equipped sixteen galleys, which sailed from Famagusta and made a wide sweep of the coasts of Egypt, Palestine, and Syria, attacking Rosetta, Alexandria, Acre, Tortosa, and Maraclea.[45] The chartering of a ship from the Genoese by Peter of Vares, Preceptor of the Temple, in February of that year, may be connected with this expedition. It was to be used between March and July, during which time it was to be loaded up in Famagusta and Limassol with the intention of going to Tortosa, Tripoli, Tyre, and Acre. A proposed division of profit suggests that the intention was to trade, but since these ports were in the hands of the Mamluks, it is possible that the attacks of that summer were intended to precede this venture.[46] The raids themselves were apparently a preliminary to a combined attack with the Mongols, for in November, Amaury of Lusignan, and the Masters of the Temple and the Hospital, with a force of about 600 knights, at least half of which were provided by the military orders, set sail for Ruad, the small island near Tortosa. From there they made raids upon the town itself, but they waited in vain for the arrival of the Mongols under the Ilkhan, Ghazan, eventually deciding that the threat of the Mamluks was too great and that therefore they had no alternative but to retire to Cyprus. The Mongol army did appear in the following February, accompanied by their vassal, the Armenian King Hetoum, but it was too late to make the proposed junction.[47]

The choice of Tortosa was nevertheless significant, for it shows the strength of Templar influence. It had been the centre of one of the Order's most important enclaves and, together with 'Atlīt, had been the last stronghold to be abandoned in 1291. As the Mamluks had dismantled 'Atlīt, Tortosa must have seemed the most practical alternative, particularly as Ruad could be used as a base. The Templars therefore followed up the raid of 1300 by establishing a considerable force on the island and by building (or rebuilding) its defences. The numbers involved show that this was a serious effort to regain a foothold in Syria, since the garrison was close to half the size of the normal complement for the twelfth-century Kingdom of Jerusalem, with 120 knights, 500 archers, and 400 servants under the Order's Marshal, Bartholomew. But the Templar force was too isolated. In 1302 the Mamluks sent a fleet of at least sixteen galleys from Tripoli and besieged the island. Although the garrison fought hard, they were eventually starved into submission. Brother Hugh of Dampierre then negotiated what was believed to be a safe-conduct, but most were killed or sent into captivity. A fleet equipped to rescue them apparently set out from Famagusta, only to find that it was too late.[48] The loss of Ruad showed the weakness of the Christian forces on Cyprus and had the Mamluks possessed a viable naval force, Cyprus itself would have been very vulnerable. As it was, in March 1302 pirates from Rhodes had seized Guy of Ibelin and his family from their castle near Limassol, and their release was secured only when James of Molay paid out a ransom of 45,000 silver pieces.[49] Experiences like these shaped the views of the Grand Master and help to explain his strong opposition to the idea of a preliminary *passagium parvum* in his *mémoire* of 1306, as well as his suspicion of an alliance with other powers such as the Armenians.

The circumstances under which the Order of the Temple was obliged to operate after 1291 were not therefore favourable. Saddled with the Bernardine vision of the perfect Christian warrior, which they could not live up to, the loss of the remains of the Holy Land emphasised the gulf between ideal and reality in a way never before experienced. Bernard had associated the Templars above all with the defence of the holy places – indeed, about half of *De laude* was taken up with a spiritual tour of these sites – so that more than any other contemporary order they could be seen to have failed at a distinct point in time. This made them vulnerable to criticism and turned upon them the searching gaze of the crusade theorists: 1291 brought the reform of the military orders to the forefront of the crusading agenda. Even so, it is clear that between 1291 and 1307 the Order attempted to fulfil its role in the conflict with the infidel as it had done in the past and that contemporaries accepted it on these terms. Moreover, the idea of a union of the orders was only one of many plans for a future ideal *regnum* in the east, plans which sought to rectify what were seen as other mistakes as well.[50] Nobody argued that the Order of the Temple was irredeemably flawed; even Pierre Dubois' demand for its abolition was evidently added to his treatise after he knew of the arrests.[51] Nobody else apparently contemplated it, as the shocked or cynical reactions of contemporary commentators demonstrate. The arrests were sudden, unexpected, and abrupt; it seems unlikely that even the French government considered them seriously more than a few months beforehand.[52] Indeed, the proposals for union implicitly accepted the propriety of the Temple, for a rotten and decaying body, addicted to heretical belief and obscene acts, such as the Templars were alleged to be in October 1307, would inevitably have spread its disease to the healthy limb of the Church with which it was supposed to be merged. The failure of the Templars to live up to the superhuman standards of St Bernard made the trial possible, but it was not in itself a cause of it.

The explanation of the Templars' demise must therefore be sought in the motives of the King of France and his government rather than in the Order itself. Philip the Fair had become king in 1285, aged only seventeen. He was heir to a long tradition, for the Capetians had occupied the throne in continuous succession since 987, and he was particularly conscious of the authority and sanctity of his famous grandfather, Louis IX, whose canonisation he obtained in 1297. Since the reign of Philip II (1180–1223) Capetian territorial gains had been enormous, turning their patrimony from a modest, landlocked demesne in the Ile-de-France into a power of European importance, encompassing both Normandy and the Toulousain. Philip IV himself was imbued with the idea of France as the chosen kingdom of God, whose rulers were especially favoured because of their fervour in the faith, ever vigilant against threats of subversion whether from within or from without.[53] Even so, before 1307, there is nothing to suggest that the French king or his advisers suspected any such threat to be contained within the Order of the Temple. If the Templars had been riddled with vice and heresy for many years before 1307, it had been very successfully concealed from the French kings, who continued to employ the Order's treasurers at Paris to oversee their demesne accounts and to make a wide variety of payments on their behalf. Delisle has demonstrated in his study of the receipts and expenses in the account of February 1288 (Candlemas 1287) that, for the first decade of the reign, the financial role of the Templars under Philip IV remained the same as that under his predecessors. His analysis shows the Templars performing nine basic financial functions for the crown: payments to *baillis* to cover their local expenses; receipt of deposits taken from the *taille* on the Jews of the Auvergne, from various *sénéchaussées*, from the counties of Chartres and Champagne, from the minting at Sommières and Paris, and from the tenth levied to pay for matters connected with the Kingdom of Aragon (with which the French had recently been at war); recovering various sums owed, left, or restored to the king; maintaining the accounts which governed the household expenses of the king and princes; payments of part of the rents, pensions, gratuities, and loans to which the royal treasury was committed; advancing money that the king loaned to his grandmother and to several barons; discharging the expenses of various diplomatic missions; sustaining the partisans and soldiers of France in the Kingdom of Navarre; and reimbursing sums loaned by Italian bankers and by French subjects to the king.[54] None of these would have been contemplated if the king had not had confidence in the Order's integrity and efficiency.

However, in about 1295, the king established a new royal treasury at the Louvre, a reorganisation of his financial administration which might suggest a diminution of the Templars' role. A more likely explanation is a growth in the scale and complication of royal finance during the reign, especially under the pressure of prolonged wars with England and with Flanders, the effects of which started to make themselves felt from the mid 1290s.[55] The two treasuries operated in co-operation thereafter, as well as in relation to other financial experts employed by the king, like the Italian bankers shown as 'Biche and Mouche'. Indeed, it is generally believed that some of the functions of the Louvre treasury were transferred back to the Temple in about 1303, albeit under the close supervision of royal officials.[56] Therefore, during 1305 and 1306, years in which some historians believe that Philip the Fair was already considering action against the Order,[57] the Paris Temple continued to operate the accounts of the *bailliages* and *prévôtés*, as well as paying out wages for soldiers employed by the crown in Picardy and Flanders.[58] In short, the developments within the royal financial administration down to 1307 offer no portents of the trial; they were prompted entirely by financial needs.

Nor can much credence be given to theories that the Templars represented some kind of political or military threat to the crown, or even that their degree of independence offended the king's concept of sovereignty. While it is true that both Philip III and Philip IV attempted to use Louis IX's confirmation of Templar possessions in 1258 as a base point after which futher acquisitions were not permitted,[59] this needs to be seen in the context of the attempts by most contemporary monarchs to reduce the proportion of lands held in mortmain by clerical institutions,[60] rather than an action aimed specifically at the Temple in France. There is no evidence of Templar opposition to the crown (in contrast to some of the French episcopacy); in June 1303, Hugh of Pairaud, Visitor in France, and the leading Templar official in the province, was listed among those supporting Philip IV in his conflict with Boniface VIII over the king's arrest and trial of Bernard Saisset, Bishop of Pamiers. The following year, the king made another general confirmation of the Order's property in France.[61] As regards a possible military threat, it is evident that the Templars under Molay had no intention of moving their headquarters from Cyprus to France,[62] while analysis of the depositions at the trial shows that those Templars who lived in French preceptories could no more muster a coherent fighting force than the Cistercians or the Franciscans. The more active soldiers were only too badly needed in the east.[63]

Nevertheless, despite all the pretensions of the French monarch in the late thirteenth century, Philip IV's inheritance had not been untroubled. He began the reign with a huge burden of debt from his father's failed crusade against Aragon in 1284–5 and, from the 1290s,

297

wars against England and Flanders added to the financial pressures, so that despite the monarchy's large resources there was always an urgent need to raise ever larger sums of money. It was the government's exactions from the clergy that provoked his first confrontation with Pope Boniface VIII in 1296–7, while his frequent interference with the coinage associated his regime indelibly with the issue of 'false money'. Seizures of the property and persons of the 'Lombards', or the Italian bankers, in 1291 and again in 1311, as well as the Jews in 1306, showed that these pressures were sufficiently powerful to persuade the government that short-term financial needs were more important than long-term planning. It is doubtful if either act was ultimately financially advantageous to the crown; in 1315, in fact, the year after Philip IV's death, the Jews had been recalled, despite being expelled 'for ever' only nine years before.[64] There are therefore obvious financial reasons for the sudden arrest of the Templars in France, for as bankers they possessed considerable liquid wealth and negotiable assets, and as landowners, fixed and movable properties in every region of France from Normandy to Provence. The careful inventories of these properties after the arrests, the sequestration and renting out of the lands, the stripping of their assets, and the continued administration and use of the Templar treasury by royal officials after October 1307, provide solid evidence of the government's material interest in the Templars, despite the strenuous denials that the government had any such intention by William of Plaisians, one of Philip's leading ministers, in 1308.[65] In addition, there was a strong motive for gaining access to the Order's cash and precious metals, for in 1306, after years of debasement, the king had ordered the re-establishment of the coinage at the standards set by Louis IX in 1266, an action which was not achievable without a greatly increased supply of specie for the recoining.[66] Many contemporaries, especially those observing events from Italy, where there was perhaps a more profound understanding of the power of money than anywhere else in the early fourteenth-century west, were quite convinced that this was the prime reason for the attack.[67] For Dante, avarice ran in the blood of the whole Capetian house from Hugh Capet onwards; Philip the Fair was the new Pilate who 'flaunts his plundering sails' into the Temple.[68]

However, motivation is seldom as straightforward as this. Investigations of the king's character in recent years suggest that, although he sought to profit from the seizures, this does not preclude the possibility that he convinced himself or had been persuaded by others of the Templars' guilt, and therefore of the imperative duty of taking action, at whatever cost. Philip maintained an aloof and stern persona intended to enhance the dignity and obligations of kingship, which in turn accords with what is known of the man, driven by a censorious morality and rigid piety which cut him off from other people, itself the product of an isolated and loveless upbringing.[69] These traits may have been intensified by the death of his wife, Jeanne of Navarre, in April 1305, aged thirty-two. This affected him deeply and he seems to have been prepared to believe that Guichard, Bishop of Troyes, a former member of the queen's entourage, had caused her death by poisoning and sorcery, for which proceedings were started in August 1308, and indeed that Guichard represented a danger to the rest of his family.[70] Therefore, if the idea had been implanted in his mind that the Templars had succumbed to heretical and sexual depravity, it would have been logical to attempt to 'purify' the realm, just as he had cleansed it of the Jews. William Jordan has shown that, although the king profited enormously from the attack on the Jews in 1306, he also believed that the Jews had regularly desecrated the host.[71] In the same way, the removal of the Templars' wealth from such polluted hands was the sacred duty of 'the most Christian king'. Given this perception of the king's cast of mind, some historians have speculated on the extent to which he was manipulated by the narrow group of ministers with which he surrounded himself and which appears to have conducted policy, including the proceedings against the Templars. The exact extent of the influence of these men is not clear, but so many of the initiatives of Philip's reign are marked by his view of the world that it is difficult to believe that he was a mere cipher. Philip did not hesitate to act in this way against the pope on the one hand, when his minister, William of Nogaret, attempted to seize Boniface VIII at Anagni in 1303 in order to answer charges in France, or against his own family on the other, when he humiliated his sons and punished their wives in the matter of the women's adultery in 1314. Nevertheless, although he was no puppet, he did present his advisers with exploitable material. While it is perhaps going too far to describe Nogaret as 'a true Rasputin',[72] the king was evidently susceptible to a certain type of allegation and his ministers must have been aware of this: a connecting strand which runs through the cases of the Templars, the Jews, Boniface VIII, and Guichard of Troyes is a belief that they were trying to undermine the true Christianity of the sacred realm of France, armed with secret and underhand means derived from their knowledge of sorcery. If the king saw the Templars as a danger to the state, it was not as a military organisation, but as a diabolical force.

One further possibility exists: that in the affair of the Templars Philip the Fair sought to achieve the crusading apotheosis to which his house claimed to have been dedicated since the time of Louis VII. Philip admired his grandfather above all and there is no doubt that the abiding theme of the saint's life was his devotion to the crusade.[73] For a king such as Philip, the concept of the *Bellator Rex* at the head of a new united military order might be thought to have some attraction, in that it would combine control of the Templars' possessions with crusading prestige in a manner which would be quite unique. Contemporaries as diverse as the English cleric and canon lawyer, Adam of Murimouth, and the Genoese merchant, Christian Spinola, believed that this was so, and in this they have been followed by some modern historians.[74] Christian Spinola thought that Philip had resented the opposition of the Temple to the proposals for a union of the orders, while Adam of Murimouth said that the king gained the condemnation of the Templars at the Council of Vienne in 1312, 'for he hoped to make one of his sons king of Jerusalem, and that all the lands and possessions of the Templars would be conceded to his son'. The burning of the Templars had been for this reason, especially James of Molay, the Grand Master. The king, though, had been frustrated by the pope, who had transferred the Temple's revenues and possessions to the Hospital.[75]

In fact, the evidence of Philip IV's interest in such a project before the Council of Vienne is rather thin, for it is largely based upon a passing reference in a letter of an Aragonese correspondent in 1308 and the report of a conversation between a French cardinal and some Aragonese envoys in 1309.[76] The idea that the king would give up his French crown for that of Jerusalem does indeed strain credibility. Despite his apparent capacity for self-delusion, it is difficult to believe that he really intended to put this into practice or that he was prepared to destroy the Temple to enable him to do so. There has been a tendency to exaggerate Philip IV's anxiety to go on crusade, for he never actually went, despite a long reign of twenty-nine years. Reasons can be found for this, but it should be pointed out that other kings in the past had managed to do so, even in the face of equally difficult domestic circumstances, and that even so unenthusiastic a crusader as Philip II had actually campaigned in the Holy Land, albeit for a relatively short period. The appointment of a cadet of the Capetian house as head of a united order might be seen as a more realistic option, but this can only be directly connected with the French court at Vienne in 1312 when the argument about the disposal of the Temple's property was at its height, and it does not need excessive cynicism to conclude that this had more relevance to an attempt to maintain the crown's grip on the Order's possessions than to serious crusading.

When the royal officials moved in on the Templar preceptories they were acting on prearranged orders sent out a month before, possibly precipitated by the chance that the Order's leaders, usually based in Cyprus, were on a visit to Paris at this time. There was no resistance because most of the Templars were unarmed and many were middle-aged or even elderly. Except for the Paris Temple itself, the houses were largely unfortified. A few Templars escaped, but most were quite unprepared and they were quickly taken away in the name of the Inquisition, imprisoned and tortured. The object was to make them confess that they had been involved in heretical initiation ceremonies in which they had denied Christ, spat on or otherwise profaned a crucifix, and then, naked, had been obscenely kissed by their receptor upon the base of the spine, the navel, and the lips. Such a ceremony was, moreover, the decadent preliminary to entry into an order in which a cult of idol worship replaced the Christian faith, and institutionalised homosexuality mocked the white garments which symbolised the supposed celibacy of the knights. Within a week, the royal officials, nominally under Inquisitorial leadership but in practice taking their orders from the French government, were able to start presenting the Templars in public, confident that most of them would admit to some or all of the charges brought against them.[77]

This confidence was not misplaced. Only four of the 138 depositions extant from the hearings in Paris between October and November 1307 show a complete denial of the accusations, and none of those who resisted was important in the Order's hierarchy. James of Molay, Hugh of Pairaud, and Geoffrey of Charney, Preceptor of Normandy, all made confessions. But, to the historian, the disjuncture between these sudden proceedings and the apparently normal relations between the Templars and the French crown since 1285 is glaring. Nowhere is this more evident than in the case of John of Tour, Treasurer of the Temple at Paris, and, like his predecessors, an apparently trusted financial adviser to the king. On 26 October 1307, he appeared before William of Paris, Papal Inquisitor in France, and made a full confession. He said he was about fifty-nine years old and had been received at the house of Maurepas (just to the southwest of Paris) by his predecessor, also called John of Tour, about thirty-two years before. The substance of his testimony was recorded by the notary in the following way:

He said also on his oath that, after making many promises concerning the observance of the statutes and secrets of the Order, the receptor led him behind the altar, and showed him a certain cross on which was depicted the image of Jesus Christ crucified, and asked whether he believed in the one whose image was pictured there, to which he replied that he did; and afterwards, on the order of the receptor, he denied Jesus Christ once only, and spat upon the cross once. He said also on his oath that after this the receptor kissed him three times, namely: firstly on the base of the spine of the back, secondly on the navel, and thirdly on the mouth. Asked concerning the vow of chastity which was enjoined on him, he said on his oath that he was prohibited from knowing women, but if any natural heat should move him, he could unite himself with his brothers, and similarly he should suffer this from them; nevertheless he said on his oath that he never did this, nor saw anyone who did. Asked on his oath whether those brothers whom he had received he had received in the same way as he had been, he said yes. Asked concerning the head of which mention was made above, he said on his oath he once saw a certain head depicted on a certain board, that he adored it in a certain chapter, and that others did similarly. Asked whether from force, or fear of tortures or prison, or for any other reason, he had spoken falsely in his deposition, he said on his oath that he had not, [that] on the contrary he had presented the pure and full truth.[78]

Yet this man, apparently irredeemably corrupt, actually appears to have been on royal financial business at the time of the arrests, for he was helping to supervise the Michaelmas session of the Norman exchequer at Rouen. Forty *livres tournois* were paid for an escort of a sergeant and four others to bring him to Paris, where he made his confession before the inquisitor.[79]

Credibility is stretched even further when the receptions of others are examined, for it seems to have been customary for the treasurers to receive new entrants in the small chapel adjacent to the treasury, which was in the tower of the Templar complex at Paris.[80] John of Tour's predecessor had received at least two men there as recently as 1301–2,[81] while he himself had used it to receive a serving brother called John of Foligny in 1304 or 1305.[82] But there is good evidence that at least from 1303, and probably from well before this time, royal officials regularly supervised accounts at the Templar treasury, to which they apparently had ready access,[83] while it is possible that other clients or their representatives visited the tower as well. John of Foligny said that he was received at dawn, so it is possible that the ceremony was performed before the arrival of such outsiders, but as a reconstruction of life in the Templar treasury at Paris in the early fourteenth century such a scenario seems improbable to say the least. Nevertheless, the testimony of John of Tour and others seems to have been the justification for condemning his predecessor as a heretic, and exhuming and burning his bones in May 1310.[84] For this to have been literally true, the first John of Tour would had to have led a remarkable double life over a period of more than a quarter of a century. While serving both the crown and the Order as treasurer, he would have been simultaneously initiating brothers, many of them in the chapel next to the tower, in ceremonies so blasphemous and obscene that, had any word of them leaked out, the whole edifice of the Order would have been brought crashing down around him.[85]

The confessions were followed by a carefully orchestrated publicity campaign and, although Pope Clement V initially objected to what he evidently regarded as a flagrant disregard of his authority, on 22 November he felt that he had little alternative but to order a general arrest of the Templars outside France on the grounds that there was an evident need for an investigation. At least by seemingly taking over the affair himself, Clement had tried to reassert the role of the papacy, even though he could do nothing to reverse the action of the French government. Although Clement's orders were received with incredulity by some rulers – among them Edward II of England and James II of Aragon – they did inaugurate a series of rather unco-ordinated actions across the other lands in which the Templars had houses and personnel.[86] With the confessions of the leaders and a subservient pope, it seems likely that the French government expected to complete the affair with the same despatch which had marked the expulsion of the Jews and the confiscation of their property the previous year. In the event the trial was greatly prolonged, first by the unexpected resistance of the leaders who revoked their confessions within a month of the pope's intervention, and then by the pope himself, who took this as a cue to suspend proceedings. It took the government six months of concerted pressure before Clement could be forced to reopen the affair, when, in July 1308, he set up two separate inquiries, one in the dioceses to examine the guilt or innocence of individuals, another in the form of a papal commission which sat at Paris, which took evidence for the Order as a whole. As a means of delaying the trial, these proved to be effective devices, for it was not until 5 June 1311 that the papal commission finally ended its hearings, while some of the provincial proceedings were incomplete even then. By this time the Templars themselves, led not by James of Molay but by Peter of Bologna, the former procurator of the Order at the papal court, had mounted an effective and sustained defence, only stifled when, in May 1310, small groups of Templars were executed as relapsed heretics in dioceses where the incumbent prelates owed their positions largely to the French crown. The end eventually came with the decree of abolition in March 1312, although this was clearly less than the king had wanted, for the Order was not condemned as such. Moreover, the bull *Ad providam* (2 May 1312) transferred the Order's property not to the French crown but to the Hospitallers, so that it could be used for the cause to which it had originally been donated, that of the Holy Land. As for the Templars themselves, a distinction was made between those who had been reconciled to the Church or against whom nothing had been found, and those claimed to have relapsed or to have remained impenitent. Most of those in the first category received pensions and some even continued to live in former Templar houses; others were sent to the houses of other orders like those of the Cistercians and Augustinians, especially in England, an arrangement which caused mutual irritation and bad feeling.[87] The relapsed and impenitent received various terms and degrees of imprisonment, generally more harsh in France than elsewhere, while the leaders were reserved for papal judgement, a decision which was to lead to the Grand Master's dramatic death by burning in 1314.

The fate of many of these individuals had originally been determined by the episcopal inquiries set up by Clement V in July and August 1308. The hearings which resulted from this are the most inadequately documented aspect of the trial in France; until recently the only published records were those of the dioceses of Elne and Nîmes.[88] However, the appearance of a critical edition of the proceedings in the diocese of Clermont in the Auvergne, which took place in June 1309, not only enables the predicament of a specific group of Templars to be studied, but also has a wider relevance for the trial as a whole.[89] Unlike many of the episcopal inquiries, this hearing, under Bishop Aubert Aycelin, was a highly efficient affair, conducted with great speed because of careful preparation beforehand. The pope had determined that eighty-eight articles should be used as the basis for the questioning in the provinces; at Clermont eighty-five of these were grouped under fifteen headings, leaving three separate questions about the circumstances of each man's reception, the origin and reason for his errors, and the nature of idol worship. This method greatly facilitated the presentation of testimony, enabling sixty-nine Templars to be heard in the space of only five days. Nor was time wasted by spending too long on each Templar: the first Templar to confess, a priest called Bernard of Villars, was taken through each group of articles in detail, providing a kind of 'model' confession, and greatly reducing the length of the testimony of the following thirty-nine Templars who had confessed. The twenty-nine who resisted were presented within an even tighter format, for all of them were heard on one day, Saturday, 7 June.

It would be expected that the course of this inquiry would favour the king; like many of the bishops, Aubert Aycelin was closely linked to the crown, for he was the nephew of Gilles Aycelin, Archbishop of Narbonne, one of the king's chief advisers. Nevertheless, he did not produce a complete set of confessions: a substantial minority resisted, amounting to nearly 43 per cent. The extent to which the confessions in the trial were determined by the control exercised over the persons of the Order by the French king's officials, or those of his relatives in Navarre and Naples, is underlined by this result. The further away from these epicentres, the less likely were inquiries to produce uniform confessions, even in a diocese such as this. It may be, as the editors suggest, that these men were not tortured, since, it is argued, the hearings were so rapid that they hardly left time for it.[90] But the case is unproven. Assuming that torture did not take place during the five days of hearings (by no means certain), there was plenty of time for it to have occurred beforehand – indeed, given the bishop's efficiency this seems the most likely time. Moreover, these men could have been tortured at a previous hearing some time in the autumn of 1307 just like their colleagues in Paris.

The confessions from hearings like this do not deviate greatly from the pattern seen in Paris, but even so, they do contain some distinctive and interesting features which highlight the methodological problems of analysing the trial depositions, as well as helping to explain why writers ever since, struck by the verisimilitude of some of the testimonies, have not been able to believe that they were fabricated, even under torture.[91] Descriptions of idols which they were supposed to have worshipped, for example, are sometimes replete with vivid detail of colour, shape, and positioning. During the proceedings in the Papal State and the Abruzzi one serving brother in Apulia claimed the Grand Preceptor of Apulia and the Abruzzi asked him if he had seen the treasure which the Templars kept at their house at Torremaggiore. When he replied that he had not, the preceptor took him 'to a certain strong and secret place, . . . and showed him many precious ecclesiastical vessels and arms; and the preceptor opened a certain reliquary which was there on the left-hand side as they entered, next to a certain drain, and genuflecting, with head uncovered and hands together, showed him a certain idol which as it seemed to him was of metal, whose form was similar to that of a boy standing up, and the height of this idol was about one cubit'.[92] The Templar could not invent something from outside his own experience, so the reliquary became an idol and the house's treasury was transformed into a mysterious sanctum.

At Clermont the records show the Templars struggling with the same problems. The priest, Bartholomew Vassales, far from being able to explain the rites and implications of the esoteric cult of which the Order was accused in its own terms, could not escape the terminology of the Church which it was supposed to be dedicated to undermining. Therefore, at his reception the Visitor, Hugh of Pairaud, had supposedly told those present: 'We are assembled here to do service to the enemy',[93] a strange way indeed to describe the alleged object of their adoration, while the form of this service was the worship of a certain head, called with stunning lack of originality, 'the idol'. The use of the term 'the enemy' to describe the Devil in fact calls to mind the theological discussions of John of Joinville and St Louis, rather than a heretical cult.[94] Surely no heresy can have attracted less convincing initiates; the contrast with real heretics like the Cathars is stark, for they had no doubt that their enemy was the Catholic Church itself, the church of the wicked, with its fraudulent and diabolical sacraments.[95] Yet if Bartholomew's terminology exposes him as a liar with a limited imagination, it equally suggests that when he describes a transgression known to have existed in the Order from evidence independent of the trial, then he is likely to be telling the truth, since he clearly found it almost impossible to make the jump from his own imprinted experience to the fantasy world created by his accusers. His description of simoniacal practice, given at the end of his deposition, clearly must be taken seriously: 'before the Visitor wished to receive him as a brother into the Order, it was necessary that he assist the said house with a census of six *setiers* of grain and release to the Visitor thirty *livres tournois*, which he did, and thus he was received'.

One further example demonstrates how the meaning of actions which almost certainly really occurred can be changed by placing them in a false context. The Templars' accusers were well aware that the Order's achievement of total secrecy over several decades at the very least would be seen as intrinsically unlikely, if not impossible. It was therefore postulated that this secrecy was the result of the creation of a climate of fear within the Order through threats and intimidation. Bernard of Villars, a priest who was Preceptor of La Roche-Saint-Paul, described what could happen to anyone whose tongue was too loose: 'he saw that brother John Culet, since it was feared that he was revealing secrets and since in certain places he spoke too much about these things, was sent to Sardinia by brother Geoffrey of Vichy, then Visitor in France, being assigned to remain there in order that he might end his days quickly and that he knew afterwards that he had not returned'.[96] There were, of course, any number of reasons why this man might have been sent to Sardinia, not necessarily disciplinary. Even had the aim been to prevent him talking too much about the Order, the 'secrets' in question need have no connection with heretical rites; an order with such widespread military, banking, and political responsibilities had much to lose if its confidentiality could not be relied upon.

Finally, these records are also significant in that most of these men later appeared in Paris before the papal commission investigating the Order as a whole, and the episcopal inquiry at Clermont makes it possible to correlate their previous stance in regard to the accusations with their role before the commission. This shows how the French government used its power over the persons of the Order to manipulate the commission's hearings in a way favourable to its own point of view. In February 1310, thirty-two of these Templars from the Auvergne province committed themselves to the defence of the Order, adhering to the general defence led by Peter of Bologna and Renaud of Provins. These can be seen as the twenty-nine who had originally denied the accusations, plus three of the others. Two of the Clermont Templars, Bertrand of Sartiges, Preceptor of Carlat, and William of Chambonnet, Preceptor of Blaudeix, were among the spokesmen for the defence.[97] This defence so alarmed Philip the Fair's government that a determined attempt was made to suppress it by means of selective executions of Templars from the province of Sens in May 1310. Many Templars were indeed intimidated, but even so the Templars who were allowed to appear after the executions were carefully selected on their past record of confession.[98] The Clermont contingent was used in exactly this way: twenty of the twenty-one who appeared in 1311 had already confessed before the bishop in 1309. The three who had confessed at Clermont, but joined the defence in Paris, were not among them.[99]

In the end, however, none of the Templars, whatever line they adopted, could prevent the suppression of the Order. Nor did the other military orders escape unscathed, for the trial undoubtedly contributed to the uncertain climate which had existed since 1291. The transfer of the Templars' possessions in itself created many problems for the Hospitallers, ranging from the pressure brought to bear by the French government for compensation and expenses, to the burden of paying out pensions to ex-Templars in dioceses from Dublin to Nicosia.[100] Final settlement with the French government was apparently made in 1318, but the achievement of full seisin of the property often took much longer: in England, for example, the king and other lords still held appreciable lands in 1338.[101] Leverage was readily available, for the destruction of the Templars did not satisfy the demands for reform of the orders, nor silence the many opinions about the best manner of crusading. Ramon Lull, for instance, had allowed himself to be convinced of the Templars' guilt, perhaps because he still saw Philip IV as the best hope of activating a crusade which would pave the way for his work of mission and re-education in Muslim countries. However, he retained his faith in the value of a united military order, although he now envisaged a master drawn from the professed knights, rather than a secular king.[102]

There was plenty of ammunition available to those who believed that the other military orders as they were then constituted were inadequate, for they had made no perceptible progress towards the recovery of the Holy Land during these years. The Hospitaller crusade of 1309–10 had been conspicuously unsuccessful, while the Order's acquisition of Rhodes between 1306 and 1310 had yet to produce any tangible benefits for the crusading movement as a whole.[103] Not surprisingly, Philip IV's ominous reference to proposed 'reform' of the Hospital in August 1312, carried with it more than a hint of menace.[104] At the end of December, Clement V issued a bull laying down a scheme for reform, reflecting the usual concerns of the secular clergy, who thought that the Order had too much independence and too many privileges, and the criticisms of the crusade theorists who had argued that the military orders were sending insufficient men and resources to the east.[105] Clement's programme was to be underpinned by an inquiry into the revenues of each of the Hospital's houses, including those received from the Temple. Manpower would be reorganised in the light of this, leaving only a small number of administrators, the aged and the sick, in the west, with the remainder being sent to the active fronts. In the end, nothing came of these plans, perhaps because of the deaths of the pope and the king in 1314, and the two-year papal interregnum which followed. Nevertheless, despite the fact that Albert of Schwarzburg, Grand Preceptor of the Hospital, extravagantly compared the transfer of Templar property to his Order to a new Donation of Constantine,[106] there is no doubt that suppression of the Templars had a negative impact upon the public perception of the Hospitallers as well, which the order did not find easy to shake off.

The Teutonic Knights were even further removed from the eastern Mediterranean action; during the thirteenth century they had increasingly concentrated upon north-eastern Europe and the Baltic. They had established themselves at Chelmo on the Vistula as long ago as

1226, had steadily taken over Prussia during the thirteenth century and, in 1308, rounded this off by seizing the valuable region of Pomerania to their rear, together with the Baltic port of Gdansk, from the Polish kingdom. Their long-term intentions had become clear when, in 1310, they moved their headquarters from a temporary base in Venice to Marienburg on the Vistula. This aggressive expansionism made them many enemies within the Christian community as well as outside it, and there had been protests about their conduct in 1298, 1300, and 1305. Their leading opponent, Frederick, Archbishop of Riga, had accused them of a whole range of offences, including attacks upon the Church, murder, and internal corruption, in addition to the allegation that they had failed to fulfil their crusading functions against the Lithuanians and the Russians. An investigation in 1312 actually led to proceedings the following year, but none of their opponents carried the weight of Philip the Fair.[107] In the event, both the Hospitallers and the Teutonic Knights survived, but the threat to them had been very real. In Iberia the kings did indeed succeed in remoulding the remains of the Temple into new viable military forces. The Aragonese king, James II, was allowed to create the Order of Montesa in 1317, modelled on the Spanish Order of Calatrava, while in Portugal King Diniz was given permission to found the Order of Christ in 1319, largely drawing on Templar property and including many former Templar personnel.

The trial of the Templars brings their history to a dramatic and tragic conclusion, which, ever since, has had direct effects upon posterity's image of the Order and its world. But it has had other, more subtle consequences for that image, for the destruction of the Order removed the chief guardians of its history, and left the documentation which monastic orders so carefully and characteristically preserve at the mercy of vicissitudes which, whatever some of the more imaginative chroniclers of the Order's fate purport to believe, could not be controlled from the grave. At some point after the suppression, the central archive of the Order, containing charters which would have been so important for the reconstruction of its activities in the east, disappeared altogether, leaving only the faintest traces of its existence. The loss for the serious historian is incalculable, but for the student of the occult and the mysterious it was a most convenient occurrence, providing scope for unbridled speculation and opportunity for unlimited publication. The sober reality of this question has, however, been examined by Rudolf Hiestand, whose convincing arguments make an appropriate conclusion to this chapter.[108]

The Templar archives must have been kept in the Temple of Solomon until 1187, but there is no evidence about their fate between the capture of Jerusalem by Saladin in October of that year and the re-establishment of the Christians in Acre in 1191. After this date it is possible that the archive was re-assembled in the Templar complex in the city: the Templar of Tyre, describing this area in 1291, says that the Order kept its treasury in the tower by the sea,[109] and it is reasonable to suppose that archives were held here too, for the evidence of possessions, mortgages, and loans was as valuable as actual liquid wealth, and would have been guarded just as carefully. However, the building of 'Atlīt in 1217–18 offered an alternative and safe centre and it is possible that at least copies of important documents were kept there, and even that the main archive itself might have been transferred there during the last years of the kingdom in anticipation of the Mamluk attack on Acre. In contrast to Acre, 'Atlīt was evacuated in an orderly manner, so there is something to be said for the view that the main archive was there in 1291. Hiestand argues that the archive survived the disasters of that year, for, on the one hand, there is evidence that a fourteenth-century copyist was able to use an original document predating the fall of Acre, while on the other, James of Molay does not seem to have made any attempt to gain papal renewal of Templar charters, an almost inconceivable omission if they had been lost in 1291. Moreover, the fact that both the Hospital and the Teutonic Knights had managed to remove their archives to Provence and Italy respectively, makes it highly unlikely that the Templars had not taken precautions of their own.[110]

Yet, today, this archive has completely vanished; only two documents survive which appear to be transcripts from originals in the Templar collection in the east, one from the County of Tripoli in 1152 and one from the Kingdom of Jerusalem in 1166. Both of these seem to have been copied for reasons which give no hint that they might be harbingers of an as yet undiscovered larger archive.[111] Theories that the archive was transferred either to the French crown or to the papacy may reasonably be dismissed, for, as has been seen, Molay had no intention of transferring the headquarters of the Order to France, nor had he any reason to bring the archive and treasure with him in 1306–7, while detailed searches of the papal archives during the last hundred years have yielded no results. So, too, can the idea that Molay had the documents burnt, an action which would be totally alien to the head of any religious order in any conceivable circumstances.[112] The Grand Master hoped that the Christians would be re-established on the mainland and he bent all his efforts to that end. Proof of their rights and possessions remained essential, especially while the clamour for a union or a restructuring of the military orders continued.

The most obvious inference, therefore, is that the archive survived the disasters of 1291 and was taken over by the Hospital in 1312; indeed, the Templar documents conserved in the western provinces of the Hospitallers are direct proof of this. It might therefore be expected that the Templars' eastern archive would be found at Malta, the last headquarters of the Hospital in the Mediterranean, where they were established in 1530. However, the only Templar documents in the Maltese archive are those which either relate to Hospitaller business and would therefore have been kept by the order in any case, or those which come from southern France and were taken to Malta in the seventeenth and eighteenth centuries as a consequence of the centralisation policies of the Grand Masters of that period. Hiestand demonstrates, too, that the Templar documents were not absorbed into the Hospitaller archive in France, despite the existence of two documents relating to the Templars' eastern affairs and the inference that a third document also existed.[113] In Hiestand's view it seems therefore that, after the evacuation to Cyprus in 1291, the Templar archive never left the island. After 1312 it was maintained there, along with the Hospitaller documents relating to the Cypriot province, until, in 1571, the Ottomans overran the island and both sets of documents were destroyed, a version of events strongly supported by the fact that the Hospital's Cypriot documents have never been found either.

For the Templars, the Holy Land had remained the centre of their attention right up to 1307; had the Order survived into the sixteenth century, it would have needed to adapt or risk appearing anachronistic in a world where the crusade remained important, but where priorities had changed. The destruction of the records of the Templars' occupation of Palestine and Syria, records which had lain largely unused and ignored since the second decade of the fourteenth century, symbolises the irrelevance of the Order to the late medieval world.

CHAPTER NINE

FROM MOLAY'S CURSE TO
FOUCAULT'S PENDULUM

When Molay and Charney burnt to death on the evening of 18 March 1314, in Paris, the Order of the Temple was effectively at an end. It is true that some knights had a few more years of life left to them, in prison, or as pensioners, or even briefly once more as fighters for the faith in new fraternities like the Order of Christ in Portugal, but there could have been few other Templars still alive when Ludolph of Sudheim found his two Palestinian veterans in the 1340s. By this time interest in religious orders had largely been replaced by enthusiam for secular knighthoods like the Order of the Garter in England (1348) and the Order of the Star in France (1351).[1] If there was any lingering nostalgia for the Templars it must soon have been overwhelmed by the harsh realities of life in the middle of the fourteenth century: the Black Death from 1348, the ravages of the seemingly endless series of wars between France and England, and the scandal of the schism in the papacy, rending the very fabric of the supposedly seamless garment of St Peter.

Nevertheless, the end of the Templars had been dramatic and for a brief period after 1314 it caught the attention of chroniclers, particularly in Italy, some of whom took the opportunity to decorate their narratives with tales of Templar vengeance. Just over a month after the executions of the leaders, on 20 April 1314, Pope Clement V died, after a long and painful illness; seven months later, Philip the Fair followed him, killed in a riding accident while hunting. Neither event is particularly surprising: Clement had been dogged by a severe internal complaint throughout his entire pontificate, while Philip IV's love of hunting amounted almost to an obsession. But this was fertile soil for legends, among which was one which demonstrates how hindsight becomes the invaluable ally of prophecy: before the flames consumed him, it was claimed, Molay had called forth his persecutors to answer for their crimes before God within the year. A variation on this story was told by the contemporary chronicler Ferretto of Vicenza, who applied the idea to a Neapolitan Templar brought before Clement V, whom he denounced for his injustice. Some time later, as he was about to be executed, he appealed 'from this your heinous judgement to the living and true God, who is in Heaven', warning the pope that, within a year and a day, he and Philip IV would be obliged to answer for their crimes in God's presence.[2]

As time passed, these events had the further effect of encouraging writers to fashion Templar history into a neat structure in which their rise and fall seemed all but inevitable. One such observer was Felix Fabri, a Dominican from Ulm in south-west Germany, who made two pilgrimages to the Holy Land in 1480 and 1483, visits which caused him to reflect upon the places he had seen and their associations. Brother Felix had evidently read William of Tyre or James of Vitry, for he was clearly influenced by them, but his verdict on the Templars owed much more to a partial view of the trial:

Albeit their beginning was holy and full of virtue, yet afterwards they degenerated from their forerunners after they waxed fat, and were spread about throughout the earth. Wherefore in the reign of Clement V, forasmuch as it became known to our people that they had gone over to the Saracens, and had fallen into many vices because of their great wealth, all of them who could be taken by Christians were slain, and not only in Asia, but also in France, they were destroyed by Philip, King of France, with the consent of the sovereign pontiff of Rome, since they were leading exceedingly disgraceful lives.

Their wealth, which he believed had been excessive, was granted partly to the Hospital and partly to other orders, including the Dominicans, who held, among other former Templar houses, those at Vienna, Strasbourg, Esslingen, and Worms. Although Felix Fabri evidently believed that the Templars had been justly condemned, he did, however, add a coda which reflected the persistence of the opposite view, that some believed them to have been the unfortunate victims of Philip the Fair's avarice.[3]

This conception of rise and fall, which can be traced in a direct line from William of Tyre, but which finds its greatest justification in the trial and suppression, has persisted ever since. In the seventeenth century, for instance, the Anglican divine Thomas Fuller (1608–61) incorporated it into his *Historie of the Holy Warre*, published in 1639:

Yea, the King and Patriarch of Jerusalem dandled this infant-order so long in their laps till it brake their knees, it grew so heavy at last; and these ungrateful Templars did pluck out the feathers of those wings which hatched and brooded them. From Alms-men they turned Lords; and though very valiant at first (for they were sworn rather to die than to flie) afterwards laziness withered their arms and swelled their bellies. They laughed at the rules of their first Institution, as at the swaddling-clothes of their infancie; neglecting the Patriarch, and counting themselves too old to be whipped with the rod of his discipline; till partly their vitiousnesse, and partly their wealth caused their finall extirpation.[4]

A more powerful voice was that of Edward Gibbon, although his grand sweep made no distinction between the Templars and the Hospitallers:

But the firmest bulwark of Jerusalem was founded on the knights of the Hospital of St John, and of the temple of Solomon; on the strange association of a monastic and military life, which fanaticism might suggest, but which policy must approve. The flower of the nobility of Europe aspired to wear the cross, and to profess the vows, of these respectable orders; their spirit and discipline were immortal; and the speedy donation of twenty-eight thousand farms, or manors, enabled them to support a regular force of cavalry and infantry for the defence of Palestine. The austerity of the convent soon evaporated in the exercise of arms: the world was scandalised by the pride, avarice, and corruption of these Christian soldiers; their claims of immunity and jurisdiction disturbed the harmony of the church and state; and the public peace was endangered by their jealous emulation. But in their most dissolute period the knights of the hospital and temple maintained their fearless and fanatic character: they neglected to live, but they were prepared to die, in the service of Christ.[5]

Sir Steven Runciman's epilogue to his three-volume *History of the Crusades* has an implicit structure which conveys a similar message. Comparing the fate of the two great military orders he concluded:

The Temple was less enterprising and less fortunate. It had always aroused more enmity than the Hospital. It was wealthier. It had long been the chief banker and money-lender in the East, successful at a profession which does not inspire affection. Its policy had always been notoriously selfish and irresponsible. Gallantly though its knights had always fought in times of war, their financial activities had brought them into close contact with the Moslems. Many of them had Moslem friends and took an interest in Moslem religion and learning. There were rumours that behind its castle walls the Order studied a strange esoteric philosophy and indulged in ceremonies that were tainted with heresy. There were said to be initiation rites that were both blasphemous and indecent; and there were whispers of orgies for the practice of unnatural vices. It would be unwise to dismiss these rumours as the unfounded invention of enemies. There was probably just enough substance in them to suggest the line along which the Order could be most convincingly attacked.[6]

As well as being presented in cyclical terms, the fate of the Templars continued to feature in the historical surveys and political debates of the sixteenth and seventeenth centuries.[7] While those imbued with chivalric nostalgia generally regretted their end, pro-monarchical writers of the *ancien régime*, such as Pierre Dupuy and Etienne Baluze, amassed valuable but strictly selective collections of documents bearing on the period intended to justify the actions of Philip the Fair's government.[8] It was, however, the appearance of Freemasonry in the eighteenth century that really revived interest in them. Through the creation of their pseudo-histories, the Freemasons established a second indispensable element in the Templar image, that of the secret society. Freemasonry began in England in the form of clubs whose members pledged mutual aid, the efficacy of which was increased by the club's exclusive nature. The exclusivity was in turn delineated by secret signs and private meetings and rituals, supposedly taken from medieval masonic lodges in which the 'secrets' of the craft had been handed down from generation to generation, thus preventing the expertise being obtained by out-siders, although by the early eighteenth century there were hardly any real masonic lodges still functioning. The beginnings of this movement in England were not initially concerned with knighthood as such, but by the 1730s, when masonry had spread to France, there had begun to develop a belief in knightly antecedents. This idea largely emanated from Andrew Michael Ramsay (1696–1743), a Scottish freemason, who, in his capacity as Chancellor of Grand Lodge in France, in 1737 outlined a supposed history of freemasonry into which the Templars later came to be incorporated as a central element. In Ramsay's version of the past, although the masons had the most ancient origins, the key period was that of the crusades, when the Christians of the Holy Land, struggling to restore the Temple in a hostile environment, devised a series of secret signs for mutual recognition and protection. These men, prominent among whom was the 'Scottish lodge', were therefore both builders and fighters for the Christian cause. It was a short step to link these to the charitable organisation of the Hospitallers.[9] This notion was particularly attractive to the French aristocracy which was already heavily addicted to pseudo-chivalric orders supposedly deriving from medieval predecessors. However, although this made a general link with the crusades, it was during the 1760s that German masons introduced a specific Templar connection, claiming that the Order, through its occupation of the Temple of Solomon, had been the repository of secret wisdom and magical powers, which James of Molay had handed down to his successor before his execution and of which the eighteenth-century freemasons were the direct heirs.[10]

This idea soon proved a bountiful source of further myths. The lodges had placed great emphasis on the legend of the murder of Hiram, King of Tyre, who had been employed by Solomon to build the Temple, but who was subsequently assassinated because he would not reveal his masonic secrets. Solomon was supposed to have sent out certain 'elect' masters to exact vengeance, an idea translated into a complicated series of 'grades of vengeance' in the masonry of the late eighteenth century. Here was the opportunity to build a whole edifice. The suppression of the Templars could be interpreted as the criminal act of a repressive religious and political establishment determined to crush an Order which preserved profound truths threatening to the prevailing authorities. The clandestine survival of the Templars through the centuries meant that the possibility of vengeance for the destruction of the Order and Molay's death in particular, remained open, just as Solomon had requited Hiram. Such a scenario appealed not only to some groups of masons themselves, but more especially to their opponents who, under the stimulus of the violence of the French Revolution in the early 1790s, seized on the idea of a secret conspiracy as an explanation for the overturning of the old order. In *Le Tombeau de Jacques Molay*, by Charles Louis Cadet de Gassicour (1769–1821), published in 1796, the last Grand Master's curse had indeed reached fruition when Louis XVI, the twenty-second successor of Philip IV, went to the guillotine from the same tower in which Molay himself, the twenty-second Grand Master, had allegedly been tortured.[11]

In the following year, a French exile, the ex-Jesuit Abbé Augustin Barruel (1741–1820) began the publication of a multi-volume work which moulded these disjointed ideas into a general historical system in which he claimed that a coherent line of anti-social teaching could be discerned stretching from the third-century Persian called Manes, whose name is given to the dualist belief of Manichaeism, down to the revolutionary Jacobins of the Terror. Among the agents for the transmission of these beliefs were the Cathar heretics of thirteenth-century Languedoc, who adhered to a form of dualism, and the Templars themselves. In the eighteenth century the promoters had been the *Philosophes*, the Freemasons and the Bavarian Illuminati.[12] Barruel's view of Templar history was based on the familiar concept of the Order's rise and subsequent decline. Ambition and debauchery had replaced their original purity, and they became tyrannical and unjust usurpers, who had had treacherous contacts with the Muslims. The chronicles of Matthew Paris showed only too clearly how they had tried to undermine the Emperor Frederick II in this way. Their end was not therefore so surprising; their guilt proven by their confessions. Here it is evident that Barruel's attitude was deeply coloured by his own experiences, for he harboured a profound bitterness at the destruction of his own order, the Society of Jesus, in 1773. 'The Jesuits have been abolished, they have not been judged; nobody has heard their case: not a single confession from their members exists against their Order. I would condemn them like the Templars, if they had provided the same proofs against themselves.' It had not, of course, ended in 1314, for after the extinction of the Order, some of the guilty Templars managed to escape proscription. Now determined upon retribution they added to 'their dreadful mysteries' a vow to avenge themselves on the kings and pontiffs who had destroyed them and upon the religion that had anathematised their dogmas. Adepts were trained and the cult and its vows transmitted from generation to generation. It was men such as these whom the masons sought to glorify as their ancestors. 'The same projects, the same means, the same horrors could not be transmitted more faithfully from fathers to children.'

So great is the appeal of a comprehensive explanation of history that writers have been attracted to it ever since, undeterred by lack of evidence. In recent times through the media of television and paperbacks, the message that the Templars fulfilled this pivotal historical role – for good or ill, depending on whether one's viewpoint is radical or conservative – has been transmitted to far greater numbers of people than ever before. However, now, as in the eighteenth century, the 'secrets' of the Templars have often been transmuted from the comparative dullness of an unspecified and vapid spiritual illumination into the much more exciting prospect of actual buried treasure. In some versions this treasure had been obtained by the Templars just before the Cathar stronghold of Montségur in the Pyrenees fell to the forces of the French crown in 1244, a fall which led to the mass burning of many of the Cathar *bonhommes* or ministers. In others, the Templars gained their allegedly vast wealth through the utilisation of the magical practices which they guarded so carefully. Not surprisingly, the Templars, too, ultimately met the same fate as the Cathars, the difference being that the last leaders were able to maintain the chain of continuity by handing on the secrets, both spiritual and material. Such links are inherently satisfying to proponents of conspiracy theories of history, for they abhor loose ends, often seeing history in terms of one vast jigsaw puzzle in which the participants leave 'clues' for latter-day Hercule Poirots to investigate.

Lack of evidence has never been a serious problem for such writers, but nevertheless during the nineteenth century some felt a compulsion to consolidate these theories by the miraculous discovery of documents and objects which seemed to authenticate the Templar role. These included a list of Grand Masters of the Temple who had occupied the office since Molay's time; caskets, coins, and medallions supposedly held by the Templars on which were carved images associated with the early Gnostic sects, which had rejected the Hebrew and Christian versions of creation; and secret 'Rules' which purported to prove that the grades within the Temple included a special class of initiates, not unlike the consoled *bonhommes* or *perfecti* of the Cathars. As most of these document and objects did not have a provenance earlier than *circa* 1800 at best, it is not surprising that William of Nogaret and his men were unable to locate any of them at the time of the trial 500 years before. Nevertheless, one writer, the Austrian orientalist, Joseph von Hammer-Purgstall, who, significantly, worked for Metternich at Vienna, in a work published in 1818 and later translated under the title *The Mystery of Baphomet Revealed*, concocted an elaborate thesis based on an interpretation of just such objects. In an historical sweep not dissimilar to that of Barruel he claimed that these showed links between subversive groups from the Gnostics down to the radicals of his own day, which his master Metternich took so seriously. The Templars were one such organisation which had threatened the social fabric, for they had worshipped an androgynous idol called 'Baphomet', the origins of which went back to pre-Christian times and which formed the centrepiece of alleged magical and occult practices. In fact, although Baphomet is occasionally referred to in the trial depositions, it is clearly an Old French corruption of Muhammad and does not have the etymology attributed to it by Hammer, who associated it with the Gnostic 'baptism of the spirit'. Although Hammer originally published his ideas in Latin in a little-known German journal, they were popularised in both France and England, where they appeared in translation and achieved wide currency.[13]

A typical example of the way that Hammer's thesis was taken seriously can be seen in Jules Loiseleur's *La Doctrine secrète des Templiers*, published in 1872, but reprinted as recently as 1975 (see plate 16)[14]. Loiseleur rejected Hammer's argument of Gnostic connections at elaborate length, but only because he wanted to replace it with his own construct, based, as he saw it, upon the Templars' own witness in the trial depositions. Loiseleur thought that the Templars were indeed guilty of heresy, thus again perpetuating the idea of a secret society in conflict with prevailing contemporary mores. This heresy was a branch of Catharism made up of an amalgam of the teaching of the Bogomils and the practices of a sect which he calls 'Luciferans' (whose existence is no longer accepted by serious historians of heresy). Medieval 'Templarism', as described by Loiseleur, recognised a duality of gods, one a superior being of the celestial world, who was pure spirit and perfect, the other an evil god, organiser of the material world, through whose fecundity seeds germinated and indeed wealth was created. The evil god was in fact the elder son of the celestial Father, having revolted against him, while the younger son was identified with Jesus Christ. An acquisitive order like the Templars was naturally attracted to the materialistic god and represented him in their idols. Jesus Christ they saw as an impostor, executed for his crimes, and not therefore worthy of man's loyalty. The insults to the cross, the denial of Christ, and the omission of the words of consecration in the mass, all of which were laid against them at the trial, were manifestations of this fundamental rejection of the idea of the divinity of Christ. For good measure, Loiseleur also believed that the Hospitallers had been infiltrated by

Plate 16 Coffret d'Essarois, attributed to the Templars in an
attempt to connect them to the worship of an imaginary idol called
'Baphomet'.

heresy, suppressed by Pope Gregory IX in about 1238, the contents of which, if they ever emerged, would serve to reinforce his arguments about the Templars.

Plot fantasies are not peculiar to the eighteenth and nineteenth centuries: in 1321 King Philip V of France had succumbed to the belief that a bizarre alliance of lepers, Jews, and Muslim rulers had conspired to take over Christendom by poisoning the wells and thus eliminating the legitimate authorities, while for much of the fourteenth century the Inquisition had pursued a non-existent organisation known as the Brethren of the Free Spirit which was supposedly spreading ideas so anarchic and pernicious that their acceptance would have produced total social breakdown.[15] However, it was during the years between 1789 and 1848, under the pressure of the need to find an explanation for unprecedentedly rapid social and political change that conspiracy theories came into their own. They were, according to J. M. Roberts, 'an aberration of maturing bourgeois society',[16] and in the Templars they found an ideal vehicle. In the hothouse atmosphere generated by the French Revolution, the belief that such a massive upheaval could only be the consequence of the actions of secret human agencies, who had long been working to undermine the very foundations of the secular and ecclesiastical establishment, had instant attraction. It appears to have been particularly satisfying to have incorporated the idea that the Templars had the continuing power to influence events even after the Order had been suppressed into a macrocosmic view of the mechanisms of historical change which reached back to the pre-Christian era.

Nevertheless, neither Barruel nor Hammer had a readership which came anywhere near that of Sir Walter Scott, and it is perhaps from his novels, *Ivanhoe* and *The Talisman*, written in the climate just described, that the most persuasive modern image of the Templars in Britain derives. In Scott's novels, the conception of an Order fallen into corruption from holy beginnings is combined with the idea of a sinister secret society in a manner more potent and dramatic than in any account before or since. Although widely popular in his own time, Scott is no longer fashionable in the late twentieth century. Even so, historical romance remains a staple of the fiction market and Scott's presentation of late twelfth-century England as a world riven by enmity between haughty Norman conquerors and a resentful Saxon populace remains one with which many people can still identify and into which they can fit his famous gallery of characters: King Richard, headstrong and at times irresponsible, but with his heart in the right place; his treacherous and scheming brother, Prince John; and Robin Hood and his men, outlaws only because they stand for the decent values of justice and integrity. This is the framework for *Ivanhoe*, published in 1819, and here the Templars have a central role.[17] In the novel, the Templar knight, Sir Brian de Bois-Guilbert, is a key figure, while in the latter part of the book the Order itself provides the setting within which the last stages of the drama are played out.

In outline, *Ivanhoe* is the story of a young knight of Saxon origins, Wilfred of Ivanhoe, who has been rejected by his fiercely patriotic father, Cedric, because of his failure to espouse in full the old Saxon cause. Cedric hopes to promote this by marrying his ward, Rowena, descended from King Alfred, to Athelstane of Coningsburgh, the highest born of the surviving Saxon nobility. Wilfred's love for Rowena is only one demonstration of his lack of regard for his father's wishes. Wilfred leaves England and fights in the crusades, where he forms a close friendship with King Richard. England without Richard, however, is an England dominated by his evil brother John and those who support him. Amongst these is the famous Templar knight, Sir Brian de Bois-Guilbert, who at this time is on a visit to England. A great tournament is held at Ashby-de-la-Zouche, presided over by Prince John. Here Bois-Guilbert demonstrates to the full his martial skills, only to be felled at the end of the first day by a mysterious entrant calling himself the Disinherited Knight (Ivanhoe) and, on the second day, by another anonymous knight dressed in black armour (King Richard), who intervenes when the Disinherited Knight is in danger of being overcome. Proceedings are cut short, however, when John receives secret news that Richard has been released from his captivity in Austria and is on his way back to England to re-establish his authority. If John is to retain power he needs to move quickly and so he at once begins plans to muster his supporters at York.

John's followers, though, have plans of their own, which divert them from their leader's purpose. Maurice de Bracy is determined to seize Rowena and take her for his wife, while the Templar has developed an aching lust for Rebecca, beautiful daughter of the Jewish money-lender, Isaac. Having kidnapped Cedric, Athelstane,

and Rowena, together with Isaac and Rebecca who are travelling
with the Saxons, De Bracy and the Templars take them to Torquil-
stone, the castle of another supporter of John, Reginald Front-de-
Boeuf, whose own interest lies in extracting large sums of money
from Isaac. But their various designs are interrupted when the castle
is put under siege by a force gathered by Locksley (Robin Hood),
who has been alerted by Gurth and Wamba, two dependants of
Cedric, who had escaped from the ambush. The siege brings the
castle down, Front-de-Boeuf is killed, De Bracy captured, and only
the Templar escapes, carrying off Rebecca to the nearby preceptory
of Templestowe (see plate 17). Unfortunately for Bois-Guilbert, the
preceptory is suffering a visitation from Lucas de Beaumanoir, the
fanatical Grand Master, who is determined to effect reforms, and
when he realises that Bois-Guilbert has Rebecca concealed in the
house, his wrath can only be diverted by the preceptor's suggestion
that Bois-Guilbert must have been bewitched. There follows the trial
and condemnation of Rebecca, but she succeeds in postponing her
execution by claiming the right to a champion to fight for her. To
Bois-Guilbert's chagrin, the Grand Master nominates him to fight
for the Temple while Rebecca is given three days to find her own
champion. At the last moment Ivanhoe appears, weary from a long
ride and still suffering the effects of a wound sustained at Ashby-de-
la-Zouche. Not surprisingly he is unhorsed in the resulting combat,
but the Templar, too, has fallen, and when Ivanhoe advances towards
him it is discovered that he is already dead, 'a victim to the violence
of his own contending passions'. King Richard appears just as the
conflict is finished and arrests Albert de Malvoisin, Preceptor of
Templestowe, one of the arch-intriguers on Prince John's behalf.
This causes a quarrel with the Grand Master, who thereupon leads
his Templars out of England to take the case before the pope. Finally,
Cedric reluctantly accepts the unreality of his hopes for the restoration of the Saxon monarchy and allows Wilfred to marry Rowena,
while Rebecca and Isaac emigrate to Muslim Granada where they
hope they will be able to live in peace.

Scott's portrayal of Brian de Bois-Guilbert is everything that
William of Tyre could have wished it to be. 'They say he is valiant
as the bravest of his Order; but stained with their usual vices, pride,
arrogance, cruelty, and voluptuousness; a hard-hearted man, who
knows neither fear of earth, nor awe of heaven.' He is indisputably

Plate 17 The Templar carrying off Rebecca, from *Ivanhoe*.

foreign, for his despotic manner and exotic entourage of Saracen servants are seen as quite out of place in the English Midlands. Indeed, he is incapable of understanding that proud Saxon serfs cannot be treated in the same way as captured Turks, whose fierceness he has tamed. Such a man is not to be restrained by the Order's Rule. ' "For my vow", said the Templar, "our Grand Master hath granted me a dispensation; and for my conscience, a man that has slain three hundred Saracens need not reckon up every little failing, like a village girl at her first confession upon Good Friday eve."' It is indeed surprising that such a person should enter the Temple at all, but it emerges that he is a 'moody and disappointed man', rejected by a Gascon lady whom he had loved, who has joined the Order in bitterness and revenge. Here, surely, is a romanticised version of Gerard of Ridefort's anger over the loss of the heiress of Botron, while the Templar arrogance bears more than a passing resemblance to Odo of Saint-Amand.

But Brian de Bois-Guilbert, although a powerful and dominant character, is not presented in isolation; his traits are intimately connected to the nature of the Order to which he belonged. This is an Order disfigured by greed and lechery, whose members may claim licence 'by the example of Solomon'. Some are tainted with heresy, others implicated in the losses sustained in the face of Saladin's attacks. Not surprisingly, such men invariably take the part of Philip II of France in his rivalry with King Richard. If this were not bad enough, Bois-Guilbert hints at more sinister designs. He tells Rebecca:

Think not we long remained blind to the idiotical folly of our founders, who forswore every delight of life for the pleasure of dying martyrs by hunger, by thirst, and by pestilence, and by the swords of savages, while they vainly strove to defend a barren desert, valuable only in the eyes of superstition. Our Order soon adopted bolder and wider views, and found out a better indemnifaction for our sacrifices. Our immense possessions in every kingdom of Europe, our high military fame, which brings within our circle the flower of chivalry from every Christian clime – these are dedicated to ends of which our pious founders little dreamed, and which we equally concealed from such weak spirits as embrace our Order on the ancient principles, and whose superstition makes them our passive tools. But I will not further withdraw the veil of our mysteries.

Into this scene steps Lucas de Beaumanoir, the Grand Master who had vowed to correct abuses, but even this is turned against the Order, for Beaumanoir is a cold-hearted bigot, devoid of ordinary human feelings. He tells his companions that he is determined to cleanse the Order:

The souls of our pure founders, the spirits of Hugh de Payen and Godfrey de Saint Omer and of the blessed Seven, who first joined in dedicating their lives to the service of the Temple, are disturbed even in the enjoyment of Paradise itself. I have seen them, Conrade, in the visions of the night – their sainted eyes shed tears for the sins and follies of their brethren, and for the foul and shameful luxury in which they wallow.

Yet Beaumanoir, too, is deformed by the sin of pride. He will not submit to the king and leaves the country rather than allow interference with the Order's privileges. His appeal to the pope echoes the words of Odo of Saint-Amand in the affair of the Assassin envoy and justifies the generalised accusation of Vincentius Hispanus. Herein lie the seeds of the Order's destruction, for the Templars exchanged humility and poverty 'for the arrogance and wealth that finally occasioned their suppression'. Whether Scott was simply writing an adventure story for boys or, as has sometimes been argued, intended to convey an anti-romantic and anti-chauvinistic message,[18] no reader of *Ivanhoe* could emerge without a vivid mental picture of the nature of the Templars, especially given the occasional parallels which can be drawn with real historical figures. Indeed, if Scott wanted to show the dangers inherent in the chivalric world the Templar is at least as important a vehicle for this as King Richard himself. Moreover, the publication of *Ivanhoe* took place in the middle of a period of intense belief in secret societies. It is not surprising to find that so many people in the nineteenth century had difficulty in accepting that there was no substance in the charges levelled against the Order in the trial, and indeed were ready to believe that the Templars really had been the custodians of what Bois-Guilbert calls 'our mysteries'.

The Templars are prominent in one other novel of Scott, which is *The Talisman*, published in 1825 as one of two 'Tales of the Crusades' (the other being *The Betrothed*).[19] This time it is actually set in Palestine, but there is no Templar to equal the importance of Brian de Bois-Guilbert in *Ivanhoe*; nevertheless, the role and attitudes of Brother Giles Amaury, the reigning Grand Master, form a motif which runs through the intrigues and bad feeling of the frustrated and demoralised crusading army, culminating in a bloody and dramatic climax. The picture which emerges serves to reinforce the image of the Order created in *Ivanhoe*, while at the same time deepening the sense that the Order had become a secret society of sinister adepts. The setting is the Third Crusade, and the central character is Richard I, presented by Scott in strongly nationalistic terms. However, at the outset of the novel Richard lies ill with fever, while the various elements of the crusading army, jealous of each other and resentful of Richard's overbearing character, swirl about him, plotting and counterplotting.

The story opens with the solitary mission of a Scottish knight, Sir Kenneth or 'the Knight of the Leopard', who has been sent by the Council of Christian princes (which at this time did not include the sick King Richard) to deliver a message to a famous hermit, Theoderick of Engaddi. The Scottish knight carries sealed letters, the chief aim of which is to propose to Saladin the establishment of a permanent peace to be followed by the retreat of the crusading armies for the east. The hermit, believed to be respected by Saladin, is to act as intermediary. During the course of the journey, Sir Kenneth meets a Saracen emir, with whom he fights an honourable combat, the consequence of which is the development of a mutual respect. The Saracen then agrees to send his own physician to treat King Richard, a task successfully accomplished with the aid of a special amulet, the talisman. The revival of the king has the effect of sharpening the rivalries in the Christian camp, for the other leaders – which include King Philip of France, Leopold, Duke of Austria, Conrade, Marquis of Montferrat, and the Grand Master – all have their own reasons for wanting the crusade to be abandoned, while in contrast Richard is equally determined to carry on and recapture Jerusalem. This is the context of the quarrel over the banners, largely engineered by Conrade of Montferrat, who thereby aims to break up the crusade. By this means he hopes to be left as governor of whatever portion of the eastern lands that Saladin might be disposed to grant him, an ambition he knows will be frustrated while Richard is still on crusade. Leopold of Austria, inflamed by wine and by the subtle deceits of Conrade, places his banner on a small hill next to that of Richard's in the middle of the camp, in token of his defiance of the king's leadership. Richard, in a characteristically towering rage, tears it down and leaves Sir Kenneth, together with his faithful hound, to guard his own banners during the following night.

Meanwhile the Saracen physician, El Hakim, has revealed to Sir Kenneth that Saladin is indeed prepared to cease hostilities and to this end proposes a marriage alliance between himself and Richard's kinswoman, the Lady Edith. Sir Kenneth is incredulous and distraught, not only because such a marriage would be across religious lines, but also because he has long been enamoured of Edith from afar, and it is in this disturbed state of mind that he is persuaded to leave his post by a message which is purported to come from Edith. The message is in fact part of a frivolous joke by Berengaria, Richard's queen, but the consequences are serious, for while Sir Kenneth is absent the banner is torn down and the hound severely wounded. Sir Kenneth is only saved from execution for his dereliction of duty by El Hakim, who is allowed by Richard to take him as his slave. Back in the Muslim camp it is revealed to Sir Kenneth that both the emir and El Hakim are actually Saladin, who now sends the knight back to the king in the guise of a Nubian slave, a present from the sultan. This is intended to provide an opportunity for Sir Kenneth to redeem himself, which he does, by first saving Richard from an Assassin dagger, and then, through his faithful dog, revealing that it was Conrade who had torn down the banner. Conrade denies it and a trial by combat is therefore arranged which takes place in an exotic setting chivalrously provided by Saladin, with the Knight of the Leopard representing Richard. Sir Kenneth duly overcomes Conrade, severely wounding him, and the marquis admits his guilt. It is then revealed that Sir Kenneth is much more than a poor Scottish knight, for he is in reality David, Earl of Huntingdon, Prince of Scotland, a rank which means he can marry Edith without fear of disparagement.

There remains, however, one climactic scene in which Saladin, having offered the crusading leaders in his tent the refreshment of a drink of iced sherbet, suddenly draws his scimitar and, with a single blow, strikes the Grand Master's head from his body before the cup can touch his lips. The incident is, as Scott himself explains in an appendix, taken directly from Gibbon's description of the execution of Rainald of Châtillon in Saladin's tent after the battle of Hattin, but with the Grand Master as villain rather than Rainald. Saladin calms the astonished crusaders by explaining why he has done this:

Not for his manifold treasons – not for the attempt which, as may be vouched by his own squire, he instigated against King Richard's life – not that he pursued the Prince of Scotland and myself in the desert, reducing us to save our lives by the speed of our horses – not that he stirred up the Maronites to attack us upon this very occasion, had I not brought up unexpectedly so many Arabs as rendered the scheme abortive – not for any of these crimes does he now lie there, although each were deserving such a doom – but because, scarce half an hour ere he polluted our presence, as the simoom empoisons the atmosphere, he poniarded his comrade and accomplice, Conrade of Montferrat, lest he should confess the infamous plots in which they had both been engaged.

The Grand Master, then, is shown to be capable of any crime to further his own ends and those of the Order, and Scott has taken care to build up a character appropriate to meet this justified death. Despite the Master's bravery in battle, King Richard had long known him as 'an idolater, a devil-worshipper, a necromancer, who practises crimes the most dark and unnatural in the vaults and secret places of abomination and darkness'. In contrast, the Hospitallers are not seen as tainted in this way, although they are mentioned in passing as being suspected of treasonable dealings with the Saracens for monetary gain. But it is the Grand Master – a man with 'a brow on which a thousand dark intrigues had stamped a portion of their obscurity' – in whom Scott is really interested. The Master's aim was to seek the advancement of the Order of the Temple 'even at the hazard of that very religion which the fraternity were originally associated to protect – accused of heresy and witchcraft, although by their character Christian priests – suspected of secret league with the Soldan, though by their oath devoted to the protection of the Holy Temple, or its recovery – the whole order, and the whole personal character of its commander or Grand Master, was a riddle, at the exposition of which most men shuddered'. As a consequence, the Templars were determined to prevent any European monarch successfully pursuing the crusade, as it would undermine the goal they shared with the Hospital, that of establishing 'independent dominions of their own'. Nothing, therefore, can be allowed to stand in the Grand Master's way. ' "May the Prophet blight them", says the chivalrous Saladin, "both root, branch and twig!" ' Here again are the ghosts of Walter Map and Matthew Paris.

The speculations about the reasons for Templar secrecy and the possible existence of an 'idol' around which a heretical cult had developed have not yet run their course even in the late twentieth century. In the debate about the authenticity of the medieval relic known as the Turin Shroud, which it has been claimed was the burial cloth of Jesus Christ on which his image was miraculously imprinted, some writers at least realised that the subject needed to be provided with a continuous historical provenance as well as being subjected to laboratory analysis, if their public were not to lose faith in it. Such an event would have seriously undermined a very active little industry, profitable to scientists, art historians, journalists, publishers, and television pundits alike. Unfortunately there are gaps in the historical record, making its existence since the time of Christ difficult to prove. These gaps become a chasm in the period between 1204, when, during the Fourth Crusade, the Latins plundered Constantinople of its huge collection of relics, including one item which might have been the Shroud, and 1389, when it was displayed by a French nobleman called Geoffrey of Charney at Troyes. In Ian Wilson's *The Turin Shroud* (1978), the Templars are once more trundled into position to provide the link just as they have been so often since the 1760s. According to Wilson, the Shroud had been held by the Templars during this period, who used it and copies made of it as the basis of secret ceremonies. They paid heavily for this ultimately, however, for it was these activities which inspired the charges of idol worship at the trial. The agents of Philip the Fair were nevertheless frustrated in that the Shroud itself eluded them, being smuggled out of the Temple before the arrests and thereafter kept in the custody of the Charney family, supposedly related to Geoffrey of Charney, Preceptor of Normandy, who was executed with Molay in 1314. In fact, not one shred of the detailed evidence cited connects the Templars with the relic, while the structure of the theory can be seen to owe a good deal to the fantasies of the late eighteenth and early nineteenth centuries.[20]

This world of conspiracy and secret societies, of masters and initiates, and its exploitation by publishers anxious to feed the public appetite for a cosmic explanation of historical change, has been the subject of a massive satire by the Italian philosopher and philologist, Umberto Eco. In *Foucault's Pendulum* (1988), three publishers' editors, Belbo, Diotallevi, and Casaubon, have been set the task of creating a series of books on the occult by their unscrupulous boss, Signor Garamond.[21] The fashion for Marxist ideology has waned and Garamond spots a gap in the market, with one set of beliefs supplanting another. 'It's a gold mine, all right. I realized that these people will gobble up anything that's hermetic, as you put it, anything that says the opposite of what they read in their books at school. I see this also as a cultural duty: I'm no philanthropist, but in these dark times to offer someone a faith, a glimpse into the beyond . . .' Garamond sees a huge audience, drawn from both the cultists and the academics: 'To work, gentlemen. There are libraries to visit, bibliographies to compile, catalogs to request.'

As they assemble material, the three begin to construct their own imaginary version of the secret history of the world, centred upon

'The Plan', as they call it. Encouraged by Casaubon, who has written a thesis on the Templars, they refine the idea of the transmission of the Templars' secret, through many generations and countries, down to the present day. Philip the Fair had naturally wished to gain access to it, for this secret was the key to power unknown in human history. 'You aim the right current, stir up the bowels of the earth, and make them do in ten seconds what it used to take them billions of years to do, and the whole Ruhr becomes a diamond mine. Eliphas Lévi said the knowledge of the universe's tides and currents holds the secret of human omnipotence.' In practice, however, it would have been little use to Philip the Fair, even had the Templars given it away.

But what stopped the Templars, once they knew the secret? The problem was how to exploit it. Between knowing and know-how there was a gap. So, instructed by the diabolical Saint Bernard, the Templars replaced the menhirs, poor Celtic valves, with Gothic cathedrals, far more sensitive and powerful, their subterranean crypts containing black virgins, in direct contact with the radioactive strata; and they covered Europe with a network of receiver-transmitter stations communicating to one another the power and the direction, the flow and the tension of the telluric currents.

I say they located the silver mines in the New World, caused eruptions of silver there, and then, controlling the Gulf Stream, shifted that precious metal to the Portuguese coast. Tomar was the distribution center; the Fôret d'Orient, the chief storehouse. This was the origin of their wealth. But this was peanuts. They realized that to exploit their secret fully they would have to wait for a technological advance that would take at least six hundred years.

Just as the supporters of the Turin Shroud apparently believe that God decided that its authenticity would be proven by technical skills only available in the twentieth century, thus neatly hoisting unbelievers on their own petard of scientific rationality, so too Eco caused the editors to fit together the disparate pieces that make up 'The Plan' with the help of the great invention of the late twentieth century, the computer. This machine is ideal for their purposes since it enables large masses of information to be readily absorbed, opening the way for the three men to make the connections so dear to the hearts of conspiracy theorists. As Casaubon says: 'If two things don't fit, but you believe both of them, thinking that somewhere, hidden, there must be a third thing that connects them, that's credulity.' Almost anything could be thrown into the pot. Casaubon's idea that they create 'a hitherto unpublished chapter of the history of magic' is therefore greeted with enthusiasm by the others. 'What if, instead, you fed it [the computer] a few dozen notions taken from the works of the Diabolicals – for example, the Templars fled to Scotland, or the Corpus Hermeticum arrived in Florence in 1460 – and threw in a few connective phrases like "It's obvious that" and "This proves that"? We might end up with something revelatory.' The possibilities were endless; they could bring in the Rosicrucians, the Comte de Saint-Germain, the Okhrana, the Assassins, the Jesuits, even Minnie Mouse. But, says, Casaubon, there was one fundamental axiom: 'The Templars have something to do with everything.'

The three men, however, underestimate the power of conspiracy theories to seduce and are themselves drawn in deeper. ' "I believe", says Casaubon, "that you reach the point where there is no longer any difference between developing the habit of pretending to believe and developing the habit of believing." ' They underestimate, too, the determination of these who are really seeking the key to the universe through the Templar secret and will do anything to fulfil the deep psychological need which demands that 'The Plan' must really exist. 'There can be no failure if there really is a Plan. Defeated you may be, but never through any fault of your own. To bow to a cosmic will is no shame. You are not a coward; you are a martyr.'

The Templar myths have therefore proved extremely durable and their contribution to the modern image of the real Templars arguably as powerful as that of their documented history between 1119 and 1314. The longevity of these myths perhaps, like Gnosticism, relates to their flexibility, for they have been used by both conservative and radical proponents of the conspiracy theory of history, by romantics imbued with nostalgia for a lost medieval past, by Freemasons seeking a colourful history to justify their penchant for quasi-religious ritual and play-acting, and by charlatans who seek profit in exploiting the gullible. When, one evening, Casaubon was carried away telling the story of the Templars, a girl in his audience was entranced. ' "It was lovely," Dolores said. "Like a movie." ' Belbo was less easily impressed. When asked, at the end of a late night drinking session, how he recognised a lunatic, he was in no doubt. 'For him, everything proves everything else. The lunatic is all idée fixe, and whatever he come across confirms his lunacy. You can tell him by the liberties he takes with common sense, by his flashes of inspiration, and by the fact that sooner or later he brings up the Templars.'

NOTES

I ORIGINS

1 Ludolph of Suchem, *Liber de Itinere Terrae Sanctae*, ed. F. Deycks, Stuttgart, 1851, ch. 41, p. 89. Such prolonged disappearances were not unique, see J.A. Brundage, 'The Crusader's Wife Revisited', *Studia Gratiana*, 14, Collectanea Stephan Kuttner 4, Rome, 1967, pp. 243–51.

2 See G.Mollat, 'Dispersion définitive des Templiers après leur suppression', *Comptes rendus des Séances de l'Académie des Inscriptions et Belles-Lettres*, Paris, 1952, p. 378. The figure for Templar houses represents a reduction of about a hundred from my original estimate, since it excludes a number of doubtful cases, particularly from France. The total was therefore probably higher in practice.

3 For the basis of these figures, see M.C. Barber, 'Supplying the Crusader States: The Role of the Templars', in *The Horns of Hattin*, ed. B.Z. Kedar, Jerusalem and London, 1992, pp. 317–19. See also A.J. Forey, *The Military Orders. From the Twelfth to the Early Fourteenth Centuries*, London, 1992, pp. 77–90.

4 Fulcher of Chartres, *Historia Hierosolymitana*, ed. H. Hagenmeyer, Heidelberg, 1913, 2.4, pp. 373–4; 3.42, p. 763.

5 Daniel. The Life and Journey of Daniel. Abbot of the Russian Land, in *Jerusalem Pilgrimage*, ed. J. Wilkinson, Hakluyt Society 167, London, 1988, pp. 126, 136, 145, 156.

6 WT, 12.7, pp. 553–5; Michael the Syrian, *Chronique de Michel Le Syrien, Patriarche Jacobite d'Antioche (1166–99)*, ed. and tr. J.-B. Chabot, vol. III, Paris, 1905 (reprint 1963), 15.11, pp. 201–3; Walter Map, *De nugis curialium*, ed. and tr. M.R. James, rev. C.N.L. Brooke and R.A.B. Mynors, Oxford, 1983, pp. 54–5. It is possible that Ernoul, whose chronicle is lost, was a fourth independent source. The account of the foundation given in the anonymous Old French compilation which Ruth Morgan called the 'abrégé' (hereafter *Ernoul-Bernard*), dating from 1232, is based upon Ernoul's work, although the source has been highly compressed and summarised, *Chronique d'Ernoul and de Bernard Le Trésorier*, ed. L. de Mas Latrie, Société de l'Histoire de France, Paris, 1871, pp. 7–9. See M.R. Morgan, *The*

Chronicle of Ernoul and the Continuations of William of Tyre, Oxford, 1973, pp. 128, 134, 178. On the relevance of the lost chronicle to the history of the Templars, see above, pp. 110–11.

7 *CG*, no. 141, p. 99.

8 *Cart.*, vol. I, no. 53, p. 145; no. 71, p. 68. *RRH*, vol. II, no. 90(a), p. 6; vol. I, no. 106, p. 25. *Ernoul-Bernard*, p. 8, hints at just such a connection, but the reference is too brief to be of much value on its own.

9 J. Chartrou, *L'Anjou de 1109 à 1151*, Paris, 1928, *pièces justificatives*, no. 37, pp. 364–7.

10 *CG*, no. 16, pp. 10–11.

11 See P.W. Edbury and J.G. Rowe, *William of Tyre, Historian of the Latin East*, Cambridge, 1988, pp. 26–31.

12 *Règle*, cl. 3, p. 14.

13 See R. Hiestand, 'Kardinalbischof Matthäus von Albano, das Konzil von Troyes und die Entstehung des Templeordens', *Zeitschrift für Kirchengeschichte*, 99 (1988), 295–325, who shows convincingly that the Council should be placed in 1129 and not in 1128 as has traditionally been the case.

14 WT, 12.13, p. 563. See H.E. Mayer, 'The Concordat of Nablus', *Journal of Ecclesiastical History*, 33 (1982), 531–43.

15 See J. Richard, 'Quelques textes sur les premiers temps de l'Eglise Latine de Jérusalem', in *Recueil Clovis Brunel*, vol. II, Paris, 1955, pp. 427–30, who shows that the letter almost certainly dates from 1120. It cannot, in any case, be later than July 1124, the date of the capture of Tyre.

16 Albert of Aix, 'Historia Hierosolymitana', in *RHCr. Occid*, vol. IV, 12.33, pp. 712–13.

17 Fulcher of Chartres, *Historia*, 1.26, p. 291. Jerusalem remained underpopulated during this period.

18 See P. Scarpellini, 'La chiesa di San Bevignate, i Templari e la pittura perugina del Duecento', in *TOI*, p. 102 and figs. 50, 51.

19 *Le Cartulaire du Chapitre du Saint-Sépulchre de Jérusalem*, ed. G. Bresc-Bautier, Documents relatifs à l'histoire des croisades publiés par l'Académie des Inscriptions et Belles-Lettres 15, Paris, 1984, no. 63, pp. 157–8; *RRH*, vol. I, no. 364, p. 95.

20 Orderic Vitalis. *The Ecclesiastical History of Orderic Vitalis*, ed. and tr. M. Chibnall, vol. VI, Oxford, 1978, pp. 308–11; on Fulk's pilgrimage, WT, 14.2, p. 633.

21 He may have been on crusade with him in 1104 and perhaps came to the east with him in 1114. On Hugh of Payns, see M.L. Bulst-Thiele, *Sacrae Domus Militiae Templi Hierosolymitani Magistri: Untersuchungen zur Geschichte des Templeordens 1118/9–1314*, Göttingen, 1974, pp. 19–29, and M.C. Barber, 'The Origins of the Order of the Temple', *Studia Monastica*, 12 (1970), 221–4. For the overall context, see T. Evergates, *Feudal Society in the Bailliage of Troyes under the Counts of Champagne, 1152–1284*, Baltimore, 1975, pp. 101–13. Evergates shows that the lands of this lordship had been

absorbed into the count's demesne by 1140. Possibly Hugh granted so much of his patrimony to the Templars that the viability of the estates as an independent lordship had been undermined. He had a son, Theobald, but he had become Abbot of Saint-Colombe-de-Sens by 1139, so there may not have been any heirs to prevent a such a takeover.

22 Bernard of Clairvaux, *Epistolae*, in *Sancti Bernardi Opera*, vol. VII, ed. J. Leclercq and H. Rochais, Rome, 1974, ep. 31, pp. 85–6.

23 *CG*, no. 2, pp. 1–2. *Cartulaire de la Commanderie de Richerenches de l'Ordre du Temple (1136–1214)*, ed. Marquis de Ripert-Monclar, Documents inédits pour servir à l'histoire du Départment de Vaucluse, Paris, 1907, pp. xxxiii–iv. This document cannot be dated later than 5 July 1131, which is the date of the death of Berengar, Bishop of Fréjus. See A.J. Forey, *The Templars in the Corona de Aragón*, London, 1973, pp. 6–9, for the dating of Templar documents in the 1120s.

24 See H.E. Mayer, 'The Succession to Baldwin II of Jerusalem: English Impact on the East', *DOP*, 39 (1985), 139–47, and R. Hiestand, 'Chronologisches zur Geschichte des Königreiches Jerusalem um 1130', *Deutsches Archiv*, 26 (1970), 22.

25 *WT*, 13.26, p. 620.

26 *RRH*, vol. I, no. 105, p. 25.

27 See J. Riley-Smith, *The Crusades. A Short History*, London, 1987, pp. 91–2.

28 *WT*, 13.15, pp. 603–4; Fulcher of Chartres, *Historia*, 3.38–9, pp. 749–56.

29 *CG*, no. 1, p. 1. Both the attribution and the authenticity of this letter have been questioned, for example by M. Melville, *La Vie des Templiers*, Paris, 1951, p. 272, n. 19, but the factual content appears accurate, while the aims accord with Baldwin II's strategy at the time. See also the discussion by P. Cousin, 'Les Débuts de l'Ordre des Templiers et Saint Bernard', in *MSB*, 49–51. He inclines to attribute it to King Fulk, although he too is very doubtful about its authenticity. On the Templar connection with St Bernard, see M.L Bulst-Thiele, 'The Influence of St Bernard of Clairvaux on the Formation of the Order of the Knights Templar', in *The Second Crusade and the Cistercians*, ed. M. Gervers, New York, 1992, pp. 57–65.

30 Bernard of Clairvaux, *Epistolae*, vol. VIII, 1977, ep. 359, p. 305.

31 *CG*, no. 59, pp. 42–3.

32 *CG*, no. 9, p. 6.

33 *CG*, no. 7, p. 5.

34 On the importance of Count Theobald, see E.M. Hallam, *Capetian France 987–1328*, London, 1980, p. 49.

35 *CG*, no. 16, pp. 10–11.

36 *CG*, no. 8, pp. 5–6; no. 12, pp. 8–10. On the chronology of these events, see Mayer, 'The Succession to Baldwin II of Jerusalem', pp. 146–7.

37 *CG*, no. 14, p. 10; no. 15, p. 10.

38 *The Anglo-Saxon Chronicle*, tr. D. Whitelock, London, 1961, pp. 194–5.

39 *Règle*, cl. 4, p. 15. See Hiestand, 'Kardinalbischof', 302–11, and

'Chronologisches', 229. Hiestand, 'Kardinalbischof', 309, points out that D'Albon placed an undated grant of a house, lands, meadows, and vines made 'in the presence of' Hugh of Payns and four other Templars in the region of Troyes, in January 1129, apparently because he too believed that the council was held at that time, CG, no. 22, p. 16.

40 Bernard of Clairvaux, *Epistolae*, vol. VII, ep. 21, pp. 71–2.

41 See *Die ursprüngliche Templerregel*, ed. G. Schnürer, Freiburg, 1903, pp. 135–53, and G. de Valous, 'Quelques observations sur la toute primitive observance des Templiers et la *Regula pauperum commilitorum Christi Templi Salomonici*, rédigée par saint Bernard au concile de Troyes (1128)', in *MSB*, pp. 32–40.

42 *Règle*, cl. 6, p. 8. If the 1129 date is accepted, then G. Schnürer's view, in 'Zur ersten Organisation der Templer', *Historisches Jahrbuch*, 32 (1911), 514, that the preface and Rule were rewritten after the council cannot be sustained. Jean Michel's record of the manner of proceeding at the council is in itself enough to explain the various changes Schnürer discerned. See Hiestand, 'Kardinalbischof', 312.

43 See P. Cousin, 'Les Débuts de l'Ordre des Templiers et Saint Bernard', in *MSB*, p. 43, n. 2.

44 *Règle*, cl. 9, pp. 21.–2.

45 *Règle*, cls. 9–71, pp. 21–70.

46 WT, 13.24, pp. 618–19.

47 WT, 13.26, p. 620. Henry of Huntingdon, *Historia Anglorum*, ed. T. Arnold, RS 74, London, 1879, pp. 250, 251, says that he returned with the Count of Anjou in 1129, although he confuses Fulk with his son, Geoffrey. This section was copied by Robert of Torigni, 'Chronicle', in *Chronicles of the Reigns of Stephen, Henry II, and Richard I.*, ed. R. Howlett, vol. IV, RS 82, London, 1889, p. 113, who nevertheless corrects this mistake, which makes it all the more probable that Hugh did travel with Fulk.

48 See *The Crusades. Idea and Reality 1095–1274*, ed. and tr. L. and J. Riley-Smith, London, 1981, p. 15.

49 Geoffrey of Clairvaux, *Vita S. Bernardi*, in *PL*, vol. 185(i), Paris, 1855, 4.1, p. 325.

50 See C.H. Lawrence, *Medieval Monasticism*, 2nd edn, London, 1989, pp. 95–7, 186–9, and Forey, *The Templars in the Corona de Aragón*, p.88.

51 See J. Riley-Smith, *The Knights of St John in Jerusalem and Cyprus c. 1050–1310*, London, 1967, pp. 40–1, 353. On the titles of the early officials of the Order, see *Records of the Templars in England in the Twelfth Century. The Inquest of 1185*, ed. B.A. Lees, British Academy Records of the Social and Economic History of England and Wales 9, London, 1935, pp. lxiii–lxv.

52 CG, no. 31, p. 24. See V. Carrière, 'Les Débuts de l'Ordre du Temple en France', *Le Moyen Age*, 18 (1914), 308–35, for the pattern of expansion.

53 CG, no. 62, p. 45.

54 CG, no. 18, p. 12; no. 47, p. 36; no. 48, p. 37.

55 CG, no. 121, p. 85; no. 132, p. 92; no. 144, p. 101; no. 150, p. 105; no. 156, p. 109; no. 165, p. 115; no. 169, p. 118; no. 170, p. 118; no. 172,

p. 120; no. 184, p. 127; no. 198, p. 138, for the charters in which he has one or more of these titles.

56 CG, no. 27, p. 19; no. 60, p. 43.

57 CG, no. 232, pp. 157–8; no. 158, p. 111; no. 200, p. 140; no. 210, p. 150.

58 CG, no. 314, p. 205.

59 See Forey, *The Templars in the Corona de Aragón*, pp. 420, 89.

60 CG, no. 408, p. 256; no. 409, p. 257; no. 390, p. 246.

61 CG, no. 364, p. 233; no. 520, p. 320.

62 For example, CG, no. 228, p. 154 (bailli); no. 408, p. 256 (master on this side of the sea); no. 464, p. 289 (master of the knights); no. 594, p. 356 (minister and servant).

63 CG, no. 113, p. 80.

64 CG, no. 329, p. 214; no. 510, p. 315; no. 50, p. 39; no. 357, p. 229; no. 527, p. 324; no. 583, p. 359; no. 177, p. 122; no. 202, p. 140; no. 520, p. 320. Moreover, although a local preceptor is not mentioned specifically, the wording of grants in several other places suggests that the Templars had been able to set up houses elsewhere during the 1130s and 1140s. See figure 2.

65 *Instrumenta Episcoporum Albinganensium*, ed. G. Pesce, Documenti del R. Archivio di Stato di Torino, Collana Storico-Archeologica della Liguria Occidentale 4, Albenga, 1935, no. 45, pp. 64–5; no. 51, pp. 70–1 (August 1144); no. 47, pp. 66–7; no. 48, pp. 67–8. In October 1143, Oberto is also described as a *conversus* of the Temple, no. 43, p. 63.

66 CG, no. 41, p. 31.

67 CG, no. 59, pp. 42–3; no. 21, pp. 15–16. The concession of Bishop Ulger could have been made at any time between the Council of Troyes in 1129 and the bishop's death in 1149. It seems more likely to have followed the issue of the bull *Milites Templi* of 1144, however, as here the pope conceded just such a limited immunity from interdicts.

68 CG, no. 226, p. 153.

69 CG, no. 29, p. 23.

70 J. Walker, 'The Patronage of the Templars and the Order of Saint Lazarus in England in the Twelfth and Thirteenth Centuries', Ph.D. thesis, University of St Andrews, 1990, pp. 156–7, 278–9, shows the overwhelming importance of the contribution of Stephen and his wife, Matilda. They were much more active than the Angevin party.

71 CG, no. 178, pp. 122–3.

72 CG, no. 232, p. 157.

73 CG, no. 20, pp. 13–15.

74 On the importance of knightly values in Italy, see J. Larner, *Italy in the Age of Dante and Petrarch 1216–1380*, London, 1980, pp. 95–102.

75 See F. Bramato, 'L'Ordine dei Templari in Italia. Dalle origini al pontificato di Innocenzo III (1135–1216)', *Nicolaus* 20 (1985), fasc. 1, 195.

76 CG, no. 85, pp. 64–5.

77 CG, no. 396, p. 249.

78 CG, no. 561, pp. 347–8.

79 See, in addition, A.J. Forey, 'Women and Military Orders in the Twelfth

and Thirteenth Centuries', *Studia Monastica*, 29 (1987), 63–6, and
M.C. Barber, 'The Social Context of the Templars', *TRHS*, 5th ser., 34
(1984), 42.

80 *CG*, no. 194, pp. 135–6.

81 *CG*, no. 221, pp. 151–2. See *Cartulario del Temple de Huesca*, ed. A. Gargallo
Moya, M.T. Iranzo Muñio, and M.J. Sánchez Usón, Textos Medievales
70, Zaragoza, 1985, no. 116, p. 118 (1189) and no. 165, pp. 176–8 (1215),
for similar endowments by both women and men.

82 See T.N. Bisson, *The Medieval Crown of Aragon. A Short History*, Oxford,
1986, pp. 15–16.

83 See E. Lourie, 'The Confraternity of Belchite, the Ribāt, and the Temple',
Viator. Medieval and Renaissance Studies, 13 (1982), 159–76, and P. Rassow,
'La cofradía de Belchite', *Anuario de historia del derecho español*, 3 (1926),
200–26, who prints and analyses the confirmation of their 'cofradia militar'
by Alfonso VII of Castile in October 1136.

84 *CG*, no. 6, pp. 3–4.

85 S.A. García Larragueta, *El Gran Priorado de Navarra de la Orden de San Juan de
Jerusalén*, vol. II, Pamplona, 1957, no. 10, pp. 15–18; *CG*, no. 40, pp. 30–1.

86 E. Lourie, 'The Will of Alfonso I, "El Batallador", King of Aragon and
Navarre: A Reassessment', *Speculum*, 50 (1975), 639–41.

87 García Larragueta, *El Gran Priorado de Navarra*, no. 13, p. 21.

88 *CG*, no. 91, p. 68. The Templars are not mentioned by name, but at this
early date their name and functions were expressed in a wide variety of
ways, see above, pp. 51–2. It is difficult to see that Ramiro could be
referring to any other body, except possibly the brothers of Belchite, south
of Zaragoza.

89 *CG*, no. 33, p. 25. This document is dated 1130 in D'Albon's version, but
there are substantial doubts about this, see Forey *The Templars in the Corona
de Aragón*, pp. 8–9.

90 *CG*, no. 72, p. 55. Dated April because Raymond Berenguer had made
other grants to the Templars on 15 April, *CG*, no. 71, pp. 53–5.

91 *CG*, no. 145, p. 102.

92 *CG*, no. 314, pp. 204–5.

93 See Forey, *The Templars in the Corona de Aragón*, pp. 20–3; Bisson, *The
Medieval Crown of Aragon*, p. 32.

94 See Forey, *The Templars in the Corona de Aragón*, p. 67, n. 43.

95 *CG*, no. 47, p. 36. The grant was confirmed by Raymond Berenguer in
1134, *CG*, no. 70, p. 53.

96 Forey, *The Templars in the Corona de Aragón*, pp. 16–17, 24.

97 See above, p. 166, the figures given for Safad in Galilee after its rebuilding
in the 1240s.

98 Lourie, 'The Will of Alfonso I', 635–51.

99 *CG*, Bullaire, no. 2, p. 373. See Forey, *The Templars in the Corona de
Aragón*, pp. 18–20.

100 The king's motives are the subject of continuing debate, for there is no
definitive answer to the problem. See A.J. Forey, 'The Will of Alfonso I of

Aragon and Navarre', *Durham University Journal*, 73 (1980–1), 59–65, and E. Lourie, 'The Will of Alfonso I of Aragon and Navarre: A Reply to Dr Forey', *Durham University Journal*, 77 (1984–5), 165–72.

101 *CG*, no. 100, p. 73.
102 *CG*, no. 94, p. 70.
103 *CG*, no. 177, p. 122.
104 *CG*, no. 553, pp. 339–40. Forey, *The Templars in the Corona de Aragón*, pp. 74–5, argues that an exchange may have taken place much earlier than this. This seems very likely, especially given the presence of a Templar preceptor at Novillas by at least 1139.
105 *CG*, no. 92, p. 69. Most royal grants in Navarre were in the form of rights over specific villages and their populations, for example, no. 211, p. 146; no. 386, p. 244; no. 404, p. 254. In Aragon, land resettlement was the most important means of increasing the value of the Templar lands, see Forey, *The Templars in the Corona de Aragón*, pp. 212–21 and Appendix 1, no. 2, pp. 368–9.
106 *CG*, no. 545, p. 334.
107 *CG*, no. 10, p. 7; no. 24, p. 17.
108 *CG*, no. 359, pp. 230–1.
109 *CG*, no. 439, p. 275.
110 *CG*, no. 363, pp. 232–3; no. 364, p. 233.
111 *CG*, no. 381, p. 241.
112 *CG*, no. 410, pp. 257–8.
113 *WT*, 14.22, pp. 659–61; *Cart.*, vol. 1, no. 116, pp. 97–8; *RRH*, no. 164, pp. 40–1. See S. Tibble, *Monarchy and Lordships in the Latin Kingdom of Jerusalem 1099–1291*, Oxford, 1989, pp. 10–11. The date is either late 1136 or early 1137.
114 *WT*, 17.12, pp. 775–7.
115 *Cart.*, vol. 1, no. 144, pp. 116–18.
116 See Riley-Smith, *The Knights of St John in Jerusalem*, pp. 52–9, and A.J. Forey, 'The Militarisation of the Hospital of St John', *Studia Monastica*, 26 (1984), 75–89. It has been argued that the Hospitaller acquisition of the fortified site of Calansue in the lordship of Bethsan in the north of the kingdom in 1128 might represent an even earlier grant of military responsibilities, Tibble, *Monarchy and Lordships*, pp. 136–9. If this were so, it suggests various possibilities, but in particular two not entirely compatible ideas. On the one hand, if it is accepted that the Hospitallers adopted military functions after the establishment of the Templars, then it strengthens the view that the Templars held fortified places in the kingdom well before 1149. On the other hand, the hints that the early Templars had been closely associated with the Hospital and may even have been an offshoot from it could indicate that the Hospitallers were as likely to have gained military responsibilities in the 1120s or early 1130s as were the Templars.
117 See J. Riley-Smith, 'The Templars and the Teutonic Knights in Cilician Armenia', in *The Cilician Kingdom of Armenia*, ed. T.S.R. Boase, Edinburgh and London, 1978, pp. 92–5.

118 WT, 13.26, pp. 620–1; 15.6, p. 683. Henry of Huntingdon, p. 251, knew of the disasters of 1129, which he attributes to the punishment of God for the crimes of the Christians.

119 Orderic Vitalis. *Ecclesiastical History*, vol. VI, pp. 496–7; WT 14.26, pp. 665–7. For the overall context, see S. Runciman, *A History of the Crusades*, vol. II, Cambridge, 1952, pp. 202–5.

120 *RRH*, no. 133, p. 33; no. 173, p. 43; no. 194, p. 48; no. 195, p. 48; no. 217, pp. 55–6; no. 226, p. 57; no. 237, p. 60. See also *CG*, no.141, p.99; no.328, p.213, n.1. The arrival of the army of Louis VII would have brought many more Templars to the east, so the 1148 council seems a reasonable divide. A grant to the Order of St Lazarus at Jerusalem, which cannot be dated earlier than April 1148, was witnessed by a further seven Templars, none of whom had appeared on previous charters in the east, *RRH*, no.252, p.63.

121 Bernard of Clairvaux, *Epistolae*, vol. VII, ep. 175, p. 393; ep. 206, p. 65.

122 The figure of 210 includes three Templars active in both the east and the west during this period (William Falco, Geoffrey Fulcher, and Osto of St Omer), but not the two Grand Masters. It is based on D'Albon's cartulary. The record of the 130 knights at Paris is *CG*, no. 448, p. 280.

123 *OR*, p. 321, for the month and the day. Hugh is last mentioned in a document which cannot be dated later than 14 April 1134, *CG*, no. 59, pp. 42–3. Robert is first shown as Grand Master in a document which can be dated between September 1137, and April 1138, *CG*, no. 141, p. 99. Hugh might therefore have died in 1134, 1135, 1136, or 1137. On Robert of Craon, see Bulst-Thiele, *Magistri*, pp. 30–40.

124 *Cartulaire de l'abbaye de Saint-Aubin d'Angers*, ed. A. de Bertrand de Broussillon, vol. II, Paris, 1903, no. 430, p. 38; Chartrou, *L'Anjou de 1109 à 1151, pièces justicatives*, no. 44, pp. 375–6. On Fulk's general policy, see H.E. Mayer, 'Angevins *versus* Normans: The New Men of King Fulk of Jerusalem', *Proceedings of the American Philosophical Society*, 133 (1989), 1–25, esp. 6–7.

125 WT, 15.6, pp. 682–3.

126 See, for example, the rise in the proportion of the Lordship of Caesarea held by the Hospitallers: 3.5 per cent in 1123 to 8.9 per cent by 1154, Tibble, *Monarchy and Lordships*, pp. 110–111. Even the tiny Order of Saint Lazarus, which was only a minor offshoot of the Temple, received six recorded grants and confirmations in the Kingdom of Jerusalem during this period, even though its own archive is incomplete, 'Fragment d'un cartulaire de l'ordre de Saint-Lazare en Terre Sainte', ed. A. de Marsy, in *AOL*, vol. II, Paris, 1884, pp. 123–7.

127 Richard of Poitou, *Chronica*, in *MGH SS*, vol.XXVI, p. 80.

128 For the loss of the Templar central archive, see above, pp. 311–13.

129 Usāmah Ibn-Munqidh, *An Arab-Syrian Gentleman and Warrior in the Period of the Crusades*, tr. P.K. Hitti, New York, 1929 (reprint 1987), pp. 163–4.

130 Alfonso Jordan died on crusade in April 1148.

131 *CG*, no. 87, pp. 66.

2 THE CONCEPT

1 See S. Shahar, 'Des lépreux pas comme les autres'. L'ordre de Saint-Lazare dans le royaume latin de Jérusalem', *Revue Historique*, 267 (1982), 19–41.

2 See F.H. Russell, *The Just War in the Middle Ages*, Cambridge, 1975, pp. 16–39.

3 See I.S. Robinson, 'Gregory VII and the Soldiers of Christ', *History*, 58 (1973), 169–92.

4 See Lourie, 'The Confraternity of Belchite', 159–76.

5 See above, pp. 26–7.

6 See A.J. Forey, 'The Emergence of the Military Order in the Twelfth Century', *Journal of Ecclesiastical History*, 36 (1985), 178–81, who argues strongly against the influence of the *ribāt*.

7 Peter the Venerable. *The Letters of Peter the Venerable*, ed. G. Constable, vol. I, Cambridge, Mass., 1967, no. 172, p. 407; no. 173, p. 411. See also V.G. Berry, 'Peter the Venerable and the Crusades', in *Petrus Venerabilis (1156–1956): Studies and Texts Commemorating the Eighth Centenary of his Death*, ed. G. Constable and J. Kritzeck, Rome, 1956, p. 144.

8 See J.A. Brundage, 'A Transformed Angel (X 3.31.18): The Problem of the Crusading Monk', in *Studies in Medieval Cistercian History presented to Jeremiah F. O'Sullivan*, Cistercian Studies Series 13, Spencer, Mass., 1971, pp. 55–62.

9 Henry of Huntingdon, 'Epistola ad Walterum de Contemptu Mundi', ed. T. Arnold, *Historia Anglorum*, RS 74, London, 1879, p. 315.

10 The problem has never been resolved. Two articles on this subject appeared almost simultaneously: 'Un document sur les débuts des Templiers', ed. J. Leclercq, *Revue d'Histoire Ecclésiastique*, 52 (1957), 81–91, and 'Lettre inédite de Hugues de Saint-Victor aux Chevaliers du Temple', ed. C. Sclafert, *Revue d'ascétique et de mystique*, 34 (1958), 275–99. Leclercq argues in favour of Hugh of Payns, whereas Sclafert believes the rubric is authentic and that the author must therefore be Hugh of St Victor. Although I was originally convinced by Leclercq's arguments, I now think it an unlikely piece of work for a man of Hugh of Payns' background. See also J. Fleckenstein, 'Die Rechtfertigung der geistlichen Ritterorden nach der Schrift "De laude novae militiae" Bernhards von Clairvaux', in *Die geistlichen Ritterorden Europas*, ed. J. Fleckenstein and M. Hellmann, Sigmaringen, 1980, pp. 9–10.

11 Bernard of Clairvaux, 'Liber ad Milites Templi de Laude Novae Militiae', in *S.Bernardi Opera*, vol. III, *Tractatus et Opuscula*, ed. J. Leclercq and H.M. Rochais, Rome, 1963, pp. 205–39. See also 'In Praise of the New Knighthood', in *The Works of Bernard of Clairvaux*, vol. VII, *Treatises*, 3, tr. C. Greenia, introd. R.J.Z. Werblowsky, Cistercian Fathers Series 19, Kalamazoo, Mich., 1977, pp. 115–71.

12 See J. Leclercq, 'Saint Bernard's Attitude toward War', in *Studies in Medieval Cistercian History* 2, ed. J.R. Sommerfeldt, Kalamazoo, Mich., 1976, p. 24.

13 See Barber, 'Social Context of the Templars', 32–7.

14 Bernard of Clairvaux, 'Apologia ad Guillelmum Abbatem'. in *S. Bernardi Opera*, vol. III, *Tractatus et Opuscula*, ed. J. Leclercq and H.M. Rochais, Rome, 1963, 10–12.24–30, pp. 101–7.

15 E. Delaruelle, 'L'idée de croisade chez saint Bernard', in *MSB*, pp. 53–67.

16 *Règle*, cl. 121, pp. 100–1. See above, p. 189.

17 *Lettres des Premiers Chartreux*, vol. I, *S. Bruno, Guiges, S. Anthelme*, Sources Chrétiennes 88, 2nd edn, Paris, 1988, pp. 154–61.

18 *Lettres des Premiers Chartreux*, pp. 115–16, for a discussion of Guigo's position on Christian warfare.

19 Anselme de Havelberg, *Dialogues*, ed. and tr. G. Salet, vol. I, Sources Chrétiennes 118, Paris, 1966, pp. 98–101.

20 See B. Smalley, 'Ecclesiastical Attitudes to Novelty c. 1100–1250', in *Studies in Church History*, 12 (1975), pp. 124–5.

21 *CG*, no. 21, p. 15. See too Elbert, Bishop of Châlons-sur-Marne (1132), no. 46, p. 35.

22 *CG*, no. 22, p. 16; no. 139, p. 97; no. 165, p. 115; no. 370, p. 236.

23 *CG*, no. 77, p. 66; no. 141, p. 99; no. 231, p. 156; no. 561, pp. 347–8.

24 *CG*, no. 33, p. 25 (for dating, see above, p. 340, n.89); no. 314, p. 204.

25 García Larragueta, *El Gran Priorado de Navarra*, no. 10, p. 16; *CG*, no. 91, p. 68.

26 *CG*, no. 307, p. 200.

27 *CG*, no. 530, pp. 326–7.

28 *CG*, no. 66, p. 50.

29 *CG*, no. 68, pp. 51–2.

30 *CG*, no. 390, p. 246.

31 *CG*, no. 40, p. 30.

32 *CG*, no. 195, p. 136.

33 *CG*, no. 359, p. 230.

34 *CG*, no. 339, pp. 220–1.

35 *CG*, no. 363, pp. 232–3.

36 *CG*, no. 17, p. 11.

37 *CG*, no. 172, pp. 119–20.

38 *CG*, no. 207, p. 144.

39 *CG*, no. 295, p. 193.

40 *Papsturkunden für Templer und Johanniter*, ed. R. Hiestand, Vorarbeiten zum Oriens Pontificius, vol. I, Abhandlungen des Akademie der Wissenschaften in Göttingen 77, Göttingen, 1972, no. 3, pp. 204–10; no. 8, pp. 214–15; no. 10, pp. 216–17; and vol. II, Abhandlungen des Akademie der Wissenschaften in Göttingen 135, Göttingen, 1984, pp. 67–103, 141.

41 D. Girgensohn, 'Das Pisaner Konzil von 1135 in der Überlieferung des Pisaner Konzils von 1409', in *Festschrift für Hermann Heimpel*, 2, Göttingen, 1972, pp. 1098–9. Hiestand, 'Kardinalbischof', 301, believes that the Templars must have been given papal recognition of some kind earlier than 1139, especially in view of the favour shown to them by Innocent II at Pisa in 1135. This may well have taken the form of the bull *Milites Templi*, now known in the version issued in 1144. Since the bull is mainly concerned

with encouraging contributions to the Templars, it would be in keeping with the example set by the pope and others attending the council, who made monetary contributions. However, it is equally likely that the schism prevented Innocent from issuing such a fundamental privilege as *Omne datum optimum*, and that he did so as soon as he was able to early in 1139.

42 See 'The Templars and the Castle of Tortosa in Syria: An Unknown Document Concerning the Acquisition of the Fortress', ed. J. Riley-Smith, *EHR*, 84 (1969), 281–2. Cf. the situation in Aragon, Forey, *The Templars in the Corona de Aragón*, pp. 159–88.

43 Bernard of Clairvaux, *Epistolae*, vol. VII, no. 175, p. 393; vol. VIII, no. 392, p. 363. Like many of Bernard's letters these are difficult to date. The Patriarch of Jerusalem is not named, but it is usually assumed that it is William of Messines, who held office from the last months of 1130 until his death in 1145. Bernard's statement at the beginning of the letter that the patriarch had been the first to send him blessings from across the sea suggests that the letter was written soon after his election. Moreover, the reference to 'the place to which you have invited us' seems to be referring to Nebi Samwil, an offer made to the Cistercians during the lifetime of Baldwin II (died August 1131). But none of this is decisive, since the carrier of the letter appears to be Andrew of Montbard, Bernard's uncle, for whose presence in the east there is no concrete evidence before 1148, while Bernard's offer of the site at Nebi Samwil to the Premonstratensians is to be found in a letter dated at late as c. 1150. The letter to the Patriarch of Antioch refers to 'Radulfus', which must mean Ralph of Domfront, Patriarch 1135–40.

44 I.S. Robinson, *The Papacy, 1073–1198. Continuity and Innovation*, Cambridge, 1990, p. 259.

45 John of Salisbury, *Policraticus: Of the Frivolities of Courtiers and the Footprints of Philosophers*, ed. and tr. C.J. Nederman, Cambridge, 1990, 7.21, pp. 168–75. Latin text, *Ioannis Saresberiensis Episcopi Carnotensis Policratici*, vol. II, ed. C.C. Webb, Oxford, 1909, pp. 692–5. See Riley-Smith, *The Knights of St John in Jerusalem*, pp. 375–420, on the problems caused by the exemptions of the military orders.

46 See L.K. Little, 'Pride Goes before Avarice: Social Change and the Vices in Latin Christendom', *American Historical Review*, 76 (1971), 16–49.

47 See B. Hamilton, *Religion in the Medieval West*. London, 1986, p. 134. A. Demurger, 'Les Templiers, Matthieu Paris et les sept péchés capitaux', in *MS*, pp. 153–68, draws attention to the moralistic stereotyping common among contemporary monastic chroniclers.

48 WT, 12.7, pp. 554–5. See above, pp.98–9.

49 See B. Z. Kedar, *Crusade and Mission. European Approaches toward the Muslims*, Princeton, 1984, pp. 104–8.

50 Isaac de l'Etoile, 'Isaac de l'Etoile et son siècle: Texte et commentaire historique du sermon XLVIII', ed. G. Raciti, *Cîteaux: Commentarii Cistercienses*, 12 (1961), 281–306. No military order is mentioned by name but the new knighthood is a clear allusion to *De laude*. It seems unlikely to have

been a reference to the Spanish Order of Calatrava as Raciti believes, since Isaac was Abbot of L'Etoile between 1147 and 1167, whereas Calatrava only received papal approval in 1164. The Templars were not, as Isaac says, engaged in 'forcing infidels to the faith', but it seems probable that Isaac believed that that was their intention. But see also Leclercq, 'St Bernard's Attitude toward War', p. 28.

51 Walter Map, *De nugis curialium*, pp. 60–3.
52 See Smalley, 'Ecclesiastical Attitudes to Novelty', pp. 113–31.
53 See Riley-Smith, *The Knights of St John in Jerusalem*, pp. 32–3.
54 *Le Dossier de l'Affaire des Templiers*, ed. and tr. G. Lizerand, Les Classiques de l'Histoire de France au Moyen Age, 2nd edn., Paris, 1964, pp. 4–5.
55 For example, Hugh of Payns, *RRH*, no. 105, p. 25 (1125), Robert of Craon, WT 17.1, p. 761 (1148), and Everard des Barres, *RRH*, no. 291, p. 73 (1152). See Hiestand, 'Kardinalbischof', 323.
56 See Russell, *The Just War*, p. 296.
57 *Le Dossier*, pp. 58–9.

3 THE RISE OF THE TEMPLARS IN THE EAST IN THE TWELFTH CENTURY

1 'Imâd ad-Din al-Isfahânî, *Conquête de la Syrie et de la Palestine par Saladin*, tr. H. Massé, Paris, 1972, pp. 30–1. English translation from *Arab Historians of the Crusades*, ed. and tr. F. Gabrieli, Eng. tr. E.J. Costello, London, 1969, p. 138.
2 See also *Cont. WT*, pp. 87–8, where the opinion is expressed that this was a tactical error by Saladin because it would invite revenge. It seems, however, to have been expected of him, see Riley-Smith, *The Knights of St John in Jerusalem*, pp. 75–6.
3 See H.E. Mayer, 'Studies in the History of Queen Melisende of Jerusalem', *DOP*, 26 (1972), 113–82.
4 WT, 21.7, p. 970.
5 *CG*, no. 448, p. 279. See above, p. 35.
6 Suger of Saint-Denis. *Abbot Suger on the Abbey Church of St Denis and its Art Treasures*, ed. and tr. E. Panofsky, 2nd edn G. Panofsky-Soergel, Princeton, 1979, pp. 112–13. Cf. the scale of royal assemblies in France up to this date, Hallam, *Capetian France*, p. 172.
7 WT, 12.7, p. 554. James of Vitry, 'Historia Hierosolimitana', ed. J. Bongars, *Gesta Dei per Francos*, vol. 1(ii), Hanover, 1611, p. 1083, interprets this as a sign of martyrdom.
8 Odo of Deuil, *De Profectione Ludovici VII in Orientem*, ed. and tr. V.G. Berry, Records of Civilization. Sources and Studies 42, New York, 1948, pp. 52–5.
9 Odo of Deuil, *De Profectione*, pp. 124–5.
10 *Ibid.*, pp. 124–7, 132–5.
11 *Etudes sur les actes de Louis VII*, ed. A. Luchaire, Paris, 1885, no. 230, p. 173; no. 236, pp. 174–5.
12 See J.F. Benton, 'The Revenue of Louis VII', *Speculum*, 42 (1967), 91.

13 WT, 17.1–2, pp. 760–2.
14 Otto of Freising and Rahewin. *Gesta Friderici I. Imperatoris auctoribus Ottone et Ragewino praeposito Frisingensibus*, ed. G.H. Pertz, in MGH SS, vol. xx, 1.58, p. 385.
15 See A.J. Forey, 'The Failure of the Siege of Damascus in 1148', *JMH*, 10 (1984), 13–23.
16 *Die Urkunden der Deutschen Könige und Kaiser*, ed. F. Hausmann, in MGH, *Diplomata*, vol. ix, Vienna, 1969, no. 197, pp. 768–9.
17 WT, 17.7, pp. 768–9.
18 'Annales Herbipolenses', ed. G.H. Pertz, in MGH SS, vol. xvi, p. 7.
19 John of Würzburg, 'Descriptio Terrae Sanctae', ed. T. Tobler, *Descriptiones Terrae Sanctae ex saec. VIII. IX. XII. et XV.*, Leipzig, 1874, ch. 5, p. 130.
20 John of Salisbury, *Historia Pontificalis*, ed. and tr. M. Chibnall, London, 1956, p. 57.
21 See J. Riley-Smith, 'Peace Never Established: The Case of the Kingdom of Jerusalem', *TRHS*, 5th ser., 28 (1978), 87–102, on the attitudes of westerners to the Holy Land and its inhabitants.
22 See Forey, 'The Failure of the Siege of Damascus', 20–1.
23 *OR*, p. 314, for the day. Everard first definitely appears as Grand Master in the papal confirmation of the grants made in 1143 by Raymond Bereguer, 30 March 1150. Here Robert of Craon is referred to as 'of good memory', *CG*, Bullaire, no. 22, pp. 386–8. Robert may have lived until early 1150, therefore, but it seems unlikely, as Andrew of Montbard, the seneschal, appears to have acted as leader in the east when Everard returned to France in the autumn of 1149. See Andrew's letter to Everard in which he refers to the battle of Inab, 29 June 1149, see below, note 25. On the career of Everard, see Bulst-Thiele, *Magistri*, pp. 41–52.
24 No new forces were raised although there was much urgent discussion involving influential figures such as St Bernard, Peter of Cluny, and Suger of Saint-Denis, see Berry, 'Peter the Venerable', pp. 158–62.
25 *RHG*, vol. xv, pp. 540–1.
26 This confirmation is dated 1154, indiction 15, *Chartes de Terre Sainte provenant de l'abbaye de Notre Dame de Josaphat*, ed. F. Delaborde, Paris, 1880, no. 29, p. 70; *RRH*, no. 291, p. 73, but Everard had already been replaced as Grand Master by Bernard of Tremelay by January, 1153, WT, 17.21, p. 790. If the indiction is correct, the year would be 1152, suggesting a scribal error. This appears to have been D'Albon's view, since he corrected the document in the manuscript notes for his uncompleted cartulary of the Temple, BN, *NAL* 70, f. 2. A dating of 1152 also fits the rather intricate chronology of the conflict between Melisende and Baldwin, as worked out by Mayer, 'Studies in the History of Queen Melisende', 170.
27 Everard was a monk at Clairvaux in 1174, BN, *Manuscrits Latin*, 14679, fols. 724–5. He was still alive in 1176, *Etudes sur les actes de Louis VII*, ed. Luchaire, Paris, 1885, no. 699, p. 319. He is not, however, recorded as Grand Master in the Obituary Roll at Reims, the only twelfth-century Master to be omitted. Bernard of Tremelay is given as 'tercius magister

Templi', p. 325. This may have been deliberate, since he had resigned, or it may reflect the haphazard construction of such rolls. Indeed, as he had become a Cistercian it is unlikely that the preceptory at Reims knew when he died.

28 Bernard of Clairvaux, *Epistolae*, vol. VIII, ep. 206, p. 65.

29 See J.-B. Jobin, *Saint Bernard et sa Famille*, Paris, 1891 pp. xxi–xxii, and Bulst-Thiele, *Magistri*, pp. 57–61.

30 *RRH*, no. 252, p. 63. He may have been the Brother Andrew referred to in St Bernard's letter to the Patriarch of Jerusalem, usually dated 1130–1, but there are problems with this dating, see above, p. 345, n.43. He is shown as a layman on a charter of Bernard II of Montbard in 1129, Jobin, *St Bernard, pièces justificatives*, no. 15, pp. 574–5.

31 *Letters of Peter the Venerable*, vol. I, no. 164, p. 397; no. 165, p. 398.

32 Bernard of Clairvaux, *Epistolae*, vol. VIII, no. 288, pp. 203–4. Bernard refers to himself as near death in this letter, but this may have been one of his earlier illnesses. The apparent reference to Gerald, Bishop of Bethlehem (1148–53), and the dangers in the east, however, suggest that it is unlikely to be before 1150. The date of 1153 is therefore the most probable.

33 Bernard of Clairvaux, *Epistolae*, vol. VIII, no. 206, p. 65; no. 289, pp. 205–6.

34 Mayer, 'Studies in the History of Queen Melisende', pp. 152–3.

35 *Ibid.*, pp. 159–60, 170. See also above, note 26.

36 See Tibble, *Monarchy and Lordships*, pp. 9–11, for overall royal policy in this area, which he believes to have been partly motivated by a desire to weaken the powerful lordship of Hebron, seen as a potential threat to the monarchy after the revolt of 1134.

37 WT, 17.12, pp. 776–7; 20.20, p. 938.

38 He appears as a witness on three Burgundian charters between 1135 and 1137, when he was still a layman, P.N.C. Persan, *Recherches historiques sur la ville de Dole*, Dole, 1812, preuves, no. 12, p. 371; BN, *Moreau* 871, *Cartulaire de l'abbaye de Rosières*, fols. 327, 329v–30. See also Bulst-Thiele, *Magistri*, pp. 53–6.

39 *OR*, p. 325, gives 16 August as the day of Bernard's death, and he was presumably killed in the engagement.

40 WT, 17.27, pp. 797–9.

41 Ibn al-Qalānisī, *The Damascus Chronicle of the Crusades*, ed. and tr. H.A.R. Gibb, University of London Historical Series 5, London, 1932, pp. 314–17; Ibn al-Athir, 'Extrait de la Chronique intitulée Kamel-Altevarykh', in *RHCr. Or.*, vol. I, Paris, 1872, pp. 490–1, who does, however, say that a Frankish attack was repulsed and that the besiegers almost gave up; Abū Shāmā, 'Le Livre des Deux Jardins', in *RHCr. Or.*, vol. IV, pp. 77–8.

42 R. Grousset, *Histoire des Croisades et du Royaume Franc de Jérusalem*, vol. II, Paris, 1935, p. 355: 'Nous apercevons déjà ici la politique cupide et violente.' In contrast, see F. Lundgreen, *Wilhelm von Tyrus und der Templerorden*, Berlin, 1911, pp. 89–93.

43 WT, 18.9, pp. 822–3; Walter Map, *De nugis curialium*, pp. 62–7.

44 Usāmah, *An Arab-Syrian Gentleman*, p. 53.

45 Lundgreen, *Wilhelm von Tyrus*, pp. 93–6.

46 Usāmah, *An Arab-Syrian Gentleman*, pp. 51–3. He does speak of 'the treasures of 'Abbas and his harem'.

47 *Hunc porro cum diebus multis predicti fratres habuissent in vinculis* . . ., p. 823. Misleadingly translated as 'a long time' in William of Tyre, *A History of Deeds done beyond the Sea*, tr. E.M. Babcock and A.C. Krey, vol. II, Records of Civilization. Sources and Studies 35, New York, 1943 (reprint 1976), p. 253.

48 *Le Dossier*, pp. 10–11.

49 See R.C. Smail, *Crusading Warfare (1097–1193)*, Cambridge, 1956, pp. 18–25, 204–15.

50 See Riley-Smith, 'The Templars and the Teutonic Knights', pp. 92–7, where he argues that 1137 is the most likely date for the Templars' first establishment in Antioch.

51 John Kinnamos, *The Deeds of John and Manuel Commenus*, tr. C.M. Brand, Records of Civilization. Sources and Studies 95, New York, 1976, p. 24.

52 Gregory the Priest, 'Chronique de Grégoire Le Prêtre', in *RHCr, Documents Arméniens*, vol. I, pp. 171–2. For Bertrand of Blancfort's letters, see above, p. 97.

53 WT, 20.26, pp. 948–50. See A.W. Lawrence, 'The Castle of Baghras', in *The Cilician Kingdom of Armenia*, ed. T.S.R. Boase, Edinburgh and London, 1978, pp. 42–3.

54 See R.W. Edwards, *The Fortifications of Armenian Cilicia*, Washington, 1987, pp. 31–3, 102, 253, and 'Baǧras and Armenian Cilicia: A Reassessment', *Revue des Etudes Arméniennes*, 17 (1983), 415–35, where he argues that very little of the castle is of Armenian construction.

55 Wilbrand of Oldenburg. 'Wilbrandi de Oldenborg Peregrinatio', ed. J.C.M. Laurent, *Peregrinatores Medii Aevi Quatuor*, Leipzig, 1864, p. 174.

56 Edwards, *Fortifications*, p. 253 and plates 246(a)–248(b), for Darbsak, and pp. 99–102 (including a plan) and plates 47(a)–52(b), for Çalan. The identification of La Roche de Roussel and La Roche Guillaume remains a matter of dispute. P. Deschamps, *Les Châteaux des Croisés en Terre Sainte*, vol. III, *La Défense du Comté de Tripoli et de la Principauté d'Antioche*, Institut Français d'Archéologie de Beyrouth. Bibliothèque Archéologique et Historique 90, pp. 128 (map), 132, places La Roche de Roussel on the coast, south of Port Bonnel (Arsouz), which was also held by the Templars, and makes La Roche Guillaume the same place as Çalan. C. Cahen, *La Syrie du nord à l'époque des croisades*, Paris, 1940, pp. 143, 512, believes that La Roche de Roussel is Çalan, and that La Roche Guillaume was nearby, an identification rather reluctantly accepted by Edwards, *Fortifications*, p. 99.

57 *Ibid.*, p. 38.

58 According to Ralph of Caen, who came to the east in 1108, and who wrote an unfinished account of the deeds of Tancred, the route from Alexandretta to Antioch was difficult, but more direct than any other leading into Syria,

'Gesta Tancredi in Expeditione Hierosolymitana', in *RHCr. Occid.*, vol. III, p. 639.

59 'The Templars and the Castle of Tortosa', ed. Riley-Smith, pp. 278–88. This document is in fact an 1157 confirmation by Raymond III, Count of Tripoli, of a grant of 1152. It survives in the form of a copy made in 1377, now in the Archivo Nacional in Madrid. The copy would have been made for the Hospitallers who had been granted the Templar properties after the suppression of 1312, and therefore probably exists only because the copyist confused Tortosa in Syria with Tortosa in Aragon, and thus believed it to be relevant to the Hospitallers in Spain, see R. Hiestand, 'Zum Problem des Templerzentralarchivs', *Archivalische Zeitschrift*, 76 (1980), 19. This underlines the problem of accurate dating in Templar history, since without it the establishment of the Templars at Tortosa could not be placed before 1169, *RRH*, no. 462, p. 121. It is therefore a rare example of the type of document which would have been kept within the central archive of the Temple.

60 *Cart.*, vol. I, no. 199, p. 154; *RRH*, no. 270, p. 68. See J. Richard, *Le Comté de Tripoli sous la dynastie toulousaine (1102–87)*, Paris, 1945, pp. 66–7.

61 Deschamps, *Les Châteaux de Croisés*, vol. III, pp. 287–91; Wilbrand of Oldenburg, pp. 169–70.

62 Deschamps, *Les Châteaux de Croisés*, vol. III, pp. 249–58, 313–16.

63 'The Templars and the Castle of Tortosa', ed. Riley-Smith, pp. 278–88.

64 Deschamps, *Les Châteaux de Croisés*, vol. III, pp. 3, 7.

65 'Chartes de Terre Sainte', ed. J. Delaville Le Roulx, *ROL*, 11, 1905–8, no. 2, 183–5. Delaville believed that Ahamant is Maan-esch-Schamich (south-east of Montréal). P. Deschamps, *Les Châteaux des Croisés en Terre Sainte*, vol. II. *La Défense du Royaume de Jérusalem*, Paris, 1939, p. 38, identifies it with Amman.

66 *Tabulae ordinis Theutonici*, ed. E. Strehlke, Berlin, 1869 (reprint 1975), no. 4, pp. 5–6; *RRH*, no. 447, p. 116.

67 WT, 21.25(26), pp. 997–8; 21.28(29), pp. 1001–2; 21.29(30), pp. 1003–4.

68 Abū Shāmā, 'Le Livre des Deux Jardins', vol. IV, pp. 203–11, who draws on a number of Muslim accounts of the siege.

69 WT, 21.29(30), p. 1003. William's statement is supported by the lack of place-name evidence for the area around Safad in Frankish sources, since these would largely have been found in Templar documents, now lost, see Tibble, *Monarchy and Lordships*, pp. 160, 163.

70 See B.Z. Kedar and R.D. Pringle, 'La Fève: A Crusader Castle in the Jezreel Valley', *Israel Exploration Journal*, 35 (1985) 164–79. Caco is usually identified with Qaqun, to the south-east of Caesarea, but this is forty-five kilometres from La Fève. Since on the night before the battle at the Springs of Cresson (1 May 1187), the Grand Master, Gerard of Ridefort, summoned Templars from Caco and they arrived by midnight, on the grounds of distance alone this identification seems unlikely. The authors' suggestion of Kh. Qara (Cara) is much more plausible (p. 169).

71 WT, 14.18, pp. 639–40. See M. Benvenisti, *The Crusaders in the Holy Land*, Jerusalem, 1972, pp. 313–16.

72 *Ibid.*, pp. 316–17.

73 WT, 10.25(26), p. 485. See C.R. Conder and H.H. Kitchener, *The Survey of Western Palestine. Memoirs of the Topography, Orography, Hydrography and Archaeology*, vol. I, London, 1881, pp. 309–10, and Benvenisti, *Crusaders*, pp. 178–9.

74 Conder and Kitchener, *Survey of Western Palestine*, vol. II, London, 1882, pp. 7–8, and Benvenisti, *Crusaders*, p. 189.

75 -WT, 17.20, p. 78.

76 *Theodericus Libellus de Locis Sanctis*, ed. M.L. and W. Bulst, Editiones Heidelbergenses 18, Heidelberg, 1976, ch. 28, p. 35. See Conder and Kitchener, *Survey of Western Palestine*, vol. III, London, 1883, pp. 207–9.

77 *Theodericus*, chs. 29, 30, pp. 36–7.

78 *Règle*, cl. 121, pp. 100–1. On the Templar presence in this region, see R.D. Pringle, 'Templar Castles on the Road to the Jordan', in *The Military Orders. Fighting for the Faith and Caring for the Sick*, ed. M.C. Barber, London, 1994, pp. 148–66.

79 *Cart.*, vol. I, no. 558, pp. 378–9; *RRH*, no. 572, p. 152.

80 Tibble, *Monarchy and Lordships*, pp. 111–12, 119–20. See also Riley-Smith, *The Knights of St John in Jerusalem*, pp. 423–50 and appendix, pp. 477–507.

81 Fulcher of Chartres, *Historia*, 1.26, p. 291.

82 *Theodericus*, ch. 17, pp. 26–7. Tr. *Jerusalem Pilgrimage*, pp. 293–4.

83 Otto of Freising, *Gesta Friderici*, 1.58, p. 385.

84 Ibn al-Athir, 'Extrait', vol. I, p. 704.

85 WT, 12.7, p. 554; Benjamin of Tudela, *Itinerary*, tr. and ed. M.N. Adler, London, 1907, p. 22, under the year 1168.

86 *Gesta Regis Henrici Secundi Benedicti Abbatis*, ed. W. Stubbs, vol. II, RS 49, London, 1867, pp. 13–14; *RRH*, no. 660, p. 176.

87 Odo of Deuil, *De Profectione*, pp. 134–5.

88 John of Würzburg, 'Descriptio', ch. 5, pp. 129–30.

89 Smail, *Crusading Warfare*, p. 90.

90 *Anglo-Saxon Chronicle*, p. 195.

91 WT, 18.14, p. 831; 18.25, p. 849; *RHG*, vol. XV, no. 34, pp. 681–2; *RRH*, no. 326, p. 84. For Bertrand's release, see John Kinnamos, *Deeds*, p. 143, 'the man in command of the knights in Palestine, whom the Latins call the Master of the Temple'. Bertrand of Blancfort first appears as Grand Master on 2 November 1156, at Acre, *RRH*, no. 322, p. 82. His predecessor, Andrew of Montbard, died on 17 January 1156, *OR*, p. 314; *RRH*, nos. 306–8, pp. 78–9. On Bertrand, see Bulst-Thiele, *Magistri*, pp. 62–74.

92 *RRH*, no. 336, p. 87.

93 WT, 21.28(29), pp. 1001–2. Pope Alexander III believed that Odo was killed in the battle, but if this is accepted then the usual dating of these events would be put into question, since the *OR*, p. 328, gives the date of Odo's death as 9 October. It seems probable that Alexander was misinformed, perhaps because death in battle accorded better with the Templar image. See D'Albon, 'La Mort d'Odon de Saint-Amand, Grand Maître du Temple', *ROL*, 12 (1909–11), 279–82. On Odo, see Bulst-Thiele, *Magistri*, pp. 87–105.

94 Abū Shāmā, 'Le Livre des Deux Jardins', vol. IV, p. 200.

95 See above, p. 189.
96 *RRH*, no. 449, p. 117.
97 The view of H.E. Mayer, *The Crusades*, 2nd edn, Oxford, 1988, pp. 120–1. Mayer thinks, however, that this was impractical as Amalric had insufficient manpower. The attitude of the Templars therefore exacerbated the problem, although it is difficult to disentangle cause and effect in their case. On the other hand, Runciman, *History of the Crusades*, vol. II, p. 180, thinks that the king was pushed into this expedition by others on his council.
98 WT, 20.10, pp. 923–5.
99 Riley-Smith, *The Knights of St John in Jerusalem*, pp. 60–3, 71–3.
100 WT, 20.5, pp. 917–18. 'Emulus' can be translated as 'enemy', but 'rival' seems to catch William's meaning more accurately.
101 Runciman, *History of the Crusades*, vol. II, p. 380. The opposite point of view is expressed by Lundgreen, *Wilhelm von Tyrus*, pp. 104–5, who thought that William might have invented the whole story.
102 WT, 18.14, p. 831.
103 *RHG*, vol. XVI, no. 125, p. 39 (1162/3); no. 195, pp. 60–1 (1163); no. 245, pp. 80–1 (1164); *RRH*, no. 399, p. 105; no. 403, p. 106; no. 406, p. 106. None of these letters is dated, so an exact chronology is not possible.
104 *RHG*, vol. XVI, no. 197, pp. 62–3; *RRH*, no. 404, p. 106; WT, 19.9, p. 875.
105 *RHG*, vol. XVI, no. 244, pp. 79–80; *RRH*, no. 407, p. 106; WT, 19.10, p. 877.
106 See above, p. 89.
107 WT, 22.2, p. 1008.
108 See 'The Templars and the Castle of Tortosa', ed. Riley-Smith, p. 282, and above, pp. 58–9.
109 WT, 12.7, pp. 554–5. A.C. Krey thought that this section might have been added later, William of Tyre, *History of Deeds done beyond the Sea*, vol. I, p. 527, n. 25.
110 See above, pp. 73–5.
111 WT, 19.11, pp. 878–9. The site has not been identified. William says vaguely 'on the borders of Arabia'. For various possibilities, see Deschamps, *Les Châteaux des Croisés*, vol. II, p. 116.
112 See above, p. 86. The incident is usually dated *c.* 1165, but William has placed it after a paragraph on the death of King William of Sicily, which occurred on 7 May 1166, so the latter year is likely.
113 WT, 20.29–30, pp. 953–5.
114 See M.G.S. Hodgson, *The Order of the Assassins*, The Hague, 1955, and C.E. Nowell, 'The Old Man of the Mountain', *Speculum*, 22 (1947), 497–519.
115 See Deschamps, *Les Châteaux des Croisés*, vol. III, pp. 4, 8, 37. See also figure 8, which shows the Assassin lands to be closely hemmed in by the castles of the military orders on the southern and western sides.
116 Walter Map, *De nugis curialium*, pp. 66–7.
117 Lundgreen, *Wilhelm von Tyrus*, pp. 110–16, 150–3.

118 Riley-Smith, 'Peace Never Established', pp. 97–8.
119 WT, 17.19, p. 786.
120 'Assises de la Cour Bourgeois', in *RHCr. Lois*, vol. II, p. 89. *Les Assises de Romanie*, ed. G. Recoura, Bibliothèque de l'Ecole des Hautes Etudes, Paris, 1930, para. 48, p. 194, which does not refer to the Templars by name. In 1188, a Templar knight, Gilbert of Ogerstan, tried to appropriate part of the Saladin tithe, which was being collected on behalf of King Henry II. Although he deserved hanging, says the *Gesta Regis Henrici Secundi*, vol. II, pp. 47–8, he was in fact handed over to the Master in London for punishment.
121 *Eracles*, vol. I(ii), p. 999.
122 Riley-Smith, *The Crusades*, pp. 75–6.
123 'Les Lignages d'Outremer', in *RHCr. Lois*, vol. II, ch. 14, pp. 452–3; *RRH* no. 52, pp. 10–11; no. 57, pp. 12–13; no. 80, pp. 18–19; no. 90, p. 21; no. 91, p. 21; no. 105, p. 25; no. 106, p. 25; no. 112, p. 27; vol. II, no. 76(a), p. 5; no. 102(a), p. 7.
124 *Tabulae ordinis Theutonici*, no. 3, pp. 3–5; *RRH*, no. 366, pp. 96–7. See Mayer, 'Studies in the History of Queen Melisende', 118–20, 179–80. Nablus owed 85 knights, Kerak and Montréal 40 knights, 'Assises de la Haute Cour', in *RHCr. Lois*, vol. I, pp. 423–4, 433. If Hebron had been included in the exchange this would have added a further 20 knights, but it is not mentioned in the document recording the transaction. By 1180 Hebron was, however, combined with Montréal, *RRH*, no. 596, p. 159.
125 *OR*, p. 313; *RRH*, no. 466, p. 122.
126 WT, 19.22, pp. 893–4.
127 *RRH*, no. 466, p. 122; no. 467, pp. 122–3.
128 WT, 20.22, p. 942; *OR*, p. 318. For the career of Philip of Nablus, see Bulst-Thiele, *Magistri*, pp. 75–86.
129 *RRH*, no. 299, pp. 76–7; no. 321, p. 82; no. 354, pp. 92–3; no. 355, p. 93; no. 366, pp. 96–7; no. 369, p. 97; no. 400, p. 105.
130 WT, 20.1, p. 913.
131 *RRH*, no. 465, p. 122.
132 See above, pp. 98–9.
133 WT, 21.25(26), p. 996. See William of Tyre, *History of Deeds done beyond the Sea*, vol. I, p. 20, for the idea that William led an attack on the military orders.
134 'The Templars and the Castle of Tortosa', ed. Riley-Smith, pp. 278–88.
135 *RRH*, no. 381, p. 100; no. 462, p. 121.
136 WT, 20.30, p. 955; 21.28(29), p. 1002.
137 WT, p. 1,002 n. ; Abū Shāmā, 'Le Livre des Deux Jardins', pp. 202–3.
138 *Cartulario del Temple de Huesca*, no. 30, p. 34; no. 31, p. 35; no. 42, p. 44; no. 51, p. 52; no. 57, p. 58; no. 58, p. 59; no. 61, p. 62; no. 65, pp. 66–7; no. 75, p. 76; no. 77, p. 78; no. 80, p. 81; no. 81, p. 82; no. 82, p. 83, showing him holding this position between 1167 and June 1180. See also J. Miret y Sans, *Les Cases de Templers y Hospitalers en Catalunya*, Barcelona, 1910, pp. 101–4, and Bulst-Thiele, *Magistri*, pp. 99–105.

139 Melville, *La Vie des Templiers*, p. 107, suggests that the election was a defeat for what she sees as the admirers of Odo of St Amand within the Order. Arnold of Torroja's activities as an arbitrator can be seen in 1181 in Antioch, WT, 22.7, pp. 1015–16, and in 1184 in Acre, *Eracles*, vol. II, pp. 2–3.

140 Ralph of Diceto, *Opera Historica*, ed. W. Stubbs, vol. II, RS 68, London, 1876, p. 32; *OR*, p. 327.

141 *Ernoul-Bernard*, p. 114, says Flemish. See also J.H. Round, 'Some English Crusaders of Richard I', *EHR*, 17 (1903), 480, who shows that there are traces of a family called 'Rideford' or 'Ridelisford' in both England and Ireland in the twelfth and thirteenth centuries. See Bulst-Thiele, *Magistri*, pp. 106–22.

142 *RRH*, no. 587, p. 156; no. 588, pp. 156–7 (1179). He may be the *Gerardus, marescalcus et camerarius*, who is signatory to a royal document at Acre in 1174, *RRH*, no. 514, p. 136.

143 *Cont. WT*, p. 46; *Ernoul-Bernard*, pp. 114, 178; *Eracles*, vol. II, 50–2.

144 *RRH*, no. 631, p. 167; vol. II, no. 637(a), p. 41.

145 *Cont. WT*, pp. 19–21; *Ernoul-Bernard*, pp. 115–19, 129; *Eracles*, vol. II, pp. 6–7.

146 *Cont. WT*, pp. 33, 46; *Eracles*, vol. II, p. 29.

147 See M.W. Baldwin, *Raymond III of Tripolis and the Fall of Jerusalem (1140–87)*, Princeton, 1936, pp. 31–46.

148 See Morgan, *Chronicle of Ernoul*, pp. 98–116. In the 1180s Ernoul was probably Balian's squire.

149 *Cont. WT*, pp. 36–7; *Ernoul-Bernard*, pp. 141–2; *Eracles*, vol. II, pp. 34–6.

150 *Cont. WT*, pp. 38–42; *Ernoul-Bernard*, pp. 143–54; *Eracles*, vol. II, pp. 36–45; 'Libellus de expugnatione Terrae Sanctae per Saladinum', ed. J. Stevenson, in Ralph of Coggeshall, *Chronicon Anglicanum, RS* 66, London, 1875, pp. 211–16; Abū Shāmā, 'Le Livre des Deux Jardins', vol. IV, pp. 261–2, who calls it 'an easy victory . . . the *préface* of future success'. Even James of Vitry, calls the action *incaute*, 'Historia Hierosolimitana', p. 1117, while Oliver of Paderborn, 'Historia regum Terre Sancte', ed. O. Hoogweg, *Die Schriften des Kölner Domscholasters*, Bibliothek des Litterarischen Vereins in Stuttgart 202, Tübingen, 1894, another writer favourable to the Templars, describes Gerard as *strenuus, sed impetuosus et temerarius*, p. 142. See also Kedar and Pringle, 'La Fève', pp. 168–9.

151 *Cont. WT*, p. 43; *Ernoul-Bernard*, pp. 156–7; *Eracles*, vol. II, p. 46.

152 *Cont. WT*, pp. 46–7; *Ernoul-Bernard*, pp. 161–2. See Morgan, *Chronicle of Ernoul*, pp. 46–50, on Bernard the Treasurer.

153 See Morgan, *Chronicle of Ernoul*, p. 136.

154 See *Das Itinerarium peregrinorum. Eine zeitgenössische Chronik zum dritten Kreuzzug in ursprünglicher Gestalt*, ed. H.E. Mayer, in *MGH Schriften*, vol. XVIII, Stuttgart, 1962, pp. 80–2.

155 *Itinerarium Peregrinorum et Gesta Regis Ricardi*, ed. W. Stubbs, vol. I, RS 38, London, 1864, p. 70; *Das Itinerarium*, pp. 313–14. Ambroise, *L'Estoire de la Guerre Sainte par Ambroise*, ed. G. Paris, Collection de documents inédits sur l'histoire de France, Paris, 1871, probably drawing on the *Itinerarium* for

this section, also presents his death as heroic when, in the heat of battle, he refused to flee, despite an opportunity to do so, p. 81. In Oliver of Paderborn's view (p. 143), he had washed away all his sins with the blood of martyrdom. See also Bulst-Thiele, *Magistri*, pp. 119–20, n. 53.

156 Roger of Howden, *Chronica*, ed. W. Stubbs, vol. II, RS 51, London, 1870, pp. 346–7; *RRH*, no. 669, pp. 178–9.

4 HATTIN TO LA FORBIE

1 Roger of Howden, *Chronica*, vol. II, pp. 324–5, 346–7; *RRH*, no. 660, p. 176; no. 669, pp. 178–9. Acre fell on 10 July and Beirut on 6 August, which are the dating limits for the first letter.

2 Beha ed-Din, *Life of Saladin*, tr. C.R. Conder, Palestine Pilgrims' Text Society 13, London, 1897, p. 117; Abū Shāmā, 'Le Livre des Deux Jardins', vol. IV, p. 313; *Ernoul-Bernard*, p. 253. *Cont. WT*, p. 55, says that Saladin was overjoyed to have in his power such rich prisoners as the King of Jerusalem and the Grand Master of the Templars. Gaza was briefly restored to the Templars by Richard I early in 1192, but under Richard's treaty with Saladin in September, its defences were demolished, *Cont. WT*, pp. 151–2. In 1250 it was generally believed among the crusaders that the Templars and Hospitallers swore an oath upon holy relics never to surrender a castle to secure anybody's release, John of Joinville, *Histoire de Saint Louis*, ed. and tr. N. de Wailly, 2nd edn, Paris, 1874, pp. 182–3. Perhaps this incident led to the introduction of this oath.

3 J. Riley-Smith, *The Feudal Nobility and the Kingdom of Jerusalem, 1174–1277*, London, 1973, p. 113.

4 *Eracles*, vol. II, p. 130; *Cont. WT*, p. 92; *Itinerarium*, p. 70; Ambroise, *L'Estoire*, p. 81, all say that he was killed in battle. Ibn al-Athir, 'Extrait', in *RMC Or.*, vol. II(i), Paris, 1887, p. 12, says that he was captured and executed. See Beha ed-Din, *Life of Saladin*, p. 215, for the date of the battle. *OR*, p. 327, gives the Kalends of October (first).

5 *Itinerarium*, p. 260. See also J. Riley-Smith, ed., *The Atlas of the Crusades*, London, 1991, p. 64.

6 See above, pp. 241–3.

7 *Itinerarium*, pp. 305–6.

8 *Itinerarium*, p. 308.

9 *Documenti sulle relazioni delle città toscane coll'Oriente cristiano e coi Turchi fino all'anno 1531*, ed. G. Müller, Florence, 1879, no. 35, pp. 58–9; *Cont. WT*, p. 92.

10 *Cartulaire de l'abbaye de Saint-Aubin d'Angers*, vol. II, no. 888, pp. 353–4, showing him as Lord of Sablé not later than 1170; *Gesta Regis Henrici Secundi*, vol. I, p. 47, for his involvement in the revolt of 1173; G. Dubois, 'Recherches sur la vie de Guillaume des Roches, sénéchal d'Anjou, du Maine et de Touraine', *BEC*, 30 (1869), 381–4, and J. Boussard, *Le Comté d'Anjou sous Henri Plantagenêt et ses fils. 1151–1204*, Paris, 1938, *Pièces justificatives*, no. 7, pp. 179–81, for arrangements with local monasteries

before his departure on crusade. On Robert, see Bulst-Thiele, *Magistri*, pp. 123-34.

11 L. Landon, *The Itinerary of King Richard I*, Pipe Roll Society n. s. 13, London, 1935, nos. 222, 223, pp. 25-6; no. 272, p. 31, for his movements in Anjou and Normandy; *Gesta Regis Henrici Secundi*, vol. II, pp. 110, 115, 119-20, 124, and Roger of Howden, *Chronica*, vol. III p. 36, for his position as justiciar of the fleet; *Itinerarium*, p. 166, and Ambroise, *L'Estoire*, p. 24, for his role as emissary to Tancred; Roger of Howden, *Chronica*, vol. III, pp. 58-9, for his place on the committee for disposing of dead crusaders' property.

12 *Eracles*, vol. II, pp. 190-1; *Cont. WT*, pp. 135-7; *Ernoul-Bernard*, pp. 284-6; *Itinerarium*, p. 35; Ambroise, *L'Estoire*, pp. 243-4. See G. Hill, *A History of Cyprus*, vol. II, Cambridge, 1948, pp. 36-8, and P.W. Edbury, 'The Templars in Cyprus', in *The Military Orders. Fighting for the Faith and Caring for the Sick*, ed. M.C. Barber, London, 1994, pp. 189-95.

13 *Ernoul-Bernard*, p. 296; *Cont. WT*, p. 155. See also Ralph of Coggeshall, *Chronicon Anglicanum*, ed. J. Stevenson, RS 66, London, 1875, p. 54.

14 'Imâd ad-Din, *Conquête*, p. 144.

15 See B. Hamilton, *The Latin Church in the Crusader States. The Secular Church*, London, 1980, pp. 201-7.

16 *RRH*, no. 851, p. 227; Innocent III, *Innocenti P.P. Registrorum*, in *PL*, vol. CCXVI, Paris, 1891, 14, no. 64, cols. 430-1.

17 On the context of this dispute, see Cahen, *La Syrie du nord*, pp. 582-621.

18 *OR*, p. 327.

19 *RRH*, no. 631, p. 167; *Cartulario del Temple de Huesca*, no. 108, p. 110; no. 109, p. 111; no. 110, p. 113; no. 114, p. 116, showing him as Master in Provence and parts of Spain between 1186 and 1189; Miret y Sans, *Les Cases*, pp. 148-9, 107-8, 156, 242-3, 334. See Bulst-Thiele, *Magistri*, pp. 134-46.

20 *RRH*, no. 740, p. 197. See Forey, *The Military Orders*, pp. 19-23, on the formation of the Teutonic Knights. Gilbert was also present when the Temple received certain *casalia* from the Abbey of St Mary of the Valley of Josaphat, June 1198, *RRH*, vol. II, no. 740(a), pp. 48-9.

21 On the family, see C.V. Langlois, *Notice sur le château de Plessis-Macé*, Angers, 1932. For the financing of Philip's crusade, see H. de Fourmont, *L'Ouest aux Croisades*, vol. III, Paris, 1867, p. 143. On Philip's career, see Bulst-Thiele, *Magistri*, pp. 147-58.

22 *RRH*, vol. II, no. 787(a), p. 51.

23 BN, *NAL* 59, fol. 70.

24 *Eracles*, vol. II, pp. 309-10.

25 Innocent III, *Innocenti P.P. Registrorum*, in *PL*, vol. CCXIV, Paris, 1890, 2, no. 189, cols. 737-8, which is a general letter to the Patriarch of Jerusalem, the Bishop of Lydda, and the Masters of the Temple and the Hospital. Grousset, *Histoire des Croisades*, pp. 189-90, surely goes beyond the facts when he describes this as 'fidèle aux traditions néfastes de son ordre – sur qui planait décidément toujours l'esprit de Hattin!' This is an example of

how, even among otherwise objective historians, the Templars seem to incite strong and often emotional reactions. In fact, the stance taken by the Grand Master might be more realistically seen as in keeping with the legalistic approach which characterised the baronage of Outremer in general.

26 *RRH*, no. 726, p. 194.

27 Innocent III. *Innocenti P.P. Registrorum*, vol. CCXIV, no. 257, cols. 816–18; *RRH*, no. 764, p. 203.

28 See above p. 108.

29 *Cart.*, vol. I, no. 1069, pp. 666–7; *RRH*, no. 751, p. 200. See Riley-Smith, *The Knights of St John in Jerusalem*, p. 444.

30 *RRH*, vol. II, no. 787(a), p. 51.

31 See above p. 101.

32 'Bulles pour l'ordre du Temple tirées des archives de Saint-Gervais de Cassolas', ed. Delaville Le Roulx, *ROL*, 11 (1905–8), no. 16, p. 419; no. 17, p. 419; BN, *NAL* 2, fols. 42, 68, 71.

33 'Bulles', ed. Delaville Le Roulx, no. 19, p. 420; no. 20, p. 420; no. 21, p. 421; no. 22, p. 421.

34 Innocent III, *Innocenti P.P. Registrorum*, in *PL*, vol. CCXV, Paris, 1891, no. 121, cols. 1217–18.

35 Honorius III, *Regesta Honorii Papae III*, ed. P. Pressutti, vol. I, Rome, 1888, no. 2114, p. 350; no. 2513, p. 415; no. 2600, p. 431. See L. Delisle, *Mémoire sur les Opérations Financières des Templiers*, Mémoires de l'Institut national de France, Académie des Inscriptions et Belles-Lettres 33 (ii), Paris, 1889, p. 28.

36 *Regesta Honorii Papae III*, vol. I, no. 673, pp. 117–18.

37 *OR*, p. 330. See Bulst-Thiele, *Magistri*, pp. 159–69, for William of Chartres.

38 *Eracles*, vol. II, pp. 322–3; *RRH*, no. 901, pp. 241–2, for the general assembly in the tent of King Andrew of Hungary which discussed the war objectives.

39 *RHG*, vol. XIX, p. 640; *RRH*, no. 902, p. 242.

40 Oliver of Paderborn. *Oliveri Paderbornensis Historia Damiatina*, ed. O. Hoogeweg, *Die Schriften*, pp. 168, 175–7; *Eracles*, vol. II, p. 326.

41 Oliver of Paderborn, *Historia Damiatina*, p. 188; James of Vitry, 'Historia Hierosolimitana', p. 1130; *OR*, p. 325. Peter of Montaigu is named as Master in September 1220, *RRH*, no. 936, p. 249.

42 Alberic of Trois Fontaines, 'Chronica a monacho novi monasterii Hoiensis interpolata', ed. P. Scheffer-Boichorst, in *MGH SS*, vol. XXIII, Leipzig, 1925, p. 909; *Gestes des Chiprois*, ed. G. Raynaud, Geneva, 1887, p. 58. See Riley-Smith, *The Knights of St John in Jerusalem*, pp. 155–6, and Bulst-Thiele, *Magistri*, pp. 170–88.

43 BN, *NAL*, 59, fols. 163–4, 188–90. See Miret y Sans, 'Itinerario del Rey Pedro I de Cataluña, II en Aragón', *Boletín de la Real Academia de Buenas Letras de Barcelona*, 3 (1905–6), p. 385; 4 (1907–8), p. 33.

44 'Gesta Crucigerorum Rhenanorum', ed. R. Röhricht, *Quinti Belli Sacri*

Scriptores Minores, Société de l'Orient latin: série historique 2, Geneva, 1879, pp. 30–1; 'Chronica regia Coloniensis', ed. R. Röhricht, *Testimonia Minora de Quinto Bello Sacro*, Geneva, 1882, pp. 150–1.

45 Oliver of Paderborn, *Historia Damiatina*, pp. 222–4; *Eracles*, vol. II, pp. 341–2; *Ernoul-Bernard*, p. 435.

46 Oliver of Paderborn, *Historia Damiatina*, pp. 181, 190–1, 194, 199–200, 205, 209–11, 252. On the way back from Burlus, however, some of the horses and mules died from lack of water.

47 *Ibid.*, pp. 254–6. On the construction of 'Atlīt, see above, pp. 161–3.

48 Roger of Wendover, *Liber qui dicitur Flores Historiarum*, ed. H.G. Hewlett, vol. II, RS 84, London, 1887; *RRH*, no. 936, p. 249.

49 Roger of Wendover, *Flores Historiarum*, vol. II, pp. 263–5; *RRH*, no. 946, p. 251.

50 *Layettes du Trésor des Chartes*, ed. M.A. Teulet, vol. I, Paris, 1863, no. 1547, p. 550.

51 *Eracles*, vol. II, pp. 355–6; *Gestes des Chiprois*, p. 20. On the context, see D. Abulafia, *Frederick II. A Medieval Emperor*, London, 1988, pp. 148–54.

52 Roger of Wendover, *Flores Historiarum* vol. II, pp. 324–7; *RRH*, no. 984, p. 260.

53 *Gestes des Chiprois*, p. 39.

54 Roger of Wendover, *Flores Historiarum*, vol. II, p. 351.

55 The point at which this occurred after Frederick's arrival is not evident, nor is it clear whether the objections were religious or political or both. Roger of Wendover, *Flores Historiarum*, vol. II, p. 351, says that the eastern leaders would not give the kiss of peace nor dine with him because of his excommunication, but they did greet him enthusiastically in the hope that through him there would be 'salvation in Israel'. A letter of the Patriarch Gerold, written the following year after relations had completely broken down, seems to imply that the real objections were to Frederick's negotiations with the Egyptian sultan, al-Kāmil, about which he consulted no one, Matthew Paris, *Chronica Majora*, ed. H.R. Luard, vol. III, RS 57, London, 1880, p. 180.

56 *Ernoul-Bernard*, p. 437.

57 See above, p. 249, and below pp. 380–1.

58 See above, p. 69.

59 *Ernoul-Bernard*, pp. 462–3.

60 *Eracles*, vol. II, pp. 372–3.

61 *Eracles*, vol. II, p. 373.

62 *Historia Diplomatica*, ed. J.-L.-A. Huillard-Bréholles, vol. III, Paris, 1852, p. 89. See P. Jackson, 'The Crusades of 1239–41 and their Aftermath', *Bulletin of the School of Oriental and African Studies*, 50 (1987), 36, who argues that the attitudes of the parties involved can be explained by seeing Frederick's primary concern as the commercial advantage of his Kingdom of Sicily rather than the strategic interests of the Kingdom of Jerusalem,

since al-Kāmil had little real power in the regions which were covered by the treaty.

63 Matthew Paris, *Chronica Majora*, vol. III, p. 182.
64 Tr. from Philip of Novara, *The Wars of Frederick II against the Ibelins in Syria and Cyprus*, tr. M.J. Hubert and J.L. La Monte, Records of Civilization. Sources and Studies 25, New York, 1936, p. 89.
65 Matthew Paris, *Chronica Majora*, vol. III, pp. 177–9.
66 Tr. *Arab Historians of the Crusades*, p. 275.
67 Bartholomew of Neocastro, *Historia Sicula*, ed. G. Paladino, in RIS, vol. XIII(iii), pp. 116–17; *RRH*, no. 998, p. 262.
68 See R. Röhricht, *Beiträge zur Geschichte der Kreuzzüge*, vol. I, Berlin, 1874, pp. 74–5, n. 202.
69 Letters of Frederick to Henry III (17 March 1229) and Richard of Cornwall (1239), describing events in the Holy Land, make no mention of a plot against his life by the military orders. Roger of Wendover, *Flores Historiarum*, vol. II, pp. 365–9, and Matthew Paris, *Chronica Majora*, vol. III, pp. 575–89.
70 *Ibid.*, p. 535. The pope wrote several times to Frederick telling him to restore the property of the orders, Potthast, nos. 8653, 8663, 8731.
71 *Ernoul-Bernard*, pp. 466–7.
72 Matthew Paris, *Chronica Majora*, vol. III, pp. 555–6.
73 The Assizes of Capua, 1220, see Abulafia, *Frederick II*, pp. 139–42.
74 *Historia Diplomatica*, vol. III, p. 267.
75 *Gestes des Chiprois*, p. 77; *Eracles*, vol. II. pp. 388–9.
76 His successor, Armand of Périgord, is titled Preceptor in Sicily and Calabria in September 1230, but cannot be identified as Grand Master until spring 1232, *Eracles*, vol. II, pp. 393–4. On him, see Bulst-Thiele, *Magistri*, pp. 188–210, who thinks that the name should more correctly be rendered Pierregort.
77 *Historia Diplomatica*, vol. III, pp. 239–41. *Datum in castris apud Avellinum, mense septembris, IV indictionis, imperii Friderici anno IX, [regni] Jerusalem IV, Sicilie XXIII*. Indiction four in Imperial dating ran from 24 September 1230, while the thirty-third year of Frederick's reign in Sicily places the document in 1230 or 1231 if the starting date is taken as 17 May 1198. However, year nine of Frederick's reign as emperor and year four as King of Jerusalem would both have ended in November 1229 (although Frederick's first proxy wedding to Isabel actually took place in August 1225). Huillard-Bréholles, in *Historia Diplomatica*, vol. III, p. 241, n. 2, shows that the circumstantial evidence strongly suggests 1230, as on 5 September 1230 Frederick was about to travel from Capua to Melfi, and Avellino would have been an obvious stopping-point. Moreover, it is inconceivable that Frederick would have been simultaneously confirming and confiscating the property of the Templars, as would have been the case if it dated from 1229.
78 *Gestes des Chiprois*, pp. 117–18.

79 *Gestes des Chiprois*, pp. 83–4; *Eracles*, vol. II, p. 394.

80 *Gestes des Chiprois*, pp. 112–13.

81 *Epistolae Saeculi XIII e Regestis Pontificum Romanorum*, ed. C. Rodenberg, in *MGH Epistolae*, vol. I, Berlin, 1883, no. 433, pp. 348–9; *RRH*, no. 1022, p. 267.

82 *Eracles*, vol. II, pp. 403–5.

83 Alberic of Trois Fontaines, 'Chronica', p. 942.

84 *RRH*, no. 1083, pp. 282–3. See S. Painter, 'The Crusade of Theobald of Champagne and Richard of Cornwall, 1239–1241', in *A History of the Crusades*, vol. II, ed. R.L. Wolff and H.W. Hazard, Madison, 1969, p. 471, n. 11, on the dating of this letter, which he believes should be 6 October 1237.

85 Alberic of Trois Fontaines, 'Chronica', p. 945; *RRH*, no. 1088, p. 284. For the Aiyūbids, see the table in Jackson, 'Crusades of 1239–41', 34.

86 *Ibid.*, 37–9.

87 Rothelin. 'Continuation de Guillaume de Tyr de 1229 à 1261, dite du manuscrit de Rothelin', in *RHCr. Occid.*, vol. II, pp. 537–48; *Eracles*, vol. II, pp. 414–15.

88 Matthew Paris, *Chronica Majora*, vol. IV, pp. 25–6.

89 J. Prawer, 'Military Orders and Crusader Politics in the second half of the XIIIth century', *Die geistlichen Ritterorden Europas*, ed. J. Fleckenstein and J. Hellmann, Sigmaringen, 1980, p. 220, believes that the unpopularity of the orders in the west began to grow from *c.* 1239–40.

90 Tibble, *Monarchy and Lordships*, pp. 135, 151.

91 *RRH*, no. 949, pp. 251–2; no. 1043, p. 272.

92 *RRH*, no. 1062, p. 277. See also Riley-Smith, *The Knights of St John in Jerusalem*, p. 446.

93 *Gestes des Chiprois*, pp. 121–2; *Eracles*, vol. II, pp. 419–20; 'Rothelin', pp. 551–3.

94 Matthew Paris, *Chronica Majora*, vol. IV, pp. 64–5; *RRH*, no. 1095, p. 285.

95 For the evidence for these manoeuvres, see Jackson, 'Crusades of 1239–41', pp. 44–6.

96 *Eracles*, vol. II, pp. 419–20; *Gestes des Chiprois*, p. 122.

97 See Riley-Smith, *The Knights of St John in Jerusalem*, pp. 172–5.

98 Matthew Paris, *Chronica Majora*, vol. IV, pp. 138–44; *Eracles*, vol. II, pp. 421–2; *Gestes des Chiprois*, pp. 122–4.

99 Matthew Paris, *Chronica Majora*, vol. IV, pp. 167–8. He repeated these charges in 1243, p. 256.

100 See P. Jackson, 'The End of Hohenstaufen Rule in Syria', *Bulletin of the Institute of Historical Research*, 59 (1986), 33.

101 *Gestes des Chiprois*, pp. 122–4.

102 'Documents relatifs à la successibilité au trône et à la régence', in *RHCr. Lois*, vol. II, pp. 399–400; *Gestes des Chiprois*, pp. 128–30.

103 Roger of Wendover, *Flores Historiarum*, vol. II, p. 345. Gregory claimed that the Templars had not resisted since, 'in accordance with the institution of their Order', they had not dared to use violence against Christians.

104 *Gestes des Chiprois*, pp. 130–6; *Eracles*, vol. II, p. 422.
105 See Jackson, 'Crusades of 1239–41', 51–2. For the fresco, see above, p. 206.
106 Matthew Paris, *Chronica Majora*, vol. IV, pp. 288–91; *RRH*, no. 1119, p. 298. The Templars had originally held a small fortress at Toron, see above, p. 88, but the Master was evidently planning a much bigger project there at this time, apparently to ensure that Jerusalem would not be lost again. However, the defeat at La Forbie in October 1244, meant that the castle was never built.
107 Matthew Paris, *Chronica Majora*, vol. IV, p. 291.
108 *Acta imperii inedita*, ed. E. Winkelmann, vol. I, Innsbruck, 1880, no. 434, pp. 369–70; *RRH*, no. 1115, p. 297.
109 See the letters in Matthew Paris, *Chronica Majora*, vol. IV, pp. 307, 339. On the options open to the Franks, see Jackson, 'Crusades of 1239–41', pp. 56–60. His conclusion is that the Templars showed flexibility in their dealings with the Muslim powers, but that 'there was no deal to be had'.
110 *Chronica de Mailros*, ed. J. Stevenson, Edinburgh, 1835, pp. 156–62; *RRH*, no. 1123, p. 299.
111 Matthew Paris, *Chronica Majora*, vol. IV, p. 141.
112 *Cart.*, vol. II, no. 2340, p. 622; *RRH*, no. 1127, pp. 299–300. This is a collective letter, but the information on Templar losses was presumably supplied by William of Rochefort. There are some doubts about the figures since a letter from the Hospitallers, Matthew Paris, *Chronica Majora*, vol. IV, p. 311, says eighteen Templars and sixteen Hospitallers escaped. See the analysis by Riley-Smith, *Ayyubids, Mamlukes and Crusaders. Selections from the Tārīkh al-Duwal wa'l-Mulūk of Ibn al-Furāt*, vol. II, ed. and tr. U. and M.C. Lyons, Cambridge, 1971, p. 173, n. 2, and pp. 174–5, n. 9. For the battle, *Eracles*, vol. II, pp. 427–31; 'Rothelin', pp. 562–6; *Gestes des Chiprois*, pp. 145–6.
113 Matthew Paris, *Chronica Majora*, vol. IV, pp. 302–3.
114 According to a letter purporting to be from William of Châteauneuf, Grand Master of the Hospital, he was killed in the battle, Matthew Paris, *Chronica Majora*, vol. IV, p. 311, but most of the evidence suggests that he was captured: a later letter of eastern leaders says that he was either captured or dead, Matthew Paris, *ibid.*, p. 342; *Eracles*, vol. II, p. 430, says he died in captivity; Matthew Paris, *Chronica Majora*, vol. IV, pp. 524–5, describes attempts to ransom him and other captives in 1246.
115 William is shown as Preceptor in Aquitaine between 1235 and 1246, BN, NAL 37, fol. 415, and NAL 38, fol. 263. He is not mentioned specifically as Grand Master until 12 May 1249, *RRH*, no. 1176, pp. 308–9. On him, see Bulst-Thiele, *Magistri*, pp. 217–24.

5 THE LAST YEARS OF THE TEMPLARS IN PALESTINE AND SYRIA

1 *Gestes des Chiprois*, p. 147.
2 Guillaume de Nangis, 'Vie de Saint Louis', in *RHG*, vol. XX, pp. 366–9.
3 Matthew Paris, *Chronica Majora*, vol. VI, p. 162; *RRH*, no. 1180, p. 309.

4 Joinville, *Histoire*, pp. 100–19.; Matthew Paris, *Chronica Majora*, vol. v, p. 147.

5 *Procès*, vol. I, pp. 43–4.

6 Other sources with less detailed accounts include 'Annales Monasterii de Burton 1004–1236', ed. H.R. Luard, *Annales Monastici*, vol. I, RS 36, London, 1864, p. 286; 'Rothelin', pp. 602–9; *Eracles*, vol. II, pp. 437–8; Guillaume de Nangis, 'Vie de Saint Louis', vol. I, p. 205; 'Epistola Sancti Ludovici Regis de Captione et Liberatione sua', ed. A. Duchesne, *Historiae Francorum Scriptores*, vol. v, Paris, 1649, pp. 428–9. This sample gives some idea of the wide interest in the incident.

7 Joinville, *Histoire*, pp. 118–21.

8 Matthew Paris, *Chronica Majora*, vol. v, pp. 147–54. According to Matthew, this was derived from information brought by a messenger to Richard of Cornwall. See Riley-Smith, in *Ayyubids*, vol. II, p. 183, n. 6, on the Christian losses.

9 Joinville, *Histoire*, pp. 134–7.

10 *Ibid.*, pp. 146–9.

11 See Riley-Smith, in *Ayyubids*, vol. II, pp. 185–6, n. 1.

12 Joinville, *Histoire*, pp. 167–87.

13 Maqrisi, *Histoire d'Egypt de Makrizi*, tr. E. Blochet, *ROL*, 11, (1905–8), 231–2; Joinville, *Histoire*, pp. 190–207.

14 *Ibid.*, pp. 206–11.

15 *Ibid.*, pp. 224–5.

16 BN, *NAL* 70, fol. 252; 52, fols. 229–30; *Layettes*, vol. II, no. 3537, p. 632. On him, see Bulst-Thiele, *Magistri*, pp. 225–31.

17 *RRH*, no. 1096, p. 285; no. 1176, pp. 308–9.

18 Joinville, *Histoire*, pp. 246–51.

19 Matthew Paris, *Chronica Majora*, vol. v, p. 257; Joinville, *Histoire*, pp. 282–3.

20 *Ibid.*, pp. 102–3.

21 *Ibid.*, pp. 280–3.

22 Abū Shāmā, 'Le Livre des Deux Jardins', in *RHCr. Or*, vol. v. Paris, 1096, p. 200; Joinville, *Histoire*, pp. 282–3.

23 BN, *NAL*, 3, fol. 258.

24 *RRH*, no. 1251, p. 328.

25 *OR*, p. 314; *Eracles*, vol. II, p. 443. On Thomas Bérard, see Bulst-Thiele, *Magistri*, pp. 232–58.

26 *Règle*, cls. 576–7, pp. 299–300. It is not dated, so placing the events here is speculative. Curzon suggests 1257.

27 *Cart.*, vol. II, no. 2902, pp. 849–63; *RRH*, no. 1269, pp. 322–3. See Riley-Smith, *The Knights of St John in Jerusalem*, pp. 447–9.

28 Matthew Paris, *Chronica Majora*, vol. v, pp. 745–6, under the year 1259, refers to the wars in the Holy Land, but gives special prominence to the conflicts between the Hospitallers and the Templars rather than to those of the maritime cities. For this war and its consequences, see J. Richard, *The Latin Kingdom of Jerusalem*, tr. J. Shirley, Amsterdam, 1979, pp. 364–71.

29 *Gestes des Chiprois*, pp. 162–4; Hayton, 'La Flor des Estoires de la Terre d'Orient', in *RHCr.*, *Documents Arméniens*, vol. II, pp. 173–4.

30 'Annales Monsteril de Burton', pp. 491–5; *RRH*, no. 1299, p. 340.

31 *Monumenta Boica*, ed. Academia scientiarum Boica, vol. XXIX(ii), Munich, 1831, pp. 197–202; *RRH*, no. 1303, p. 341.

32 *Flores Historiarum*, ed. H.R. Luard, vol. II, RS 95, London, 1890, pp. 451–2; *RRH*, no. 1290, pp. 337–8.

33 'Menkonis Chronicon', ed. L. Weiland, in *MGH SS*, vol. XXIII, Leipzig, 1925, pp. 547–9; *RRH*, no. 1288, p. 337; 'Lettre des Chrétiens de Terre-Sainte à Charles d'Anjou', ed. Delaborde, *ROL*, 2 (1894), 206–15; *RRH*, vol. II, no. 1291(a), p. 83.

34 'Rothelin', p. 637.

35 On the events of this period, see Jackson, 'The Crisis in the Holy Land in 1260', *EHR*, 95 (1980), 481–513.

36 Abū Shāmā, 'Le Livre des Deux Jardins', vol. V, p. 204; Ibn al-Furāt, *Ayyubids*, vol. II, pp. 49, 195–6; *Eracles*, p. 445; *Gestes des Chiprois*, pp. 163–4.

37 *Gestes des Chiprois*, p. 167; Maqrisi, *Histoire des Sultans Mamelouks de l'Egypte*, ed. and tr. M.E. Quatremère, vol. I(i), Paris, 1837, pp. 194–7.

38 *Diplomatic Documents (Chancery and Exchequer)*, ed. P. Chaplais, vol. I (1101–1271), London, 1964, nos. 385, 386, pp. 264–6; *RRH*, no. 1325, pp. 346–7.

39 *RRH*, vol. II, no. 1332(a), p. 88; *Cart.*, vol. III, no. 3128, p. 99; no. 3172, p. 115; no. 3206, pp. 131–2.

40 On papal policy during this period, see N. Housley, *The Italian Crusades: The Papal–Angevin Alliance and the Crusades against Christian Lay Powers, 1254–1343*, Oxford, 1982.

41 'Emprunts de Saint-Louis en Palestine et en Afrique', ed. G. Servois, *BEC*, 19 (1858), 116–17, no. 1, pp. 123–5; *RRH*, no. 1339, p. 351.

42 'Emprunts', ed. Servois (1858), *Appendice*, no. 5, pp. 290–3; *RRH*, no. 1347, pp. 352–3. See above, pp. 266–7.

43 *RRH*, no. 1348, p. 353.

44 *Gestes des Chiprois*, p. 191; *Eracles*, vol. II, p. 457. The abandonment of Baghras caused some controversy within the Order, since the decision had already been taken and implemented by the local commander before receiving the message from the Master. This conduct is described in the *Catalan Rule*, Archivo de la Corona de Aragón, Barcelona, *Cartas reales*, 3344, fols. 53a–57b. Partial text in, 'Un nouveau manuscrit de la Règle du Temple', ed. J. Delaville Le Roulx, *Annuaire-Bulletin de la Société de l'Histoire de France*, 26(ii) (1889), cl. 48, pp. 208–11.

45 *Gestes des Chiprois*, p. 199; *Eracles*, vol. II, p. 460; Ibn al-Furāt, *Ayyubids*, vol. II, p. 143, on the fall of Chastel-Blanc. The author believed that its capture was the key to the control of Tripoli itself.

46 See above, p. 89.

47 See above, p. 88.

48 See C.N. Johns, *Guide to ʿAtlīt*, Jerusalem, 1947, p. 18.

49 Oliver of Paderborn, *Historia Damiatina*, pp. 254-6. See also above, p. 129.
50 Oliver of Paderborn, *Historia Damiatina*, pp. 169-72.
51 See C.N. Johns, 'Excavations at 'Atlīt (1930-1)', *The Quarterly of the Department of Antiquities in Palestine*, 2 (1932-3), p. 41, for earlier occupation.
52 Johns, *Guide to 'Atlīt*, pp. 38-41.
53 Burchard of Mount Sion, 'Descriptio Terrae Sanctae', ed. J.C.M. Laurent, *Peregrinatores Medii Aevii Quatuor*, Leipzig, 1864, ch. 10, pp. 82-3.
54 *RRH*, no. 1233, p. 324. See Tibble, *Monarchy and Lordships*, pp. 111, 144-6. The village had been sold to the Hospitallers in 1232 for 16,000 *besants, Eracles*, vol. II, p. 398, but appears to have been one of the components in a rationalisation of properties of the two orders before 1255.
55 *Eracles*, vol. II, p. 398. See also Johns, *Guide to 'Atlīt*, p. 26.
56 *RRH*, no. 1450, pp. 378-9. See also Tibble, *Monarchy and Lordships*, pp. 147-8, and Johns, *Guide to 'Atlīt*, p. 29. The definition of 'canton' is not known, but a reasonable guess might equate it to a substantial village and its adjacent land.
57 'De constructione castri Saphet', ed. R.B.C. Huygens, in *Studi Medievali*, ser. 3, 6 (1965), 378-87. On the history and importance of this castle, see M.-L. Favreau-Lilie, 'Landesausbau und Burg während der Kreuzfahrerzeit: Safad in Obergalilaea', *Zeitschrift des Deutschen Palästina-Vereins*, 96 (1980), 67-87.
58 R.D. Pringle, 'Reconstructing the Castle of Safad', *Palestine Exploration Quarterly*, 117 (1985), 142.
59 Ibn al-Furāt, *Ayyubids*, vol. II, p. 89.
60 *Gestes des Chiprois*, pp. 180-1; *Eracles*, vol. II, pp. 454-5. Ibn al-Furāt, *Ayyubids*, vol. II, pp. 95-6, denies that there was a formal safe-conduct and claims that, in any case, the terms of the surrender were broken by the Templars, who tried to bring out prohibited articles.
61 Burchard of Mount Sion, 'Descriptio', ch. 4, p. 34.
62 *Cart.*, vol. IV, no. 3308, p. 292.
63 'Majus Chronicon Lemovicense', in *RHG*, vol. XXI, pp. 773-4; 'Chronicon Sampetrinum', ed. B. Stübel, *Geschichtsquellen der Provinz Sachsen*, vol. I, Halle, 1870, pp. 93-4.
64 See Tibble, *Monarchy and Lordships*, pp. 99-168.
65 *Ibid.*, pp. 173-4. Tibble draws attention to the possibility that Julian may have only leased the lordship to the Templars, but it seems most probable that they did indeed purchase it, *RRH*, vol. II, no. 1303(a), p. 84.
66 *Eracles*, vol. II, p. 445; *Gestes des Chiprois*, p. 162.
67 *RRH*, no. 1319, pp. 344-5.
68 Ibn al-Furāt, *Ayyubids*, vol. II, pp. 110-12.
69 *Gestes des Chiprois*, pp. 191-2. The ramifications of these claims are considerable and the arguments put forward very technical. Both could make a case in law, but it is not clear what practical value the Templars saw in supporting Maria at this juncture, unless they knew her already to be in contact with Charles of Anjou. In theory, Hugh was a better potential leader against the Mamluks than Maria. See J.L. La Monte, *Feudal Monarchy*

in the Latin Kingdom of Jerusalem, Cambridge, Mass., 1932, pp. 75–9, for the detailed circumstances.

70 Eracles, vol. II, p. 463. See also the letter of Hugh Revel in 'Six lettres relatives aux Croisades', ed. P. Riant, in AOL, vol. I, Paris, 1881, no. 5, pp. 390–1.

71 I registri della cancelleria angioina, ed. R. Filangieri, vol. IX, Naples, 1957, no. 258, p. 261; no. 288, pp. 264–5; Gestes des Chiprois, p. 202. For his biography, see Bulst-Thiele, Magistri, pp. 259–90.

72 Chronique de la Maison de Beaujeu, ed. M.-C. Guigue, Collection Lyonnaise 4, Lyon, 1878, pp. 1–8, 50–1; I registri della cancelleria angioina, vol. IX, no. 288, pp. 264–5; Codice Diplomatico sui rapporti Veneto-Napoletani durante il Regno di Carlo I d'Angiò, ed. N. Nicolini, RCI 36, Rome, 1965, no. 205, pp. 217–18; Gli Atti Perduti della Cancelleria Angioina, ed. C. de Lellis, vol. I(i), RCI 25, Rome, 1939, no. 445, p. 545; Gestes des Chiprois, p. 201.

73 See above, n. 69.

74 Chronique de la Maison de Beaujeu, pp. 7–8; Joinville, Histoire, pp. 238–9.

75 Cartulaire de l'Eglise Collégiale Notre-Dame de Beaujeu, ed. M.-C. Guigue, Lyon, 1864, p. 59; Gestes de Chiprois, p. 164; RRH, no. 1378, p. 359.

76 Gestes des Chiprois, pp. 201–2; Eracles, vol. II, p. 463; RRH, no. 1387, p. 361.

77 Eracles, vol. II, p. 449.

78 James of Aragon, The Chronicle of James I, King of Aragon, surnamed the Conqueror, tr. J. Forster, vol. II, London, 1883, p. 639; J.-B. Martin, Conciles et Bullaire du diocèse de Lyon, Lyon, 1905, no. 1642, p. 402; no. 1763, pp. 418–19.

79 James of Aragon, Chronicle, vol. II, pp. 646–55.

80 Eracles, vol. II, p. 468.

81 Eracles, vol. II, pp. 474–5. He had, however, been involved in other quarrels, apart from that with the Temple.

82 Gestes des Chiprois, p. 206.

83 Gestes des Chiprois, pp. 206–7; Eracles, vol. II, pp. 478–9.

84 Documents en Français des Archives Angevines de Naples (Règne de Charles Ier), ed. A. de Boüard, vol. I, Paris, 1933, no. 136, pp. 147–8.

85 Gli Atti Perduti della Cancelleria Angioina, no. 445, p. 545.

86 RRH, no. 1413, pp. 366–7.

87 Gestes des Chiprois, p. 207; Amadi. Chroniques d'Amadi et de Strambaldi, ed. R. de Mas Latrie, vol. I, Collection de documents inédits sur l'histoire de France, Paris, 1891, p. 214; Florio Bustron, Chronique de l'Île de Chypre, ed. R. de Mas Latrie, Collection de documents inédits sur l'histoire de France. Mélanges historiques 5, Paris, 1886, p. 116.

88 Gestes des Chiprois, pp. 214–17; Amadi, Chroniques, pp. 214–15.

89 Eracles, vol. II, pp. 468–9.

90 Gestes des Chiprois, p. 204.

91 Gestes des Chiprois, pp. 210–12; RRH, no. 1444, pp. 375–7.

92 Gestes des Chiprois, pp. 218–19; Amadi, Chroniques, pp. 216–17; RRH, no. 1466, pp. 382–3.

93 *Gestes des Chiprois*, p. 227.
94 *RRH*, vol. II, no. 1402(b), p. 95.
95 'Lettres inédits concernant les croisades', ed. C. Kohler and C.-V. Langlois, *BEC*, 52 (1891), 47–8, 55–6; *RRH*, no. 1404, p. 364.
96 *RRH*, vol. II, no. 1447, p. 377. Text of the treaty from Ibn 'Abd az-Zahir, tr. in *Arab Historians of the Crusades*, pp. 325–6. He was secretary to Baybars and Kalavun.
97 *Gestes des Chiprois*, pp. 234–7; Abu'l Feda, 'Annales', in *RHCr. Or.*, vol. I, pp. 162–3; Maqrisi, *Histoire des Sultans Mamelouks*, vol. II(i), pp. 101–4.
98 *RRH*, no. 1480, p. 386; no. 1505, pp. 391–2.
99 *Acta Aragonensia*, ed. H. Finke, vol. III, Berlin, 1922, no. 5, pp. 8–11.
100 *Gestes des Chiprois*, p. 238.
101 *Gestes des Chiprois*, pp. 238–40; Amadi, *Chroniques* pp. 218–19.
102 Ludolph of Suchem, *Liber*, ch. 26, pp. 42–3.
103 *Gestes des Chiprois*, pp. 240–3; Amadi, *Chroniques*, pp. 219–20; Maqrisi, *Histoire des Sultans Mamelouks*, vol. II(i), pp. 110–12; *RRH*, no. 1508, p. 392.
104 *Gestes des Chiprois*, pp. 245–51; Amadi, *Chroniques*, pp. 222–4.
105 See above, pp. 240–1.
106 *Gestes des Chiprois*, pp. 255–7.
107 *Gestes des Chiprois*, pp. 164, 227, 257; BN, *NAL* 46, fols. 196–7; *Procès*, vol. II, p. 313. See too Bulst-Thiele, *Magistri*, pp. 291–4.
108 W. Müller-Wiener, *Castles of the Crusaders*, tr. J.M. Brownjohn, London, 1966, pp. 69–70, for plans.
109 Oliver of Paderborn, *Historia Damiatina*, p. 256, had described 'Atlīt as 'the bulwark (*antemurale*) of the city of Acre', but with Acre gone one of its most important functions had disappeared.
110 *Gestes des Chiprois*, pp. 258–9; Florio Bustron, *Chronique*, p. 127; Abu'l Feda, 'Annales', p. 164.
111 *Gestes des Chiprois*, p. 258.

6 TEMPLAR LIFE

1 *Anonymous Pilgrim V.2*, tr. A. Stewart, *Anonymous Pilgrims, I-VII (11th and 12th centuries)*, Palestine Pilgrims' Text Society 6, London, 1894, pp. 29–30.
2 Guiot de Provins, 'La Bible', in *Les Oeuvres de Guiot de Provins, poète lyrique et satirique*, ed. J. Orr, Manchester, 1915, pp. 62–4. Tr. from A. Luchaire, *La Société Français au temps de Philippe-Auguste*, Paris, 1909, p. 216.
3 For the context of such illustrations, see E. Siberry, 'Victorian Perceptions of the Military Orders', in *The Military Orders. Fighting for the Faith and Caring for the Sick*, ed. M. C. Barber, London, 1994, pp. 365–72.
4 *De laude*, p. 221.
5 See above, pp. 111–12.
6 *Procès*, vol. I, pp. 44–5.
7 The translations in chapters 6 and 7 are from *The Rule of the Templars. The*

NOTES TO PAGES 182-8

French Text of the Rule of the Order of the Knights Templar, tr. J.M. Upton-Ward, Woodbridge, 1992.

8 Nevertheless, it does not follow that, for this reason, the French Rule predates the Latin Rule as Prutz argued, see Schnürer, 'Organisation', pp. 311–16. For views on dating see S.S. Rovik, 'The Templars in the Holy Land during the Twelfth Century', D. Phil. thesis, Oxford, 1986, pp. 101–5, and Bulst-Thiele, *Magistri*, p. 62, n. 2.

9 See M. Bennett, '*La Règle du Temple* as a military manual, or How to deliver a cavalry charge', in *Studies in Medieval History presented to R. Allen Brown*, ed. C. Harper-Bill, C. Holdsworth, and J.L. Nelson, Woodbridge, pp.7–19.

10 See above, p. 219.

11 See above chapter 5, n. 44.

12 *Papsturkunden für Templer und Johanniter*, vol.1, no. 3, pp. 206–7; *Règle*, cl. 675, p. 344.

13 See above, pp. 282–3.

14 'Un nouveau manuscrit', ed. Delaville Le Roulx, p. 186.

15 *Règle*, cl. 11, p. 23.

16 See Rovik, 'The Templars in the Holy Land', p. 105; Forey, *The Templars in the Corona de Aragón*, p. 282, 302, n. 167. *La Règle des Templiers*, ed. and tr. L. Dailliez, Nice, 1977, pp. 12–13, cites fourteen manuscripts.

17 'Un nouveau manuscrit', ed. Delaville Le Roulx, p. 186.

18 *Règle*, cls. 387–91, pp. 216–18; cl. 418, p. 228; cl. 550, p. 288. These clauses show that the requirement of secrecy was in force from at least the 1160s and probably earlier. It was not a new introduction in the last years of the Order's existence in Outremer.

19 *Règle*, cl. 326, p. 189.

20 See above, p. 307.

21 *Règle*, cls. 77–9, pp. 75–7.

22 *Procès*, vol. II, pp. 289–90, 294; vol. I, pp. 40, 538.

23 *Règle*, cl. 84, pp. 78–9; cl. 78, pp. 76–7; cl. 98, p. 86.

24 See E.M. Hallam, 'Royal Burial and the Cult of Kingship in France and England, 1060–1330', *JMH*, 8 (1982), 359–80.

25 *Règle*, cls. 198–9, pp. 142–3.

26 *Règle*, cls. 198–223, pp. 142–52.

27 *Papsturkunden für Templer und Johanniter*, vol. I, no. 3, p. 206.

28 *Procès*, vol. II, pp. 224–5.

29 *Règle*, cl. 223, p. 152.

30 *Règle*, cls. 79–98, pp. 77–86.

31 See above, p. 158.

32 *Gestes des Chiprois*, pp. 163–4; Urban IV. *Les Registres d'Urbain IV*, ed. J. Guiraud, vol. IV, BEFAR ser. 2, Paris, 1906, no. 2858, p. 27; Clément IV. *Les Registres de Clement IV*, ed. E. Jordan, vol. I, BEFAR ser. 2, Paris, 1893, nos. 21–3, pp. 8–9; no. 836, pp. 326–7.

33 See S. Lewis, *The Art of Matthew Paris in the Chronica Majora*, Aldershot, 1987, fig. 48, p. 91; fig. 153, p. 239; fig. 182, p. 289; and see plate 6.

34 See Scarpellini, 'La chiesa di San Bevignate', no. 92, p. 133.

35 *Règle*, cls. 99–119, pp. 86–100; cls. 130–1, pp. 105–6.

36 *Règle*, cls. 120–29, pp. 100–5; cls. 132–7, pp. 106–9.

37 *Règle*, cls. 169–79, pp. 127–33; cls. 190–7, pp. 138–41.

38 *Règle*, cls. 180–1, p. 134; cl. 328, p. 190.

39 See above, p. 70.

40 *RRH*, no. 322, pp. 82–3; no. 403, p. 106; no. 404, p. 106. *RHG*, vol. XVI, no. 125, p. 39; *RRH*, no. 399, p. 105, for his mission to France. WT, 19.18, p. 887, for his part in the embassy to Egypt. He had certainly been in the Order since 1151, *RRH*, no. 266, p. 67, and probably since before 1144, see *CG*, no. 328, p. 213, n. 1. *Papsturkunden für Templer und Johanniter*, vol. II, no. 24(a) and (b), pp. 235–6, for his position in the west. On him see E.G. Rey, 'Geoffrey Foucher. Grand-Commandeur du Temple, 1151–70', *Revue de Champagne et de Brie*, 6 (1894), 259–69.

41 *Règle*, cls. 138–40, pp. 110–12. Cf. visual evidence for the Latin east in D.C. Nicolle, *Arms and Armour of the Crusading Era 1050–1350*, 2 vols., New York, 1988, pp. 318–35, 583–627, 807–11.

42 The dictionary definition of a squire is 'a young man of noble birth, who attended upon a knight', but this is misleading in this context. A rough modern equivalent might be a stable-lad or a caddie, neither of whom are necessarily young or trainees, but rather provide specific skills which contribute to the effectiveness of the front-line operators.

43 For example, the Armenian, Malih, who attacked Templar castles in Cilicia in 1169/71, is described by WT, 20.26, pp. 948–9, as a former Templar, and the Syrian who is alleged to have betrayed Safad in 1266 was a Templar sergeant, *Gestes des Chiprois*, p. 180.

44 *Règle*, cl. 337, p. 194; cl. 431, p. 234; cls. 435–6, pp. 236–7. The offence was equally serious the other way round, i.e. a knight who pretended to be a sergeant. The reasons for this can only be guessed at, but it might well imply a more elaborate attempt to cover one's identity, cl. 446, p. 241.

45 *Règle*, cl. 586, pp. 304–5.

46 See M.C. Barber, *The Trial of the Templars*, Cambridge, 1978, p. 54, and also above, p. 229.

47 *Règle*, cl. 175, p. 130; cl. 325, p. 189; cl. 300, p. 178.

48 *Règle*, cl. 499, p. 264; cl. 647, p. 332.

49 Riley-Smith, *The Knights of St John in Jerusalem*, pp. 239–40.

50 *Der Untergang des Templer-Ordens*, ed. K. Schottmüller, Berlin, 1887, vol. II, pp. 207, 216, 217, 347, 368. There is even a hybrid term, *sergiens*, pp. 215–16. Usage illustrated in J.F. Niermeyer, *Mediae Latinitatis Lexicon Minus*, Leiden, 1976, p. 962, includes serf, servant, *ministerialis*, and sergeant (foot or mounted).

51 *Règle*, cls. 148–9, pp. 115–17; cls. 156–68, pp. 120–7. See also Bennett, 'La Règle du Temple', pp. 17–18. Cls. 419–21, pp. 229–30, show the specific circumstances in which a Templar could leave the field.

52 *De laude*, p. 221.

53 John of Würzburg, 'Descriptio', ch. 5, p. 130; *Theodericus*, ch. 17, p. 27. See also above, p. 82.

54 R.D. Pringle, 'A Templar Inscription from the Haram Al-Sharif in Jerusalem', *Levant*, 21 (1989), 197–201; Z. Jacoby, 'The Workshop of the Temple Area in Jerusalem in the Twelfth Century: Its Origin, Evolution and Impact', *Zeitschrift für Kunstgeschichte*, 45 (1982), 325–94. It is possible that the workshop appertained to the Temple, but there is no direct evidence of this. It took commissions from a wide range of patrons, including royalty and the Hospitallers.

55 Deschamps, *Les Châteaux des Croisés*, vol. III, pp. 156, 250, 252, 254, 257. See also figure 5, p. 83. There was a similar chapel at the Order's castle at Çalan in the Amanus Mountains, where it occupied an important position in the inner bailey. Below the nave is a vaulted crypt, see Edwards, *Fortifications*, pp. 101–2.

56 James of Vitry. *Lettres de Jacques de Vitry: (1160/1170–1240), évêque de Saint-Jean-d'Acre*, ed. R.B.C. Huygens, Leiden, 1960, no. 2, pp. 93–4.

57 See Johns, *Guide to 'Atlît*, pp. 52–5. The idea that the round or polygonal shape is in imitation of the Dome of the Rock, or the Temple of the Lord, as the Christians called it, seems unlikely, as this area of the Temple platform was held by the Canons of the Temple of the Lord. Moreover, a design based upon a central sanctuary accords more closely with the Church of the Holy Sepulchre.

58 See Pringle, 'Reconstructing the Castle of Safad', pp. 147–8. Ibn al-Furāt, *Ayyubids*, vol. II, p. 105, for the statues.

59 See E. Lambert, *L'Architecture des Templiers*, Paris, 1955, pp. 61–91. For an example of a plain Templar church based on a simple axial design, see R. Gem, 'An Early Church of the Knights Templars at Shipley, Sussex', in *Anglo-Norman Studies*, vol. VI, *Proceedings of the Battle Conference 1983*, ed. R.A. Brown, Woodbridge, 1984, pp. 238–46, who dates it *c.* 1140.

60 See F. Laborde, 'L'église des Templiers de Montsaunès (Haute-Garonne)', *Revue de Comminges*, 92 (1979), pp. 496–500, and plan.

61 *Papsturkunden für Templer und Johanniter*, vol. I, no. 3, pp. 207–8.

62 *Règle*, cls. 268–71, pp. 164–71.

63 *Règle*, cl. 585, p. 304.

64 Examples are William of St John, titular Archbishop of Nazareth, 1288–90, Hamilton, *The Latin Church*, p. 279, and Humbert, Bishops of Banyas, in 1272, Bulst-Thiele, *Magistri*, p. 254, n. 87. The Rule, however, makes clear provision for such promotions, cl. 434, pp. 235–6.

65 'Bulles pour l'ordre du Temple', ed. Delaville Le Roulx, no. 21, p. 421 (September, 1206).

66 *Règle*, cl. 269, p. 165.

67 *Règle*, cl. 354, p. 202.

68 *Le Procès des Templiers d'Auvergne (1309–11): Edition de l'interrogatoire de juin*

1309, ed. R. Sève and A.-M. Chagny-Sève, Mémoires et documents d'historie médiévale et de philologie, nouvelle collection, Paris, 1987, pp. 113, 119. The Rule also refers to secular priests, who serve the house 'out of charity', cl. 525, pp. 276–7.

69 *Procès*, vol. I, p. 43.

70 See Hallam, 'Royal Burial', p. 372.

71 Matthew Paris, *Chronica Majora*, vol. IV, p. 11. The Templars had moved to this site in 1161, having been established previously at Holborn. The Round Church predates the consecration in 1185 by the Patriarch Heraclius, see *Records of the Templars in England in the Twelfth Century*, pp. xxxix, liii, lxxxvii, 163.

72 *Procès*, vol. I, pp. 143, 419; 'Les Chemins et pelerinages de la Terre Sainte', ed. H. Michelant and G. Raynaud, *Itinéraires à Jérusalem*, Geneva, 1882, p. 180.

73 See F. Tommasi, 'I Templari e il culto delle reliquie', in *MS*, pp. 208–9.

74 *Procès*, vol. I, pp. 646–7.

75 *Der Untergang*, ed. Schottmüller, vol. II, p. 136.

76 Ludolph of Suchem, *Liber*, cap. 19, p. 29. According to Ludolf, its imprint in wax was efficacious against storms at sea. See Tommasi, 'I Templari', pp. 203–4.

77 Matthew Paris, *Chronica Majora*, vol. IV, p. 641; vol. VI, p. 142. See Bulst-Thiele, *Magistri*, p. 254, n. 87.

78 Lambert, *L'Architecture des Templiers*, pp. 84–91; *Procès*, vol. I, p. 502.

79 See Tommasi, 'I Templari', p. 197.

80 *The Trial of the Templars in the Papal State and the Abruzzi*, ed. A. Gilmour-Bryson, Studi e Testi 303, Città del Vaticano, 1982, pp. 264–7. This was the region where, in 1264, at Bolsena, a German priest had claimed that the host had begun to bleed, staining the mass cloth, a revelation which led to the establishment of the Feast of *Corpus Domini*. On the Templar churches in Italy and their decoration, see F. Bramato, *Storia dell'Ordine dei Templari in Italia. Le Fondazione*, Rome, 1991, pp. 175–82.

81 See G. Dickson, 'The Flagellants of 1260 and the Crusades', *JMH*, 15 (1989), 227–67. See U. Nicolini, 'Bonvicino', in *Dizionario biografico degli Italiani*, vol. XII, Rome, 1970, pp. 471–2.

82 See P. Deschamps and M. Thibout, *La Peinture murale en France. Le Haut Moyen Age et l'Epoque Romane*, Paris, 1951, pp. 133–7. As in a modern military chapel, the suspension of war trophies and shields added to the impact of the frescoes. According to Matthew Paris, *Chronica Majora*, vol. V, p. 480, it was the custom of the Templars to hang as many shields as they could around the walls of their buildings, 'in accordance with their custom beyond the sea'.

83 See D.H. Farmer, *The Oxford Dictionary of Saints*, Oxford, 1978, pp. 69–70.

84 See P. Deschamps and M. Thibout, *La Peinture murale en France au début de l'époque gothique*, Paris, 1963, pp. 27, 131, 137, 140, 153.

85 Laborde, 'L'église des Templiers', 93 (1980), 48–50, 227–41, 339–45.
86 See P. Raspa and M. Marchesi, 'Note sull'architettura di San Bevignate', in *TOI*, pp.79–92.
87 See Scarpellini, 'La chiesa di San Bevignate', pp. 93–158.
88 *Règle*, cl. 75, pp. 72–3.
89 Scarpellini, 'La chiesa di San Bevignate', p. 129, suggests that the source of this theme might have been the mosaic decoration from the apse of St John the Evangelist at Ravenna (now lost). This showed an episode in the life of Galla Placida, in which the empress and her family were carried safely through a sea voyage.
90 *Règle*, cl. 56, p. 58.
91 See F. Tommasi, 'L'Ordine dei Templari a Perugia', *Bollettino della Deputazione di Storia Patria per l'Umbria*, 78 (1981), pp. 71–2. See above, p.143.
92 Oliver of Paderborn, *Historia Damiatina*, p. 171.
93 *Règle*, cl. 279, p. 170.
94 *Règle*, cls. 279–313, pp. 170–83.
95 *Règle*, cl. 146, p. 115; cl. 300, p. 178.
96 *Règle*, cl. 313, pp. 182–3.
97 *Règle*, cl. 309, p. 181.
98 See R.D. Pringle, *The Red Tower (al-Burj al-Ahmar): Settlement in the Plain of Sharon in the time of the Crusaders and Mamluks (AD 1099–1516)*, British School of Archaeology Monographs Series 1, London, 1986, pp. 128, 178–9, 185–6.
99 James of Vitry, *The Exempla or Illustrative Stories from the Sermones Vulgares*, ed. T.F. Crane, New York, 1890, no. 85, pp. 38–9.
100 *Règle*, cls. 184–6, pp. 135–6; cl. 192, p. 139; cl. 196, pp. 140–1.
101 *Règle*, cl. 283, p. 171; cl. 305, pp. 179–80; cl. 315, pp. 183–4; cl. 319, pp. 185–6; cl. 606, pp. 313–14.
102 *Règle*, cl. 294, pp. 175–6.
103 *Procès*, vol. II, p. 160; *Règle*, cl. 501, pp. 264–5.
104 *Règle*, cl. 367, p. 207.
105 *Règle*, cl. 285, p. 172.
106 *Règle*, cls. 340–65, pp. 195–206.
107 *Règle*, cl. 343, p. 197.
108 *Règle*, cls. 346–8, pp. 198–200.
109 *Règle*, cl. 349, p. 200.
110 *Règle*, cl. 431, p. 234.
111 *Règle*, cls. 657–86, pp. 337–50. Cf. the reception of a Hospitaller, Riley-Smith, *The Knights of St John in Jerusalem*, pp. 232–3.
112 *Règle*, cl. 70, p. 69. These clauses imply that women had been more closely associated with the Templars during the 1120s, perhaps helping with the care of pilgrims.
113 *Règle*, cl. 679, pp. 346–7.
114 See above, pp. 25–6, 257.

115 *Règle*, cl. 433, p. 235.
116 See Forey, 'Women and Military Orders', pp. 63-7, and *Records of the Templars in England*, pp. lxi-lxii. On this issue see the discussion by H.J. Nicholson, 'Templar Attitudes towards Women', *Medieval History*, 1 (1991), 74-80.
117 Joinville, *Histoire*, pp. 282-3; *Gestes des Chiprois*, p. 147, says she was sent to Acre and then ʿAtlīt.
118 *Règle*, cl. 14, pp. 25-6. Repeated in the French translation. On the age of recruits, see A.J. Forey, 'Recruitment to Military Orders (Twelfth to mid-Fourteenth Centuries)', *Viator*, 17 (1986), 148-53.
119 *Provins. Histoire et cartulaire des Templiers de Provins*, ed. V. Carrière, Paris, 1919, no. 12, pp. 49-50.
120 *Procès*, vol. I, p. 415; vol. II, pp. 352, 390.
121 *Rorgo Fretellus de Nazareth et sa description de la Terre Sainte. Histoire et edition du texte*, ed. P.C. Boeren, Amsterdam, 1980, pp. XVIII, 54, 72-7. For similar examples in Aragon, see Forey, *The Templars in the Corona de Aragón*, p. 285 and Appendix I, no. 13, p. 380. See also above, p. 37.
122 See E. Magnou, 'Oblature, classe chevaleresque et servage dans les maisons méridionales du Temple au XIIme siècle', *Annales du Midi*, 73 (1961), 390-1.
123 *Règle*, cl. 11, p. 23; *Papsturkunden für Templer und Johanniter*, vol. I, no. 3, p. 208. See A.J.Forey, 'Novitiate and Instruction in the Military Orders during the Twelfth and Thirteenth Centuries', *Speculum*, 61 (1986), 1-17.
124 *Règle*, cl. 14, p. 26.
125 See Barber, *Trial*, p. 54, and above, p. 229.
126 *Règle*, cl. 97, p. 85.
127 See S. Painter, *William Marshal*, Baltimore, 1933, pp. 284-5.
128 *Gestes des Chiprois*, pp. 117-18. Tr. from Philip of Novara, *The Wars of Frederick II*, pp. 169-70.
129 *Règle*, cl. 338-9, pp. 194-5.
130 *Règle*, cl. 93, p. 83. Facilities may have been provided at designated houses. Two examples were at Eagle (Lincolnshire) and at Denney (Cambridge-shire) in the English province, see *Records of the Templars in England in the Twelfth Century*, p. clxxx, and *The Victoria History of the Counties of England*, ed. L.F. Salzman, *A History of Cambridgeshire and the Isle of Ely*, vol. II, London, 1948, pp. 259-62.
131 *Règle*, cls. 438-9, pp. 237-8; cl. 672, p. 343.
132 *Règle*, cls. 190-7, pp. 138-41.
133 *Règle*, cl. 443, pp. 239-40. See Shajar, 'Des lépreux', pp. 29-30.
134 *Catalan Rule*, fols. 10a-11b; 'Un nouveau manuscrit', ed. Delaville Le Roulx, cl. 14, pp. 197-8. This obligation appears to have applied only to Templars serving in the east, since there was a leper brother among those held in the Temple at Paris during the trial in 1310, *Procès*, vol. I, p. 159.
135 *Catalan Rule*, fol. 11b; 'Un nouveau manuscrit', ed. Delaville Le Roulx, cls. 16-17, pp. 198-9.

136 *Règle*, cl. 188, p. 137.

137 *Règle*, cl. 370, pp. 208–9.

138 *RRH*, vol. II, no. 614(b), p. 40 (March 1182).

139 John of Würzburg, 'Descriptio', ch. 5, p. 130.

140 *Le Dossier*, pp. 6–7.

141 For example, *Procès*, vol. I, pp. 192, 370, 430, 528, 550; *Der Untergang*, ed. Schottmüller, vol. II, p. 247; *Papsttum und Untergang des Templerordens*, vol. II, ed. H. Finke, Münster, 1907, no. 48, p. 72.

142 *Procès*, vol. I, pp. 400–1.

143 *Procès*, vol. II, p. 259.

144 *Règle*, cls. 386–415, pp. 216–27.

145 *Règle*, cls. 224–32, pp. 153–4. The last section of the Rule, added in the middle of the thirteenth century, lists these offences with practical examples, as well as the offence of lying at reception, cls. 544–85, pp. 285–304, and see above, pp. 224–7.

146 *Règle*, cl. 423, pp. 230–1.

147 *Règle*, cl. 418, p. 229.

148 *Règle*, cl. 554, pp. 289–90.

149 *Règle*, cl. 428, pp. 232–3.

150 See Barber, *Trial*, pp. 238–40.

151 *Règle*, cl. 429, p. 233. There is, however, the interesting case of one Bartholomew, described by Gerard of Nazareth, Bishop of Latakia (1139–61). This man abandoned his wife and went on pilgrimage to the east, where he joined the Templars. He appears, nevertheless, to have devoted himself to the care of lepers in Jerusalem, while at the same time torturing his body with fasts and vigils. He eventually left the Templars – it is not clear whether he had permission or not – and became a monk on the Black Mountain at Antioch. See B. Z. Kedar, 'Gerard of Nazareth, a Neglected Twelfth-Century Writer in the Latin East. A Contribution to the Intellectual and Monastic History of the Crusader States', *DOP*, 37 (1983), p. 72.

152 *Règle*, cl. 437, p. 237.

153 See A. Spicciani, 'Papa Innocenzo IV e I Templari', in *MS*, pp. 56–7.

154 *Règle*, cls. 451–67, pp. 242–50. The section of the Rule added in the mid thirteenth century lists thirty-one different offences with examples, cls. 587–622, pp. 305–22.

155 *Règle*, cl. 451, pp. 242–3; cl. 468, p. 250; cl. 470, p. 251; cl. 472, pp. 251–2; cl. 477–8, pp. 253–4; cl. 481, p. 255.

156 *Règle*, cl. 474, p. 252; cls. 486–7, pp. 257–8. See, for example, the case of Adam of Wallaincourt, who had joined the Carthusians (which certainly fitted the definition of a more severe order), but later regretted his decision, *Procès*, vol. I. p. 204. However, contrary to the belief of the anonymous pilgrim, *Règle*, cl. 512, p. 271, allows for cats and dogs to be driven away if they were interfering with a brother eating his bread.

157 *Règle*, cl. 476, p. 253.

158 *Règle*, cls. 496–7, pp. 262–3.

159 *Règle*, cls. 493, p. 261; cl. 502, pp. 265–6.

160 *Règle*, cl. 532, p. 279. This conduct was important not only in itself, but also 'to set a good example to secular people', cl. 340, p. 195.

161 *Règle*, cls. 315, pp. 183–4; cl. 317, pp. 184–5.

162 *Règle*, cl. 638, p. 328.

163 *Règle*, cl. 605, p. 313. See also the case of the Commander in Cyprus, who caused the death of a horse which had been given into the care of the house for treatment. The horse had to be destroyed after the commander had fallen with it while chasing a hare, cl. 606, p. 289.

164 *Calendar of the Close Rolls, Edward I.*, vol. III, AD 1288–1296, London, 1904, p. 289.

165 *Règle*, cls. 558, pp. 291–2; cl. 592, p. 308; cl. 625, p. 322.

166 See above, pp. 229–31.

167 Walter Map, *De nugis curialium*, pp. 72–3.

168 See J.H. Lynch, *Simoniacal Entry into the Religious Life from 1000 to 1260*, Columbus, Ohio, 1976, pp. 190–2. On the issue of simony and military orders, see Forey, 'Recruitment', pp. 155–7.

169 *Cartulaires des Templiers de Douzens*, ed. P. Gérard and E. Magnou, Collection de documents inédits sur l'histoire de France 3, Paris, 1965, Cartulaire A, no. 199 [198], pp. 171–2. See also Magnou, 'Oblature', pp. 387–8.

170 *Règle*, cl. 224, p. 153.

171 See J.A. Brundage, 'The Crusader's Wife: A Canonistic Quandary', *Studia Gratiana*, 12, Collectanea Stephan Kuttner 2, Rome, 1967, pp. 434–5.

172 *Règle*, cls. 544–49, pp. 285–88. See Lynch, *Simoniacal Entry into Religious Life*, pp. 216–17.

173 This was probably Reginald of Vichiers, who was Preceptor of Acre in 1240, *RRH*, no. 1096, p. 285. William of Sonnac, Armand of Périgord's immediate successor, was Preceptor of Aquitaine in the mid 1230s and therefore not present in the east when the matter seems to have arisen.

174 See above, pp. 230–1.

175 *Calendar of the Close Rolls, Edward I.*, vol. V, AD 1302–7, London, 1908, p. 339.

176 *Catalan Rule*, fols. 35b–37a; 'Un nouveau manuscrit', ed. Delaville Le Roulx, cl. 31, pp. 201–2.

177 WT, 20.26, p. 949. See above, p. 79.

178 *Eracles*, vol. II, p. 467.

179 *Règle*, cl. 603, p. 312.

180 Matthew Paris, *Chronica Majora*, vol. V, p. 387.

181 *Règle*, cl. 569, pp. 296–7.

182 *Règle*, cl. 418, p. 229. See C. Davies, 'Sexual Taboos and Social Boundaries', *American Journal of Sociology*, 87 (1982), 1032–63, for prohibitions against various kinds of sexual activity, which consequently implicitly recognise that they were occurring.

183 *Règle*, cls. 236, p. 156; cl. 452, p. 243.

184 *Règle*, cls. 572–3, pp. 297–8. A very similar story was told by the knight, Hugh of Faure, during the trial in 1311. He may have heard talk of it, or taken it directly from the Rule, *Procès*, vol. II, p. 223.

185 *Le Procès des Templiers d'Auvergne (1309–11)*, p. 148.

186 For example, J.R. Strayer, *The Reign of Philip the Fair*, Princeton, 1980, p. 291. However, his claim that the Templars 'were unchaste and that they often engaged in homosexual practices goes without saying' far surpasses anything to be found in the existing evidence.

187 The rarity of confessions such as that of William of Born goes some way towards confirming the view put forward by J. Boswell, *Christianity, Social Tolerance and Homosexuality*, Chicago, 1980, pp. 295–8, that Christian society was becoming increasingly intolerant of homosexuality in the thirteenth century. However, as suggested above, pp. 306–7, the issue may be one of the methodology applied to the analysis of the depositions rather than of social change.

7 THE TEMPLAR NETWORK

1 *Procès*, vol. II, pp. 330–1.

2 Barber, *Trial*, p. 54.

3 A. Trudon des Ormes, 'Listes des maisons et de quelques dignitaires de l'ordre du Temple, en Syrie, en Chypre et en France, d'après les pièces du procès', *ROL*, 5 (1899), 440–2; *Records of the Templars in England in the Twelfth Century*, pp. xxxii–xxxiii, on the baillia in England.

4 Matthew Paris, *Chronica Majora*, vol. IV, p. 291. These figures have often been quoted as if they have some objective basis. It can be seen from the context that they have no validity as a means of estimating the wealth of the military orders. See also, above, pp. 1–2.

5 See above, p. 62.

6 See A.J. Forey, 'The Military Orders in the Crusading Proposals of the Late-Thirteenth and Early-Fourteenth Centuries', *Traditio*, 36 (1980), 327–33, and A.J. Forey, *The Military Orders*, pp. 204–20, for criticism of the military orders' use of their resources.

7 See A.J. Forey, 'The Order of Mountjoy', *Speculum*, 46 (1971), 250–66, for the troubled history of this Order. Salimbene de Adam, *Cronica*, ed. G. Scalia, vol. I, Scrittori d'Italia 233, Bari, 1966, p. 255, quoting letters from Robert of Nantes, Patriarch of Jerusalem, on the fate of the members of St Lazarus at La Forbie. Cf. the problems of the Hospitallers, Riley-Smith, *The Knights of St John in Jerusalem*, pp. 439–43, and of the military orders in general, Forey, *The Military Orders*, pp. 128–32.

8 Figures gathered by R. Fossier, *Peasant Life in the Medieval West*, tr. J. Vale, Oxford, 1988, pp. 140–1, 118. See also P. Contamine, *War in the Middle Ages*, tr. M. Jones, Oxford, 1984, pp. 96–7, whose figures suggest that Fossier's estimates represent only the lower end of the market. In the Holy

Land in 1251 Louis IX reckoned a knight's horse at eighty *livres*. Joinville, *Histoire*, pp. 278–9.

9 Contemporary conditions have been described as 'a crisis of feudalism' by G. Duby, *The Three Orders. Feudal Society Imagined*, tr. A. Goldhammer, Chicago and London, 1980, p. 326, which, in Fossier's view, provoked 'an intense seigneurial reaction' (p. 141). This manifested itself on Templar estates in the application of tough administrative methods in regard to both tenants and neighbours, see Barber, 'Social Context of the Templars', 44–5. Cf. the problems of the Templars in Aragon where, by the later thirteenth century, the opportunities for expansion were negligible, yet the demands on resources remained heavy, Forey, *The Templars in the Corona de Aragón*, pp. 57–62, 140–1.

10 See Tibble, *Monarchy and Lordships*, pp. 186–8, and Riley-Smith, *Feudal Nobility*, pp. 28–32.

11 C. Duffy, *The Military Experience in the Age of Reason*, London, 1987, pp. 11, 159.

12 See the section on logistics in *The New Encyclopaedia Britannica. Macropaedia*, 15th edn, vol. XXIX, London, 1986, pp. 693, 695. For the Templars themselves, see A. Demurger, *Vie et mort de l'Ordre du Temple*, Paris, 1985, pp. 163–226. Cf. F. Tallett, *War and Society in Early-Modern Europe, 1495–1715*, London, 1992, pp. 50–68.

13 See Spicciani, 'Papa Innocenzo IV', pp. 49–55.

14 It is clear that Thomas Bérard had been accustomed to raise loans from Italian merchants in Acre, see above, p. 156.

15 Innocent IV. *Les Registres d'Innocent IV*, vol. I, ed. E. Berger, BEFAR ser. 2, Paris, 1884, no. 2692, p. 401 (1247); vol. II, 1887, no. 4398, p. 55 (1249). Cf. the situation after the suppression of the Templars. 'To a greater extent than historians have commonly recognised, the direction and tempo of the crusading movement in the second quarter of the fourteenth century were dictated by the condition and interaction of Hospitaller and papal finances', N. Housley, *The Later Crusades. From Lyons to Alcazar, 1274–1580*, Oxford, 1992, p. 217.

16 Innocent IV. *Les Registres d'Innocent IV*, vol. III, no. 6237, p. 159; no. 6256, pp. 162–3.

17 See above, p. 35, and Hiestand, 'Kardinalbischof', pp. 321–2.

18 See above pp. 97, 115, 147. For the 1237 engagement, Abu'l Feda, 'Annales', p. 112, and Matthew Paris, *Chronica Majora*, vol. III, pp. 404–6. The Darbsak defeat was so serious that Henry III made a special grant of 500 marks to the Master of the Temple in England to help pay for the ransom of those captured there, *Calendar of the Patent Rolls, 1232–47*, London, 1906, p. 207.

19 'Emprunts', ed. Servois, Appendice, no. 4, p. 292; *RRH*, no. 1347, pp. 352–3.

20 See W.C. Jordan, *Louis IX and the Challenge of the Crusade*, Princeton, 1979, pp. 65–104, for a detailed examination of the complexities of crusade finance.

21 *RHG*, vol. xv, pp. 540–1. See above, p. 70.
22 *CG*, no. 589, p. 362.
23 Gerald of Wales, 'De Principis Instructione Liber', ed. G.F. Warner, *Giraldi Cambrensis Opera*, vol. viii, RS 21, London, 1891, dist. 2, ch. 23, pp. 201–2.
24 Matthew Paris, *Chronica Majora*, vol. iv, p. 416.
25 *Procès*, vol. ii, p. 305; vol. i, pp. 44–5. See above, p. 181.
26 *Papsttum und Untergang*, ed. Finke, vol. ii, pp. 334–5.
27 See Barber, 'Supplying the Crusader States', pp. 320–1.
28 *Règle*, cl. 432, pp. 234–5; cl. 436, pp. 236–7. On the supply of recruits, see Forey, 'Recruitment', pp. 157–62.
29 See above, pp. 185, 190–1. This figure might seem high, but other sources confirm that numbers on this scale were needed for serious campaigning, see Contamine, *War in the Middle Ages*, p. 67. See also the importance of horses to the Hospitallers, Riley-Smith, *The Knights of St John in Jerusalem*, pp. 318–20.
30 See *The New Encyclopaedia Britannica. Macropaedia*, vol. xxix, p. 688.
31 Odo of Deuil, *De Profectione*, pp. 134–5.
32 'Imâd ad-Din, in Abū Shāmā, 'Le Livre des Deux Jardins', pp. 271–2.
33 *Itinerarium*, vol. i, pp. 291–4, 299, 303–4. Compare the problems of seventeenth-century armies, G. Perjés, 'Army Provisioning, Logistics and Strategy in the Second Half of the 17th Century', *Acta Historia Academiae Scientarium Hungaricae*, 16 (1970), 1–51, especially 14–19, on the provision of fodder.
34 *The New Encyclopaedia Britannica. Macropaedia*, vol. xx, p. 706.
35 *Règle*, cl. 596, pp. 309–10.
36 *Règle*, cl. 103, p. 90; cl. 135, pp. 108–9 (buying); cls. 114–15, pp. 96–7 (foals).
37 *RHG*, vol. xix, p. 640.
38 *Règle*, cl. 84, p. 78; cl. 609, p. 314.
39 *Documenti del commercio veneziano nei secoli XI-XIII*, ed. R. Morozzo della Rocca and A. Lombardo, vol. i, *RCI* 28, Rome, 1940, no. 158, pp. 155–6. On this family, see G. Luzzatto, 'Capitale e lavoro nel commercio veneziano dei secoli XI e XII', in *Studi di Storia Economica Veneziana*, Padua, 1954, pp. 108–116. Luzzatto describes them as *mercanti-armatori*.
40 Joinville, *Histoire*, pp. 70–1.
41 WT, 11.21, p. 526; Fulcher of Chartres, *Historia*, 3.25, pp. 657–8.
42 See J. Pryor, 'Transportation of horses by sea during the era of the Crusades', *Mariner's Mirror*, 68 (1982), 15–19. See also Forey, *The Templars in the Corona de Aragón*, p. 325 and Appendix 1, no. 30, p. 402, for horses sent from Aragon to the east.
43 *Documenti del commercio veneziano nei secoli XI-XIII*, vol. ii, no. 487, pp. 27–8.
44 *Acta imperii inedita*, vol. i, no. 139, p. 117; *Cart.*, vol. ii, no. 1464, pp. 186–7; no. 2067, pp. 462–4. See Barber, 'Supplying the Crusader States', pp. 322–3.
45 On the importance of Marseille, see D. Abulafia, 'Marseilles, Acre and the

Mediterranean, 1200–1291', in *Coinage in the Latin East: The Fourth Oxford Symposium on Coinage and Monetary History*, ed. P.W. Edbury and D.M. Metcalf, *British Archeological Reports*, International Series 77, Oxford, 1980, 19–39.

46 *Procès*, vol. I, p. 458. There is a hint that such officials were found not only in the ports, but operated throughout the system. See the references in Burgundy in the middle of the thirteenth century, J. Richard, 'Les Templiers et les Hospitaliers en Bourgogne et en Champagne méridionale', in *Die geistlichen Ritterorden Europas*, ed. J. Fleckenstein and M. Hellmann, Sigmaringen, 1980, p. 233.

47 See D. Abulafia, 'Southern Italy and the Florentine Economy, 1265–1370', *Economic History Review*, ser. 2, 33 (1981), pp. 377–88, and 'The Crown and the Economy under Roger II and his successors', *DOP*, 37 (1983), pp. 1–14. Wheat produced in Sicily and Apulia stood up to long voyages better than that grown further north and was therefore especially important as a source of supply for the Holy Land.

48 Ramon Muntaner, *Crónica Catalana*, ed. and tr. A. de Bofarull, Barcelona, 1860, pp. 368–9. English tr. from *The Chronicle of Muntaner*, tr. Lady Goodenough, Hakluyt Society 50, vol. II, London, 1920–1, pp. 467–8.

49 See Bramato, 'L'Ordine Templare nel Regno di Sicilia nell'età Svevo-Angioina', in *MS*, pp. 121–38.

50 Martin da Canal, *Les Estoires de Venise. Cronaca veneziana in lingua francese dalle origini al 1275*, ed. A. Limentani, Civiltà Veneziana, Fonti e Testi 12, Florence, 1972, pp. 108–9.

51 Matthew Paris, *Chronica Majora*, vol. III, p. 556.

52 See Abulafia, *Frederick II*, pp. 139–42.

53 *Historia Diplomatica*, vol. II(i), p. 224; *Acta imperii inedita*, vol. I, no. 246, pp. 225–6 (1223). For the grants and concessions of 1209 and 1210, *Historia Diplomatica*, vol. I, pp. 144–5; *Acta imperii inedita*, vol. I, no. 102, pp. 88–9; no. 106, p. 93.

54 See above, pp. 132–5.

55 On relations with Frederick II, see Bramato, 'L'Ordine Templare', pp. 107–112.

56 R. Bevere, 'Notizie storiche tratte dai documenti conosciuti col nome di "Arche in carta bambagina"', *Archivio Storico per le Province Napoletane*, 25, (1900), pp. 403–4.

57 See Bramato, 'L'Ordine Templare', pp. 112–13.

58 *Syllabus Membranarum ad Regiae Siclae archivum pertinentium*, ed. A.A. Scotti, vol. I, Naples, 1824, fasc. I, no. 10, p. 8.

59 See Barber, 'Supplying the Crusader States', p. 325, n. 44. See *I registri della cancelleria angioina*, vol. XXVI, 1979, no. 735, p. 207, where special permission is given to the Temple to resell grain. For Templar agricultural production in this region, see Bramato, *Storia dell'ordine dei Templari in Italia*, pp. 167–75.

60 *I registri della cancelleria angioina*, vol. XI, 1958, no. 143, p. 55, and Roger of Wendover, *Flores Historiarum*, vol. II, p. 345, for slaves of the Templars in

Apulia and Sicily. They may have been used particularly for domestic tasks, as they were in many Italian and Spanish households in the later middle ages, see I. Origo, 'The Domestic Enemy: The Eastern Slaves in Tuscany in the Fourteenth and Fifteenth Centuries', *Speculum*, 30 (1955), 321–66. For slaves in the Aragonese houses, see Forey, *The Templars in the Corona de Aragón*, pp. 285–6.

61 *Historica Diplomatica*, vol. III, pp. 73–5; Roger of Wendover, *Flores Historiarum*, vol. II, p. 345.

62 For Ayas as a centre of the slave trade, see R. Irwin, 'The Supply of Money and the Direction of Trade in Thirteenth-Century Syria', in *Coinage in the Latin East*, ed. P.W. Edbury and D.M. Metcalf, Oxford, 1980, p. 84.

63 See J. Richard, 'The Eastern Mediterranean and its Relations with its Hinterland (11th–15th Centuries)', in *Les Relations entre l'Orient et l'Occident au Moyen Age*, Variorum. Collected Studies 69, London, 1977, pp. 1–18.

64 'Actes passés en 1271, 1274 et 1279 à l'Aïas (Petite Arménie) et à Beyrouth par devant des notaires génois', ed. C. Desimoni, in *AOL*, vol. I, Paris, 1881, no. 4, p. 495.

65 Ramon Muntaner, *Crónica Catalana*, pp. 368–9. *The Chronicle of Muntaner*, tr. Goodenough, pp. 466–9.

66 See D. Jacoby, 'Crusader Acre in the Thirteenth Century: Urban Layout and Topography', *Studi Medievali*, 20 (1979), 1–46 and map.

67 *Theodericus*, cap. 40, p. 43.

68 See D. Jacoby, 'Les communes italiennes et les ordres militaires à Acre: aspects juridiques, territoriaux et militaires (1104–1187, 1191–1291)', in *Etat et colonisation au Moyen Age et à la Renaissance*, ed. M. Balard, Lyon, 1989, pp. 204–6.

69 *Gestes des Chiprois*, pp. 252–3.

70 See Johns, *Guide to 'Atlīt*, p. 50.

71 See above, pp. 270–1. The percentage is based on one complete year.

72 See Forey, *The Templars in the Corona de Aragón*, p. 324.

73 *RRH*, vol. II, no. 1303(a), p. 84.

74 See Forey, *The Templars in the Corona de Aragón*, pp. 322–4.

75 *RRH*, no. 1303, p. 341. See above, pp. 156–7. The division of the post of Visitor in the west at about this time may have been the consequence of the problems faced by Thomas Bérard in the east during his Mastership, see above, p. 245. On the lead taken by the military orders in sending letters to the west, see S. Lloyd, *English Society and the Crusade 1216–1307*, Oxford, 1988, pp. 24–9, and Appendix 1, pp. 248–52.

76 *Règle*, cl. 87, p. 80.

77 See above, p. 19.

78 *RRH*, no. 1303, p. 341; *Procès*, vol. II, pp. 295–6; *Conciliae Magnae Britanniae et Hiberniae*, ed. D. Wilkins, vol. II, London, 1737, p. 337. See Trudon des Ormes, 'Listes', pp. 440–2, and chart.

79 *The Trial of the Templars in the Papal State and the Abruzzi*, pp. 29–30, 131–3, 173, 188–9, 201–2, 250. His powers sometimes encompassed Hungary as well, which reinforces the view that this meant primarily Dalmatia.

In 1194 the Templars of Albenga made a sale with the permission of 'master Gaimard, preceptor of all the houses of the Temple in Italy', *Instrumenta Episcoporum Albinganensium*, no. 36, pp. 54-5. On the early development of the Temple in Italy, see Bramato, 'L'Ordine dei Templari in Italia', 183-221.

80 Forey, *The Templars in the Corona de Aragón*, pp. 328-9. See also *Documents concernant les Templiers*, ed. J. Delaville Le Roulx, Paris, 1882, no. 34, p. 45, showing a Visitor for the houses of the Temple in the Kingdoms of France and England (August 1290). This reorganisation may have been precipitated by the schism in the provincial government of Spain. In 1244 the brothers of Castile and León supported one commander, while those of Portugal accepted another. This had only been resolved by the rather cumbersome method of calling both claimants to appear before the Master in the Holy Land, *Règle*, cl. 582-3, pp. 302-3.

81 *RRH*, no. 815, p. 218; see K.M. Setton, *The Papacy and the Levant (1204-1571)*, vol. I, Philadelphia, 1976, p. 28, n. 9; Innocent III. *Innocenti P.P. Registrorum*, in *PL*, vol. CCXVI, no. 137, col. 324; W. Miller, *The Latins in the Levant. A History of Frankish Greece (1204-1566)*, London, 1908, p. 70.

82 This version dates from *c.* 1388 and cannot be regarded as the definitive word on the subject. It is unlikely, however, that the proportions of the fees owed are wildly inaccurate. See *Crusaders as Conquerors. The Chronicle of the Morea*, tr. H.E. Lurier, Records of Civilization. Sources and Studies 69, New York and London, 1964, pp. 126-8.

83 On the pattern of military orders in Iberia, see A.J. Forey, 'The Military Orders and the Spanish Reconquest in the Twelfth and Thirteenth Centuries', *Traditio*, 40 (1984), 197-234, and Forey, *The Military Orders*, pp. 25-32.

84 James of Aragon, *Chronicle*, vol. I, pp. 18-24, 210-16, 252-8, 266-9, 305; vol. II, pp. 668-71. For the context of these events, see Bisson, *The Medieval Crown of Aragon*, pp. 58-63.

85 See E. Lourie, 'Free Muslims in the Balearics under Christian Rule in the Thirteenth Century', *Speculum*, 45 (1970), 625-9, 644-5. On Templar concessions to the Muslim population in Aragon, see Forey, *The Templars in the Corona de Aragón*, pp. 200-1 and Appendix, no. 24, pp. 395-7. The colonisation of lands in Aragon, shown by Forey, was paralleled by a similar process in Portugal. See, for example, the charter for Castelo Branco in 1213, *Portugaliae Monumenta Historia, Leges et consuetudines*, vol. I, Libson, 1856, pp. 566-7. For the distribution of Templar lands in Portugal, see A.H. Oliveira Marques, *Historia de Portugal*, 11th edn, vol. I, Lisbon, 1983, fig. 21, p. 143.

86 See Forey, *The Templars in the Corona de Aragón*, pp. 31-6.

87 For the Templars in Lorraine, H. von Hammerstein, 'Der Besitz der Tempelherren in Lotharingen', *Jahrbuch der Gesellschaft für lothringische Geschichte und Altertumskunde*, 7 (1895), 1-29, who lists the places where the Templars held property together with documentary extracts. The Order

appears to have established at least three houses in Lorraine (Metz, Gelu-court, and Pierrevillers). Further east, see the establishment of Tempelburg, near Falkenburg, from c. 1290, H. Lüpke, 'Das Land Tempelburg. Eine historisch-geographische Untersuchung', *Baltische Studien*, 35 (1933), pp. 43–97.

88 See M. Starnawska, 'Notizie sulla composizione e sulla struttura dell'Ordine del Tempio in Polonia', in *MS*, pp. 143–52.

89 See K. Eistert, 'Der Ritterorden der Tempelherren in Schlesien', *Archiv für Schlesische Kirchengeschichte*, 14 (1956), p. 8.

90 *Schlesisches Urkundenbuch, 1231–1250*, ed. W. Irgang, vol. ii, Vienna, Cologne, and Graz, 1977, no. 219, p. 133.

91 *Documenti del commercio veneziano nei secoli XI-XIII*, vol. ii, no. 798, pp. 321–2; *Deliberazioni del Maggior Consiglio di Venezia*, ed. R. Cessi, vol. ii, Bologna, 1931, no. 33, p. 51. The Templars had paid compensation for the damage to Segna.

92 For example, *Urkunden zur Reichs-und Rechtsgeschichte Italiens*, ed. J. Ficker, vol. iv, Innsbruck, 1874, no. 430, pp. 441–2 (1259). See Dickson, 'The Flagellants', pp. 243–5.

93 A. Luttrell, 'Two Templar-Hospitaller Preceptories North of Tuscania', *Papers of the British School at Rome*, 39 (1971), 90–124.

94 *Cart.*, vol.i, no. 1069, pp. 666–7; *RRH*, no. 751, p. 200; *Procès*, vol. i, p. 100.

95 *Records of the Templars in England in the Twelfth Century*, pp. 1–135. The Inquest says that it was made in 1185, although the returns may have been irregular. Internal evidence suggests that they had been largely sent in by c. 1190, pp. xvii–xviii. Detailed study of a specific region, that of Essex, shows how the Templars had acquired a landed base in the county superior to that of the Hospitallers and how effectively they exploited it. See M. Gervers, '*Pro defensione Terre Sancte*: The Development and Exploitation of the Hospitallers' Landed Estate in Essex', in *The Military Orders. Fighting for the Faith and Caring for the Sick*, ed. M.C. Barber, London, 1994, pp. 3–20.

96 See Barber, 'Supplying the Crusader States', pp. 318–19. The existence of houses staffed by only small numbers of Templars is tacitly confirmed by the Rule, which sets down that chapter-meetings should be held whenever there were four or more brothers assembled, *Règle*, cl. 385, p. 215. See also J.E. Burton, 'The Knights Templars in Yorkshire in the Twelfth Century: a Reassessment', *Northern History. A Review of the History of the North of England and the Borders*, 27 (1991), 39–40 and n. 63. In 1308, there were nine preceptors and nineteen other Templars in Yorkshire, with no more than four men in any one house. See too the structure of Templar houses in south-western France, A.-M. Legras, *Les Commanderies des Templiers et des Hospitaliers de Saint-Jean de Jérusalem en Saintonge et en Aunis*, Paris, 1983, p. 12 and map, p. 19.

97 *Procès*, vol. II, pp. 423–515. See also B. Alart, 'Suppression de l'ordre des Templiers en Roussillon', *Bulletin de la Société Agricole, Scientifique et Littéraire des Pyrénées-Orientales*, 15 (1867), 28–30.

98 See R.W. Emery, *The Jews of Perpignan in the Thirteenth Century*, New York, 1959, pp. 98–9.

99 See above, p. 208.

100 *OR*, pp. 303–36.

101 *CG*, no. 341, p. 221.

102 *CG*, no. 228, p. 154; no. 133, p. 93.

103 See Brundage, 'The Crusader's Wife', pp. 431–33.

104 See above, p. 21.

105 *CG*, no. 306, p. 199.

106 *CG*, no. 17, pp. 11–12.

107 *CG*, no. 141, p. 99.

108 *CG*, no. 275, p. 180.

109 *CG*, no. 205, p. 143; no. 314, p. 205; no. 353, p. 227. On Osto, see *Records of the Templars in England in the Twelfth Century*, pp. xxxix, xliv, xlviii–liv. He may have been Master in England in the early 1150s. He was still alive in 1174.

110 *CG*, no. 375, p. 239.

111 *WT*, 17.18, p. 785; 21.5, p. 967 (Walter, Prince of Galilee); 10.9, p. 464; 11.5, pp. 502–3 (Hugh of St Omer). On this family, see A. Giry, 'Les châtelains de Saint-Omer, 1042–1386', *BEC*, 35 (1874), 325–55.

112 See *Cartulaire de la Commanderie de Richerenches*, pp. cxl–cxliii.

113 *CG*, no. 189, p. 129.

114 *CG*, no. 371, p. 237.

115 *Cartulaire de la Commanderie de Richerenches*, no. 87, pp. 162–6; *CG*, no. 598, pp. 368–71.

116 See *Cartulaire de la Commanderie de Richerenches*, p. cxxix. On the social background of Templars, see Forey, 'Recruitment', pp. 143–4.

117 *Layettes*, vol. I, no. 237, p. 100. See J. Dunbabin, 'From Clerk to Knight: Changing Orders', in *The Ideals and Practice of Medieval Knighthood*, vol. II, *Papers from the Third Strawberry Hill Conference 1986*, ed. C. Harper-Bill and R. Harvey, Woodbridge, 1988, pp. 26–39.

118 *Règle*, cl. 69, p. 68.

119 See Magnou, 'Oblature', p. 381.

120 *Cartulario del Temple de Huesca*, no. 138, pp. 143–5. See also no. 61, pp. 62–3; no. 181, pp. 201–2.

121 See Magnou, 'Oblature', pp. 394–5.

122 See *Provins*, pp. xlviii–ii. On the key importance of the Champagne-Burgundy region to the Templars, particularly as a source of recruits, see Richard, 'Les Templiers', pp. 231–42.

123 *CG*, no. 9, p. 6. See above, p. 13.

124 *Provins*, no. 89, pp. 108–9.

125 *Provins*, no. 82, pp. 103–4; no. 83, pp. 104–5; no. 91, p. 110; no. 8, p. 47; no. 78, p. 100; no. 138, pp. 142–3. See also p. lxxxv.

126 *Provins*, no. 89, pp. 108–9.

127 *Provins*, no. 98, p. 113.

128 See H. d'Arbois de Jubainville, *Histoire des Ducs et des Comtes de Champagne*, vol. III, Paris, 1861, *pièces justificatives*, no. 160, p. 477.

129 *Ibid.*, vol. V, no. 1859, p. 256. See *Provins*, pp. lvii–lix.

130 See Barber, 'Social Context of the Templars', pp. 44–5.

131 *Provins*, no. 7, pp. 46–7; no. 89, pp. 108–9; *Procès*, vol. II, pp. 350, 381, 395; *Der Untergang des Templer-Ordens*, vol. II, pp. 39–40.

132 *Provins*, no. 64, pp. 90–1.

133 E.-G. Léonard, *Introduction au Cartulaire Manuscrit du Temple (1150–1317) constitué par le Marquis d'Albon*, Paris, 1930, pp. 125–8.

134 See M. Borracelli, 'La Magione Templare di Frosini e l'importanza delle strade che vi convergevano', in *MS*, pp. 311–30, and maps.

135 *Regesto del Capitolo di Lucca*, ed. P. Guidi and O. Parenti, RCI 6, Rome, 1910, no. 925, p. 404.

136 See T. Szabò, 'Templari e viabilità', in *MS*, pp. 297–307.

137 *Cartulario del Temple de Huesca*, no. 82, pp. 83–4. See also no. 167, pp. 179–80 (an exchange); no. 198, pp. 225–6 (a settlement of a dispute). The great increase in land values which irrigation brought made such arrangements particularly desirable, see Forey, *The Templars in the Corona de Aragón*, pp. 240–1.

138 *Cartulario del Temple de Huesca*, no. 10, pp. 15–16; no. 161, pp. 172–3.

139 'Emprunts', ed. Servois, 'Appendice', no. 5, pp. 290–3; *RRH*, no. 1347, pp. 352–3. This does not represent the full extent of the patriarch's requirements, but only those which he expected could be accomplished directly by the Templar bank in Paris. See also above, p. 159

140 Matthew Paris, *Chronica Majora*, vol. V, p. 478, for Henry staying at the Parisian Temple. See R. Cazelles, *Nouvelle histoire de Paris de la fin du règne de Philippe Auguste à la mort de Charles V 1223–1380*, Paris, 1972, plate 9 (top), (between pages 152 and 153). See H. de Curzon, *La Maison du Temple de Paris. Histoire et description*, Paris, 1888, esp. pp. 71–147, where he attempts a reconstruction of the enclosure.

141 For example, see above, p.25.

142 Delisle, *Mémoire*, no. 5, pp. 97–8.

143 *Chartes et documents poitevins du XIIIe siècle en langue vulgaire*, ed. M.S. La Du, vol. II, Archives historiques du Poitou 58, Poitiers, 1963, no. 412, p. 341.

144 *Rotuli Litterarum Patentium*, ed. T.D. Hardy, vol. I(i), London, 1835, pp. 48b, 54b; *Foedera, Conventiones, Literae et Cuiuscunque Generis Acta Publica*, ed.T.Rymer, 3rd edn, vol. I(ii), The Hague, 1745, pp. 65, 84, 120–1. For the use made of the London Temple by the English kings, particularly in the services provided for the Wardrobe and the Exchequer, see A. Sandys, 'The Financial and Administrative Importance of the London Temple in the Thirteenth Century', in *Essays in Medieval History presented to Thomas Frederick Tout*, ed. A.G. Little and F.M. Powicke, Manchester, 1925, pp. 147–62. See also Forey, *The Templars in the Corona de Aragón*,

Appendix I, no. 18, pp. 385–6, for the deposit of jewels by James I of Aragon.

145 Joinville, *Histoire*, pp. 224–7.

146 Delisle, *Mémoire*, no. 8, pp. 99–102. See the analysis in J. Piquet, *Des Banquiers au Moyen Age. Les Templiers. Etude de leurs Opérations financières*, Paris, 1939, pp. 38–45.

147 Delisle, *Mémoire*, pp. 73–86; no. 29, pp. 162–210. See also Piquet, *Des Banquiers*, pp. 119–46.

148 The desk was nevertheless open on a number of feast days which the Rule lays down should be observed by the Templars, *Règle*, cl. 75, pp. 72–3.

149 See above, p. 67.

150 See above, pp. 151–2.

151 'Récit du XIIIe siècle sur les translations faites en 1239 et en 1241 des saints reliques de la Passion', ed. N. de Wailly, *BEC*, 39 (1878), no. 39, 410; Delisle, *Mémoire*, p. 17.

152 *Rotuli Litterarum Clausarum*, ed. T. Hardy, vol. I, London, 1833, p. 148b; *Rotuli Litterarum Patentium*, vol. I(i), pp. 135a, 141a, 152a–153b. For Templar financial activities in England, see T.W. Parker, *The Knights Templars in England*, Tucson, Arizona, 1963, pp. 58–80. See Forey, *The Templars in the Corona de Aragón*, Appendix I, no. 23, pp. 394–5, for a loan contracted by James I of Aragon.

153 Delisle, *Mémoire*, no. 4, pp. 96–7.

154 *Calendar of the Close Rolls. Edward I*, vol. v, 1302–7, pp. 172–3, 343.

155 J.W. Baldwin, *The Government of Philip Augustus. Foundations of French Royal Power in the Middle Ages*, Berkeley and London, 1986, p. 248.

156 Rigord. *Oeuvres de Rigord et de Guillaume le Breton*, ed. H.-F. Delaborde, vol. I, Société de l'Histoire de France, Paris, 1882, pp. 103–4.

157 On Haimard, see Baldwin, *Government of Philip Augustus*, pp. 57, 118–19.

158 See Delisle, *Mémoire*, pp. 61–73.

159 BN, *NAL*, fol. 400; *RRH*, no. 1318, p. 344; Léonard, *Introduction*, p. 114; *Procès*, vol. II, pp. 192, 298.

160 Strayer, *Reign of Philip the Fair*, pp. 144–5.

161 *OR*, pp. 324–5. See Delisle, *Mémoire*, pp. 121–2, for a full list of the *curiales* at this session.

162 Delisle, *Mémoire*, pp. 35, 37; P. Durrieu, *Les Archives angevines de Naples*, vol. I, BEFAR 46, Paris, 1886, p. 97; *Histoire de l'Ile de Chypre*, ed. L. de Mas Latrie, vol. I, Paris, 1852, p. 86.

163 H. de L'Epinois, 'Comptes relatifs à la fondation de l'Abbaye de Maubuisson', *BEC*, 19 (1858), 550–67; Delisle, *Mémoire*, pp. 32–3.

164 See J.M. Powell, *Anatomy of a Crusade 1213–1221*, Philadelphia, 1986, pp. 15–32.

165 See Delisle, *Mémoire*, pp. 21–2, 25.

166 Honorius III. *Regesta Honorii Papae III*, vol. I, no. 2620, p. 435; *Epistolae Saeculi XIII e Regestis Pontificum Romanorum*, ed. C. Rodenberg, vol. I, no. 124, pp. 89–91.

167 See Robinson, *The Papacy*, pp. 257-9. He comments that they fulfilled the same role in the *curia* as the Cluniacs had done under Urban II, Paschal II, and Calixtus II. Initially, however, the Templars in Italy seem to have been uncertain where their loyalties lay. Rahewin lists the Master of the Temple on the Aventine Hill (the Templar preceptory at Rome) and his brothers as among the supporters of Alexander's rival, the anti-pope, Victor IV, in February, 1160, Otto of Freising and Rahewin, *Gesta Friderici I.*, 4.67, p. 482. For the Templar house on the Aventine Hill, see Bramato, *Storia*, pp. 112-14.

168 See above, n. 92. After Bonvicino's death a similar role was filled by William Charnier, Preceptor of the Temple in the Patrimony of St Peter, who was apparently also based at Perugia, Tommasi, 'L'Ordine dei Templari', Appendice 1, no. 7, p. 51. See also M.L. Bulst-Thiele, 'Templer in königlichen und päpstlichen Diensten', in *Festschrift Percy Ernst Schramm*, vol. 1, pp. 303-4.

169 See Delisle, *Mémoire*, pp. 29-30, and illustrative documents, no. 18, pp. 112-13; no. 19, pp. 113-14; no. 20, pp. 114-15; no. 21, pp. 115-16.

170 *Papsttum und Untergang des Templerordens*, vol. II, no. 74, p. 114.

171 See Piquet, *Des Banquiers*, p. 225. For earlier royal charters to the Templars in England, see *Records of the Templars in England in the Twelfth Century*, pp. 137-44. For privileges in England, see T.W. Parker, *The Knights Templars in England*, Tucson, Ariz., 1963, pp. 25-31.

172 Delisle, *Mémoire*, pp. 87-8.

173 See T.P. McLaughlin, 'The Teaching of the Canonists on Usury', *Medieval Studies*, 1 (1939), 81-147; 2 (1940), 1-22.

174 *Foedera*, vol. 1(ii), p. 141.

175 See W.L. Warren, *Henry II*, London, 1973, pp. 72, 90, for their guard of castles in the very sensitive area of the Norman Vexin in 1158-9, following the attempt by Henry II and Louis VII to resolve their long-standing differences.

176 *Rotuli Litterarum Patentium*, vol. 1(i), pp. 119a, 121b.

177 For example, see above, p. 353, n.120; *Catalan Rule*, fols. 49b-51a; 'Un nouveau manuscrit', ed. Delaville Le Roulx, cl. 42, pp. 205-6, for the false seal.

178 *Règle*, cls. 329-331, pp. 190-1.

179 See above, p. 112.

180 Gervase of Canterbury, *The Gesta Regum with its Continuation*, ed. W. Stubbs, RS 73, London, 1880, p. 222. According to the annals of Dunstable, however, the figure was £1,000, 'Annales Prioratus de Dunstaplia', ed. H.R. Luard, *Annales Monastici*, vol. III, RS 36, London, 1866, p. 222. On the circumstances which led to these events, see F.M. Powicke, *King Henry III and the Lord Edward*, Oxford, 1947, pp. 439-40.

181 Walter of Hemingborough, *Chronicon de Gestis Regum Angliae*, ed. H.C. Hamilton, vol. II, English Historical Society 14, London, 1849, pp. 273-4.

182 Bernat Desclot, *Chronicle of the Reign of King Pedro III of Aragon, AD 1276-1285*, tr. F.L. Critchlow, Princeton, 1928, pp. 201-2.

8 THE END OF THE ORDER

1 *Decrees of the Ecumenical Councils*, ed. N.P. Tanner, vol. I, London, 1990, pp. 336-43.

2 For a full study of contemporary perceptions of the Temple, see H.J. Nicholson, *Templars, Hospitallers and Teutonic Knights. Images of the Military Orders, 1128-1291*, Leicester, London, and New York, 1993.

3 James of Vitry, *Historia Hierosolimitana*, vol. I(ii), pp. 1083-4.

4 James of Vitry, *Exempla*, no. 86, p. 39.

5 Wolfram von Eschenbach, *Parzival*, tr. A.T. Hatto, Harmondsworth, 1980, p. 239.

6 See J.A. Brundage, *Law, Sex and Christian Society in Medieval Europe*, Chicago and London, 1987, p. 403 and n. 415.

7 See S. Schein, *Fideles Crucis. The Papacy, the West and the Recovery of the Holy Land 1274-1314*, Oxford, 1991, pp. 74-111.

8 See N. Housley, *The Avignon Papacy and the Crusades 1305-1378*, Oxford, 1986, on the range and diversity of crusading projects in the fourteenth century. The crusade continued to be important to western Christians and, indeed, this helps to explain why the position of the Temple remained an issue of debate.

9 See Forey, 'Military Orders', pp. 317-45, and S. Schein, 'The Templars: The Regular Army of the Holy Land and the Spearhead of the Army of its Reconquest', in *MS*, pp. 15-25. On the position of the Templars and Hospitallers from 1274 onwards, see Housley, *The Later Crusades*, pp. 204-33.

10 *Le Dossier*, pp. 2-15.

11 Molay clearly had no direct experience of the discussions at Lyon, since he apparently believed that the council had been attended by St Louis, who had died in 1270, *Le Dossier*, pp. 2-3.

12 Pope Nicholas IV had in fact told the prelates to hold synods to discuss the question of union, among other relevant issues, Potthast, vol. II, nos. 23781, 23784, 23786, 23787, 23803. On these, see Schein, *Fidelis Crucis*, pp. 75-6, 91-2.

13 J.N. Hillgarth, *Ramon Lull and Lullism in Fourteenth-Century France*, Oxford, 1971, pp. 66-74.

14 Ramon Lull, *Liber de Fine*, ed. A. Madre, *Raimundi Lulli Opera Latina*, Corpus Christianorum. Continuatio Mediaevalis 35, Turnhout, 1981, pp. 270-1.

15 *Papsttum und Untergang des Templeordens*, vol. II, no. 75, p. 118.

16 C.J. Tyerman, 'Sed Nihil Fecit? The Last Capetians and the Recovery of the Holy Land', in *War and Government in the Middle Ages*, ed. J. Gillingham and J.C. Holt, Woodbridge, 1984, p. 170. Some of the theories had practical possibilities, but Molay was well aware how little had actually been achieved.

17 See Housley, *The Avignon Papacy*, p. 3.

18 *Vitae Paparum Avenionensium*, ed. E. Baluze, new edn. G. Mollat, vol. III, Paris, 1927, no. 32, pp. 145-9.
19 See above, p. 294.
20 See above, pp. 120-2.
21 See above, pp. 293-4.
22 *OR*, p. 319. There is no mention of Theobald Gaudin after 1291, while the first definite reference to Molay as Master is 8 December 1293, *Calendar of the Close Rolls, Edward I.*, vol. III, AD 1288-96, p. 339. The Templar of Tyre says that he succeeded Theobald Gaudin, *Gestes des Chiprois*, p. 329. For Molay's life, see M.C. Barber, 'James of Molay, the Last Grand Master of the Temple', *Studia Monastica*, 14 (1972), 91-124; Bulst-Thiele, *Magistri*, pp. 295-359; and J. Fried, 'Wille, Freiwilligkeit und Geständnis um 1300. Zur Beurteilung des letzten Templergrossmeisters Jacques de Molay', *Historisches Jahrbuch*, 105 (1985), 388-425.
23 *Procès*, vol. II, p. 139.
24 *Procès*, vol. II, pp. 224-5, 290, 207-8. On the election, see above, pp. 186-7.
25 *Gestes des Chiprois*, pp. 329-30.
26 Amadi, *Chroniques*, pp. 280-1. This is an anonymous Italian translation of a lost French source.
27 See above, p. 172.
28 *Histoire de l'Ile de Chypre*, ed. Mas Latrie, vol. II(i), pp. 108-9, which consists of summary of instructions by the king to his envoy in Rome outlining the history of the Order's opposition to him. It is undated, but Mas Latrie places it before May 1306, since the attack of Amaury of Lusignan is not mentioned. It could in fact relate to any period of Henry's reign up to that date.
29 Boniface VIII. *Les Registres de Boniface VIII*, ed. G. Digard, vol. II, BEFAR, ser. 2, Paris, 1884, no. 2348, pp. 37-9; no. 2439, pp. 38-9 (1298).
30 Florio Bustron, *Chronique*, pp. 137-8; Amadi, *Chroniques*, p. 248. On these events, see P. W. Edbury, *The Kingdom of Cyprus and the Crusades, 1191-1374*, Cambridge, 1991, pp. 109-31.
31 'Allocution au Roi Henri II de Lusignan', ed. L. de Mas Latrie, *Revue des Questions Historiques*, 43 (1888), 524-41.
32 Pierre Dubois, *De Recuperatione Terre Sancte*, ed. C.V. Langlois, Collection de Textes pour servir à l'étude et à l'enseignement de l'histoire, Paris, 1891, pp. 13-14. See Barber, *Trial*, pp. 15-16.
33 *Procès*, vol. II, p. 139. See also above, p. 234.
34 *Der Untergang des Templer-Ordens*, vol. II, pp. 166-218. See Barber, 'Supplying the Crusader States', pp. 320-1.
35 *Acta Aragonensia*, vol. I, Berlin, 1908, no. 17, pp. 26-7.
36 *Ibid.*, vol. III, no. 18, pp. 31-2.
37 Molay's letter to James II is the one fixed point in this visit. The letter to Peter of St Just is dated only by the day of the month. Evidence that he went to Paris and London comes from Templar witnesses at the trial, but their memories may not have been entirely accurate. They range from John

of Stoke, who said that he saw him in England in 1294, to Peter of St Just, Preceptor of Correus in Picardy (not the same man to whom Molay wrote in 1294), who said that he had been received by Molay in the Templar chapel in Paris on the Feast of St John the Baptist, ten years before the trial, i.e. 1297. He was probably correct about the feast, since the Parisian Templars were accustomed to hold a key chapter meeting at this time of year, which Molay would almost certainly have attended had he been in the west, but the preceptor may have been mistaken about the year. *Conciliae Magnae Britanniae*, vol. II, pp. 387–8; *Procès*, vol. I, p. 475. See also *Der Untergang des Templer-Ordens*, vol. II, p. 192.

38 Boniface VIII. *Les Registres de Boniface VIII*, ed. A. Thomas, vol. I, Paris, 1884, no. 487, pp. 169–70. This was to last until such time as the Holy Land had been recovered.

39 *Histoire de l'Ile de Chypre*, ed. Mas Latrie, vol. II(i), pp. 91–2; L. de Mas Latrie, 'Rapport sur le recueil des archives de Venise intitulé "Libri pactorum", ou "Patti"', *Archives des Missions Scientifiques*, 2 (1851), 365.

40 Mas Latrie, *Histoire de l'Ile de Chypre*, vol. II,(i), pp. 97–8.

41 Boniface VIII. *Les Registres de Boniface VIII*, vol. I, no. 489, p. 170. See also letters to the Kings of Sicily and France, and the King of the Romans.

42 *Calendar of the Close Rolls, Edward I.*, vol. III, AD 1288–96, p. 511.

43 Bulst-Thiele, *Magistri*, Anhang I, no. 8, pp. 366–7; *Calendar of the Close Rolls, Edward I.*, vol. I, AD 1302–7, pp. 137–8. The importance that Molay attached to Edward I's support can be seen in his anxiety to keep the king informed of developments in the east, see also William Rishanger, *Chronica monasterii S. Albani*, ed. H.T. Riley, RS 28, London, 1865, pp. 400–1 (1299), and Bulst-Thiele, *Magistri*, Anhang I, no. 7, p. 366 (1301).

44 James Doria, 'Annales Ianuenses', in *Annali genovesi de Caffaro e dei suoi continuatiori*, ed. C. Imperiale de Sant'Angelo, vol. V, Rome, 1929, p. 167. See also Schein, *Fidelis Crucis*, p. 82.

45 Amadi, *Chroniques*, pp. 236–7; *Gestes des Chiprois*, pp. 303–5.

46 'Actes passés à Famagouste de 1299 à 1301 par devant le notaire génois Lamberto di Sambuceto', ed. C. Desimoni, in *AOL*, vol. II(ii), no. 74, Paris, 1884, pp. 42–3. See Richard, 'The Eastern Mediterranean', p. 36, n. 109.

47 Amadi, *Chroniques*, pp. 237–8; *Gestes des Chiprois*, pp. 305–6; Marino Sanudo, *Liber secretorum fidelium crucis*, in *Gesta Dei per Francos*, ed. J. Bongars, vol. II, p. 242; Florio Bustron, *Chronique*, p. 132. Molay took the potential alliance with the Mongols very seriously for he made efforts to raise additional funds from the western houses to finance the expedition, *Acta Aragonensia*, vol. I, no. 55, pp. 78–9. For a short while the plan excited widespread enthusiasm in the west, see Housley, *The Later Crusades*, p. 23.

48 Amadi, *Chroniques*, pp. 238–9; Florio Bustron, *Chronique*, p. 133; *Gestes des Chiprois*, pp. 309–10, giving 1303 as the year that Ruad was lost. In 1301 Molay had explained to James II of Aragon how he had garrisoned Ruad in

anticipation of the arrival of the Mongols, *Papsttum und Untergang des Templerordens*, vol. II, no. 3, pp. 3–4.

49 Amadi, *Chroniques*, p. 238; Florio Bustron, *Chronique*, p. 134.

50 See S. Schein, 'The Future *Regnum Hierusalem*. A Chapter in Medieval State Planning', *JMH*, 10 (1984), 95–105.

51 *Vitae Paparum Avenionensium*, vol. III, pp. 161–2. Dubois then purported to believe that the apostasy and hypocrisy of the Order had been obvious from the beginning. See Pierre Dubois, *The Recovery of the Holy Land*, tr. W.I. Brandt, Records of Civilization. Sources and Studies 51, New York, 1956, pp. 6–8. Brandt dates the treatise as a whole to 1306, giving the death of Edward I on 7 July 1307, as the terminal date. The section on abolition is an addition to this and the reference to the Order's apostasy suggests strongly that it was written very soon after the arrests in October, probably in early 1308.

52 The pope claimed that he had discovered the matter at the time of his coronation at Lyon in November 1305, but the issue does not seem to have been high on the French agenda until the spring of 1307, see Barber, *Trial*, pp. 48, 73.

53 See J.R. Strayer, 'France: The Holy Land, the Chosen People, and the Most Christian King', in *Medieval Statecraft and the Perspectives of History. Essays by Joseph R. Strayer*, ed. J.F. Benton and T.N. Bisson, Princeton, New Jersey, 1971, pp. 300–14.

54 Delisle, *Mémoire*, pp. 53–5, and no. 27, pp. 133–60.

55 Even before the wars, royal demesne income was rising, as the figures for the period 1286 to 1290 show. From 1292 Philip IV made strenuous efforts to increase all forms of royal income. See Strayer, *Reign of Philip the Fair*, p. 143 and n. 4, pp. 148–9.

56 Strayer, *Reign of Philip the Fair*, p. 174, is puzzled by this decision, which he thinks came at a bad time, given the acute problems arising from relations with Flanders and the papacy during 1303. But he himself offers a reasonable answer: 'One can only conclude that Philip did not think that he was making a drastic change.' Similarly, perhaps, the establishment of the Louvre treasury in 1295 was not such a major change as it has sometimes been portrayed.

57 For example, G. Mollat, *The Popes at Avignon 1305–1378*, tr. J. Love, London, 1963, pp. 232–3.

58 Delisle, *Mémoire*, pp. 56–8. See, for example, no. 33, pp. 226–7, covering the period January 1305 to November 1306.

59 H. Prutz, *Entwicklung und Untergang des Tempelherrenordens*, Berlin, 1888, no. 3, p. 297, for Louis' confirmation; nos. 10–13, pp. 302–3, for Philip IV's acts. *Lettres inédites de Philippe Le Bel*, ed. A. Baudouin, Mémoires de l'Académie des Sciences, Inscriptions et Belles-Lettres de Toulouse, ser. 8, 8, Toulouse, 1886, no. 184, pp. 211–13, for the prohibition on *mainmorte*.

60 See, for example, Edward I's legislation on this subject in England in the

Statute of Mortmain (1279). On its implications, see P. Heath, *Church and Realm 1272–1461*, London, 1988, pp. 36–9.

61 Prutz, *Entwicklung*, no. 21, pp. 307–8.

62 See H.C. Lea, *A History of the Inquisition of the Middle Ages*, vol. III, New York, 1889, pp. 248–9.

63 See Barber, *Trial*, p. 54, and 'Supplying the Crusader States', pp. 320–1,on the age structure of the Templars in France.

64 *Ordonnances des Roys de France de la troisième race*, ed. E. de Laurière, vol. I, Paris, 1723, pp. 595–7.

65 *Le Dossier*, pp. 114–15.

66 See Barber, *Trial*, pp. 38–9.

67 See, for example, Giovanni Villani and Guglielmo Ventura di Asti.

68 Dante, *Purgatorio*, Canto 20, lines 91–3.

69 See E.A.R. Brown, 'The Prince is Father of the King: The Character and Childhood of Philip the Fair of France', *Medieval Studies*, 49 (1987), 282–334.

70 See A. Rigault, *Le Procès de Guichard, Evêque de Troyes (1308–13)*, Paris, 1896.

71 W.C. Jordan, *The French Monarchy and the Jews. From Philip Augustus to the Last Capetians*, Philadelphia, 1989, pp. 191–4, 209–12.

72 R.-H. Bautier, 'Diplomatique et histoire politique: ce que la critique diplomatique nous apprend sur la personnalité de Philippe le Bel', *Revue historique*, 259 (1978), p. 27.

73 See Jordan, *Louis XI*, pp. 3–13, 220.

74 Adam of Murimouth, *Continuatio Chronicarum*, ed. E.M. Thompson, RS 93, London, 1889, pp. 16–17; *Papsttum und Untergang des Templerordens*, vol. II, no. 34, p. 51. See Hillgarth, *Ramon Lull*, pp. 94–5, and N. Cohn, *Europe's Inner Demons*, London, 1976, pp. 81–2.

75 Adam of Murimouth was, however, writing after the event with what appears to be a generalised knowledge only, since the Templars were not condemned by the pope, but suppressed, and James of Molay was not executed until 1314, after it had already been decided to transfer the goods to the Hospital.

76 *Papsttum und Untergang des Templerordens*, vol. II, no. 75, p. 118; no. 101, p. 183.

77 See Barber, *Trial*, pp. 45–71.

78 *Procès*, vol. II, pp. 315–16.

79 Delisle, *Mémoire*, p. 72 and n. 2.

80 See above, p. 267.

81 *Procès*, vol. I, pp. 353, 589.

82 *Procès*, vol. I, p. 598, according to his own witness. He also received a Templar in the main chapel at Paris in about 1294, *Procès*, vol. I, p. 597. See *Der Untergang des Templer-Ordens*, vol. II, p. 35, for the witness of John of Foligny, who says that it took place in the oratory of the chapel which he describes as 'a secret place'.

83 See Strayer, *Reign of Philip the Fair*, pp. 174-5.

84 *Chronique Latine de Guillaume de Nangis de 1113 à 1300 avec les continuations de cette chronique de 1300 à 1368*, ed. H. Géraud, vol, I, Société de l'Histoire de France, Paris, 1843, p. 381.

85 The case of John of Tour is only one of many in the trial which demonstrate the truism that an unsupported confession never provides a solid basis for conviction, even when not the product of excruciating tortures, verbal intimidation, and harsh imprisonment.

86 See, for example, the fitful progress of the trial in Aragon, A.J. Forey, 'The Beginnings of the Proceedings against the Aragonese Templars', in *God and Man in Medieval Spain. Essays in Honour of J.R.L. Highfield*, ed. D.W. Lomax and D. Mackenzie, Warminster, 1989, pp. 81-96.

87 See R. Hill, 'Fourpenny Retirement: The Yorkshire Templars in the Fourteenth Century', in *Studies in Church History*, 24 (1987), pp. 123-8. Pope John XXII found the problem particularly vexatious, and as late as 1324 he withdrew pensions from ex-Templars living as laymen in Castile, León, and Portugal, see Mollat, *Comptes Rendus*, pp. 376-80.

88 *Procès*, vol. II., pp. 421-515; L. Ménard, *Histoire civile, ecclésiastique et littéraire de la ville de Nismes*, vol. I, Paris, 1750, *preuves*, no. 136, pp. 166-95.

89 *Le Procès des Templiers d'Auvergne (1390-11)*, ed. Sève and Chagny-Sève.

90 *Ibid.*, pp. 50-1.

91 For example, Prutz, *Entwicklung*, p. 231.

92 *The Trial of the Templars in the Papal State and the Abruzzi*, p. 133.

93 *Le Procès des Templiers d'Auvergne (1309-11)*, pp. 150-2.

94 Joinville, *Histoire*, pp. 24-5.

95 Rainerius Sacconi, *Summa de Catharis et Pauperibus de Lugduno*, in *Un Traité néo-manichéen du XIIIe siècle: Le Liber de duobus principiis, suivi d'un fragment de rituel cathare*, ed. A. Dondaine, Rome, 1939, p. 64. Rainier was a former Cathar, who had entered the Dominican Order. He was inquisitor in Lombardy between 1254 and 1259.

96 *Le Procès des Templiers d'Auvergne (1309-11)*, p. 116.

97 *Ibid.*, pp. 65-6; *Procès*, vol. I, pp. 58-9, 126.

98 See Barber, *Trial*, p. 161.

99 *Le Procès des Templiers d'Auvergne (1309-11)*, pp. 70-1.

100 Mollat, 'Dispersion définitive des Templiers', 377-8.

101 See the Hospitaller extent of that year, *The Knights Hospitallers in England*, ed. L.B. Larking and J.M. Kemble, Camden Society, old series 65, London, 1857, pp. 212-13.

102 Hillgarth, *Ramon Lull*, pp. 98-113.

103 See N. Housley, 'Clement V and the Crusades of 1309-10', *JMH*, 7 (1982), 29-43.

104 *Le Dossier*, p. 200.

105 See A. Luttrell, 'Gli Ospitalieri e l'eredità dei Templari', in *MS*, pp. 76-8.

106 *Papsttum und Untergang des Templerordens*, vol. II, no. 116, p. 220. In fact,

rich as the Templar lands were, the actual transfer initially caused great problems for the Hospital. See, for example, the situation in Essex, *The Cartulary of the Knights of St John of Jerusalem in England. Secunda Camera. Essex*, ed. M. Gervers, Records of Social and Economic History, new series 6, Oxford, 1982, pp. xlvii–xlix.

107 See Housley, *The Avignon Papacy*, pp. 267–81, and W. Urban, *The Livonian Crusade*, Washington, 1981, pp. 29–62. Housley, *The Later Crusades*, pp. 326–7, points to the disputes within the Teutonic Order concerning overall aims, but suggests that the trial of the Templars helped to clarify the knights' intentions by demonstrating the vulnerability of the Grand Master at Venice, and thus hastening the move to Marienburg.

108 Hiestand, 'Problem', 17–38.

109 *Gestes des Chiprois*, p. 253.

110 Hiestand, 'Problem', 19, 35–6.

111 On the 1152 document, see above, p. 350, n.59.

112 This idea has more in common with the modern habit of shredding documents to foil an advancing enemy or a police raid than with the attitudes which prevailed inside a medieval monastic order.

113 Hiestand, 'Problem', 23–25.

9 FROM MOLAY'S CURSE TO *FOUCAULT'S PENDULUM*

1 See Y. Renouard, 'L'Ordre de la Jarretière et l'Ordre de l'Etoile', *Le Moyen Age*, 55 (1949), 281–300, and M. Keen, *Chivalry*, New Haven and London, 1984, pp. 179–99, on the differences between the military orders and the new secular knighthoods. Renouard thinks that one of the reasons for the foundation of the latter was in reaction to the failures of the military orders.

2 Ferretto of Vicenza, 'Historia rerum in Italia gestarum ab anno 1250 ad annum usque 1318', in RIS, vol. IX, pp. 1017–18. Ferretto wrote *c*. 1328. See Lea, vol. III, pp. 326–7, for the various versions of this.

3 Felix Fabri. *The Book of the Wanderings of Brother Felix Fabri (c. 1480–83)*, tr. A. Stewart, vol. II, Palestine Pilgrims' Text Society 9, London, 1893, pp. 320–1.

4 T. Fuller, *The History of the Holy War*, London, 1840, p. 71 (originally 1639). See also pp. 92, 191, 271–3, 242–7.

5 E. Gibbon, *The History of the Decline and Fall of the Roman Empire*, vol. VII, ed. F. Fernández-Armesto, London, 1990, p. 304 (originally 1788).

6 Runciman, *History of the Crusades*, vol. III, pp. 435–6.

7 See P. Partner, *The Murdered Magicians. The Templars and their Myth*, Oxford, 1981, pp. 90–7. and A. Wilderman, *Die Beurteilung des Templerprozesses bis zum 17. Jahrhundert*, Freiburg, 1971, on attitudes towards the Templars at this period. Wildermann provides a systematic analysis of all the important writers, arranged by country, from the time of the trial down to Pierre Dupuy.

8 *Histoire de l'Ordre Militaire des Templiers ou Chevaliers du Temple de Jérusalem*, ed. P. Dupuy, Brussels, 1751 (originally published 1654, three years after Dupuy's death); *Vitae Paparum Avenionensium*, originally two vols., Paris, 1693.

9 On Ramsay, see J.M. Roberts, *The Mythology of the Secret Societies*, London, 1972, pp. 35–8, and Partner, *The Murdered Magicians*, pp. 103–6. For the most comprehensive explanation of these developments, see R. Le Forestier *La Franc-Maçonnerie templière et occultiste au XVIIIe et XIXe siècles*, ed. A. Faivre, Paris, 1970.

10 Partner, *The Murdered Magicians*, pp. 110–14, traces the invention of the Templar connection to Germany, c. 1760.

11 C.L. Cadet de Gassicour, *Le Tombeau de Jacques Molai*, Paris, 1796, esp. pp. 10–11, where Templars, disguised as masons, collect Molay's ashes, before setting up four lodges dedicated to vengeance on the race of the kings of France and the pope. See A.A. Mola, 'Il Templarismo nella Massoneria fra Otto e Novecento', in *MS*, p. 266.

12 A. Barruel, *Mémoires pour servir à l'histoire du Jacobinisme*, vol. I, Vouillé, 1973, pp. 456–77 (originally 4 vols., 1797–8). See Roberts, *Mythology*, pp. 188–202, and Partner, *The Murdered Magicians*, pp. 131–3. A later manifestation can be found in the works of the French bishop, Mgr Besson, who, while making the usual clerical denunciation of Freemasonry, ascribed its origins to the Templars, adepts of a Satanist cult, *Oeuvres pastorales*, vol. I, Paris, 1879, p. 217.

13 J. von Hammer-Purgstall, 'Mysterium Baphometis revelatum', *Fundgruben des Orients*, 6 (1818), 1–120, 445–99. Hammer's views, however, were not accepted without challenge, even in his own day, see F.J.M. Raynouard, 'Etude sur "Mysterium Baphometi revelatum"', *Journal des Savants* (1819), 151–61, 221–9.

14 J. Loiseleur, *La Doctrine Secrète des Templiers*, Paris and Orléans, 1872, especially pp. 43–8, 140–8, for his overall conclusions.

15 See M.C. Barber, 'Lepers, Jews and Moslems: The Plot to Overthrow Christendom in 1321', *History*, 66 (1981), 1–17, and R.E. Lerner, *The Heresy of the Free Spirit*, Berkeley and London, 1972.

16 Roberts, *Mythology*, p. 2.

17 Sir Walter Scott, *Ivanhoe. A Romance*, 1819.

18 See, for example, J.E. Duncan, 'The Anti-Romantic in *Ivanhoe*', in *Walter Scott. Modern Judgements*, ed. D.D. Devlin, London, 1968, pp. 142–7.

19 Sir Walter Scott, *The Talisman*, 1825.

20 I. Wilson, *The Turin Shroud*, Harmondsworth, 1979 (revised edn of 1978 publication), pp. 193–237. See M.C. Barber, 'The Templars and the Turin Shroud', *The Catholic Historical Review*, 68 (1982), 206–25. Another book of this genre that has received widespread attention is M. Baignent, R. Leigh, and H. Lincoln, *The Holy Blood and the Holy Grail*, London, 1976. For example, p. 34: 'it was with the Templars that our inquiries began to yield concrete documentation and the mystery began to assume far greater proportions than we had ever imagined'.

21 U. Eco, *Foucault's Pendulum*, London, 1989 © English translation Harcourt Brace Jovanovich. Quotations from pp. 261–2, 452–3, 49, 375, 467, 619, 94, 67.

BIBLIOGRAPHICAL ORIENTATION

There is no central core of documents upon which a study of the Templars can be based, primarily because of the loss of the main archive of the Order in the east. This archive was probably destroyed when the Ottoman Turks took Cyprus in 1571. The definitive analysis of this subject is that of Rudolf Hiestand (*Archivalische Zeitschrift*, 1980). Information on the Templars' activities in the Levant must therefore largely be derived from charters collected by other institutions which had dealings with the Templars, particularly ecclesiastical bodies like the Hospitallers and the canons of the Holy Sepulchre, and the Italian trading communities; from limited references in legal texts; and from the accounts of chroniclers and visiting crusaders and pilgrims. The only document emanating from the Order itself which provides substantial evidence is the Rule, particularly in the form of its several extensions in French in the twelfth and thirteenth centuries.

Among the chroniclers of the Latin east two stand out as sources from Templar history: William of Tyre and the 'Templar of Tyre'. William's history of the Kingdom of Jerusalem up to 1184 provides vital information about the Templar role and the environment within which the Order operated. However, the archbishop's bias against the mature Order together with his powerful presentation of its history within a preformed structure of its rise and fall mean that a conscious effort of will is needed to avoid, on the one hand, total acceptance of his views or, on the other, too extreme a reaction against them. In the thirteenth century there are many references to the Templars in the compilation known as the *Gestes des Chiprois*, but the most useful is the section apparently composed by one of the Order's paid administrators (perhaps secretary to the Grand Master, William of Beaujeu) known as the 'Templar of Tyre', covering the crucial years between 1249 and 1309. This includes material ranging from the Templars' role in the many political conflicts in the east during this period to a valuable description of the Order's thirteenth-century head-quarters in Acre. In addition, most visitors to the east who set down their impressions include references to the Templars, not only because the Order's prominence in eastern affairs was so obvious to them, but also in some cases because the Templars seem to have made efforts to impress them for propaganda purposes. There is substantial material in the accounts of John of Würzburg,

394

Theoderich, Oliver of Paderborn, and John of Joinville, as well as the anonymous member of the entourage of the Bishop of Marseille who wrote up the role of the bishop in stimulating the rebuilding of Safad from 1240. Muslim sources are of more limited value, for it is evident that the crusades occupy a much less important place in the history of Islam than they do in the Christian heritage; nevertheless, the dramatic and colourful language of a writer such as 'Imâd-ad-Din does provide an important insight into the way that the Order was regarded by its religious opponents.

The Rule, originally granted to the Order at the Council of Troyes in 1129 in the form of 72 clauses in Latin, had expanded to 686 clauses by c. 1267, written in French to facilitate understanding among brethren with only limited Latin. Military and disciplinary needs made such additions necessary since the Latin Rule was more strongly influenced by the cloister than the battlefield. Sections on the military hierarchy, the conduct of conventual life, chapter-meetings, and the application of a complex system of penances were added in the period before 1187, probably between the 1140s and the early 1160s, although not all the new sections are likely to have been contemporaneous. Further explanation of the penance system enlarged the Rule still more in the middle of the thirteenth century. In using accounts of actual incidents from Templar history to demonstrate his points, the author of this last section provides information about Templar activities not found elsewhere. Even later is a section of the Rule in Catalan, which incorporates a unique account of the loss of Baghras in 1268.

Documentation of the Templars' role in the west is more abundant, although it remains diffuse. Valuable cartularies have been published for specific houses such as Provins, Richerenches, Douzens, and Huesca among others, while some idea of the administration of a province and the complex of lands and rights which this encompassed can be gained from the inquest ordered by the Master of the Temple in England in 1185. Moreover, the obituary roll kept by the preceptory at Reims reveals a much fuller picture of the house's relationship to the local community than might at first sight appear to be likely, as well as giving the day of death of most of the Grand Masters. The attempt by the Marquis d'Albon to compile a general collection of Templar charters and bulls was cut short by his premature death, but he did publish a substantial volume for the period up to 1150, while the remains of his collection, together with his letters and notes, are deposited in the Bibliothèque Nationale. The chief value of these documents is for the study of the Order's houses in France, as can be seen in the list and analysis published by E.-G. Léonard in 1930. At the end of his volume D'Albon also collected together the important papal bulls relevant to the Order, but this has now been superseded by the two volumes edited by Rudolf Hiestand which appeared in 1972 and 1984.

Even in the west, however, there are serious gaps in the Templar record: little is known of Templar shipping, surely more important in the thirteenth century than the sources indicate, while the Order's financial system is insufficiently documented. In the case of the latter, the pioneering work of Léopold Delisle published in 1889 has been the foundation of subsequent research. Not only did he analyse the basic elements of Templar banking, but he also published

documents of fundamental importance. Nevertheless, one of these documents –
the surviving folios of the *Journal du Trésor* of 1295–6 – demonstrates the
problems involved. Here, there appears a tantalising glimpse of the Templar
bank at Paris fulfilling its daily functions, but the period covered is less than
seventeen months.

Strong opinions about the Order were not of course confined to those who
either lived in or visited the crusader states. Bernard of Clairvaux's treatise, *De
laude novae militiae*, remains the most famous and dramatic characterisation of
the Order and set the standard by which its member would be judged. However,
many western writers, both among St Bernard's contemporaries and afterwards,
were anxious to give their opinions of the Templars' performance, albeit in
more piecemeal and prosaic terms. The best-known of these – and the one which
has had the greatest influence on later historians – is Matthew Paris. Although
his prejudices were honed by informants who were often hostile to the Templars,
he is nevertheless valuable not only as a reflection of an aspect of public opinion,
but also because he incorporated much information about events in the east,
including letters from the leaders at the front-line. In addition to references by
chroniclers, from the time of the Council of Lyon in 1274 debate was stimulated
about the nature and aims of the crusades, which inevitably involved reconsider-
ation of the role of the military orders. The views of Fidenzio of Padua, Ramon
Lull, Charles II of Anjou, Pierre Dubois, and the Templar Master, James of
Molay, all incorporate opinions about the Temple, as do the reports solicited by
Pope Nicholas IV from the clergy in 1291. Much of the debate revolved around
the question of whether a union of the Temple and the Hospital would benefit
the crusade.

Sources for the trial are substantial, partly because its proceedings were
recorded by efficient notaries, who have left a mass of depositions, and partly
because the matter excited so much controversy that it produced many bulls,
letters, ambassadors' reports, and chronicle references. The main body of
depositions for the proceedings in Paris can be found in the two volumes
published by Jules Michelet in 1841, which incorporated the records of the initial
proceedings in Paris in October and November 1307, and of the papal commission investigating the Order as a whole, which sat between 1309 and 1311, as
well as those of the episcopal inquiry in Roussillon in 1310. Materials for the
study of the papal inquiry in Poitiers in 1308, the proceedings in Brindisi, the
Papal State, and Cyprus in 1310, and an undated report of the English inquiry,
apparently intended for the Council of Vienne, were published by Konrad
Schottmüller in the second volume of his study of the Templars' fall (1887).
More recently, important new materials have been published for the proceedings
in the Auvergne by Roger Sève and Anne-Marie Chagny-Sève (1987) and in the
Papal State and the Abruzzi by Anne Gilmour-Bryson (1982). Equally valuable
are the reports on the trial by the Aragonese ambassadors, which are among the
fundamental collection of documents assembled by Heinrich Finke (1907). The
trial culminated in the suppression of the Temple at Vienne (1311–12), the

documents for which are now available in English translation edited by Norman Tanner (1990). Most convenient is the representative collection of trial documents assembled by George Lizerand (1923).

Written sources remain the basis for any reconstruction of Templar history, but they can be supplemented by illustrations and material remains. For instance, the Temple compound at Paris no longer exists but an idea of its appearance and plan can be gained from engravings made in the eighteenth century, or later copies of these engravings now in the Cabinet des Estampes of the Bibliothèque Nationale. Time and new wars have had their effects upon many of the eastern castles: 'Atlīt, largely dismantled by the Mamluks, is now an Israeli naval base, the ruins of Safad are buried beneath a public park, Beaufort has suffered from the effects of recent regional conflicts, while Baghras has been undermined by a combination of earthquakes and neglect. In the west the Temple Church in London was fire-bombed in 1941, which caused considerable damage to the effigies on the floor beneath. Even so, significant remains of castles and churches do survive. In Iberia, for example, the Temple church at Segovia is still impressive despite the alteration in its appearance caused by the addition of a later tower, while there are important castle remains at Miravet, Peñíscola, Almourol, and Tomar, among others. Two churches at Cressac (Charente) and San Bevignate, Perugia (Umbria), although fairly plain architecturally, contain impressive schemes of fresco decoration. Judging by the faded remnants of fresco in the church at the small preceptory at Montsaunès (Haute-Garonne), programmes of this kind may well have been more common in Templar churches than is now apparent. Such decoration can offer important insights into the Templar self-image.

These uneven sources have produced a vast secondary literature. Some idea of its scope can be obtained from the two standard bibliographies by M. Dessubré (Paris, 1928) and Heinrich Neu (Bonn, 1965). However, the subject has moved on since the Neu's publication. There are good general surveys by Marie Luise Bulst-Thiele, *Sacrae Domus Militiae Templi Hierosolymitani Magistri* (1974), and Alain Demurger, *Vie et mort de l'ordre du Temple* (1985), and a concise and analytical introduction to the history of the military orders by Alan Forey, *The Military Orders* (1992). The strange 'afterhistory' of the Order has been surveyed by Peter Partner in *The Murdered Magicians* (1980). Studies of particular regions within the Templar 'empire' offer scope for an interesting variety of approaches: two quite different but equally effective examples are Alan Forey's detailed investigation of the Templars in Aragon (1973) and the examination of the history and art of the Templar church of San Bevignate at Perugia by Mario Roncetti, Pietro Scarpellini, and Francesco Tommasi in *Templari et Ospitalieri in Italia* (1987). Excellent use of Templar sources has also been made to elucidate specific aspects of the subject in recent periodical literature. See, for instance, Joshua Prawer's attempt to chart the changes in public attitudes towards the military orders in the second half of the thirteenth century, 'Military Orders and Crusader Politics' (1980), the study of the castle of La Fève through a combination of written sources and field survey by Benjamin Kedar and Denys Pringle (1985), the overturning of the conventional wisdom on the dating of the Council of Troyes by Rudolf Hiestand, 'Kardinalbischof Matthäus von Albano' (1988), and the use of the Rule as a source for Templar military practices by Matthew Bennett (1989). Finally, an idea of the lines of research currently being pursued can be obtained from the published proceedings of the international conference held on the Templars at Poggibonsi-Siena in 1987, which have been edited by Giovanni Minnucci and Franca Sardi (1989).

LIST OF REFERENCES

SOURCES

Abu'l Feda, 'Annales', in *RHCr. Historiens Orientaux*, vol. I

Abu Shāmā, 'Le Livre des Deux Jardins', in *RHCr. Historiens Orientaux*, vols. IV, V

Acta Aragonensia, ed. H. Finke, 3 vols., Berlin and Leipzig, 1908–22

Acta imperii inedita, ed. E. Winkelman, vol. I, Innsbruck, 1880

'Actes passés à Famagouste de 1229 à 1301 par devant le notaire génois Lamberto di Sambuceto', ed. C. Desimoni, in *AOL*, vol. II(ii), Paris, 1884

'Actes passés en 1271, 1274 et 1279 à l'Aïas (Petite Arménie) et à Beyrouth par devant des notaires genois', ed. C. Desimoni, in *AOL*, vol. I, Paris, 1881

Adam of Murimouth, *Continuatio Chronicarum*, ed. E.M. Thompson, RS 93, London, 1889

Alberic of Trois Fontaines, 'Chronica a monacho novi monasterii Hoiensis interpolata', ed. P. Scheffer-Boichorst, in *MGH SS*, vol. XXIII

Albert of Aix, 'Historia Hierosolymitana', in *RHCr. Occidentaux*, vol. IV

'Allocution au Roi Henri II de Lusignan', ed. L. de Mas Latrie, *Revue des Questions Historiques*, 43 (1888)

Amadi. *Chroniques d'Amadi et de Strambaldi*, ed. R. de Mas Latrie, vol. I, Collection de documents inédits sur l'histoire de France, Paris, 1891

Ambroise. *L'Estoire de la Guerre Sainte par Ambroise*, ed. G. Paris, Collection de documents inédits sur l'histoire de France, Paris, 1871

The Anglo-Saxon Chronicle, tr. D.W. Whitelock, London, 1961

'Annales Herbipolenses', ed. G. Pertz, in *MGH SS*, vol. XVI

'Annales Monasterii de Burton 1004–1263', ed. H.R. Luard, *Annales Monastici*, vol. I, RS 36, London, 1864

'Annales Prioratus de Dunstaplia', ed. H.R. Luard, *Annales Monastici*, vol. III, RS 36, London, 1866

'Anonymous Pilgrim V.2', tr. A. Stewart, *Anonymous Pilgrims (11th and 12th Centuries)*, Palestine Pilgrims' Text Society 6, London, 1894

Anselme de Havelberg, *Dialogues*, ed. and tr. G. Salet, vol. I, Sources Chrétiennes 118, Paris, 1966

Arab Historians of the Crusades, ed. and tr. F. Gabrieli, Eng. tr. E.J. Costello, London, 1969

'Assises de la Cour des Bourgeois', in *RHCr. Lois*, vol. II

'Assises de la Haute Cour', in *RHCr. Lois*, vol. I

Les Assises de Romanie, ed. G. Recoura, Bibliothèque de l'Ecole des Hautes Etudes, Paris, 1930

Gli Atti Perduti della Cancelleria Angioina, ed. C. de Lellis, vol. I(i), *RCI* 25, Rome, 1939

Bartholomew of Neocastro, *Historia sicula*, ed. G. Paladino, in *RIS*, vol. XIII(iii)

Beha ed-Din, *Life of Saladin*, tr. C.R. Conder, Palestine Pilgrims' Text Society 13, London, 1897 (reprint 1971)

Benjamin of Tudela, *Itinerary*, tr. and ed. M.N. Adler, London, 1907

Bernard of Clairvaux, 'Apologia ad Guillelmum Abbatem', in *S. Bernardi Opera*, vol. III, *Tractatus et opuscula*, ed. J. Leclercq and H.M. Rochais, Rome, 1963

'Liber ad milites Templi de laude novae militiae', in *S. Bernardi Opera*, vol. III

Epistolae, in *Sancti Bernardi Opera*, vols. VII, VIII, Rome, 1974–7.

'In Praise of the New Knighthood', in *The Works of Bernard of Clairvaux*, vol. VII, *Treatises*, 3, tr. C. Greenia, intr. R.J.Z. Werblowsky, Cistercian Fathers Series 19, Kalamazoo, Mich., 1977

Bernat Desclot, *Chronicle of the Reign of King Pedro III of Aragon, AD 1276–1285*, tr. F.L. Critchlow, Princeton, 1928

Bibliothèque Nationale, *Manuscrits Latin 14679*

Moreau 871, Cartulaire de l'Abbaye de Rosières

Nouvelles Acquisitions Latines, 2, 3, 37, 38, 46, 59, 70

Boniface VIII. *Les Registres de Boniface VIII*, ed. A. Thomas vols. I, II, BEFAR ser. 2, Paris, 1884

'Bulles pour l'ordre du Temple tirées des archives de Saint-Gervais de Cassolas', ed. J. Delaville Le Roulx, *ROL*, 11 (1905–8)

Burchard of Mount Sion, 'Descriptio Terrae Sanctae', ed. J.C.M. Laurent, *Peregrinatores Medii Aevi Quatuor*, Leipzig, 1864

Calendar of the Close Rolls, Edward I., vol. III, AD 1288–96, London, 1904; vol. V, AD 1302–7, London, 1908

Calendar of the Patent Rolls preserved in the Public Record Office, Henry III, 1232–47, London, 1906

Cartulaire de l'abbaye de Saint-Aubin d'Angers, ed. A. de Bertrand de Broussillon, vol. II, Paris, 1903

Le Cartulaire du Chapitre de Saint-Sépulchre de Jérusalem, ed. G. Bresc-Bautier, Documents relatifs à l'histoire des croisades publiés par l'Académie des Inscriptions et Belles-Lettres 15, Paris, 1984

Cartulaire de la Commanderie de Richerenches de l'Ordre du Temple (1136–1214), ed. Marquis de Ripert-Monclar, Documents inédits pour servir à l'histoire du Départment de Vaucluse, Paris, 1907 (reprinted 1978)

Cartulaire de l'Eglise Collégiale Notre-Dame de Beaujeu, ed. M.-C. Guigue, Lyon, 1864

Cartulaire général de l'Ordre des Hospitaliers de Saint-Jean de Jérusalem, 1100–1310, ed. J. Delaville Le Roulx, 4 vols., Paris, 1894–1905 (reprint 1980)

Cartulaire général de l'Ordre du Temple 1119?–1150. Recueil des chartes et des bulles relatives à l'ordre du Temple, ed. Marquis d'Albon, Paris, 1913

Cartulaire des Templiers de Douzens, ed. P. Gérard and E. Magnou, Collection de documents inédits sur l'histoire de France 3, Paris, 1965

Cartulario del Temple de Huesca, ed. A. Gargallo Moya, M.T. Iranzo Muñio, and M.J. Sánchez Usón, Textos Medievales 70, Zaragoza, 1985

The Cartulary of the Knights of St John of Jerusalem in England. Secunda Camera. Essex, ed. M. Gervers, Records of Social and Economic History, n.s. 6, Oxford, 1982

Catalan Rule. Archivo de la Corona de Aragón, Barcelona, Cartas reales 3344

Chartes de documents poitevins du XIIIe siècle en langue vulgaire, ed. M.S. La Du, vol. II, Archives historiques du Poitou 58, Poitiers, 1963

Chartes de Terre Sainte provenant de l'abbaye de Notre Dame de Josaphat, ed. F. Delaborde, Paris, 1880

'Chartes de Terre Sainte', ed. J. Delaville Le Roulx, *ROL*, 11, 1905–8

'Les Chemins et les pelerinages de la Terre Sainte', ed. H. Michelant and G. Raynaud, *Itinéraires à Jérusalem*, Geneva, 1882

Chronica de Mailros, ed. J. Stevenson, Edinburgh, 1835

'Chronica regia Coloniensis', ed. R. Röhricht, *Testimonia Minora de Quinto Bello Sacro*, Geneva, 1882

'Chronicon Sampetrinum', ed. B. Stübel, *Geschichtsquellen der Provinz Sachsen*, vol. I, Halle, 1870

Chronique Latine de Guillaume de Nangis de 1113 à 1300 avec les continuations de cette chronique de 1300 à 1368, ed. H. Géraud, vol. I, Société de l'Histoire de France, Paris, 1843

Chronique de la Maison de Beaujeu, ed. M.-C. Guigue, Collection Lyonnaise 4, Lyon, 1878

Clement IV. *Les Registres de Clement IV*, ed. E. Jordan, vol. I, BEFAR ser. 2, Paris, 1893

Codice Diplomatico sui rapporti Veneto-Napoletani durante il Regno di Carlo I d'Angiò, ed. N. Nicolini, RCI 36, Rome, 1965

Conciliae Magnae Britanniae et Hiberniae, ed. D. Wilkins, vol. II, London, 1737

La Continuation de Guillaume de Tyr (1184–1197), ed. M.R. Morgan, Documents relatifs à l'histoire des Croisades publiés par l'Académie des Inscriptions et Belles-Lettres 14, Paris, 1982

Crusaders as Conquerors. The Chronicle of the Morea, tr. H.E. Lurier, Records of Civilization. Sources and Studies 69, New York and London, 1964

The Crusades. Idea and Reality 1095–1274, ed. and tr. L. and J. Riley-Smith, London, 1981

Daniel. 'The Life and Journey of Daniel, Abbot of the Russian Land', ed. J. Wilkinson, *Jerusalem Pilgrimage*, Hakluyt Society 167, London, 1988

Dante Alighieri, *The Divine Comedy*, Cantica II, *Purgatory*, tr. D. Sayers, Harmondsworth, 1955

'De constructione castri Saphet', ed. R.B.C. Huygens, *Studi Medievali*, ser. 3, 6 (1965)

Decrees of the Ecumenical Councils, ed. N.P. Tanner, vol. I, London, 1990

Deliberazioni del Maggior Consiglio di Venezia, ed. R. Cessi, vol. II, R. Accademia dei Lincei. Commissione per gli atti delle Assemblee Costituzionali Italiane, Bologna, 1931

Diplomatic Documents (Chancery and Exchequer), ed. P. Chaplais, vol.I, 1101–1272, London, 1964

'Un document sur les débuts des Templiers', ed. J. Leclercq, *Revue d'Histoire Ecclésiastique*, 52 (1957)

Documenti del commercio veneziano nei secoli XI-XIII, ed. R. Morozzo della Rocca and A. Lombardo, 2 vols., RCI 28, Rome 1940

Documenti sulle relazioni delle città toscane coll'Oriente cristiano e coi Turchi fino all'anno 1531, ed. G. Müller, Florence, 1879

Documents concernant les Templiers extraits des archives de Malte, ed. J. Delaville Le Roulx, Paris, 1882

Documents en Français des Archives Angevines de Naples (Règne de Charles Ier), ed. A. de Boüard, 2 vols., Paris, 1933

'Documents relatifs à la successibilité au trône et à la régence', in *RHCr. Lois*, vol. II

Le Dossier de l'Affaire des Templiers, ed. and tr. G. Lizerand, Les Classiques de l'Histoire de France au Moyen Age, 2nd edn, Paris, 1964

'Emprunts de Saint Louis en Palestine et en Afrique', ed. G. Servois, *BEC* 19, 1858

Epistolae Saeculi XIII e Regestis Pontificum Romanorum, ed. C. Rodenberg, in *MGH Epistolae*, vol. I, Berlin, 1883

'Epistola Sancti Ludovici Regis de Captione et Liberatione sua', ed. A. Duchesne, *Historiae Francorum Scriptores*, vol. V, Paris, 1649

Eracles. L'Estoire d'Eracles Empereur et la Conqueste de la Terre d'Outremer, in *RHCr. Occidentaux*, vols. I, II

Ernoul-Bernard. Chronique d'Ernoul et de Bernard le Trésorier, ed. L. de Mas-Latrie, Paris, 1871

Etudes sur les actes de Louis VII, ed. A. Luchaire, Paris, 1885

Felix Fabri. *The Book of the Wanderings of Brother Felix Fabri (c. 1480–1483)*, tr. Stewart, vol. II, Palestine Pilgrims' Text Society 9, London, 1893

Ferretto of Vicenza, 'Historia rerum in Italia gestarum ab anno 1250 ad annum usque 1318', in RIS, vol. IX

Flores Historiarum, ed. H.R. Luard, vols. II, III, RS 95, London, 1890

Florio Bustron, *Chronique de l'île de Chypre*, ed. R. de Mas Latrie, Collection de documents inédits sur l'histoire de France. Mélanges historiques 5, Paris, 1886

Foedera, Conventiones, Literae et Cuiuscunque Generis Acta Publica, ed. T. Rymer, 3rd edn, vol. I(ii), The Hague, 1745

'Fragment d'un cartulaire de l'ordre de Saint-Lazare en Terre Sainte', ed. A. de Marsy, in *AOL*, vol. II, Paris, 1884

Fulcher of Chartres, *Historia Hierosolymitana*, ed. H. Hagenmeyer, Heidelberg, 1913

Geoffrey of Clairvaux, *Vita S. Bernardi*, in *PL*, vol. 185(i)

Gerald of Wales, 'De Principis Instructione Liber', ed. G.F. Warner, *Giraldi Cambrensis Opera*, vol. VIII, RS 21, London, 1891

Gervase of Canterbury, *The Gesta Regum with its Continuation*, ed. W. Stubbs, RS 73, London, 1880

'Gesta Crucigerorum Rhenanorum', ed. R. Röhricht, *Quinti Belli Sacri Scriptores Minores*, Société de l'Orient latin: série historique 2, Geneva, 1879

Gesta Regis Henrici Secundi Benedicti Abbatis: The Chronicle of the Reigns of Henry II and Richard I, AD 1169–1192, known commonly under the name of Benedict of Peterborough, ed. W. Stubbs, 2 vols., RS 49, London, 1867

Gestes des Chiprois, ed. G. Raynaud, Geneva, 1887

Gregory the Priest. 'Chronique de Grégoire Le Prêtre', in *RHCr. Documents Arméniens*, vol. I

Guillaume de Nangis, 'Vie de Saint Louis', in *RHG*, vol. XX

Guiot de Provins, 'La Bible', in *Les Oeuvres de Guiot de Provins, poète lyrique et satirique*, ed. J. Orr, Manchester, 1915

Hayton, 'La Flor des Estoires de la Terre d'Orient', in *RHCr. Documents Arméniens*, vol. II

Henry of Huntingdon, *Historia Anglorum*, ed. T. Arnold, RS 74, London, 1879

'Epistola ad Walterum de Contemptu Mundi', in *Historia Anglorum*, ed, T. Arnold

Histoire de l'Ile de Chypre, ed. L. de Mas Latrie, vol. II, Paris, 1852

Histoire de l'Ordre Militaire des Templiers, ou Chevaliers du Temple de Jérusalem. Depuis son Etablissement jusqu' à sa Decadence et sa Suppression, ed. P. Dupuy, Brussels, 1751 (originally published 1654)

Historia Diplomatica, ed. J.-L.-A. Huillard-Bréholles, vols. I, II, Paris, 1852

Honorius III. *Regesta Honorii Papae III*, ed. P. Pressutii, vols. I, II, Rome, 1888–95

Ibn al-Athir, 'Extrait de la Chronique intitulée Kamel-Altevarykh', in *RHCr. Orientaux*, vols. I, II(i)

Ibn al-Furāt. *Ayyubids. Mamlukes and Crusaders. Selections from the Tārīkh al-Duwal wa'l-Mulūk of Ibn al-Furāt*, text and tr. U. and M.C. Lyons, historical intr. J. Riley-Smith, 2 vols., Cambridge, 1971

Ibn al-Qalānisī, *The Damascus Chronicle of the Crusades*, ed. and tr. H.A.R. Gibb, University of London Historical Series 5, London, 1932

'Imâd ad-Din al-Isfahânî, *Conquête de la Syrie et de la Palestine par Saladin*, tr. H. Massé, Paris, 1972

Innocent III. *Innocenti P.P. Registrorum*, in *PL*, vols. 214–16.

Innocent IV. *Les Registres d'Innocent IV*, ed. E. Berger, vols. I–III, BEFAR, ser. 2, Paris, 1884–97.

Instrumenta Episcoporum Albinganensium, ed. G. Pesce, Documenti del R. Archivio di Stato di Torino, Collana Storico-Archeologica della Liguria Occidentale 4, Albenga, 1935

Isaac de l'Etoile. 'Isaac de l'Etoile et son siècle: Texte et commentaire historique du sermon XLVIII', ed. G. Raciti, in *Cîteaux: Commentarii Cisterciensis*, 12, 1961

Das Itinerarium peregrinorum. Eine zeitgenössische Chronik zum dritten Kreuzzug in ursprünglicher Gestalt, ed. H.E. Mayer, in *MGH Schriften*, vol. XVIII, Stuttgart, 1962

Itinerarium Peregrinorum et Gesta Regis Ricardi, ed. W. Stubbs, vol. I, RS 38, London, 1864

James of Aragon. *The Chronicle of James I, King of Aragon surnamed the Conqueror*, tr. J. Forster, 2 vols., London, 1883

James Doria, 'Annales Ianuenses', in *Annali genovesi de Caffaro e dei suoi continuatiori*, ed. C. Imperiale de Sant'Angelo, vol. V, Rome, 1929

James of Vitry, 'Historia Hierosolimitana', ed. J. Bongars, *Gesta Dei per Francos*, vol. I(ii), Hanover, 1611

The Exempla or Illustrative Stories from the Sermones Vulgares, ed. T.F. Crane, New York, 1890

Lettres de Jacques de Vitry: (1160/1170–1240), évêque de Saint-Jean-d'Acre, ed. R.B.C. Huygens, Leiden, 1960

Jerusalem Pilgrimage 1099–1185, ed. J. Wilkinson, with J. Hill and W.F. Ryan, The Hakluyt Society 167, London, 1988

John of Joinville, *Histoire de Saint Louis*, ed. and tr. N. de Wailly, 2nd edn, Paris, 1874

John Kinnamos, *The Deeds of John and Manuel Comnenus*, tr. C.M. Brand, Records of Civilization. Sources and Studies 95, New York, 1976

John of Salisbury, *Historia Pontificalis*, ed. and tr. M. Chibnall, London, 1956

Ioannis Saresberiensis Episcopi Carnotici Policratici, vol. II, ed. C.C. Webb, Oxford, 1909

Policraticus. Of the Frivolities of Courtiers and the Footprints of Philosophers, ed. and tr. C.J. Nederman, Cambridge, 1990

John of Würzburg, 'Descriptio Terrae Sanctae', ed. T. Tobler, *Descriptiones Terrae Sanctae ex saec. VIII. IX. XII. et XV.*, Leipzig, 1874

The Knights Hospitallers in England, ed. L.B. Larking and J.M. Kemble, Camden Society, old series 65, London, 1857

Layettes du Trésor des Chartes, ed. M.A. Teulet, vols. I, II, Paris, 1863

'Lettre des Chrétiens de Terre-Sainte à Charles d'Anjou', ed. H. Delaborde, *ROL*, 2 (1894)

'Lettre inédite de Hugues de Saint-Victor aux Chevaliers du Temple', ed. C. Sclafert, *Revue d'ascétique et de mystique*, 34 (1958)

'Lettres inédites concernant les croisades', ed. C. Kohler and C.-V. Langlois, *BEC*, 52 (1891)

Lettres inédites de Philippe Le Bel, ed. A. Baudouin, Mémoires de l'Académie des Sciences, Inscriptions et Belles-Lettres de Toulouse, ser. 8, 8, Toulouse, 1886

Lettres des Premiers Chartreux, vol. I, *S. Bruno, Guigues, S. Anthelme*, Sources Chrétiennes 88, 2nd edn, Paris, 1988

'Libellus de expugnatione Terrae Sanctae per Saladinum', ed. J. Stevenson, in Ralph of Coggeshall, *Chronicon Anglicanum*, RS 66, London, 1875

'Les Lignages d'Outremer', in *RHCr. Lois*, vol. II

Ludolph of Suchem, *Liber de Itinere Terre Sancte*, ed. F. Deycks, Stuttgart, 1851

'Majus Chronicon Lemovicense', in *RHG*, vol. xxi

Maqrisi. *Histoire d'Egypt de Makrizi*, tr. E. Blochet, *ROL*, 6 (1898); 8 (1900–1); 9 (1902); 10 (1903–4); 11 (1905–8) *Histoire des Sultans Mamelouks de l'Egypte*, ed. and tr. E. Quatremère, vols. i, ii, Paris, 1837–45

Marino Sanudo, *Liber secretorum fidelium crucis*, in *Gesta Dei per Francos*, ed. J. Bongars, vol. i, Hanover, 1611

Martin da Canal, *Les Estoires de Venise. Cronaca veneziana in lingua francese dalle origini al 1275*, ed. A. Limentani, Civiltà Veneziana, Fonti e Testi 12, Florence, 1972

Matthew Paris, *Chronica Majora*, ed. H.R. Luard, vols. iv–vi, RS 57, London, 1880

'Menkonis Chronicon', ed. L. Weiland, in *MGH SS*, vol. xxiii, Leipzig, 1925

Michael the Syrian. *Chronique de Michel Le Syrien. Patriarche Jacobite d'Antioche (1166–99)*, ed. and tr. J.-B. Chabot, vol, iii, Paris, 1905

Monumenta Boica, ed. Academia scientiarum Boica, vol. xxix(ii), Munich, 1831

'Un nouveau manuscrit de la Règle du Temple', ed. J. Delaville Le Roulx, *Annuaire-Bulletin de la Société de l'Histoire de France*, 26(ii) (1889)

'Obituaire de la Commanderie du Temple de Reims', ed. E. de Barthèlemy, in *Mélanges historiques. Collection des Documents inédits*, vol. iv, Paris, 1882

Odo of Deuil, *De Profectione Ludovici VII in Orientem*, ed. and tr. V.G. Berry, Records of Civilization. Sources and Studies 42, New York, 1948

Oliver of Paderborn, 'Historia regum Terre Sancte', ed. O. Hoogweg, *Die Schriften des Kölner Domscholasters*, in Bibliothek des Litterarischen Vereins in Stuttgart 202, Tübingen, 1894 *Oliveri Paderbornensis Historia Damiatina*, ed. O. Hoogweg, *Die Schriften*

Orderic Vitalis. *The Ecclesiastical History of Orderic Vitalis*, ed. and tr. M. Chibnall, vol. vi, Oxford, 1978

Ordonnances des Roys de France de la troisième race, ed. E. de Laurière, vol. i, Paris, 1723

Otto of Freising and Rahewin, *Gesta Friderici I. Imperatoris auctoribus Ottone et Ragewino praeposito Frisingensibus*, ed. G.H. Pertz, in *MHH SS*, vol. xx

Papsttum und Untergang des Templerordens, ed. H. Finke, vol. ii, Münster, 1907

Papsturkunden für Templer und Johanniter, ed. R. Hiestand, Vorarbeiten zum Oriens Pontificius, vols. i and ii. Abhandlungen der Akademie der Wissenschaften in Göttingen 77, 135, Göttingen, 1972–84

Peter the Venerable. *The Letters of Peter the Venerable*, ed. G. Constable, vol. i, Cambridge, Mass., 1967

Philip of Novara, *The Wars of Frederick II against the Ibelins in Syria and Cyprus*, tr. M.J. Hubert and J.L. La Monte, Records of Civilization. Sources and Studies 25, New York, 1936

Pierre Dubois, *De Recuperatione Terre Sancte*, ed. C.V. Langlois, Collection de textes pour servir à l'étude et à l'enseignement de l'histoire, Paris, 1891 *The Recovery of the Holy Land*, tr. W.I. Brandt, Records of Civilization. Sources and Studies 51, New York, 1956

Portugaliae Monumenta Historica. Leges et consuetudines, vol. I, Lisbon, 1856

Procès des Templiers, ed. J. Michelet, 2 vols., Collection de documents inédits sur l'histoire de France, Paris, 1841

Le Procès des Templiers d'Auvergne (1309–11): Edition de l'interrogatoire de juin 1309, ed. R. Sève and A.-M. Chagny-Sève, Mémoires et documents d'histoire médiévale et de philologie, nouvelle collection, Paris, 1987

Provins. Histoire et cartulaire des Templiers de Provins, ed. V. Carrière, Paris, 1919 (reprint 1978)

Rainerius Sacconi, 'Summa de Catharis et Pauperibus de Lugduno', in *Un Traité néo-manichéen du XIIIe siècle: Le Liber de duobus principiis, suivi d'un fragment de rituel cathare*, ed. A. Dondaine, Rome, 1939

Ralph of Caen, 'Gesta Tancredi in Expeditione Hierosolymitana', in *RHCr. Occidentaux*, vol. III

Ralph of Coggeshall, *Chronicon Anglicanum*, ed. J. Stevenson, RS 66, London, 1875

Ralph of Diceto, *Opera Historica*, ed. W. Stubbs, vol. II, RS 68, London, 1876

Ramon Lull, 'Liber de Fine', ed. A. Madre, *Raimundi Lulli Opera Latina*, Corpus Christianorum. Continuatio Mediaevalis 35, Turnhout, 1981

Ramon Muntaner, 'Crónica Catalana, ed. and tr. A. de Bofarull, Barcelona, 1860

The Chronicle of Muntaner, tr. Lady Goodenough, vol. II, Hakluyt Society 50, London, 1920–1

'Récit du XIIIe siècle sur les translations faites en 1239 et en 1241 des saintes reliques de la Passion', ed. N. de Wailly, *BEC*, 39 (1878)

Records of the Templars in England in the Twelfth Century. The Inquest of 1185, ed. B.A. Lees, British Academy Records of the Social and Economic History of England and Wales 9, London, 1935

Regesta Pontificum Romanorum, ed. A. Potthast, 2 vols., Berlin 1873–5

Regesta Regni Hierosolymitani, ed. R. Röhricht, 2 vols., Innsbruck, 1893–1904

Regesto del Capitolo di Lucca, ed. P. Guidi and O. Parenti, vol. I, RCI 6, Rome, 1910

I registri della cancelleria angioina, ed. R. Filangieri, vols. IX, XI, XXVI, Naples, 1957–79

La Règle des Templiers, ed. and tr. L. Dailliez, Nice, 1977

La Règle du Temple, ed. H. de Curzon, Société de l'Histoire de France, Paris, 1886

Richard of Poitou, *Chronica*, in *MGH SS*, vol. XXVI

Rigord. *Oeuvres de Rigord et de Guillaume le Breton*, ed. H.-F. Dalaborde, vol. I, Société de l'Histoire de France, Paris, 1882

Robert of Torigni, 'Chronicle', ed. R. Howlett, *Chronicles of the Reigns of Stephen, Henry II, and Richard I.*, vol. IV, RS 82, London, 1889

Roger of Howden, *Chronica*, ed. W. Stubbs, vols. II, III, RS 51, London, 1870

Roger of Wendover, *Liber qui dicitur Flores Historiarum*, ed. H.F. Hewlett, vol. II, RS 84, London, 1887

Rorgo Fretellus de Nazareth et sa description de la Terre Sainte. Histoire et edition du texte, ed. P.C. Boeren, Amsterdam, 1980

Rothelin. 'Continuation de Guillaume de Tyr de 1229 à 1261, dite du manuscrit de Rothelin', in *RHCr. Occidentaux*, vol. II

Rotuli Litterarum Clausarum, ed. T.D. Hardy, vol. I, London, 1833

Rotuli Litterarum Patentium, ed. T.D. Hardy, vol. I(i), London, 1835

The Rule of the Templars. The French Text of the Rule of the Order of the Knights Templar, tr. J.M. Upton-Ward, Woodbridge, 1992

Salimbene de Adam, *Cronica*, ed. G. Scalia, vol. I, Scrittori d'Italia 233, Bari, 1966

Schlesisches Urkundenbuch, 1231–1250, ed. W. Irgang, vol. II, Vienna, Cologne, and Graz, 1977

'Six lettres relatives aux Croisades', ed. P. Riant, *AOL*, vol. I, Paris, 1881

Suger of Saint-Denis. *Abbot Suger on the Abbey Church of St.-Denis and its Art Treasures*, ed. and tr. E. Panofsky, 2nd edn G. Panofsky-Soergel, Princeton, 1979

Syllabus Membranarum ad Regiae Siclae archivum pertinentium, ed. A.A. Scotti, vol. I, Naples, 1824

Tabulae ordinis Theutonici, ed. E. Strehlke, Berlin, 1869 (reprint 1975)

'The Templars and the Castle of Tortosa in Syria: A Unknown Document Concerning the Acquisition of the Fortress', ed. J. Riley-Smith, *EHR*, 84 (1969)

Theodericus Libellus de Locis Sanctis, ed. M.L. and W. Bulst, Editiones Heidelbergenses 18, Heidelberg, 1976

The Trial of the Templars in the Papal State and the Abruzzi, ed. A. Gilmour-Bryson, Studi e Testi 303, Città del Vaticano, 1982

Der Untergang des Templer-Ordens, ed. K. Schottmüller, vol. II, Berlin, 1887 (reprint 1970)

Urban IV. *Les Registres d'Urbain IV*, ed. J. Guiraud, vol. IV, BEFAR ser. 2, Paris, 1906

Die Urkunden der Deutschen Könige und Kaiser, ed. F. Hausmann, in *MGH Diplomata*, vol. IX

Urkunden zur Reichs-und Rechtsgeschichte Italiens, ed. J. Ficker, vol. II, Innsbruck, 1874

Die ursprüngliche Templerregel, ed. G. Schnürer, Freiburg, 1903

Usāmah ibn-Munqidh, *An Arab-Syrian Gentleman and Warrior in the Period of the Crusades*, tr. P.K. Hitti, New York, 1929 (reprint 1987)

Vitae Paparum Avenionensium, ed. E. Baluze, new edn G. Mollat, vol. III, Paris, 1927

Walter of Hemingborough, *Chronicon de Gestis Regum Angliae*, ed. H.C. Hamilton, vol. II, English Historical Society 14, London, 1849

Walter Map, *De nugis curialium*, ed. and tr. M.R. James, rev. C.N.L. Brooke and R.A.B. Mynors, Oxford, 1983

Wilbrand of Oldenburg. 'Wilbrandi de Oldenborg Peregrinatio', ed. J.C.M. Laurent, *Peregrinatores Medii Aevi Quatuor*, Leipzig, 1864

LIST OF REFERENCES

William Rishanger. *Chronica monasterii S. Albani. Willelmi Rishanger . . . Chronica et annales*, ed. H.T. Riley, RS 28, London, 1865
William of Tyre. *Guillaume de Tyr, Chronique*, ed. R.B.C. Huygens, 2 vols., Corpus Christianorum. Continuatio Mediaevalis 63 and 63A, Turnhout, 1986
A History of Deeds done beyond the Sea, tr. E.A. Babcock and A.C. Krey, 2 vols., Records of Civilization. Sources and Studies 35, New York, 1943 (reprint 1976)
Wolfram von Eschenbach, *Parzival*, tr. A.T. Hatto, Harmondsworth, 1980

SECONDARY WORKS

Abulafia, D. 'Marseilles, Acre and the Mediterranean, 1200–1291', in *Coinage in the Latin East: The Fourth Oxford Symposium on Coinage and Monetary History*, ed. P.W. Edbury and D.M. Metcalf, British archaeological reports, International Series 77, Oxford, 1980, pp. 19–39
'Southern Italy and the Florentine Economy, 1265–1370', *Economic History Review*, ser. 2, 33 (1981), pp. 377–88
'The Crown and the Economy under Roger II and his Successors', *DOP*, 37 (1983), pp. 1–14
Frederick II. A Medieval Emperor, London, 1988
Alart, B. 'Suppression de l'ordre des Templiers en Roussillon', *Bulletin de la Société Agricole, Scientifique et Littéraire des Pyrénées-Orientales*, 15 (1867), 25–115.
Albon, Marquis d'. 'La Mort d'Odon de Saint-Amand, Grand Maître du Temple', *ROL*, 12 (1909–11), 279–82
Arbois de Jubainville, H. d'. *Histoire des Ducs et des Comtes de Champagne*, vols. III, V, Paris, 1861–3.
Baignent, M., R. Leigh, and H. Lincoln. *The Holy Blood and the Holy Grail*, London, 1976
Baldwin, J.W. *The Government of Philip Augustus. Foundations of French Royal Power in the Middle Ages*, Berkeley and London, 1986
Baldwin, M.W. *Raymond III and the Fall of Jerusalem (1140–87)*, Princeton, 1936
Baratier, E., G. Duby, and E. Hildesheimer. *Atlas Historique. Provence. Comtat Venaissin. Comté de Nice. Principauté de Nice. Principauté de Monaco*, Paris, 1969
Barber, M.C. 'The Origins of the Order of the Temple', *Studia Monastica*, 12 (1970), 219–40
'James of Molay, the Last Grand Master of the Temple', *Studia Monastica*, 14 (1972), 91–124
The Trial of the Templars, Cambridge, 1978
'Lepers, Jews and Moslems: The Plot to Overthrow Christendom in 1321', *History*, 66 (1981), 1–17
'The Templars and the Turin Shroud', *The Catholic Historical Review*, 68 (1982), 206–25
'The Social Context of the Templars', *TRHS*, 5th ser., 34 (1984) 27–46

408

'Supplying the Crusader States: The Role of the Templars', in *The Horns of Hattin*, ed. B.Z. Kedar, Jerusalem and London, 1992, pp. 314–26

Barruel, A. *Mémoires pour servir à l'histoire du Jacobinisme*, 2 vols., Vouillé, 1973 (originally in 4 vols., 1797–8, revised 1818)

Bautier, R.-H. 'Diplomatique et histoire politique: ce que la critique diplomatique nous apprend sur la personnalité de Philippe le Bel', *Revue Historique*, 259 (1978), 3–27

Bennett, M. '*La Règle du Temple* as a military manual, or How to deliver a cavalry charge', in *Studies in Medieval History presented to R. Allen Brown*, ed. C. Harper-Bill, C. Holdsworth, and J.L. Nelson, Woodbridge, 1989, pp. 7–19

Benton, J.F. 'The Revenue of Louis VII', *Speculum*, 42 (1967), 84–91

Benvenisti, M. *The Crusaders in the Holy Land*, Jerusalem, 1972

Berry, V.G. 'Peter the Venerable and the Crusades', in *Petrus Venerabilis (1156–1956): Studies and Texts Commemorating the Eighth Centenary of His Death*, ed. G. Constable and J. Kritzeck, Rome, 1956, pp. 141–62

Besson, L.F.N. *Oeuvres pastorales*, vol. I, Paris, 1879

Bevere, R. 'Notizie storiche tratte dai documenti conosciuti col nome di "Arche in carta bambagina"', *Archivio Storico per le Province Napoletane*, 25 (1900), 241–75, 389–407

Bisson, T.N. *The Medieval Crown of Aragon. A Short History*, Oxford, 1986

Bleis, H. 'La place prise par l'abbaye de Clairvaux, au temps de Saint Bernard, dans la rivalité entre le Comte de Champagne et le Duc de Bourgogne' in *MSB*, pp. 28–31

Borracelli, M. 'La Magione Templare di Frosini e l'importanza delle strade che vi convergevano', in *MS*, pp. 311–30

Boswell, J. *Christianity, Social Tolerance, and Homosexuality*, London and Chicago, 1980

Boussard, J. *Le Comté d'Anjou sous Henri Plantagenêt et ses fils, 1151–1204*, Paris, 1938

Bramato, F. 'L'Ordine dei Templari in Italia. Dalle Origini al pontificato di Innocenzo III (1135–1216)', *Nicolaus*, 20 (1985), fasc. I, 183–221

'L'Ordine Templare nel Regno di Sicilia nell'età Svevo-Angioina', in *MS*, pp. 107–41

Storia dell'ordine dei Templari in Italia. Le Fondazione, Rome, 1991

Brown, E.A.R. 'The Prince is Father of the King: The Character and Childhood of Philip the Fair of France', *Medieval Studies*, 49 (1987), 282–334

Brundage, J.A. 'The Crusader's Wife: A Canonistic Quandary', *Studia Gratiana*, 12, Collectanea Stephan Kuttner 2, Rome, 1967, 427–41

'The Crusader's Wife Revisited', *Studia Gratiana*, 14, Collectanea Stephan Kuttner 4, Rome, 1967, 243–51

Medieval Canon Law and the Crusader, Madison, 1969

'A Transformed Angel (x 3.31.18): The Problem of the Crusading Monk', in *Studies in Medieval Cistercian History presented to Jeremiah F. O'Sullivan*, Cistercian Studies Series 13, Spencer, Mass., 1971, pp. 55–62

Law, Sex and Christian Society in Medieval Europe, Chicago and London, 1987

Bulst-Thiele, M.L. 'Templer in königlichen und päpstlichen Diensten', in *Festschrift Percy Ernst Schramm*, vol. I, Wiesbaden, 1964, pp. 289–308

Sacrae Domus Militiae Templi Hierosolymitani Magistri: Untersuchungen zur Geschichte des Templeordens 1118/9–1314, Göttingen, 1974

'The Influence of St Bernard of Clairvaux on the Formation of the Order of the Knights Templar', in *The Second Crusade and the Cistercians*, ed. M. Gervers, New York, 1992, pp. 57–65

Burton, J.E. 'The Knights Templar in Yorkshire in the Twelfth Century: A Reassessment', *Northern History. A Review of the History of the North of England and the Borders*, 27 (1991), 26–40

Cadet de Gassicour, C.L. *Le Tombeau de Jacques Molai*, Paris, 1796

Cahen, C. *La Syrie du nord à l'époque des croisades*, Paris, 1940

Carrière, V. 'Les Débuts de l'Ordre du Temple en France', *Le Moyen Age*, 18 (1914), 308–35

Cazelles, R. *Nouvelle histoire de Paris de la fin du règne de Philippe Auguste à la mort de Charles V 1223–1380*, Paris, 1972

Chartrou, J. *L'Anjou de 1109 à 1151*, Paris, 1928

Cohn, N. *Europe's Inner Demons*, London, 1976

Conder, C.F. and H.H. Kitchener. *The Survey of Western Palestine. Memoirs of the Topography, Orography, Hydrography and Archaeology*, 3 vols., London, 1881–3

Contamine, P. *War in the Middle Ages*, tr. M. Jones, Oxford, 1984

Cousin, P. 'Les Débuts de l'Ordre des Templiers et Saint Bernard', in *MSB*, pp. 41–52

Curzon, H. de *La Maison du Temple de Paris. Histoire et description*, Paris, 1888

Davies, C. 'Sexual Taboos and Social Boundaries', *American Journal of Sociology*, 87 (1982), 1032–63

Delaruelle, E. 'L'idée de croisade chez saint Bernard', in *MSB*, pp. 53–67

Delisle, L. *Mémoire sur les Opérations Financières des Templiers*, Mémoires de l'Institut national de France, Académie des Inscriptions et Belles-Lettres vol. 33 (ii), Paris, 1889

Demurger, A. *Vie et mort de l'Ordre du Temple*, Paris, 1985

'Les Templiers, Matthieu Paris et les sept péchés capitaux', in *MS*, pp. 153–68

Deschamps, P. *Les Châteaux des Croisés en Terre-Sainte*, vol. II, *La Défense du Royaume de Jérusalem*, Paris, 1939

Les Châteaux des Croisés en Terre Sainte, vol. III, *La Défense du Comté de Tripoli et de la Principauté d'Antioche*, Paris, 1973

Deschamps, P. and M. Thibout, *La Peinture murale en France. Le Haut Moyen-Age et l'Epoque Romane*, Paris

La Peinture murale en France au début de l'époque gothique, Paris, 1963

Dessubré, M. *Bibliographie de l'Ordre des Templiers*, Paris, 1928 (reprint 1966)

Dickson, G. 'The Flagellants of 1260 and the Crusades', *JMH*, 15 (1989), 227–67

Dubois, G. 'Recherches sur la vie de Guillaume des Roches, sénéchal d'Anjou, de Maine et de Touraine', *BEC*, 30 (1869), 377–424

Duby, G. *The Three Orders. Feudal Society Imagined*, tr. A. Goldhammer, Chicago and London, 1980

Duffy, C. *The Military Experience in the Age of Reason*, London, 1987

Dunbabin, J. 'From Clerk to Knight: Changing Orders', in *The Ideals and*

Practice of Medieval Knighthood, vol. II, *Papers from the Third Strawberry Hill Conference 1986*, ed. C. Harper-Bill and R. Harvey, Woodbridge, 1988, pp. 26–39

Duncan, J.E. 'The Anti-Romantic in *Ivanhoe*', in *Walter Scott. Modern Judgements*, ed. D.D. Devlin, London, 1968, pp. 142–7

Durbec, J.-A. 'Introduction à une liste des biens du Temple saisis en 1308 dans la region des Alpes-Maritimes', *Nice Historique*, 54 (1951), 45–52

'Les Templiers en Provence. Formation des Commanderies et répartition géographique des leurs biens', *Provence Historique*, 9 (1959), 3–37, 97–132

Durrieu, P. *Les Archives Angevines de Naples. Etude sur les Registres du Roi Charles I (1265–1285)*, vol. I, BEFAR 46, Paris, 1886

Eco, U. *Foucault's Pendulum*, tr. W. Weaver, London, 1989

Edbury, P.W. *The Kingdom of Cyprus and the Crusades, 1191–1374*, Cambridge, 1991

Edbury, P.W. and J.G. Rowe. *William of Tyre. Historian of the Latin East*, Cambridge, 1988

Edbury, P.W. 'The Templars in Cyprus', in *The Military Orders. Fighting for the Faith and Caring for the Sick*, ed. M.C. Barber, London, 1994, pp. 189–95

Edwards, R.W. 'Bağras and Armenian Cilicia: A Reassessment', *Revue des Etudes Arméniennes*, 17 (1983) 415–55

The Fortifications of Armenian Cilicia, Washington, 1987

Eistert, K. 'Der Ritterorden der Tempelherren in Schlesien', *Archiv für Schlesische Kirchengeschichte*, 14 (1956), 1–23

Emery, R.W. *The Jews of Perpignan in the Thirteenth Century*, New York, 1959

Evergates, T. *Feudal Society in the Bailliage of Troyes under the Counts of Champagne, 1152–1284*, Baltimore, 1975

Farmer, D.H. *The Oxford Dictionary of Saints*, Oxford, 1978

Favreau-Lilie, M.-L. 'Landesausbau und Burg während der Kreuzfahrerzeit: Safad in Obergalilaea', *Zeitschrift des Deutschen Palästina-Vereins*, 96 (1980), 67–87

Fleckenstein, J. 'Die Rechtfertigung der geistlichen Ritterorden nach der Schrift "De laude novae militiae" Bernhards von Clairvaux', in *Die geistlichen Ritterorden Europas*, ed. J. Fleckenstein and M. Hellman, Sigmaringen, 1980, pp. 9–22

Forey, A.J. 'The Order of Mountjoy', *Speculum*, 46 (1971), 250–66

The Templars in the Corona de Aragón, London, 1973

'The Military Orders in the Crusading Proposals of the Late-Thirteenth and Early-Fourteenth Centuries', *Traditio*, 36 (1980), 317–45

'The Will of Alfonso I of Aragon and Navarre', *Durham University Journal*, 73 (1980–1), 59–65

'The Militarisation of the Hospital of St John', *Studia Monastica*, 26 (1984), 75–89

'The Failure of the Siege of Damascus in 1148', *JMH*, 10 (1984), 13–23

'The Military Orders and the Spanish Reconquest in the Twelfth and Thirteenth Centuries', *Traditio*, 40 (1984), 197–234

'The Emergence of the Military Order in the Twelfth Century', *Journal of Ecclesiastical History*, 36 (1985), 175–95

'Recruitment to Military Orders (Twelfth to mid-Fourteenth centuries)', *Viator*, 17 (1986), 139–71

'Novitiate and Instruction in the Military Orders during the Twelfth and Thirteenth Centuries', *Speculum*, 61 (1986), 1–17

'Women and Military Orders in the Twelfth and Thirteenth Centuries', *Studia Monastica*, 29 (1987), 63–92

'The Beginnings of the Proceedings against the Aragonese Templars', in *God and Man in Medieval Spain. Essays in Honour of J.R.L. Highfield*, ed. D.W. Lomax and D. Mackenzie, Warminster, 1989, pp. 81–96

The Military Orders. From the Twelfth to the Early Fourteenth Centuries, London, 1992

Fossier, R. *Peasant Life in the Medieval West*, tr. J. Vale, Oxford, 1988

Fourmont, H. de *L'Ouest aux Croisades*, vol. III, Paris, 1867

Fried, J. 'Wille, Freiwilligkeit und Geständnis um 1300. Zur Beurteilung des letzten Templergrossmeisters Jacques de Molay', *Historisches Jahrbuch*, 105 (1985), 388–425

Fuller, T. *The History of the Holy War*, London, 1840 (originally Cambridge, 1639)

García Larragueta, S.A. *El Gran Priorado de Navarra de la Orden de San Juan de Jerusalén*, vol. II, Pamplona, 1957

Gem, R. 'An Early Church of the Knights Templars at Shipley, Sussex', in *Anglo-Norman Studies*, vol. VI, *Proceedings of the Battle Conference 1983*, ed. R.A. Brown, Woodbridge, 1984, pp. 238–46

Gervers, M. 'Pro defensione Terre Sancte: The Development and Exploitation of the Hospitallers' Landed Estate', in *The Military Orders. Fighting for the Faith and Caring for the Sick*, ed. M.C. Barber, London, 1994, pp. 3–20

Gibbon, E. *The History of the Decline and Fall of the Roman Empire*, vol. VII, ed. F. Fernández-Armesto, London, 1990 (originally 1788)

Girgensohn, D. 'Das Pisaner Konzil von 1135 in der Überlieferung des Pisaner Konzils von 1409', in *Festschrift für Hermann Heimpel*, vol. II, Göttingen, 1972, pp. 1063–1100

Giry, A. 'Les châtelains de Saint-Omer, 1042–1386', *BEC*, 35 (1874), 325–55

Grousset, R. *Histoire des Croisades et du Royaume Franc de Jérusalem*, vols. II, III, Paris, 1935

Gwynn, A. and R.N. Hadcock. *Medieval Religious Houses. Ireland*, London, 1970

Hallam, E.M. *Capetian France 987–1328*, London, 1980

'Royal Burial and the Cult of Kingship in France and England, 1060–1330', *JMH*, 8 (1982), 359–80

Hamilton, B. *The Latin Church in the Crusader States. The Secular Church*, London, 1980

Religion in the Medieval West, London, 1986

Hammer-Purgstall, J. von 'Mysterium Baphometis revelatum', *Fundgruben des Orients*, 6 (1818), 1–120, 445–99

Hammerstein, H. von, 'Der Besitz der Tempelherren in Lotharingen', *Jahrbuch der Gesellschaft für lothringische Geschichte und Altertumskunde*, 7 (1895) 1–29

Heath, P. *Church and Realm 1372–1461*, London, 1988

Hiestand, R. 'Chronologisches zur Geschichte des Königreiches Jerusalem um 1130', *Deutsches Archiv*, 26 (1970), 220–9
'Zum Problem des Templerzentralarchiv', *Archivalische Zeitschrift*, 76 (1980), 17–37
'Kardinalbischof Matthäus von Albano, das Konzil von Troyes und die Entstehung des Templeordens', *Zeitschrift für Kirchengeschichte*, 99 (1988), 295–325
Hill, G. *A History of Cyprus*, vol. II, Cambridge, 1948
Hill, R. 'Fourpenny Retirement: The Yorkshire Templars in the Fourteenth Century', in *Studies in Church History*, 24 (1987), pp. 123–8
Hillgarth, J.N. *Ramon Lull and Lullism in Fourteenth-Century France*, Oxford, 1971
Hodgson, M.G.S. *The Order of the Assassins*, The Hague, 1955
Housley, N. *The Italian Crusades. The Papal–Angevin Alliance and the Crusades against Christian Lay Powers, 1254–1343*, Oxford, 1982
'Clement V and the Crusades of 1309–10', *JMH*, 7 (1982), 29–43
The Avignon Papacy and the Crusades 1305–1378, Oxford, 1986
The Later Crusades. From Lyons to Alcazar, 1274–1580, Oxford, 1992
Irwin, R. 'The Supply of Money and the Direction of Trade in Thirteenth-Century Syria', in *Coinage in the Latin East*, ed. P.W. Edbury and D.M. Metcalf, Oxford, 1980
Jackson P. 'The Crisis in the Holy Land in 1260', *EHR*, 95 (1980), 481–513
'The End of Hohenstaufen Rule in Syria', *Bulletin of the Institute of Historical Research*, 59 (1986), 20–36
'The Crusades of 1239–41 and their Aftermath', *Bulletin of the School of Oriental and African Studies*, 50 (1987), 32–60
Jacoby, D. 'Crusader Acre in the Thirteenth Century: Urban Layout and Topography', *Studi Medievali*, 20 (1979), 1–45
'Les communies italiennes et les ordres militaires à Acre: aspects juridiques, territoriaux et militaires (1104–1187, 1191–1291)', in *Etat et colonisation au Moyen Age et à la Renaissance*, ed. M. Balard, Lyon, 1989, pp. 193–214
Jacoby, Z. 'The Workshop of the Temple Area in Jerusalem in the Twelfth Century: Its Origin, Evolution and Impact', *Zeitschrift für Kunstgeschichte*, 45 (1982), 325–94
Jobin, J.-B. *Saint Bernard et sa Famille*, Paris, 1891
Johns, C.N. 'Excavations at 'Atlīt (1930–1)', *The Quarterly of the Department of Antiquities in Palestine*, 2 (1932–3), 41–104
Guide to 'Atlīt, Jerusalem, 1947
Jordan, W.C. *Louis IX and the Challenge of the Crusade*, Princeton, 1979
The French Monarchy and the Jews. From Philip Augustus to the Last Capetians, Philadelphia, 1989
Kedar, B. Z., 'Gerard of Nazareth, a Neglected Twelfth-Century Writer in the Latin East. A Contribution to the Intellectual and Monastic History of the Crusader States', *DOP*, 37 (1983), 55–77
Crusade and Mission. European Approaches to the Muslims, Princeton, 1984

Kedar, B.Z. and R.D. Pringle. 'La Fève: A Crusader Castle in the Jezreel Valley', *Israel Exploration Journal*, 35 (1985), 164–79

Keen, M. *Chivalry*, New Haven and London, 1984

Knowles, D. and R.N. Hadcock, *Medieval Religious Houses. England and Wales*, London, 1953

Laborde, F. 'L'église des Templiers de Montsaunès (Haute-Garonne)', *Revue de Comminges*, 92 (1979), 335–73, 487–507; 93 (1980), 37–51, 227–41, 335–55

Lambert, E. *L'Architecture des Templiers*, Paris, 1955

La Monte, J.L. *Feudal Monarchy in the Latin Kingdom of Jerusalem*, Cambridge, Mass., 1982

Landon, L. *The Itinerary of King Richard I*, Pipe Roll Society n.s. 13, London, 1935

Langlois, C.V. *Notice sur le château du Plessis-Macé*, Angers, 1932

Larner, J. *Italy in the Age of Dante and Petrarch 1216–1380*, London, 1980

Lawrence, A.W. 'The Castle of Baghras', in *The Cilician Kingdom of Armenia*, ed. T.S.R. Boase, Edinburgh and London, 1978, pp. 34–83

Lawrence, C.H. *Medieval Monasticism*, 2nd edn, London, 1989

Lea, H.C. *A History of the Inquisition of the Middle Ages*, vol. III, New York, 1889

Leclercq, J. 'St Bernard's Attitude toward War', in *Studies in Medieval Cistercian History*, vol. II, ed. J.R. Sommerfeldt, Kalamazoo, Mich., 1976, pp. 1–39

Monks and Love in Twelfth-Century France. Psycho-Historical Essays, Oxford, 1979

Le Forestier, R. *La Franc-Maçonnerie templière et occultiste au XVIIIe XIXe siècles*, ed. A. Faivre, Paris, 1970

Legras, A.-M. *Les Commanderies des Templiers et des Hospitaliers de Saint-Jean de Jerusalem en Saintonge et en Aunis*, Paris, 1983

Léonard, E.-G. *Introduction au Cartulaire Manuscrit de Temple (1150–1317) constitué par le Marquis d'Albon*, Paris, 1930

L'Epinois, H. de 'Comptes relatifs à la fondation de l'Abbaye de Maubuisson', *BEC*, 19 (1858) 550–67

Lerner, R.E. *The Heresy of the Free Spirit*, Berkeley and London, 1972

Lewis, S. *The Art of Matthew Paris in the Chronica Majora*, Aldershot, 1987

Little, L.K. 'Pride Goes before Avarice: Social Change and the Vices in Latin Christendom', *American Historical Review*, 76 (1971), 16–49

Lloyd, S. *English Society and the Crusade 1216–1307*, Oxford, 1988

Loiseleur, J. *La Doctrine Secrète des Templiers*, Paris and Orléans, 1872 (reprint 1975)

Lourie, E. 'Free Muslims in the Balearics under Christian Rule in the Thirteenth Century', *Speculum*, 45 (1970), 624–49

'The Will of Alfonso I, "El Batallador", King of Aragon and Navarre; A Reassessment', *Speculum*, 50 (1975), 635–51

'The Confraternity of Belchite, the Ribāt, and the Temple', *Viator. Medieval and Renaissance Studies*, 13 (1982), 159–76

'The Will of Alfonso I of Aragon and Navarre: A Reply to Dr Forey', *Durham University Journal*, 77/2 (1984–5), 165–72

Luchaire, A. *La Société Français au temps de Philippe-Auguste*, Paris, 1909

Lüpke, H. 'Das Land Tempelburg. Eine historisch-geographische Untersuchung', *Baltische Studien*, 35 (1933), 43–97

Lundgreen, F. *Wilhelm von Tyrus und der Templerorden*, Berlin, 1911

Luttrell, A. 'Two Templar-Hospitaller Preceptories North of Tuscania', *Papers of the British School at Rome*, 39 (1971), 90–124

'Gli Ospitalieri e l'eredità dei Templari', in *MS*, pp. 67–86

Luzzatto, G. 'Capitale e lavoro nel commercio veneziano dei secoli XI e XIII', in *Studi di Storia Economica Veneziana*, Padua, 1954, pp. 89–116

Lynch, J.H. *Simoniacal Entry into Religious Life from 1000 to 1260*, Columbus, Ohio, 1976

McLaughlin, T.P. 'The Teaching of the Canonists on Usury', *Medieval Studies*, 1 (1939), 81–147; 2 (1940), 1–22

Magnou, E. 'Oblature, classe chevaleresque et servage dans les maisons méridionales du Temple au XIIme siècle', *Annales du Midi*, 73 (1961), 377–97

Martin, J.-B. *Conciles et Bullaire du diocèse de Lyon*, Lyon, 1905

Mas Latrie, L. de 'Rapport sur le recueil des archives de Venise intitulé "Libri pactorum", ou "Patti"', *Archives des Missions Scientifiques*, 2 (1851), 261–300, 341–85

Histoire de l'Ile de Chypre, vol. 1, Paris, 1861

Mayer, H.E. 'Studies in the History of Queen Melisende of Jerusalem', *DOP*, 26 (1972), 95–182

'The Concordat of Nablus', *Journal of Ecclesiastical History*, 33 (1982), 531–43

'The Succession to Baldwin II of Jerusalem: English Impact on the East', *DOP*, 39 (1985), 139–47

The Crusades, 2nd edn, Oxford, 1988

'Angevins versus Normans: The New Men of King Fulk of Jerusalem', *Proceedings of the American Philosophical Society*, 133 (1989), 1–25

Melville, M. *La Vie des Templiers*, Paris, 1951

Ménard, L. *Histoire civile, ecclésiastique et littéraire de la ville de Nismes*, vol. 1, Paris, 1750

Miller, W. *The Latins in the Levant. A History of Frankish Greece (1204–1566)*, London, 1908

Minnucci, G. and F. Sardi. *I Templari: Mito e Storia. Atti del Convegno Internazionale di Studi alla Magione Templare di Poggibonsi-Siena, 29–31 Maggio 1987*, Siena, 1989

Miret y Sans, J. 'Itinerario del Rey Pedro I de Cataluña, II en Aragón', *Boletín de la Real Academia de Buenas Letras de Barcelona*, 3, (1905–6), 365–87; 4, (1907–8), 15–36

Les Cases de Templars y Hospitalers en Catalunya, Barcelona, 1910

Mola, A.A. 'Il Templarismo nella Massoneria fra Otto e Novecento', in *MS*, pp. 259–78

Mollat, G. 'Dispersion définitive des Templiers après leur suppression', *Comptes Rendus des Séances de l'Académie des Inscriptions et Belles-Lettres*, Paris, 1952, pp. 376–80

The Popes at Avignon 1305–1378, tr. J. Love, London, 1963

Morgan, M.R. *The Chronicle of Ernoul and the Continuations of William of Tyre*, Oxford, 1973

Müller-Wiener, W. *Castles of the Crusaders*, tr. J.M. Brownjohn, London, 1966

Neu, H. *Bibliographie der Templer-Ordens 1927–1965*, Bonn, 1965

The New Encyclopaedia Britannica. Macropaedia, 15th edn, vols.20, 29, London, 1986

Nicholson, H.J. 'Templar Attitudes towards Women', *Medieval History*, 1 (1991), 74–80

Templars, Hospitallers and Teutonic Knights. Images of the Military Orders, 1128–1291, London, 1993

Nicolini, U. 'Bonvicino', in *Dizionario biografico degli Italiani*, vol. VII, Rome, 1970, pp. 471–2

Nicolle, D.C. *Arms and Armour of the Crusading Era 1050–1350*, 2 vols., New York, 1988

Niermeyer, J.F. *Mediae Latinitatis Lexicon Minus*, Leiden, 1976

Nowell, C.E. 'The Old Man of the Mountain', *Speculum*, 22 (1947), 497–519

O'Callaghan, J.F. *A History of Medieval Spain*, Ithaca and London, 1975

Oliveira Marques, A.H. *Historia de Portugal*, 11th edn, vol. 1, Lisbon, 1983

Origo, I. 'The Domestic Enemy: The Eastern Slaves in Tuscany in the Fourteenth and Fifteenth Centuries', *Speculum*, 30 (1955), 321–66

Painter, S. *William Marshal*, Baltimore, 1933

'The Crusade of Theobald of Champagne and Richard of Cornwall, 1239–41', in *A History of the Crusades*, vol. II, ed. R.L. Wolff and H.W. Hazard, Madison, 1969, pp. 463–85

Parker, T.W. *The Knights Templars in England*, Tucson, Ariz., 1963

Partner, P. *The Murdered Magicians. The Templars and their Myth*, Oxford, 1981

Perjés, G. 'Army Provisioning, Logistics and Strategy in the Second Half of the Seventeenth Century', *Acta Historica Academiae Scientarium Hungaricae*, 16 (1970), 1–51

Persan, P.N.C. *Recherches historiques sur la ville de Dole*, Dole, 1812

Piquet, J. *Des Banquiers au Moyen Age. Les Templiers. Etude de leurs Opérations financières*, Paris, 1939

Powell, J.M. *Anatomy of a Crusade 1213–1221*, Philadelphia, 1986

Powicke, F.M. *King Henry III and the Lord Edward*, Oxford, 1947

Prawer, J. 'Military Orders and Crusader Politics in the Second Half of the XIIIth Century', in *Die geistlichen Ritterorden Europas*, ed. J. Fleckenstein and M. Hellmann, Sigmaringen, 1980, pp. 217–29

Pringle, R.D. 'Reconstructing the Castle of Safad', *Palestine Exploration Quarterly*, 117 (1985), 139–49

The Red Tower (al-Buri al-Ahmar): Settlement in the Plain of Sharon at the Time of the Crusaders and Mamluks (AD 1099–1516), British School of Archaeology Monographs Series 1, London, 1986

'A Templar Inscription from the Haram al-Sharif in Jerusalem', *Levant*, 21 (1989), 197–201

'Templar Castles on the Road to the Jordan', in *The Military Orders. Fighting for the Faith and Caring for the Sick*, ed. M.C. Barber, London, 1994, pp. 148–66

Prutz, H. *Entwicklung und Untergang des Tempelherrenordens*, Berlin, 1888

Pryor, J. 'Transportation of Horses by Sea during the Era of the Crusades. Part I: To c. 1225. Part II: 1228–85', *Mariner's Mirror*, 68 (1982), 9–27, 103–25

Raspa, P. and M. Marchesi. 'Note sull'architettura di San Bevignate', *TOI*, pp. 79–92

Rassow, P. 'La cofradía de Belchite', *Anuario de historia del derecho español*, 3 (1926), 200–26

Raynouard, F.J.M. 'Etude sur "Mysterium Baphometi revelatum"', *Journal des Savants* (1819), 151–61, 221–9

Renouard, Y. 'L'Ordre de la Jarretière et l'Ordre de l'Etoile', *Le Moyen Age*, 55 (1949), 281–300

Rey, E.G. 'Geoffrey Foucher. Grand-Commandeur du Temple, 1151–70', *Revue de Champagne et de Brie*, 6 (1894), 259–69

Richard, J. *Le Comté de Tripoli sous la dynastie toulousaine (1102–87)*, Paris, 1945

'Quelques textes sur les premiers temps de l'Eglise Latine de Jérusalem', in *Recueil Clovis Brunel*, vol. II, Paris, 1955, pp. 420–30

'The Eastern Mediterranean and its Relations with its Hinterland (11th–15th Centuries)', in *Les Relations entre l'Orient et l'Occident au Moyen Age*, Variorum. Collected Studies 69, London, 1977, pp. 1–39

The Latin Kingdom of Jerusalem, tr. J. Shirley, Amsterdam, 1979

'Les Templiers et les Hospitaliers en Bourgogne et en Champagne méridionale', in *Die geistlichen Ritterorden Europas*, ed. J. Fleckenstein and M. Hellmann, Sigmaringen, 1980, pp. 231–42

Rigault, A. *Le Procès de Guichard, Evêque de Troyes (1308–13)*, Paris, 1896

Riley-Smith, J. *The Knights of St John in Jerusalem and Cyprus c. 1050–1310*, London, 1967

The Feudal Nobility and the Kingdom of Jerusalem, 1174–1277, London, 1973

'The Templars and the Teutonic Knights in Cilician Armenia', in *The Cilician Kingdom of Armenia*, ed. T.S.R. Boase, Edinburgh and London, 1978, pp. 92–117

'Peace Never Established: The Case of the Kingdom of Jerusalem', *TRHS*, 5th ser., 28 (1978), 87–102

The Crusades. A Short History, London, 1987

ed., *The Atlas of the Crusades*, London, 1991

Roberts, J.M. *The Mythology of the Secret Societies*, London, 1972

Robinson, I.S. 'Gregory VII and the Soldiers of Christ', *History*, 58 (1973), 169–92

The Papacy 1073–1198. Continuity and Innovation, Cambridge, 1990

Röhricht, R. *Beiträge zur Geschichte der Kreuzzüge*, vol. I, Berlin, 1874

Roncetti, M., P. Scarpellini, and F. Tommasi. *Templari e Ospitalieri in Italia. La chiesa di San Bevignate a Perugia*, Milan, 1987

Round, J.H. 'Some English Crusaders of Richard I', *EHR*, 17 (1903), 475–83

Rovik, S.S. 'The Templars in the Holy Land during the Twelfth Century', unpublished D. Phil. thesis, University of Oxford, 1986

Runciman, S. *A History of the Crusades*, vols. II, III, Cambridge, 1952–4

Russell, F.H. *The Just War in the Middle Ages*, Cambridge, 1975

Sandys, A. 'The Financial and Administrative Importance of the London Temple in the Thirteenth Centurty', in *Essays in Medieval History presented to Thomas Frederick Tout*, ed. A.G. Little and F.M. Powicke, Manchester, 1925, pp. 147–62

Scarpellini, P. 'La chiesa di San Bevignate, i Templari e la pittura perugina del Duecento', in *TOI*, pp. 93–158

Schein, S. 'The Future *Regnum Hierusalem*. A Chapter in Medieval State Planning', *JMH*, 10 (1984), 95–105

'The Templars: The Regular Army of the Holy Land and the Spearhead of the Army of its Reconquest', in *MS*, pp. 15–25

Fideles Crucis. The Papacy, the West and the Recovery of the Holy Land 1274–1314, Oxford, 1991

Schnürer, G. 'Zur ersten Organisation der Templer', *Historisches Jahrbuch*, 32 (1911), 298–316, 511–46

Scott, Sir W. *Ivanhoe. A Romance*, 1819

The Talisman, 1825

Setton, K.M. *The Papacy and the Levant (1204–1571)*, Philadelphia, 1976

Shahar, S. 'Des lépreux pas comme les autres. L'ordre de Saint-Lazare dans le royaume latin de Jérusalem', *Revue historique*, 267 (1982), 19–41.

Siberry, E. 'Victorian Perceptions of the Military Orders', in *The Military Orders. Fighting for the Faith and Caring for the Sick*, ed. M.C. Barber, London, 1994, pp. 365–72

Smail, R.C. *Crusading Warfare (1097–1193)*, Cambridge, 1956

Smalley, B. 'Ecclesiastical Attitudes to Novelty *c.* 1100–1250', in *Studies in Church History*, 12 (1975), pp. 113–31

Spicciani, A., 'Papa Innocenzo IV e I Templari', in *MS*, pp. 41–65

Starnawska, M. 'Notizie sulla composizione e sulla struttura dell'Ordine del Tempio in Polonia', in *MS*, pp. 143–51

Strayer, J.R. 'France: The Holy Land, the Chosen People, and the Most Christian King', in *Medieval Statecraft and the Perspectives of History. Essays by Joseph R. Strayer*, ed. J.F. Benton and T.N. Bisson, Princeton, 1971, pp. 300–14

The Reign of Philip the Fair, Princeton, 1980

Szabò, T. 'Templari e viabilità', in *MS*, pp. 297–307

Tallett, F. *War and Society in Early-Modern Europe, 1495–1715*, London, 1992

Tibble, S. *Monarchy and Lordships in the Latin Kingdom of Jerusalem 1099–1291*, Oxford, 1989

Tommasi, F. 'L'Ordine dei Templari a Perugia', *Bollettino della Deputazione di Storia Patria per l'Umbria*, 78 (1981), 1–79

'I Templari e il culto delle reliquie', in *MS*, pp. 191–210

Trudon des Ormes, A. 'Listes des maison et de quelques dignitaires de l'ordre du Temple, en Syrie, en Chypre et en France, d'après les pièces du procès', *ROL*, 5 (1897), 389–459; 6 (1898) 156–213; 7 (1900) 223–74, 504–89

Tyerman, C.J. 'Sed Nihil Fecit? The Last Capetians and the Recovery of the Holy Land', in *War and Government in the Middle Ages*, ed. J. Gillingham and J.C. Holt, Woodbridge, 1984, pp. 170–81

Urban, W. *The Livonian Crusade*, Washington, 1981

Valous, G. de, 'Quelques observations sur la toute primitive observance des Templiers et la *Regula pauperum commilitonum Christi Templi Salomonici*, rédigée par saint Bernard au concile de Troyes (1128)', in *MSB*, pp. 32–40

The Victoria History of the Counties of England, ed. L.F. Salzman, *A History of Cambridgeshire and the Isle of Ely*, vol. II, London, 1948

Walker, J. 'The Patronage of the Templars and the Order of Saint Lazarus in England in the Twelfth and Thirteenth Centuries', unpublished Ph. D. thesis, University of St Andrews, 1990

Warren, W.L. *Henry II*, London, 1973

Wildermann, A., *Die Beurteilung des Templerprozesses bis zum 17. Jahrhundert*, Freiburg, 1971

Wilson, I. *The Turin Shroud*, Harmondsworth, 1979

INDEX

H Hospitaller, Order of St John
T Templar, Order of the Temple
TK Teutonic Knight, Teutonic Order

Albizzo Guidi, banker, 297
Albon, Marquis d', historian, 338 n. 39,
340 n.89, 347 n. 26, 395
Alcacer do Sal, 128
Alcanadre, River, 266
Alcántara, Order of, 34, 246
Aleppo, 12, 65, 70, 156, 232
Aleth, mother of Bernard of Clairvaux, 71
Alexander III, Pope, 59, 125, 275–6, 351 n.
93, 385 n. 167
Alexander IV, Pope, 157, 244, 276
Alexander Nevsky, Great Prince of
Vladimir, 157
Alexandretta, 349 n. 58; Gulf of, 79
Alexandria, 96, 138, 148, 293
Alfonso I, 'the Battler', King of Aragon,
26–31, 40, 52, 54, 340 n. 100
Alfonso III, King of Aragon, 176
Alfonso VI, King of Castile, 32, 246
Alfonso VII, King of Castile, 28, 30, 32,
34, 340 n. 83
Alfonso-Jordan, Count of Toulouse, 37,
51, 214, 342 n. 130
Ali, cousin of Muhammad, 100
Alice, Queen-Dowager of Cyprus, Regent
of Jerusalem, 142–3
Almenar de Soria, 34
Almohades, Berber dynasty, 246
Almoravides, Berber dynasty, 32, 246
Almourol, T castle, 246, 397, plate 15
almsgiving, 16, 185, 187, 210–11, 218,
258, 264
Alphonse, Count of Poitiers, 152
Alps, 157, 250
Altabella, donor to the T of Huesca, 266
Amadeus of Morestello, Master of the T in
England, 157
Amalric, King of Jerusalem, 65, 73, 86,
95–107, 109, 122, 125, 136, 352 n. 97
Amalric of Nesle, Patriarch of Jerusalem,
103
Amanus Mountains, 35, 77, 79, 97, 286,
369 n. 55
Amaury de la Roche, Master of the T in
France, 159, 266, 274, 288
Amaury of Lusignan, Lord of Tyre,
289–90, 293, 387 n. 28
Amman, see Ahamant
Amur, River, 137
Anacletus II, Antipope, 56
Anagni, 299
Anceau of Brie, 134
Ancessa, church, 31
Ancona, marches of, T sub-Province, 245
Andrew, St, 167
Andrew, T knight, 12

Andrew II, King of Hungary, 127, 357 n.
38
Andrew of Montbard, Seneschal and
Grand Master of the T, 35, 70–2, 75, 79,
97, 189, 233, 345 n. 43, 347 n. 23, 348 n.
30, 351 n. 91
Angers, monastery of St Nicholas, 123
Angevin rulers of Sicily, 170, 173, 175,
192, 240, 251, 289
Anglo-Saxon Chronicle, 14, 95
Anjou, 13, 119, 123, 275
Anno of Sangerhausen, Grand Master of
the TKs, 155, 158
Ansell of Quincy, donor to the T, 263
Anselm, Bishop of Havelberg, 50
Anterius, Bishop of Valania, 108
Antioch, 2, 35–7, 65, 67, 70, 71, 77, 79,
94, 97, 113, 121–2, 129, 137, 140, 155–6,
160, 163, 187, 212, 219, 233, 240, 243,
349 n. 50, 349 n. 58, 354 n. 139
Apologia to William of St Thierry by
Bernard of Clairvaux, 45
apostasy, see desertion
Apulia, 132, 212, 238–40, 244, 250, 264,
306, 378 n. 47, 379 n. 60
Arabia Petraea, 75
Aragon, 2, 20, 21, 23, 26–32, 34, 36, 52,
109, 171, 230, 240, 246, 249, 261, 265,
285, 296, 300, 341 n. 105, 345 n. 42, 350
n. 59, 376 n. 9, 377 n. 42, 379 n. 60, 380
n. 85, 391 n. 86, 396–7
Aragon, River, 30, 266
Arames, 164, 364 n. 54
Archibald of Bourbon, 66
Archive of the T, 89, 311–13, 342 n. 128,
350 n. 59, 394
Arezzo, T preceptory, 265
al-'Arīmah, T castle, 81–2, 97–8, 124, fig.
6
Armand of Périgord, Preceptor of the T in
Sicily and Calabria, Grand Master,
136–9, 141–5, 147, 165, 225–6, 230, 359
n. 76, 361 nn. 106 and 114, 374 n. 173
Armenia, Kingdom of, see Cilicia
Armenian Church, 121
Armenians, 121, 286, 294, 349 n. 54; see
also Cilicia
Arnold of Bedocio, 'minister' of the T,
20
Arnold, Abbot of Morimond, 12–13
Arnold of Sournia, 56
Arnold of Torroja, Master of the T in
Spain and Provence, Grand Master, 109,
251, 254, 354 n. 139
Arnoul of Wisemale, Preceptor of T of
Reims, Royal Treasurer, 274

INDEX

Humbert V, Lord of Beaujeu, 170
Humbert of Pairaud, Master of the T in England, 288
Hungarians, Hungary, 245, 275, 379 n. 79
Hungary, T Province, 244–5
Huntingdonshire, 223

Ibelin, castle, 73
Ibelin family, 110, 113, 136
Iberia, 2, 19–20, 26, 34, 183, 244, 246, 310, 380 n. 83, 397
Ibn al-Furāt, Egyptian chronicler, 167
Ibn al-Qalānisī, Damascene chronicler, 74–5
idol worship, 301–2, 306–7, 321, 331
Ile-de-France, 20, 295
Illuminati of Bavaria, 319
'Imād-ad-Dīn, secretary and chancellor to Saladin, chronicler, 64, 120, 235, 395
Inab, battle of (1149), 70, 347 n. 23
Indus, River, 137
Inés, wife of Bartholomew of Milagro, 261
Innocent II, Pope, 30, 56–8, 344–5 n. 41
Innocent III, Pope, 41, 121–2, 124–7, 223–5, 251, 275
Innocent IV Pope, 145, 220, 231–2, 239, 249, 293
Inquest of T lands in England (1185– c.1190), 251, 381 n. 95, 395
Inquisition, 229, 234, 301–2
Iran, 137
Ireland, 354 n. 141
irrigation, 266, 383 n. 137
Isaac, Abbot of L'Etoile, 61–2, 346 n. 50
Isaac, in Ivanhoe, 324–5
Isabel of Hainault, Queen of France, 169
Isabel, Queen of Jerusalem, 122, 169
Isabel of Brienne, Queen of Jerusalem, 131–2, 359 n. 77
Italians, Italy, 2, 19, 25, 109, 132–3, 135, 169, 176, 192, 200, 240–1, 245–6, 250–1, 275–6, 296, 298, 339 n. 74, 370 n. 80, 376 n. 14, 379 n. 60, 380 n. 79, 385 n. 167, 394
Itinerarium, 113, 117, 235, 354 n. 155
Ivanhoe, by Sir Walter Scott, 323–8

Jabala, 140, 243
Jacobins, 319
Jacob's Ford, 86, 95
Jaffa, 3, 88, 118, 133–4, 144, 155, 160
Jalāl-ad-Dīn, Khorezmian Shah, 137
James the Less, St, 167
James, St, 271; Epistle of, 56
James I, King of Aragon, 170–1, 246, 249, 384 nn. 144 and 152

James II, King of Aragon, 249, 287, 291, 303, 310, 387 n. 37, 388 n. 48
James II, King of Mallorca, 278–9
James of Mailly, Marshal of the T, 111
James of Molay, Grand Master of the T, 1, 63, 77, 181–2, 185–6, 199, 218, 234, 243, 283–94, 297, 300, 304, 312, 314–15, 318, 320, 332, 386 nn. 11 and 16, 387 nn. 22 and 37, 388 nn. 43, 47 and 48, 390 n. 75, 393 n. 11, 396
James of Vitry, Bishop of Acre, 130, 194, 209, 280–1, 315, 354 n. 150; see also Exempla; History of Jerusalem
Jaulan, 158
Jean Michel, scribe at the Council of Troyes, 9, 15, 338 n. 42
Jeanne of Navarre, Queen of France, 300
Jebail, 109
Jericho, 88–9
Jerome, St, 47, 203, 206
Jerusalem, Chancellor of the Kingdom of, 130
Jerusalem, City of, 2, 3, 7, 9, 11, 14, 25, 27, 38, 40, 51–3, 55–6, 62, 68, 88, 90–3, 106, 113, 115–18, 126, 128, 133–4, 143–5, 155, 185, 190–1, 194, 199, 213–14, 230, 236, 281, 311, 336 n. 17, 373 n. 151; al-Aqsa mosque, 7, 10, 36, 90–3, 113, 193–4, 311, 318, plate 4, fig. 7; 'Beautiful Gate', 90; Citadel (Tower of David), 90; Damascus Gate, 8; Dome of the Rock, 7, 90, 114, 369 n. 57, plate 4, fig 7; Holy Sepulchre, Church of, 46–8, 52, 116, 133, 195, 226, 369 n. 57; Jaffa Gate, 90; St Stephen's Church, 8; Street of the Chain, 90; Workshop in the Temple Area, 194, 369 n. 54
Jerusalem, Kingdom of, 3, 9, 17, 18, 34–7, 51, 65–6, 71, 94, 99, 105–6, 109, 113–14, 118, 122–3, 137, 147, 155–6, 169–70, 182, 230, 259, 274, 285–6, 294, 300, 311, 316, 341 n. 116, 342 n. 126, 358 n. 62, 359 n. 77, 394
Jesus, Society of, 319, 334
Jews, 165, 296, 298–300, 304, 323
Jezreel Valley, 87, 161, 164
John, St, 206; Gospel of, 56
John the Baptist, St, 271
John, Archbishop of Braga, 33–4, 54
John of Brienne, King of Jerusalem, 122–3, 127–8, 130–1
John of Carcella, T knight, 171
John Cenaud, Preceptor of the T of La Fouilhouze, 198, 290
John Comnenus, Byzantine Emperor, 77
John Culet, T brother, 307

Maria of Montferrat, Queen of Jerusalem, 122–3

Marienburg, TK castle, 310, 392 n. 107

Marittima, T sub-Province, 245

Marj Ayun, battle of (1179), 86, 95, 109

Marmoutier, Abbey of, 13; T preceptory, 21

al-Marqab, H castle, 101, 116, 124–5, 133, 168, 175, 251

married brothers (fratres conjugati), 18

Marseille, 138, 153, 237–8, 240–1, 250

Martha, sister of Mary and Lazarus (New Testament), 47

Martin IV, Pope, 276

Mary, sister of Martha and Lazarus (New Testament), 47

Mary Magdalene, 167, 204

Mas-Deu, T preceptory, 51, 54–5, 254

Mas Latrie, Louis de, historian, 387 n. 28

Massa Marittima, 265

Matilda of England, Empress, 14

Matilda, Queen of England, 339 n. 70

Matilda, Queen of Portugal, 33

Matthew, St, 167; Gospel of, 54–5, 260

Matthew Paris, chronicler of St Albans, 134–5, 139, 142–4, 147, 149–50, 171, 181, 188, 227, 229–30, 234, 319, 331, 362 n. 8, 396; see also Chronica Majora

Matthew du Remois, Cardinal-Bishop of Albano, 14

Matthias, St, 271

Maubuisson, Abbey of, 275

Maurepas, T preceptory, 302

Maurice de Bracy, in Ivanhoe, 324–5

Mayer, Hans, historian, 72, 352 n. 97

Mediterranean Sea, 169, 237, 250, 266, 277, 309, 312

Melfi, 359 n. 77

Melisende, Queen of Jerusalem, 12, 18, 65, 71–2, 106, 347 n. 26

Melun, 25

mercenaries, 70, 94, 166

Merle, T castle, 88

Messina, T preceptory, 238–9

Metternich, Prince Klemens, Austrian Foreign Minister and Chancellor, 320

Metz, 25; T preceptory and church, 202, 381 n. 87

Michael, St, 194, 271

Michael the Syrian, Jacobite Patriarch of Antioch, chronicler, 6, 7, 10

Michelet, Jules, historian, 396

Milan, 1

Miles of Montbard, 71

Milites Templi (1144), 56, 58, 60, 339 n. 67, 344 n. 41

Militia Dei (1145), 58, 60

Milon, Bishop of Thérouanne, 23

Minnie Mouse, 334

Minnucci, Giovanni, historian, 398

Miño, River, 32

Miravet, T castle, 246, 249, 397, plate 14

Moisy, T preceptory, 264

Mondego, River, 32

Mongay, T castle, 29

Mongols, 137, 145, 155–9, 168, 175, 202, 240, 244, 250, 293–4, 388 nn. 47 and 48

monophysite heresy, 121

Monreal del Campo, confraternity (militia), 26–7

Montaigu, T preceptory, 264

Montaperti, battle of (1260), 276

Montbellet, T church, 202

Montbouy, T preceptory, 243

Mont-de-Soissons, T preceptory, 264

Monte Gargano, 265

Montelopio, T preceptory, 265

Montesa, Order of, 310

Montferrand, 35

Montfort, castle of the TKs, 156, 160

Montréal, castle, 86, 116, 350 n. 65, 353 n. 124

Montroque, 174

Montsaunès, T preceptory, 195, 202–3, 397, fig. 10

Montségur, castle, 320

Monzón, T castle, 29, 246, 249

Moral, 258

Morea, 2, 19, 127; Chronicle of the, 245–6, 380 n. 82

Morgan, Ruth, literary historian, 335 n. 6

Mortmain, Statute of (1279), 390 n. 60

'Mouche', see Musciatto Guidi

Mount Calvary, 46

Mount Carmel, 88, 160–1, 163–4, 198

Mountjoy, Order of, 230

Mount of Olives, 46

Mount Quarantene, 88–9

Mount Sinai, 202

Mount Tabor, 147, 161, 167

Mozi of Florence, banking house, 273

al-Mu'azzam, ruler of Damascus, 127, 129, 161

Muhammad, 100, 147, 166, 227, 321

Muret, battle of (1213), 246

Musciatto Guidi, banker, 297

al-Muwaylih, 75

al-Muzaffer Mahmūd, ruler of Hamah, 137–8

The Mystery of Baphomet Revealed by Joseph von Hammer-Purgstall, 320

INDEX

Osto of St Omer, T knight, 35, 51, 259, 342 n. 122, 382 n. 109
Otto, Bishop of Freising, 68, 93
Ottoman Turks, 312, 394
Oultrejourdain, 86, 100, 106
Ourique, battle of (1139), 32
Ouvèze, River, 52
Ovid, 74

Pagan the Butler, Lord of Oultrejourdain, 106
Paganus, Burgundian knight, see Hugh of Payns
Palau, T preceptory, 23
Palestine, 2, 36, 127–30, 145, 155, 158, 164, 176, 229, 268, 272, 288, 293, 313, 316, 351 n. 91; see also Holy Land
Palmae, 68
Pandolf, Papal Legate in England, 275
Papal reform, 38–40, 223
Papal Schism, 314
Papal State, 200, 396; see also Patrimony of St Peter
Paphos, T preceptory, 173
Paris, 35, 42, 66, 159, 200, 229, 233–4, 291, 301–6, 308, 314, 342 n. 122; Louvre, 297, 389 n. 56; St Victor, Abbey of, 268; T preceptory, 195, 243, 250, 266–71, 291, 297–8, 301–3, 372 n. 134, 383 n. 139, 387 n. 37, 390 n. 82, 396; university, 63
Paris, Bibliothèque Nationale, 395; Cabinet des Estampes, 397
Paris, Prévôt of, 270
Partner, Peter, historian, 397
Parzival of Wolfram von Eschenbach, 281
Paschal II, Pope, 385 n. 167
Passagium parvum, 286, 294
Paterno, 136
Patrimony of St Peter in Tuscia, T sub-Province, 245
Patzinaks, 66
Paul, St, 55, 115, 203
Paul of Segni, Bishop of Tripoli, 173
Payen of Montdidier, Master of the T in France, 20, 244
Pelagius, Cardinal-Bishop of Albano, 128–30, 140, 275
Pelagius, Archbishop of Braga, 33–4
penances, 17, 179, 182–3, 191, 202, 210, 213, 219–22, 395
Peñíscola, T castle, 249, 397
Perpignan, T preceptory, 254, 279
Persia, 100
Perugia, 251, 276, 385 n. 168; Porta Sole, 200; San Bevignate, T church, 10, 143,

180, 187, 200, 203–7, 397, plates 10, 11, 12; San Guistino d'Arno, 203
Peter, St, 57, 62, 115, 167, 203
Peter Abelard, 61
Peter, Count of Alençon, 153
Peter II, King of Aragon, 246
Peter III, King of Aragon, 278
Peter of Bologna, Procurator of the T at the Papal Court, 251, 305
Peter of Erlant, Bishop of Limassol, 290
Peter of Fontaines, Procurator of the T Preceptor in Sicily and Apulia, 172
Peter of Limoges, Archbishop of Caesarea, 225
Peter of Montaigu, Grand Master of the T, 128–31, 134–6, 161, 357 n. 41
Peter of Peraverde Ultramontanus, Grand Preceptor of the T in Apulia and the Abruzzi, 306
Peter of Rovira, Master of the T in Provence, 21, 258–60
Peter of St Just, Preceptor of the T of Correus, 387 n. 37
Peter of St Just, Preceptor of the T of Graynane, 291
Peter of Sevrey, Marshal of the T, 177
Peter of Vares, T Preceptor, 293
Peter the Venerable, Abbot of Cluny, 41, 49, 71, 347 n. 24
Peter of Vieille Bride, Grand Master of the H, 141
Peter of Villaplana, T brother, 125
Peter's Pence, 275
Petra, 86
Petronilla of Aragon, 28
Philip, St, 167, 200
Philip of Alsace, Count of Flanders, 115
Philip II, King of France, 117, 119, 131, 169, 257, 273–5, 295, 301, 327, 329
Philip III, King of France, 276, 279, 298
Philip IV, the Fair, King of France, 63, 184, 257, 277, 279, 285, 287, 289, 291, 295–301, 309, 314–15, 317–18, 332–3, 388 n. 41, 389 nn. 55 and 56
Philip V, King of France, 323
Philip of Milly, Lord of Nablus, Grand Master of the T, 86, 100, 106–7, 186, 353 n. 128
Philip of Novara, chronicler, 134, 142, 216–17
Philip of Plessis, Grand Master of the T, 123, 126–7, 356 nn. 21 and 25
Philistines, 73
Philosophes, 319
Phoenicians, 163
Picardy, 6, 106, 259, 297, 387 n. 37

435

INDEX

Tortosa (Syria), 140, 293–4; T castle 81, 89, 94, 103, 107–8, 113, 124, 133, 175, 178, 194, 243, 283, 286, 350 n. 50, fig. 4; diocese, 83; Notre-Dame, Cathedral of, 81; St Helen, Gate of, 81
torture, 301–2, 305–6, 391 n. 85
Toulousain, 24–5, 295
Toulouse, 1, 20–1, 202, 214
Tournai, 1
Tours, 21
Trani, 1; T preceptory, 238
Transjordan, 145
Trapesak, see Darbsak
Tréfols, T preceptory, 264
Treviso, 25
trial of the Ts, 1, 34, 42, 181, 183, 192, 198, 200, 210, 215, 218, 227–8, 229, 234, 249, 276, 288, 290–1, 295–309, 372 n. 134, 387 n. 37, 389 n. 51, 391 nn. 85 and 86, 392 n. 7, 396–7
Trinity, Order of, 227
Tripoli, town and county, 2, 35, 37, 65, 79–83, 94, 97–8, 101, 111, 113, 123–5, 129, 133, 155–6, 160–1, 163, 173–6, 187, 192, 212, 218–19, 222, 243, 293–4, 311, 363 n. 45
Troyes, Council of (1129), 8–10, 13–20, 33, 44, 50, 56, 68, 71, 232, 246, 258, 332, 336 n. 13, 338 nn. 39 and 42, 339 n. 67, 395, 398
Troyes, T preceptory, 51
True Cross, 115–16, 130, 189, 195, 200, 272
Tudela, 26
Tūrān-Shāh, Sultan of Egypt, 152, 154
Turcomans, 158, 166, 188, 287
Turcopoles, 166, 189
Turin Shroud, 331–3
The Turin Shroud by Ian Wilson, 332
Turks, 149, 151, 181, 193, 235, 326
Tuscany, 204, 243, 264–5; T sub-Province, 245
Tyre, 2, 9–10, 12, 36, 65, 71, 101, 114–16, 129, 135–6, 143, 167, 173, 219, 243, 293, 336 n. 15

Ulger, Bishop of Angers, 23, 50–1, 339 n. 67
Ulm, 315
Umbria, 200, 204, 251
Union of the Military Orders, 77, 283–5, 295, 300, 386 n. 12, 396
USA, 231
Unur, Muʿīn-ad-Dīn, Turkish ruler of Damascus, 69

Urban II, Pope, 2, 14, 40, 50, 59, 385 n. 167
Urban III, Pope, 115, 233
Urban IV, Pope, 159, 188, 274
Uriah, Hittite Solider (Old Testament), 60
Urraca, Queen of Castile, 27
Usāmah Ibn-Munqidh, Damascene chronicler, 36, 75–6
usury, 231–2, 277

Valania, 107–8, 124–5, 140, 168, 218, 251
Valania, Bishop of, 125
Valencia, 27, 246, 249, 279
Vaour, T preceptory, 215
Varenne, River, 263
Vassayll, T sergeant and sea-captain, 240
Vaucluse, 254, 260
Venetians, Venice, 12, 126–7, 143, 155–6, 173, 237, 245, 250–1, 287, 293, 310, 392 n. 107; T preceptory, 251
Vermandois, bailli of, 270
Verona, 109
Vetralla, T preceptory, 251
Vexin, 385 n. 175
Via Cassia, 251
Victor IV, Antipope, 385 n. 167
Vienna, 120; T preceptory, 315
Vienne, Council of (1311–12), 280, 285, 300, 396–7
Vietnam War, 231
Vignale, T preceptory, 265
Villa Sicca, village, 34
Villel, T castle, 249
Vincentius Hispanus, canon lawyer, 282, 328
Virgin Mary, 81, 203–4, 271
Vistula, River, 309
Viterbo, 200, 251
Vox in excelso (1312), 280

Walter of Avesnes, 138, 161
Walter IV, Count of Brienne and Jaffa, 138, 145
Walter of Châtillon, 151
Walter, Prince of Galilee, 382 n. 111
Walter Map, Archdeacon of Oxford, 6–7, 61–2, 75–6, 103, 223, 230, 331
Walter of Mesnil, T knight, 101, 104, 125
Walter, Castellan of Saint-Omer, Prince of Galilee, 259–60
Walter, Abbot of Saint-Vaast, 23–4, 31
Walter, Canon of Valania, 108
Wamba, Saxon serf in Ivanhoe, 325
Wardrobe of the English Crown, 383 n. 144
Warmund of Picquigny, Patriarch of Jerusalem, 7–9, 12, 14, 51
Warrêton-Bas, castellany, 259

440